Theory and Methods in Comparative Policy Analysis Studies

Volume One

Volume One of the *Classics of Comparative Policy Analysis*, "Theory and Methods in Comparative Policy Analysis Studies", includes chapters that apply or further theory and methodology in the comparative study of public policy, in general, and policy analysis, in particular.

Throughout the volume the chapters engage in theory building by assessing the relevance of theoretical approaches drawn from the social sciences, as well as some which are distinctive to policy analysis. Other chapters focus on various comparative approaches based on developments and challenges in the methodology of policy analysis. Together, this collection provides a comprehensive scholastic foundation to comparative policy analysis and comparative policy studies.

"Theory and Methods in Comparative Policy Analysis Studies" will be of great interest to scholars and learners of public policy and social sciences, as well as to practitioners considering what can be learned or facilitated through methodologically and theoretically sound approaches.

The chapters were originally published as articles in the *Journal of Comparative Policy Analysis* which in the last two decades has pioneered the development of comparative public policy. The volume is part of a four-volume series, *the Classics of Comparative Policy Analysis* including Theories and Methods, Institutions and Governance, Regional Comparisons, and Policy Sectors.

Each volume showcases a different new chapter comparing domains of study interrelated with comparative public policy: political science, public administration, governance and policy design, authored by the JCPA co-editors Giliberto Capano, Iris Geva-May, Michael Howlett, Leslie A. Pal and B. Guy Peters.

Iris Geva-May has been recognized by Thomson Reuters for having pioneered the field of comparative policy analysis since 1998, when she founded the now high indexed *Journal of Comparative Policy Analysis*. She serves as its Founding Editor and the Founding President of the Scholarly Society for International Comparative Policy Analysis (ICPA-Forum). She has published among others *The Logic and Methodology of Policy Analysis, An Operational Approach to Policy Analysis (with Wildavsky), International Library of Policy Analysis Series, Routledge Handbook of Comparative Policy Analysis*, and *Policy Analysis as a Clinical Profession*. She is Professor Emerita at Simon Fraser University, Vancouver, Canada and currently an Honorary Visiting Professor at SPPA, Carleton University, Ottawa, Canada, and the Wagner School NYU, USA.

B. Guy Peters is Maurice Falk Professor of Government at the University of Pittsburgh, USA, and an Honorary Editor of the *Journal of Comparative Policy Analysis*. He is also the Founding President of the *International Public Policy Association* and Editor of the *International Review of Public Policy*. Among his seminal publications are as follows: *Comparative Politics Theory and Methods, Institutional Theory in Political Science, The Politics of Bureaucracy: A Comparative Perspective, An Advanced Introduction to Public Policy,* and *The Next Public Administration*.

Joselyn Muhleisen serves as the Awards Coordinator for the International Comparative Policy Analysis Forum and the *Journal of Comparative Policy Analysis*. She is a Doctoral Lecturer at the Marxe School of Public and International Affairs, Baruch College, City University of New York (CUNY), USA. She earned her doctorate in political science from The Graduate Center, CUNY, USA. She is the former Assistant Director of the European Union Studies Center, CUNY, USA. She has published work about the development of comparative policy analysis and its relationship to international studies.

Theory and Methods in Comparative Policy Analysis Studies
Volume One

Edited by
Iris Geva-May, B. Guy Peters and Joselyn Muhleisen

With

Foreword by Laurence E. Lynn, JCPA Founding Co-Editor

Introduction to the Series, Iris Geva-May, JCPA Founding Editor, B. Guy Peters Co-Editor, Joselyn Muhleisen Co-Editor

And

Part 2, New Contribution: Two Ships in the Night: Comparative Politics and Comparative Policy Analysis—Making the Linkage, B. Guy Peters, JCPA Co-editor and Iris Geva-May, JCPA Founding Editor

Sponsored by

LONDON AND NEW YORK

First published 2020
by Routledge
2 Park Square, Milton Park, Abingdon, Oxon, OX14 4RN

and by Routledge
52 Vanderbilt Avenue, New York, NY 10017

Routledge is an imprint of the Taylor & Francis Group, an informa business

© 2020 The Editor, Journal of Comparative Policy Analysis: Research and Practice

All rights reserved. No part of this book may be reprinted or reproduced or utilised in any form or by any electronic, mechanical, or other means, now known or hereafter invented, including photocopying and recording, or in any information storage or retrieval system, without permission in writing from the publishers.

Trademark notice: Product or corporate names may be trademarks or registered trademarks, and are used only for identification and explanation without intent to infringe.

British Library Cataloguing-in-Publication Data
A catalogue record for this book is available from the British Library

ISBN13: 978-1-138-33273-7

Typeset in Times
by codeMantra

Publisher's Note
The publisher accepts responsibility for any inconsistencies that may have arisen during the conversion of this book from journal articles to book chapters, namely the inclusion of journal terminology.

Disclaimer
Every effort has been made to contact copyright holders for their permission to reprint material in this book. The publishers would be grateful to hear from any copyright holder who is not here acknowledged and will undertake to rectify any errors or omissions in future editions of this book.

 Printed in the United Kingdom
by Henry Ling Limited

Contents

Citation Information viii
Notes on Contributors xi
Foreword to the Book Series*: The Classics of*
Comparative Policy Analysis xiv
Laurence E. Lynn, Jr.

PART 1
An Introduction to the Classics of Comparative Policy Analysis Book Series
1

Why the Classics of Comparative Policy Analysis Studies? 3
Iris Geva-May, B. Guy Peters and Joselyn Muhleisen

PART 2
Lesson Drawing Relationships: Comparing Associated Disciplines and Comparative Policy Analysis
11

Two Ships in the Night: Comparative Politics and Comparative Policy Analysis – Making the Linkage 13
B. Guy Peters and Iris Geva-May

PART 3
The Classics: Theory and Methods in Comparative Policy Analysis Studies
29

1 Comparative Policy Analysis: Déjà Vu All Over Again? 31
 Peter Deleon and Phyllis Resnick-Terry

2 Compared to What? The Multiple Meanings of Comparative Policy Analysis 43
 Beryl A. Radin, & David L. Weimer

3 The Problem of Policy Problems 59
 B. Guy Peters

4 Twenty Years of Comparative Policy Analysis: A Survey of the Field and a Discussion of Topics and Methods — 81
   Iris Geva-May, David C. Hoffman, & Joselyn Muhleisen

5 Comparative Logic Versus Problem Logic? An Introduction — 99
   Monika Steffen

6 Comparing Complex Policies: Lessons from a Public Health Case — 105
   Monika Steffen

7 Understanding Policy Change as an Epistemological and Theoretical Problem — 129
   Giliberto Capano

8 The Dependent Variable Problem in the Study of Policy Change: Understanding Policy Change as a Methodological Problem — 154
   Michael Howlett and Benjamin Cashore

9 Mechanisms of Policy Change: A Proposal for a Synthetic Explanatory Framework — 168
   José Real-Dato

10 The Matching Problem within Comparative Welfare State Research: How to Bridge Abstract Theory and Specific Hypotheses — 195
   Sabina Stiller and Kees van Kersbergen

11 The Dependent Variable Problem within the Study of Welfare State Retrenchment: Defining the Problem and Looking for Solutions — 212
   Christoffer Green-Pedersen

12 Policy Innovations: Towards an Analytic Framework — 224
   Sami Mahroum

13 Exploring the Concept of Governability — 240
   Jan Kooiman

14 The Role and Impact of the Multiple-Streams Approach in Comparative Policy Analysis — 260
   Daniel Béland & Michael Howlett

15 Differences That Matter: Overcoming Methodological Nationalism in Comparative Social Policy Research — 267
   Scott Greer, Heather Elliott, & Rebecca Oliver

16 Europeanization as a Methodological Challenge: The Case of Interest Groups — 289
   Sabine Saurugger

17 How to Construct a Robust Measure of Social Capital: Two Contributions — 311
   Gert Tinggaard Svendsen and Christian Bjørnskov

18	Cultural Theory: The Neglected Variable in the Craft of Policy Analysis *Iris Geva-May*	329
19	Cultures of Public Policy Problems *Robert Hoppe*	349
20	Toward Cultural Analysis in Policy Analysis: Picking Up Where Aaron Wildavsky Left Off *Brendon Swedlow*	368
21	Metachoice in Policy Analysis *Aidan R. Vining and Anthony E. Boardman*	384
22	Introduction: The OECD and Policy Transfer: Comparative Case Studies *Leslie A. Pal*	395
23	Learning Transferable Lessons from Single Cases in Comparative Policy Analysis *Amanda Wolf & Karen J. Baehler*	401
	Index	417

Citation Information

The chapters in this book were originally published in the *Journal of Comparative Policy Analysis*. When citing this material, please use the original page numbering for each article, as follows:

Chapter 1
Comparative policy analysis: Déjà vu all over again?
Peter Deleon, Phyllis Resnick-Terry
Journal of Comparative Policy Analysis, volume 1, issue 1 (September 1998) pp. 9–22

Chapter 2
Compared to What? The Multiple Meanings of Comparative Policy Analysis
Beryl A. Radin, David L. Weimer
Journal of Comparative Policy Analysis, volume 20, issue 1 (2018) pp. 56–71

Chapter 3
The Problem of Policy Problems
Guy B. Peters
Journal of Comparative Policy Analysis, volume 7, issue 4 (December 2005) pp. 349–370

Chapter 4
Twenty Years of Comparative Policy Analysis: A Survey of the Field and a Discussion of Topics and Methods
Iris Geva-May, David Hoffman, Joselyn Muhleisen
Journal of Comparative Policy Analysis, volume 20, issue 1 (2018) pp. 18–35

Chapter 5
Comparative logic versus problem logic? An introduction
Monika Steffen
Journal of Comparative Policy Analysis, volume 7, issue 4 (December 2005) pp. 261–266

Chapter 6
Comparing complex policies: Lessons from a public health case
Monika Steffen
Journal of Comparative Policy Analysis, volume 7, issue 4 (December 2005) pp. 267–290

Chapter 7
Understanding Policy Change as an Epistemological and Theoretical Problem
Giliberto Capano
Journal of Comparative Policy Analysis, volume 11, issue 1 (March 2009) pp. 7–31

Chapter 8
The Dependent Variable Problem in the Study of Policy Change: Understanding Policy Change as a Methodological Problem
Michael Howlett, Benjamin Cashore
Journal of Comparative Policy Analysis, volume 11, issue 1 (March 2009) pp. 33–46

Chapter 9
Mechanisms of Policy Change: A Proposal for a Synthetic Explanatory Framework
José Real-Dato
Journal of Comparative Policy Analysis, volume 11, issue 1 (March 2009) pp. 117–143

Chapter 10
The Matching Problem within Comparative Welfare State Research: How to Bridge Abstract Theory and Specific Hypotheses
Sabina Stiller, Kees van Kersbergen
Journal of Comparative Policy Analysis, volume 10, issue 2 (June 2008) pp. 133–149

Chapter 11
The Dependent Variable Problem within the Study of Welfare State Retrenchment: Defining the Problem and Looking for Solutions
Christoffer Green-Pedersen
Journal of Comparative Policy Analysis, volume 6, issue 1 (April 2004) pp. 3–14

Chapter 12
Policy Innovations: Towards an Analytic Framework
Sami Mahroum
Journal of Comparative Policy Analysis, volume 15, issue 2 (2013) pp. 182–197

Chapter 13
Exploring the Concept of Governability
Jan Kooiman
Journal of Comparative Policy Analysis, volume 10, issue 2 (June 2008) pp. 171–190

Chapter 14
The Role and Impact of the Multiple-Streams Approach in Comparative Policy Analysis
Daniel Béland, Michael Howlett
Journal of Comparative Policy Analysis, volume 18, issue 3 (2016) pp. 221–227

Chapter 15
Differences That Matter: Overcoming Methodological Nationalism in Comparative Social Policy Research
Scott Greer, Heather Elliott, Rebecca Oliver
Journal of Comparative Policy Analysis, volume 17, issue 4 (2015) pp. 408–429

Chapter 16
Europeanization as a methodological challenge: The case of interest groups
Sabine Saurugger
Journal of Comparative Policy Analysis, volume 7, issue 4 (December 2005) pp. 291–312

Chapter 17
How to construct a robust measure of social capital: Two contributions
Gert Tinggaard Svendsen, Christian Bjørnskov
Journal of Comparative Policy Analysis, volume 9, issue 3 (September 2007) pp. 275–292

Chapter 18
Cultural theory: The neglected variable in the craft of policy analysis
Iris Geva-May
Journal of Comparative Policy Analysis, volume 4, issue 3 (November 2002) pp. 243–265

Chapter 19
Cultures of public policy problems
Robert Hoppe
Journal of Comparative Policy Analysis, volume 4, issue 3 (November 2002) pp. 305–326

Chapter 20
Toward cultural analysis in policy analysis: Picking up where Aaron Wildavsky left off
Brendon Swedlow
Journal of Comparative Policy Analysis, volume 4, issue 3 (November 2002) pp. 267–285

Chapter 21
Metachoice in policy analysis
Aidan R. Vining, Anthony E. Boardman
Journal of Comparative Policy Analysis, volume 8, issue 1 (March 2006) pp. 77–87

Chapter 22
Introduction: The OECD and Policy Transfer: Comparative Case Studies
Leslie A. Pal
Journal of Comparative Policy Analysis, volume 16, issue 3 (2014) pp. 195–200

Chapter 23
Learning Transferable Lessons from Single Cases in Comparative Policy Analysis
Amanda Wolf, Karen J. Baehler
Journal of Comparative Policy Analysis, volume 20, issue 4 (2018) pp. 420–434

For any permission-related enquiries please visit:
http://www.tandfonline.com/page/help/permissions

Contributors

Karen J. Baehler is Scholar in Residence in the School of Public Affairs at American University, Washington D.C., USA.

Daniel Béland is the Director of the McGill Institute for the Study of Canada and James McGill Professor in the Department of Political Science at McGill University, Montreal, Canada.

Christian Bjørnskov is a Professor of Economics in the Department of Economics at Aarhus University, Denmark, and an Affiliated Researcher at the Research Institute of Industrial Economics (IFN) in Stockholm, Sweden.

Anthony Boardman is the Van Dusen Professor of Business Administration in the Strategy and Business Economics Division at the University of British Columbia, Vancouver, Canada.

Giliberto Capano serves as co-Editor of the *Journal of Comparative Policy Analysis*. He is a Professor of Political Science and Public Policy at the University of Bologna, Italy. His most recent books are *Making Policies Work* (Edward Elgar 2019), *Designing for policy effectiveness* (Cambridge 2018), and *Changing Governance in Universities* (Palgrave 2016).

Benjamin Cashore is a Professor of Environmental Governance & Political Science at the Yale University's School of Forestry and Environmental Studies, New Haven, USA. He is courtesy joint appointed in Yale's Department of Political Science and is a Senior Research Fellow at Yale MacMillan Center for International and Area Studies. He is the Director of the Governance, Environment and Markets (GEM) Initiative at Yale and is the Joseph C. Fox Faculty Director of the Yale International Fox Fellows Program.

Peter deLeon is a Professor of Public Policy in the School of Public Affairs at the University of Colorado at Denver, USA, and was recently given the honour of Distinguished Professor.

Heather Elliott is an Associate Professor at the University of Alabama School of Law, Tuscaloosa, USA.

Iris Geva-May has been recognized by Thomson Reuters for having pioneered the field of comparative policy analysis since 1998, when she founded the now high indexed *Journal of Comparative Policy Analysis*. She serves as its Founding Editor and the Founding President of the Scholarly Society for International Comparative Policy Analysis (ICPA-Forum). She has published among others *The Logic and Methodology of Policy Analysis, An Operational Approach to Policy Analysis (with Wildavsky), International Library of*

Policy Analysis Series, Routledge Handbook of Comparative Policy Analysis, and *Policy Analysis as a Clinical Profession*. She is Professor Emerita at Simon Fraser University, Vancouver, Canada and currently an Honorary Visiting Professor at SPPA, Carleton University, Ottawa, Canada, and the Wagner School NYU, USA.

Christoffer Green-Pedersen is a Professor of Political Science at Aarhus University, Denmark.

Scott Greer is a Professor of Health Management and Policy, Global Public Health, and Political Science (by courtesy) at the University of Michigan, Ann Arbor, USA.

David C. Hoffman is an Associate Professor at the Marxe School of Public and International Affairs at Baruch College at City University of New York (CUNY), USA.

Robert Hoppe is Emeritus Professor of Policy and Knowledge at the University of Twente, Enschede, the Netherlands.

Michael Howlett serves as co-Editor of the *Journal of Comparative Policy Analysis*. He is Burnaby Mountain Professor and Canada Research Chair (Tier 1) in the Department of Political Science at Simon Fraser University, Vancouver, Canada. His most recent books are *Designing Public Policies* (Routledge 2019) and *Making Policies Work* (Edward Elgar 2019).

Kees van Kersbergen is a Professor in the Department of Political Science at Aarhus University, Denmark.

Jan Kooiman was a Professor of Public Organizations and Management at the Faculty of Business Administration of the Erasmus University Rotterdam, the Netherlands.

Laurence E. Lynn, Jr. is the Founding Co-editor of the *Journal of Comparative Policy Analysis*. He is the Sydney Stein, Jr. Professor of Public Management Emeritus at the University of Chicago, USA. He chaired the Masters in Public Policy Program at Harvard's Kennedy School of Government. He has been a Fellow of the National Academy of Public Administration and of the Council on Foreign Relations, as well as APPAM President. He has been honored by Lifetime Academic Achievement Awards by the American Political Science Association, American Society for Public Administration, and the Public Management Research Association. He published, among others, *Public Management as Art, Science, and Profession* from the Academy of Management, *Oxford Handbook of Public Management*, and (with Hill) *Public Management: Thinking and Acting in Three Dimensions*.

Sami Mahroum is a Professor at the Faculty of Social Sciences and Solvay Business School at the Free University of Brussels, and the Director of Research and Strategy for Dubai Future Labs.

Joselyn Muhleisen serves as the Awards Coordinator for the International Comparative Policy Analysis Forum and the *Journal of Comparative Policy Analysis*. She is a Doctoral Lecturer at the Marxe School of Public and International Affairs, Baruch College, City University of New York (CUNY), USA. She earned her doctorate in political science from The Graduate Center, CUNY, USA. She is the former Assistant Director of the European Union Studies Center, CUNY, USA. She has published work about the development of comparative policy analysis and its relationship to international studies.

Rebecca Oliver is an Assistant Professor of Political Science at Murray State University, USA.

Leslie A. Pal is a Chancellor's Professor in the School of Public Policy and Administration at Carleton University, Ottawa, USA.

CONTRIBUTORS

B. Guy Peters is Maurice Falk Professor of Government at the University of Pittsburgh, USA, and an Honorary Editor of the *Journal of Comparative Policy Analysis*. He is also the Founding President of the *International Public Policy Association* and Editor of the *International Review of Public Policy*. Among his seminal publications are as follows: *Comparative Politics Theory and Methods, Institutional Theory in Political Science, The Politics of Bureaucracy: A Comparative Perspective, An Advanced Introduction to Public Policy*, and *The Next Public Administration*.

Beryl A. Radin is a member of the faculty at McCourt School of Public Policy of Georgetown University in Washington, DC. An elected member of the National Academy of Public Administration, she is the former President of the Association of Public Policy and Management. She also served as a Special Advisor to the Assistant Secretary for Management and Budget of the US Department of Health and Human Services and other agencies. She is the Editor of the Georgetown University Press book series, Public Management and Change, and the author of several books, including *Policy Analysis in the Twenty-First Century: Complexity, Conflict, and Cases; Beyond Machiavelli: Policy Analysis Reaches Midlife*, and *Federal Management Reform in a World of Contradictions*.

José Real-Dato is a Full Professor and teaches Political Science and Public Administration at the Universidad de Almeria, Spain.

Phyllis Resnick-Terry is the Lead Economist for the Colorado Futures Center at the Colorado State University, USA. Additionally, she is an independent consultant with a practice that focuses on economic forecasting, revenue and fiscal sustainability studies for state and local governments, and economic impact studies.

Sabine Saurugger is a Professor of Political Science and Honorary Fellow of the Institut universitaire de France (IUF), and the Dean of Research at Sciences Po Grenoble, France.

Monika Steffen is CNRS Senior Research Fellow (Centre National de la Recherche Scientifique), CERAT-PACTE in the Institut d'Etudes Politiques at Universite Pierre Mendes, Grenoble, France.

Sabina Stiller is a Researcher in the Amsterdam Institute for Advanced Labour Studies at the University of Amsterdam, the Netherlands.

Brendon Swedlow is a Professor in the Department of Political Science at the School of Public and Global Affairs, as well as Faculty Associate at the College of Law & Institute for the Study of the Environment, Sustainability, and Energy at Northern Illinois University, DeKalb, USA.

Gert Tinggaard Svendsen is a Professor of Public Policy in the Department of Political Science at the University of Aarhus, Denmark.

Aidan R. Vining is the Centre for North American Business Studies (CNABS) Professor of Business and Government Relations in the Beedie School of Business at Simon Fraser University, Vancouver, Canada.

David L. Weimer is the Edwin E. Witte Professor of Political Economy at the University of Wisconsin-Madison, USA.

Amanda Wolf is a Senior Lecturer in the School of Government at the Victoria University of Wellington, New Zealand.

Foreword to the Book Series: The Classics of Comparative Policy Analysis

LAURENCE E. LYNN, JR.
Founding co-Editor, *Journal of Comparative Policy Analysis*
Sydney Stein, Jr. Professor of Pubic Management Emeritus
The University of Chicago, USA

The Classics of Comparative Policy Analysis Series is both a record of and a milestone in the development of the theories and methods not only of comparative public policy analysis but, as well, of comparative studies in public affairs-related disciplines and professions, which the *Journal of Comparative Policy Analysis (JCPA)* has advanced. Having been present at the founding of the field of public policy analysis in the 1960s and of comparative policy analysis studies through the *JCPA* in 1998, and having been contributed to a field of research, public governance, which is heavily influenced by comparative perspectives, I am pleased that this series calls attention to the extent to which public affairs research has been influenced by the intellectual ambitions of the kinds of scholarship represented in the four volumes of this series.

Publication of this series of research papers that appeared in volume 20:1 of the *JCPA*, 2018, marks and celebrates the twentieth anniversary of the journal. Selections of classic papers provide not only models for scholars, they are of immense value to teachers in creating reading lists and study assignments. As well, they reinforce awareness of the dimensions and content of a vital field of public affairs research.

Especially welcome are new chapters in each volume authored by the *JCPA* co-editors, highlighting the emerging symbiotic relationships between established disciplines and professions and comparative policy studies. These developments advance the fulfillment of an early intention of the policy analysis movement: promoting the integration of the social sciences in public affairs research. Also important in this regard is the attention in the *Classics of Comparative Policy Analysis* to recent development in research fields, such as policy design and governance, harkening back to the emergence in the original policy analysis movement of implementation studies and program evaluation, with their comparative bent. These newer research studies now appear not only in *JCPA* but in a patulous number of public affairs-oriented academic journals and conference agendas.

It is noteworthy that the *Classics of Comparative Policy Analysis Series* appears in unsettled and unsettling times in national and international affairs. The intellectual developments celebrated in this series have been taking place in a relatively stable and liberal global order. Beginning in the aftermath of World War II, various forms of international cooperation gradually took shape, including regional and the United Nations-sponsored governance and shared sovereignty institutions. This order is now challenged by the seemingly ascendant emergence of nationalism and authoritarianism in many of the world's largest and oldest nations and democracies. These developments threaten the rule of law and the rule of reason, both of which have largely come to be taken for granted in the teaching and research of public affairs-oriented disciplines and professions. Activism and tribalism are competing with analysis and democratic deliberation in the shaping of public policy, and it appears at the expense of fairness and social justice and institutional stability.

But the current political context could also provide opportunities for comparative policy studies. Its scholars have perspectives, models, and methods, as well as the disposition, to study the dynamics of instability, changing institutional and organizational environments and their consequences for policymaking and public administration. For example, researchers on federalism, already informed by comparative studies at subnational levels of governance and international institutions, have the tools to address new questions posed by evolving patterns of governance.

As depicted by Geva-May, Peters, and Muhleisen in their introduction to the series and evident throughout the four volumes, the comparative perspective is producing the kinds of intellectual capital that may be of unique value in policy formulation and design. Lesson drawing is increasingly appropriate in an era of worldwide reinventing of governance. Through the publication of this series, and through papers accepted for publication in future volumes of the *JCPA*, the journal will continue to be a pilot light for imaginative and pathbreaking research that sustains the momentum of the development of comparative policy studies.

Part 1

An Introduction to the Classics of Comparative Policy Analysis Book Series

Why the Classics of Comparative Policy Analysis Studies?

IRIS GEVA-MAY, B. GUY PETERS AND JOSELYN MUHLEISEN

The Classics of Comparative Policy Analysis is a collection of the most representative articles in the *Journal of Comparative Policy Analysis (JCPA)* on its twentieth anniversary. The *JCPA* has "pioneered the domain of comparative policy analysis" studies since 1998[1] and is still the only journal explicitly devoted to promoting comparative policy studies. The articles published in the *JCPA* have become classics in the field of comparative policy analytic studies, and have established it as a distinctive field of study since (Thomson Reuters 2008; Radin 2013; Geva-May, Hoffman and Muhleisen 2018). The papers published over the last two decades in *JCPA* are explicitly comparative and could be viewed as cornerstones of comparative public policy analysis theory, methodology, policy inter-disciplinarity, and inter-regional scholarship. Contributors include founders of the field of policy analysis, comparative politics, and comparative public administration and management from which comparative policy analysis (CPA) has derived: Peter deLeon, Duncan McRae, Laurence E. Lynn, B. Guy Peters, Beryl Radin, David Weimer, Frans Van Nispen, Yukio Adachi, as well as second- and third-generation policy analysis scholars who have set high scholarship bars in advancing the field.

The term "comparative" has normatively been associated with descriptive accounts of national similarities or dissimilarities with respect to content or to features of the public policy process requiring information sharing. At the research level, it has traditionally been concerned with cross-national generalizations or explanations of differences among policies. As the founding editors of the *JCPA* declare in the first volume, "JCPA seeks to go beyond these confines and offer an intellectual arena for analyzing comparative explanatory frameworks and research methods, testing models across spatial structures … and comparing different instruments for achieving similar ends".[2]

The collections of articles included in the volumes of this series support the aim and scope of the *JCPA* to establish points of reference for aspects of comparative policy analytic studies. The four volumes compile, respectively, those foundation articles which contribute to the four main aspects of CPA scholarship advanced by the *JCPA*: (a) Apply or develop comparative methodologies and theories; (b) Investigate valid and reliable means of performing inter-regional or inter-social units comparisons; (c) Investigate the connection among public policy, institutions, and governance factors that can explicate similarities or differences in policymaking; (d) Finally, they focus on the application or utilization of comparative public policy analysis in a variety of policy sectors such as immigration, technology, healthcare, welfare, education, economics, and many others.

Although the chapters included in each volume are classified according to a specific overarching topic, we do find overlaps between, for instance, regional comparisons and methodology or theories, or linkages to institutions as independent variables and policy sectors as dependent variables – thus transcending the single focus of the research presented in each of the volumes.

There is one more aspect that has been explicitly covered neither in the *JCPA* (except for its anniversary Vol 20:1) nor as a separate volume in the present series: the linkages among comparative public policy and the more established fields of comparative politics (political science) and public administration, as well as the newly emerging (or diverging) domains such as governance – from public administration and policy design – from public policy. To open a window to further comparisons among inter-related public domains we introduce a new chapter in Part II of each volume. Authored by the *JCPA* co-editors, the four chapters embrace the notion that the established political science and comparative politics, as well as public administration and comparative public administration, have much to offer to policy studies and to the developing field of CPA studies. It is also noteworthy that the comparative policy analytic studies domain is seen as a source of lesson drawing for the increasing interest in policy design and in governance. The cross-fertilization between these domains can range anywhere between theoretical, conceptual, methodological, and empirical. Identifying points of similarity or difference in enhancing lesson drawing, adaptation, transfer and borrowing, or missed opportunity thereof.

These fundamentals common to all domains of study are addressed by Guy Peters and Geva-May who note down the prospective gift of (comparative) political science to CPA and reciprocal missed opportunities in Volume One; Capano contributes a new chapter on governance, regimes, and comparative public policy in Volume Two; Leslie Pal writes about comparative public administration and comparative public policy in Volume Three; while Howlett addresses the newly emerging branch of policy design and what can be derived from comparative public policy in Volume Four.

In today's politics and policymaking, the reality of global policy convergence, economic competition, and political fads, the cross-national sources of information have proliferated to the extent that any policy analyst, public policy scholar, or policy decision-maker in any given country is bound to be aware of developments that happen in a different "social unit" as Ragin and Zaret (1983) label units of social analysis. Comparisons between social units may be nations or institutions, or points of reference such as policy goals, actor interference, market failures, or intervention in public policy issues of concern. The main reason is lesson drawing in order to maximize utility of policy solutions, avoid failure, or utilize information to seek advantage. Comparative cross-national policy analysis can extend insights, perspectives, or explanations that otherwise would be difficult or impossible to obtain. Lesson drawing (Rose 1991; Geva-May 2004), transfer, borrowing, adoption or adaptations, or sheer inspiration (DeLeon 1998; Geva-May 2002a) increases effectiveness and efficiency, and avoids fallacies. Notwithstanding this stipulation, there is a word of warning: CPA done badly has an immediate effect on the public, and can be financially wasteful or dangerous to the social units and populum immediately involved. Furthermore, it can be detrimental to the credibility of policymaking, as well as to policy analysis as a practical and scholarly domain.

One more contention is that in the *Classics of Comparative Policy Analysis Studies* the terms policy analysis, policy studies, and policy analytic studies are often used by authors interchangeably for a number of reasons: Foremost, because these domains are often similar in their possible points of linkage to the comparative aspects that they cover. Additionally, in today's third generation of policy analysis studies, the borderlines between policy studies, policy design, and policy analysis have frequently blurred and the terminology used has often been transposable. The terms used contain a wider perception of public policy within which domains and sub-domains complement one another despite their very distinct roles. Except for those actually studying or working in these sub-fields, the scholarly work refers to them frequently interchangeably.

We selected the articles in the series not only by thematic relevance and excellence, but also based on how they serve the aim and scope of the *JCPA* (Geva-May and Lynn 1998) which set clear intellectual avenues towards the development of the field beyond the mere prevalent perception of "comparative" as the comparison of two objects – whether institutions or regions. Proven valid enough to have served as scholarly cornerstones in the development of comparative policy studies for two decades, each respective *JCPA* aim drives the focus of each respective volume in the series. **Volume One** presents selections focused on **comparative theory and methodology** development, and comparative **theory testing**: two central aims of the *JCPA*. **Volume Two** addresses **institutions and questions about modes and types of governance** which speaks about the aim of examining the inter-relations between institutions and policy analysis either as dependent or independent variables. **Volume Three** builds on comparative empirical research, as well as lesson drawing and extrapolation, and evaluates comparative research methods through articles on regional policy differences or similarities. **Volume Four** touches on almost all the aims of *JCPA* through studies of specific policy sectors – healthcare, immigration, education, economics, welfare, technology, etc., – particularly allowing for lesson drawing, extrapolation, and possible avoidance of failures within sectors.

Volume One: Theory and Methodology

CPA depends upon the various theoretical and methodological approaches to public policy. The same theoretical perspectives such as the advocacy-coalition framework, multiple-streams models, and agenda-setting are important for understanding national and international policymaking and public policy comparatively. These are applied through lesson drawing and policy transfer, for instance, among others, by Pal (2014), and Wolf and Baehler (2018).

Of particular interest are the linkages of policy theories with various academic disciplines, including economics, political science, sociology, and law, all of which bring their own theoretical perspectives to bear on public policy. Each of the articles included in the first volume demonstrates the need to make difficult theoretical and methodological choices in the study of CPA.

Perhaps the most important aspect of these articles is that the researcher had to make a conscious choice about theory and method, and had to justify those choices. The articles also indicate how they frame policy problems and how they overcome methodological challenges in CPA (Ira Sherkansky 1998; Hoppe 2002; Green-Pedersen 2004; Peters 2005; Saurugger 2005; Stiller and van Kersbergen 2008; Capano 2009; Howlett and Cashore 2009; Greer et al. 2015; among others). In doing so, many address another aim of the *JCPA*: the evaluation of comparative research methods. One way to both evaluate the aptness of research methods and to test theory is to conduct empirical studies. For example, Green-Pedersen contends with the dependent variable problem in the context of social welfare research (Green-Pedersen 2004).

Volume Two: Comparative Policy Analysis and Institutions

"Evidence-based policymaking" is more difficult than sometimes assumed, depending, as it does, on understanding both the dynamics of public policy and the institutional contexts. Despite this difficulty, there has been a surge of interest in policy designed on the basis of "scientifically" demonstrated effectiveness and the ability to identify those successful policies within various structures.

Drawing on the larger institutionalism and governance literatures, many selections in the second volume are concerned with distinct forms of governance and types of political institutions. Governance and institutions are treated both as independent and dependent variables (Weimer and Vining 1998; Ng 2007; Radaelli 2008). The latter make an important distinction between first-order and second-order instruments. The first are those known to policy analysts, the second less transparent depend on features of institutions that "facilitate or constrain" the adoption of first-order policies. The authors contend that in order to make meaningful comparisons, it is important to analyze the usefulness of policy analysis against the analysis of the institutional features that condition policy choice. While public policy scholars and politicians have given increasing attention to new, innovative governance apparatuses, empirical work basically intends to document whether these instruments are effective in specific jurisdictions and institutional contexts and what can be extrapolated from one milieu to another.

One of the chief institutional explanations of policy variation is the nature of political and bureaucratic institutions within which the policies are developed or implemented. CPA has also considered the influence of particular governance arrangements, for example, public-private partnerships on policy outcomes (Vining and Boardamn 2018). But governance structures and institutions are also reflective of the societies, cultures, and polities that constitute them (Hoppe 2002; Geva-May 2002b). Other studies focus on the determinants of certain governance mechanisms, such as privatization (Breen and Doyle 2013), and the impact of the participation of certain societal groups in the policymaking process (Heidbreder 2015). Thus, public policy, institutions, and society are in complex and reciprocal relationships that require a great deal of care to properly disentangle and analyze.

Major themes that underscore several contributions in the volume on institutions and governance will be unsurprising to policy scholars; many selections are especially concerned with effectiveness, efficiency, and mechanisms of compliance (Lee and Whitford 2009; Ross and Yan 2015).

Volume Three: Comparative Inter-regional Policy Analysis Studies

The selections included in this volume make policy comparisons within and across regions. In fact, CPA studies are mostly regarded as comparisons across political systems, whether they are countries, provinces, cities, or another jurisdiction. Likewise, much of the policy analytic research focuses on how policies have fared in specific jurisdictions (Laguna 2011; Saetren 2015) and which factors that contribute to a policy's success can potentially be applied in other contexts.

This mode of analysis brings CPA closer to comparative politics and sociology, and focuses on many of the variables used in the other social sciences to explain observed similarities or differences in the policy choices made by different political systems. The policy choices of federalist systems, for example, are compared by Radin and Boase (2000); Boushey and Luedtke (2006); Sheingate (2009); and Capano (2015). The latter, for instance, compare the Canadian and US federal systems in order to identify similarities and differences between them that explicate the divergence in their social and economic policies. The argument is based on two typologies – Lowi's typology refers to different types of policies, and Deil Wright's typology refers to different models of intergovernmental systems. Here, we also glance at how other theories and related typologies can be applied to CPA across units of comparative analysis.

Focusing on regional comparisons can offer a solid methodological basis for comparative studies by eliminating sources of variation and allowing scholars to isolate more clearly the influence of independent variable(s). To the extent that countries in a region share culture, language, history, or institutional design, inter-regional studies can also target alternate explanations for policy differences. Alternatively, where there is a high degree of policy similarity in very different countries, the existence of a regional power or institution may explain policy convergence. Several studies included in this volume take this approach when considering the phenomenon of Europeanization, for instance, which considers both regional and institutional policy determinants (Mendez et al. 2008; Raedelli 2008; Sarugger 2005). Many contributions compare the policies or policymaking process in a domain across jurisdictions (Ng 2007; Smith and Williams 2007). Other scholars rather focus on tendencies towards regional agglomeration (May et al. 2005) or policy convergence (Clavier 2010).

The *JCPA* has contributed substantially to the body of inter-regional comparative public policy literature and has devoted a number of Special Issues to the topic. This is reflected in the diversity of regions addressed by this volume's selections: Latin America, North America, East Asia, Southeast Asia, Southern Africa, the Baltic states, the Nordic states, Western Europe, Central Europe, Eastern Europe, and Europe as a whole. Dedicated to CPA, the wide range of cases published in the *JCPA*, and the attempt to understand policy and policymaking in many contexts, has served as a major object of interest among authors, readers, and researchers of comparative inter-regional studies.

Volume Four: Comparing Policy Sectors

Our volume on comparative policy sectors focuses on the major areas of strength in the *JCPA*: markets, money and economy, healthcare, welfare, education, migration, and biotechnology policy. These articles explicitly compare policies within policy sectors. The reader can readily identify the marked differences between more technical domains such as technology (Allison and Varone 2009), and more politicized domains such as immigration (Scholten and Timmermans 2010; Geddes and Scholten 2015), healthcare (Marmor et al. 2010), and higher education (Levy and Zumeta 2011).

Many of the articles in this volume deal with comparisons of differences and similarities in various policy disciplines and sectors within and among political systems. For example, Gornick and Heron (2006) compare working time policies across eight European countries, the US, and Japan. Sheingate (2009), on the other hand, compares biotechnology policy decision-making in the European Union and the US, which are treated in his analysis as different styles of federalist regimes.

The absence of papers that explicitly compare *across* policy sectors is noteworthy in the *JCPA*. This is why the *JCPA* anniversary Special Issue Vol. 20:1 and Part One of each volume in this series have been devoted to the comparison of policy, politics, and administration studies. Yet, we still do not find comparative papers between healthcare and immigration, or policy analysis and psychology, or medicine, or law (Geva-May 2005).

To some extent, this phenomenon represents the difficulties of scholars to master the details of any other policy domain, much less several that might be appropriate for comparison. This does not come as a surprise. To cite Gary Freeman (1985), indeed, the differences across domains within a single country would, on average, be greater than differences between the same domain across countries. That was a rather bold claim, but there are some reasons to expect policy domains to be significantly different, and therefore more difficult to compare. For example, some policy domains – such as defense or taxation – tend to be dominated by the government itself, while others – education, social policy – tend to have significant direct influence by citizens. Still other policy domains such as health and technology will be dominated by expert professionals who can reduce some of the role of government in policy. We could add to this list of variables, but the fundamental point remains that the nature of the policy does influence the ways in which policy is made and implemented. That said, differences across political systems do continue to show up in these domains, and it remains crucial for the student and the researcher of CPA to be sensitive to several sources of variation in process and outcomes.

In sum, the four volumes in the *Classics of Policy Analysis Studies* seek to present scholars the most salient work that the *JCPA* has covered in the last two decades and illustrate the multiple levels of study on which we can pursue the intellectual dialogue on comparative public policy. First, the series offers a centralized resource of work that furthers the aims of the new discipline of CPA and the inter-related fields of political science, sociology, and economics. Second, it contributes to the database of knowledge by investigating, applying, or developing theories and methodologies that ensure the validity and reliability of the comparative policy studies. Third, it extends case studies that enrich the ongoing discussions about what can be learned through comparative policy analytic studies to increase efficiency, effectiveness, transparency, and equity in public policy.

We wish the readers of the *Classics of Comparative Policy Analysis Studies* an interesting journey, from which they can adopt, adapt, borrow, transfer, extrapolate, or be inspired for their comparative studies.

Notes

1. Thomson Reuters. (2008). *Whos Who*.
2. Geva-May, I., & Lynn, E. L, Jr. (1998). Comparative policy analysis: Introduction to a new journal. *JCPA*, *1*(1), 1.

References

Allison, C. R., & Varone, F. (2009). Direct legislation in North America and Europe: Promoting or restricting biotechnology? *Journal of Comparative Policy Analysis, 11*(4), 425–449.

Boushey, G., & Luedtke, A. (2006). Fiscal federalism and the politics of immigration: Centralized and decentralized immigration policies in Canada and the United States. *Journal of Comparative Policy Analysis, 8*(3), 207–224.

Breen, M., & Doyle, D. (2013). The determinants of privatization: A comparative analysis of developing countries. *Journal of Comparative Policy Analysis: Research and Practice, 15*(1), 1–20.

Boardman, A. E., Greenberg, D.H., Vining, A.R. & Weimer, D.L. *Cost-Benefit Analysis: Concepts & Practices*, 2018, Cambridge University Press: Cambridge, UK.

Capano, G. (2009). Understanding policy change as an epistemological and theoretical problem. *Journal of Comparative Policy Analysis, 11*(1), 7–31.

Capano, G., Howlett, M., & Ramesh, M. (2015). Bringing governments back in: Governance and governing in comparative policy analysis. *Journal of Comparative Policy Analysis: Research and Practice, 17*(4), 311–321.

Clavier, C. (2010). Bottom–up policy convergence: A sociology of the reception of policy transfer in public health policies in Europe. *Journal of Comparative Policy Analysis, 12*(5), 451–466.

DeLeon, P., & Resnick-Terry, P. (1998). Comparative policy analysis: Déjà vu all over again?, *Journal of Comparative Policy Analysis: Research and Practice*, 1:1, 9–22.

Dunn, W. N. (2008, 2015). *Public Policy Analysis: An Introduction* (4 ed.). Upper Saddle River, NJ: Pearson Prentice Hall.

Freeman, G. P. (1985). National styles and policy sectors: Explaining structured variation. *Journal of Public Policy, 5*(4), 467–496.

Geddes, A., & Scholten, P. (2015). Policy analysis and Europeanization: An analysis of EU migrant integration policymaking. *Journal of Comparative Policy Analysis: Research and Practice, 17*(1), 41–59.

Geva-May, I. (Ed.) (2005). *Thinking Like a Policy Analyst: Policy Analysis as a Clinical Profession*. New York: Palgrave Macmillan.

Geva-May, I. (2002a). Comparative studies in public administration and public policy. *Public Management Review, 4*(3), 275–290.

Geva-May, I. (2002b). From theory to practice: Policy analysis, cultural bias and organizational arrangements. *Public Management Review, 4*(4), 581–591.

Geva-May, I. with Wildavsky, A. (1997, 2001, 2011). *An Operational Approach to Policy Analysis: The Craft: Prescriptions for Better Analysis*. Kluwer Academic Publishers.

Geva-May, I., & Lynn, L. E. Jr. (1998). Comparative Policy Analysis: Introduction to a New Journal. *Journal of Comparative Policy Analysis, 1*(1).

Geva-May, I., Hoffman, D. C., & Muhleisen, J. (2018). Twenty years of comparative policy analysis: A survey of the field and a discussion of topics and methods. *Journal of Comparative Policy Analysis: Research and Practice, 20*(1), 18–35.

Green-Pedersen, C. (2004). The dependent variable problem within the study of welfare state retrenchment: Defining the problem and looking for solutions. *Journal of Comparative Policy Analysis: Research and Practice, 6*(1), 3–14.

Greer, S., Elliott, H., & Oliver, R. (2015). Differences that matter: Overcoming methodological nationalism in comparative social policy research. *Journal of Comparative Policy Analysis: Research and Practice, 17*(4), 408–429.

Heidbreder, E. G. (2015). Governance in the European Union: A policy analysis of the attempts to raise legitimacy through civil society participation. *Journal of Comparative Policy Analysis: Research and Practice, 17*(4), 359–377.

Hoppe, R. (2002). Cultures of public policy problems. *Journal of Comparative Policy Analysis: Research and Practice, 4*(3), 305–326.

Howlett, M., & Cashore, B. (2009). The dependent variable problem in the study of policy change: Understanding policy change as a methodological problem. *Journal of Comparative Policy Analysis, 11*(1), 33–46.

Laguna, M. I. (2011). The challenges of implementing merit-based personnel policies in Latin America: Mexico's civil service reform experience. *Journal of Comparative Policy Analysis, 13*(1), 51–73.

Lee, S. Y., & Whitford, A. B. (2009). Government effectiveness in comparative perspective. *Journal of Comparative Policy Analysis, 11*(2), 249–281.

Leslie A. Pal (2014). Introduction: The OECD and policy transfer: Comparative case studies. *Journal of Comparative Policy Analysis: Research and Practice, 16*(3), 195–200.

Levy, D. C., & Zumeta, W. (2011). Private higher education and public policy: A global view. *Journal of Comparative Policy Analysis: Research and Practice, 13*(4), 345–349.

Marmor, T. R. (2010). Introduction: Varieties of comparative analysis in the world of medical care policy. *Journal of Comparative Policy Analysis, 12*(1–2), 5–10.

May, Peter, Jones B. D., Beem, B. E., Neff-Sharum, E. A. & Poague, M. K. (2005). Regional Policy Agglomeration: Arctic Policy in Canada and the United States, *Journal of Comparative Policy Analysis: Research and Practice,* 7(2), 121–136.

Mendez, C., Wishlade, F., & Yuill, D. (2008). Made to measure? Europeanization, goodness of fit and adaptation pressures in EU competition policy and regional aid. *Journal of Comparative Policy Analysis, 10*(3), 279–298.

Ng, M. K. (2007). Sustainable development and governance in East Asian world cities. *Journal of Comparative Policy Analysis, 9*(4), 321–335.

Peters, G. B. (2005). The problem of policy problems. *Journal of Comparative Policy Analysis, 7*(4), 349–370.

Radaelli, C. M. (2008). Europeanization, policy learning, and new modes of governance. *Journal of Comparative Policy Analysis, 10*(3), 239–254.

Radin, B. A. (2013). *Beyond Machiavelli: Policy Analysis Reaches Midlife.* Georgetown University Press.

Radin, B., & Boase, A. (2000). Federalism, political structure, and public policy in the United States and Canada, *Journal of Comparative Policy Analysis: Research and Practice, 2*(1), 65–89.

Ragin, C. C. (1994). Introduction to qualitative comparative analysis. *The Comparative Political Economy of the Welfare State, 299*, 300–309.

Ragin, C. and Zaret, D. (1983) Theory and Method in Comparative Research: Two Strategies. *Social Forces, 61* (3), 731–754.

Rose, R. (1991). What is lesson-drawing? *Journal of Public Policy, 11*(1), 3–30.

Ross, T. W., & Yan, J. (2015). Comparing public–private partnerships and traditional public procurement: Efficiency vs. flexibility. *Journal of Comparative Policy Analysis: Research and Practice, 17*(5), 448–466.

Rothmayr Allison, C., & Varone, F. (2009). Direct legislation in North America and Europe: Promoting or restricting biotechnology?. *Journal of Comparative Policy Analysis, 11*(4), 425–449.

Saurugger, S. (2005). Europeanization as a methodological challenge: The case of interest groups. *Journal of Comparative Policy Analysis, 7*(4), 291–312.

Scholten, P., & Timmermans, A. (2010). Setting the immigrant policy agenda: Expertise and politics in the Netherlands, France and the United Kingdom. *Journal of Comparative Policy Analysis, 12*(5), 527–544.

Sheingate, A. D. (2009). Federalism and the regulation of agricultural biotechnology in the United States and European Union. *Journal of Comparative Policy Analysis, 11*(4), 477–497.

Smith, A. J., & Williams, D. R. (2007). Father-friendly legislation and paternal time across Western Europe. *Journal of Comparative Policy Analysis, 9*(2), 175–192.

Stiller, S., & van Kersbergen, K. (2008). The matching problem within comparative welfare state research: How to bridge abstract theory and specific hypotheses. *Journal of Comparative Policy Analysis: Research and Practice, 10*(2), 133–149.

Thomson Reuters (2008). Iris Geva-May, *Who's Who.*

Vining, A. R., & Weimer, D. L. (1998). Informing institutional design: Strategies for comparative cumulation. *Journal of Comparative Policy Analysis, 1*(1), 39–60.

Wolf, A., & Baehler, K. J. (2018). Learning transferable lessons from single cases in comparative policy analysis. *Journal of Comparative Policy Analysis: Research and Practice, 20*(4), 420–434.

Part 2
Lesson Drawing Relationships: Comparing Associated Disciplines and Comparative Policy Analysis

Two Ships in the Night: Comparative Politics and Comparative Policy Analysis – Making the Linkage

B. GUY PETERS AND IRIS GEVA-MAY

This chapter embraces the notion that political science and especially the comparative politics domain have much to offer to policy studies and the developing field of comparative policy analysis studies.[1,2] Their respective characteristic contribution and cross-fertilization can range anywhere between theoretical, conceptual, methodological, or empirical. Identifying points of similarity or difference for lesson drawing, adaptation, transfer and borrowing, or missed opportunity thereof is at the heart of comparative studies and applies as much for political science as to public policy and policy comparisons in the public domain. At times we will use political science and politics interchangeably as relating to the same field. The same is the case for comparative policy studies and policy analysis.

Comparative Policy Analysis and Linkages to Other Comparative Domains

The need for a strong linkage between points of relevance in political science, or the comparative study of politics and government, and the comparative analysis of public policy should be obvious to even those not involved in these fields of inquiry. Policies are made by governments and within institutions with administrative and bureaucratic power. Those policies may be influenced by, and implemented by, a host of private sector actors (see Vining and Weimer, 1998, 2015; Donahue and Zeckhauser, 2011; Torfing et al., 2011), but in the end the responsibility for public policy resides in the public sector. And perhaps most fundamentally politics is, as Harold Lasswell famously argued, ultimately about "who gets what", and public policies are the action through which governments and their allies in the private sector determine who gets what. In this context, one of the tenets of policy analysis is to start with mapping the actors ("who") and their politics, and provide systematically obtained policy alternatives ("what") which would be feasible given who the actors are. The interconnection between knowledge of actors and policy analysis outputs is obvious to any seasoned policy analyst, considering policy recommendations with any chances of being adopted and implemented. Have these dimensions and others been compared and cross-shared between political science and policy analysis/studies? In this chapter we will try to identify the relevant possible answers.

Although the linkage between the above two dimensions of comparative analysis (who gets what) may be obvious to more casual observers, they do not appear to always be quite so obvious to professionals in either academic camp – comparative politics and comparative policy analysis. At one point in the development of these disciplines and/or sub-disciplines, there was a close linkage between policy and comparative politics. For example, there has been a huge literature on the Welfare State, comparing the development of this collection of policies across time and countries.[3] Likewise, much of the early quantitative analysis of public policies was comparative, but limited to states and cities in a number of countries. In this respect the Journal of Policy Analysis , has opened the door since 1998 to additional points at issue such as, comparative development or application of of methodologies and theories, comparisons within disciplinary sectors, and significance of institutions and governments for policy making.

The fundamental argument of this chapter is that these forms of comparative analysis have drifted apart, and that the separation, albeit not final divorce, of these strands of research has weakened both (for a more optimistic view, see Tosun and Workman, 2018). Given that this paper is intended for readers of a policy and policy analysis volume, there will be more discussion of strands of research in comparative politics that should and could have more to say about public policy and policy analysis, and which should be valuable in these domains, as well. Scholars of policy cannot be absolved entirely when attempting to explain this separation.

Much of this paper will be critical, and may appear excessively so, and some of the generalizations made may appear far too sweeping for such large fields of research. The purpose of these sweeping generalizations is to emphasize the points being made, and not to denigrate the research that is the exception to the generalizations. Even with the counter examples for the most extreme cases, we do believe the basic characterizations of these literatures are correct and are useful for understanding how comparative politics and policy analysis/studies interact, or do not.

Also, these ships passing in the night are not the only ones in the social sciences. Perhaps as a product of increased specialization and the massive literatures in each sub-field, the opportunities for cross-fertilization across academic fields are being missed on a regular basis. Even within political sciences, take, for instance, the separation between American politics and comparative politics which appears to make an artificial separation and to diminish both fields. The same is true for comparative politics, and comparative public policy and policy analysis.

Approaches to Comparative Politics and the Relationship to Policy

The development of theory in comparative politics has been characterized by concentration on a number of alternative explanations for political phenomena. Some of compared phenomena in politics have been persistent forms of explanation, while others represent more fad and fashion. But for each we can ask to what extent the approach does, and could, provide explanations for political phenomena. Although there are some exceptions, the general observation one must make is that these theoretical approaches have generally been little concerned with public policy, even though they would certainly have had the capacity to provide some explanations had the scholars involved been more interested in making those connections. What are these common points of reference?

Institutionalism and Public Policy

Beginning with Aristotle, the study of institutions has been central to the study of comparative politics. Much of the early versions of comparative politics and comparative public administration were focused on the description of regimes and their respective organizational templates, institutions in formal and legal terms, with an assumption that what was written down in constitutions would actually happen in practice (see Apter, 1991). With the rebirth of this approach in the new institutionalism (March and Olsen, 1984; Peters, 2018), there is no reliance on formal structures to define institutions. That said, however, there is still no linkage with the outcomes of politics, i.e. policies, as might be expected, which would be desirable for both comparative politics and policy studies.

Much of the contemporary literature on institutionalism deals with internal compliance of the members of the institution and ways in which decisions are made rather than with the outputs of the institution, i.e. policies. For example, the original version of "New Institutionalism" (March and Olsen, 1984) argued that individual members of an institution would behave according to a "logic of appropriateness" that they learned as they were socialized into the institution. That logic of appropriateness may address some issues of the mission of the institution, and what tasks it should (must) perform but the fundamental issue is compliance. While public policy sees institutions as producers of policies, they do not borrow from political science the various aspects of institutionalism in analyzing and designing policies.

Rational choice versions of institutions (Shepsle, 2006), on the other hand, tend to be concerned with how decisions are made within the institution. For example, the logic of veto points (Tsebelis, 2002) is that the more steps that a decision must go through within an institution, or within a set of institutions, the less likely there is to be a positive outcome. Fritz Scharpf (1988) similarly notes that institutions with multiple veto players tend to make decisions, if at all, by the lowest common denominator. Although rarely taken up in policy studies or comparative policy analytic studies, this veto point argument is very similar to the clearance point argument that Pressman and Wildavsky (1974) made about policy implementation. In short, the designers of political institutions and policy scholars should be very careful because those structures shape to some degree the choices made within them.

The rational choice literature on institutions says little about the substance of the decisions being made, but focuses primarily on the capacity of institutions to make innovative decisions, the speed of making decisions, and the stability of the decisions once made. The "oversight" of ignoring policy choices is baffling given that ultimately choices pertain to the actions these institutions produce and assign, that is, the policies that are developed, recommended, or implemented by or within them. Considerations such those raised by Tsbelis and by Scharp (1997) are important points of reference in the selection of policy solutions that would be compatible with the institutional voting, towards the legitimation of policy recommendation and implementation. Elinor Ostrom (1990) and her colleagues (Cole and McGinnis, 2014) work on designing institutions, or allowing institutions to evolve, is an exception in that it has focused on a variety of common pool resources such as water, fish, and natural resources, touching on policymaking, and how to overcome collective action problems such as the tragedy of the commons.

One major exception to the above generalizations about the lack of concern by institutionalism with public policy can be found in historical institutionalism. Although the discussions of historical institutionalism is largely in terms of structure, the major content of studies in this tradition are of specific policies. Beginning with Peter Hall's discussion of the persistence of economic policies, the basic argument has been that policies persist (Hall, 1993). Whether this is because of simple inertia or the positive feedback that the programs create for both ordinary citizens and political elites (Pierson,

2000), policies do tend to survive (Geva-May 2001). These arguments have been replicated by policy scholars as regards the difficulties to propose or implement "termination" policy solutions when policies become obsolete, wasteful, or dangerous. That said, the historical institutionalist literature often contains a conflation of institution and policy, with institutions largely being defined as a policy rather than as a political structure distinct from that policy, and policy studies remaining within the boundaries of the domain without reference to institutionalism.

Another important contrary example was the Weaver and Rockman book (1993; see also Pal and Weaver, 2003), asking the very basic question of whether differences in institutions do make a difference in policies. While they only examined a narrow range of institutional differences – presidential versus parliamentary governments – this analysis is important for linking institutional differences to policy – in contrast to much of the comparative politics literature on presidentialism (Linz, 1990; Chaisty, Cheeseman and Power, 2014) that looks primarily at the effects on the stability of regimes.[4]

Much of the institutional literature in comparative politics that deals with presidents and prime ministers concentrates on the political dynamics of those institutions. For example, there is a massive literature on how coalitions are formed, maintained, and then dissolved (see Müller and Strom, 2003). In that literature public policy represents a potential means of bargaining among political actors, but there is little interest in what actually happens in policy terms as a result of the coalition politics, or whether the policy will materialize and resolve a policy problem at street level (Peter Hupe, 2019) and policy choices. In this case the degree of congruence of the formal and informal institutions of governance defines the capacity to make and implement policies, as well as to some extent the content. And perhaps more importantly this literature can link policy and institutions more broadly with patterns of governance in contemporary states.

But what would we expect the comparative study of institutions to tell us about public policy. At the simplest level the differences between types of institutions such as presidential and parliamentary governments should produce different types of policies. Those differences may not be in the details of policy but perhaps in more general patterns, e.g., policy styles (see below). Likewise, understanding the ideational content of institutions may be able more precisely to explain the policy choices made by institutions (see Beland and Cox, 2013). Institutions are the carriers of ideas and may indeed be ideas converted into structures (Berman, 2013). Indeed, outside the scope of comparative politics there is an increasing literature in public policy which deals with the cultural bias inherent in policy analysis and policymaking and dictated by the values, norms, and risk perceptions within the individual institutions, or social units within and outside governments.

Recommendations of "stepping stones for implementation" incorporated in policy alternatives, or the design of a policy in support of the implementation of policy solution add another important potential linkage between the comparative politics literature on institutions and public policy (Pressman and Widawsky, 1974; Geva-May with Wildavsky, 1997; Geva-May, 2019; Ingram, 1990). While we may be able to design a wonderful policy in the abstract, attempting to do so without recognizing the role that institutions will play in the adoption and especially the implementation of the policy is likely to be unsuccessful. Likewise, any academic attempting to understand policy formulation without reference to institutional framework of these policies is also likely to be disappointed.

Interest Intermediation and Public Policy

A second major strand of theorizing in comparative politics has been focused on patterns of linkage between social actors and the public sector. The dominant strand of theorizing of this type was corporatism (Rokkan, 1967; Schmitter, 1974) then followed by the spread of network models of governance and policymaking (Sorensen and Torfing, 2007). These several varieties of theorizing, along with pluralist models in the Anglo-American systems (Lowi, 1972; McFarland, 200x), have all ascribed an important role to interest groups in the processes of governing and policymaking, albeit conceptualizing those roles very differently. Although the heyday of interest in corporatism has largely passed, there is still substantial interest in the ideas of corporatism and pluralism and the manner in which they affect governance (Oberg et al., 2011). In addition, the network model has become very central in thinking about governance processes and the ways in which social actors are engaged in governing. In all these approaches to comparative politics social actors are crucial for shaping policies these groups bargain and engage in political conflict in order to shape the content of policies.

Despite the importance of interest groups and their role in governing, the linkages between political science and public policy have not been as strong as might be expected. For example, although much of the corporatist literature was based on the involvement of social actors in policy processes, referred to in policy studies as stakeholders, often it did not take the next step of seeing if that involvement actually mattered. That often appeared more assumed than investigated directly. Policy studies literature, whether policy analysis, evaluation, or design, gives particular emphasis on stakeholders involvement and acceptance of policies (Weiss 1983; Geva-May and Wildavsky 1997; Geva-May 2020). This literature has not been taken up by comparative politics, and the knowledge cross-fertilization appears to have been unambiguously missed.

One of the major exceptions to that generalization was the "micro-corporatism" literature that examined policy processes at a very local level and often did track the influence of groups on choices – often at the implementation stage. The other major exception to that generalization is the pluralist literature that has focused on the role that big business and the wealthy have had on policy. This was central to Lowi's work and has gained new prominence as levels of inequality in industrialized societies have continued to increase. But much of the pluralist work has been on the United States and ignored the effects of different forms of interest intermediation on policy choices.

As the interest intermediation literature has morphed from corporatist and pluralist conceptions to network, and a significantly greater concern with public policy and indeed with comparative policy. The failure of much of the work on the role of interest groups to address substantive policy issues more explicitly is very unfortunate. There are a number of obvious hypotheses about the effects of groups and group access on policy that could have been asked. Again, the process questions were asked and answered very effectively, but the effects on the substance of policy was not traced very effectively. For example, did the openness of corporate pluralist systems to a wide range of ideas and influences improve the quality of the decisions made, or was this important primarily for democratic reasons? And did the tripartite bargaining associated with economic policy under corporatism create policy choices that were significantly different from those which might have been made using economic experts? On the other hand, while the policy process is interesting and important, it does not answer many questions about the substance of policy which are key in policy studies and policy analysis. Thus, although public policy analysis considers interest groups in the analytic process and formulation of policies, it has not reached out to pluralist conceptions to network to borrow or adapt.

Development Studies and Public Policy

Another major strand of research in comparative politics has been the study of political development, including a large number of studies of democratization. In some ways the development literature taken broadly has had a strong policy focus, especially concerned with how to move societies from one level of development to another. Some of the development questions have been at a large societal level, while others have been at a very local level, examining the effects of a new well-being on local economic life and the status of women in local society, for example.

The literature on political development, however, has had somewhat less concern with policy choices, other than major choices about economic policy (which may be imposed by donors). There has been some concern with the development of policymaking capacity in transitional countries, but relatively little on the choices that are made and the success of the choices. In particular, much of the development literature – especially that in fragile states – tends to ignore the role of public bureaucracies in implementing policy, while the comparative aspect of implementation is key for effectiveness and efficiency of policies driving the success, or lack thereof, in development studies.

Governance and Public Policy

Governance has become an important approach to comparative politics, although perhaps more in Europe than in North America (see Pierre and Peters, 2000; Peters and Pierre, 2016). While the meaning of the term governance has been the subject of significant debate the most fundamental research question is determining how, and how well, societies are capable of steering themselves towards collective goals. We tend to think of the State and its policies, as being the major actor in that governance, but there are also important private sector actors involved in the process.

Given that governance is concerned with the capacity to set goals, formulate policies, and then implement those policies (Peters and Pierre, 2016), the governance literature should have a great deal of relevance for comparative public policy. Indeed, the conception of process within some governance models is extremely similar to the process models that exist in policy studies and policy analysis solution predictions, as is the concept of goal specification and attainment through policy analysis or design. The governance approach to comparative politics, however, does tend to consider an array of factors in those processes, and mainly focus on general patterns of steering than on specific pieces of policy.

While the typical discussion may assume that governance is the independent variable and public policy is the dependent variable, the reverse may be equally true. That is, how can public policy build the capacity to govern? The most obvious example is the success of the mixed-economy Welfare State in Europe and the increased legitimacy and governance capacity of these governments (see Scharpf, 2010). This discussion of governance capacity is closely related to the very long-term discussion of effectiveness and legitimacy for governments, and the capacity to use effective public policies for state building (see Lipset, 1959).

If in the 1960s "speaking truth to power" (Wildavsky, 1998, 2017) was referring to providing policy solutions to government level actors in support of effective and efficient governance, the third-generation policy analysis has diverted supporting the structures and mission of social units other than the government: agencies, public institutions, NGOs, and so on. Yet, the same themes and concerns run across the smaller pieces of policymaking, analysis, formulation, and design within the smaller "social units". What can be derived from the two different scopes of politics and policy studies, for one another, may be a missed opportunity in lesson drawing for both.

Comparative Political Economy and Public Policy

One reason for the divergence of comparative politics and comparative policy analysis/studies is the growth of interest in comparative political economy. If one picks any book on comparative political economy or any syllabus for a course on that topic, the proximity to policy studies can be seen readily. There are questions about the roots of economic policy and also at times the foundations of social policies. Although there are a range of research questions in this field, the principal concerns have been on the effects of economic policies on economic growth and also the effects of economic policy on inequality. And sometimes the direction of causality is reversed, and there are studies of how openness to trade, for example, affects policy choices (Rogowski, 1987).

What differentiates this body of literature from comparative policy studies? Perhaps the simplest is nothing except the label. But at another level there are some important differences. Perhaps the most important difference is the level of interest in, and detailed analysis of, specific public policies. Most comparative political economy studies adopt rather broad conceptualizations of a policy and are not concerned with the details that might engage the interest of a student of public policy. But, while some policy scientists might consider that the manner in which political economy deals with policy borders on the superficial, political economists are able to provide some interesting explanations for the linkage of policies and outcomes.

Public Policy Studies and the Role of Comparative Politics

Although we have been placing much of the onus for the absence of stronger and more fruitful connections between comparative politics and policy studies on the students and scholars of comparative politics, policy studies have not been blameless. The most obvious component of this blame is not the failure to consider context in much of the basic research and theorizing about public policy, especially in the subfields of policy analysis, design, and formulation. For example, much of the discussion of policy instruments and policy design is relatively context-free, and assumes (implicitly if not explicitly) that instruments are essentially the same no matter where they are employed. However, some instruments may simply be unavailable in some settings, e.g., authority-based instruments depend on the legitimacy of the government that is attempting to utilize them while these instruments may be of little use in poor countries. A relatively significant difference is in the policy analysis process. A primary requirement for any policy analysis is the mapping of the context of the policy problem. Notwithstanding, the first generation of policy analysis devoted less emphasis on the setting where the policy problem occurred. The stages approach to policy analysis were mostly presented as applicable in any context. This might be the reason why, despite its obvious contribution to policy making, it has taken more than a decade to adopt (or rather, adapt) this domain of study to the North of the US, in Canada, or across the Atlantic, in Europe.

Perhaps even more egregious is the manner in which the policy cycle models and their components are used without much attention to context as if that process were the same in almost any setting. This has been central to political science discussions of public policy (Jann and Wegrich, 2007). While that may be true in some stylized manner, certainly the involvement of actors and the relative importance of various stages will vary across systems. For an extreme example, the policy process in authoritarian regimes will not be nearly as concerned with issues of legitimation of policies, or the openness of the policy agenda to new ideas, as will be process in democratic regimes. Indeed, much of the policy process literature is written with an assumption of something like a functioning democracy (but see Truex, 2014).

Another large body of literature in public policy studies has been concerned with policy transfer or policy diffusion (Marsh and Sharman, 2009; but see Karch, 2006; Hadjisky, Pal and Walker, 2017). While at the borderline of comparative studies, this literature is almost by definition transnational, it has not always been as comparative as it might have been intended. There has been somewhat greater concern with the characteristics of policies that can facilitate successful diffusion than there has been on the characteristics of political systems that can make the transfer work.[5] Again, there are notable exceptions. The scope of comparative policy analytic studies is to mostly enhance inter- and intra-social units comparisons from which lessons can be drawn. By definition, this implies that on analysis of selected variables – policy parameters, causality and effect assessment, context, and actors investigation – degrees of dissemination and transfer do have to take place (Geva-May and Lynn, 1998; see also Rose 1993).

But to return to a discussion of comparative politics and public policy, it is also remarkable the extent to which studies of the policy process (to the extent that they have actually existed within this comparative politics) have addressed at all the models of policy coming out of policy studies. For example, the Advocacy Coalition Framework has been used in a number of countries to describe and to explain policy change, but most of this work has been country by country, policy by policy rather than examining the comparative dimension of the analysis.[6] The same is the case with the Policy Streams model (Kingdon, 1984; Geva-May 2004), of which one stream is the political one, and which is widely utilized in policy studies, but has received meagre, if any, attention in comparative politics.

Best Practice

Lest this essay appear totally negative, we should also mention some examples of work on comparative policy and comparative politics that have made significant advances in integrating the concerns of these two field of research. Some studies of comparative public policy have attempted to integrate political factors directly into the analysis of policy, and to make the linkages with existing strands of theory in comparative politics, or to develop theory based on some extension policy concerns.

Several major research projects also have integrated public policy and comparative political analysis directly. Perhaps the best example is the Comparative Agendas Project (Baumgartner, Green-Pedersen and Jones, 2006). This body of work began in the United States (Baumgartner and Jones, 1983) but the ideas and methods of research have now been diffused to a large number of countries around the world. Further, in this research project, the concern with public policy is central to the research questions, and with the diffusion, the results coming from the project are directly comparative.

The study of policy styles is another example of research that has explicitly attempted to link patterns of policymaking with comparative politics (see Richardson, 1982; Howlett and Tosun, forthcoming).[7] The policy styles are a product of active versus reactive policymaking, and consensus versus imposition policymaking. Instead of examining specific policy choices, this research has attempted to explain patterns of response to policymaking challenges. For example, policy in Germany (Dyson, 1982) is described as a search for a rationalist consensus. While it can be argued that developing a sweeping characterization of policymaking in a country ignores many nuances, it does link factors in comparative politics directly with policy choices.

Another example of best practice in linking comparative public policy and comparative politics to be mentioned here (there are of course others) is the study of the Welfare State. This is a huge and rich comparative literature beginning in the 1960s (Esping Andersen, 1990). But it is also important to consider how and when the economic and political foundations of the Welfare State began to be challenged, there was a revival in this literature focusing on reform and the politics of reform (see Stiller and van Kersbergen, 2008). With its expansion beyond its original heartland in Western Europe, the study of the Welfare State provided comparable models in Asia and Latin America (Huber and Stephens, 2012; Holliday, 2000).

In the last two decades, *the Journal of Comparative Policy Analysis* has been a hub for comparative policy scholarship reporting on numerous studies and comparative statistics. Many of these are explicitly or implicitly involve comparative methods, theories, or references to the politics of policy analysis, policy design, policy implementation, or policymaking.

In all these examples, and there could be more, characteristics of political systems are linked directly to policy choices being made. These examples focus less on micro-level behaviors of individuals and more on structural or even cultural characteristics of political systems (Geva-May and Drake, forthcoming, 2020). As such they are less based on agency than on structure for the explanations of policy, although certainly agency could be introduced.

Explaining the Low Level of Connection between Comparative Politics and Comparative Public Policy

The discussion above has gone through a number of areas of comparative politics and public policy, and has made a number of rude and hyperbolic comments about them. In this section of the paper we will attempt to understand why this seemingly natural alliance between the two areas of research has been so weak, with the two fields often not appearing to know that they could benefit by the alliance. While some of the failures to connect more effectively may be a function simply of the ignorance of the other field, there may be more compelling academic reasons as well.

Coming from the perspective of policy studies, a significant share of this literature focused on the processes by which policies are made. This may be the conventional stages model of policy (Palumbo, 1987), or it may be more theoretical perspectives such as the advocacy coalition (Jenkins-Smith et al., 2018) or policy streams (Kingdon, 1984) frameworks or the stages approach to policy analysis (De Leon, 1999; Geva-May with Wildavsky, 1997; Geva-May, 2020; Bardach, 2018), but however conceptualized, the process is central to much of policy studies. On the other hand, contemporary political science has had difficulty in dealing with process. Most of research in the discipline relates to and attributes to individuals or institutions or the environment to some dependent variable, and tends to ignore the process through which those connections occur.[8]

Methodological Individualism and Public Policy

Even with the resurgence of institutional analysis in comparative politics, the dominant intellectual approach in political science in general and comparative politics in particular is individualistic. The dominant approaches of rational choice and various forms of behavioralism all focus on the behavior of individuals rather than on collective actors. On the one hand, this is very appropriate, given that individuals make decisions within those collectivities. To argue otherwise would be to anthropomorphize organizations and institutions. But on the other hand, as March and Olsen (1987) and other institutionalists have argued, it may be difficult to understand the behavior of individuals without understanding the organizational matrix within which they are embedded. And for policy scholars this individual behavior often creates collective action problems that will require policy interventions which policy analysis "creates"[9] and extends.

The role of institutions and organizations should be especially important for understanding public policy. Policy analysis gives particular attention to the "context" or environment within the problem situation occurs and where the problem solution through action, i.e. policy, is required. As Charles Goodsell (2011) and others have pointed out, organizations are vessels that hold ideas and that use those ideas to influence the behavior of their members. In theoretical terms, this role of ideas within organizations is most apparent in historical institutionalism (see above), but can be found in a wide range of studies of public policy. Thus, policymakers are not atomistic actors pursuing their own goals, guided by their own opinions, but are having their views and behaviors shaped by their institutions. In turn, institutions and organizations, or "social units" are shaped by the policies that they produce.

To the extent that contemporary comparative politics is concerned with public policy, it has been mainly interested in the attitudes of citizens and their policy preferences (see Dalton, 2014). Especially in democratic regimes these preferences are inherently important, but they do not go very far in explaining what policies may actually be selected and what happens when they are implemented. We know that there are many slippages in the process that links popular preferences, voting and policy outcomes, but there has been relatively little analysis of these linkages in the comparative politics literature.[10] Take for instance Puttman (1993) who examines institutions in terms of political cultural biases and the characteristics of regimes but does not specifically make the linkage to the policies Italian governments create.

Following from the above, for much of contemporary comparative politics, public policy is more relevant as an independent variables than as a dependent variable, that is, politics affect the type of policy created. For example, as well as attempting to understand policy choices, comparative political economy also examines the influence of policies (and their consequences) on domestic politics. Likewise, policy choices tend to mobilize interest groups or social movements and may also feed back into agenda-setting processes within government.[11]

Comparative Methodologies and Comparative Policy

As well as the issues of the substantive focus of research, changes in methodologies have tended to push public policy out of comparative politics. While there are any number of excellent large-N quantitative studies of public policy that have been done comparatively (see, for example, the discussion in Amenta and Hicks, 2010), policy studies often appear to require very detailed qualitative analyses of process and the impacts of policy choices as shown in the *JCPA* publications (1998–2019). Policy studies require the triangulation of methods and types of tools in order to validate and explicate quantitative findings. Therefore, the comparative method as described by Lijphart (1971; but see Gupta, 2012) that utilizes case selection as the fundamental source of experimental variance, and control of extraneous variance, appears especially well suited for the study of public policy. Given that a good deal of comparative policy research uses a small number of cases, the careful selection of those cases can enhance the power of the analysis.

It is to some extent the nature of policy studies that any selection of cases must be made on the basis of the policies adopted in that country. If a country does not have policy X, then there is little chance to study it (except as a negative case of something that should have happened but did not (see Mahoney and Goertz, 2004). This style of research approaches sampling on the dependent variable, which some comparative scholars tend to treat as an "inferential felony" (Geddes, 1994). Some may argue that case selection is not as relevant for policy studies as for comparative politics, and hence making comparative inferences is much less possible. Thus, one could maintain that comparative policy studies may be limited simply by the nature of policy choices made in different settings. Policy scholars would disagree that most of the comparative policy analytic studies are case studies, i.e., whether cases from which inferences or lesson drawing can be extrapolated, or comparisons between components of the policy process and their respective treatment can be policy goals, policy solutions, policy interventions, policy implementation facilitation, and others.

Despite the development of qualitative methodologies (see Thomann, 2017) that can work effectively with bodies of data larger than the usual case study, much of comparative politics remains focused on the use of statistical methods. As noted above, there is a good deal of comparative policy analysis that employs those same statistical methods, but a much larger promotion of policy research utilizes qualitative methods, or both, as part as the tenet of evidence-based policy analysis supporting transparent and accountable policymaking. In large part because policy analysis is client(s), actors, oriented and thus it is imperative to trace carefully the ways in which participants in the policy process interact in the making and execution of often complex public policies.

The good news from the methodological front is that the increased interest in experiments as a method of research may help to pull together policy studies and comparative politics. Nevertheless, although policy experiment and control groups have been rarely utilized in policy research because detrimental outcomes would affect a large population, this trend is slowly changing (for instance, see JCPA, Vol 22, Special Issue on Policy Experimentation).[12] Leaving aside the important questions of external validity, experimental methodologies have become a means of research with stronger claims for assessing causation than are available for many statistical methodologies. And especially for field experiments, there may be a greater capacity to include policy context directly in the analysis. Experiments may not be capable of the fine-grained analysis of process (and causation) that can come from methods such as process-tracing, but they do offer a possible comparative route undertaken in both domains.

Summary and Conclusions

As forecasted at the beginning, this article has been rather critical and pointed to a number of problems in the connections, or lack of connections, between comparative politics and comparative public policy. Although comparative politics and comparative policy studies might be seen to be natural allies in understanding how governments make and implement policies, in reality these areas of research have been characterized by indifference or occasionally hostility. And in passing we must also comment that the same has been true of comparative politics and comparative public administration or comparative public administration and comparative policy studies.

The more important question may be how to move these areas of inquiry closer together, given that they can both benefit from such a rapprochement. There is no magic solution for this problem for both areas of study, but just some rather straightforward attempts on the part of both camps to engage the other would help. The *Journal of Comparative Policy Analysis* provides one forum for the increased interaction of these two camps of scholars, and the increased internationalization of policy studies is also assisting in this effort. We can only hope that the potential for greater mutual recognition and involvement will be fulfilled.

Notes

1 Originated in the United States due to developments that took place in the early 1960s, policy analysis has become a field of social scientific inquiry, whose main rationale has been to support the tenets of democratic societies through systematic, evidence- based, transparent, efficient, and accountable policy making. Policy analysis was meant to "Speak Truth to Power," in the words of Wildavsky (1978, 2017), that is, provide evidence based solutions to immediate policy problems and advise those making policy decisions. While much of the evidence sought in policy analysis relies on an investigation of aspects such as institutional or political suitability not much has been transferred in theoretical terms, from political science or public administration in the "doing" of policies through policy analysis and design.
2 In ancient Greek "Analysis" means *breaking down into components*. The policy analysis process is fundamentally seen in literature as comprising of a number of core iterative stages and elements and relating to a myriad of interdisciplinary fields. In its search for policy problem solutions which are evidence based it is understood that it would reach out to information normatively found in other domains of study such as public administration, political science, governance and so on.; (Dunn, 1995; deLeon, 1997; Geva-May with Wildavsky, 1997; Bardach, 2011).
3 While that literature is far from dead, being animated in part by the numerous threats to the continuation of the Welfare State as we know it (see Van Kersbergen and Vis and Hemerijck, 2014) it is by no means as central in either comparative politics or policy analysis as it once was.

That said, there has been some geographical expansion of interest in the Welfare State, notably in Asia (Holliday, 2000).
4 This is hardly an unimportant question: by examining differences among presidential systems and the effects of institutional choice, what could be gained is also an understanding of the effects on policy.
5 Implicitly if not explicitly policy students have accepted Gary Freemen's notion that policy areas are much more different than are political systems. Even if that is true, there may still be good reasons to include differences among the political systems in the analysis.
6 As is true for all the gross generalizations being made in this paper, there are exceptions here. See, for example.
7 Van Waarden (1995) has discussed the persistence of these policy styles even as both the politics of these systems and the policymaking challenges they face are changing.
8 The major exception would be case-based research, especially that using process tracing, which is more sensitive to process. But that research is generally denigrated by the mainstream of the political science discipline. Also, social movement theory also contains more of a notion of process than is characteristic of most of the discipline.
9 Policy analysis is defined by Wildavsky as "creating a problem that can be solved", that is framing the policy problem in such a way as to drive a possible (rather than unfeasible) solution.
10 Richard Rose's analysis of party government (1976), and the literature that has followed (Blondel and Cotta, 2000; Mair, 2008) that do attempt to make that linkage. That said, these studies are more concerned with policy in the abstract, being interested in political parties control the policy rather than in the substance of the policy.
11 Aaron Wildavsky once argued (1998, 2017) that policy was its own cause, with each policy being made creating the need for new policies. In some instances policies create need for their own revisions, while in other cases a policy abstract will impact ongoing programs in other policy domains.
12 Guest Editor: Xufeng Zou, Tsingua University, Beijing.

References

Amenta, E. and A. Hicks (2010) Research Methods, in F. G. Castles, S. Leibfried, A. Lewis, H. Obinger and C. Pierson, *Oxford Handbook of the Welfare State* (Oxford University Press, p. 105–120).
Apter, D. E. (1991) Institutionalism Reconsidered, *International Social Science Journal* 129, 453–81.
Baumgartner, F., C. Green-Pedersen and B. D. Jones (2006) Comparative Studies of Policy Agendas, *European Journal of Public Policy* 13, 959–74.
Beland, D. and R. H. Cox (2013) The Politics of Policy Paradigms, *Governance* 26, 193–5.
Berman, S. (2013) Ideational Theorizing in the Social Sciences Since "Policy Paradigms, Social Learning and the State", *Governance* 26, 217–37.
Chaisty, P., N. Cheeseman and T. Power (2014) Rethinking the "Presidentialism Debate": Conceptualizing Coalitional Politics in Cross-Regional Perspective, *Democratization* 21, 72–94.
Cole, D. H. and M. D. McGinnis (2014) *Elinor Ostrom and the Bloomington School of Political Economy* (Lanham, MD: Lexington Books).
Collins, K. (2006) *Clan Politics and Regime Transition in Central Asia* (Cambridge: Cambridge University Press).
Dalton, R. J. (2014) *Citizen Politics: Public Opinion and Political Parties in Advanced Industrial Democracies*, 6th ed. (London: Sage).
Donahue, J. D and R. J. Zeckhauser (2011) *Collaborative Governance: Private Roles for Public Goals in Turbulent Times* (Princeton, NJ: Princeton University Press).
Dyson, K. (1982) West Germany: The Search for a Rationalist Consensus, in J. J. Richardson, ed. *Policy Styles in Western Europe* (London: George Allen & Unwin, p. 17–46).
Esping Andersen, G. (1990) *The Three Worlds of Welfare Capitalism* (Princeton, NJ: Princeton University Press).
Geddes, Barbara (1994). *Politician's Dilemma: Building State Capacity in Latin America*. University of California Press.

Geddes, B. (2003) *Paradigms and Sand Castles: Theory Building and Research Design in Comparative Politics* (Ann Arbor: University of Michigan Press).

Geva-May, I. (2002b). Cultural theory: The Neglected Variable in the Craft of Policy Analysis. *Journal of Comparative Policy Analysis: Research and Practice* 4(3), 243–265.

Geva-May, I. (2002a). From Theory to Practice: Policy analysis, cultural bias and organizational arrangements. *Public Management Review* 4(4), 581–591.

Geva-May, I. (2004). Riding the Wave of Opportunity: Termination in Public Policy. *Journal of Public Administration Research and Theory* 14(3), 309–333.

Geva-May, I. (2020). *The Logic and Methodology of Doing Policy Analysis in the 21st Century* (New York: Routledge).

Goodsell, C. T. (2011) *Mission Mystique: Belief Systems in Public Agencies* (Washington, DC: CQ Press).

Gupta, K. (2012) Comparative Public Policy: Using the Comparative Method to Advance Our Understanding of the Policy Process, *Policy Studies Journal* 40, 11–26.

Hadjisky, M., L. A. Pal and C. Walker (2017) *Public Policy Transfer: Micro-Dynamics and Macro-Effects* (Cheltenham: Edward Elgar).

Holliday, I. (2000) Productivist Welfare Capitalism: Social Policy in Asia, *Political Studies* 48, 706–27.

Howlett, M. and J. Tosun (forthcoming) *Policy Styles and Policy-Making: Exploring the National Dimension* (London: Routledge).

Huber, E. and J. D. Stephens (2012) *Democracy and the Left: Social Policy and Inequality in Latin America* (Chicago: University of Chicago Press).

Hupe, P. (2019) *Handbook on Street-Level Bureaucracy* (Cheltenham: Edward Elgar).

Ingram, H. (1990). Implementation: A Review and Suggested Framework. In Lynn, N.B. & Wildavsky, A. (Eds.), Public Administration: The State of the Art. Chatham (NJ: Chatham House).

Jann, W. and K. Wegrich (2007) Theories of the Policy Cycle, in F. Fischer, G. J. Miller and M. S. Sidney, eds. *Handbook of Public Policy Analysis* (Boca Raton: CRC Press, p. 43–62).

Jenkins-Smith, H., D. Nohrstedt, C. M. Weible and K. Ingold (2018) The Advocacy Coalition Framework: An Overview of the Research Program, in C. M. Weible and P. A. Sabatier, eds. *Theories of the Policy Process*, 4th ed. (Boulder, CO: Westview Press, p. 183–224).

Karch, A. (2006) *Democratic Laboratories: Policy Diffusion among the American States* (Ann Arbor: University of Michigan Press).

Kingdon, J. (1984) *Agendas, Alternatives and Public Policies* (Boston: Little, Brown).

Linz, J. J. (1990) The Perils of Presidentialism, *Journal of Democracy* 1, 51–69.

Lipset, S. M. (1959) Some Social Requisites of Democracy: Economic Development and Political Legitimacy, *American Political Science Review* 53, 69–105.

Lowi, T. J. (1972) Four Systems of Politics, Policy and Choice, *Public Administration Review* 32, 298–310.

Mahoney, J. and G. Goertz (2004) The Possibility Principle: Choosing Negative Cases in Comparative Research, *American Political Science Review* 98, 653–69.

Mair, P. (2008) The Challenge to Party Government, *West European Politics* 31, 311–24.

March, J. G. and J. P. Olsen (1989) *Rediscovering Institutions: The Organizational Basis of Politics* (New York: Free Press).

March, J. G. and J. P. Olsen (1989) *Rediscovering Institutions: The Organizational Basis of Political Life* (New York: Free Press).

Marsh, D. and J. C. Sharman (2009) Policy Diffusion and Policy Transfer, *Policy Studies* 30, 269–88.

Oberg, P.-O., T. Svensson, P. M. Christiansen, A. S. Nørgaard, H. Rommetvedt and G. Thesen (2011) Disrupted Exchange and Declining Corporatism: Government Authority and Interest Group Capability in Scandinavia, *Government and Opposition* 48, 365–91.

Ostrom, E. (1990) *Governing the Commons: The Evolution of Institutions of Collective Action* (Cambridge: Cambridge University Press).

Pal, L. A. and R. K. Weaver (2003) *The Government Taketh Away: The Politics of Pain in the United States and Canada* (Washington, DC: Georgetown University Press).

Palumbo, D. J. (1987) *The Politics of Program Evaluation* (Newburry Park, CA: Sage).

Peters, B. G. (2010) *Institutional Theory in Political Science: The "New Institutionalism"* (London: Continuum).

Peters, B. G and J. Pierre (2016) *Governance and Comparative Politics* (Cambridge: Cambridge University Press).

Pierre, J. and B. G. Peters (2000) *Governance, Politics and the State* (Basingstoke: Macmillan).

Pierson, P. (2000) Increasing Returns, Path Dependence, and the Study of Politics, *The American Political Science Review*, 94, 251–267.
Pressman, J. L. and A. Wildavsky (1974) *Implementation* (Berkeley: University of California Press).
Richardson, J. J. (1982) *Policy Stes in Western Europe* (London: George Allen & Unwin).
Rogowski, R. (1987) Political Cleavages and Changing Exposure to Trade, *American Political Science Review* 81, 1121–37.
Rokkan, S. (1967) Norway: Numerical Democracy and Corporate Pluralism, in R. A. Dahl, ed. *Political Oppositions in Western Democracies* (New Haven, CT: Yale University Press, p. 70–115).
Rose, R. (1976) *The Problem of Party Government* (London: Macmillan).
Rose, R. (1993) *Lesson-Drawing in Policy Analysis: A Guide to Learning across Time and Space* (Chatham, NJ: Chatham House).
Scharpf, F. W. (1988) The Joint Decision Trap: Lessons from German Federalsim and European Integration, *Public Administration* 66, 239–78.
Scharpf, F. W. (2010) *Community and Autonomy: Institutions, Policies and Legitimacy in Multi-level Europe* (Frankfurt: Campus Verlag).
Shepsle, K. A. (2006) Rational Choice Institutionalism, in R. A. W. Rhodes, S. A. Binder and B. A. Rockman, eds., *Oxford Handbook of Political Institutions* (Oxford: Oxford University Press, p. 23–38).
Stiller, S. and K. Van Kersbergen (2008) The Matching Problem Within Comparative Welfare State Research, *Journal of Comparative Policy Analysis* 10, 133–49.
Thomann, E. (2017) QCA for Comparative Policy Analysis, Paper presented at International Conference on Public Policy, Singapore, June.
Tosun, J. and S. Workman (2018) Struggle and Triumph in Fusing Policy Process and Comparative Research, in C. M. Weible and P. A. Sabatier, eds., *Theories of the Policy Process*, 4th ed. (Boulder, CO: Westview Press, p. 329–362).
Truex, R. (2014) Consultative Authoritarianism and Its Limits, *Comparative Political Studies* 50(3), 329–361.
Tsebelis, G. (2002) *Veto Players: How Political Institutions Work* (Princeton, NJ: Princeton University Press).
Weaver, R. K. and B. A. Rockman (1993) *Do Institutions Matter?: Government Capabilities in the United States and Abroad* (Washington, DC: The Brookings Institution).
Wildavsky, A. (1998, 2017) Policy as Its Own Cause, in Wildavsky, *The Art and Craft of Policy Analysis*, Reissued (London: Macmillan).
Wleziien, C. and S. N. Soroka (2012) Political Institutions and the Opinion-Policy Link, *West European Politics* 35, 1407–32.

Part 3
The Classics: Theory and Methods in Comparative Policy Analysis Studies

Comparative Policy Analysis: Déjá vu All Over Again?

PETER DELEON AND PHYLLIS RESNICK-TERRY

ABSTRACT *During the 1970s and early 1980s, many policy analysts were engaged in comparative policy analysis. For a variety of reasons, the most important of which being a general neglect of the particular policy contexts, the use of comparative policy analysis fell largely into disuse. There are now a number of emerging reasons why a renaissance in comparative policy analysis seems much more propitious: a growing number of transnational policy issues; advances in communication technologies, such that physical distances have been "virtually" eliminated; and new conceptual bases. All of these combine to produce a new demand for comparative policy studies.*

Introduction

The policy sciences, like most human activities, can be viewed as running in trends or emphases (see, deLeon, 1988; for examples). Harold D. Lasswell (1951), often thought to be one of the originators of the policy sciences, linked them closely to the democratic orientation, perhaps out of reaction to his earlier rejection of the totalitarian (or what he called the "garrison") state (Lasswell, 1941). In the late 1990s, a trend emphasizing democracy and policy analysis has clearly re-emerged (see, e.g., Dryzek and Torgerson, 1993; Schneider and Ingram, 1997). Peter deLeon, in his description of the evolution of the policy sciences (1988), noted how various intellectual (and maybe practical) orientations seemed to favor one particular phase of the policy process (e.g., implementation) over the others (termination). These general observations serve as prelude to yet another orientation or feature in the policy sciences' on-going development, namely, comparative policy analysis.

Few would argue de novo against the idea of comparative policy analysis. Taken on a national scale, public policies usually entail large programs; national health plans or social welfare or national security programs typically come one to a nation. Yet national programs are often the unit of analytic attention. So to obtain more "data points" from "naturally occurring experiments," one would readily turn to multinational examples of specific programs as analytic grist, that is, comparative policy analysis, if one hopes to assess different kinds of programs.

Comparative policy analysis is hardly a foundling gleam in anyone's eye. In the 1970s, many scholars turned to the inductive comparison of similar policy issues among different nations. Their idea, of course, was to see if particular policies' patterns transcended individual nations. The purpose was to assess if specific policies could be seen as having a "life of their own," a life pattern that evolved analogously out of the programmatic requirements in spite of their respective nations' differing politics, structures, and cultures. Secondarily, one could inquire as to the comparative effectiveness of similar programs (e.g., deLeon (1979) compared the developmental pace of six nations' nuclear reactor systems) in hopes of disseminating or sharing "successful" programs or, conversely, avoiding particular national follies (Hall, 1980).

A few notable endeavors in this approach should be recognized. Heidenheimer, Heclo, and Adams (1975, 1983) reviewed a series of domestic policy issues (e.g., housing, tax structures, and local governmental policies) across Western European nations and the United States to derive a series of policy patterns and contrasts. To the authors' admitted surprise (in the preface to the second edition), the American Political Science Association designated their *Comparative Public Policy* as the best book that year on *national* policy, with the following citation:

> Their work should provide a major stimulus to cross-national comparative studies of public policy. It helps to expand the perceptions of students of national policy by comparing policies of the United States and selected Western European nations in health, education, [and other government activities]. Cross-national policy research is still in its infancy in our profession; the...award will be well-used if it stimulates the development of this field. (Anonymous, *PS* 1976, p. 441).

T. Alexander Smith wrote in the introduction to his *The Comparative Policy Process* (1975, p. v) that "This book was written with the conviction that students of comparative politics devote insufficient attention to theorizing about the policy process. As a result there has been much unsystematic talk about policy, or policies, but little in the way of theoretic conceptualization." Rather than looking at governmental functions (Heidenheimer, Heclo, and Adams, 1975), Smith partially drew upon Theodore Lowi's typology (e.g., the politics of distribution and redistribution) to examine programs among the major western democratic states. His conclusions were more nation-specific than comparative in content.

Specific issue-areas seemed to be amendable to comparative policy studies. For instance, comparative discussions of national defense postures and energy programs were easy to locate (e.g., Murray and Viotti, 1982; Smart, 1982), although one might have questioned if they were more descriptions of specific national policies than legitimately comparative in nature. And one might easily claim that the highly influential Princeton/ SSRC series on Political Development of the 1960s, with its deep genuflection to structural-functionalism, fell into much the same comparative policy boat, only this time looking at the less developed nations of the world (see the final volume in the series for an overview; Binder et al., 1971).[1]

Yet, for reasons we shall discuss momentarily, the study of comparative policy analysis fell into disfavor in the 1980s, and published research in this area virtually ceased. Currently, however, there has been a renaissance in comparative studies, as policy scholars again turn overseas as a source of inspiration and insight. This essay addresses this re-emerging development in the policy sciences to ask, as sage (and Hall of Fame catcher) Yogi Berra once inquired (admittedly in another ballpark), is comparative policy analysis a relevant development to the contemporary policy tool kit or, as he so aptly phrased it, perhaps it is simply "déjà vu all over again"?[2]

As a means to this end, this essay will examine more closely exactly what led to the demise of comparative policy research in the 1980s, then what evidence indicated a return to comparative research in the 1990s, finally inquiring as to the likelihood that comparative policy research will remain a more prominent feature in the policy sciences discipline than its lamented 1970's brethren.

What went wrong?

The apparent hibernation of comparative policy analysis in the early 1980s can largely be attributed to the recognition on the part of the policy research community that the fundamental basis of policy research—the contextuality of the specific problem—really did make a difference, indeed, such a difference that seemingly "simple" comparisons were, upon reflection, seriously problematic. For instance, what comparisons can one make between the two great western democracies (the United States and Great Britain) knowing that they have two different forms of democratic governance in addition to different "constitutions" and social structures? Is it any wonder, then, that policy comparisons between the British National Health Service and the American medical system flounder on both the rocks of the nations' respective practice and social theory (Levine (1979); for an exemplary instance, see Heclo, 1974)?

In one sense, this recognition has a very salutary effect. Americans, for instance, no longer could assume that its democratic form of government was, ipso facto, the only form of government for the other nations of the world. The predictable result, of course, is what Fareed Zakaria (1997) recently described as "The Rise of Illiberal Democracy" around the world.[3] Hence, the initial American tendency to export American democracy whole cloth to the newly emerging nations of the former Soviet Union soon was tempered by an understanding that American and Russian (to pick one nation) democracies did not have to be identical. From a policy perspective, the acknowledgment that not all polities have interchangeable parts or conveniently identical systems implied that comparative policy analysis was not the ready remedy it appeared to be.

Obviously, this realization made itself clear on the more programmatic levels as well. As an example, during the search for an American "health program," policy scholars were actively visiting such nations as Canada (single payer system), Great Britain (national health service), Germany (health maintenance organizations), and Holland (a variation on a national health service) to understand what they might bring to the American health care arena. Many of these national health plans were considered during the Clinton Administration's attempt to set forth an American health plan. As we know, none to these plans were translated into the US health context. For whatever peculiar constellation of reasons, including a reaction against government service in general (see Skocpol, 1997), the American political and social contexts made the health policy transplantation impossible to effect. Similar observations can be made regarding energy, public education, criminal justice, and social welfare programs. The tacit explanation, as foreseen by Lasswell, was quite straightforward: context counts.

A second possible reason for the demise of comparative policy studies falls in the less practical and more conceptual camp (although, of course, the two are hardly disjoint).

Part of the early blush of comparative policy analysis was a product of some scholars' enthusiasm for a theoretic policy loadstone, what Dror (1971) called the "mega-policy" sciences. How, they asked, does a political system recognize and execute a policy, i.e., what generalized condition underlies policymaking? In retrospect, the logic was understandable: government functions the world over (and, by extension, government policies) were roughly analogous. Therefore, akin to some of the social science theories then extant (e.g., structural-functionalism and group theory), it was argued that national policies could be studied under one mega-policy umbrella.

We have already discussed how this perspective was found to be impossible to adduce on a policy level because of the peculiarities of different nations and their programmatic exigencies. It was even more beyond the intellectual pale on a conceptual level. Nobody seems to have offered a workable conceptual framework for understanding comparative policy analysis, although not without some serious attempts (for one attempt, see Hofferbert, 1990). More to the point, few, if any, saw a compelling reason for aggregating national policies as if they were somehow homogeneous. Certainly there was no call for a "universal" policy regime and, hence, little clarion for comparative policy analysis. The result, not surprisingly, was that most policy scholars simply backed away from proposing a theoretic approach.

In short, while comparative policy studies initially held out great promise, the results were much more lacking. Nor was there a particularly great demand for them; European and Asian policy scholars were more interested in American—not comparative—cases and approaches (e.g., regulatory policies or PPBS), while American policy researchers turned almost as one to internal American issues. Even books that were nominally comparative in nature were collections of national studies, with perhaps a comparative epilogue (see Wagner, et al. (1991), especially the concluding chapter). The question, then, was not so much potential substance of comparative policy research; it was more a case of whether the marginal costs of very demanding research tasks were worth the marginal returns, especially since the demand for such goods was not particularly high.

Traces of a comparative renaissance

By the early 1990s, the policy sciences' community began to sense the distinct appearance of a new turn to comparative policy studies for a number of different reasons, some technical, some theoretical, one perhaps ideological in nature, and some even practical (perhaps necessary).

Surely the most obvious and integrated reason is that the physical world is becoming increasingly an example of what journalists call a "global village." The ideological barriers that once stood between many of the world's nations have dissolved, to be replaced by an apparent economic imperative towards an internationalized economy. One does not need to project an "end to history" to realize that one very generalized form of economy— capitalism—is ameliorating many of the former ideological obstructions between nations and, in turn, making comparative policy analysis more plausible. Even as the People's Republic of China stubbornly retains its political communism (with all its authoritarian trappings), its economy is moving (and is being moved) to a "socialist capitalism" as it tries to engage itself in the accoutrements of international trade. Moreover, political unions, such as the European Union and NAFTA within the near future, have led to an additional lowering (if not elimination) of trade barriers. Robert Reich's *The Next American Frontier* (1983) was only one small flagstone in the newly emerging international economic highway.[4]

Just as important to a growing American (and European) presence in the world is that being "global" is not a one-way street, a latter-day imperialism as it were. While American and European markets are eagerly reaching out for foreign products and manpower, other nations, such as the Japanese, are investing heavily within the United States and Europe, as well as in the developing world (Ensign, 1992). While investment trends ebb and flow with national economic cycles, it is hard to imagine any nation proclaiming itself to be autarkic. The economic competition will almost certainly lend itself to a comparison of policies as a means of identifying (and obtaining) greater effectiveness. Furthermore, the increasing number of mergers between corporations from different nations will only serve to magnify these trends, as such issues as comparative investment and regulatory policies loom large in importance.

These movements are accelerated by breathtaking advances in telecommunications, such as electronic mail, making international markets as (if not more) accessible as the local merchant.[5] In the words of *The Economist* (1995, p. 1), this condition represents "the death of distance...[that] will probably be the single most important economic force shaping society in the first half of the next century."[6] Markets that used to be limited to electronic communications now can literally remain "on line" twenty-four hours a day, just as individuals can remain in easy contact with one another, separated only slightly by time zones, not geography. Communications-wise, the world is an unquestionably a smaller place. While these observations are financially oriented, economics do not exist is a vacuum; thus, one can posit that, as commercial ties broaden, some of the psychological and political barriers between people and nations have also been reduced and, most likely, changed.

In virtually the same breathe, new conceptual theories have been forwarded that potentially bridge national differences. The most obvious example is the "new institutionalism" (see, for example, March and Olson, 1989). Perhaps just as precarious from a theoretic perspective as structural-functionalism in the 1960s (e.g., what distinguishes a "new" from an "old" institution?), the new institutionalism operates on the axiom that institutions make a difference and that analogous institutions may be found "making a difference" in nations throughout the world (Steinmo et al., 1992; Immergut, 1998). Thus, the proponents of institutional analysis claim that, for instance, comparative health policies may be usefully studied as an institutional issue (Immergut, 1992). A contrasting view is presented by David Imbeau and Robert McKinlay (1996), who suggest that governments might be compared by examining their respective national activities rather than their analogous institutions. Lastly, scholars such as Elinor Ostrom (1990,1998) have focused their theoretic lenses on less-than-national issues—in her case, the procedures posed by regulating "common pool resources"—and compared national respective examples in order to construct a mid-range but still comparative theory dealing with localized rule-making and enforcement.

Capacities (e.g., communication proximity) and theory are a powerful duo, but they are greatly abetted by the growing recognition of an informal international consortium of what Anne Schneider and Helen Ingram have felicitously described as "pinching ideas" (1988). That is, the argument once held that cultural and national perspectives ameliorated the idea of borrowing policies and even specific programs from other nations. Of late, however, nations are more willing to compare and even "borrow" innovations and ideas; Hillary

Rodham Clinton's task force on American national health care reform is just one of many obvious examples, although it argued to the negative, i.e., rather parochially, contending that the United States would not wish to mimic the British, Germans, or Canadians (Skocpol, 1997). Again, the study of institutions as a unit of analysis has supported this tendency.

One emerging policy area for comparative analysis deals with participatory policy analysis. Europeans such as Ortwin Renn and his colleagues (1993, 1995; also see Mayer, 1997) have contributed significantly to American research in participatory policy analysis, bringing national examples (e.g., participatory experiments in Holland (Renn et al., 1995) as well as active comparison (e.g., comparing citizen panels in Germany and New Jersey (1993)). While one must certainly be careful of not eradicating political, social, and cultural differences in participatory analysis, the cross-fertilization among European and American scholars in this area appears to be synergistic and growing (cf. Renn et al., 1993 or 1995; with Kathlene and Martin, 1991).

These instances of "policy pinching" have proliferated—perhaps appropriately—even down to the local levels. In municipalities across the United States, planners are discussing mechanisms and processes for adopting European-style urban planning concepts into their designs for American cities. The challenge before these planners is to combine the unique cultural values of their citizens (for instance, their headlong rush to suburbia) with the benefits of a European model that relies more upon public transportation and a strong central city than suburbanization and its accompanying reliance upon the automobile.

One city widely recognized for its achievements in this area is Portland, Oregon. This northwestern city "pinched" the European model of a centralized city and then developed an efficient light rail public transportation system to facilitate easy access to the downtown area. The light rail transit system has resulted in the maintenance of a less-automobile congested downtown in the face of a national trend towards suburbanization. While many European cities have achieved this result by actually banning some automobile uses in the center city, Portland planners were sufficiently cognizant of its citizens' life style revolving around personal mobility to recognize that the "stick" approach to resticting mobility would not work, or at least would be widely unpopular. Instead, these planners have been able to achieve the same results for their downtown areas with the "carrot" (public transit) approach.[7] Explicit recognition of the ability to incorporate cultural variables into the analysis has aided the resurrection of a comparative policy approach as a pertinent policy tool (Downs, 1994; Orfield, 1994).

Although some scholars justifiably continue to argue that the results of comparative analyses provide no meaningful insights due to the idiosyncratic (that is to say, the contextual) nature of the analytic beast, others have attempted to reap some benefits from using the technique. This is especially true at the local level, with works such as Meyer (1993) on local economic development and Cullingworth (1993) on local land use planning and the use of zoning demonstrate forays back into the comparative approach to urban policy evaluation.

However, the local level is not the only one to which comparative analysis is being employed. Recently, national environmental policies have been studied and evaluated under the microscope of comparative analysis techniques. In their studies of national level environmental policies, both Harrison (1995) and Shaw (1991) were able to draw tentative conclusions concerning enforcement mechanisms, institutional arrangements, and the use of taxes as a pollution abatement policy. Harrison's (1995) comparison of the American deterrence style of environmental enforcement with the Canadian cooperative style resulted in conclusions that demonstrated, contrary to prior wisdom in the area, the American deterrence-based model was actually more effective in achieving compliance with regulations in the paper mill industry. Furthermore, Harrison's analysis allowed her to conclude that a mixed enforcement scheme preferable to either the cooperative or the deterrent only approaches could perhaps exist. Harrison summarized her study: "While this study represents only a first step in a research agenda to more systematically compare the effectiveness of different enforcement approaches, one can speculate about whether it would be possible to combine the strengths of both models. A compromise solution may be to administratively separate the functions of technical support and enforcement" (Harrison, 1995, p. 241).

Comparative analysis in the environmental area has yielded other conclusions that hold promise for improving national policy. Shaw (1991) studied the ability of pollution taxes to reduce successfully the levels of water pollution in major rivers in Germany and the Netherlands. Similar to Harrison's (1995) conclusions about appropriate enforcement mechanisms, Shaw's analysis concluded concerning the institutional arrangement most effective in supporting a system of pollution taxes, that "It may be inferred that a strong sense of mission and purpose from the central authority coupled with regional control constitutes the best recipe for success in a pollution tax system" (Shaw, 1991, p. 130). Again, however, one needs to recognize that even here, the realization that contextual issues need to be accounted for is key to successful policy "pinching."

Comparative analyses have presented some interesting, almost tantalizing results for both local and national level policies. However, the increasingly practical side of the equation is that there are now policies that simply must be international in scope, and therefore demand a type of comparative policy analysis. Issues range from international energy to terrorism to—most trenchantly—international environmental concerns. All of this genre of policies have one central feature in common: while they are necessarily national in origin, they have transnational (i.e., externality) effects, in other words, their effects cross-national borders (such as acid rain). Thus, they increase in scope and thereby necessitate a more global or international policy approach, such as that used by the 1987 Montreal Convention dealing with the reduction in the release of ozone depleting chlorofluorocarbons (CFCs) into the atmosphere (Benedick, 1991). We need, then, to take a moment to discuss some of the research into national environmental programs that must work cooperatively with other nations if they are to be effective.

Although not generally thought of as the natural resource issue with the largest externality problem, Kamieniecki and Sanasarian (1990) demonstrate the importance of addressing deforestation from a comparative perspective. The authors argue that the potential worldwide effects of forest depletion, including threats to ecosystem maintenance and national economies as well as the loss of the medicinal value of trees, watershed, lumber, fuel, and food supplies places deforestation in the category of natural resource problems requiring a better integrated, global policy response.

To date, most attempts at comparative analysis of the deforestation problem have been incomplete, addressing only comparisons between western, industrialized nations and taking into account only a few aspects of cultural or legal/political factors. Kamieniecki and Sanasarian (1990) argue that a more complete comparative analysis could be performed by incorporating theories of comparative politics (e.g., radical or economic development theories) into the policy analytic endeavors. By relying on the theories of comparative politics, one can more clearly see the motives of developing nations and enter the particular cases of countries such as Indonesia and those of Africa and Latin America into the analysis.

This sort of comparative analysis allows for broader generalizations across nations, better understanding of one's own system, opportunities for cross-disciplinary studies, and most importantly from our perspective, the provision of tools for dealing with policy issues with transnational effects (Kamieniecki and Sanasarian, 1990). The strength of this sort of comparative analysis is neatly summed up in the authors' conclusion:

> While it may be easier from a theoretical and methodological standpoint to restrict comparative analysis to Western nations, studies involving Third World and communist countries have the potential of highlighting certain causes and possible solutions previously overlooked. Theories of the state can be an extremely valuable guide in this regard. If important theoretical and methodological difficulties that tend to plague comparative studies between the United States and nonwestern nations can be minimized, the findings from such research can greatly broaden understanding of natural resource issues and suggest alternative policy approaches to addressing these issues (Kamieniecki and Sanasarian, 1990, p. 339).

One does not have to think too long to generate a list of other environmental and resource policy issues that would benefit from this type of analysis. A short list might include the management of common property resources such as international fisheries, the prevention of global climate change, the reduction of acid rain, and the protection of endangered species and the maintenance of biodiversity. Incorporating an explicit comparative approach, such as that of Kamieniecki and Sanasarian, should lead us to better, more comprehensive policy recommendations and results.

Conclusion: A new avenue or another dead end?

In concluding, let us propose two "generations" of comparative policy analysis research. The first generation largely took place in the 1970s and early 1980s; as we have seen, it was more noted for dead ends (or, more generously, missed avenues). The second generation is contemporaneous and would appear to be (at least potentially) more fruitful on many fronts, at least potentially because of what it learned from the first generation's shortfalls.

In laying out the development of the second generation of comparative policy analysis, several road signs point to the emergence of a renewed and valuable policy tool for a number of reasons. The most important is the increasing globalization of policy issues and, concomitantly, communications capabilities. From a communications perspective, today's world is unquestionably "smaller" and more immediate, making it more likely that analogous programs will be entered into a common pool of policy knowledge. Enhanced communications makes the policy interchange more likely, first on an informal, electronic mail basis, but subsequently in terms of journals and books, whose circulations are likewise enlarged by these networks. With these conditions, a shared globalization of policy research inevitably occurs. These trends are reinforced by a growing number of policy issues that by their very nature transcend national boundaries; some are seen as threats (e.g., terrorism and environmental perils) while others are perceived as opportunities (commercial activities, biodiversity, and agricultural goods or services), with a few being either (the development and utilization of energy resources). And, finally, one needs to acknowledge the growing number of commercial interactions, which generally are preceded by a comparison of different nations' regulatory, social, and political statutes. These activities provide a valuable market for comparative policy analyses outside the typical academic studies and government audits. In brief, the second comparative policy generation reflects a more genuine and wide-spread demand (business and government) for the insights one might glean from comparative policy research.

These possibilities—in some cases, imperatives—need, however, to "learn" something from the first generation's attentions to comparative policy analysis. First, there is the key question of context: what works in (say) Malaysia might not work in Massachusetts. To use Ostrom's (1990) example of common pooled resources, local governing autonomy might be more plausible in the United States and less likely in France due to variances in their respective political cultures (e.g., decentralized vs. centralized). Merging companies might discover that differences in government policies require delicate negotiations and compromise. These are major, often foreseeable issues; smaller ones—such as adjustments in working hours, labor unions, or company benefits—could also cause initial (and maybe permanent) obstacles. These can occur even between relatively sophisticated partners; Japanese financial investments in both the developing world and the United States can hardly be characterized as a string of unbroken successes (Ensign, 1992). One, then, needs to be cautious in "pinching idea" whole cloth; as David Vogel (1986) has cautioned us, there are "national styles" (in his case, national styles refers to regulatory policies). Moreover, there is little chance for an appeal to a recognized decision "authority." Careful comparative policy analysis therefore needs to identify born the commonalities and the distinctions among the different parties The concept that *context* counts has become a guiding principle in the second "generation" of comparative policy analysis.

A second possible "lesson" learned, one closely aligned with the first, has to do with the scope of expectations. In part, the first generation's initial emphasis on comparative policy was to develop overarching policy models and paradigms. Since then, a certain amount of moderation or temperance have taken place. Scholars and analysts now realize that comparative research can yield interesting, although limited observations without being forced to pretensions of mega-policy models. Few contemporary authors are engaged in the latter exercises. In contrast, many policy authors are testing discrete hypotheses in specified settings (e.g., various pollution incentives versus disincentives or the effectiveness of different forms of citizen participation) to understand their ability to operate effectively in other policy settings. This is not to imply that policy scientists should neglect general theorizing; rather, it is to suggest that there are other worthy grails besides the silver chalice.

Some years back, I suggested the metaphor of policy research as displaying two vectors, a supply side (that is, analysts having the capability and willingness to engage in public policy research) and a demand counterpart (some client wanted and were willing to pay for that research); both, I proposed, were simultaneously necessary for the policy sciences to flourish (deLeon, 1988). Without ascribing any mystical relevance to this supply/demand notion, the metaphor would seem to indicate one reason why the first generation of comparative policy research was deficient. The first generation's supply side of the equation was fraught with multiple difficulties, perhaps being complex beyond the analyst's modeling capabilities; and the demand side was largely lacking, as few outside the academy seemed particularly interested. Now, in the second generation, we find a very different constellation. On the supply side, a more global policy community has some of the tools and interests to compare notes, while (hopefully) keeping its contextual reservations well in hand. The demand side is equally invigorated; clients from both the public and private sectors are asking for high quality comparative research because their futures are relying upon the analyses. The comparisons might be more limited (Swedish efforts to decommission civilian nuclear power reactors being studied to advise American efforts to do the same) but the limited scope does not detract from the concept that comparative policy analysis is playing a growing role in the policy research community.

We observed early on that the policy sciences, in their development, are occasionally given to the pursuit of certain emphases. We have little way of knowing with confidence that the second generation of comparative policy analysis will be any more durable and affecting than the first. However, as outlined above, the conceptual (e.g., a focus on the new institutionalism), situational (a greater latitude for "pinching" policy ideas and innovations from other societies), technical (the communications breakthrough that continue to "downsize" the world), and practical (transnational issues, such as environmental and commercial) components seem much more propitious for the current generation's ultimate tenure. This will not necessarily be easy, as analysts might well have to develop new sets of skills and knowledge bases necessary for cross-national research.

The occasional (one might opine "inevitable") policy blunder that somehow arises from comparative policy research might blunt the comparative analytic agenda. However, the "globalization" of national interests will almost motivate the "demand" side of the supply/demand "policy equation" towards the inclusion of comparative policy analysis as part of the contemporary analytic approach.

Acknowledgments

We are grateful to our colleague Jeffrey A. Romine for his assistance in preparing this essay.

Notes

1. Under the "Truth in Advertising" rules, author deLeon must admit to having actively engaged in comparative policy analysis research during the late 1970s; see deLeon (1979, 1980); also deLeon and Cyr (1975).
2. The complete Berra lexicologist should begin with Blount (1984).
3. Also see Thomas Carothers* "Democracy without Illusions" (1997); a counterpoint is Deputy Secretary of State Strobe Talbott's "Democracy and the National Interest" (1996).
4. Reich and the internationalization of the American economy are hardly without their critics. See Greider (1997) and Kuttner (1997).
5. As an example of the mixed blessing variety: a recent issue of *The Economist* (Anonymous, 1997a) claims that e-mail has revolutionized the international market in sexual goods and services.
6. Also see *The Economist's* Telecommunications Survey for 1997 (Anonymous, 1997b); both were written by Francis Cairncross, who also has authored *The Death of Distance* (1997).
7. To be sure, Portland planners did implement another major big "stick," that is, strict regional boundaries to curtail the future expansion of Portland.

References

Anonymous. *PS* (1976). 9(4), 441.
Anonymous. (1995). "Telecommunications: The Death of Distance." *The Economist* (September), Special Telecommunications Survey, 1–28.
Anonymous. (1997a). "The Sex Industry: Giving the Customer Want He Wants." *The Economist* (February), 21–23.
Anonymous. (1997b). "Telecommunications: A Connected World." *The Economist* (September), Special Telecommunications Survey, 1–27.
Benedick, Richard E. (1991). *Ozone Diplomacy*. Cambridge, MA Harvard University Press.
Binder, Leonard et al. (1971). *Crises and Sequences in Political Development*. Princeton, N J: Princeton University Press.
Blount, Roy. (1984). "Yogi." *Sports Illustrated* 60 (April), 84–88.
Cairncross, Francis. (1997). *The Death of Distance*. Cambridge, MA: Harvard Business School Press.
Carothers, Thomas. (1997). "Democracy Without Illusions." *Foreign Affairs* 76(1) (January/February), 85–99.
Cullingworth, J.B. (1993). *The Political Culture of Planning: American Land Use Planning in Comparative Perspective*. London: Routledge.
deLeon, Peter. (1979). *The Development and Diffusion of the NuclearPowerReactor: A Comparative Analysis*. Cambridge, MA: Ballinger.
deLeon, Peter. (1980). "Comparative Technology and Public Policy." *Policy Sciences* 11 (3) (February), 285–309.
deLeon, Peter. (1988). *Advice and Consent: The Evolution of the Policy Sciences*. New York: The Russell Sage Foundation.
deLeon, Peter and Arthur Cyr. (1975). "Comparative Policy Analysis." *Policy Sciences* 6(4) (December), Special Issue.
Downs, Anthony. (1994). *New visions for Metropolitan America*. Washington, DC: The Brookings Institution.
Dror, Yehezkel. (1971). *Design for the Policy Sciences*. New York: American Elsevier.
Dryzek, John D. and Douglas Torgerson. (1993). "Democracy and the Policy Sciences." *Policy Sciences*, 26(3) (Autumn), 127–138.
Ensign, Margee. (1992). *Doing Good or Doing Well: Japan's Foreign Aid Program*. New York: Columbia University Press.
Greider, William. (1997). *One World, Ready or Not: The Manic Logic of Global Capitalism*. New York: Simon & Schuster.
Hall, Peter. (1980). *Great Planning Disasters*. Berkeley: University of California Press.
Harrison, Kathryn. (1995). "Is Cooperation the Answer? Canadian Environmental Enforcement in Comparative Context." *Journal of Policy Analysis and Management* 14(2) (Spring), 221–244.
Heclo, Hugh. (1974). *Modern Social Policies in Britain and Sweden: From Relief to Income Maintenance*. New Haven, CT: Yale University Press.
Heidenheimer, Arnold J., Hugh Heclo, and Carolyn Teich Adams. (1975,1983). *Comparative Policy Analysis*. 1st and 2nd eds. New York: St. Martin's Press.
Hofferbert, Richard I. (1990). *The Reach and Grasp of Policy Analysis: Comparataive Views of the Craft*. Tuscaloosa: University of Alabama Press.
Imbeau, David M. and Richard D. McKinlay (Eds.). (1996). *Comparing Government Activity*. New York: St. Martin's Press.
Immergut, Ellen M. (1992). "The Rules of the Game: The Logic of Health Policy-Making in France, Switzerland, and Sweden." In Sven Steinmo, Katheen Thelen, and Frank Longstreth (eds.), *Structuring Politics: Historical Institutions in Comparative Anaysis*. New York: Cambridge University Press, chap. 3.
Immergut, Ellen M. (1998). "The Theoretical Core of the New Institutionalism." *Politics & Society* 26(1) (March), 5–30.
Kamieniecki, Sheldon and Eliz Sanasarian. (1990). "Conducting Comparative Research on Environmental Policy." *National Resource Journal* 30(2), 321–339.
Kathlene, Lyn and John A. Martin. (1991). "Enhancing Citizen Participation: Panel Designs, Perspectives, and Policy Formulation." *Journal of Policy Analysis and Management* 10(1) (Winter), 46–63.
Kuttner, Robert. (1997). *Everything for Sale: The Virtues and Limits of Markets*. New York: New York Times Books.
Lasswell, Harold D. (1941). "The Garrison State." *American Journal of Sociology* 46(4) (January).

Lasswell, Harold D. (1951). "The Policy Orientation." In Daniel Lerner and Harold D. Lasswell (eds.), *The Policy Sciences*. Palo Alto, CA: Stanford University Press.

Levine, Robert A. (Ed.). (1979). *Evaluation Research and Practice: Comparative and International Perspectives*. Beverly Hills, CA: Sage Publications.

March, James G. and Johan P. Olson. (1989). *Rediscovering Institutions: The Orgizational Basis of Politics*. New York: The Free Press.

Mayer, Igor. (1997). *Debating Technolgoies: A Methodology Contribution to the Design and Evaluation of Participatory Policy Analysis*. The Hague, Netherlands: Tilburg University Press.

Meyer, Peter B. (Ed.) (1993). *Comparative Studies in Local Economic Development: Problems in Policy Implementation*. Westport, CT: Greenwood Press.

Murray, Douglas J. and Paul R. Viotti (Eds.). (1982). *The Defense Policies of Nations: A Comparative Study*. Baltimore: The Johns Hopkins Press.

Orfield, Myron. (1994). *Metropolitan Politics: The Regional Agenda for Community and Stability*. Washington, DC: The Brookings Institution.

Ostrom, Elinor. (1990). *Governing the Commons*. New York: Cambridge University Press.

Ostrom, Elinor. (1998). "A Behavioral Approach to the Rational Choice Theory of Collective Action." *American Political Science Review* 92(1) (March), 1–22.

Reich, Robert. (1983). The *Next American Frontier*. New York: Times Books.

Renn, Ortwin, Thomas Webler, Horst Rakel, Peter Dienel, and Braden Johnson. (1993). "Public Participation in Decision-Making: A Three-Step Procedure." *Policy Sciences* 26(3), 189–214.

Renn, Ortwin, Thorns Webler, and Peter Wiedemann (Eds.). (1995). *Fairness and Competence in Citizen Participation*. Boston: Kluwer Academic Publishers.

Schneider, Anne L and Helen Ingram. (1988). "Systematically Pinching Ideas: A Comparative Approach to Policy Design." *Journal of Public Policy* 8(1), 61–80.

Schneider, Anne L. and Helen Ingram. (1997). *Policy Design for Democracy*. Lawrence: University of Kansas Press.

Shaw, Christopher L. (1991). "Green Taxes, Blue Taxes: A Comparative Study of the Use of Fiscal Policy to Promote Environmental Quality." *National Resources Forum* 15(2), 123–131.

Skocpol, Theda. (1997). *Boomerang: Health Care Reform and the Turn Against Government*. New York: W.W. Norton.

Smart, Ian (Ed.). (1982). *World Energy Policy*. Baltimore: The Johns Hopkins Press for the Royal Institute for Intemationl Affairs.

Steinmo, Sven, Katheen Thelen, and Frank Longstreth (Eds.). (1992). *Structuring Politics: Historical Institutions in Comparative Anaysis*. New York: Cambridge University Press.

Talbott, Strobe. (1996). "Democracy and the National Interest." *Foreign Affairs* 75(6) (November/December), 47–63.

Vogel, David. (1986). *National Styles of Regulation*. Ithaca, NY: Cornell University Press.

Wagner, Peter, Carol Hirschon Weiss, Björn Wittrock, and Hellmut Wollmann (Eds.). (1991). *Social Sciences and Modern States*. New York: Cambridge University Press.

Zakaria, Fareed. (1997). "The Rise of Illiberal Democracies." *Foreign Affairs* 76(6) (December), 22–43.

Compared to What? The Multiple Meanings of Comparative Policy Analysis

BERYL A. RADIN, & DAVID L. WEIMER

ABSTRACT *What is comparative public policy? How can it contribute to better public policy? These questions seem fundamental to the mission of the* Journal of Comparative Policy Analysis. *Some scholars have addressed the first question, which usually places comparative policy analysis in an institutional context, emphasizing comparisons across countries. However, fewer scholars have addressed the second, which lies at the heart of the comparative enterprise. As a result, the boundaries of this analytic effort are unclear and attempts to evaluate work that is defined as "comparative" are sometimes controversial. In this essay, we first sketch the history of the development of policy analysis in the United States. This historical review provides a sense of how comparative analysis fits into the development of the field, how the field has ignored some opportunities to think about comparative analysis, and offers some insight into how comparative policy analysis can contribute to better public policy. It then turns to possible avenues for comparison to identify the opportunities and limitations of the comparative approach.*

Introduction

The *Journal of Comparative Policy Analysis* (JCPA) is now celebrating its 20th anniversary. The journal has taken its place in a rather crowded field of periodicals and has managed to survive and grow with a title that seems to evoke interest yet escape clear definition. Actually the term "comparative" is deceptively simple. While a majority of readers of the journal tend to associate "comparative" with analyses that involve more than one country, it is clear that the term – and, most importantly, the field of comparative policy analysis – is extraordinarily complex.

More than ten years before the first JCPA issue saw the light of day, Arthur Cyr and Peter deLeon (1975) edited an issue of *Policy Sciences* that focused on comparative policy analysis. In their introductory article to the issue, Cyr and deLeon offered advice to those who sought to analyze public policy issues from a cross-national perspective. They used the specific articles in the issue to emphasize three factors that they ascribed to the relative dearth of comparative studies. First, they argued that comparative research is particularly difficult to conceptualize, organize, and implement. Second, they found that the seeming replacement of the field of public administration with public policy confused the issue. And third, they linked the lack of attention to comparative work to the professional training orientation of public policy programs.

Cyr and deLeon offered alternative arguments that they thought would lure their colleagues to undertake comparative studies. They found that such efforts hold considerable promise for both the academician and the policy maker and could uncover specific policy payoffs for the student of similar programs in several countries. Anticipating a more globalized society, they thought that such information could assist in the development of beneficial interdependencies between countries.

The JCPA has emphasized the comparison of similar policies in multiple countries. Table 1, based on a review of abstracts of articles appearing up to Volume 19, Issue 2, shows that half of the articles published involved multi-country comparisons.[1] Indeed, the proportion has increased from 45 per cent for the first ten volumes to 56 per cent subsequently. As the proportion of single-country studies has remained constant at 30 per cent, the increase in multi-country articles has come at the expense of theoretical or other types of articles. Similar to research into comparative public administration (Fitzpatrick et al. 2011), the majority of the multi-country articles employ qualitative methods; most of the large-n studies use existing data sets.

While Cyr and deLeon's concerns continue today, a number of additional questions have been raised that have contributed to an even more complex definitional situation. We suggest that at least three questions should be asked before approaching a comparative policy analysis. First, why do you want to do a comparison? Are you looking for new ideas or do you have an expectation of finding a solution that can be applied in diverse settings? Do you think that the person you want to advise is looking for new ideas or are you searching for new ways of enriching the research and theory on the topic? Are you looking for ways to move along the stages of the policy process – e.g. to move from an adopted policy to implementation?

Second, what do you want to compare? Are you assuming that there will almost always be a number of topics available for comparison? Comparing countries is not the only possible focus of this topic. Federalist systems, as well as unitary systems that delegate

Table 1. Number (%) of JCPA articles by type

	Volumes 1–10	Volumes 11–19.2	Total
Theory and other	43 (26)	27 (14)	70 (20)
Single country	49 (30)	57 (30)	106 (30)
Multiple countries	74 (45)	106 (56)	180 (50)
Total	166	190	356

some policy making to local or regional bodies, allow one to compare activity that comes from separate subnational governments to try to determine whether one is more effective in achieving desired goals than another. One could also compare policy responses to problems in different industrial sectors with an eye toward borrowing promising alternatives across sectoral lines.

Third, what do you think will emerge from your comparison? Are you assuming that the insights that come from your comparative analysis will be new and of interest to the political actor you are advising? Do you expect that your findings would inform alternatives or recommendations? Are you looking for ways to expand the research on a topic and contribute to knowledge through production of articles or other publications?

The articles that have appeared in JCPA over the years suggest that there are many ways to answer these questions. Some of the work that is defined as "comparative" is broad and embedded in the very structure and values found in different governmental systems. Thus, one might expect that findings would emerge in democratic systems that are different from those inferred from autocratic systems. Or that shared power systems would create different information than those with parliamentary systems.

Other work is narrow and focuses on technical issues related to the detailed implementation of a policy. And both broad and narrow approaches usually exist in a constantly changing context and environment. These contributions also suggest that there is not a clear set of expectations about the field of policy analysis itself. The lack of universal agreement about the goals and techniques in policy analysis as a broad field makes it difficult to figure out what adding "comparative" to the quest actually means.

This article proceeds from an acceptance of this diversity to attempt to focus on these issues through two lenses. The first is a historical lens that draws on the experience of the policy field within the United States over time to illustrate the development of what is now called "comparative analysis". The second conceptual lens focuses on the different things that we may want to compare and how they can contribute to better public policy. Neither lens provides a clear pathway to effectiveness but rather each contributes to an attempt to map the development and alternatives that might be helpful to policy analysts who wish to contribute to or benefit from comparative work.

"Comparative" in US Policy Analysis

Policy analysis as a modern profession arose in the latter part of the twentieth century in the United States. Its evolution can be traced through three phases (Radin 2017b).[2]

The Beginnings

While the development of a formal field called "policy analysis" emerged in the United States in the 1960s, it is clear that this field was both ancient and new. As Herbert Goldhamer (1978) noted in *The Adviser*, advising decision makers and rulers was an ancient art. But it was the growth of democratic governmental forms that actually led to the modern version of that relationship. Originally, the parliamentary system in the British Commonwealth built in the advising relationship by assuming that top-level elite bureaucrats would play the advising role. And lawyers played that role in the United States in the period during and after the New Deal. The field that we have called policy analysis actually emerged in the United States after World War II. The activity in the early years of policy analysis was based in the Department of

Defense, where new analytic techniques developed by statisticians and operations researchers during World War II showed that it was possible to apply principles of rationality to strategic decision making (Hitch 1953; Radin 2013). These principles seemed to be so obvious to these early analysts that they ignored the possibility of using them as a way to compare different decision processes. Interestingly, the initial use of operations research by the US military during World War II was comparative in origin, motivated by observation of British success in its use during the Battle of Britain (Fortun and Schweber 1993).

The optimism that emerged from the early practitioners identified top officials of the federal government as the clients for the analysis (especially the Secretary of Defense), highlighted analysis of possible new policies (e.g. formulation of policies), was linked to the budget process undertaken by the Executive Branch (rather than the Congress), was undertaken by individuals who were disproportionately trained as economists, and employed techniques of operations research, cost-effectiveness and cost–benefit analysis, and program budgeting and systems analysis (PPBS). Like Machiavelli, these advisors focused rather narrowly on the authority of the "prince".

It was not always clear that the agenda of the analysts corresponded to the more complex agendas of their clients, which stayed within the early confines of the authority of the top officials but reflected more complex sets of goals. Top officials sought to control the fragmented and diffuse organizational program units that were theoretically viewed as under their control. They attempted to improve efficiency in the way that resources were allocated and programs implemented. And they also believed that an increased use of knowledge and information would produce better decisions (Radin 2013). Although decision makers acknowledged the importance of the shared powers system in the United States (particularly the struggle for control by the executive branch over the Congress), that acknowledgement was rarely made explicit in the work they commissioned from their analytic staffs. It was possible to compare approaches to policy problems across institutions explicitly, but this was rarely done. This was an example of failure to use comparative analysis techniques.

Although others beyond the Defense Department were also concerned about similar agenda items, the early experience of the field stayed largely in the defense arena until Lyndon Johnson became president. Israeli defense analyst Yehezkel Dror joined some Americans in conceptualizing the field and American economist Alice Rivlin connected with some former Department of Defense analysts (all known as the Whizz Kids) to apply the concepts and techniques to areas related to poverty and social policy (Radin 2013, p. 17). But it was rare for analysts to compare the use of the techniques in defense to those in poverty and social policy areas or to compare the experience with the techniques in Israel or other countries with that in the US.

By 1965, President Johnson ordered the Bureau of the Budget (the forerunner of the current Office of Management and Budget) to issue a directive to all federal departments and agencies calling on them to embark on the PPBS route and establish central analytic offices that would present budgets using the PPBS format. Johnson's action introduced a new set of dynamics. It shifted the expectations from a set of analytic procedures in a single sector (defense) to a realization that the very structure of the US system (shared powers) meant that cabinet officials and the executive branch did not have the unified powers found in a parliamentary system. One can view this transfer of PPBS from defense to domestic policy as an example of comparative public policy. The failure to consider the differences between these sectors meant that PPBS could not achieve the same success in the domestic applications as it had in defense (Wildavsky 1969). Making an intergovernmental comparison, the Ford Foundation funded efforts to implement PPBS in a number of states and local government (Hatry 1971). The critiques of the diffusion of PPBS only scratched the surface; more explicitly, comparative research might have identified more positive findings about how to organize more effective analytical offices.

Policy Analysis Grows and Diversifies

Despite the failings of PPBS, it seems to have opened the door for the rapid spread of policy analysis across the domestic federal agencies. Within a decade policy analysis units could be found throughout the federal government. Where the policy analysis staffs had once been found only at the top reaches of the federal agencies, they were now found throughout the federal structures, located at specific program units and reflecting the diverse perspectives of those in the federal agencies. Those who were concerned about specialized program elements did not always garner the attention of generalist appointees at the top of the organization. Where the original units had enjoyed a monopoly on analytic activity (and the deference that followed that monopoly), frequently they were being challenged by staff who were unwilling to defer to the centralized unit in the offices of the cabinet department's secretary or agency head (Radin 2013, p. 33).

While the separate bureaucratic locations of multiple analytic approaches might have been treated as a potential source for comparative approaches to policy problems, there was little attention to that potential. Instead, policy analysis units in a number of federal agencies became highly fragmented. Staff of these units were familiar with the techniques and language of the original units and were likely to provide competing policy advice that was packaged in the language and form of policy analysis. Further, the analytic activities undertaken by these units took on the coloration of the agencies and policy issues they addressed. These staff members stayed in offices with responsibility for specific programs and took on the characteristics of policy area specialists.

The diffusion of the practice of policy analysis led to its transformation. Although some analysts continued to concentrate on the formulation of new policies, others considered implementation and evaluation. The original focus on technical and political skills continued (Meltsner 1976), but analysts were also chosen for their organizational, evaluation, and issue-specific skills and knowledge. Clients also diversified: while some analysts continued to work directly for those officials at the top reaches of the organization, others focused on more complex institutional processes and organizational maintenance that frequently involved multiple actors (Radin 2016).

Analysts who focused on domestic policies found themselves in environments where the federal role in policy implementation was limited. The discretion underlying the activities of states and localities in a federal system was crucial in the implementation process and these non-federal actors varied tremendously in both their administrative capacities and the way they interpreted their authority and responsibility. Despite an explosion of academic literature on the "implementation problem" (Pressman and Wildavsky 1973; Bardach 1977; Sabatier 1986), policy analysts rarely focused on the differences between the activities of non-federal actors and how their different types of capabilities and discretion contributed to variation in outcomes.

In addition, policy analysts were increasingly found in a wide variety of settings, including think tanks, which trace their origins to the philanthropically supported

Progressive Era Municipal Bureaus, specialized units serving state and local legislatures, congressional committees, and interest groups. The variable cultures of the agencies and differences in policy issues had an impact on the way that policy analysis was undertaken. Agencies with scientifically trained staff were often attracted to more technical analytical approaches, while agencies that were supported by strong interest groups were likely to be more sensitive to maintaining their support.

Through the remainder of the twentieth century policy analysis did seem to be moving toward a professional identity. It had its own professional association, Association for Public Policy Analysis and Management (APPAM), journals (including JCPA), a range of university-based professional schools, and individual practitioners (largely in federal government agencies) who identified themselves as policy analysts (Radin 2013, pp. 26–27). During this growth period, while some analysts continued to identify with the analytical technician role that emerged with the new profession in the 1970s and 1980s, others sought ways to accommodate new techniques and values within the burgeoning field. By the end of the twentieth century the optimism that had surrounded the early years of the field was muted. Few analysts were searching for techniques that would allow them to devise a comparative perspective on these developments within the US context. At this point it appeared that the policy analysis field took at least two forms: one focused on the practice of policy analysis while the second emphasized the academic and research side of the enterprise.

There were attempts to move discussion about the field of policy analysis beyond experiences within the United States. British academics Brian Hogwood and Lewis Gunn expressed their concerns in *Policy Analysis for the Real World*:

> Although our primary interest was in producing policy analysis materials for British students, our experience has made us aware of the limitations of much American literature for American students, particularly those who have previously thought of policy analysis as merely American politics rehashed, or as arcane mathematical techniques ... Much of the literature about particular techniques concentrates on technical points and assumes that the "optimal" decision will automatically be taken and enforced by a single, authoritative decision maker. (Hogwood and Gunn 1984, pp. v–vi)

The appearance of the JCPA in 1998 was almost a voice in the wilderness. It defined itself as "the only explicitly comparative journal of policy analytic studies" that sought to stimulate the growth of an international community of scholars who research the challenges and benefits of global inter- and intra-policy making. While its definition of "comparative" was not narrow – the journal "aims to capture differences or similarities in policy issues as well as the role of comparative policy analysis both within and between social units" – it did seem to rely on the definition found in the political science community; that is, comparative meant focusing on experiences in at least two countries. It was not always clear what the journal expected from its authors and a fairly wide range of articles appeared within it.

Facing Globalization

The advent of the twenty-first century suggested that the growing interest and concerns about globalization generated new interest in something defined as comparative policy analysis across the world. A range of developments included a broad scope of subjects: types of policy issues, diverse relationships between analysts and clients, types of analysis required, time frames imposed, the stage of the policy process where it occurs, where in the system it occurs (e.g. inside or outside of government), the structure of government involved, placement of analysis in central agencies versus program offices, career or political staff, skill sets required, and the boundaries between policy analysis and public management.

Activity emerged in practice settings, sometimes as the renaming of existing data and planning offices to call them policy analysis organizations. In some settings career staff who traditionally acted as advisors to the government became the core of the policy analysis enterprise. The demise of the Soviet Union provided the impetus in some nations for a unit that would provide advice on alternatives to previous approaches. In some other settings, policy analysis units were established within autocratic governments that provided an impression of openness (Radin 2017a, p. 57).

Training in policy analysis spread widely outside the United States. But while teachers and researchers seemed to be using the same English terms, they often defined them in quite different ways – cultural differences seemed to blur concepts. Such adaption is certainly necessary for preparing policy analysts to function effectively in their national contexts. Nonetheless, it does pose a barrier to comparative policy research when concepts take on different meanings in different countries.

Does the US Experience Help Answer Questions about Comparison?

The US experience with comparative analysis does not tell a clear story. At times opportunities for comparative analysis were present but analysts did not pursue them. There were other times when analysts identified similarities that were either quite dissimilar or operated in very different contexts that diminished the lessons from comparison (Radin 2017b). To increase the chances that we will have answers to these questions in the future, we turn to the question: what aspects of public policy can be usefully compared?

We begin this discussion by acknowledging the differences between policy analysis as a profession and disciplinary research. This dichotomy sets the scene for our expectations about comparative analysis. There are limitations in both areas but there appear to be more opportunities for the researcher than for the analyst. We identify the primary dimensions of comparison and their possibilities and limitations as they attempt to contribute to the development of better public policy.

Policy Analysis as Profession Rather than Discipline

Unlike many academic disciplines, the policy analysis field does not operate as an independent and separate effort. As many have noted, policy analysis involves a conversation between an analyst and a decision maker or actors in a decision-making process. As the previous discussion suggests, that relationship has changed significantly over the years. Yet the literature about the field has rarely focused on the client role. Instead, attention has been concentrated on the methodologies and theories employed by the analyst. Growing complexity of policy problems and the development of multiple analytical approaches have led to tensions between the analyst and the client. Indeed, it is not always clear what it means to be a client of policy analysis (Radin 2016; Vining and

Weimer 2017). Is the decision maker someone who has authority or influence on a particular policy question? Is the client someone who is affected by the policy decision? Are there multiple players within a network involved in various decision-making processes?

The occasional incompatibility between professional responsibility to a particular client and conventional analytical practice may result in an inadequate differentiation between the two (Radin 2016, 2017a). Analysts may forget that they have not been provided with an opportunity to influence decisions and believe that their technical expertise should be the sole basis for decisions. And the complexity of policy problems leads them to focus on existing research sources. They may ignore the political and organizational context in which decisions are made, e.g. ignoring the limitations of already decided policies on implementation possibilities. In reaction, decision makers may view the analyst as insensitive to the constraints they experience and why they need analysis to justify – not to change – their already determined decisions.

It is not clear whether there is a natural interest in comparative work among clients. Clients are sometimes so focused on the difficulties of surviving in their own environment that they are skeptical of looking at other approaches, be they in the neighboring state or in another country. If they do look elsewhere for ideas, it might be as a result of a personal relationship with others in their field or some other somewhat idiosyncratic interest. As a result, there might be skepticism when an analyst suggests an alternative that seems to have emerged from another planet. As the policy analyst must serve the client, lack of client interest in comparison to dampen any interest in comparison on the part of the analyst.

Possible Avenues for Comparative Policy Research

Policy analysts fundamentally address the question: compared to what? Beyond the immediate and narrow focus on comparing alternatives to current policy, policy analysts can potentially improve their contributions through a number of broader comparisons. That is, they can potentially gain useful ideas, information, and insights from research or experience drawn from other contexts. Scholars who seek to inform policy analysts about alternatives, ways of assessing them, or simply frameworks for conceptually ordering a complex world can also gain from comparison. But what are the avenues for comparison? We focus on several categories: policy process research, policy-relevant research, policy ideas, policy research, and policy transfer.

Harold Lasswell (1971) famously distinguished between knowledge of and knowledge in the policy process (Weimer 2008). Both are important but our primary concern is knowledge in the policy process. That is, how can analysis improve the content of public policy? Nonetheless, effective comparison often requires knowledge of policy processes and the context that defines them. That is, how do political processes affect the choice, content, and implementation of public policies?

Table 2 sketches avenues for improving public policy in terms of knowledge of, and knowledge in, the policy process as well as how directly the avenue contributes to actual changes in public policy. We begin with knowledge of the policy process. At the most general level, *political science*, broadly defined to include political economy and political sociology, offers comparisons of different governance regimes that facilitate understanding of the policy process. Although studies of specific institutions or political phenomena can usefully inform policy analysts especially in their predictions of political feasibility, we do

Table 2. Comparative avenues for improving public policy

	Knowledge of the policy process	Knowledge in the policy process
General research	Political science	Policy-relevant research Policy ideas
Policy-focused research	Policy process research	Policy research
Professional practice	Policy analysis methods	Policy transfer

not explicitly consider this avenue here. We do consider *policy process research*, which usually looks across the institutions of governance within countries and introduces concern about how policy processes shape policy content. We also consider *policy analysis methods*, which help professional analysts systematically design and assess policy alternatives. We then consider what we define as knowledge *in* the policy process. At the most general level, science in many disciplines produces *policy-relevant research* that can inform policy design, often crystalized as *policy ideas*, and analysis. *Policy research* focuses more explicitly on public policy problems and alternatives for addressing them. It is often a key resource for informing *policy transfer*, the adaption of policy alternatives to specific applications. One can think of policy transfer as the potential payoff to society from better policy resulting from knowledge in the policy process. We discuss policy process research, policy-relevant research, policy ideas, policy research, policy analysis methods, and policy transfer as possible comparative avenues for improving public policy.

Policy Process Research

The comparative study of political systems can be traced all the way back to Aristotle's assessment of the constitutions of city states. The comparative cross-national study of contemporary policy processes poses two challenges. First, modern government is very complex and diverse. Understanding policy-making processes typically requires detailed knowledge of both formal and informal institutions. Few scholars can competently develop such knowledge for more than a few countries. Second, delving beneath the surface of policy adoption into the substantive content and implementation of policy places yet more demands on researchers. The challenge is finding ways of coordinating the creation of knowledge by multiple researchers, each with deep understanding of the social and political circumstances of one or perhaps a few countries.

Three approaches to meeting this challenge have been pursued. First, common conceptual frameworks can coordinate research by individual scholars. For example, Elinor Ostrom (1990) demonstrated truly comparative research on governance of common property resources. Researchers have employed the broader framing of her approach, institutional rational choice (Kiser and Ostrom 1982), to frame natural resource issues in a variety of settings. Similarly, the advocacy coalition framework (Sabatier and Jenkins-Smith 1988; Real-Doto 2009) has been used to frame long-term policy change in different contexts.

Beyond these widely recognized policy processes frameworks, a systematic framework for at least identifying relevant features of policy systems would potentially be useful in helping to make research more comparable. For example, assessment of the attributes of intra- and inter-organizational property rights relevant to policy issues as suggested in the first issue of the JCPA is one way of increasing the chances that decentralized research efforts would facilitate useful comparison (Vining and Weimer 1998). Although a common framework is desirable, it is unlikely that any particular one will always best facilitate useful comparison. Also, commitment to a particular framework may shift effort away from learning about the substance of policy issues to the assessment of the framework itself. It is not clear how far a highly theoretical approach takes us: witness the extensive development and empirical testing of punctuated equilibrium theory (Jones and Baumgartner 2005) with almost no payoff in terms practical implications for policy analysts beyond that analysts should expect punctuations (Weimer and Vining 2017, p. 268).

Second, project organizers can recruit experts with country- or sector-specific expertise to do parallel assessments of policy processes. For example, projects have recruited country experts to do comparative studies of the changes in property rights systems in post-communist countries (Weimer 1997) and assisted reproductive policies in Canada and European countries (Bleiklie et al. 2004). One of the most ambitious efforts recruited experts to assess governance of the steel, health, and financial sectors in European countries (Bovens et al. 2001). These projects draw on the depth of knowledge of the recruits to provide broader cross-national comparison. Success depends on substantial effort being devoted to the use of common frameworks and the development of common approaches so that the collections become more than the sum of their parts.

Third, comparison of policy processes, including the role of policy analysis, can be facilitated by recruiting experts within specific countries to follow a template through which they address a common set of topics. This is the approach followed by the International Library of Policy Analysis edited by Iris Geva-May and Michael Howlett and published by the University of Bristol's Policy Press in association with the International Comparative Policy Association and JCPA. The series already covers a dozen countries with more volumes planned. The similar structures of the volumes allow for the identification of similarities and differences across countries (Radin 2017b). One can imagine that as these volumes accumulate, they will provide "data" for more systematic cross-national assessments of the role of policy analysis in policy processes.

Policy-Relevant Research

Turning to knowledge in the policy process, researchers in many fields make contributions to knowledge potentially relevant to public policy. Although they may be driven by a desire to contribute to a better society, these researchers often do not relate their findings to specific public policies. For example, better understanding of the link between early childhood nutrition and subsequent cognitive development creates knowledge that could be used to inform policy design whether or not the researchers themselves seek to do so. Such research may be relatively context free, providing generalization but little guidance on application across different political, economic, and social systems. The internationalization of science facilitates broad dissemination of findings. The challenge for policy researchers is translating the knowledge into policies that can be applied in specific contexts.

Policy Ideas

General approaches to specific policy problems, or even concepts of governance more generally, often diffuse with limited assessment. Nonetheless, such ideas, often based in disciplinary theories, can be highly influential in shaping policy. For example, the

Keynesian perspective on macroeconomics achieved dominance among developed countries following World War II (Hall 1989). Ideas based on general theories with clearly hypothesized cause and effect are more likely to diffuse within epistemic communities (Strang and Meyer 1993); ideas that can be framed relatively simply may be more likely to gain public support for their application (Kangas et al. 2014). International organizations and transnational networks increasingly appear to be playing a role in the diffusion of policy ideas (Stone 2004; Lee and Strang 2006).

The abstraction of policy ideas offers both advantages and disadvantages. Even more so than general findings from policy research, novel policy ideas do not come with information that informs detailed policy designs. Indeed, they may diffuse widely well before evidence about their impacts can be gathered and interpreted. Consequently, analysts often have to create policies consistent with the ideas from scratch. However, by requiring explicit policy design to fit the local context, efforts to employ them may help analysts avoid complacency about appropriate fit that may arise when borrowing working policies from other contexts.

Policy Research

Extant policy research seeks to inform public policies by providing evidence relevant to the framing of public policy problems or their solutions. As inherently empirical, it is context specific. For example, it may explore the causes and consequences of teen pregnancy in a particular community. Or it may evaluate a particular intervention intended to reduce the likelihood of pregnant teens in a particular school district dropping out of school before they earn high school diplomas. Assuming internal validity, such findings can usually be reasonably assumed to predict the consequences of continuation of policies in the particular contexts in which they were evaluated, although changing circumstances could intervene to undercut even these predictions. Predictions about the consequences of expanding, shrinking, or incrementally modifying policies in the studied context are likely to be less reliable.

Comparative approaches to policy research can be thought of as increasing the external validity of research by expanding the contexts in which the same, or very similar, policies are evaluated. Although policy research is often observational rather than experimental, researchers may nonetheless be able to increase external validity through the judicious choice of contexts to compare (Cook 2014). However, because policies are often complex bundles of rules and incentives, identifying contexts that offer a favorable tradeoff between internal and external validity may be difficult.

External validity aside, two features of policy research as it is commonly practiced tend to hinder its usefulness to policy analysts (Weimer 2009). First, policy researchers often take a narrow approach to policy impacts, focusing on maximizing the internal validity of inferences about the primary impact of the policy. Policy researchers in academia are often driven in this direction by a desire to publish in disciplinary journals that frequently favor narrow findings produced by novel methods over the more comprehensive assessment produced by more mundane approaches. Although policy analysts want more confident inferences about primary impacts, they also want to know the full range of impacts, even those that were not the focus of evaluative research.

Second, policy research often ignores the costs, broadly defined, of policies. What resources would be needed to implement the policy successfully in a similar context? How were they combined? Answering these questions takes on even greater importance as analysts seek to use the findings to predict the consequences of the policy in less similar contexts. However, gathering such information is itself costly and often excluded from publications.

Policy Analysis Methods

The most basic framework for structuring policy analysis in response to a perceived policy problem includes the identification of relevant goals, the specification of policy alternatives, the systematic prediction and valuation of the impacts of alternatives in terms of goals, and a recommendation based on an explicit comparison of the impacts of the alternatives. Often the predictions employ social science theory and empirical methods. Usually analysts must argue for appropriate valuation metrics, though the protocols of cost–benefit analysis provide commonly accepted ways to assess impacts in terms of economic efficiency. Professional training in policy analysts can be thought of as developing the collection of craft skills for applying this framework.

On the surface, these craft skills would seem to be universal in the sense of applying in any public policy context. However, their execution is actually quite contextual (Weimer 2012). For example, analysts addressing the same policy problem in different countries might very well place different weights on goals or even select different sets of goals because of constitutional or cultural differences. Further, the choice of policy alternatives may also reflect such differences, as well as differences in experience with and public acceptability of various types of policy instruments. Even predicting impacts with generic tools, such as economic theory and statistical methods, require context-specific information to apply theory effectively and interpret empirical findings. Of course, assessing the likelihood of successful implementation is inherently contextual, usually requiring the identification of specific actors who must make contributions to implementation success. For all these reasons, an effective analyst in one country would not necessarily be effective in some other country without explicit attention to how context shapes the use of the universal craft skills.

The importance of context for the effective practice of policy analysis has implications for the training of new policy analysts. Along with the universal craft skills, neophyte analysts should also learn about how to assess and adapt to the contexts in which they are likely to practice. Such learning, like that in other crafts, usually requires hands-on experience to gain tacit knowledge. With a plethora of potential clients and a relatively transparent political system, programs in the United States can usually provide experience through client-oriented projects. Comparable experience may be more difficult to provide in countries with more closed and less transparent political systems. The appropriate professional ethics, in terms of duties to both client and society, may also differ, and, if not carefully considered, expose novice analysts to personal risk.

Policy Transfer

A fundamental task of policy analysts is the identification and crafting of viable and potentially desirable alternatives to current policies. Doing so almost always involves some comparison, if only implicitly through the observation of a single policy implemented in a different context. The process has been called "systematic pinching" (Schneider and Ingram 1988) and "tinkering" (May 1981): analysts identify a working model in some other context, identify its essential elements, and modify the essential elements to craft additional alternatives (Weimer

1993). At one extreme, a novel policy that has not been formally evaluated provides the starting point; at the other extreme, a policy has been implemented and formally evaluated in many contexts. With a fortunate bounty of evaluations of a policy, analysts may benefit from meta-analyses that integrate findings across evaluations to arrive at effect sizes that can be used to predict policy impacts. One example is the approach taken by the Washington State Institute for Public Policy to support cost–benefit analyses of social programs based on US evaluations (Lee et al. 2012), an approach being promoted across US states by the Pew-MacArthur Results First Initiative. Another example is the systematic reviews complied by the Campbell Collaboration, which often include evaluations from many countries (Shadish et al. 2005).

At least three meanings of comparative pinching seem relevant to the work of policy analysts: comparing policies across countries, sub-national governments, or industrial sectors. By far the most common interpretation of comparative policy involves multiple countries. However, the most practical comparisons often involve assessing policies in different contexts within the same country. Less attention has been given to comparing across industrial sectors.

In the overview for a recent issue of the JCPA focusing on comparative studies, Ted Marmor (2017) reviews the opportunities and challenges to cross-national policy comparisons. He notes that cross-national comparisons may allow analysts to understand their own circumstances more clearly by putting them into a broader perspective. Comparisons may also serve as "quasi-experiments" for making inferences about what might work in one's own context. Against these opportunities, however, he cautions against both "naïve transplantation" of what appear to be best practices and the opposite "fallacy of comparative difference", which rejects the value of comparison if there are any cross-national differences; as such differences are ubiquitous, the fallacy precludes any cross-national learning about policy.

Marmor offers four rules for cross-national comparisons. First, the purpose of the comparison should be clear. Comparisons of policy-making processes seek different information than comparisons of the operations of actual policies. Second, as policy contexts differ across industrial sectors even within the same country, careful consideration has to be given to the nature of the sector in making comparisons. Third, operational definitions – rather than marketing labels – are needed to facilitate meaningful comparisons. Fourth, "[there] is the need to understand the country-specific constellation of dominant values, political institutions, and the role of organized interests in the policy domain when assessing the chances of failure or success of given reform proposals" (Marmor 2017, p. 315). Taken together, the third and fourth rules point to the fundamental problem faced by policy analysts seeking to learn about policy designs or their likely impacts from cross-national policy comparisons: the myriad potentially meaningful differences between countries as well as inevitable differences in the details of even nominally similar policies. Indeed, in the face of differing contexts, it would be surprising if nominally similar policies were not modified to accommodate them, whether by initial intention or adaptive response.

One approach to reducing the number of differences across contexts is to make comparisons across sub-national rather than national governments (Snyder 2001). Doing so has long been common in the United States where states have been famously called the "laboratories of democracy". The use of comparative case studies has been a common methodology in this situation (Agranoff and Radin 1991). The opportunity for subnational comparisons seems most obvious in federal systems in which the sub-national units have formal authority over some issues. Nonetheless, unitary governments often create differences in the content or timing of policy because they decentralize some decisions to regional or local administrative units. The sweet spot would seem to be a very comparable context with some policy variation. Further, analysts are likely to be better able to follow Marmor's rules when pinching from parallel sub-units than across national borders because of the greater similarity in contexts. Further, closer proximity may enable them to observe policies on site or learn about them through national policy networks.

Borrowing policies across industrial sectors within a country eliminates cross-national differences but introduces contextual differences because of variation in the issues that the policies address. A policy instrument that works well in one context may not do so in another. For example, a public–private partnership may work well when the private firm and government share profit maximization as the primary goal, future costs are fairly certain, and the costs of monitoring the quality of output are low. However, if the government does not have profit maximization as its primary goal, future costs are highly uncertain, or if the quality of output is costly to monitor, then it may not work well or even end catastrophically with the private partner ending the partnership through bankruptcy (Vining and Weimer 2016). As policy analysts often substantively specialize, not only may they not know where to look for promising policies in other sectors, but they may have difficulty identifying key factors in the apparent success of the policies they decide to consider borrowing.

Conclusion

Although policy analysts are most directly concerned about what we have labeled policy transfer, policy scholars usually contribute to this process indirectly through their policy research. Helping analysts understand differences in policy processes can potentially enable them to identify more relevant sources for policy transfers and the political differences that may be relevant to transfer. Comparative policy research, which links policy content and context to outcomes, can point analysts to potential policy transfers. Its usefulness usually depends on careful consideration of the context in which the studied policy operates. JCPA authors can make more valuable contributions to good public policy by clarifying what they are comparing and providing information relevant to policy transfer.

How can editors and reviewers increase the chances that a retrospective on the JCPA done 10 or 20 years from now will laud its contributions to better public policy? First, they should continue to provide a home for research that compares policy outcomes across countries – half of JCPA articles fall into this category. Although such research can contribute to theory, its inherent value is as a resource for policy transfer.

Second, they should encourage research that makes comparisons across sub-national governments, a category of research currently relatively scarce in JCPA. By holding national constitutional and some aspects of culture constant, they offer the possibility of more confident inferences about policy impacts. JCPA has had a few articles that make sub-national comparisons across countries with respect to urban problems. In some circumstances, such comparisons might provide some of the internal validity of sub-national comparisons with possibly greater external validity in terms of the countries included.

Third, they should encourage research on policy processes that recognizes the role of the policy analyst. Contributions to understanding policy processes can easily find homes in disciplinary journals, especially in political science. However, these contributions often do not identify a role for policy analysis. Providing an understanding of when and how policy analysis can make a difference would potentially help guide the application of policy analysis where it would have the greatest impact.

Notes

1. The review only included items published as articles and only included symposia introductions if they were published in the article section. It is based on a review of abstracts with follow-up reading of the articles if the content was not clear. The classification into theory (and other), single-country, and multi-country articles involved some discretion. For example, articles that focused on international organizations such as the Organisation for Economic Co-operation and Development or the European Union were classified as multi-country. Single-country articles included a few that made sub-national comparisons and one that compared policy issues.
2. Because the formal field called "policy analysis" emerged from US experience, we are using that experience to illustrate possibilities that might have emerged earlier as "comparative analysis".

References

Agranoff, R. and Radin, B. A., 1991, The comparative case study approach in public administration, in Perry, J., editor. *Research in Public Administration*, **1**(1), pp. 203–231.
Bardach, E., 1977, *The Implementation Game: What Happens after a Bill Becomes a Law* (Cambridge: MIT Press).
Bleiklie, I., Goggin, M. L. and Rothmayr, C. (Eds), 2004, *Comparative Biomedical Policy: Governing Assisted Reproductive Technologies* (New York: Routledge).
Bovens, M., 'T Hart, P. and Peters, B. G. (Eds), 2001, *Success and Failure in Public Governance: A Comparative Analysis* (Northampton, MA: Edward Elgar).
Cook, T. D., 2014, Generalizing causal knowledge in the policy sciences: External validity as a task of both multiattribute representation and multiattribute extrapolation. *Journal of Policy Analysis and Management*, **33**(2), pp. 527–536. doi:10.1002/pam.21750
Cyr, A. and deLeon, P., 1975, Comparative policy analysis. *Policy Sciences*, **6**(4), pp. 375–384. doi:10.1007/BF00142380
Fitzpatrick, J., Goggin, M., Heikkila, T., Klingner, D., Machado, J. and Martell, C., 2011, A new look at comparative public administration: Trends in research and an agenda for the future. *Public Administration Review*, **71**(6), pp. 821–830. doi:10.1111/puar.2011.71.issue-6
Fortun, M. and Schweber, S. S., 1993, Scientists and the legacy of World War II: The case of operations research (OR). *Social Studies of Science*, **23**(4), pp. 595–642. doi:10.1177/030631293023004001
Goldhamer, H., 1978, *The Adviser* (New York: Elsevier).
Hall, P. A. (Ed), 1989, *The Political Power of Economic Ideas: Keynesianism across Nations* (Princeton, NJ: Princeton University Press).
Hatry, H. P., 1971, Status of PPBS in local and state governments in the United States. *Policy Sciences*, **2**(2), pp. 177–189. doi:10.1007/BF01411222
Hitch, C., 1953, Sub-optimization in operations problems. *Journal of the Operations Research Society of America*, **1**(3), pp. 87–99. doi:10.1287/opre.1.3.87
Hogwood, B. and Gunn, L., 1984, *Policy Analysis in the Real World* (Oxford: Oxford University Press).
Jones, B. D. and Baumgartner, F. R., 2005, *The Politics of Attention: How Government Prioritizes Problems* (Chicago: University of Chicago Press).
Kangas, O. E., Niemelä, M. and Varjonen, S., 2014, When and why do ideas matter? The influence of framing on opinion formation and policy change. *European Political Science Review*, **6**(1), pp. 73–92. doi:10.1017/S1755773912000306
Kiser, L. L. and Ostrom, E., 1982, Three worlds of Action: A metatheoretical synthesis of institutional rational choice, in: E. Ostrom (Ed) *Strategies of Political Inquiry* (Beverly Hills: Sage), pp. 179–222.
Lasswell, H. D., 1971, *A Pre-View of the Policy Sciences* (New York: American Elsevier).
Lee, C. K. and Strang, D., 2006, The international diffusion of public-sector downsizing: Network emulation and theory-driven learning. *International Organization*, **60**(4), pp. 883–909. doi:10.1017/S0020818306060292
Lee, S., Aos, S., Drake, E., Pennucci, A., Miller, M. and Anderson, L., 2012, Return on investment: Evidence-based options to improve statewide outcomes. *Olympia: Washington State Institute for Public Policy*.
Marmor, T. R., 2017, Comparative studies and the drawing of policy lessons: Describing, explaining, evaluating, and predicting. *Journal of Comparative Policy Analysis*, **19**(4), pp. 313–326.
May, P. J., 1981, Hints for crafting alternative policies. *Policy Analysis*, **7**(2), pp. 227–244.
Meltsner, A. J., 1976, *Policy Analysis in the Bureaucracy* (Berkeley, CA: University of California Press).
Ostrom, E., 1990, *Governing the Commons: The Evolution of Institutions for Collective Action* (New York: Cambridge University Press).

Pressman, J. L. and Wildavsky, A., 1973, *Implementation: how Great Expectations in Washington are Dashed in Oakland; Or, Why It's Amazing that Federal Programs Work at All.*. (Berkeley: University of California Press).
Radin, B. A., 2013, *Beyond Machiavelli: Policy Analysis Reaches Midlife* (Washington, DC: Georgetown University Press).
Radin, B. A., 2016, Policy analysis and advising decisionmakers: Don't forget the decisionmaker/client. *Journal of Comparative Policy Analysis: Research and Practice*, **18**(3), pp. 290–301. doi:10.1080/13876988.2016.1175191
Radin, B. A., 2017a, Reflections on a half century of policy analysis, in: M. Brans, I. Geva-May and M. Howlett (Eds) *Routledge Handbook of Comparative Policy Analysis* (London: Rutledge), pp. 85–99.
Radin, B. A., 2017b, Book review. *Journal of Comparative Policy Analysis*, **19**(1), pp. 87–89. doi:10.1080/13876988.2017.1286018
Real-Dato, J., 2009, Mechanisms of policy change: A proposal for a synthetic explanatory framework. *Journal of Comparative Policy Analysis*, **11**(1), pp. 117–143. doi:10.1080/13876980802648268
Sabatier, P. and Jenkins-Smith, H., 1988, An advocacy coalition model of policy change and the role of policy-oriented learning. *Policy Sciences*, **21**(2–3), pp. 129–168. doi:10.1007/BF00136406
Sabatier, P. A., 1986, Top-down and bottom-up approaches to implementation research: A critical analysis and suggested synthesis. *Journal of Public Policy*, **6**(1), pp. 21–48. doi:10.1017/S0143814X00003846
Schneider, A. and Ingram, H., 1988, Systematically pinching ideas: A comparative approach to policy design. *Journal of Public Policy*, **8**(1), pp. 61–80. doi:10.1017/S0143814X00006851
Shadish, W. R., Chacón-Moscoso, S. and Sánchez-Meca, J., 2005, Evidence-based decision making: Enhancing systematic reviews of program evaluation results in Europe. *Evaluation*, **11**(1), pp. 95–109. doi:10.1177/1356389005053196
Snyder, R., 2001, Scaling down: Subnational comparative method. *Studies in Comparative International Development*, **36**(1), pp. 93–110. doi:10.1007/BF02687586
Stone, D., 2004, Transfer agents and global networks in the 'transnationalization' of policy. *Journal of European Public Policy*, **11**(3), pp. 545–566. doi:10.1080/13501760410001694291
Strang, D. and Meyer, J. W., 1993, Institutional conditions for diffusion. *Theory and Society*, **22**(4), pp. 487–511. doi:10.1007/BF00993595
Vining, A. R. and Weimer, D. L., 1998, Informing institutional design: Strategies for comparative cumulation. *Journal of Comparative Policy Analysis*, **1**(1), pp. 39–60. doi:10.1080/13876989808412615
Vining, A. R. and Weimer, D. L., 2016, The challenges of fractionalized property rights in public-private hybrid organizations: The good, the bad, and the ugly. *Regulation & Governance*, **2**(10), pp. 161–178. doi:10.1111/rego.12086
Vining, A. R. and Weimer, D. L., 2017, Policy analysis: A valuable skill for public administrators, in: J. C. N. Raadschelders and R. Stillman II (Eds) *Foundations of Public Administration* (Irvine, CA: Melvin and Leigh), pp. 162–176.
Weimer, D. L., 1993, The current state of design craft: Borrowing, tinkering, and problem solving. *Public Administration Review*, **53**(2), pp. 110–120. doi:10.2307/976703
Weimer, D. L. (Ed), 1997, *The Political Economy of Property Rights: Institutional Change and Credibility in the Reform of Centrally Planned Economies* (New York: Cambridge University Press).
Weimer, D. L., 2008, Theories of and in the policy process. *Policy Studies Journal*, **36**(4), pp. 489–495. doi:10.1111/psj.2008.36.issue-4
Weimer, D. L., 2009, Making education research more policy analytic, in: G. Sykes, B. Schneider and D. N. Plank (Eds) *Handbook of Education Policy Research* (New York: Routledge), pp. 93–100.
Weimer, D. L., 2012, The universal and the particular in policy analysis and training. *Journal of Comparative Policy Analysis*, **14**(1), pp. 1–8. doi:10.1080/13876988.2011.646819
Weimer, D. L. and Vining, A. R., 2017, *Policy Analysis: Concepts and Practice*, 6th ed. (New York: Routledge).
Wildavsky, A., 1969, Rescuing policy analysis from PPBS. *Public Administration Review*, **29**(2), pp. 189–202. doi:10.2307/973700

The Problem of Policy Problems

B. GUY PETERS

ABSTRACT *Although conceptions of policy design have well-developed conceptions of the instruments used to address public problems, they have much less developed conceptions of those problems themselves. This article proposes one analytic scheme for understanding the nature of policy problems and issues, and begins to relate the choice of instruments to the nature of the underlying problems for society.*

Policy design involves developing models of causation, instrumentation, and evaluation (Linder and Peters 1984, 1989, Ringeling 2005), and then finding ways of linking those three models. As the literature on policy design has been developing, the principal emphasis has been placed on the nature of policy instruments or "tools", and on the political process of linking instruments and policy evaluations. That is, scholars and practitioners have gained a reasonably good knowledge of the consequences of selecting one type of instrument, and scholars are beginning to have the capacity to advise decision makers about when, and under what circumstances, to select one tool or another to maximize certain values.

By contrast, the literature linking policy problems and tools has been less well developed. While the long-term goal of such an analytic effort should be to catalogue differing kinds of problems and link them logically, and empirically, with appropriate forms of policy instruments, the objective here is more modest. It involves developing an analytical framework for understanding relevant variations in problems and offering some early thoughts in tying problem characteristics to policy tools. Throughout the paper, examples of policy problems are highlighted, and these examples are drawn disproportionately from social policy.[1]

The analytic framework for dealing with issues of design developed in this paper is general, and can be applied to any political system. In this paper, however, I will be paying some particular attention to the European Union and the particular policy-making style of that system (see, for example, Wallace and Wallace 2000, Steunenberg and van Vught 1998). The EU has been described, among other ways, as a regulatory state (Majone 1996) that tends to intervene more through legal instruments than through monetary tools. There are, of course, some important European spending programs but law tends to be the dominant tool. Further, the political process of the EU is more complex than most, in part because of the continuing importance of the member nations in making, and then implementing, the decisions of the Union. Indeed, while the analytic focus here is on the possibilities of design, much of the decision making in the EU approximates the randomness and serendipity of the garbage can model (Cohen, March and Olsen 1971, Peters and Pierre 2005) and other approaches to policy based on bounded rationality.

Another important element of policy making in the European Union is the role of the bureaucracy as a central player. Bureaucracies are often under-rated in terms of their impact on policy choices, but this is especially true in the EU (see Peters 1992). This importance is manifested in the definition of policies and the construction of the agenda for policy making. This style of making policy helps to create the famous democratic deficit in the Union, but it also produces substantial internal conflicts over policy, and a particular style of policy. In particular, the multiple DGs that may contend for control of some policy areas (Patterson 1998), and the right of initiating policy given to the Commission, create policy-making processes different from those found in "normal" political systems.

Policy Instruments and Design: A Brief Review of Literature

Although a great deal of research is still needed in the areas of policy instruments and evaluation, there is a substantial extant body of knowledge. For example, the tools literature has progressed from its roots in implementation (Bardach 1980, Hood 1986, Salamon and Lund 1989), through critiques of these models based on ideas of autopoesis and self-referentiality (Ringeling and Van Nispen 1998, in 't Veld 1991), and then a reformulation of the tools approach taking into account critiques of more traditional approaches to instruments (Peters and Van Nispen 1998). There is at present a further round of development in the implementation approach of instrument theories, taking into account changes in the environment of public policies, as well as an improved understanding of the interactions of the various tools in the delivery of services (Salamon 2000). Similarly, Ingram and Schneider (1997) in their discussion of policy design have pointed to the need for would-be designers to consider the nature of the populations addressed by instruments, rather than just examining the instruments in isolation. Timmermans *et al.* (1998) also place the study of policy instruments within a broad design context, focusing on the institutional context and the roles of actors involved in designing.

The instruments literature has also performed a rather effective job in cataloging the characteristics of policy instruments. The political nature of instruments has been contrasted with their more utilitarian role in the delivery of public services (Peters 2000). The value biases embedded in each type of instrument have been identified and discussed (Zito *et al.* 2000). Several also have demonstrated the pervasive impact of national political cultures on the choice of tools (Howlett 1991; see Trebilcock 2005), helping to identify biases in the manner in which tools are selected. That finding, in turn, highlights the emphasis in this growing body of literature on the *conscious* selection of instruments, as opposed to their selection merely on the basis of custom, familiarity and institutional inertia (Linder and Peters 1998, 1990).[2]

The tools literature has made substantial progress in characterizing the modes of intervention in the economy and society, and the notion of policy design has become a standard component of the general literature on public policy. What has been less well developed in the available literature, however, is an analytic understanding of the policy problems that are being "solved" through the employment of those instruments. Even if we are now capable of understanding more thoroughly the characteristics of policy instruments, that knowledge might be of relatively little utility (practically or even theoretically) if we do not understand the situations into which they are being used to implement public policies. The intention of producing desired programmatic results through well chosen instruments might be unfulfilled if there is no appropriate linkage with the problems being addressed. Therefore, this paper begins to explore more fully the nature of policy problems. The ultimate end of the analysis is both to understand the nature of the problems, as well as the ways in which they may be matched with particular instruments and particular forms of evaluation to round out more fully a model of policy design.

The most fundamental point to be made in this paper, therefore, is that the contingent relationship argued to exist between problems and instruments is crucial to the enterprise of policy design. In a more recent discussion of the instruments literature (Linder and Peters 1998), we have described the answers that some respondents gave to our survey investigation concerning policy instruments as "contingentist". These respondents argued that the real answer to any question about which instrument to select for a problem was that "It depends". They argued that there was no single instrument that should be selected for all situations, and that there is a need to select carefully on the basis of the particular problem being addressed (see also Bagchus 1998). The contingentists were not, however, given the opportunity to develop their own ideas about the factors on which tools choice should depend; we will be beginning some of that inquiry in this paper.

The present inquiry concerning policy problems more implicitly makes the same statement about contingent relationships. If we were to understand completely the characteristics of the range of available tools there still would not be an algorithm for mapping tools into problems; the answer about in what circumstances to employ each tool is always, fundamentally, "It depends". For the purposes of this paper, perhaps the most fundamental characteristic is the ability to utilize private as well as public sector instruments in the delivery of the policy, and through that mixture begin to address the collective nature of both problems and instruments. Therefore, we need to consider carefully the nature of policy problems that make them more amenable to interventions using mixtures of both public and private sector actors. There will be relatively few answers to these basic questions of contingent relationships between problems and instruments provided here; rather the attempt is to develop the correct questions that would then guide in the selection of instruments, and to conduct a preliminary exploration of those questions in relation to the changing nature of social policy problems in the United States and in Europe.

The Changing Nature of Social Problems

The collection of programs and issues usually referred to as social policy help to make the point that the functional titles that are usually used to describe policy are inadequate for effective analysis. There is as much variance within this category of policy as there is between some aspects of "social policy" and other policy areas. For example, providing public pensions is a relatively simple and mechanical exercise of determining eligibility and writing checks. On the other hand, providing personal social services such as counseling or adoption services involves a great deal of personal interaction and personal judgment on the part of professionals. If health services are included as a part of social services then the mix becomes even more complex, with a policy area dominated by professionals and technical expertise, as well as delivered through complex organizational structures such as hospitals. These examples might be extended, but the basic point is that functional titles are a starting point for the analysis rather than an ending point if we want to develop a more effective analytic approach to policy.

Although there is an established literature on social policy in the welfare states of Europe (and some other parts of the world as well – see Mesa-Lago 1994) the economic and social transformations of the late twentieth century, continuing into the twenty-first, have altered the discourse about social policy, and also changed the nature of the problems themselves. Globalization, for example, has required thinking more creatively about the role of the welfare state in national systems of production (Fitzpatrick 2003). Further, the continuing demographic crisis in many societies requires rethinking work and retirement, and even forces societies committed to substantial leisure time to reconsider the role of work in contemporary economies.

For the European Union social policy to some extent resides at the periphery of its competencies. The economic basis of the Union does not appear to give Brussels much authority over issues of social policy, but the intimate connection of the welfare state to employment, especially after Lisbon, means that the EU does have an increasing role in social policy issues. Further, given the importance of the Lisbon agenda on employment and its linkage with the open method of co-ordination and social policy, the EU has become important for redefining social policy issues in many countries. While social policy and labor market policy have always been closely connected that linkage is now more manifest and co-ordination among these areas of policy will be crucial to the success of both (Peters forthcoming).

Policy Problems

Defining policy problems in a way that can be effective for policy design appears to be a two-step process. The first stage in the process is defining what the problem is about; is it a problem of agriculture, environment, or whatever. This can be a difficult question politically and even empirically, and it is often a crucial question for the resolution of the issue, and for the type of government response. For example, is the problem of how to fertilize Midwestern farmland properly a question of agricultural productivity and/or environmental protection? Depending on how that question is answered, different organizations in government will be given greater or lesser roles in resolving the problem, and different modalities of involvement will be invoked. Further, if a *"wrong"* definition of the problem is made it may mean that the ultimate "solution" for the problem will be delayed. Another confounded characteristic of defining the policy problem is that the most important problems themselves are becoming less clearly defined. For example, conventional economic problems are now transforming into "competitiveness" problems that involve not only finance but also labor, environmental, and education issues. Likewise, poverty – which was itself somewhat difficult to define in other than very nominal terms – has been redefined as social exclusion, and now includes a range of behavioral as well as economic variables as part of the syndrome to be explored.

The second stage of the analytic process is to develop a set of dimensions that can be used to characterize problems. Although it is important (at least in practical terms) to link a problem with an agency or ministry, and to assign a functional name to that problem, that may be inadequate for policy design purposes. For this task, a clearer analytic understanding of the problem is necessary in order to understand that the problems that are defined as being within the control of one ministry or another may themselves be very different. Therefore, a good deal of this paper will be concerned with a preliminary discussion of characteristics that appear useful for describing problems and for linking them with instruments.

Stage One: What is the Problem?

The existing literature on the social construction of policy problems and on policy framing has done a useful service in pointing to the politics involved in problem definition (Rochefort and Cobb 1994). First, we have seen how important the minimal capacity to name a problem is for even recognizing its existence, and then beginning to address the problem through the public sector. Problems of spousal abuse and child abuse, for example, had to be conceptualized in that way before they could be taken into the political arena for some form of resolution (Nelson 1984). Until there is a label that can be attached to an issue, it is difficult to feed into the political process for any sort of resolution or even discussion; indeed without that label the question is not really an issue.

The agenda-setting literature in political science (Cobb and Elder 1983, Baumgartner and Jones 1993, Kingdon 1994) also is closely connected with these constructivist arguments about issues and problems. Again, the assumption that policy problems must be recognized and identified in order to be usable within the political process is central. The agendas literature argues that problems (or opportunities) present themselves rather independently, although there is ample room for the role of the policy entrepreneur in the process. This entrepreneur will identify and process the issues so that those issues can proceed onto some active agenda within the political system. Further, the agenda-setting literature tends to focus somewhat more on the organizational basis of politics and the roles that those structures play in sorting and advocating items for an agenda. Any definition of an issue will advantage some organizations rather than others so that this may become a locus for bureaucratic politics. As Petracca (1992, p.4) argues, "how an issue is defined or redefined, as the case may be, influences: (1) the type of politicking which will ensue around it; (2) its chances of reaching the agenda of particular political institution; and (3) the chances of a policy outcome favorable to advocates of the issue". In short, problem definition will set the stage for the final determination of the policy and therefore is crucial for shaping the final resolution of "the problem".

Schon and Rein (1994) have extended this argument somewhat by their discussion of "policy framing". They argue that perhaps the most crucial stage of the policy process is the juncture at which the issue is "framed", or defined in political terms. This framing defines who the participants will be, who the winners and losers may be, what the range of conflict may be, and a whole range of other components of the debate over the issue.³ Once framed, the issue is difficult to reframe in the policy debate with the consequence that initial choices have an enduring impact in the political process. That having been said, reframing is actually one of the mechanisms for resolving (seemingly) intractable policy problems that Schon and Rein develop (see also Hisschemoller and Hoppe 1995).⁴

The agendas and framing literatures go some distance in the identification of policy problems as a crucial aspect of the *political* process, but do not do a great deal in explaining how to deal with issues in the policy process per se. That is, once the issue has arrived on the agenda and must be dealt with, how will decision makers process them, and how do they then move into the mode of designing government interventions to correct the real and/or perceived defect in the society or economy. The psychological and sociological elements of the problem may have been defined well, but that information does not necessarily enable governments to make good public policy decisions about how to solve the problem that has been constructed. Indeed, the social construction of the problem that is crucial for its political selection on the agenda may mask more than it reveals about the underlying problem.

Stage 2: Framing the Problem for Solution

We will now transfer attention to the second stage of the process of defining the problems that governments are addressing. This is the stage in which that problem, having been identified, comes to be understood in a manner that will prepare it for solution. This stage in the policy process has subjective and political elements, just as did the first stage, but at this stage there is arguably a larger objective component to the issue. Further, having been defined in a manner that tends to assign it to a particular organization within the public sector, that organization will itself have to differentiate the issue beyond the simple functional label that has been attached to it. It will, in short, have to develop and design policy instruments to address the problem.

We will be arguing here that the labeling of a policy problem as being "health", "environmental", "agricultural" or whatever, tends to mask a good deal of the complexity contained within the problem, and ultimately may limit the capacity of the public sector to solve the problem. By labeling the problem in that particular way, the political process tends to assume that there is some defined set of tools that the policy organization in question tends to bring to bear on the problem and which in turn simplifies the problem of policy choice. On the contrary, however, this labeling tends to ignore the high level of variance within policy areas. While much of the literature in political science and public policy tends to define environmental policy as social regulatory policy (May 2000), the reality is that – to an increasing degree – the applicability of the social regulatory label depends on the policy subfield being addressed. In water pollution control, for example, point source discharges are dealt with differently than non-point source water pollution runoff; point sources are dealt with in direct regulatory fashion and non-point sources are generally not – at least at the federal level in the US. Thus, even if organizations within a particular government department might like to address all their problems in a particular way, the reality is that they cannot and do not (no matter how hard they may try!).

The basic point being made here is that the names emblazoned on government buildings are an inadequate guide for the internal differences and complications involved in the policies that they administer and the problems that they confront.[5] Therefore, as we begin to conceptualize the numerous factors that might be utilized to define problems, we need to think about a broad range of variables, rather than confining our attention to those familiar labels of policy areas and government departments. The labels certainly are very useful at the first stage, as the means of linking problems and organizations, but they quickly lose that utility once the second stage of designing policies is reached.

For that second stage a more variable approach appears to be required, an approach that forces consideration of a number of factors in the single definition of a problem. This inherent eclecticism may appear to be a shotgun approach to a highly complex question, and to some extent it is. Still, the level of theoretical and practical guidance available in addressing policy problems does not appear to permit more than this wide-open attack on the issue at the initial stages. Therefore, the remainder of this paper will contain a discussion of categories of variables that might be included in a classification of policy problems. We will conclude with some (extremely preliminary) ideas about how to link those variables with the instruments that may be used to implement any programs designed to resolve problems.

The above having been said, there are several extant schemes that provide some beginning to the analysis of policy problems. In particular the Thompson and Tuden (1959) scheme, and that developed by Charles Perrow (1970), to characterize decision making in organizations actually may be useful places at which to begin thinking about characterizing policy problems. Both schemes are concerned with the nature of the knowledge decision makers have about the questions they are facing, as well as the degree of agreement on preferences for the outcomes of the process. In the one scheme (Thompson and Tuden 1959), the argument is based on the degree of agreement on the causation of the phenomenon in question, combined with the degree of agreement about goals. In the other, problems are characterized more in terns of uncertainty so that designs of processes (as well as the designs of the policies themselves) must consider the degree of robustness required. Still another approach is offered by Gormley (1986) and focuses on the complexity and salience of the problems addressed, and their influence of the politics associated with crafting policy solutions.

All of these existing schemes highlight the interaction of aspects of the environment of designing, but as interesting as these schemes are they may understate the complexity of that context and also use far too many variables (at least for such a preliminary stage of the investigation). These are insightful looks at some of the intricacy of problems, but are only part of the nature of problems that need to be explored. Therefore, we will continue to opt for a more open-ended enumeration of the attributes of policy problems in the hope of even over-specifying their nature so that some future reduction of these attributes can simplify the problem for both the analyst and the practical policy maker.

Characteristics of Policy Problems

As I begin to examine policy problems, I will not develop a taxonomy of problems per se but rather will develop a set of variables that can characterize the problems. The analytic problem then is to think about what is really the problem, and what factors determine the applicability of one tool or another. The attributes of problems that should be considered in such an analysis are both objective and subjective; they are both "natural" and socially constructed; they are both mutable and immutable. The outcome of our enumeration will provide a start, but only a start. Indeed, as we begin to make even a partial catalog of the attributes we find that each of the variables appears to have sub-variables that define it, and the problem becomes increasingly complex. We will outline seven variables related to policy problems, some of which may be related to one another, and others which possess "sub-attributes" that are subject to differing interpretations in relation to policy instrument selection. The first three variables discussed relate clearly to the problems themselves, and appear as though they may influence the selection of policy instruments that focus more on process than substance. The second set of variables relates more to the nexus or connection between problem characteristics and instrument choice, and they tend to be somewhat more substantive in their implications.

Rochefort and Cobb (1994) proposed a set of attributes of issues when discussing agenda setting that are not too dissimilar from a list that might be developed for characterizing policy problems. This list was: *causality, severity, incidence, proximity, novelty, crisis and the availability of solutions.* Another characteristic, the problematic nature of the population, seems more relevant to agenda setting per se than to objective policy. Nevertheless, some of the problem attributes discussed below raise similar concerns about the nature of the population being served, and include those clientele questions in the mix of problem characteristics.

Solubility

The first, and perhaps most basic, issue to be addressed in looking at policy problems is whether they can be "solved" or not. That is no simple question, given both the number of problems that are addressed by government and the difficulty of some of those problems.[6] Further, we are aware of the political realities of policy making that require the advocate of a "solution" to act as if that program was indeed *the* answer to the problem, if for no other reason than failure to do so would almost certainly ensure that the program would not be adopted. We can imagine the success of a program advocate who begins by arguing that this may or may not really solve the problem, but it is worth a try anyway. The political reality is that programs and instruments have to be oversold simply to have any realistic opportunity for adoption. This is true even though for many of the issues confronting government there is far from any clear idea about either cause or solution (Nelson 1978).

What we are referring to here is whether a problem can be argued to have a finite and definable solution or whether it is likely to appear again and again on the agenda of government. At one level some procedural issues in government, for example, budget decisions about how much to spend, return to the agenda on an annual (or even more frequent) basis. On a more substantive level, however, some issues appear to return frequently for adjustment and for reconsideration. The absence of durable solutions for some problems implies that they will be chronic questions that will be "solved" again and again, and really not solved at all (see Sieber 1981). The implication is that these problems may be best addressed through policy instruments that allow sufficient flexibility to revise and adapt specific solutions relatively easily on an ongoing basis.

We should note, however, that the absence of durability in a particular set of solutions may be a function either of the politics surrounding the issue or of the more programmatic nature of the issues.[7] Even if a problem has a simple programmatic solution (the technology for abortion, for example, is relatively simple and well known), political considerations *may* not permit the issue to rest. On the other hand, the technology available for addressing the problem, or the nature of the operational environment of a program, may change sufficiently often to force frequent revisions. Even social policies such as pensions that might once have been considered "solved" now have to be reopened as a result of demographic and financial change (Fawcett 2005).

Is there any way to predict *a priori* whether a problem is likely to be acute or chronic? As with much of the rest of this discussion, this kind of analysis is necessarily at a preliminary stage; however, several other variables appear to be useful in making such a prediction. One would be the degree of value dissensus in the policy area, and the degree to which the issue touches on fundamental moral and political values. This is clearly true for certain obviously moral issues (Tatalovich and Daynes 1997) that are reconsidered regularly for political reasons, e.g. abortion in the United States, but certain environmental issues may also have strong moral overtones that lead them to be the subjects of continuing debate and discussion. For example, the debate over genetically modified crops in Europe has assumed some of the element of moral argument. In American environmental policy, the "rights" of *individuals* to use their property as they see fit carries moral connotations that are stronger than the rights of large corporate entities to produce products as they wish (Epstein 1985). Thus, in this sense, the target audience of a policy may have moral implications that affect the degree to which the problem may be subject to durable solution, and this susceptibility to policy change may in turn influence the choice of appropriate policy instruments.

Policy durability may also be affected by variables that are more programmatic in nature. Many social programs, for example, and especially those designed to reduce poverty, have been argued "not to work" or to have required excessive expenditures for the benefits produced (Kenworthy 1999). In such a case as poverty it is difficult to separate the political from the programmatic causes for the problem being made chronic, but the justification for its frequent reconsideration at least is phrased in programmatic terms. In either case, however, the fundamental ideological contests taking place in this policy area appear to require almost constant tinkering, or perhaps threats of termination, of the programs in order for any advancement to occur. European social policy has not had the same dissensus at the national level, but when some aspects of labor market policy are debated in Brussels fundamental differences in national styles emerge, and policy making difficulties escalate.

Another aspect of the chronic nature of a problem may be the availability of a technology that can indeed "solve" the problem once and for all. Take, for example, the problem of children who are not immunized against all the basic childhood diseases. While there can be financial questions about this issue, there is a simple technology and there is a basic agreement that children should be immunized against a range of serious diseases.[8] On the other hand, public programs designed to eradicate poverty, or even those designed to educate students, may be much less certain about the methodology to be used, or the real effectiveness of the methodology that has customarily been employed. Likewise, when governments take it upon themselves to "eradicate" drug use they enter an area of behavior with numerous possible causes and also numerous possible remedies, none of which has been fully verified.

Chronic problems are also those that are heavily dependent upon external factors, and especially external factors that are themselves highly variable. The economy is an obvious case of a chronic policy problem that confronts governments. Even when those governments believed that they could manage the economy successfully, they did not act as if they could do so with a single dose of Keynesian, or monetarist, or supply-side medicine. Rather, there was almost constant adjustment of those policy instruments to correspond to changes in economic performance, or predictions of economic performance.[9] Economic policy has the further characteristic that one round of interventions may produce the need for the next; curing inflation may only lead to the need to combat unemployment, and then perhaps back to fighting inflation yet again.

One interesting way of coping with problems that are insoluble, or that are perceived to be insoluble, is to rely more on procedure than on substance. While procedures rarely solve other than procedural issues, they can be a means of forcing the regular and thorough reconsideration of a policy problem, and hence allow for some systematic adjustment. At the extreme, the weekly meetings of the Federal Reserve Board are a procedural device that ensures the regular reconsideration of monetary policy, and economic policy more generally. At less of an extreme, the requirement for regular review of the Social Security program addresses a problem that was once considered solved but is now much less of a given in American policy (Wildavsky 1998).

Another way to cope with policy issues that are insoluble for political reasons is to attempt to depoliticize them, or to transfer them to non-majoritarian institutions. Majone (2001) has argued on behalf of such solutions in the European Union, and to some extent more generally, as a means of providing predictability for policies – credible commitment – and of removing some of the sharper alterations in policy that can produce dysfunctional consequences. Of course, in a system that already is perceived to have a democratic deficit relying on non-majoritarian institutions may not be the wisest course of action for enhancing legitimacy.

Complexity

The second attribute of policy problems that I will examine is their complexity. This term is used in several ways in the policy literature, and we will be doing the same here. Initially, we will want to differentiate *political* complexity from *programmatic* complexity,[10] and then we will want to differentiate between at least two forms of programmatic complexity. By *political complexity* we mean the number of political interests and actors involved in the problem, and hence the degree of difficulty in negotiating agreements among the parties involved. One of the characteristics of policy making in the contemporary environment is the difficulty in restraining involvement, and hence the increasing difficulty in reaching solutions (Gray 1998). Or, as Charles Jones (1982) has put it with respect to the United States, "iron triangles have become big sloppy hexagons". It is not necessarily the case that this form of political complexity must induce policy failure – the Scandinavian countries appear capable of governing effectively even with a wide range of interests involved. Still, wider involvement of interests increases the load on the decision-making apparatus of the political system, and may complicate discussions and resolution of policy instrument related issues.

Programmatic complexity refers to several aspects of a policy problem. One would be its technical content. Problems vary markedly in the extent to which the average citizen in the street is capable of understanding the issues and, more importantly, capable of intervening effectively in the decision-making process. Most citizens feel perfectly capable of discussing the education of their children, or zoning for their neighborhood (even though there are experts in these fields as well) but feel much less efficacious in discussing complex technical issues associated with global warming, acid rain, or nuclear power generation. Further, the real knowledge bases in the latter areas are, *ceteris paribus*, more demanding than in the former areas, so that even if citizens have opinions they are unlikely to be effective participants in the process unless they also have substantial technical expertise.

Another way to think of complexity is in terms of multiple causation. As noted already, we have conceptualized the policy design process as the marrying of models of causation, instrumentation, and evaluation (Linder and Peters 1984). The problem is that for many public problems there are competing models of causation, and hence competing experts. In water pollution control, for example, there has been an historic tendency for civil and environmental engineers to conceptualize environmental problems as largely technological in nature. This kind of conceptual model dominated the early establishment of technology based treatment controls in the United States, for example. Over the last decade and half, however, this technological perspective has been increasingly challenged by biologists and toxicologists who have conceived of environmental problems as problems of behavior and ecological balance, with the result that there has been a move toward more preventively oriented policy solutions. For a policy area such as crime, there are multiple ways of conceptualizing the root causes of the problem and hence no clear way of addressing the problem.

This discussion of complexity demonstrates that it is a multi-faceted concept that yields differing implications for policy design and instrument choice, depending on the forms of complexity that are evident in any particular policy problem situation. When complexity is conceived of in political terms, it appears that policy design efforts should enable processes that are: (1) flexible enough to respond to varying interests; (2) understood by all those involved; (3) defined in terms of specific processes for overcoming stalemate and disagreement. These processes, it seems, may incorporate both public and private sectors in the formulation and implementation phases of the policy process, while reserving authoritative mechanisms for public sector intervention when they are necessary to overcome stalemate and/or inaction.

It can also be argued that programmatic complexity that assumes a highly technical form should be inversely correlated with political complexity. That is, as problems become more technical, and hence more dominated by experts and information, it becomes more difficult for other groups of actors, such as interest groups, to intervene effectively into the policy process. Of course, there has been significant growth in expertise among the groups opposed to the dominant directions of policy in industrialized democracies – environmentalists and other social movements can now muster a wealth of technical information as well as people. Based at least in part on these successes, advocates of deliberative democracy are attempting to open up decision making, even when there are apparently high technical hurdles to be jumped (Elster 1998). Further, governments are themselves developing policy tools that enable counter-expertise to be applied during the policy process, e. g. the hiring of paid public intervenors in regulatory hearings (Gormley 1986). Even so, it is necessary to recognize that high levels of technical content can create obstacles for widespread participation and that the scope of political conflict often can be minimized by placing greater emphasis on expertise in making decisions and defining the relevant issues in technical rather than distributive terms.

And finally, when problem complexity is viewed in terms of competing models of causation, it is necessary to recognize that the policy instruments chosen are likely to depend on the model(s) of causation that are viewed as predominant. In practical terms, this may mean that policy instrument choice will vary over time as differing conceptions of the causal processes underlying specific problems gain and lose support. We see this dynamic in water pollution control, for example, as older technology based conceptions of water pollution problems have given way to more process oriented approaches such as watershed protection activities that are directed toward changing behaviors of those affecting water quality within particular geographically defined watersheds. The result here (and likely elsewhere as well) is a layering of policy instruments "on top of one another", as instruments conceived under previously accepted models of causality are supplemented with new instruments that are based on more recent conceptions of problem causation. The end result here, of course, is not the selection of one policy instrument over another, but rather an increasingly complex admixture of policy instruments built on the foundations of changing conceptual understandings of causal processes underlying the problems in question.

That redundancy in instruments and approaches to policy can be, and often is conceptualized as, wasteful. On the other hand, however, it can also be seen as a highly rational approach to problems, especially when those problems are complex and perhaps less well understood than they might be. Just as triangulation is a useful approach to building social theory, so too may multiple methods and instruments be useful for coping with complex problems. For example, if we accept that the socio-economic processes undergirding continuing poverty are not understood adequately then using multiple instruments may be the best way of combating the problem.[11]

The Question of Scale

A third attribute of problems that is worth considering here is the scale of the question confronting government. That is, what is the magnitude of the problem, and the range of effects that it produces. Phrased somewhat differently, can the problem be disaggregated into smaller components, or is it of such a nature that it requires comprehensive solution or nothing at all. Further, is the problem amenable to digesting large levels of input at once, or is it more incremental and cumulative in nature. Some examples may help clarify the nature of the term "scale" as applied to policy problems.

The term of scale was first used with respect to public policy by Paul Schulman (1980). He argued that some policy problems were inherently large-scale and therefore required an "all or nothing" approach to solving the problem. The principal example given was the space program. It would do NASA little or no good to get a man half way to the moon; the project was such that partial solutions were, in essence, failures. As a less extreme example, it would do the Army Corps of Engineers little or no good to build half a dam over a river; they have to complete the task or not start in the first place if they are to be successful, and economical, in the use of scarce resources. An even less extreme example in environmental policy may be the "third generation" problem of global warming, in which small reductions in greenhouse gas emissions may do little to address the problem, absent a more complete and comprehensive effort. In short, these large-scale problems cannot be readily disaggregated, although greenhouse gas emissions reductions may appropriately take place in phases, but probably still requires major interventions to be resolved.

Antithetical examples might be the "war on cancer", or the proposed "war on AIDS". While these problems are of substantial concern to those affected by them, they appear to be susceptible to disaggregation into smaller scales (Rettig 1977, Rushefsky 1986, Perrow 1990). As a result, the appropriate method of policy attack appears to be incremental, with the accumulation of scientific evidence, careful medical trials, trial and error, and the like. Any attempt to introduce very high levels of resources in short bursts into the policy area could lead to "choking" on the resources (Hogwood and Peters 1985) and potentially little real contribution to the resolution of the underlying policy problems. These problems are very amenable to disaggregation, with individual scientists, engineers, and policy makers able to make their own contributions to the resolution (relatively) independent of the actions of others. Indeed, many scientists would argue that this is only way for real progress to be made.

Perhaps more than any other aspect of policy problems the issue of scale can be misunderstood and can lead to inefficient and ineffective use of resources. When a problem is identified there is always a desire to apply the "war" metaphor and to create the moral equivalent of war. In some instances that may be appropriate. Poverty is a sufficiently complex (see above) and intertwined set of problems that the only way to address it may be through "war". Indeed, the failure of the War on Poverty may be the result of failure to apply the metaphor with enough zeal, and over a sufficiently long period of time, rather than an inadequacy of the metaphor in this particular case. This also points out the extent to which this particular attribute of policy problems, like all others, is at least in part a consequence of framing and political construction (Schon and Rein 1994).

European policy making presents some interesting challenges for understanding the concept of scale, especially at the implementation stage. The style of policy making in Europe tends to be large scale, at least in terms of gaining compliance among the member states. This style can be contrasted with that in other multilevel governance arrangements (see Hooge and Marks 2003) in which the components of the union are granted more latitude in interpreting central government policy, and are more autonomous. The drive for conformity has to some extent been lessened by the adoption of the Open Method of Coordination (Borras and Jacobsson 2004) and its emphasis on benchmarks and standards rather than regulations, so that the scale of the policy system may be lessening.

We turn now to a second set of problem attributes – ones that move beyond mere characterization of problems, and make more conscious attempts to explicate the relationships between problems and instrument choice. To some extent all the attributes of problems we have presented here are related to instrument choice, but this second set of attributes should be seen as more proximate to that crucial choice in the implementation process.

Divisibility

The fourth attribute of policy problems that we will discuss is their "divisibility". We noted above that some small-scale problems can be disaggregated, but here we are talking more about the nature of the goods required to "solve" the problem. In a sense, we are talking here about the classic economic concern over market failures, and most specifically about the classic economic distinction between public goods and private goods (Buchanan 1987). Similarly, James Q. Wilson (1980) has constructed a typology of policies based largely upon the extent to which benefits and costs are concentrated or diffuse, a distinction somewhat akin the economists' conceptions of jointness in goods.

The Wilson typology is intended to explain the politics of policy, but the basic idea involved is also applicable to more substantive issues about policy problems. That basic idea is that problems that entail collective action and produce diffuse benefits may be more difficult to solve than those problems for which the benefits are more immediate and more appropriable to individuals. The reasons for this increased difficulty are fundamentally political, and relate to generating and maintaining support for policies that yield only indirect benefits to particular constituencies. In politics, however, the nature of the goods being produced may not be so firmly established as economists would tend to believe, so that a fundamental question for the political entrepreneur advocating government action to address a problem requiring the development of public goods is to construct the issue as if the goods were less indivisible and hence of greater benefit to particular constituencies.[12]

One problem with this form of analysis is that it appears to lead to problems being solved that are not problems *per se* but rather are better conceptualized as opportunities for public action that may confer differential benefits on one or another segments of society. That is, if a small group is able to mobilize support for a policy idea that will confer benefits on them while diffusing the costs of those benefits widely, the political imbalance is likely to swing in the direction of government adopting the policy. This process – in many cases – becomes somewhat analogous to Lowi's (1972) distributive politics, in which the policy instrument becomes direct or indirect government subsidies for the development of policies that are at least justified by language consistent with the concept of public goods. This style of policy making has been very evident in making tax policy, as well as when providing certain types of supports for business, public works, and agriculture (Bonser, McGregor and Oster 1996). In some ways the real question that arises in these cases is why are there not more programs like this created in the public sector, and why do programs like this ever get terminated given that the political climate for them is so supportive (Mucciaroni 1990)?

So, what are the implications of these public goods related problems for the selection of policy instruments? The first and clearest implication is that these problems appear to require government interventions in some form if the collective action problems which give rise to them are to be overcome. What is far less clear, however, is whether any particular form of intervention is preferable to another. As is indicated above, the subsidies can take many forms – direct provision of governments services (for example roads), tax benefits (such as credits and deductions), grant subsidies to nongovernmental organizations or lower levels of government (for example grants for wastewater treatment works), and creating government sanctioned monopolies (electric utilities, and so on). While each of these forms of intervention appears to carry some relatively obvious advantages and disadvantages in terms of both efficiency and accountability, more analytical work is required in order to determine more specifically how these differing forms of government action can be best applied to differing kinds of problems.

Monetarization

This awkward term is intended to capture the question of whether the policy problem being considered is phrased in monetary or non-monetary terms, or whether in principle money can be utilized to solve, or at least ameliorate, the problems identified. While monies can be, and are, used as discussed above to address "indivisible" problems associated with collective goods, the concept here is broader and also includes problems that are divisible. For example, it is clear that some *divisible* problems, such as the danger of poverty after retirement from employment or reducing health risks associated with lead piping materials in low income households, can be (and have been) addressed successfully simply by using money. Other problems, such as civil rights, gender equality, or even reducing automobile use may not be so amenable to being addressed simply by spending money. Rather, these problems may require other forms of government action, and perhaps broad societal changes, to be implemented. The policy question here is whether the difficulties identified can be addressed successfully through financial instruments and, if not, what sort of other interventions can be used to address the issues.

As is the case with the divisibility question noted above, the idea of monetarization noted here asks a question directly about the nature of the instruments that can be employed effectively to address an issue, but the importance of the variable in defining a policy problem may extend beyond that. The question here is also about the capacity of government to confer status on groups, or to control certain undesirable behaviors through education or other means, or to cope with the increasing range of issues that appear to be defined as public problems.[13] Money as a fungible resource makes the interventions of government apparently easier, but it may make the choices too easy. That is, given the general theme of this paper, there is a temptation to throw money at problems and hope that they go away. Further, conferring of status, rights and other non-monetary benefits on members of society is in part a role of the public sector but perhaps is primarily a task for the private sector. If the general public is opposed to granting these rights, then the state will not have the capacity to enforce legislation that confers these benefits on members of society, nor to adjudicate all the cases that may arise from those rights. Furthermore, to the extent the problems addressed suggest a need for further educational or socialization efforts, it is clear that these efforts will require involvement from nongovernmental sectors of society to be successful.

Most of the politics within the European Union has been about issues that are primarily monetized, or about bargainable issues. These policy concerns of the EU have left the primary responsibility for most issues of status, for example immigration, to the member countries. Gender has to some extent become an EU issue, but still is not so central as the economic issues that have comprised the foundation of the Union. This differential focus for policy may well be functional given that the national governments still have greater legitimacy in most of the member countries than does the EU.

Scope of Activity

Another potential variable of concern in understanding differences among policy problems and the appropriate instruments of government to address them relates to the scope of activity or behaviors that contribute to the creation of the problem. In general, where the numbers of people, activities, or organizations involved with a problem is defined and relatively small, the likelihood that direct *regulatory* intervention by governmental bodies will be successful is increased. By contrast, public sector action can become quite difficult and resource intensive in cases where many very different forms of activity must be controlled or changed, and government chooses to seek resolution of the problem through direct regulation.

Most fundamentally, this concern with the scope of the problem relates to the capacity of government. When government regulation is applied to relatively small numbers of similar activities it has a reasonable chance for success. However, when the activities to be controlled and/or altered are numerous and highly differentiated, the capacity of government to deal with them is likely to be strained, and this strain is likely to make non-regulatory solutions more desirable by comparison. For example, ensuring the safety of nuclear energy facilities appears to be amenable to successful regulation (although successful and effective regulation is certainly not guaranteed!). There are only so many nuclear energy facilities to be regulated and they pose at least somewhat similar risks and concerns. By contrast, it would be far more difficult to regulate directly the manner in which people cook their food in an effort to reduce the potential emission of particulate matter into the air. For, in this case, there are hundreds of thousands of mealtime activities to be regulated each day, and they may take many different forms (charcoal grills, gas stoves, electric stoves, wood stoves, and so on). An effort to accomplish this kind of regulation would significantly tax the capabilities of any government that sought to carry it out. Consequently, it would probably be appropriate to explore other approaches to addressing this problem.

In cases where direct government regulation is infeasible or prohibitively expensive, other policy instruments need to be explored. One approach would be to apply regulatory solutions to different (although related) sets of activities. Using the example above, we might apply regulations to the manufacture of cooking stoves and grills that would require that appliances used for cooking remove particulate matter prior to emission into the air. This kind of regulation would be applied to a smaller number of regulated entities and might require the installation of similar technologies in each case. This in fact, is somewhat like the rationale behind the Corporate Average Fuel Economy (CAFÉ) standards used in the United States to reduce air emissions from automobiles (although the limits of this approach are now becoming more apparent, as the number of vehicle miles driven continues to contribute to air pollution problems in some areas). Another approach would be to move toward non-regulatory mechanisms such as economic incentives or educational efforts. In these cases, for example, taxes might be applied to cooking appliances according to the extent to which they include devices for minimizing particulate emissions, or educational programs for users of cooking appliances might help people understand which cooking appliances are environmentally friendly or they may provide guidance on how to avoid cooking on days in which particulate matter in the air is of concern.

The point here is that the relationship between policy problems and instrument selection is related to the capacity of governments to carry out differing activities. In general, direct regulation requires significant resources for standard setting, monitoring, and enforcement, and sufficient resources are likely to be available only in those cases where the numbers and types of activities regulated are limited to a reasonable number. Where these conditions are not met, alternative policy instruments should perhaps be considered. In environmental policy, these alternatives may include economic instruments designed to make polluting activities more expensive and educational activities that enable consumers and the public to make environmentally friendly decisions – in other words sticks and sermons.

In the European Union the scope question is now assuming an interesting dimension with the increasing utilization of "soft law" as a means of making interventions (Morth 2003). To some extent the use of this and other informal instruments for regulation now permit the EU to intervene effectively in policy areas that might have been difficult if using more formal means of regulation. This means that the EU has been able to expand its sphere of influence into areas that are certainly related to its formal mandates but more difficult to control and to regulate. Further, it has been able to do so in a manner that lessens the sense of intrusiveness that some citizens have found so problematic in their involvement with the Union.

Interdependencies

Policy problems also vary in the extent to which they are confined, or confinable, to a single policy domain. At this point we come full circle and return to thinking about the impact of those names on government buildings. Some problems facing government clearly correspond to the domains of a single building; providing social insurance pensions in the United States falls within the domain of the Department of Health and Human Services (actually now the independent Social Security Administration). Other policy problems, for example the control of non-point source water pollution flowing after rainstorms to rivers, lakes and streams, require the involvement of, and co-ordination with, a number of departments, agencies, and even levels of government.

The degree of interdependence characterizing any particular problem influences the capacity of government to solve the problem, as well as the range of appropriate policy instruments. The political requirements of co-ordination and forming coalitions across a range of organizations will mean that more interdependent problems are likely to be more difficult to resolve. Further it may mean that organizations are less likely to be able to solve them through existing routines. In addition, if the problems are large scale, there is a danger that a number of different organizations will attempt to parcel out components among themselves, thereby reducing the overall effectiveness of the interventions.[14] These problems then become a domestic analogue of the "joint decision trap" that Fritz Scharpf (1988) discussed in reference to international politics, with decisions perhaps being made at the level of the lowest common denominator.

The other rather obvious point here is that interdependent policies are more subject to debates over framing, and hence may be more contentious. Some of this contention over policies may represent sincere intellectual differences of opinion about the way in which the problem should be defined, while another part may be a function of attempts to utilize the problem to acquire more budgetary and personnel resources for each department advocating an alternative "frame" for the issue. The need to mobilize political support for programs will also tend to push the definition of programs toward those using instruments that are more appropriable for private benefits. Likewise, there is a strong political push to ignore identification of the interconnections of policies when possible, given that such involvement of multiple actors makes the program less easily captured by departments.

It appears that over time the degree to which problems can be confined to a single domain is diminishing. Agricultural price supports, for example, might once have been solely the concern of a department of agriculture, but as these commodities become more linked to international trade these supports become the concern of departments of foreign affairs, international trade, and similar organizations.[15] Agriculture policy also now involves numerous, often rancorous, involvements with environmental policy organizations in and out of government. Similarly, educational policy now has a major impact on international competitiveness, and hence education ministries must now co-ordinate more with departments of labor, trade and industry and international affairs if they are to do their jobs effectively.

The overall point here is that policy problems that have foundations and implications for many governmental units are likely to experience more difficulty and controversy in the selection and implementation of instruments than policy problems that are clearly within the jurisdiction of a single organization of government. Instrument choice, in this context, can become quite politicized and complex, as competing organizations incorporate arguments about appropriate instruments into larger arguments about how to frame the problem and whether the problem is best addressed by one agency or another. The end results in these situations may often be policy instrument choices that grow incrementally and in haphazard fashion out of bureaucratic turf battles rather than out of clear-headed analyses of the policy problem being addressed.

Summary

This discussion of the seven characteristics of policy problems is but an inadequate beginning to an interesting, and we believe important, extension of the current literature on policy design, as well as that on policy instruments as the most well-established component of that literature. The discussion also provides some beginning steps in providing a systematic foundation for changes that are now taking place in the area of water pollution control in the US. These first steps suggest that the current move toward decentralized and non-regulatory policy instruments in non-point water pollution control may find grounding in the political and causal complexity of the problems involved, their broad scope, and their significant policy interdependence. However, what these very preliminary insights do more conclusively is to force some consideration of policy problems faced by government as questions that have basic attributes which influence how they must be approached by would-be policy formulators. The presence of these multiple attributes of problems also requires additional thinking about how to compile and perhaps weight, the multiple attributes that will characterize any one problem. As noted, thinking about the attributes of problems goes well beyond the usual way in which policy expertise is organized, for example on the basis of functional policy areas, and requires more analytic thinking.

These underlying characteristics that must be addressed are, we argue, most important for the selection of policy instruments for intervention. This paper has focused on the nature of the problems themselves, and has only begun to discuss directly the contingent relationships between instruments and these problems. That relationship does exist, however. For example, if we rely upon several of the attributes we discussed above it is clear that "treasure" based tools – to use one of Hood's (1986) categories – are more appropriate for some problems than for others. Likewise, the "chronic" problems we have identified may be more amenable to being addressed by instruments relying more heavily on "organization" – another of Hood's (1986) categories – than on instruments that have a less enduring nature. We could go on with the examples, but the basic point here is that we have begun to use these categories to categorize problems and to make the links with instruments, and that the exercise will bear fruit in the future.

Notes

1. An earlier version of this paper, focusing on environmental policy in the United States was co-authored with Dr. John Hoornbeek (Peters and Hoornbeek 2003).
2. This distinction, in turn, mirrors the distinction between the consequentialist approach to institutional choices, as opposed to a dependence upon routine and symbols in that selection in the more sociological literature on institutions.
3. Although particularly well stated and argued, some aspects of the Schon and Rein argument are not entirely novel. For example, there is a strong link to the social constructionist approach in sociology (Best 1989). Also, Lowi's (1972) and Wilson's (1980) seminal discussions of public policy tend to have some of the same aspects of defining the problem in terms of winners and losers, and even in terms of the arenas within which the problem is addressed.
4. This argument is not dissimilar to the historical institutionalist arguments (Thelen, Steinmo, and Longstreth 1992; King 1995).
5. This has been referred to as "brass plaque institutionalism", meaning that institutions are defined by the brass plaques on their buildings.
6. As has been noted (Hogwood and Peters 1983), few problems in government of any consequence are ever really solved. Still, there are marked differences in the extent to which they are likely to require reconsideration.
7. As has been noted when discussing policy failures there is an important difference between the political and the programmatic elements of policy problems. See Bovens, t'Hart and Peters (1998).

8. This leaves aside some religious groups who do not believe in immunizations, as well as some medical evidence about the risk/benefit ratios of some of the standard shots children receive.
9. This may be thought of as a chronic problem in one way, although the choice of the basic technology or technologies may be done on a more discrete basis. That is, after the choice to have a Federal Reserve and to use money supply as a major economic instrument, the rest is simply playing with the one instrument, rather than selecting multiple instruments in independent decisions.
10. For a discussion of these terms in relationship to policy failure see Bovens, t'Hart and Peters (1998, 2001).
11. For example, in addition to using the conventional cash transfers, we can think of using tax-based instruments (Earned Income Tax Credit (EITC) in the United States for example) for assisting the working poor, and better coordinating these programs with active labor market policy.
12. This argument represents, of course, the rather famous point from Lindblom about the use of "partisan analysis" in selling programs to different constituencies. Likewise, the constructivist arguments inherent in framing (see Gottweiss 2005) demonstrates the need to sell programs to constituencies in their own terms.
13. One of the ironies of contemporary political life is that the problem-solving capacity of government is consistently being denigrated but yet more and more issues appear to be defined as public issues.
14. This is in part the reason that governments create new organizations to address large scale problems, e.g. the Office of Economic Opportunity (OEO) in the United States as a vehicle for creating and implementing programs of the War on Poverty; or even the current efforts in the United States to develop a Department of Homeland Security.
15. The central role of agricultural products in the North American Free Trade Agreement (NAFTA) deliberations are indicative of the expansion of this policy issue.

References

Bagchus, R., 1998, The Trade-off Between Appropriateness and Fit of Policy Instruments, in: B. G. Peters and F. K. M. Van Nispen (Eds) *Public Policy Instruments* (Cheltenham: Edward Elgar).
Bardach, E., 1980, Implementation and the study of implements. Paper delivered at annual meeting of the American Political Science Association, Washington, DC.
Baumgartner, F. R. and Jones, B. D., 1993, *Agendas and Instability in American Politics* (Chicago: University of Chicago Press).
Bonser, C. F., McGregor, E. B. and Oster, C. V., 1996, *Policy Choices and Public Action* (Upper Saddle River, NJ: Prentice-Hall).
Borras, S. and Jacobssen, K., 2004, The open method of coordination in the European Union. *European Journal of Public Policy*, **11**, 185–208.
Bovens, M. A. P., 't Hart, P. and Peters, B. G., 1998, The study of policy disasters, in: P. Gray (Ed) *Public Policy Disasters in Western Europe* (London: Routledge).
Bovens, M. A. P., 't Hart, P. and Peters, B. G., 2001, *Policy Success and Failure*, 2 vols. (Cheltenham: Edward Elgar).
Buchanan, J. M., 1987, *Public Finance in the Democratic Process* (Chapel Hill, NC: University of North Carolina Press).
Cobb, R. W. and Elder, C. D., 1983, *Participation in American Politics: The Dynamics of Agenda-Building* (Baltimore: Johns Hopkins University Press).
Cohen, M. D., March, J. G. and Olsen, J. P., 1971, A garbage can mode of organizational decision-making. *Administrative Science Quarterly*, **17**, 1–25.
Elster, J., 1998, *Deliberative Democracy* (Cambridge: Cambridge University Press).
Epstein, R. A., 1985, *Takings* (Cambridge, MA: Harvard University Press).
Fawcett, H., 2005, Pensions policy, in: B. G. Peters and J. Pierre (Eds) *Handbook of Public Policy* (London: Sage).
Fitzpatrick, T., 2003, *After the New Social Democracy: Social Policy for the 21st Century* (Manchester: University of Manchester Press).
Gormley, W. T., 1986, Institutional Policy Analysis: A Critical Review. *Journal of Policy Analysis and Management*, **6**, 153–169.

Gottweiss, H., 2005, The constructivist approach, in: B. G. Peters and J. Pierre (Eds) *Handbook of Public Policy* (London: Sage).
Gray, P., 1998, *Public Policy Disasters in Europe* (London: Routledge).
Hisschemoller, M. and Hoppe, B., 1995, Coping with intractable controversies: the case for problem structuring in policy design and analysis. *Knowledge and Policy*, **8**, 40–60.
Hogwood, B. W. and Peters, B. G., 1983, *Policy Dynamics* (Brighton: Wheatsheaf).
Hogwood, B. W. and Peters, B. G., 1985, *The Pathology of Public Policy* (Oxford: Oxford University Press).
Hood, C., 1986, *The Tools of Government* (Chatham, NJ: Chatham House).
Hooge, E. and Marks, G., 2003, Unraveling the central state, but how? Types of multi-level governance. *American Political Science Review*, **97**, 233–243.
Howlett, M., 1991, Policy instruments, policy styles and policy implementation: national approaches to theories of instrument choice. *Policy Studies Journal*, **19**, 1–21.
Ingram, H. and Schneider, A. L., 1997, *Policy Design for Democracy* (Lawrence, KS: University Press of Kansas).
Jones, C. O., 1982, *Congress* (Homewood, IL: Richard D. Irwin).
Kenworthy, L., 1999, Do social welfare policies reduce poverty: a cross-national assessment. *Social Forces*, **77**, 1119–1139.
King, D. S., 1995, *Actively Seeking Work* (Chicago, IL: University of Chicago Press).
Kingdon, J., 1994, *Agendas, Alternatives and Public Policies*, 2nd edn. (New York: Harper Collins).
Linder, S. H. and Peters, B. G., 1984, From social theory to policy design. *Journal of Public Policy*, **4**, 237–259.
Linder, S. H. and Peters, B. G., 1989, Instruments of government: perceptions and contexts. *Journal of Public Policy*, **9**, 35–58.
Linder, S. H. and Peters, B. G., 1998, The study of policy instruments: four schools of thought, in: B. G. Peters and F. K. M. Van Nispen (Eds) *Public Policy Instruments* (Cheltenham: Edward Elgar).
Linder, S. H. and Peters, B. G., 1990, An institutional approach to the theory of policymaking: the role of conscious choice in policy formulation. *The Journal of Theoretical Politics*, **2**, 59–83.
Lowi, T. J., 1972, Four Systems of Policy, Politics and Choice. *Public Administration Review*, **52**, 298–310.
Majone, G., 1996, *Regulating Europe* (Oxford: Oxford University Press).
Majone, G., 2001, Nonmajoritarian institutions and the limits of democratic governance. *Journal of Institutional and Theoretical Economics*, **157**, 57–78.
May, P., 2000, Social Regulation, in: L. M. Salamon (Ed.) *The Handbook of Policy Instruments* (New York: Oxford University Press).
Mesa-Lago, C., 1994, *Changing Social Security in Latin America: Towards Alleviaing the Costs of Economic Reform* (Boulder, CO: Lynne Reinner).
Morth, U., 2003, *Soft Law in Governance and Regulation: An Interdisciplinary Approach* (Cheltenham: Edward Elgar).
Mucciaroni, G., 1990, Public choice and the politics of comprehensive tax reform, *Governance*, **3**, 1–32.
Nelson, B. J., 1984, *Making an Issue of Child Abuse: Political Agenda Setting for Social Problems* (Chicago, IL: University of Chicago Press).
Nelson, R. R., 1978, *The Moon and the Ghetto* (New York: W. W. Norton).
Patterson, L. A., 1998, Agricultural Policy Reform in the European Union: A Three-level Game Analysis. *International Organization*, **51**, 135–165.
Perrow, C., 1970, *Organizational Analysis: A Sociological Perspective* (Belmont, CA: Wadsworth).
Perrow, C., 1990, *The AIDS Disaster* (New Haven, CT: Yale University Press).
Peters, B. G., 1992, Bureaucratic politics in the European Community, in: A. Sbragia (Ed) *Euro-Politics* (Washington, DC: The Brookings Institution).
Peters, B. G., 2000, The politics of policy instruments, in: L. M. Salamon (Ed) *The Handbook of Policy Instruments* (New York: Oxford University Press).
Peters, B. G., forthcoming, *Coordinating the European Union: The Union Itself* (Lanham, MD: Rowman and Littlefield).
Peters, B. G. and Pierre, J., 2005, *Governing Complex Societies* (Basingstoke: Palgrave).
Peters, B. G., and Van Nispen, F. K. M. (Eds), 1998, *Public Policy Instruments* (Cheltenham: Edward Elgar).
Petracca, M. P., 1992, Issue definitions, agenda-building and policymaking. *Policy Currents 2*, **1**, 4.

Rettig, R., 1977, *Cancer Crusade* (Princeton, NJ: Princeton University Press).
Ringeling, A., 2005, Instruments in Far; Elements of Policy Design, in: P. Eliadis, M. Hill and M. Howlett (Eds) *Designing Government* (Montreal: McGill/Queens University Press).
Ringeling, A. and Van Nispen, F. K. M., 1998, On instruments and instrumentality: a critical assessment, in: B. G. Peters and F. K. M. Van Nispen (Eds) *Public Policy Instruments* (Cheltenham: Edward Elgar).
Rochefort, D. A. and Cobb, R. W., 1994, *The Politics of Problem Definition* (Lawrence, KS: University Press of Kansas).
Rushefsky, M., 1986, *Making Cancer Policy* (Albany, NY: State University of New York Press).
Salamon, L. M., 2000, *The Handbook of Policy Instruments* (New York: Oxford University Press).
Salamon, L. M. and Lund, M., 1989, *Beyond Privatization: The Tools of Public Policy* (Washington, DC: The Urban Institute).
Scharp, F. W., 1988, The joint decision trap: lessons from German federalism and European integration. *Public Administration*, **66**, 239–278.
Schon, D. A. and Rein, M., 1994, *Frame Reflection: Solving Intractable Policy Controversies* (New York: Basic Books).
Schulman, P., 1980, *Large-Scale Policymaking* (New York: Elsevier).
Sieber, S., 1981, *Fatal Remedies* (New York: Plenum).
Steunenberg, B. and van Vught, F., 1997, *Political Institutions and Public Policy* (Dordrecht: Kluwer).
Tatalovich, R. and Daynes, B., 1997, *Social Regulatory Policy*, 2nd edn. (Boulder, CO: Westview).
Thelen, K., Steinmo, S. and Longstreth, F., 1992, *Structuring Politics: Historical Institutionalism in Comparative Politics* (Cambridge: Cambridge University Press).
Thompson, J. D. and Tuden, A., 1959, *Strategy, Structure and Process in Organizational Design, in Comparative Studies in Administration* (Pittsburgh, PA: University of Pittsburgh Administrative Studies Center).
Timmermans, A., Rothmayr, C., Serduelt, U. and Varone, F., 1998, The design of policy instruments: perspectives and contexts. Paper presented at Annual Meeting of the Midwest Political Science Association Chicago, April 23–25.
Trebilcock, M., 2005, Choosing Policy Instruments: A Retrospective, in: P. Eliadas, M. Hill and M. Howlett (Eds) *Designing Government* (Montreal: McGill/Queens University Press).
in 't Veld, R., 1991, Autopoesis, configuration and steering: impossibility theory or dynamic steering theory, in: in 't Veld *et al.* (Eds) *Autopoesis and Configuration Theory* (Dordrecht: Kluwer).
Wallace, H. and Wallace, W., 2000, *Policy-Making in the European Union* (Oxford: Oxford University Press).
Wildavsky, B., 1998, Looming liabilities, *National Journal*, January 17, 102–105.
Wilson, J. Q., 1980, *The Politics of Regulation* (New York: Basic Books).
Zito, A., Jordon, A., Rudiger, K. W. and Wirzel, K. W., 2003, Policy Innovation or 'Mudding Through': New Environmental Policy Instruments in the United Kingdom. *Environmental Politics*, **12**, 179–200.

Twenty Years of Comparative Policy Analysis: A Survey of the Field and a Discussion of Topics and Methods

IRIS GEVA-MAY, DAVID C. HOFFMAN, & JOSELYN MUHLEISEN

ABSTRACT *Comparative policy analysis has emerged as a distinct field of study in the past two decades, however only one journal is explicitly devoted to its study: the* Journal of Comparative Policy Analysis: Research and Practice *(JCPA). This article performs a content analysis of abstracts in the field of comparative policy analysis to determine the contours of the field. First, the paper charts the development of comparative policy analysis and compares the trajectories of comparative politics, comparative public administration and comparative policy analysis. Second, the paper analyzes the results of the abstract coding to reveal the methods employed, countries studied, the number of countries studied and the countries of the authors' institutions. The results from JCPA and other journals in the Elton B. Stephens Co. (EBSCO) Academic Complete database are compared to distinguish the dominant role that JCPA plays in the field. Finally, it discusses the major trends in the work published in comparative policy analysis, the limitations of the current publications and further areas for development. A clear finding is that the field of comparative policy analysis is on a sharp upward trajectory.*

Introduction

In her 2013 article "Policy Analysis Reaches Midlife", and her seminal second book titled *Beyond Machiavelli: Policy Analysis Reaches Midlife*, Beryl Radin traces the development of the policy studies and policy analysis field and highlights the *Journal of Comparative Policy Analysis: Research and Practice* (*JCPA*) and its mission statement as important stepping-stones in the development of the field. To date, *JCPA* is still the only journal exclusively devoted to comparative policy studies. Founded 20 years ago, the mission of *JCPA* has been advanced with the support of leading scholars and dedicated editorial board members, such as Laurence E. Lynn Jr., first co-editor, Peter deLeon, Duncan McRae, David Weimer, Beryl Radin, Frans VanNispen, Yukio Adachi, Claudia Scott, Allan Maslove and others in the US, Canada, Europe, Australia/New Zealand and Asia. In recent years it has increased from three to five issues per annual volume. There are about 120 articles submitted each year. In 2016 the *JCPA* acceptance rate was 21 per cent, there were 443 citations of its articles, and the impact factor increased from 0.612 to 1.07 within one year (Thompson Reuters SSI Citation Index, June 2017). This shows that an increasing number of policy researchers and scholars from many policy domains are engaging in comparative studies, and indicates the standing of JCPA in this field. New comparative policy books are in process or have been recently published and more courses in comparative public policy are being offered around the world. This trajectory in comparative policy studies is also evident in the establishment of the International Comparative Policy Analysis Forum (ICPA-Forum) with over 1,400 international members and around 50 institutions involved in a scholarly network advancing comparative studies. The ICPA-Forum also partners with ten scholarly associations to offer awards to outstanding comparative work.

In an effort to take stock of where the field of comparative policy analysis has been and where it is going, this paper reports the results of a content analysis of *JCPA*, the field's flagship journal, and compares the results to a broader analysis of comparative public policy articles indexed on the Elton B. Stephens Co. (EBSCO) Academic Complete database. This analysis categorizes research articles published over the last two decades in comparative policy analysis by topic, methodology, countries studied and countries of the authors' institutional affiliations. It reveals some strengths and weaknesses of the field as a whole, and sheds light on *JCPA*'s place within it. We also trace the development of comparative policy analytic studies in contrast to comparative political science and comparative public administration. We begin with a brief survey of the history of the field, move on to a discussion of its scope and importance, review the results of the content analysis, and then make suggestions for some new directions that comparative policy analysis in general, and *JCPA* in particular, might head in the future.

The Development of Comparative Policy Analysis as a District Field of Study

The field of comparative policy analysis developed out of the older and more general field of policy analysis, also drawing on research traditions in public administration and comparative politics. Policy analysis originated in the United States because of developments in the early 1960s. It is a relatively new area of social scientific inquiry, whose main rationale is the need and requirement for democratic societies and their elected policy makers to be systematic, evidence-based, transparent, efficient and accountable. Policy analysis is a craft, which "Speaks Truth to Power", in the words of Wildavsky (1979), a pioneer of the policy analysis field. Policy analysis has been defined in at least six ways: (1) "A type of quantitative analysis involving comparisons and interactions of values and politics" (Lindblom 1958, pp. 280–312), (2) creating problems that can be solved (Wildavsky 1979, p. 1), (3) the use of reason and evidence to choose the best policy among a number of alternatives (MacRae and Wilde 1979, p. 14), (4) a "profession-craft clustering on providing systematic, rational, and science-based help with decision-making" (Dror 1983, p. 79), (5) a problem-solving process (Bardach 1992, p. 1), (6) client-oriented advice relevant to public decisions (Weimer and Vining 1989, p. 1; 2010).

Initially, the movement started with the notion that the key objective of public service was to design, enact and implement better public policies – meeting the Kaldor–Hicks criteria for economic efficiency as Lindblom (1958) first asserted. A major cornerstone in policy analysis has been the principle that decision making should be evidence-based, verifiable and evaluable, transparent and accountable and implementable to meet democratic principles, meet social and economic needs, and be answerable to the public (Brans et al. 2016). Evidence-based policy making also implies, by definition, looking for evidence "elsewhere" for historical, international, disciplinary, or other comparisons of data, facts and events. This requirement appears to have been the reason for the divergence of the new comparative policy analysis field from the policy analysis domain.

Although policy analysis has been in existence for more than half a century, the *comparative* field in policy analysis, which examines similarities and differences between the policies of different nations or sub-national political units, has been around only since the 1990s. In the 1970s and 1980s we witness the re-initiation of discussions about scientific comparative research design or methodologies, and their logics and limitations. Nevertheless, these debates do not include "comparative public policy" as perceived today. We witness an attempt in Dierkes et al.'s (1987) contribution, *Comparative Policy Research: Learning from Experience*, in which Wildavsky is a contributor. The realization that policy literature written about the US did not apply directly to other countries was one of the factors that led to the creation of *comparative* policy analysis. Hogwood and Gunn (1984) pointed to the difficulty of even teaching the concepts and practice to UK students mainly because of the need to translate the strategies and techniques developed in the US to other contexts. They conclude, "this [policy analysis] literature fails to discuss the use and limits of policy analysis techniques" (vi).

At its inception, comparative policy analysis, as a modern research tradition, joined comparative politics and comparative public administration as a field of political science that uses the comparative method. While comparative politics has been a domain of study since the late 1800s and comparative public administration since the 1950s, scholars doing comparative policy analysis in the 1980s did not identify as part of a distinct field of study. John Stuart Mill's *A System of Logic*, first published in 1843, is widely considered to be the first systematic formulation of the modern comparative method for social sciences research (Mill 1843). The comparative method began to be systematically applied in the modern academic study of politics being conducted in 1968 when the journal *Comparative Politics* was established by the Graduate School in the University Center at City University of New York and where Harold Lasswell published his "The Future of the Comparative Method" – as the lead article of the first issue of the journal. Comparative policy analysis became a domain in the 1990s because (i) there were more publications identifying as part of an explicit field and (ii) scholars began investigating and developing specific theories and methodologies (Lasswell 1968).

Comparative policy analysis shared a developmental trajectory with both comparative politics and comparative public administration, as Beryl Radin argues (2013a) but has tended to thrive as comparative public administration stalled. Comparative public administration uses the comparative method to study bureaucratic institutions and identify policies that are applicable in different political contexts. Substantively, public administration focuses almost exclusively on the public bureaucracies of the executive branch and the implementation stage of policy, drawing a distinction between administration and politics. After World War II, scholars began to use comparative studies to answer questions about development and find administrative strategies that would work in different countries. In 1960 the comparative administration group was created and its Chairman, Fred W. Riggs, used it to push forward a scholarly agenda for the field. Comparative public administration experienced a boom in the 1960s and several journals were formed to advance the field. However, in the 1970s funding and academic support ended and the discipline floundered (Heady 2001). Reflecting this decline in interest, *The Journal of Comparative Administration* was renamed *Administration & Society* in 1973. In the late 1980s and 1990s neoliberal economic principles changed the approach to government in the United Kingdom and United States. Instead of privatizing public authorities and services, governments embraced mechanisms that provide competition, applied market principles, and focused on efficiency and rightsizing. International development organizations projected neoliberalism globally as part of the Washington Consensus. The new ideas about government were embodied in the New Public Management literature and this scholarship led to a slight resurgence of comparative public administration in the 1990s. Since that period, the discipline of comparative public administration has been stagnant. According to Jreisat, many scholars avoid cross-cultural studies or any study in which the units of comparison are not functional equivalents (2002). This is a significant shortcoming of comparative public administration as the interdependence that results from globalization necessitates such comparisons. As comparative policy analysis is not limited to focusing on the unit of bureaucratic administration, it has taken up the challenge of analyzing how policies work in dissimilar environments.

The rise in output in the comparative policy analysis field and the concurrent decline of output in comparative administration are borne out by data gathered from the EBSCO Academic Complete database and from Google Books. Figures 1 and 2 show the growth of literature on Comparative Public Policy and the decline of literature in Comparative Public Administration. Figure 1 is a comparison of the number of articles indexed in the EBSCO Academic Complete database per year with the words "comparative administration" and "comparative policy" in their titles or abstracts from 1969 to 2015. Figure 2 shows the result of a Google Books N-gram search for "comparative policy" and "comparative administration". The chart represents the percentage of two word combinations in the "Google Million", a randomly sampled set of books published between 1500 and 2008, comprising the target phrases.[1] In Figure 3 another Google Books N-gram search shows how much more frequent the phrase "comparative politics" is than either "comparative policy" or "comparative administration". However, of course there is ample comparative work that may not be explicitly labelled comparative. Unfortunately our search strategy does not capture those studies that perform comparative work without using the term comparative. Although there is much that these searches do not capture, we believe they show strong trends in a fair sampling of overall publications. The graphs look different because they show data from different samples and

Figure 1. A comparison of the number of articles indexed in the EBSCO Academic Complete database per year with the words "comparative administration" and "comparative policy" in their titles or abstracts from 1969 to 2015.

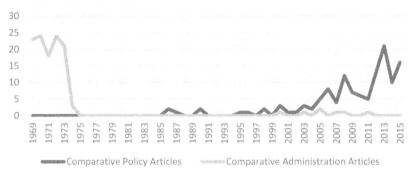

Figure 2. Relative usage rates of "comparative policy" and "comparative administration" by year in the "Google Million" Database. The y-axis represents the percentage of two-word phrases in the corpus comprised by the target phrase. Although these two phrases will certainly not capture all the references to these fields, they are essentially a random sample of all references which can be expected to capture about the same portion of the total over time

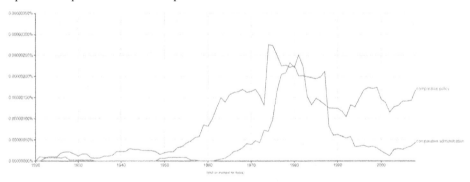

measure the prevalence of "comparative policy" in different samples, but the overall trend that they show is the same: there is more discourse about comparative policy now than ever before. We believe the fact that the same trend is apparent in different samples measured by different methods adds robustness to the finding.

The Importance and Limitations of Comparative Policy Analysis

Why do we compare public policies? We do so to be more effective and efficient, avoid the replication of failures, to maximize our use of resources, to save time and to be

Figure 3. Relative usage rates of "comparative politics", "comparative policy" and "comparative administration" by year in the "Google Million" Database

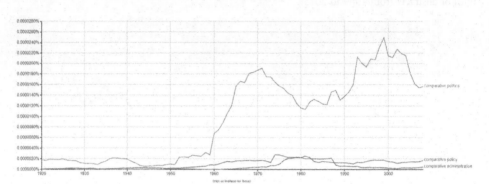

inspired by those similarities that allow for degrees of lesson drawing. Comparative policy analysis contributes to saving precious time and resources in an era when challenges need to be faced at optimal speed and level (Wildavsky 1979; Neustadt and May 1986; Rose 1991; Rose and Mackenzie 1991; Weimer 1993; Geva-May and Wildavsky 1997; Ostrom 1998; Weimer and Vining 1999).

It is natural to pursue comparisons within the field of policy analysis for many reasons. De facto comparisons, implicit or explicit, have always pervaded the work of social scientists. The basic research methods advocated in experimental designs are comparative in that they use control and experiment groups. To cite Swanson (1971, p. 145), "Thinking without comparisons is unthinkable and in the absence of comparisons, so are all scientific thought and scientific research". Comparison is an innate cognitive attribute of humans that we apply in our daily lives, in our professional activities, or as producers or consumers of products. Public policy can be viewed as one such product. Further, there are political, cultural, sociological, economic and other terms of reference within different contexts. What may be considered successful in one country may be assessed harshly in another due to different values as social controls.

But context and policy transfer, policy borrowing, or lesson drawing *can be* compatible between social units, while transferring, borrowing or lesson drawing are determined with a view of the country's particular structure, culture and politics (Geva-May 2002), because "the commonalities are more important than the differences" (Ingraham 1996, p. 4). The value of comparative policy studies lies in

> crossing national boundaries [and] expand[ing] the number of programs that can be observed in action... the fact that they are foreign introduces an element of speculation whether they can transfer. But speculation is bounded, for experience elsewhere provides palpable evidence how programs actually work. (Rose 1993, p. 110)>

Comparisons are needed in today's public policy analytic world for at least four reasons. First, *access*: in the global village age, distance has been made less significant through communication technology and transportation systems. Public policies are more visible, as are their successes or failures, which can be adopted or avoided, as would any tangible product. Second, *economic path dependence or interdependence* among national actors because of economic considerations – markets, customers, firms, legal systems and transactions – which affect the welfare or even survival of other entities. Third, in the global village governments are faced with *similar national policy problems* that usually have similar triggers and outcomes and lead to similar socio-economic, structural and technological challenges and dilemmas. Loss or gain of human capital, population aging and skilled workforce scarcity, safety and security, healthcare access and so on, are only a few examples of such policy problems. Finally, *cross-national problems* constantly emerge and reveal the extent of interdependence. Take for instance cross-border legal or illegal migration from one country to another affecting the welfare or socio-political canvas of the target state; or environmental policies: whether or not countries adhere to the Kyoto Accord, their policies affect other countries' pollution levels – air simply cannot be stopped at a jurisdiction's borders. As long as there are governments and public services or institutions faced with similar emerging global issues, there are, as Rose (1991) contends, "lessons to be drawn".

Comparative policy studies are often perceived as international comparisons between two or more nations. Indeed, the comparative case study is a significant method utilized in the field, as will be discussed in the results of our coding. However, the logic of the comparison being drawn is important. Comparative means that contributions should clearly contribute to comparative lesson drawing based on circumstances in which the domains compared have some potentially manipulable policy, program or institutional variables in common.

The "Aims and Scope" statement of *JCPA* embodies, to a large extent, the dimensions of the field of comparative policy analysis. These are:

(1) Drawing lessons based on circumstances in which compared policy issues share manipulable policy, program or institutional variables;
(2) Contribution to comparative theory development;
(3) Presentation of theory-based empirical research;
(4) Comparative evaluations of research methods;
(5) Comparative practice implications of theory-based research; and
(6) Uses of conceptual heuristics to interpret practice. (Geva-May and Lynn 1998)

Comparative methodology does have its limitations. The methods first explicated in Mill's *A Theory of Logic* are difficult to apply in the social sciences in general and in comparative public policy analysis in particular, because it is problematic to find sufficiently similar cases to compare, and because of resources, timeliness and other practical constraints. This leads to problems of randomization versus purposive limitations. Gerring (2006) addresses these limitations in his work on case study selection. Public policy comparisons also face the problem that policies or governmental structures – for instance in education, immigration and transportation – are typical of the cultural or structural context in which they emerge. In Lasswell and Kaplan's view (1950), "context is all-important". Additionally, we need to acknowledge that public policy does not occur in laboratory conditions, and that there are limitations attached to the difficulty to observe and rigorously compare these "contexts" as control groups or experimental groups for ethical and practical reasons; the target units of comparison are purposive rather than random, and they are affected by volatile events, agendas and timelines, unexpected natural or economic developments, political changes, and so on. While in social science research we acknowledge external interfering variables, the volatility of public policy implies significant interference of external and unexpected variables. What we are studying in comparative public policy analysis are not control and experimental groups but rather "naturally occurring experiments"; that is, what happens in a certain "social unit", and what lessons can be drawn from that jurisdiction to others.

Recognizing the limitations we have just discussed, we need to define what comparative policy analysis means given contextual differences. Accordingly, in comparing and lesson drawing there are nuances on the comparative spectrum ranging from full Transfer, Borrowing, Adoption, Adaptation, to "Pinching" (Deleon and Resnick-Terry 1998; Geva-May 2002), or in Rose's (1991, 1993) words, from Copying, Emulation, Hybridization, to mere Synthesis or Inspiration – depending on the respective culture or system of said social units. This view of the nuanced nature of comparative public policy accounts for the perception that there must be core commonalities among aspects of policy problems, which are more similar than different and that they can be taken up at distinct levels. To address the validity of the comparison, one needs to identify the comparable common core aspects, which dictate the search for comparative information. The contextual differences would then shape the degree to which lessons are drawn ranging from adoption to sparking a creative signal, which can lead to the creation of a policy solution that otherwise would not have been reached.

Content Analysis Study of *JCPA* and Comparative Policy Analysis Articles in the EBSCO Academic Database

In order to discover trends within the domain of Comparative Public Policy Analysis as a scholarly domain, we conducted a content analysis of two sets of refereed articles (a) 356 non-forum articles that have appeared in *JCPA* between 1998 and 2016, and (b) a set of 144 articles contained within the EBSCO Academic Search Complete database published between 1976 and 2016 that were returned when the phrases "comparative policy analysis" or "comparative public policy" were entered (this set of articles was not inclusive of the *JCPA* articles). Although there is undoubtedly more literature that is substantially about comparative policy than was captured by our search (a Google Scholar search for "comparative policy" yields more than 18,000 hits), our search provides a sample of the overall literature of a manageable size that provides a window on the total output. For both these sets of articles, we used the program NVIVO to code each article for (1) Year of Publication, (2) Policy Area, (3) Country of the Authors' Institutions, (4) Number of Countries Studied, (5) Names of Countries Studied, (6) Journal of Publication, and (7) Methodology and/or Theory. These categories were chosen because they could be detected by reading the abstracts of the articles in most cases, and because they could provide useful information about the type of work that is and is not being produced in the comparative policy field. Not all the data collected figure into the present analysis. Here we concentrate on the results concerning year published, policy area, countries studied and methodology/theory. Categories under the headings of Policy Areas Studied and

Methodology Employed were arrived at inductively. They certainly do not represent the only ways of classifying articles, and further useful distinction might well be made. All coding judgments have been reviewed by at least two coders, and none by more than three. All discrepancies were resolved in conference between coders. We believe that we have gathered evidence to strongly support a number of important claims about the growth of the field of comparative policy analysis, and about what is being published both in the pages of *JCPA* and more broadly.

The Growth of the Field of Comparative Policy Analysis

There are strong indications that general interest in the field of comparative policy analysis is increasing. As shown by Figure 1, even excluding *JCPA*, which is not indexed by EBSCO, the number of journal articles published whose titles and abstracts contain some combination of the terms "comparative policy" or "comparative public policy" has increased dramatically over the course of the last 15 years. These results should be viewed in light of the fact that the overall number of academic journals indexed in EBSCO has probably increased as a whole, a fact that needs to be controlled for in future analysis. Also it should be noted that there are many journals, *JCPA* among them, that are not included in the EBSCO database.

JCPA remains central to the field as the only journal devoted solely to comparative policy analysis. Even while the overall number of publications in the field of public policy analysis has been on the rise, very few journals in our EBSCO sample have yielded more than two hits in the search. Of the 88 journals in the sample that had published at least one article in comparative policy analysis between 1976 and 2016, only four had published five or more articles, while the vast majority, 75 journals, had published only one. *The Journal of European Public Policy* and *Politics & Policy* had ten comparative articles apiece. Also competitive were the *Journal of Policy & Practice in Intellectual Disabilities* (eight articles) and *Policy Studies* (five articles), and *Comparative Political Studies* and *Social Policy and Administration* with four articles each.

Next we turn to a more detailed analysis of what has been published in *JCPA*.

The Journal of Comparative Policy Analysis: *Publication Trends*

Our content analysis revealed a number of distinct publishing trends in *the Journal of Comparative Policy Analysis*.

Policy Areas Studied. JCPA has a very strong history of publication in the area of economic and financial policy, on the one hand, and of welfare states and social subsidies, on the other. Figure 4 shows the number of articles by topic published in JCPA between 1998 and 2016, and the percentage of the total output each topic represents. There has also been a strong interest in international agreements and organizations, the environment, education, healthcare and immigration. Comparatively little has been published about criminal justice, economic development, foreign policy, human rights, NGOs and arts and culture. At first glance it would appear that *JCPA* has not much partaken in the trend of publishing centered on the key term "globalization". However, such a view would not take into account frequent publication on a number of overlapping topics, including "convergence" and "Europeanization". (Note: Policy areas were coded in a non-mutually exclusive way to allow for one article to count in

Figure 4. *JCPA* articles published in common policy areas, 1998–2016

Policy Areas Studied	Percentage	Articles
Markets, Money and the Economy	19%	68
Welfare, Social Services, and Poverty	14%	49
Health, Healthcare, and Medicine	11%	40
Local and Regional Government & Policy	11%	38
International Relations and Organizations	10%	37
Environment	9%	32
Education	9%	31
Media & Communication	6%	20
Science & Technology	6%	20
Immigration and Migration	5%	19
Regulation & Deregulation	5%	18
Privatization and Public Private Partnerships	4%	16
Disasters	3%	9
Globalization	3%	9
Development of Underdeveloped Regions	2%	7
Human Rights	2%	6
NGOs and Non-Profits	1%	5

two or more areas. In addition, 21 per cent of articles had one or more areas not captured in the list and were categorized as "other". Many of these articles were devoted to building theory or frameworks.)

Countries Studied. While *JCPA* has published work about countries on all five continents, studies have tended to focus on the most economically developed countries. The United States is the single most studied country, with 52 articles including it in comparisons, and Europe is the most studied region. Central America, the Caribbean, Africa, the Middle East and Central Asia have received relatively sparse coverage. Two international organizations frequently determined the set of countries compared, the European Union (21 articles, 6 per cent) and the Organization for Economic Co-operation and Development (OECD) (nine articles, 3 per cent). Countries named in EU or OECD studies are not included in the totals used for Figure 5 because it was frequently difficult to determine the sub-set of member states that were being studied.

Methodology and Theory. Figure 6 shows a breakdown of the methodologies employed in the *JCPA* articles. The single largest methodological category was the case study, which represented 62 per cent of the total sample. Relatively few articles (2 per cent) drew upon interview or ethnographic methods. A sizable portion (42 per cent) of the articles attempted to employ or develop a theoretical or methodological framework, but a greater portion (58 per cent) of articles compared practices and outcomes without advancing a theoretical framework.

Methodology was assessed in a way that does not involve mutual exclusion: a single article could be fit into more than one category as was appropriate. Descriptions are as follows:

Figure 5. Articles per country in *JCPA*

Figure 6. *JCPA* article methodology, 1998–2016

Methodology Employed	Percentage	Articles
Case-Based & Historical	62%	219
Theory and Framework Pieces	42%	150
Quantitative Analysis	15%	55
Textual & Content Analysis & Qualitative	10%	34
Survey Created for this Research	3%	11
Ethnography and Interview	2%	7

Case-Based and Historical: Articles in this category draw conclusions by comparing different countries, localities and policy regimes, often over a period of time. They do not attempt to delimit any set of texts or sources for analysis, but rather freely mix scholarship, journalism, government reports and other sources.

Theory and Framework Pieces: Articles in this category have the advancement of a theoretical or methodological framework as one of their aims, as opposed to providing insight into specific cases or answering an empirical question. Frequently they advance this theoretical or methodological objective by employing some other more specific method. For instance, theoretical perspectives are often advanced through comparative case studies.

Quantitative Analysis: Articles in this category employ descriptive statistics, significance testing, regression and cluster analyses, and other statistical methods.

Textual and Content Analysis and Qualitative Research: Articles in this category delimit a set of texts – such as speeches, newspaper articles or legislation – for specific analysis, and then employ methods like content and rhetorical analysis to draw conclusions.

Survey Created for this Research: The authors of articles in this category created and conducted surveys specifically for the articles.

Ethnography and Interview: Articles in this category employ ethnographic fieldwork and in-depth interview to draw conclusions.

Comparative Policy Analysis Articles in the EBSCO Academic Complete Database

A search of the EBSCO Academic Complete database for articles in comparative policy analysis yielded 144 hits for the search period 1976 to 2016, exclusive of review pieces. The first hit was in 1986. Although the date range of the search is broader than the publication period of *JCPA*, we believe that this provides a robust comparison to the field of comparative policy analysis as it exists beyond *JCPA*. Figures 7 and 8 show policy areas and countries studied in the EBSCO sample, respectively. Figure 9 shows the methodology used in the studies in the EBSCO sample.

Policy Areas Studied. In general, the strengths and weaknesses in *JCPA*'s coverage are echoed in the EBSCO sample. In the matter of policy areas studied, the top four topics are the same in both the *JCPA* and the EBSCO analysis, although in a slightly different order. There is relatively more attention to health and healthcare in the EBSCO sample (24 per cent) than in *JCPA* (11 per cent), although health is by no means a neglected topic in *JCPA*. Both the *JCPA* and the EBSCO samples lack much coverage in the areas of criminal justice, human rights, arts and culture, and developmental aid, for instance.

Figure 7. EBSCO articles published in common policy areas, 1976–2016

Policy Area Studied	Percentage	Articles
Health, Healthcare, and Medicine	24%	34
Markets, Money and the Economy	19%	28
Welfare, Social Services, and Poverty	15%	22
Local and Regional Government & Policy	13%	18
Education	10%	15
International Relations and Organizations	9%	13
Science & Technology	8%	12
Environment	7%	10
Human Rights	6%	8
Regulation & Deregulation	4%	6
Media & Communication	3%	5
Immigration and Migration	3%	4
Globalization	2%	3
Privatization and Public Private Partnerships	2%	3
Criminal Justice	1%	2
Development of Underdeveloped Regions	1%	2
NGOs and Non-Profits	1%	2

*Policy areas are not exclusive categories. That is, each of the total 144 articles coded from the EBSCO database may have been coded as studying multiple policy areas.

Figure 8. Articles per country in the EBSCO sample

Figure 9. EBSCO methodology, 1976–2016

Methodology Employed	Percentage	Article
Historical and Case-Based	53%	76
Theory and Framework Pieces	42%	60
Quantitative Analysis	19%	28
Textual, Content & Qualitative Analysis	11%	16
Ethnography and Interview	8%	11
Survey Created for this Research	3%	5

Countries Studied. The results of the EBSCO analysis also look very similar to those of the *JCPA* analysis in what they reveal about the countries that have been studied. Again, North America and Europe predominate, and Central America, Africa, the Middle East and Central Asia are the least studied regions. A number of new countries – like Iran, Haiti and Cuba – do show up in the EBSCO articles, but these are mostly from comparative policy briefs published in a single issue of one journal, the *Journal of Policy & Practice in Intellectual Disabilities*, in 2008. (See Appendix 2 for a full list of the countries studied in the EBSCO sample.)

Methodology and Theory. The results of the analysis of methodology and number of countries studied were much the same for the EBSCO and *JCPA* samples. A greater percentage (8 per cent) of articles in the EBSCO sample employed ethnographic and interview techniques than in *JCPA* (2 per cent), but these methods still ranked toward the bottom of the list.

Conclusions

Comparative policy analysis has emerged as a separate field in order to achieve what the "old" social sciences research did not: to extend robust, actionable findings grounded in comparison to decision makers and to the scholarly community. The comparative policy analysis domain has gained momentum, as Figure 1 shows, post-1998 as the field of comparative administration declined. *JCPA* is the only journal of comparative public policy devoted entirely to the publication of articles on comparative policy analysis. Its emergence coincided almost exactly with the rise of interest in the field of comparative policy analysis we see in Figures 1 and 2. It channels a multitude of policy disciplines, regional cases and methodological and theoretical approaches.

Although we cannot know exactly the publication output of the entire comparative policy analysis field, *JCPA*'s output accounts for a sizable portion of it. *JCPA* published over 350 articles between 1998 and 2016 while the entire EBSCO database shows 144 articles for all journals over this period of time (with ten appearing before 1998). According to Routledge's database, in 2015 there were over 30,000 full-text downloads of articles from the *JCPA*. This is an increase of 29.6 per cent on the total from the previous year and an increase of *86* per cent on the total from 2012. At present, the *JCPA* publishes five issues per annual volume – that is about 600 pages of refereed studies of comparative policy analytic work. *JCPA* promised to advance comparative studies beyond comparisons of two national entities and address, apply or develop comparative methodologies and theories. About 40 per cent of *JCPA* articles feature a comparison of more than two countries. Prominent theoretical frameworks that have been highlighted in *JCPA* are path dependence, multiple streams and convergence (Coleman 2001; Kuipers 2009; Clavier 2010; Happaerts and Van Den Brande 2011). In 2016 a special issue edited by Beland and Howlett addressed the contributions of the multiple-streams approach to comparative policy analysis (Beland and Howlett 2016). *JCPA* should continue to build on these strengths, but might also encourage the development of thought with other prominent frameworks such as punctuated equilibrium theory and policy diffusion (Jones and Baumgartner 2005; Berry and Berry 2007; Shipan and Volden 2012). The journal might also feature less prominent and experimental designs, like qualitative comparative analysis (QCA), so far only addressed by Rizova (2011), and a special issue edited by Marleen Brans and Valerie Pattyn (2017).

JCPA also has as part of its mission the comparison and development of methodologies useful in comparative analysis and has published work that employs a wide variety of methodological approaches. But some approaches are used far more than others, and *JCPA* should encourage the building of methodological capacity for rigorous qualitative analysis, and research based on interviews and ethnography. Case studies are the prominent approach and represent 62 per cent of the articles analyzed. This reinforces the "natural experiments" perception of the policy analytic studies' comparative methodology. The addition of a section devoted exclusively to statistics in 2014 has helped to increase the prevalence of quantitative approaches. These studies more often rely on publicly available data, often from national governments and multinational organizations like the OECD and EU, than on data generated by surveys designed by the researchers. A few exceptions to this rule are Benito and Brusca (2004), Avrami and Rimmerman (2005) and Varma and Kapur (2013). Although Fischer and Maggetti (2017) recently made the case for the usefulness of the controversial qualitative comparative analysis, large-*n* qualitative methods are used more rarely than case studies or statistical analysis. The addition of the Comparative Statistics section of the journal did seem to somewhat increase the overall number of quantitative studies. There remains a dearth of work that employs interview or ethnographic methods, although these methods are not completely absent from the pages of *JCPA*, as exemplified by the recent work of Maybin (2015) and Escobar (2015). Both of these articles occurred in the special issue on "Professional Knowledge and Policy Work" which attempted to pursue inquiry into how policy is subjectively perceived in addition to traditional analysis of which policies are most effective according to objective measures. We suggest that an understanding of "policy-perception" is critical to an understanding of policy success and failure.

JCPA promised to be international in scope and indeed it has published articles about five continents, but the developed world is studied far more than the developing world. The predominance of authors from the developed world most likely reflects the nascent status of the field of comparative policy analysis and comparative policy analysis studies in much of the developing world (Muhleisen and Mukherjee 2016). Increasing awareness means that the *JCPA* should seek to publish more comparative policy analytic studies from Central Asia, the Middle East, Africa, Central America and the Caribbean. Steps have been taken already to expand JCPA's geographic reach. Five years ago the *JCPA* initiated the Best Comparative Paper Award at the Network of Institutes and Schools of Public Administration in Central and Eastern Europe (NISPAcee) for papers presented at the NISPAcee annual conference. Since then, *JCPA* has published a special issue on "Policy Analysis in Eastern Europe", and another special issue is forthcoming on comparative public policy methodology in the former Soviet satellite state public policies. The special issue is based on a recent workshop at the School of Higher Economics, Moscow. Several institutions in Eastern Europe have become members of the ICPA-Forum seeking to engage in collaborative research and publications. *JCPA* should extend such efforts to Africa, Central Asia and the Near East, Central America and other under-studied regions.

There is a certain fit between the geographical and methodological trends at *JCPA*. The developed nations which are studied most frequently tend to have relatively open governments that produce reliable data for quantitative analysis and keep publicly accessible records, they have free presses that report on policy developments with some degree of objectivity, they have developed academic establishments to coordinate and oversee research. Consequently, historical, case-based, qualitative and quantitative methods can be used with relative ease. On the other hand, many of these characteristics – and consequently the data available to researchers – are less prevalent in the countries scholars have neglected. The presence of such public data and independent journalistic and academic establishments is likely to be correlated with democracy and GDP. Consequently, a greater emphasis would need to be placed on fieldwork to draw meaningful conclusions about the effects of policy.

As noted in the content analysis, *JCPA* has a strong record of publication in the areas of economic and financial policy, welfare and social subsidies, and health. It is fairly strong on international agreements and organizations, the environment, education and immigration/migration. But there are many important questions of policy that fall beyond this scope. Christos Kassimeris' (2006) effort to advance a framework for comparing foreign policies is one of just a handful of articles on this topic, and while there is at least one study of military spending (Dicle and Dicle 2010), there is no comparative work on the outcomes of military intervention. There is no work on the effectiveness of economic and other sanctions as a tool of international diplomacy. Although social welfare, healthcare and environmental policies all have a basis in a fundamental set of human rights, there is little work dealing explicitly with human rights policies as such, although Montefrio (2014) and Golder and Williams (2006) are part of a small number who do make contributions in this area. There is little to nothing on crime and criminal sentencing, prison and incarceration, and racial bias and discrimination, despite a wealth of raw data in these fields.

As the leading journal in the field of comparative policy analysis, *JCPA* should continue to encourage pioneering work. The content analysis revealed that the strengths and weaknesses of *JCPA* are similar to the strengths and weaknesses of the comparative policy analysis field at large in terms of topics studied and methods employed. *JCPA* could maintain its leadership position in the field of comparative policy analysis by encouraging work about neglected regions and topics, and by building bridges to those who practice academic disciplines not normally associated with comparative policy analysis. Special issues of the journal might explore human rights, international development or military intervention. Editors might reach out to researchers in the discipline of anthropology, who are increasingly engage in policy-relevant work in many geographic regions where *JCPA* is at its weakest. The American Anthropology Association has an entire section called the Association for the Anthropology of Policy, and journals like *Anthropology in Action* are devoted to publishing policy-relevant finding of anthropologists. Scholars and researchers in the fields of criminal justice, who are increasingly relying on cross-jurisdictional comparisons, might also make important contributions (Reichel 2010). And efforts similar to those that resulted in more attention being paid to Eastern Europe might be made in other geographic regions.

Note

1. Google's description of the Google Million: "The 'Google Million'. All are in English with dates ranging from 1500 to 2008. No more than about 6000 books were chosen from any one year, which means that all of the scanned books from early years are present, and books from later years are randomly sampled. The random samplings reflect the subject distributions for the year (so there are more computer books in 2000 than 1980)." Retrieved from https://books.google.com/ngrams/info on 8 October 2016.

References

Avrami, S. and Rimmerman, A., 2005, Voting intentions of Israeli legislators regarding proposed disability and social welfare laws. *Journal of Comparative Policy Analysis: Research and Practice* **7**(3), pp. 221–232. doi:10.1080/13876980500209421

Bardach, E., 1992, *Problem Solving in the Public Sector*. (Berkeley, CA: UC Berkeley, GSPP).

Béland, D. and Howlett, M., 2016, The role and impact of the multiple-streams approach in comparative policy analysis. *Journal of Comparative Policy Analysis: Research and Practice* **18**(3), pp. 221–227. doi:10.1080/13876988.2016.1174410

Benito, B. and Brusca, I., 2004, International classification of local government accounting systems. *Journal of Comparative Policy Analysis: Research and Practice* **6**(1), pp. 57–80. doi:10.1080/1387698042000222790

Berry, F. S. and Berry, W. D., 2007, Innovation and diffusion models in policy research, in: P. A. Sabatier (Ed) *Theories of the Policy Process* (Colorado: Westview).

Brans, M., Geva-May, I. and Howlett, M., 2016, Introduction, in: M. Brans, I. Geva-May and M. Howlett (Eds) *The Routledge Handbook of Comparative Policy Analysis* (New York: Routledge).

Brans, M. and Pattyn, V., 2017, Validating methods for comparing public policy: Perspectives from academics and "pracademics". Introduction to the Special Issue. *Journal of Comparative Policy Analysis: Research and Practice*, **19**(4), pp. 303–312.

Clavier, C., 2010, Bottom–Up policy convergence: A sociology of the reception of policy transfer in public health policies in Europe. *Journal of Comparative Policy Analysis: Research and Practice* **12**(5), pp. 451–466. doi:10.1080/13876988.2010.516509

Coleman, W. D., 2001, Agricultural policy reform and policy convergence: An actor-centered institutionalist approach. *Journal of Comparative Policy Analysis: Research and Practice* **3**(2), pp. 219–241. doi:10.1080/13876980108412661

Deleon, P. and Resnick-Terry, P., 1998, Comparative policy analysis: Déjà vu all over again? *Journal of Comparative Policy Analysis: Research and Practice* **1**(1), pp. 9–22. doi:10.1080/13876989808412613

Dicle, B. and Dicle, M. F., 2010, Military spending and GDP growth: Is there a General causal relationship? *Journal of Comparative Policy Analysis: Research and Practice* **12**(3), pp. 311–345. doi:10.1080/13876981003714644

Dierkes, M., Weiler, H. N. and Antal, A. B., 1987, *Comparative Policy Research: Learning from Experience*. (Aldershot: Gower).

Dror, Y., 1983, *Public Policy Making Reexamined*. (Dunn, WN: Transaction Publishers).

Escobar, O., 2015, Scripting deliberative policy-making: Dramaturgic policy analysis and engagement know-how. *Journal of Comparative Policy Analysis: Research and Practice* **17**(3), pp. 269–285. doi:10.1080/13876988.2014.946663

Fischer, M. and Maggetti, M., 2017, Qualitative comparative study of policy analysis and the processes. *Journal of Comparative Policy Analysis: Research and Practice* **17**(4), pp. 345–361.

Gerring, J., 2006, *Case Study Research: Principles and Practices*, 1st ed. (New York: Cambridge University Press)

Geva-May, I., 2002, Cultural theory: The neglected variable in the craft of policy analysis. *Journal of Comparative Policy Analysis: Research and Practice* **4**(3), pp. 243–265. doi:10.1080/13876980208412682

Geva-May, I. and Lynn Jr., L. E., 1998, Aims and scope. *Journal of Comparative Policy Analysis*, **1**, pp. 5–8. doi:10.1023/A:1010006610304

Geva-May, I. and Wildavsky, A., 1997, *An Operational Approach to Policy Analysis: The Craft. Prescriptions for Better Analysis*. (Boston: Kluwer Academic Publishers).

Golder, B. and Williams, G., 2006, Balancing national security and human rights: Assessing the legal response of common law nations to the threat of terrorism. *Journal of Comparative Policy Analysis: Research and Practice* **8**(1), pp. 43–62. doi:10.1080/13876980500513335

Happaerts, S. and Van Den Brande, K., 2011, Sustainable development and transnational communication: Assessing the international influence on subnational policies. *Journal of Comparative Policy Analysis: Research and Practice* **13**(5), pp. 527–544. doi:10.1080/13876988.2011.605946

Heady, F., 2001, *Public Administration: A Comparative Perspective*, 6th ed. (New York: Dekker)

Hogwood, B. W. and Gunn, L. A., 1984, *Policy Analysis for the Real World*. (Oxford: Oxford University Press).

Ingraham, P., 1996, *A Laggard's Tale: civil Service and Administrative. Building A Government that Works*. (Washington, DC: Brookings Institution Press).

Jones, B. D. and Baumgartner, F. R., 2005, A model of choice for public policy. *Journal of Public Administration Research and Theory* **15**(3), pp. 325–351. doi:10.1093/jopart/mui018

Jreisat, J. E., 2002, *Comparative Public Administration and Policy*. (Boulder, CO: Westview Press).

Kassimeris, C., 2006, A depiction of the foreign policy behaviour of dyadic case studies based on the 'Triangle Model.'. *Journal of Comparative Policy Analysis: Research and Practice* **8**(3), pp. 271–281. doi:10.1080/13876980600858549

Kuipers, S., 2009, Paths of the past or the road ahead? Path dependency and policy change in two continental European welfare states. *Journal of Comparative Policy Analysis* **11**(2), pp. 163–180. doi:10.1080/13876980902887998

Lasswell, H. D., 1968, The future of the comparative method. *Comparative Politics* **1**(1), pp. 3–18. doi:10.2307/421372

Lasswell, H. D. and Kaplan, A., 1950, *Power and Society: A Framework for Political Inquiry*. (New Haven, CT: Yale University Press).

Lindblom, C. E., 1958, Policy analysis. *American Economic Review*, **48**(3), pp. 298–312.

MacRae, D. and Wilde, J. A., 1979, *Policy Analysis for Public Decisions*. (North Scituate, MA: Duxbury Press).

Maybin, J., 2015, Policy analysis and policy know-how: A case study of civil servants in England's department of health. *Journal of Comparative Policy Analysis: Research and Practice* **17**(3), pp. 286–304. doi:10.1080/13876988.2014.919738

Mill, J. S., 1843, *A System of Logic, Ratiocinative and Inductive: being A Connected View of the Principles of Evidence and the Methods of Scientific Investigation*. (London: John W. Parker).

Montefrio, M. J. F., 2014, State versus indigenous peoples' rights: Comparative analysis of stable system parameters, policy constraints and the process of delegitimation. *Journal of Comparative Policy Analysis: Research and Practice* **16**(4), pp. 335–355. doi:10.1080/13876988.2014.938912

Muhleisen, J. and Mukherjee, I., 2016, Policy analysis: A rich array of country and comparative insights. *Asia Pacific Journal of Public Administration* **38**(3), pp. 204–210. doi:10.1080/23276665.2016.1217663

Neustadt, R. E. and May, E. R., 1986, *Thinking In Time: The Uses Of History For Decision Makers*. (New York, NY: Simon and Schuster).

Ostrom, E., 1998, A behavioral approach to the rational choice theory of collective action: Presidential address, American political science association, 1997. *American Political Science Review* **92**(1), pp. 1–22. doi:10.2307/2585925

Radin, B. A., 2013a, *Beyond Machiavelli: policy Analysis Reaches Midlife*, 2nd ed. (Washington, DC: Georgetown University Press).

Radin, B. A., 2013b, Policy analysis reaches midlife. *Central European Journal of Public Policy*, **7**(1), pp. 8–27.

Reichel, P., 2010, *Comparative Criminal Justice Systems*. (Oxford Bibliographies). http://oxfordindex.oup.com/view/10.1093/obo/9780195396607-0075

Rizova, P. S., 2011, Finding testable causal mechanisms to address critical public management issues, *Journal Of Comparative Policy Analysis* **13**(1), 105–114. doi:10.1080/13876988.2011.538544

Rose, R., 1991, What is lesson-drawing? *Journal of Public Policy* **11**(1), pp. 3–30. doi:10.1017/S0143814X00004918

Rose, R., 1993, *Lesson-Drawing in Public Policy: A Guide to Learning across Time and Space*. (Chatham, NJ: Chatham House).

Rose, R., James, W. and Mackenzie, M., 1991, Comparing forms of comparative analysis. *Political Studies* **39**(3), pp. 446–462. doi:10.1111/j.1467-9248.1991.tb01622.x

Shipan, C. R. and Volden, C., 2012, Policy diffusion: Seven lessons for scholars and practitioners. *Public Administration Review* **72**(6), pp. 788–796. doi:10.1111/j.1540-6210.2012.02610.x

Swanson, G., 1971, Frameworks for comparative research: Structural anthropology and the theory of action, in: I. Vallier (Ed) *Comparative Methods in Sociology* (Berkeley: University of California Press), pp. 141–202.

Varma, R. and Kapur, D., 2013, Comparative analysis of brain drain, brain circulation and brain retain: A case study of Indian Institutes of Technology. *Journal of Comparative Policy Analysis: Research and Practice* **17**(4), pp. 315–330. doi:10.1080/13876988.2013.810376

Weimer, D. L., 1993, The current state of design craft: Borrowing, tinkering, and problem solving. *Public Administration Review*, pp. 110–120. doi:10.2307/976703

Weimer, D. L. and Vining, A. R., 1989, *Policy Analysis: Concepts and Practice*. (Englewood Cliffs, NJ: Prentice-Hall).

Weimer, D. L. and Vining, A. R., 1999, *Policy Analysis: Concepts and Practice*. (Englewood Cliffs, NJ: Prentice-Hall).

Weimer, D. L. and Vining, A. R., 2010, *Policy Analysis: Concepts and Practice*. (Englewood Cliffs, NJ: Prentice-Hall).

Wildavsky, A., 1979, *Speaking Truth to Power: the Art and Craft of Policy Analysis*. (Boston: Little, Brown).

Comparative Logic versus Problem Logic? An Introduction

MONIKA STEFFEN

During the past two decades, profound transformations have affected public policies on national as well as international levels. In most countries, the regional and local levels have become important in both policy elaboration and conduct. International institutions, actor networks and policy communities have gained considerable influence. Policy ideas and recommendations are traveling across national borders and supra-national regions have been built up or given stronger competency. The European Union (EU), the Association of South East Asian Nations (ASEAN) and the South American market union (MERCOSUR) constitute examples of such supra-national bodies that have become new sources of legitimacy, often with legal competency, especially in economic and financial matters. In the context of globalization, it becomes increasingly difficult to draw the borderlines and distinguish national policy making from other sources, factors and inputs. Whilst there is little doubt on the reality of these multifold changes, it is less clear how these empirical changes affect the methods of and theoretical approaches to comparative policy analysis. What are the new challenges for research?

Furthermore, new priorities have emerged in most fields of public policy, in connection with changing patterns of public and private demands and interests. In established policy sectors, traditional belief systems and policy paradigms have evolved and enhanced changes in the dominant networks of actors and modes of governance. One of the most obvious examples is provided by the health sector, where the central aim of public policies shifted from the accessibility of medical services to cost containment. Controlling the medical profession and surveying public health risks became new priorities in a sector that was formerly dominated by the interests of an organized profession. Extremely complex policy issues have thus arrived on the public agendas of most countries, such as environmental issues, religious issues, the restructuring of welfare states, the security of modern information technology, or the reorientation of educational policies and professional training tracks in response to changing employment patterns. Consequently, international, national and local authorities are confronted with the need to solve increasingly complex problems, most of them concerning several policy sectors simultaneously.

The range of actors and interests involved tends to become larger and less homogeneous. Non-governmental organizations are taking an increasing part in public policy making and implementation. Economic business and actors are increasingly becoming an inherent part of public policies, politics and polities (Hall and Soskice 2001). The problem for comparative policy analysis is how to compare what is extremely diverse. How to draw up coherent research designs between countries and between policy sectors when the national aggregation of actors and interests are homogenous only at an extremely abstract level? How should the intermediate layers of policy making (such as branches of businesses, patterns of public–private collaboration on regional or inter-regional levels, technological clusters, or professional organizations) be treated, especially in terms of theory?

The literature of the 1980s and 1990s elaborated "national models" aimed at understanding public policies within their national environment. A typical example of this approach was the opposition between the French centralized Fordist model and the German decentralized consensual model (Maurice *et al.* 1982, Jobert and Steffen 1994). The research agenda focusing on national models and differences was fueled by the extensive development of comparative studies in the field of social security systems and policies. The efforts were particularly systematic in the European welfare states (Flora 1986, Esping-Anderson 1990, Ferrera and Rhodes 2000), which were examined and compared through common research designs. Subsequently, comparisons were aimed at the different capacities of national economies and polities to respond to the challenges of globalization (Crouch and Streeck 1996, Boyer and Hollingworth 1997, Scharpf and Schmidt 2001). Surprisingly, many European comparisons, especially in the field of social policies, pay little attention to the specific effects of European integration on national policy systems. To what extent do the "national" models remain pertinent today, in the light of the growing complexity of public problems and their changing links to geographical territories?

The overriding question is how the available theoretical framework and knowledge can be used and adopted to analyze recent evolutions and draw up adequate research designs for new cases of comparative public policy analysis? When it comes to complex issues, such as environmental, transportation, health or retirement policies, to what extent should comparative analysis focus on *national* cases and levels? Or, should it rather concentrate on policy *sectors* or on precise policy *problems?* And, finally, how can these approaches be combined?

Many comparative policy analyses share, at least in part, three characteristics. First, some studies focus on policy elaboration, taking into account less systematically the processes of implementation, learning and policy change. This may bias the theoretical statements drawn from the comparative results. Second, empirical observations still tend to concentrate on the national capacities of problem definition and resolution. Nevertheless, at the intellectual level policy construction and problem solving is most often embedded in infra- or supra-national networks, data systems and decision-making. Third, the interpretation of results often remains limited to an item to item comparison of the particular cases under review, without constructing more general statements that would also be applicable to cases or policy areas other than those included in the particular comparison. This point addresses a major difficulty of comparative methodology and interpretation, which is the combination of the different kinds of factors, for example of a political, cultural, institutional, technical or economic nature. The interpretation of comparative results ought to aim to produce a set of coherent causal explanations that are sufficiently "subtle" to explain each individual case of the comparison, and at the same time sufficiently general to transcend them all and contribute to theory.

The interesting problem concerning the selection of discriminating factors (at both stages: the comparative research design and the interpretation of results) is that the independent or dependent nature of factors is not given in advance, at least not definitively. The national policy-making system acts in general as an independent factor, which explains the national differences between countries, even between very similar or neighboring countries. This certainty, however, is only relative. It is valid under "normal" circumstances, when stability dominates, but it may lose its validity when policies change. This happens under the pressure of new needs and interests as well as being due to international references or benchmarking. Another reason may be policy failure or acute crisis. Change proceeds by incremental adjustment or by structural and radical reform. Especially in this latter case, the dynamics of change in one policy area can lead to a major reorientation, with spillover effects in other sectors or at various levels of the general political system. This was illustrated in France during the 1990s by the HIV/blood transfusion crisis (Steffen 1999). In such cases, the normally independent factors may become dependent factors and vice versa. When comparative policy analysis observes changing policy patterns, it may reveal a potentially unstable and shifting hierarchy of explanatory factors.

A single special issue cannot address the entire range of interesting questions raised by the comparative analysis of public policies. An extensive literature is available, including teaching books (Peters 1998) and theoretical frameworks (Geva-May 2001) based on extensive field research and systematic comparison of numerous cases (Bovens *et al.* 2001). The specific aim of this collection is to provide different methodological approaches to the recent developments in public policies. It presents a selection of original research articles from different policy sectors, countries and regional areas. The authors review their own methodological approaches, results and interpretations and focus on questions with potential added value given the present state of art in the discipline. They reassess central aspects of case methodology, of intermediate levels of policy analysis and of the use and the limits of national models in the context of internationalization and the growing complexity of public policies.

The first two articles examine European policies, with the underlying assumption that "Europe" constitutes a specific policy-determining factor. The first article, by Monika Steffen, presents an apparently classical example of a comparative case study, the management of the AIDS epidemic in four European countries. The particular methodological interest of the case is that it presents all the characteristics of a "complex" policy problem. It involves several sectors of public policies, uncertainty over future developments, departure from previous policy paths and a close mix of public and private dimensions. The case focuses on public health policies, a field outside the mainstream of health policy and politics, with a different structure of problems, institutions, interests and intellectual paradigms. It reveals a specific public/private frontier in each national case and illustrates how cultural dimensions can act in public policy. The methodological approach, inspired by Weberian theory, allows the schematization of exclusively qualitative data, such as values and co-ordination capacities, and the assessment of comparative policy change.

The second article, by Sabine Saurugger, introduces the methodological treatment of change. She focuses on Europeanization as a methodological problem. While the theories and concepts of Europeanization are prominent issues in a number of research agendas, the methodological challenges of empirical research have been less considered. The article proposes a research design capable of solving the three main problems: first, the complex interdependence between national and European levels that characterize the processes of Europeanization; second, the difficulty of distinguishing between "European" and "domestic" variables; and, third, the measurement of change. The underlying case studies, on interest groups in the EU, show the necessity of long-term micro-studies in order to identify national and sectoral policy styles, traditions and changes. Only then can one distinguish "European" impacts from Europeanization.

The following two articles take into account policy makers, as initiators or users of comparative policy analyses, and discuss links to methodological issues. The third article, by Richard Burkhauser and Dean Lillard, analyzes major international data collection systems. All economically developed countries undertake surveys and systematic data collection on the economic and social situation of their citizens, in terms of income, employment, retirement, entry and exit movements in the labor market. These longstanding data systems were initially purely national and served, among others, the purpose of evaluating public policies. During the last twenty-five years, projects were launched to make data collection and presentation internationally comparable within the EU, the OECD or by country clusters. The article analyzes the methodological difficulties of data harmonization and ways by which they can be resolved.

In contrast, the fourth article, by Ted Marmor, Richard Freeman and Kieke Okma, reaches a negative conclusion on similar questions. The authors document the failure of comparative research in the field of health care policy. A considerable gap exists "between promises and effective performance," because of rhetorical distortion, misdescription and superficiality in the terms of comparison. The article reviews the international comparative literature on health care policy and explores the methodological questions raised by the weakness of the outcome. The second focus is on cross-national policy learning. The authors analyze the methodological pitfalls of the enterprise and examine how competent learning could effectively take place from one nation to another in the health care sector. In their perspective, neither the promises of comparative policy scholarship nor the claims of convergence among OECD health care systems have been met. Both remain unrealistic aims. The reason is that the rare good comparative books, based on adequate approaches, are purely academic with little chance of reaching the desks of policy makers. These studies are necessarily limited to a small number of countries and to specific health policy problems, which may not be within the immediate interest of policy makers.

The fifth and last article, by Guy B. Peters clarifies what appear as implicit assumptions in the articles by Steffen, Marmor *et al.* and to a lesser degree also Saurugger. It provides the theoretical foundation to a new perspective: comparative policy analysis needs to turn to policy content and to the very "nature of the policy problems governments are confronted with". Peters argues that policies are not undifferentiated, as many scholars of comparative politics seem to assume. On the contrary, the "policies themselves" may be the principal source of variance. The article develops a set of analytic dimensions that can be used to characterize policy "problems". The seven variables proposed to qualify policy problems combine what the literature on agenda setting and policy framing: the objective (substantial, technical, "natural") dimensions of a problem and its subjective (socially constructed) dimensions. The aim in comparative policy studies should be to establish the links between the different types of policy problems on the one hand and the instruments at disposal to actually solve them on the other. While the instruments and their use will of course differ according to the national, and probably also sectoral contexts, the characteristics of the policy problem remain the same. This new approach, which is illustrated here by the empirical case of water pollution in the US, explains why certain problems are more difficult to solve than others.

This special issue opens with a comparative case study on an extremely complex policy and closes with a theoretical approach to policy "problems", considered as the core variable of comparative policy analysis. The collection thus hopes to contribute to the promotion of theoretical and methodological discussion on comparative approaches. Unfortunately, the limited space did not allow broadening the selection of articles and subjects to include, for example, the specific situation of Third World, emerging countries or macro-studies. The latter are best adapted to test a limited number of factors (ideally only one) with the assumption that it would always trigger identical effects. As the articles here show, this is not the case in public policies, where similar factors can produce different effects and vice versa. With this special issue, the Journal has also widened its international authorship, in particular towards the work of French political scientists who until now have been under-represented in English-speaking policy journals.

References

Boven, M., t'Hart, P. and Peters, B. G. (Eds), 2001, *Success and Failure in Public Governance. A Comparative Analysis* (London: Edward Elgar Publishers).
Boyer, R. and Hollingsworth, J. R. (Eds), 1997, *Contemporary Capitalism – The Embeddedness of Institutions* (Cambridge: Cambridge University Press).
Crouch, C. and Streeck, W. (Eds), 1996, *Les Capitalismes en Europe* (Paris: Edition La Découverte).
Esping-Anderson, G., 1990, *The Three Worlds of Welfare Capitalism* (Cambridge: Polity Press).
Ferrera, M. and Rhodes, M. (Eds), 2000, *Recasting the European Welfare States* (London and Portland: Frank Cass Publishers).
Flora, Peter (Ed.), 1986, *Growth to limits. The European Welfare States since World War II*, Vol. 4 (Berlin: de Gruyer).
Hall, P. and Soskice, D. (Eds), 2001, *Varieties of Capitalism – The Institutional Foundations of Comparative Advantage* (Oxford: Oxford University Press).
Jobert, B. and Steffen, M. (Eds), 1994, *Les politiques de la santé en France et en Allemange* (Paris: Observatoire Européen des Politiques Sociales/Espace Social Européen).
Lallement, M. and Spurk, J., 2003, *Stratégies de la comparaison internationale* (Paris: Édition du CNRS).
Maurice, M., Sellier, F. and Silvestre, J. J., 1982, *Politique d'éducation et organisation industrielle en France et en Allemagne* (Paris: Presses Universitaires de France).

Peters, B. G., 1998, *Comparative Politics – Theory and Methods* (Hampshire: Macmillan Press).
Scharpf, F. W. and Schmidt, V. (Eds), 2001, *Welfare and Work in the Open Economy* (Oxford and New York: Oxford University Press).
Steffen, M., 1999, The Nation's Blood. Medicine, Justice and the State in France, in: E. Feldman and R. Bayer (Eds) *Blood Feuds: Aids, Blood, and the Politics of Medical Disaster* (Oxford and New York: Oxford University Press), pp. 95–126.

Comparing Complex Policies: Lessons from a Public Health Case

MONIKA STEFFEN

ABSTRACT *The article presents the methodological approach to a comparative case study in a regional group of countries, comparing a set of public health policies in four European welfare states. The policy problem, fighting the AIDS epidemic, is extremely complex and fast moving. It involves many policy areas as well as important private life dimensions and introduces changes in national as well as sectoral policy making. The results show four distinct policy patterns, but bring together Britain and Germany on the one hand and Italy and France on the other, although France follows a unique path with extensive policy learning and major institutional reforms. They suggest hypotheses on how culture acts in the formation of public policies. The analysis binds together internal case commonalities and the comparative logic.*

Introduction

Why do neighboring countries with similar political, economic and social systems have varying success in responding to an identical policy problem? Which key variables should be taken into account when a comparative analysis concerns a new policy field, on which theoretical knowledge is not yet available? The new problem may be extremely complex and policy making may involve several sectors and distinct actor networks. What are the relevant theoretical and comparative frameworks we need for such cases? And how should we proceed when interpreting the many comparative results and drawing general conclusions aiming at theoretical statements? The AIDS policy case provides a particularly interesting example in these respects. An identical public health problem appeared simultaneously in many countries, confronting policy makers, institutions and beneficiaries in different national systems with the same unprecedented challenges. Conditions for comparison seem to be both optimal and extremely complex.

Methodological difficulties originate from several sources, especially the cross-sectoral dimensions of the policy problem and its dynamics of change. The AIDS epidemic is an unusual and fast-moving problem. It has been a source of controversy, and even crisis, and it introduced important innovations in all policy fields concerned with the problem. The question here is which changes need to be compared, and at which point in time the analysis needs to begin? Should the events triggered by the discovery of the new disease in 1981 be taken into consideration in the same way as the political crisis sparked off ten years later in France by the "contaminated blood affair"? How far back do we need to go in the history of the political treatment of sexually transmitted diseases, homosexuality or drug addiction in order to be able to observe the role of path dependency and identify effective changes, via crises or incremental adjustments? How can the identified dynamics of changes be attributed to either the national context or the internal case characteristics?

Fighting and managing the epidemic involved many different policy fields that up to then had little, if any contact, such as the prevention of sexually transmitted diseases, the security of the blood and plasma supply, the treatment of injecting drug use, the policies of health and sexual education, clinical research and the provision of specialized medical care. Furthermore, AIDS involves private life issues and questions of social solidarity. The phenomenon involves several public policies and the society in its most profound dimensions, including cultural attitudes to sex, disease and death, as well as a trans-sector and trans-national dimension. How can "a" policy encompassing a wide range of measures and involving rapidly changing issues be compared?

A rather obvious answer would be to turn to comparative health policy studies. Their focus, however, is the control of health expenditure, whilst AIDS policies have not been subject to such considerations, which were even deliberately excluded. Hence, the case of AIDS *contrasts* with the major challenges running through the health sector. Not only did no effective medical treatment exist when the disease appeared, but all new drugs were made available as quickly as possible, at least in all European welfare states, without any restrictions to AIDS patients likely to derive some medical benefit from them. In fact, comparative analysis becomes difficult when it concerns *public* health policies, because the latter involve a different set of actors and interests compared to health policies in the common but restricted medical sense. Three main differences can be mentioned. First, public health issues and policies are situated at the intersection of private and public life. Individual and collective dimensions are closely linked, as shown in the struggle against tobacco and alcohol abuse or sexually transmitted diseases (Bayer 1991, Feldman and Bayer 2004). Second, the successful management of public health issues depends directly on government action and on the rapidity and coherence thereof, as shown in the recent cases of epidemics in Europe and Asia, for example foot-and-mouth disease, severe acute respiratory syndrome, and avian influenza. Third, the role of the medical profession, which is dominant in the polities of "the medical care state" (Moran 1999), is limited when it comes to public health policy making and implementation.

Furthermore, the struggle against AIDS contributed to important structural changes in health policy. Under the pressure of the epidemic, the position of public health, traditionally weak and marginal compared to the prevailing curative medicine, was consolidated in each individual country and at the international level, particularly at the level of the European Union (Steffen 2005). Public health policies have thus shifted from the periphery of the "medical care state" towards the center of public attention. Last but not least, doctor/patient relations have become more democratic. Militant organizations representing the interests of AIDS patients and at-risk persons have imposed themselves as unavoidable interlocutors of medical institutions and the public authorities (Epstein 1996, Pinell 2002, Barbot 2002). The comparative analysis of public health policies can therefore contribute to a new and more comprehensive concept of health policy itself.[1]

This article presents a comparative case study conducted in four European countries: the United Kingdom, Germany, France and Italy. The choice is limited to Europe in order to insure a sufficient degree of comparability between the national cases, all committed to the European standards of social security and welfare and sharing a similar cultural and political inheritance.[2] The aim of this article is to present the methodological approach and discuss the comparative results thus obtained. The first section sets out the choice of the national cases. The second defines the "typical" dimensions of the complex policy problem to be handled. It looks at the ways comparability can be constructed despite multi-sided policy content and timing. The third section presents selected parts of the country stories, focusing on how the national cases responded to the most critical and typical challenges: initiating government action, building up consensus and co-ordination capacities, and developing health and sexual education. The fourth section discusses the explanatory factors, including invalidated hypotheses and unexpected elements that may contribute to explaining the national successes and failures.

Selecting Country Cases: A Multi-polar and Proximity Choice

The literature provides no model describing contemporary management of epidemics in developed countries. The threat seemed to have disappeared with the improvement in living conditions, vaccinations and antibiotics. Historical comparative studies establish the predominance of national and sectoral path dependency. Baldwin (1999) explains public health policies by the historical compromises, laid down in each country during nineteenth and early twentieth century, between private individual rights on the one hand and the power of public authorities to limit personal freedom in order to protect public health on the other.

The international statistics show a direct relationship between the spread of the disease and poverty, underdevelopment and violence, such as war or forced migration. As with all other health indicators, the spread of HIV/AIDS reflects the lack of resources for the health sector, unequal access to services and poor organization of the nation's health systems (Ghorbarah and Huth 2004). The striking differences between Western and Eastern Europe, with an extremely rapid growth in the incidence of HIV/AIDS in most former socialist countries,[3] illustrate the impact of change and instability on public health conditions and management (Steffen 1999).

According to the World Heath Organization and the Joint United Nations Program on HIV/AIDS (UNAIDS), the prevalence of HIV infection ranges from close to ninety adults in one thousand in sub-Saharan Africa, to six in South and Central Asia, Eastern Europe and North and South America, but only three in the European Union and one in Australia and New Zealand.[4] In fact, the European Union (before extension to 25 members) constitutes the only *major*[5] exception in the dark picture of the spread of AIDS in the world. The present study was therefore limited to Western European countries, which have a similar level of social, political and cultural development, along with health coverage and social welfare for their entire populations. This choice takes into account both the strong institutional path dependency and the cultural embeddedness of public health policies, on the one hand, and the existence of full health and welfare coverage, on the other.

The number of countries to be included in a comparison depends on a trade-off between an in-depth analysis of a particular policy case, limited to a few countries, ideally only two, and an analysis aiming at the impact of a particular factor, tested in a large variety of cases, ideally all EU member states plus Switzerland, Norway, Australia, New Zealand, Japan, and so on. For the present study, focusing on an unprecedented and complex policy case, only the first option seems eligible. The number of national cases included was, however, enlarged to four in order to avoid the bias often observed in bi-national comparisons, with one national case being constructed in relation to, and most often in contrast with the other (Boyer 2002). We selected France, the UK, Italy and Germany because[6] they are neighboring countries with a comparable size of population, demography being an intrinsically important criterion for epidemics, but they coped differently in managing the epidemic.

While the specialized AIDS literature did not propose any convincing hypothesis about policy developments and outcomes,[7] early comparative studies of political scientists linked them to general features of sectoral or general policy making (Fox et al. 1989, Fee and Fox 1992). The selection of countries in this study therefore takes into account the institutional organization of the health sector, basic features of the political system and the transmission models of the epidemic.

The two theoretical models of the health care sector are represented: the Beveridgian type of national health system (the UK, Italy) and the Bismarckian type of health insurance system (France, Germany). Each of these two contrasting models provides a different institutional position of prevention in relation to care. In the national health systems, prevention is part of the institutional apparatus and is largely funded and regulated by the same authorities, whereas the competence of the health insurance funds is generally limited to medical care, leaving preventive services outside the main structures of the sector, under the responsibility of other authorities and most often local ones. Theoretically, the organization of the health sector should therefore influence the capacity to manage a public health problem, a factor to be tested in the AIDS case.

Two countries have a centralized public policy system (France, the UK) and two a decentralized system, both formally and in practice (Germany and Italy). The degree of (de)centralization of public, social, artistic and economic life is accurately reflected in the spread of the epidemic, which is a reminder of the "political" nature of any public health problem.[8] In the UK and in France, three-quarters of the population with HIV live in the London area and in the Paris area and Provence-Alpes-Côte d'Azur, respectively, while in Italy and Germany the five regions most affected in each country account for hardly two-thirds of the HIV-positive population.[9]

The selected countries also include different models of the spread of the epidemic. Although transmission patterns are changing at present, the policy problem has been dominated in Italy by drug abuse while in the UK and, to a lesser extent, in Germany homosexual transmission has been predominant. The French epidemic has three distinct social and geographic poles, with interacting effects: a primarily drug abuse related epidemic in the South, a homosexuality related epidemic in Paris, and a heterosexual epidemic in the overseas territories and in groups from mainland France in contact with these extra-European areas.

The epidemiological transmission models form part of the policy problem, because they present particular constraints for policy implementation. Transmission related to homosexuality is the easiest to prevent, because the gay community is well structured and politically motivated to collaborate with the public authorities. Heterosexual transmission is more difficult to control since it concerns mainly the underprivileged, in particular migrant groups among which prevention policies encounter problems linked to weak social integration, a lack of "civic literacy" (Milner 2002) and even language problems. An epidemic related to injecting drug use is the most difficult to contain. Addicts are in an extremely marginal social position, engaged in a health-damaging lifestyle and are difficult for public institutions to reach. Hence, according to the particular profile of their epidemic, the national cases are confronted with a more or less difficult task. Yet, after twenty years of struggle against the epidemic, the figures also indicate the output of more or less effective policies.

Table 1 shows notable differences within Western Europe, with extreme variations between the North and the South of the continent. Whilst the North/South differences have been studied in terms of governance, social capital and political culture (Inglehart 1990, Rokkan 1999), the AIDS situation suggests a surprising link between public health and religious traditions. Countries with a Protestant tradition seem to have a better capacity in conducting prevention policies than those of the Catholic tradition.[10] Since the churches had little impact on public AIDS policies, explanation calls for a more complex set of indirect factors.[11]

The Construction of a Comparable Policy Problem

The comparability of the research subject requires us to draw boundaries in the multi-sided AIDS field, in order to master the empirical diversity and complexity. The general methodological question is how to exclude extraneous factors. The choice in this study was to limit the subject to policy issues that fall within the sphere of public health or are directly related to it. Sex education at school is therefore included in the analysis but policies regarding homosexual identity are not. The latter constitute a set of policies differing substantially from health policies in terms of goals, interests, institutions and actors. Legal recognition of homosexual couples enters within the frame of analysis only when it concerns, for example,

Table 1. HIV/AIDS incidence per 10,000 adults (cumulated, December 1999*)

Portugal	83	Netherlands	25	**United Kingdom**	16
Spain	75	Denmark	21	**Germany**	13
Switzerland	65	Luxembourg	20	Ireland	13
France	60	Belgium	20	Sweden	13
Italy	47	Greece	19	Norway	10
Austria	27	Iceland	16	Finland	6

*Completed new data series are either not yet available, or if so, they are biased by the different national test policies linked to anti-retroviral therapy.

the transferability of social rights to the unemployed partner, enabling him or her to be a beneficiary of medical insurance. Even within this "reduced" frame, a wide variety of national and sectoral configurations still remains that also need to be reduced in order to obtain a limited number of comparable categories. This can be achieved with a classical Weberian approach of constructing ideal types. The method consists in retaining the *real* policy content and timing, but without taking into account all the specific variations and particularities observed. The aim is to identify the *general* properties of the fight against AIDS, which then help to assess the differences between empirical cases.

Defining a Typical Policy Content

Political responses to AIDS were extremely numerous and diverse, ranging from the delivery of medical services at home to the installation of condom vending machines in public places, from legislative measures banning any discriminatory act towards persons with HIV to health reforms in prisons and, more generally, efforts to improve the medical coverage of marginalized populations: drug addicts, the homeless and illegal immigrants. Faced with the empirical diversity of measures and policies in each country, two methodological options exist. Either we can focus on an irreducible diversity, which would make it difficult to explain policy changes, learning and trends towards convergence, or we can reduce it and construct analytical categories. In fact, all the empirically observed measures can be classified in analytical categories that allow a comparative approach.

A first category of measures concerns the creation and development of an expertise system. The adaptation of health statistics to the specific AIDS requirements falls into this category, including the confidentiality of data and the controversial question of compulsory or voluntary registration of either acute cases of disease or of positive test results. At present, several approaches coexist in Europe. The registration of seropositive cases was practiced from the outset in the UK, where it was voluntary and effective, in Germany, where it was compulsory but ineffective – hence a revision of institutional practices – and in Italy, where it was practiced unequally, depending on the region – leading to a difficult and still ongoing harmonization. By contrast, in France statistics on seropositive cases were excluded until recently by political decision aiming to "prevent social stigmatization" of people with HIV/AIDS. Drive for change originated from two convergent sources. First, the European Union is striving to harmonize national systems and to make epidemiological data comparable throughout its member states (Steffen 2004). Second, all experts are currently pushing for a reorientation of the registration system to include and focus on HIV infection, rather than clinical AIDS diagnoses that are no longer considered as relevant for the management of the epidemic because effective medicines are now available. Supported by the general access to early medication, a supra-national public health policy is thus developing and imposing its logic on national policy actors.

A second category comprises measures promoting "solidarity" with victims of the epidemic. It encompasses all the adjustments in the system of medical and social care, including comprehensive services such as home care, therapeutic apartments, networks of care-givers including psychological support and the participation of voluntary workers. In those countries that have a clear institutional break between the social and medical domains the implementation of these comprehensive actions is impeded by a compartmentalization of services, financing, administrative competencies and professional nomenclatures, a problem that was particularly acute in France and Italy. For marginalized groups such as drug addicts and people living in extreme poverty, the aim is to complete traditional social services by a comprehensive medical and preventive approach, including free medical care with individual follow-up and free provision of condoms and clean syringes.

The policy of solidarity with AIDS victims thus has two sides to it that mobilize separate networks of actors and institutions. One side focuses on the "individual" and respect for her or his private life and right to a normal social life, as defended by militant homosexuals. This aspect, which depends primarily on general laws guaranteeing civic and democratic rights, has been the easiest to implement throughout Western Europe. No noteworthy difference exists between the four countries studied. By contrast, the second part consists mainly in a re-medicalization of social work to meet the specific needs of the underprivileged. The implementation depends mainly on local authorities and implies the effective collaboration of a plurality of professions and combined sources of funding. Under the pressure of AIDS, the authorities in big cities revived one of their traditional missions, that of providing medical and preventive services to the underprivileged on their territories. It is likely that professional paradigms and local initiatives constitute a main factor explaining different national achievements in managing the epidemic in marginal populations. Two institutional configurations should facilitate such successful local strategies: political–administrative decentralization and comprehensive health systems that favor collaboration with their environment.

A third category of measures concerns prevention in the two areas of individual and community behavior: sexual practices and drug use. Despite their different nature, they constitute a similar policy problem. In both cases, public authorities have to conduct policies aimed at modifying behaviors, and are therefore obliged to *accept* behaviors formerly considered as amoral or illegal, e.g. homosexuality, injecting drug use, prostitution and multiple partner sex. The main policy tools are the promotion of condom use and the public provision of sterile syringes or, alternatively, substitutive medications such as methadone. The effective collaboration with the representatives of the concerned communities is necessary because only insiders are familiar with the relevant practices and languages. National capacities for implementation of such measures are obviously not equal. They depend on previous policies and experiences with health and sex education, and on the legal and medical treatment of drug addiction. Only a strong political consensus and government engagement can impose such new policies against existing professional interests, social attitudes and public opinion.

A last category groups together measures of prevention of and compensation for transmission of HIV via medical treatment. In the four countries, the iatrogenic infection of hemophiliacs and other patients with HIV led to closer control over blood transfusion, organ donation systems and more generally the safety of medicinal drugs and products. The result was strict selection of blood donors and the creation of independent agencies, at national and EU levels, to control sectoral agents and interests. Donated blood and derived products lost their traditional sacred aura and became assimilated into ordinary medicine.[12] The hemophiliacs' legal struggle together with the AIDS activism of the homosexual organizations had a common effect: public responsibility for medicine and patients' rights were considerably enhanced, especially in those countries where they had been weak.

Typical Policy Timing

These policies developed with different timing in the different sectors and countries. The complex time schedules also need to be reduced to a standardized chronology for the purpose of comparison. The factor "time" is important in practical as well as theoretical terms. The struggle against an epidemic is contingent on quick intervention, in the earliest possible phases before large-scale expansion. Hence, rapid and coherent government action seems most crucial for success. In terms of comparative methodology, policy timing and changes can only be assessed with reference to a general type of chronology. The empirical data from the four countries allows the identification of four ideal-typical policy sequences that can be used as an analytical tool to compare the cases.

The initial phase is a period of recognition marked by uncertainty. It lasted four years, from 1981 to 1984. It ended when a test for screening became available. At the time, the only experts familiar with the strange disease were the clinicians who treated the first patients, militant homosexuals who defended the interests of the many patients in their ranks, and public health professionals, generally epidemiologists who were trying to ascertain the extent of the problem and the routes of transmission. This group dominated the initial stage characterized by two contrasting attitudes: the experts' activism and the political authorities' wait-and-see approach.

The following phase is a period of policy debate and controversy. It is very short, typically only a few months during 1985. Opinions differed on the use of the screening test. During this stage, the network of actors expanded: experts, jurists and political and administrative authorities defended their views on screening policies. The media fuelled the controversy and gave the disease an exceptional status. The topic was whether existing laws on epidemics and (sexually) transmitted diseases were to be applied to AIDS patients or whether AIDS should be excluded from their sphere of application, and whether a liberal preventive policy should be adopted that would be based on exclusively voluntary screening and health education. The stormiest and most prolonged debate took place in France, owing to a context marked by the new political experience of "cohabitation"[13] and unusually frequent elections. Germany experienced a similar, but extremely brief, political controversy which, in contrast to the French case, left no lasting trace in the national policy.

The most visible phase of anti-AIDS policies corresponds to the vast public information and education campaigns. Each country devoted four or five years to these campaigns, starting in 1984 in the earliest cases: the UK, Germany and Scandinavian countries. At the other extreme the southern European countries, although plagued by an epidemic related to drug use, were late: eight to ten years in Italy, and even fifteen in Spain, Portugal and Greece. France launched its mass prevention campaigns from 1988 onwards, but had to change their orientation, judged ineffective in the mid-1990s. The social sciences were mobilized during this period to provide expertise in the two areas of sexual practices and social communication. The period experienced the typical division of labor. The public authorities carried out campaigns "for all", aimed at promoting the general use of condoms and positive social attitudes towards HIV carriers, whilst the targeted campaigns for specific groups were delegated to private AIDS organizations, working with public finance and under public control.

The final and still continuing phase corresponds to institutional consolidation.[14] Sectoral institutions took over and could manage the problem in a "business as usual" way. This process is pragmatic and general. Public health institutions have been modernized and institutionally and financially strengthened. Certain public policies have been reoriented and given prevention and public health objectives, the most illustrative case being "reduction of health risks" as the new priority of the policies fighting drug addiction. Medical care institutions have reinforced their usual curative role, thanks to the arrival of a new generation of medicinal drugs in 1996–97. This modified radically the struggle against AIDS: the screening test is perceived no longer as a vehicle of political or social risk, but as a window to lifelong therapeutic care. The epidemic has become a new chronic disease.

AIDS arrived as an "ill-structured problem" (Simon 1973) to established policy-making systems and health systems alike, all confronted with the same complex challenges. The above section has retraced how the multifold reality can be analytically reduced to a small number of comparable categories and indicators. The following section presents the country stories in a selective manner, according to the set of hypotheses drawn from this analytical framework.

Selected Country Stories

The major challenge for governments was to conduct a wide-ranging prevention policy based on *non-medical* measures. The capacity to do this should be linked with the respective positions of the medical profession and the public authority in national (and sectoral) decision-making systems. Furthermore, since the struggle against an epidemic can only be successful if it is simultaneously and consistently waged in all the areas concerned by the routes of transmission, effective co-ordination between governmental, administrative, professional and associative actors, and across sectoral boundaries and legal competencies should constitute a discriminating factor. The obstacles to be overcome in each country can be expected to be more numerous when the health policy system is fragmented and when "public health" ranks low in the scale of public values and priorities. Last, but not least, the successful implementation of a participative and educational approach implies the delivery of explicit prevention messages that clearly describe the risky situations along with the ways of avoiding them. This depends on the existence of professional competencies for health and sex education, including for drug addicts, and on a strong political consensus on these measures.

Policy Initiation and Government Involvement

The initial French expert group remained isolated, with only a tenuous link with the *Direction générale de la santé*, the weakest part of the Health Ministry. Neither the medical authorities nor the government showed any interest in the new disease until a US research team claimed the paternity of the virus discovery (Seytre 1993). AIDS entered the French policy agenda as a matter of national interest in the field of science and industry. In Germany, the local health authorities of Berlin informed the federal health authorities about the first cases. The Federal Ministry of Health reacted immediately by setting up a consultative structure bringing together public health authorities, medical specialists and representatives of gay organizations. In the UK a similar bottom-up process channeled the information from London genito-urinary clinics up to the highest levels of the National Health Service (NHS). The government and medical authorities, convinced of the emergency, called for rapid action. In Italy, gay men launched the very first prevention campaigns, on a local basis, whilst the central health administration initiated its action with systematic testing in prisons, hospitals and care centers for drug addicts.

The attitude of the medical profession constituted a major difference between the countries. Although public health was a marginal sector in all countries, the lack of interest of the French medical elite had more crucial consequences than elsewhere. Because the medical elite holds a central position in French health policies and politics (Immergut 1992, Jobert and Steffen 1994), its attitude legitimized the politicians and intellectuals in their common strategy of minimizing the public health risk and exaggerating a hypothetical political risk of stigmatization. In Italy, by contrast, a group of medical professors pushed for the creation of the National AIDS Commission. This body was and still is responsible for drafting Italian policy on HIV/AIDS. The first national anti-AIDS plans became law in 1990, but implementation was hampered by institutional conflict. Regional and municipal health agencies opposed the alliance between the central administration, the government and part of the medical elite. The regions even fought the issue in the constitutional court, arguing that health programs were within regional competence, whilst private organizations contested the allocation of resources that reserved up to 85 per cent for public hospital wards.

In the UK eminent public health specialists pushed the reluctant Conservative government into action, using the powerful argument of the financial burden if the epidemic was not stopped immediately (Berridge 1996). In the British system the institutional structure of the NHS and the political level of decision making are linked through the position of the Chief Medical Officer, an independent person whose role is to advise the Minister of Health. During the early AIDS years this strategic position was held by an epidemiologist, assisted by a clinical specialist in sexually transmitted disease, in charge of the practical problems and implementation. The combined approach of institutional and medical management of public health resulted in an efficient model for AIDS prevention.

In Germany politicians made the strategic choices via the Permanent Conference of Health Ministers, a standing committee of regional ministers and the federal minister, reflecting the left- and right-wing majorities in the regional parliaments. The health ministers declared AIDS to be a major public health problem requiring an urgent response in the form of a national priority program. They brought the matter to the parliament and mobilized the public health agencies under their authority. Reluctant local or regional administrations were officially encouraged to implement the new prevention policies. These regional dynamics proved very helpful when medical and political opposition at national level, concerning prevention strategies for drug addicts, had to be overruled.

Consensus Building and Co-ordination

In the UK and Germany the controversies and choices relating to AIDS were debated in parliament, which granted an indisputable legitimacy to the anti-AIDS policies. Parliamentary commissions monitored, evaluated, reinforced and sometimes amended the policies adopted. The Italian Parliament was less involved, but it discussed and voted the successive anti-AIDS programs. The French Parliament, in addition to its voiceless role in health policy at that time, had no active part in framing the response to the AIDS problem. A 1987 law gave exclusive competence to the central government.

In all countries, controversy and political conflict arose over two issues, both related to the application of previously existing law. The first issue was the question of screening, whether tests should be carried out systematically in certain situations or whether this should only be done with the explicit consent of the individual. In the UK the screening debate was dominated by professional arguments and remained limited to epidemiologists, who were divided over the usefulness of systematic testing as a scientific means to monitor the epidemic. In Italy, systematic screening of hospital patients, intravenous drug users (IDUs) and prison inmates had been initiated by the competent administrations. It was combated by the National AIDS Commission whose medical experts imposed voluntary testing on the professionals and on the Ministry of Justice. Outside the commission the screening issue raised little public debate.

It was only in France, and to a lesser degree in Germany, that screening provoked major political controversies, in both cases as part of electoral politics in the mid-1980s. In Germany the Bavarian CSU party (*Christliche Soziale Union*) demonstrated its independence from the Christian Democrats by taking advantage of regional authority over the health sector. Bavaria thus applied existing regulations on epidemics and transmitted diseases to AIDS, despite the liberal option taken in the national policy and the opposition of the Health Ministers' Conference. The issue generated heated debates between specialists on constitutional and administrative law as well as court procedures to clarify institutional authority. The conflict subsided after the 1986 general election, however, when the newly elected federal parliament engaged in an active AIDS policy with a four-year emergency program (1986–90) supported by all parties, including the CSU. In France the AIDS issue coincided with the unprecedented context of "cohabitation" and the rise of the extreme right-wing National Front. AIDS became extremely politicized and decisions on prevention were systematically delayed until after the next election. As an example, two laws, one forbidding advertisements for condoms and the other the sale of syringes, had to be amended, which was only decided, respectively, in 1987 and 1988. As the National Front's anti-AIDS crusade included systematic screening and quarantine for people infected with HIV, all other political parties, the intellectuals and the media mobilized to "fight against discrimination". Although the National Front withdrew from this unfruitful battleground, as with the Bavarian CSU, this argument remained and shaped the subsequent public AIDS campaigns:

the government rejected targeted campaigns, subordinating the technical requirements of public health to the political value of universalism and "solidarity".

The second controversial issue was the introduction of comprehensive prevention strategies to reduce health risks resulting from injecting drug use, including substitute medication for addicts. In most countries the medicalization of drug policies was not readily accepted because professional paradigms had moved away from medicine towards psychotherapeutic approaches since the 1970s, and because of the high electoral sensitivity and public demands for repressive action. AIDS experts and pressure groups insisted that policies penalizing drug consumption had to be abandoned if the preventive strategies were to be implemented. In the four countries, consensus building in the drug field depended mainly on professional agreement and practice. When the epidemic arrived, substitutive medication was strictly prohibited by professional rules in Germany and France, whilst it was still in marginal use in the UK and Italy. Hence, these two latter countries encountered fewer difficulties in developing methadone treatment and risk reduction strategies.

The UK could furthermore rely on a useful precedent. "Harm" reduction strategies aimed at reducing the social consequences of addiction, such as delinquency, were already developing in local initiatives that brought together voluntary organizations and social services (Berridge 1996). With AIDS these networks extended or reoriented their activity toward "health" risk reduction. Already in the mid-1980s needle exchange programs and comprehensive programs for primary medical care for addicts were launched under the responsibility of the local NHS units. In Italy professional consensus and effective implementation suffered from a private/public split. During the 1980s a growing part of the surveillance and management of addiction was contracted out to private organizations. The care institutions linked with Catholic charities maintained their traditional commitment to abstinence, in both drug use and sex, whereas those linked with local governments or the political Left promoted risk reduction strategies, including needle, condom and methadone provision. Contradictory messages were thus being delivered to people at risk, politicians and public opinion, whilst coherent prevention strategies developed only in favorable local circumstances.

In Germany health professionals from the drug and public health fields implemented risk reduction, with support from the regional and local health authorities and financial help from the statutory health insurance funds. The latter estimated that methadone provision to IDUs was less expensive than long-term care for new cases of HIV infection and hepatitis B. The strongest opposition originated from conservative medical circles and the national medical commission responsible for clinical classifications of medicines. This resistance was progressively undermined as practical reform dynamics grew at regional and local levels, and finally overcome when jurisprudence established that the existing restrictions on methadone and needle provision did not apply to "prevention and public health policies".

The specificity of the French case was a combined political *and* professional opposition to risk reduction. The professionals caring for drug addicts constituted an extremely isolated corporatist network that defied supervision by the health ministry and cultivated an impervious barrier against medical authorities (Bergeron 1999). They were committed to a particular psychoanalytical paradigm and affiliated to a unique national organization that acted as a guardian of this exclusive approach. The medical AIDS risk was ignored as alien to their professional concern. When growing numbers of IDUs arrived in hospitals with full-blown AIDS, hospital doctors tried, unsuccessfully, to change the situation. The strength of the political opposition was illustrated when a newly appointed health minister was dismissed from office in July 1988, after having announced his intention to introduce methadone and needle exchange programs. Finally, the first programs were launched outside the professional and institutional structures, by a humanitarian medical organization in 1990, with a single mobile street unit operating in Paris and modest financial support from *Direction générale de la santé*. It was only in the aftermath of the contaminated blood trial that the Henrion Commission was set up (1995) and the abstinence alliance and theory was questioned for the first time.

For co-ordination and implementation, Britain could rely on the local units of the NHS, and Germany on the local public health offices (*Gesundheitsämter*), each of them staffed with a co-ordinator for AIDS prevention for at least five years. Italy mainly needed to extend the provision of condoms, clean syringes and free medical care for addicts. This became more effective on a nation-wide scale once the primary health care centers (*Unità Sanitarie Locali*) had been officially charged with the financial co-ordination of AIDS prevention in the course of the general health reforms in the mid-1990s. France had first to overcome the professional and then the political resistance, and finally to remove serious contradictions remaining in implementation of policies.[15] The two laggards reached European standards only at the end of the 1990s.[16]

Health and Sex Education

Everywhere prevention of the sexual HIV risk was based on a political compromise: non-application of public health regulations to AIDS so that at-risk people would adopt new patterns of behavior. The urgency to act against an epidemic that could affect the entire population provided legitimacy to a highly pragmatic approach. Instead of fighting deviant behavior, public authorities undertook to *socialize* it. The new behavioral patterns, known as "safer sex" (and "safer shooting" when referring to injecting drug users), were promoted with public money and support, not only via advertising but also through sex education delivered in schools in order to reach all young people.

The educational approach to the sexual risk confronted all governments with a difficult question: should the public campaigns be targeted at specific risk groups, which in fact meant gay men, or should they address the general population? The uncomfortable problem was the official recognition of homosexuality. The forced alliance between gay activists and state authorities was delicate. The French government was unwilling to deal with this "private" issue and left it to the French AIDS prevention agency, which was set up in 1989 for the purpose, and became the battlefield for conflict with and between gay organizations.[17] The British public health authorities, having acknowledged that homosexuality represented a major transmission route, requested the active collaboration of gay organizations but imposed a subordinate position on them. The issue was less acute in Germany and Italy owing to decentralization, which tends to limit national controversy, and two national particularities. In Italy, the IDU-dominated epidemic did not open a window of opportunity for homosexuality to enter the agenda. In Germany the well-established tradition of lay-group participation in all medical–social policies (Jobert and Steffen 1994) provided an operational pattern applicable to collaboration with the gay organizations.

Concerning public prevention campaigns, the French case stands out as an exception. The "AIDS" and "condom" themes were carefully separated. Condom use was made attractive by an image of spontaneous free sex, "without constraints" (Mossuz-Lavau 1991), in the tradition of the 1968 political philosophies, whilst the AIDS theme was exclusively attached to the idea of solidarity and universalism, in line with the classical repertoire of French social policies. References to the person's responsibility towards his or her partner, to illness and the acute risk of death, frequent in the other countries, was deliberately excluded. The French idea was to avoid concern in public opinion and stigmatization for people at risk of HIV infection. It was only in 1994 that the public campaigns mentioned the word "health" for the first time.[18] The non-targeted approach and the supporting actor alliances were criticized for inefficiency in an official report (Montagnier 1993) in the direct aftermath of the "contaminated blood" trials. The AIDS prevention agency, guardian of the universalistic approach, was closed down in 1995 and its competency relocated within the Ministry of Health as part of broader prevention policies including all transmitted diseases.

Initially, in all national cases the pre-existing structures of health education appeared unable to respond to the AIDS challenge. They were either completed or replaced by new agencies. Only the UK had a body of professional health educators with experience in sex education, most of them from family planning. The newly created Health Education Authority could therefore rely on *trained professionals* with experience in public health and sexual behavior. In France, the other extreme example, the dominant players in sex education for the youth were *militant volunteers* from family planning organizations who focused exclusively on girls and oral contraception. These women campaigners originating from the battle for legal abortion (obtained in 1976) fought for a long time (like the professionals working with drug addicts) against a reorientation in their field. They rejected prevention of sexually transmitted diseases and condom use as alien and even counterproductive to their concern. In Germany, on the other hand, experience acquired from intensive work on AIDS has been formalized and constituted as a university discipline and professional training on sexual health pedagogy.

The comparison suggests that the ability to conduct policies aimed at sexual behaviours reflects previous policy tracks and depends on the public authorities' recognized legitimacy in setting norms on private behaviors. In this respect the UK was able to rely on its past accomplishments. Vast campaigns to prevent sexually transmitted diseases had already been run after the Second World War, with methods close to those used today. In Italy, where the implementation of AIDS prevention is still geographically uneven (less developed in the South), the fight against the epidemic has enabled the public authorities to make a breach in the Catholic Church's monopoly[19] on sexual morals and impose their authority over this field as part of public health. Germany benefited from stable and consensual collaboration with gay organizations and public health professionals, as well as active support from the Protestant organizations. In France, the state imposed its central authority on autonomous professionals and militant groups, but only after long hesitation and critical policy failures.

The observed differences in policy approaches to sexual health education, combined with a possible relation between religious traditions and more or less successful AIDS prevention, as suggested in Table 1, opens an interesting research agenda.[20] In searching for a possible hypothesis one can look at policy problems with a similar structure and comparable public–private embeddedness. Both sexual education and religious instruction confront governments with the challenge of making public policies in a field protected as private life. Table 2 illustrates an interesting correspondence between the national capacity to teach the prevention of sexually transmitted diseases and the capacity to deal with religious instruction at school. It suggests a hypothesis. Given the long path dependency of public health policies, as well as their content in modern AIDS prevention based on education and tolerance, one can assume that countries with a *policy pattern* available that proved workable in similar circumstances have an advantage over those that lack such patterns in their policy repertoires. Most probably, the political approach to religious practice provides a historical matrix for policies in the field of sexual behaviors. Countries of Protestant tradition, which had to accept religious diversity and elaborate the rules for power sharing between the state (or monarch) and the churches, may have such historical advantage. The evidence from this study is that, in all four countries, sexual education followed closely the patterns of religious instruction.

Table 2 also contains a methodological lesson. It shows that *contrasting* conditions can lead to similar results (and vice versa). The strict separation between the state and religious authorities in the French case and the continuous, though indirect, influence of the latter in Italy *both* hamper the conduct of public policies when moral and private implications exist. Problem-based policy comparisons must therefore carefully contextualize each factor.

Comparative Results and Interpretation

European policy and health systems have faced the new challenges with different inputs and outcomes. Two decades after the outbreak of the epidemic, the prevalence of HIV infection is still up to four times higher in France and Italy than in Germany and the United Kingdom. In particular, the UK and to a lesser degree Germany have managed to avoid the large-scale contamination of drug addicts witnessed in Italy and also in France.[21]

The countries differ mainly in the following respects: early or late government intervention, more or less coherent implementation, and the values mobilized in the fight against AIDS. France stands out by its extremely conflictual policy style, and Italy in contrast by the absence of public controversy. The many comparative results have been schematized in Table 3, which reveals clear similarities between the UK and Germany. France and Italy share certain factors of failure but also important policy changes and improvements in a second phase, from the mid-1990s onwards. Despite a common policy problem to be solved, each country follows its own model of policy making, implementation and change.

Table 2. Religious instruction and sex education in public schools

	France	Italy	UK	Germany
Religious classes	Forbidden by law*	Yes	Yes	Yes
Financing of religious classes	Not relevant*	The state, for Catholicism only	The counties	The *Länder*
Participation in religious classes	Not relevant	Theoretically voluntary. In practice everyone attends	Systematic classes. Parents can remove their children.	Systematic classes. Parents can remove their children.
Sex education/ AIDS classes	Theoretically compulsory	Provided for in AIDS laws. Weak application	Systematic classes. Parents can remove their children.	Systematic classes. Parents can remove their children.
Effective offer of sex education classes	Depends on the head of the school	Depends on the school head, and local on authorities moral issues	Systematic classes. Parents can remove their children.	Systematic classes. Parents can remove their children.

*Except in Alsace-Lorraine (state financed) where the German system remained after 1918.

Table 3. Political and instituting national differences

	UK	Germany	France	Italy
Political Rhetoric	Weak	Limited	(1) Strong (2) Became weak	Absent
Professional forums	Open and collaborative	Open and collaborative	(1) Extremely closed (2) Opening	(1) Two networks: AIDS, IDU (2) Better co-ordinated
Co-ordination and local initiative	Very strong	Strong	(1) Extremely weak (2) Considerably strengthened	(1) Average (2) Strengthened
Practical policies construction	(1) Strong (2) Reinforced	Fairly strong	(1) Extremely weak (2) Substantially reinforced	(1) Average (2) Strengthened
Beneficiaries' participation	Fairly strong	(1) Strong (2) Reinforced	(1) Limited and conflictual (2) Improved and pacified	(1) Average (2) Being raised
Values emphasized in the fight against AIDS	Public health protection and pragmatic approaches	Public health protection and pragmatic approaches	(1) Political values: universalism, solidarity, individual freedom (2) Effective public health management, group specific prevention	(1) Social inclusion, family life (2) Public health, prevention

(1) Initial situation (**Phase 1**).
(2) Situation after learning (**Phase 2**).

The theoretical models describing the institutional organization of the European welfare states and the medical care system, opposing a Bismarckian and a Beveridgian type, proved irrelevant in the public health case. The success or failure of the different countries in their public health and prevention policies is contingent above all on their capacity of co-ordination, at all levels, from the highest political level including the cabinet down to the practical level of local implementation. The UK and Germany both had such capacities, whilst France and Italy encountered huge difficulties. Their decision-making and implementation systems were fragmented, by professional corporatism in France, by localism and the split between the AIDS and IDU policy communities in Italy.

Political consensus-building was rapid in the UK, less straightforward in the two decentralized countries of the study, Germany and Italy, and extremely lengthy in France, characterized by the combined effects of an extremely weak public health administration and an unfavorable political context. Furthermore, the agents of co-ordination were not the same in the different countries. In the UK the key part was played by the executives of the NHS, that is senior civil servants with medical titles; in Italy by a group of medical university professors in collaboration with the Liberal party and senior officials at the Health Ministry; and in Germany by politicians, that is the federal plus the fifteen regional health ministers. With the exception of France, the national parliaments legitimized the policy choices and evaluated the results. The French ad hoc agency entrusted with the prevention policy lacked the institutional position and political legitimacy to co-ordinate national policies.

The national/local relationship has proved to be a key factor in policy implementation. Italy suffered from regionally unequal policy developments, but the initiatives of local public and private agents compensated for national shortcomings, at least in the main cities of the North. The UK could activate the public and private networks of co-operation around the local units of the National Health Service. Germany relied on its 400 or so local public health offices, each of which was staffed with a specific AIDS co-ordinator. In France, on the other hand, as a ploy to exclude local councilors from the National Front, the 1987 law confined competence on AIDS policy to the central government. It was only with the reorientation of AIDS policies in the mid-1990s that a system of contracting took over. Since then, the devolved social administrations at regional and district level negotiate with local public or private organizations and finance them on the basis of local programs targeted at specific risk groups.

The (de)centralization factor produces opposite results according to the surrounding institutional networks and practices. Like the Bismarckian and Beveridgian models, (de)centralization does not operate with direct or independent impact on public health policies. In Germany, decentralization favored the mobilization of all available resources and helped to overcome specific national veto points. Even the Bismarckian sickness funds provided support for prevention among drug addicts. In Italy, by contrast, decentralization expressed the weakness of national policy conduct, the lack of public interest and the rather formal political consensus. In the United Kingdom, centralized policy making, at the level of government as well as of the NHS, provided a coherent set of measures, identifiable leadership and good conditions for nation-wide implementation. In France, on the other hand, exclusive centralized competency allowed ideological and corporatist policy making to continue, despite the inadequate content for public health.

Table 3 isolates the factors explaining the national differences. Political rhetoric refers to the discourse politics of political parties, eventually also the intellectuals and media that played a major part in problem framing in the French case, the parliamentary assemblies, and the government. This level becomes most active in election periods and when laws, for example in the case of anti-IDU legislation, are to be revised. Professional forums designate the level where organized professions and scientific experts intervene, for whom the new policies around AIDS constitute interests to be defended, such as the safeguard or extension of their field. Coordination and local initiatives point to the structures, such as official commissions, advisory councils or appointed personalities in charge of making policies coherent. The level of practical policy construction brings together the administrations, civil servants, specialists and institutions that elaborate the practical policy recipes and the procedures for implementation. The health ministry and administration constitute the central part at this level. Beneficiary participation refers to the conditions of efficient reception of the measures, messages and programs. In the AIDS case, the organization and participation of the beneficiaries is crucial to the success of prevention, since contamination can only be avoided through the adequate behavior of the people at risk. The values emphasized in the fight against AIDS designate the more general references under which the specific measures are labeled as legitimate goals for society. They have to be in line with the general repertoire of political values and, in fact, express the scale of priorities in a given society and policy system. Whereas from the outset AIDS was defined as a major public health risk in the UK and Germany, up to the mid-1990s it was treated as a marginal problem, at best an additional aspect of drug addiction in Italy, and as a problem of social exclusion, a risk of a political nature, in France. The intellectual framing of the problem proved most important because it set the frame for policies.

The identified factors form coherent and interdependent sets of *policy patterns*, each of them revealing the internal logic of national cases. Hence, strong political rhetoric goes hand in hand with closed professional communities, low levels of beneficiary participation and a weak capacity in practical policy-building. In this case, particular professional groups penetrate and dominate the policy-building level very easily, especially in circumstances of high political controversy. The pattern describes the French case: the health ministry was unable to impose its authority on the professionals of the blood transfusion sector and those in charge of drug addicts, and unable to convince the government of the urgent public health risk. Conversely, a strong policy-building capacity goes together with open professional communities, active beneficiary participation and values directly oriented towards public health. In this case the politicization of issues is unlikely or remains limited. The British and German cases correspond to this pattern. The Italian case presents a low-profile pattern, without political controversy, but with great difficulties in mobilizing sufficient public resources and competency to fight a nation-wide epidemic.

The study has allowed a comparative assessment of change. Policies were completed or revised, especially in France after the tainted blood scandal that reshaped the perception of public health risks and responsibilities. The French government conducted a series of structural reforms, unequaled in the other European countries, with goals that transcended the AIDS problem and instituted public health as a new policy sector.[22] Table 3 shows the comparative extent of institutional and political learning processes. The UK and Germany only reinforced those areas that had already proved to be effective, i.e. practical policy-building and collaboration with beneficiaries, respectively. Italy activated its theoretically well-conceived policy when the conditions for implementation improved, after general political changes (*mani polite*) and the general reforms in the public administration, including the health sectors.

France was an exception. Here the learning process was most thorough and took place in *two stages*. The first stage, from 1986 to 1992, consisted in mobilizing the public authorities, which responded by setting up a national agency, but continued to base their action on traditional policy references (individual freedom, social exclusion, universalism). The second phase followed an acute political crisis that stripped the political class and medical institutions of their legitimacy. It resulted in an accelerated learning process during which new intellectual references were adopted. "Public health" was defined as the state's responsibility. The French model of radical change through crisis contrasts with the model in the other countries where change is pragmatic, incremental and selective, related only to certain aspects. The French case provides an example where the internal logic of a policy problem imposed major changes on the national policy-making system, and even the political system.[23] Convergence with others countries can thus be reached by reversing independent and dependant factors in the a-typical national case.

Conclusion

This article pursued a twofold ambition, an analytical one aiming at the understanding of a public health policy, and a methodological one explaining the construction of a comparative framework for complex policy cases. The AIDS case allowed the observation of the emergence of new public health policies, involving policy institutions, social contexts and cultural norms.

The analysis thus contributes to a more comprehensive approach to comparative health policy. The results show that neither the theoretical models guiding policy analyses in the (medical) health care sector, such as the Bismarckian or Beveridgian type of institutional arrangements, nor the common classifications of policy systems, such as (de)centralization, explain policy developments in public health. The latter are linked to a broader set of variables:

- the functioning of the (democratic) political system, in terms of participation and education;
- the effective implementation of welfare state policies, in terms of comprehensive care for the most vulnerable groups; and
- good governance, in terms of pragmatic problem-orientated approaches and effective co-ordination.

The fight against AIDS required the substitution of technical approaches, with public health objectives, identical in all countries, for earlier conceptualizations formulated in terms of philosophical principals, ethics or morality that expressed strictly national convictions. The French case illustrated how abstract political values can lead to bad case management and failure in public policy. Simultaneously, it also illustrated how a centralized system of policy making can learn, and implement major reforms.

The case constituted a fertile example for a comparative methodology. The sudden appearance of an epidemic acted as an "intervening factor" (Peters 1998), an exogenous event that imposed constraints on all its environments. It was a real shock to Western societies, a historical watershed encompassing a large number of dependent and independent variables in a short space of time. It is therefore an ideal gateway to study how different national systems deal with multi-sided problems and how they learn from and adapt to new challenges. The struggle against the disease covers twenty years of fast-moving history, and hence binds together policy making, implementation and changes. Moreover, since it involves sex and blood, the case brings cultural dimensions and social attitudes into comparative policy analysis. Other public policies, however, share such characteristics: environmental, educational and most social policies as well as the fight against urban delinquency. Hence, the methodological approach applied here in a public health case seems applicable to the international comparison of many other policies.

Most public health cases can be seen as "complex policy problems" according to the indicators defined by Peters.[24] They have connections with many policy sectors, actors and interests; most of them have moral implications; they can potentially affect the entire population; they cannot be eliminated definitively; solutions exist but require continuous policy involvement. The comparison of AIDS policies suggests a theoretical conclusion concerning the (in)compatibilities between certain types of policy problems and certain types of policy regimes or patterns: Public health and any similarly structured problems are difficult to manage in "centralized policy systems", a term which should refer not exclusively to centralized administration or decision making but also to homogenous belief systems, because the latter form part of governance mechanisms. Such unchallenged professional paradigms, political ideologies or policy references represent serious handicaps whenever complex policy problems are to be treated, because they do not spontaneously engage in transversal and pragmatic approaches and they are unable to respond to new moral or private implications. The particular difficulty for public health and similarly structured policy problems is that solutions continue nevertheless to depend on direct government engagement.

Notes

1. It is probably this difficulty of comparing *complex* policies that explains the persisting cleavage between two categories of scientific work, although both are based on the same theoretical models using neo-institutional approaches. Studies known as "comparative health policy analysis" focus on the conflictual relations between public authorities and the medical profession, while comparative work on "welfare state policies" is limited to the modes of financing and the financial regulation of the medical care sector. For a review of comparative health policy studies, cf. Marmor, Freeman and Okma in this collection.
2. Other developed democracies, such as the USA, Australia, Canada and Japan, have been deliberately excluded from this study. For these case studies, cf. Kirp and Bayer (1999).

3. In the Russian Federation, the annual incidences of new cases of HIV/AIDS infection jumped from 1.1 per million in 1994 to 609.2 in 2001, and remained at high levels with 350.7 in 2002 and 275.5 in 2003, the absolute number of cases representing less than 700 in 1994 but 268,400 in 2003.
4. Figures on December 31, 2002, UNAIDS/WHO.
5. HIV infection rates equal to or lower than the EU mean are observed only in New Zealand and Australia, small isolated countries compared to the world's population masses and flows, and in the North Africa–Middle-East region where statistics do not necessarily reflect the reality and where sexual relations are severely controlled (UNAIDS, Annual reports).
6. Including important practical reasons, such as knowledge of the language.
7. These studies insisted on the impact of the degree of organization and mobilization of the gay community, a factor that does not explain the national differences within Europe.
8. A thesis already developed by the founders of social medicine in the nineteenth century, notably Dr Virchow in Germany (Rosen 1974: 62).
9. The epidemiological data on Europe used in this article originates from the official statistics of the *European Center for the Epidemiological Monitoring of AIDS*, WHO and UNAIDS Collaborating Center, Paris: Institut de Veille Sanitaire.
10. The relationship suggested by Table 1 is too regular to be ignored. The irregularities are the fact of countries having a relatively small population and an internationally attractive center for at-risk groups: Amsterdam for the Netherlands, Geneva and Zurich for Switzerland, Copenhagen for Denmark. The only real exception is Ireland, where the traditionally restrictive access to oral contraception enhances general condom use and, consequently, a preventive effect against HIV transmission, a situation that Ireland shares with only Japan (Kirp and Bayer 1992).
11. A hypothesis will be formulated below, in the last section of the article.
12. The contaminated HIV/blood part of the AIDS policy story cannot be included in this article. For details of the French case and an international comparison, cf. Steffen in Feldman and Bayer (1999), and Chapter V in Bovens, t'Hart and Peters (2001).
13. The sharing of power (in a presidential regime) between the state president and a parliamentary majority from the two main rival political parties, respectively.
14. The expression preferred in the specific AIDS literature is "normalization" (Rosenbrock *et al.* 2000).
15. The over-the-counter sale of syringes had been legal since mid-1987 but syringe possession still continued to be an official "indicator of illegal consumption" in the mid-1990s, and the police continued to arrest IDUs near pharmacies.
16. In 1994 France had only 77 "experimental" authorizations for methadone treatment, extended to 300 patients at the end of 1996, compared to a range of 15,000 to 20,000 in Germany, Italy and the UK since the early 1990es. In 2000, finally, France had caught up, with a total of 48,000 addicts under substitutive treatment.
17. The Agency had seven directors in its six years of existence.
18. "The Sida, une priorité de santé publique" ("AIDS, a public health priority").
19. The church/state separation, that deprived Catholicism of its "Chiesa della stato" status, dates only from 1984.
20. This article however cannot address the possible impacts of religious attitudes (towards responsibility, sexuality, the body, illness, etc.). This would require new studies and quantitative and socio-psychological methods. This article focuses on the methodology of comparative policy analysis; it tries to explain policy matters with policy factors.
21. The number of AIDS cases transmitted via IDU amounted to 1,187 in the United Kingdom, to 3,349 in Germany, to 12,800 in France and to 30.027 in Italy (December 2003). At the same date, HIV prevalence was estimated at 1 per cent among drug users in Manchester, compared to 30–40 per cent in many French and 65 per cent in Italian cities.
22. Even the French constitution was amended to make politicians and public administrators accountable, personally in terms of penal law, for illness and accidents linked to decisions made during their term of office.
23. The constitution was modified in order to reform the special law court reserved for judging of members of government for action or negligence in office.
24. Cf. his contribution to this volume.

References

Baldwin, Peter, 1999, *Contagion and the State in Europe, 1830–1930* (Cambridge: Cambridge University Press).

Barbot, Jannine, 2002, *Les malades en mouvement: la médecine et la science à l'épreuve du Sida* (Paris: Balland).

Bayer, Ronald, 1991, *Private Acts, Social Consequences. AIDS and the Politics of Public Health* (New Brunswick, NJ: Rutgers University Press, 2nd edn, with a new Afterword).

Bergeron, Henri, 1999, *L'État et la toxicomanie. Histoire d'une singularité française* (Paris: Presses Universitaires de France).

Berridge, Virgina, 1996, *AIDS in the UK. The Making of Policy, 1981–1994* (New York and Oxford: Oxford University Press).

Bovens, Marc, t'Hart, Paul and Peters, Guy (Eds), 2001, *Success and Failure in Public Governance: A Comparative Analysis* (London: Edward Elgar).

Boyer, Robert, 2002, Variétés du capitalisme et théorie de la regulation. *L'Année de la Régulation*, **6**, 125–194.

Fee, Elizabeth and Fox, Daniel M. (Eds), 1992, *The Making of a Chronic Disease* (Berkeley, CA: University of California Press).

Feldman, Eric and Bayer, Ronald (Eds), 1999, *Blood Feuds. AIDS, Blood and the Politics of Medical Disaster* (New York: Oxford University Press).

Feldman, Eric and Bayer, Ronald (Eds), 2004, *Conflicts over Tobacco Policy and Public Health* (Cambridge, MA: Harvard University Press).

Fox, Daniel M., Day, Patricia and Klein, Rudolf, 1989, The power of professionalism: policies for AIDS in Britain, Sweden, and the United States. *Daedalus*, **118**(2) 93–112.

Ghorbarah, Hazem A. and Huth, Paul, 2004, Comparative public health: the political economy of human misery and well-being. *International Studies Quarterly*, **8**, 73–94.

Epstein, Steven, 1996, *Impure Science: AIDS, Activism and the Politics of Knowledge* (Berkeley, CA and London: University of California Press).

Immergut, Ellen, 1992, *Heath Politics. Interests and Institutions in Western Europe* (Cambridge and New York: Cambridge University Press).

Inglehart, Ronald, 1990, *Culture Shift in Advanced Industrial Society* (Princeton, NJ and Oxford: Princeton University Press).

Jobert, Bruno and Steffen, Monika (Eds), 1994, *Les politiques de la santé en France et en Allemagne* (Paris: Observatoire de la Protection Sociale, Paris, Espace Social Européen).

Kirp, David L. and Bayer, Ronald (Eds), 1992, *AIDS in the Industrialized Democracies. Passions, Politics, and Policies* (New Brunswick, NJ and New York: Rutgers University Press).

Milner, Henry, 2002, *Civic Literacy. How Informed Citizens Make Democracy Work* (Medford, MA: Tufts University Press).

Montagnier, Luc, 1993, *Rapport sur le Sida*, Rapport au Premier Ministre, au Ministère des Affaires sociales, de la Santé et de la Ville, et au Ministère délégué à la Santé. 1 December, Paris.

Moran, Michael, 1999, *Governing the Health Care State. A Comparative Study of the United Kingdom, the United States and Germany* (Manchester and New York, Manchester University Press).

Mossuz-Lavau, Jannine, 1991, *Les Lois de l'amour. Les politiques de la sexualité en France (1950–1990)* (Paris: Payot).

Peters, Guy B., 1998, *Comparative Politics. Theory and Methods* (London: Macmillan).

Pinell, Patrice, 2002, *Une épidémie politique. La lutte contre le Sida en France, 1981–1996* (Paris: Presses Universitaires de France).

Rokkan, Stein, 1999, *State Formation, Nation-Building, and Mass Politics in Europe. The Theory of Stein Rokkan. Based on his Collected Works*, edited by Peter Flora, with Stein Kunhle and Derek Urwin (Oxford and New York: Oxford University Press).

Rosen, George, 1974, *From Medical Police to Social Medicine: Essays on the History of Health Care* (New York: Science History Publications).

Rosenbrock, Rolf, Shaeffer, D., Dubois-Abser, F., Moers, M., Pinell, P. and Serbon, M., 2000, The normalisation of AIDS in Western European countries. *Social Sciences and Medecine*, **50**, 1607–1629.

Simon, Herbert A., 1973, The structure of ill-structured problems. *Artificial Intelligence*, **4**, 181–201.

Steffen, Monika, 1999, The response to AIDS in Eastern and Western Europe, in: Jak Jabes (Ed) *Public Administration and Social Policies in Central and Eastern Europe* (Prague: NISPAcee).

Steffen, Monika, 2004, AIDS and health policy responses in European welfare states. *Journal of European Social Policy*, **14**(2), 159–175.

Steffen, Monika (Ed), 2005, *Health Governance in Europe. Issues, Challenges and Theories* (London and New York: Routledge).

Seytre, Bernhard, 1993, *Sida: les secrets d'une polémique* (Paris: Presses Universitaires de France).

Understanding Policy Change as an Epistemological and Theoretical Problem

GILIBERTO CAPANO

ABSTRACT *Change is the fundamental focus of those who are interested in studying public policy. As a result of the multidimensional nature of policy dynamics, policy change is a very ambiguous area of academic study, and one full of pitfalls. All aspects of policy change have been dealt with, all the possible independent variables have been examined (ideas, interests, institutions, socio-economic structures, political institutions, internationalization, individual entrepreneurship, social culture and values, and so on), and a great many theoretical frameworks, combining diverse causal mechanisms, have been proposed. However, when choosing certain independent variables, or the specific design of the dependent variable, or a particular sequence of causal factors, policy scholars make a series of strong epistemological and theoretical choices which they are often not conscious of (as revealed by the fact that their frameworks and theories may be incoherent and characterized by evident shortcomings). In this paper, I am going to present the kind of analytical questions which need to be resolved from the epistemological and theoretical points of view, in order to grasp the essence of policy change and the potential consequences of the aforesaid choices. I shall then review the way in which the most important policy/change frameworks (Multiple Stream Approach, Punctuated Equilibrium Framework, Advocacy Coalition Framework, and Path Dependency Framework) have attempted to solve the epistemological and theoretical puzzle, the degree to which they are coherent, and the pros and cons of the solutions they adopt. Finally, I conclude by presenting a number of recommendations for further theoretical reflection and empirical investigation regarding the epistemological and theoretical coherence and effectiveness of theories of policy change.*

1. Introduction

Change is the core business of all sciences, from biology and genetics to anthropology and sociology. The question is: why, when, and how does change occur, and what does such change really mean? Trying to provide answers to such questions is the unending task of all involved in the field of scientific study, and this is also true when it comes to explaining policy change. In order to define what policy change consists of, and to understand and explain why, when and how policies change, one is faced with, and may have to solve, the same analytical problems encountered when handling the phenomenon of change in other scientific subjects.

Too often, both policy scholars and political scientists treat change in a rather mechanical manner, without actually being aware of the epistemological and theoretical nature of the choices they have made when opting for a given direction rather than another. The *explanandum* (change) is too frequently defined in an ambiguous manner, or its complexity is played down (when the contents of law or policy programmes are employed as a proxy for policy change). Too often the *explanans* (the independent variable or set of con-causal factors) is chosen in the biased belief that what really matters is that "theory must be validated". Too often we do what we are supposed to do without really reflecting on "what we are actually doing". The truth is that when designing a theory (or theoretical framework) of social, political, and policy change, we first need to solve (or decide on) certain structural epistemological and theoretical (and sometimes methodological) puzzles. There is a plentiful selection of studies from various academic fields examining the question of whether the process of change should be considered evolutionary or revolutionary, reversible or irreversible, linear or non-linear, contingent or partially determined, etc.

What we have here is the construction of a theoretical framework involving a combination of intertwined epistemological and theoretical choices. There are a variety of such combinations, but each combination implies a different theoretical perspective on policy change, a different perception of what the object of analysis is, and, of course, a different understanding of the explanation for this policy change. All scholars interested in policy change should be aware of the intrinsic logic ingrained in each specific combination.

The current paper aims to analyze the aforementioned topics by focusing on:

1. the kind of analytical questions which need to be resolved from the epistemological and theoretical points of view in order to grasp the essence of policy change and the potential consequences of the aforementioned choices (sections 2 and 3);
2. the way in which the most important policy/change frameworks have solved the epistemological and theoretical puzzle, the degree to which they are coherent, and the pros and cons of the solution they adopt (section 4);
3. some recommendations for further theoretical reflection and empirical investigation regarding the epistemological and theoretical coherence and effectiveness of theories of policy change (section 5).

Thus I am not proposing a new model for policy change analysis, but am simply trying to focus on the problematic aspects of existing research into policy change. My objective is to encourage policy scholars to reinforce their own awareness of what they are doing: this is necessary in order to strengthen those theories of policy change – such as Multiple Streams Approach (MSA), Punctuated Equilibrium Framework (PEF), Advocacy Coalition Framework (ACF), Path Dependency Framework (PDF) – which genuinely consider public policy as a complex phenomenon and not simply as an output of macro-factors.

2. Epistemological Choices in the Study of Policy Change

A given entity (society, human behaviour, policy, political party) "changes" when, between time t and time $t1$, there is empirical evidence that it has undergone changes to its properties (shape, state or quality). It is clear that in order to understand the nature of such changes, it is also necessary to understand and explain the persistence of the object of analysis. From this point of view, any theory of change (in whatever field) should be able to account for both "constancy and change" (Hernes 1976). Thus each scientific theory attempts to explain both the normal functioning of its subject matter, and the changes to that subject matter. From this point of view, each scientific theory needs to be of a "developmental" nature. So, theories of change do not exist by themselves in that they not only focus on change, but they also should account for the persistence, and the deeply-rooted patterns, of behaviour. Therefore, there is no separation between "normal" theories and theories of change. While this may be considered a rather banal argument, too often this simple remark is forgotten, creating considerable ambiguity about what theories really are or should do. Furthermore, it is impossible to explain persistence without providing an account of those changes that the objects of analysis need to undergo in order to survive in a changing environment. Thus to focus theoretically on change simply provides an analytical tool with which to get a better understanding and explanation of how given entities (human life, molecular cells, society, political parties, policies, etc.) develop.

More than 20 theories of social and political development have been provided in various different academic fields: this extreme epistemological and theoretical pluralism can be summed up by four ideal-type theories of social and political development (Van de Ven and Poole 1995): life-cycle theories, evolution theories, dialectic theories, teleological theories. For each of these types of theory, Van de Ven and Poole propose a list of constitutive, intrinsic elements. For the purposes of the present paper, I point out the more important of such elements. Table 1 below illustrates the four theories plus a further fifth ideal type of development theory – the theory of chaos and complexity – which has been developed over the last 30 years (Waldrop 1992, Eve et al. 1997, Wimmer and Kossler 2006) and has been recently observed to be of considerable interest for political science (Ma 2007) and public management (Farazmand 2003) as well.

This ideal-typical classification can help enlighten the spectrum of epistemological and theoretical problems which have to be dealt with and, if possible, solved in order to interpret and explain social change in general, and thus also policy change. Given that they are ideal types, it is of course unlikely that there will be a complete fit with existing theories and frameworks of change. As a rule, existing theorizations (especially political science and public policy theories and frameworks) consist of a hybridization of different elements from the above-listed types. However, the ideal-type classification is extremely useful when reflecting on the constitutive epistemological and theoretical choices which have to be made when constructing a framework for the analysis of policy change. It reveals the constitutive features of the puzzle which policy scholars are called upon to work out when explaining change. It shows the complexity of the set of choices to be made before commencing any concrete analysis of policy change.

Table 1. Ideal types of social and political development

	Life cycle	Evolution	Dialectic	Teleology	Chaos and complexity theory
Key metaphor	Organic growth	Competitive Survival	Opposition, conflict	Purposeful co-operation	On the edge of chaos
Logic	Prefigured sequence with compliant adaptation	Natural selection among competitors in a population	Contradictory forces	Envisioned end state; equi-finality	Co-evolution of different part of the system
Way of event progression	Linear	Recurrent, cumulative and probabilistic sequence of variation, selection and retention events. *Disconnected linearity*	Recurrent, discontinuous unpredictable sequence of confrontation, conflict and synthesis between contradictory values and events.	Recurrent, discontinuous unpredictable sequence of goal setting, implementation and adaptation of means to reach the desired end state. *Disconnected linearity*	Uncertain, unpredictable, non-linear
Motors of change	Prefigured program/rule regulated by nature or institutions	Competition; scarce sources; learning and imitation	Conflict and confrontation between opposing interests or values	Goal enactment, consensus on means, co-operation	Self-organized innovation; agency; chance and contingency
Speed of change	Not prefigured	Not prefigured	Not prefigured	Not prefigured	Not prefigured
Scope of change	Not prefigured	Not prefigured	Not prefigured	Not prefigured	Not prefigured
Outcome of change	Irreversible	Not prefigured	Not prefigured	Not prefigured	Irreversible
Independent variables	Exogenous	Not prefigured	Endogenous	Not prefigured	Not prefigured

Adapted and updated from Van de Ven and Poole (1995).

Making an epistemological choice simply means *deciding on the viewpoint to be taken when considering reality*. Thus in order to study and explain policy change, we first need to resolve certain epistemological problems regarding:

- the way of event progression, that is, of development and change (i.e. whether change is to be assumed to be linear or non-linear);
- the dynamics of development (i.e. whether change is to be assumed to be evolutionary or revolutionary);
- the motors of change.

The Way of Event Progression

Unlike other scholars (Nisbet 1972, Baumgartner and Jones 2002, Cashore and Howlett 2007), I personally believe that there are two aspects of the directionality of a process, that is, of its progression of events. The first, and fundamental, aspect is that of the "way", of the characteristics of the path of the process. It can be linear or non-linear. The other aspect of event progression is what I refer to as the "logic of direction", which indicates whether the process is cumulative or adaptive. The first aspect is a matter of epistemological judgement, while the second one, as we shall see, is more a matter of theoretical choice.

Linear policy development means the presence of unitary sequences of events that are strictly related to each other, and that follow a pre-designed programme or project. There is no turning back in the case of such linear policy development. In the public policy field, there are no pure linear perspectives on change. From this point of view, simple linearity is as uncommon in theories of political and policy development as it is in pure historical models. It is disputable whether the most highly reputed models of policy change and development, especially those based on path dependence, may be defined as being linear. We shall be examining this argument below. It should be said that teleological ideal-type theories of development – i.e. functionalism (Merton 1968), social constructivism (Berger and Luckmann 1966), adaptive learning (March and Olsen 1976) – which influence theories of policy change, albeit partially, are linear, but their linearity is of a different kind: teleological social development, in fact, is characterized by a repetitive sequence of steps (goal formulation, implementation, evaluation and eventual goal change) by which public policy is designed to achieve the envisaged end-state (the final goal may be modified by the actors in question, but there is nevertheless a form of linearity in the policy process, due to the envisaged nature of this goal). Even if there is a recurrent, discontinuous re-designing of the said sequence, it is nevertheless strongly committed towards the "linear" achievement of an established goal (end-state).

Non-linearity means that policy progression does not follow a pre-established sequence, and that there is not necessarily any causal link between the steps or stages. Furthermore, non-linearity also means that the continuous change in any one factor or variable may lead, albeit not necessarily, to deep changes in the behaviour of the entire system. Some sequential causal connections may be hypothesized (for example "increasing returns", positive or negative feedback, lock-in effects, etc.): even if the sequence is not pre-established, a form of linearity emerges as a result of cumulative, stochastic sequences. So, from this point of view, evolutionary ideal types could be affected by a kind of "disconnected linearity" (even if this is a matter of theoretical choice). Thus non-linearity is intrinsic to two of the five ideal-type theories: the dialectic theories and theories of chaos and complexity. I believe that this is no coincidence, since both these types assume a non-equilibrium perspective (meaning that stability and change are intrinsically interwoven, and that they have to be considered together from a processual perspective, whereas equilibrium or stability are not of theoretical importance).

Therefore, the choice between linearity and non-linearity (or, more realistically, between the degree of linearity/non-linearity, if they are conceived as extreme poles of a single continuum) is the first that policy scholars are called to make. It is clear that this choice determines how reality is handled, and how events are linked to each other and thus ordered. It should be pointed out that there is no particular pre-structured relationship between the ways of event progression and the content of its logic. A linear process can be either cumulative or adaptive; and the same is true of non-linear event progression.

The Dynamics of Development

The dynamics of policy development may be intrinsically evolutionary or revolutionary. By "evolutionary" we mean that they involve a process of continuous adaptation. This process of adaptation, which is of an incremental, gradual nature, may be slow but may also at times be rapid – as in the case of the punctuated equilibrium model as applied in the fields of biology and palaeontology (Eldredge and Gould 1972). Here the real dimension is *tempo* (Howlett and Ramesh 1992, Roberts 1998): evolutionary changes can be so fast that they may seem to be revolutionary, but in reality they represent a certain continuity with the past rather than any true novelty.[1]

Policy developments may also be revolutionary, that is, characterized by radical, discontinuous, unpredictable breaks from the past (Gerlach and Hines 1973, Van de Ven and Poole 1995). In such cases, changes really are innovative departures from previous directions, and as such constitute original new solutions to policy problems.

Generally speaking, the life cycle and evolutionary ideal types are characterized by the first type of dialectical process, while the teleological and chaotic ideal types are characterized by a revolutionary process. This distinction is not made very clear in existing theories of policy change, even if all the more important such theories (in particular ACF, PEF and MSA) attempt to include both categories of policy development, and even if too often the term "revolutionary" is misunderstood as simply being a rapid process within evolutionary dynamics. So, policy scholars first have to choose between an evolutionary and a revolutionary perspective:[2] should they opt for the former, they then have to decide on the *time* dimension.

However, even if the two different perspectives can both be accommodated at the theoretical and empirical level, the nature of this arrangement (whereby revolution and evolution are linked together) is based on an epistemological choice regarding the prevalence of one of the two. The theoretical and empirical consequences of this choice will be the specific design of research regarding, respectively: the reconstructive description of policy developments (focusing, for example, either on the cumulative effects of slow, incremental change or on dramatic, radical changes to policy); the nature of the descriptive reconstruction (thick or thin depending on the epistemological bias); the relationships between incremental and radical changes and between the different time scales involved; the types of policy changes chosen for the analysis; the level of abstraction; the definition of stability and persistence; the definition of adaptation. Indeed, one decision, albeit of an epistemological nature, can have a surprising number of effects on the framework and contents of research.

The Motors of Change

The decision regarding the motors of policy development (the generating forces leading to change) is an essential epistemological choice (with certain theoretical consequences regarding the construction of the causality mechanisms). The proposals contained in Table 1 have to be calibrated on the definition of the object of analysis (which in our case is public policy). Which motors cause policies to change? The ideal types underline how: competition, learning and imitation are characteristic of evolutionary dynamics; conflict is inherent in dialectic models; institutional rules are strictly associated with a linear process; consensus and cooperation are the drivers of teleological dynamics; chaotic theories of change are characterized by several apparently contradictory forces such as self-organization, contingency and agency. We know perfectly well that, very often, existing theories of change tend to blend different "generating forces"; however, the ideal-typical exercise teaches us that each general principle possesses its own underlying logic.

This assumption has to be fully understood given that, in reality, many theoretical frameworks for social and policy change combine different epistemological motors. For example, ACF combines institutional rules, competition, conflict and learning, while PEF brings together agency and contingency, imitation and rules. Hence the necessary epistemological choice is that of clarifying the logical relationships between the chosen general motors and generating forces.

3. Theoretical Choices made when Studying Policy Change

To make theoretical choices means deciding *how to develop the epistemological premises when choosing how to study the research object*. In other words, a theoretical framework designed to explain policy developments, needs to be constructed on the basis of certain conjectural assumptions – that is specific choices – regarding the following constitutive elements which have to be logically linked together:

- the definition of policy development and change (what is the real object?);
- the type of change (incremental or radical?);
- the output of change (is it reversible or irreversible?);
- the level of abstraction and the structure/agency dilemma;
- the causal mechanisms, the explanatory variables, and the configurative dimensions.

Definition of Policy Development and Change

The decision in question here is to define what public policy means, and, in particular, to decide how policy change is to be defined. In other words, we need to clarify what the real object of the analysis is, that is, what is to be described and explained. This may seem a rather simple recommendation, but all too often this theoretical choice is forgotten or is not completed. As Hogwood and Peters (1983: 25) pointed out, "all policy is policy change": so the definition of what is change represents a strategic issue for the researcher. It really makes a substantial difference if policy change is defined in terms of the transformation of the definition of the issues in question, or as the structure and content of the policy agenda, or in terms of the content of the policy programme, or as the outcome of implementation of policy. It is very dangerous to reduce policy change (that is policy *tout court*) to a specific area of the ongoing process of policy making. It is clear that there may well be suitable ways of rendering the concept of policy change operational, such as the tripartition of policy change suggested by Hall (1993) and by Sabatier and Jenkins Smith (1993), or the taxonomy by which Cashore and Howlett (2007) design six possible orders of policy change.

However, such complex conceptual and empirical efforts need to avoid the risk of "reductionism". For example, nothing can guarantee that a profound change in the policy instrument or in the policy's core elements is going to modify the effectiveness of those services provided to the public, or that even a significant change in the definition of the issue in question is going to ensure a similar change in the legislative framework of the policy field, and so on. This is one of the more problematic issues for scholars working in the public policy field: it is not easy to convincingly explain the ongoing process of public policy (with all its various steps) using the same theoretical framework for all the different components of the process itself. From this point of view, further reflection on the instrumental efficacy of the heuristic stage is probably required (DeLeon 1999).

The Type of Change (Incremental or Radical)

While the definition of the object of change helps us decide about what is being changed (the policy process or part thereof, or the content of policy – i.e. values, strategies, instruments), we also need to "measure" the entity of change: in other words, we need to discover the degree of change. Hence the classical dichotomy between incremental (first-order, prescribed, evolutionary, momentum, single-loop learning, continuous) change and radical (third-order, paradigmatic, constructive, revolutionary, transformative, double-loop learning, quantum, discontinuous) change. Such definitions are characterized by their focus on the mode of change. However, as policy scholars are well aware, it is not easy to define the real meaning of the two forms of change (incremental vs. radical). Change is clearly incremental when it represents a marginal shift from the status quo, while radical change is any profound shift from the present situation. However, this general understanding of the difference between the two needs to be put into context, and several other aspects need to be considered. Studies have shown that the most important aspects are:

- the level of abstraction, since the same change may appear radical from a micro perspective, but incremental from a macro perspective (Knill and Lenschow 2001);
- the *tempo*/speed dimension. The temporal dimension helps us to better define and specify the nature of change. Sometimes what may seem a radical change is

simply an incremental change that has come about very rapidly; likewise, what seems to be an incremental change may really be a radical transformation that has occurred very slowly (Durant and Diehl 1989, Roberts 1998);
- the logic of event progression (of direction) that is the cumulative or adaptive nature of change.[3] In the first case, the diachronic sequence of change is conducive to a different policy paradigm; in the second case, the sequence of change is a simple process of adaptation of the present features of policy to the changes in the external environment;
- the scope of change, that is, whether change involves a part or all of the policy field (Roberts 1998). This dimension can be very useful not only in distinguishing which part of the policy is changing (the values, or strategies, or tools in question, for example), but may also help us understand whether changes are occurring in a specific sub-system of the policy field (for example, higher education policy may undergo changes in different sub-fields, such as the academic profession, the structure of teaching, institutional governance, etc.).[4]

The Output of Change: Reversibility/Irreversibility

Can a process of change and its outputs (and subsequent outcome) be reversed? It is unclear whether this question is epistemological or theoretical; I personally would opt for the latter, given that, as Table 1 above shows, it is impossible to fill in the boxes of all the ideal types for this particular dimension. In fact, it is only possible to provide a clear solution to this dichotomy in the case of linear models and chaotic models. It is intrinsic for linear models that changes be irreversible, because they postulate mechanical reactions based on a clear, direct cause/effect correlation which develops in a pre-established manner. On the other hand, the structural non-linearity of chaos theory defines change as being irreversible, since from this epistemological perspective what "emerges" as a transformation of the previous situation is ontogenetically different from its own antecedent, and thus it is impossible to reproduce the initial conditions, due also to influence that chance has on the process of change (Prigogine 1997, Mattausch 2003).

However, for other ideal types, the reversibility/irreversibility dilemma cannot be epistemologically postulated. It is a matter of theoretical choice. For example, if we take evolutionary models of public policy, on the one hand we discover the existence of a strictly path-dependent framework (David 1985, Pierson 2000a, 2000b), which theoretically presupposes the irreversibility of policy sequences and trajectories; however, on the other hand, we have punctuated-equilibrium models which state that changes may be reversible, because the new policy strategy adopted can be reversed when it proves no longer capable of adequately responding to the problem for which it was designed to be a solution (Haydu 1988, Baumgartner and Jones 2002, Morgan and Kubo 2005). Nevertheless, it may be also be a matter of empirical observation and inference, and of the comparison of results obtained through a process of implementation. For example, the dialectic view (Marxist or pluralistic models) of political and policy development maintains that the irreversibility/ reversibility problem has no theoretical solution: it is the ongoing conflict of interests that produces outcomes which can be subsequently reversed (and thus we can only try to "explain" when and why outputs are irreversible or have been reversed).

The Level of Abstraction and the Structure/Agency Dilemma

In designing a theoretical framework to explain policy development, decisions have to be made about the micro/macro problem and the structure/agency relationship. However, before making such decisions, the reductionism problem has to be resolved. In the public policy field, one has to decide whether to embrace a "co-evolutive" (emergentist) or a "reductionist" perspective. This alternative is not generally dealt with in public policy studies, for understandable reasons. Nevertheless, something needs to be said about this dilemma in order to clarify the theoretical and empirical implications of choosing one or the other of the two perspectives. The embracing of reductionism means that we assume it to be possible to explain policy development simply by focusing on a specific part thereof, at a specific individual analytical level, and on certain forms of interaction with the external environment (that is, with political, societal and economic institutions). Thus policy change is studied either at the macro level (where policy change is perceived as an output of a macro factor such as political competition, economic trend, public opinion) or at the micro level (the in-depth reconstruction of a specific policy development). Nevertheless, we need to avoid reducing all features of policy development to those displayed at one specific level. Such a reduction may well provide a useful simplification of reality, but it also entails the danger of over-emphasizing certain features rather than others.

From this point of view, and assuming that each level of analysis displays different patterns and can be analyzed using different kinds of theoretical approach, the "emergentist" perspective proves very useful, and as such should be taken seriously.[5] Clearly, this does not necessarily mean accepting a systemic, holistic perspective, that is, an approach to policy change which focuses on the co-evolution of all its various components (at all levels of analysis) and of their relations with the external environment: indeed, this would be a very lengthy and expensive business. However, if only one level of analysis is chosen (for example, policy development in environmental policy at either the national or local level), then policy scholars should try to avoid ontological reductionism. This attempted clarification may well slow down the accumulation of knowledge and the generalization of theoretical frameworks.

The micro/macro problem is accompanied by the structure/agency dilemma. Choices regarding the theoretical relationships between structures (institutions, patterns of behaviour, collective units) and individual preferences and actions, determines the level of analysis and the type of change analyzed. This chain of theoretical choices should be intrinsically coherent; the well-known theoretical proposals regarding "micro/macro" linkage (Alexander 1982) and "structure, action and structuration" (Giddens 1984) should really be considered together with the micro-foundation problem theorized by Coleman (1986), and in particular his statement that: "the satisfactory social theory must attempt to describe behaviour of social unit, not merely that of individuals, that it must nevertheless be grounded in the behaviour of individuals; and the central theoretical challenge is to show how individual actions combine to produce a social outcome" (Coleman 1986: 363).

Taking this challenge seriously means reflecting on the fact that too much structuralism[6] (whereby all individual policy actions are determined by institutionalized factors – rules, patterns of behaviour, cultures) is intrinsically deterministic and conducive to an incrementalist view of change. On the other hand, the overemphasizing of the independence of agency, contingency and chance is conducive to an excessive openness and randomness of the policy process and to the intrinsic weakness when making ex ante hypotheses.

So, the effort to conciliate such theoretical issues in the public policy sphere is indeed not a simple task, if one thinks that only one of the more reputed theories of policy change (ACF) tries to inter-relate, in an ordered way, the macro perspective (macro dimensions such as the socio-economic environment, public opinion, etc.), the "meso" perspective (policy development within a specific policy sub-system), the micro perspective (individual preferences and behaviour), and the "structuration" problem (through the use of the belief system as a theoretical device with which to describe the combination of individual preferences and collective actions).

Causal Mechanisms, Explanatory Variables, and Configurative Dimensions

The first issue here is the choice of causal logic. In short, one has to choose between a more positivist, fundamentally "nomothetic" notion of causality, and a more complex notion of causality based on the pursuit of causal combinations. So while on the one hand there is a linear-additive view of causality, which assumes that there is a clear separation between independent and dependent variables (thus permitting the "net effect" of the independent variable), on the other hand, there is the viewpoint which focuses on the search for possible combinations of causal conditions capable of generating a specific outcome, and thus "once these combinations are identified it is possible to specify the contexts that enable or disable specific individual causes" (Ragin 2006: 640). The important thing here is to understand that the choice of a linear-additive form of causality means focusing on "why" something happens, whereas the choice of a combinative causality means focusing on "how" something happens.

In public policy theory, the linear/combinative-conditional causality dichotomy would appear to have been finally resolved, since the most highly reputed, widespread models of policy change are based on a combination of conditioning factors and parameters. However, it should be said that there are different applications of the combination of causal conditions, and that those models which emphasize institutional factors (such as rules, political parties and ruling coalitions) are based on a kind of hierarchy of conditions that assumes, maybe unconsciously, the search for a "net effect".

Thus the first decision to be made here is whether the analysis of policy development and change should be based on linear causality or on conditional causality. This choice is intrinsically linked with another problematical issue: that is, whether the independent variables/causal conditions are to be assumed to be endogenous or exogenous. The most sophisticated models of policy change and development, due to their underlying combinative causal logic, tend to design causal mechanisms which mix (but too often simply sum up) both types of explanatory variable. In this case, the real analytical problem from the point of view of the framework's theoretical coherence, is the feedback interaction between the endogenous and exogenous sets of factors. The feedback sequence and loops make the difference here.

Last, but not least, there is the question of the type of explanatory variable. Many factors are assumed to influence and co-determine policy change and development: institutional arrangements and rules, critical junctures, ideas, interests, networks, single individuals, and so on. In order to deal with this issue, I propose five broad configurations of policy settings (each of which favours a specific dimension of policy or specific combinations of explanatory variables). This way of perceiving public policies can be conceptualized as the following particular combinations and configurations of variables, which define a specific constitutive dimension of policies. So from this point of view, policies:

a) are *arenas of power*, which means that they are the context within which self-interested actors behave in order to maintain, or to increase, their own power, resources or benefits;
b) are *institutions*, which means that they are historically entrenched frameworks full of formal rules, historically established practices, interactions, routines, cognitive maps and values. Like every institution, through their institutionalized elements policies "are maintained over long periods of time without further justification or elaboration, and are highly resistant to change" (Zucker 1987: 446);
c) are *ideational forums* in which different ideas about what should be done and which values should be pursued are developed and interact, and often come into conflict with each other;
d) are primary targets *of the influence of political institutions*, which means that they are constantly subjected to the intervention of political institutions;
e) are *sets of networked relationships*, sometimes strongly institutionalized, between diverse policy actors (interest groups, social movements, political parties, experts, etc.) and political institutions. From this point of view, they may be defined also as *networked arenas*.

Public policy is therefore a complex phenomenon in which institutionalized elements, formal rules, ideas, interests, and political institutions interact, often through structured networks. This means that when choosing explanatory variables a decision has to be made as to the specific configurative dimension to favour, or to the mix of different factors when designing con-causal explanatory mechanisms.

4. Policy-Change Frameworks: Which Kind of Epistemological and Theoretical Coherence?

How have theories of policy change solved, or rather tried to solve, the aforementioned long list of epistemological and theoretical dilemmas? In order to answer this question, the first thing is to choose which frameworks are to be analyzed. Personally, I think that the focus ought to be on those theories committed to grasping the multidimensional character of public policies. This means focusing on those theories based upon a synthesis of other theoretical frameworks which in turn generally concentrate on certain specific dimensions of policy developments. This is the case, for example, with those theoretical perspectives which focus on specific individual elements of policy developments, such as: institutions and institutionalization, strategic actors (rational choice theory), political parties (party government models); socio-economic events (characteristic of many macro-structural and functionalist approaches, especially during the 1960s and 1970s); interest groups (pluralist theories); networks (following an approach – network analysis – which was developed from the 1980s on), and ideas and paradigms (fashionable during the 1990s). Each of these perspectives observes policy development in terms of certain specific, sometimes single, elements, and can be very interesting and potentially very parsimonious. However, an understanding of the "heterarchic" nature of public policy and of its combination of powering and puzzling (Heclo 1974) may call for a more complex framework, one that is capable of encapsulating the intrinsic complexity of policy development. Clearly this is once again a question of choice; in this case, the choice of a complex (multidimensional) framework means a greater depth of understanding, to the detriment of parsimony.

I am thus going to follow the proposal made by Peter John (1998, 2003), that is, to consider those approaches which account for most of the components of policy change and development.[7] Thus the most important theoretical frameworks on which to focus, in order to evaluate the way they solve the long list of epistemological and theoretical puzzles mentioned above – are the Multiple Stream Approach (MPS) – which, however, focuses strictly on change rather than on development – the PEF and the ACF. However I think that another framework ought to be mentioned here, that is, PDF. The Path Dependency Framework is the most frequently used framework when studying policies from the historical-institutionalist perspective. Although it does not strictly belong to the specific literature on policy change, we ought to analyze PDF simply because of its popularity, and because the other three frameworks in question are only partially able to take account of the historical perspective.

Table 2 represents an attempt at summarizing the characteristics of the aforementioned four frameworks in relation to the basic epistemological and theoretical problems presented and discussed in the previous sections.[8]

The Multiple Stream Approach

The MSA defines public policy as the world of "structural" ambiguity (Zahariadis 2003). From the epistemological point of view, MSA, together with PDF, is the closest of the four frameworks to the epistemological character of chaos and complexity theory. In fact, MSA adopts a non-linear logic of policy development, a revolutionary dynamics, and gives importance to the role of chance and individual behaviour in generating change. Change is unpredictable. As with chaos theory, it adopts a co-evolutionary perspective, meaning that policies are seen as "complex adaptive systems" (Kingdon 1995: 224). This is where the substantial incongruence of the MSA approach lies. A complex adaptive system means a system (a policy in our case) that adapts through the reciprocal adaptation of all its own components (Axelrod and Cohen 2000); the MSA, on the contrary, assumes that there is only a contingent confluence of the three streams of policy, politics and problems, even if the political stream provides several constraints that limit the independence of the other two streams (Kingdon 1984: 217). How do the various components of a policy co-evolve if the three constitutive elements are supposed to be substantially independent? In other words, if the political stream is significantly constraining the

Table 2. Epistemological and theoretical choices in four frameworks of policy change

Epistemological choices	MSA	PEF	ACF	PDF
Way of event progression	Non-linearity (ambiguous and unpredictable)	Disconnected linearity (partially predictable)	Linearity (partially predictable)	Non-linearity
Dynamics of development	Not prefigured but predominantly evolutionary	Evolutionary (sequence slow/rapid changes)	Not prefigured	Disconnected evolution
Motors of change	Partially constrained chance and entrepreneurship	External crisis, partisan change, conflict	External factors, partisan change, confrontation, learning	Increasing returns; history
Theoretical choices				
Definition of policy development and change	Particularly focused on agenda setting. No distinction among different types of policy change	Particularly focused on punctuations in agenda setting, in policy image construction, and in legislative behaviour	Covering the entire process. Tripartition of content of changes (based on a tripartition of policy beliefs)	Covering the entire process
Type of change (incremental or radical)	Not prefigured even incremental oriented	Structural link between both types	Both	Both
The output of change	Not prefigured	Reversible	Reversible	Irreversible
The level of abstraction	Co-evolutive perspective	Macro	Linking macro, meso and micro levels	Co-evolutive perspective
The structure-agency dilemma	Structural prevalence but with room for individualistic strategic behaviour	Structural prevalence	Linking constantly structure and agency	Structural prevalence
Causal mechanisms	Random combinative causality mixing exogenous and endogenous variables, but the exogenous ones seem prevalent	Combinative causality with the prevalence of exogenous variables	Combinative causality – the composition of which depends on the type of change. Major changes are exogenously determined.	Combinative causality; historical paths; critical junctures.

(continued)

Table 2. (*Continued*)

Epistemological choices	MSA	PEF	ACF	PDF
Explanatory variables	Critical external events (technological change, electoral victory, systemic or international crisis) plus the eventual role of single individuals	Critical external events; institutional arrangements; cycles of public attention; dynamics of processing information	Critical events, ideas and beliefs competition, learning.	Self-organized innovation, chance, contingency
Configurative dimensions	Semi-chaotic mix of 3 dimensions (policy as arena of power, as ideational forum, and as target of political institutions' influence)	Involving all five configurations but under the prevalent influence of political institutions	Focused on the interaction of three configurative dimensions: policy as arena of power, as set of networks and as ideational forum	Prevalence of the institutional configuration

other two streams, this indicates a kind of hierarchy among the three streams. If so, the presumed ambiguity of policy making and the intrinsically chaotic nature of the "primeveral soup" is a misleading metaphor. To be coherent from the "complex adaptive systems" perspective we need to assume that the various parts of the policy arena constitute a driver of change by directly influencing other components. From this point of view, the MSA is affected by a contradiction between its basic epistemological and theoretical choices and the combination thereof.

It should also be pointed out that the logic of the model is particularly suitable for analyzing certain stages or specific parts of policy development. The fact that change is conceptualized as a discrete event (that is, something that happens at a specific moment in time) makes the MSA more useful when analysing agenda setting and the formulation stage. It is more difficult to apply it to the implementation stage, that is, during the process by which change is operationalized and institutionalized. This fits perfectly with the absence of a typology of the content of change, which is left to the individual choice of the scholar using the framework.

Furthermore, it is flexible enough, when it comes to the majority of the theoretical choices involved (especially those regarding outcome type, causal mechanisms, the structure/agency relationship and the explanatory variable), to provide users with considerable room for manoeuvre and substantial options when formulating their analyses. Obviously the strength of this framework lies in its basic simplicity (semi-independent streams, partially constrained chance and contingency, policy entrepreneurs), which provides a highly original, counterintuitive tool with which to construct and interpret reality. In fact, this is the real point I want to make. The MSA adopts a complexity and chaos perspective and a non-linear, unpredictable perspective. However, from this point of view, all its complexity potentialities have yet to be theoretically developed, especially in relation to the process of interaction between streams and their external environment, and to the mutual adaptation of the three streams (which can only be conceived as independent of one another for the purposes of analytical clarity!). The MSA focuses strictly on policy change, and not on the dynamics of the policy process and of general policy development. It could probably offer greater interpretive and explanatory potential if it were remodelled to cover other stages and elements of policy dynamics other than just the events constituting the change. In order to do so, we would need to find some continuative, structural, institutionalized connections between the three streams. If this were achieved, then the adopted approach may provide better internal incoherence. This would help reduce both the excessive role played, in the MSA, by external factors in determining the opportunities for change and the prevalence of the political stream over the policy and problematic streams.

However, even without this kind of theoretical evolution, which would allow a broader empirical use to be made of the framework, the MSA preserves its importance and even a certain fascination, particularly given that the emphasis is on the individual's role as a driver of change. However, the flexibility of this approach tends to encourage the inappropriate use of its basic concepts (especially those of policy window and policy entrepreneur), which are very often defined in a purely descriptive way or to explain marginal/residual variance.[9]

The Punctuated Equilibrium Framework

The PEF has acquired a considerable reputation over the last decade, thanks to the scientific studies and achievements of Baumgartner and Jones, and to their ability to institutionalize their research in the form of the Policy Agenda Project. The PEF combines a number of different concepts borrowed from other frameworks and subjects. It tries to preserve a mix of stability (conceived as incremental adaptations) and radical change: this is because, from the epistemological point of view, it is a characteristic evolutionary conceptualization, featuring a disconnected linearity which develops according to structured sequences involving different institutional venues. The PEF accepts some of the assumptions inherent to chaos and complexity theories, especially when it is observed that "punctuated-equilibrium theory predicts a form of systems-level stability, but it will not help us to make point-specific predictions for particular policy issues" (True *et al.* 2006: 20). This observation shows that the PEF is consciously committed to explain the systemic level of stability and change from an evolutionary perspective. The choice regarding the level of abstraction is quite clear. What this means is that even if the PEF sometimes suggests that we take into consideration those policy entrepreneurs and small changes capable of generating large-scale transformations through a bandwagon effect, it is more interested in the structural dynamics of interactions at the systemic level. Thus it is no coincidence that it has specifically focused on agenda setting, and more recently on the legislative stage and outputs, which are the best objects to analyze from a systemic, macro perspective.

The PEF also places particular emphasis on the importance of the institutional setting in influencing policy dynamics and the possible output of the process of change. Institutions are conceived as strictly conservative: thus pressure towards major change can only be exogenously derived, thus creating opportunities for those (individuals and interest groups) who are pursuing policy innovation. This choice in favour of the conservative role of institutions – conceived as the structural driver of policy stability – means that policy development is simply based on homeostatic dynamics, that is, on passive reactions to external challenges and transformations (Cashore and Howlett 2007). It is here that the fundamental epistemological and theoretical incoherence of the PEF lies. In fact, a coherent evolutionary perspective would require specification of the features of the sequence of variation, selection and retention. Translated into a policy language, this means that the PEF's assumption that there are no real feedback effects from policy dynamics that affect and re-model both external structural dynamics (the socio-economic environment, political competition, etc.) and the institutional arrangements involved in policy-making, is a questionable one. In other words, in order to achieve evolutionary coherence, the real problem is that of focusing on the internal feature of the policy field in order to identify those characteristics capable of inter-relating with the external environment in an active manner through the dynamics of reciprocal influence.

We should not forget that evolution is not simply an adaptation to inputs from the external environment, but a process by which systems also influence external sources and the external environment. Furthermore, the lack of focus on the internal features of policy making (content, values, tools, strategies) prevents us from identifying those elements which are less likely to disappear, those which are more likely to change, and those that are more likely to persist.

However, the decision to analyze policy dynamics at the systemic level is a clear choice which prevents any coherent evolutionary reasoning. Furthermore, what emerges is that the PEF is not really interested in policy development, but simply in identifying the temporal distribution of punctuations. This means that policy development is seen as a sequence of discrete decisions. Basically, policy is not analyzed from the point of view of its internal diachronic complexity, but simply as an output of the complex political and institutional dynamics by which information is processed and political attention is allocated (Jones and Baumgartner 2005). This is because the PEF is not particularly interested in analysing the content and quality of policy change. From this point of view, therefore, the evolutionary perspective is only evoked by the PEF.

The Advocacy Coalition Framework

The ACF is probably the most ambitious of the various frameworks designed to explain policy development and change. It is characterized by a combination of features from at least three different epistemological ideal types. Like the life-cycle model, it is a linear framework; its motors of change are competition, learning and imitation, as with the evolutionary models; and finally – albeit to a slighter, more secondary degree – it assumes confrontation and conflict between different ideas and values, as stated by the dialectic ideal type. Thus, from an epistemological point of view, the ACF is a clear example of "eclecticism". From the theoretical point of view, it is the only framework which links all three levels of abstraction, constantly connecting individual behaviour and structural elements (through the *system of beliefs*). Furthermore, it takes the ideational approach seriously, giving it a pivotal role as a driver of change to ideas, values and beliefs. Finally, the ACF distinguishes between different types of change. Its coherence seems to be sound, even if constructed on an eclectic basis.

I believe that two major points of possible theoretical incoherence ought to be examined. Firstly, there is the problem of causal mechanisms, and then, more importantly, that of the relationship between endogenous and exogenous variables. The proposed theoretical solution is that the necessary condition for major change is a transformation in the external factors (the socio-economic system, public opinion, governing coalitions, other policy subsystems). This means that radical changes are exogenously driven, even if the external changes do not necessarily produce an internal transformation within policy making (Sabatier and Jenkins Smith 1999). Despite this clarification (the fact that external factors do not determine, but only strongly influence, major changes), the structuralist point of view remains untouched upon. This point of view sees the causal mechanism as being asymmetrically designed. If only minor changes result from a learning process within the policy-making sphere, then this means that there is a clear distinction between external and internal factors in terms of causal potential: in other words, it is the former variables that make the real difference, whereas endogenously driven variance is only marginal. This shortcoming has not really been corrected by the recent modifications made to the model (Sabatier and Weible 2007), whereby two alternative paths leading to major policy change have been proposed, namely internal shocks and negotiated agreements. Both these paths seem to be exogenously driven. "Policy shocks" are usually important when an external factor or actor – either public opinion or government – is mobilized by its perception of specific events. The "negotiated agreement" path – whereby a consensual decision is reached within a policy subsystem after years of infighting – may be chosen under strong pressure from the external environment (government or public opinion) which refuses to accept the damaging stalemate any longer.

From this point of view, the ACF also suffers from the same problem as that afflicting both the PEF and the MSA: external factors are prevalent and not enough theoretical attention is paid to feedback effects from the internal dynamics of policy making and from external factors. Little attention is paid to the fact that the policy networks and advocacy coalitions not only compete with each other inside the policy subsystem, but they also try to manipulate external change to their own advantage (Mawhinney 1993, Capano 1996) and are also capable of "manipulating" internal crises. So, from this point of view, the ACF conceives of major changes in a reactive/adaptive way.

Secondly, in the case of the ACF, the ideational approach is less important than it assumes. Beliefs are not really drivers of change, but rather the adhesive binding together of advocacy coalitions. They are dealt with as structural components of the model. This would appear to be an important theoretical assumption, as it indicates that what keeps the members of networks together are shared values and beliefs, and not only shared material interests. Nevertheless, beliefs are not deemed to be drivers of change, but, somewhat paradoxically, factors of stability (and thus of incremental change). Radical, paradigmatic changes can only be produced by external alterations or pressures (especially changes in government or in the public's perceptions and emotions). So the balance between "to power" and "to puzzle" is structurally biased in favour of the former.

The Path Dependency Framework

The PDF has been discussed at length in policy studies (Kay 2005, Howlett and Rayner 2006). It is judged to be a-systematic, idiosyncratic, and above all to be capable of explaining stability rather than change. Such negative opinion is significant, but epistemologically biased. The real hidden feature of path dependency frameworks is that they belong to the chaos and complexity epistemological perspective. I realize that such a classification is arguable: however, if we compare the last columns in Table 1 (chaos and complexity theories) and Table 2 (PDF), a number of similarities emerge. The PDF, contrary to popular belief, is non-linear: it does not follow a preordained scheme of events; in fact, even when a policy trajectory is assumed, nobody can foresee if it will persist or will change path. Initial conditions are important, but they do not determine the outcome: it is what happens in the middle that in fact determines the real outcome. The PDF is therefore unpredictable, being strongly based on contingency, chance and increasing returns. The concept of increasing returns is what specifically links the PDF to chaos and complexity theory: that means the irreversibility of the process' output and outcome (Pierson 2000a).

The only incoherent aspect of PDF compared with its epistemological premises is the fact that in spite of its claimed focus on small changes – even at the local and individual levels – the majority of PDF scholars adopt a structural perspective which leaves little room for individual actors. This is a considerable problem since it is conducive to the risk of historical (structural) determinism. More specifically, as Thelen (1999) and Mahoney (2006) have pointed out, the PDF is characterized on the one hand by excessive contingency at the initial stage of the sequence (when the mix of initial conditions is being formulated), since the framework assumes that chance, minor events and marginal factors can trigger off a new path; on the other hand, the PDF is overly deterministic in the design of the sequences' development (as a result of increasing returns and lock-in effects). Clearly the PDF's response could be that, given the chaotic and complex nature of policy making, the stability achieved by policy is only of an apparent nature, since something could happen to change the path at any moment.

So, paradoxically, the PDF is more in keeping with an ideal type of epistemological family than the other frameworks. This is where the PDF's real problem lies, I believe. In being coherent with its chaos/complexity epistemological premises, PDF has accepted the irreversibility of output and outcome. This epistemological condition is not difficult for the PDF to share, as its history causes it to assume the uniqueness of historical events. However, irreversibility does not fit in with the reality of policy development, where very often policy content, solutions, strategies and principles can be reversed within the space of a few years or decades. So it seems that the irreversibility clause makes the PDF a useful approach to the analysis of specific policy developments and change only, or to the understanding of radical, epoch-making events and turning points only. In order to avoid this extreme confrontation between chance and necessity, the PDF should try to concentrate more on "de-locking" factors (Castaldi and Dosi 2006), which require theoretical assumptions and hypotheses about the motors of chance and contingency.

5. Grasping Reality: A Decalogue to Alleviate the Sufferings of Policy Scholars

The above analysis reveals that frameworks of policy change and development are designed by policy scholars in an eclectic way. Eclecticism may well compromise theoretical accuracy, but sometimes it can be the only practicable way forward. Furthermore, a considerable quantity of theoretical dullness, ambiguity, incoherency and shortcomings are seen to debilitate the study of policy change.

Summing up the results of my synthetic analysis, I would like to make the following recommendations.

1. Policy scholars should be more aware of the epistemological choices they make. We borrow a great many concepts from other subjects, and too often we do so without any proper contextualization of the new concepts in relation to the object of our analysis. Evolution, punctuated equilibrium, policy entrepreneur, etc., have been created for other objects of research in other fields. We must clearly define what they mean in the field of policy research if we are to avoid the danger of their metaphorical usage.
2. Stability and change should be clearly connected at the theoretical and empirical levels. Too often, these two elements of policy development are dealt with separately. Policy is an ongoing phenomenon, and stability and change constantly co-exist.
3. The object of analysis has to be properly defined. Too often, policy means too many things to different people. At the same time, we have to avoid the reductionist problem: for example, if a framework focuses on agenda setting or on implementation, this has to be made clear.
4. The kind of change to be explained has to be clearly defined. The content of the change in question has to be declared. They may be changes in: the process; the policy actors' relationships; the basic policy values and goals; policy strategies; policy instruments; policy definitions; the institutional arrangements of a policy field. All these changes are different from each other, and as such may imply different causal mechanisms and a different impact on reality.
5. The reversibility/irreversibility dichotomy should be properly defined and analyzed. The real problem is that in order to resolve this dilemma, we need to study the concrete impact of policy change, that is, we need to discover how it is actually implemented. This recommendation calls for more attention to be paid not only to the implementation stage of policies but also to a broad-ranging comparison of thick reconstructions of single cases. This, in turn, means a greater focus on micro-level analyses.
6. The possibility that a general explanatory theory for policy change is not ontologically viable has to be carefully evaluated. The consequence of this is that different frameworks of change can be designed for different types of change, and for different levels of abstraction.
7. More care needs to be taken with regard to the endogenous/exogenous dichotomy. The strength and fascination of the policy perspective lies in the fact that policies (in the sense of arenas, institutions, networks, ideational *fora*) have their own lives, their own internal logic and goals: they not only passively adapt to external inputs, but indeed they actively influence external factors.

From this point of view, the potential capacity of "endogeneity" requires further theoretical and empirical analysis.

8. The fact that policies possess different components means that they are necessarily multi-driven. They are composed of several different factors: ideas, interests, institutions, actors, different types of rationalities, different individual motivations. Thus combinative causality is unavoidable. However, this should not be a simple list of variables and factors, but needs to be designed to show the possible interdependencies and mutual compatibilities among con-causal factors. The configurative nature of policy dynamics must be considered as an inescapable characteristic.

9. Time and history do matter, and as such they cannot be omitted. Timing is an essential discriminatory factor with regard to the nature of change and the essence of the process of change. History means that policies are not developed within *a vacuum*. History means that policies are contextualized in a place, that they come from a past, that they have taken up time. Those not entirely convinced by historical-institutionalism and by the PDF should bear in mind the influence that historical processes and sequences have had on the policy development and change in question. From this point of view, the "configurational" logic of the framework of policy change should include an historical perspective.

10. Chance should be taken into careful consideration. I am perfectly aware of the fact that chance may represent a considerable problem for many approaches, and that from the positivist perspective chance is the "devil". As Boudon (1986: 173) underlines, "in the social sciences, chance is generally thought to be a very unwelcome guest, ubiquitous but studiously concealed, ignored and even denied the right to exist by virtually everyone". Nevertheless, it exists, and we cannot pretend that things are otherwise. It is the real challenge to the social sciences, and thus to policy studies. I would therefore suggest we seriously consider Boudon's (1986: 179) suggestion that "we must see chance not as a substance, a variable or a set of variables, but as a structure which is characteristic of certain sets of causal chains as perceived by an observer". Chance is a structural aspect of ongoing reality. It deserves attention, and even if it may seem paradoxical, it deserves a theoretical analysis of those forms it takes. If we bear in mind chance, we can avoid the continuous risk of the strong determinism that is intrinsic to all theoretical analysis within the social sciences.

Policy scholars are required to borrow a variety of different theoretical and epistemological concepts and perspectives. The object of our research is ambiguous, multifaceted, ubiquitous and evasive. We are perfectly aware that it does not really exist and that it depends on the design of our research. The subjective nature of public policy not only generates extreme fragmentation in definitions and approaches, but also leads to the creation of highly competitive frameworks, and the radical fragmentation of different theoretical conceptualizations and veins of research. The danger is that we may well run aground in a veritable Tower of Babel, and this does not bode well for the future development and the reputation of public policy.[10] It is of essential importance that a greater degree of epistemological and theoretical awareness be developed in the case of policy studies. I genuinely believe that serious reflection on the abovementioned points would really help to improve theoretical reflection and empirical research in the field of policy change and development.

Notes

1. The original model of punctuated equilibrium does not discard the evolutionary model, but focuses on the "time scale" of evolution as observed both in paleontology (Laporte 1982) and biology (Mayr 1982). Furthermore, it has to be underlined that, as Gould and Eldredge (1977) pointed out, in fact, punctuation is the result of a species variation within a population in isolation, where less competition creates the condition for unique forms of adaptation to spread rapidly through the isolated population. As a result of this process, in a "geological instant" – 10,000 to 50,000 generation – a new species may emerge. So it is a problem of time scale. This is because Gould and Eldredge themselves confirmed that arguing in favour of punctuated equilibrium does not represent a departure from the classic evolutionary model (1977).
2. Gersick (1991), in an outstanding article on punctuated equilibrium, makes the mistake of defining punctuation as a revolutionary form of change, because he underestimates the time *dimension* and treats the punctuated equilibrium model as the opposite of evolutionary theory, rather than as a sub-type thereof, as it should be, at least according to the proponents of this approach mentioned in the previous footnote.
3. Let me remind the reader that in section 2 I distinguished between the way and the logic of event progression (that is directionality).
4. This dimension also reveals the considerable difficulties encountered when defining the "field" and when trying to understand policy change across multiple policy sectors. Moreover, policy issues are very often tackled by strategies covering different policy fields.
5. The study of emergence, which is the basilar concept in chaos and complexity approaches, has been a relevant topic in many fields, including philosophy (Goldstein 2000), sociology (Buckley 1967, Eve *et al.* 1997), and organization science (Dansereau *et al.* 1999).
6. A structural perspective can be adopted from different epistemological perspectives. For example, both rationalists and constructivists (such as Douglas North, and March and Olsen, respectively) can be defined as strongly structuralist.
7. I have deliberately left out a highly reputed framework such as the IAD (institutional analysis and development framework) proposed by Elinor Ostrom, which in my opinion, even though it is extremely sophisticated, tends to over-emphasize the role of institutional rules in decision making. In doing so, such a model focuses on the institutional dimension of policies, while at the same time tending to portray policies simply as a succession of separate choices. I have likewise excluded another, commonly used theoretical approach to political decision making, namely the "veto players theory": this latter theory is not really concerned with grasping the complexity of policy making, but focuses in particular on the influence that institutional rules and actors' sources have on shaping the dynamics and content of decision making. So from a policy perspective, it seems to be far too restrictive compared to the broad perspective we need to adopt when analyzing the multidimensional nature of policy development and change.
8. However, it is clear that the same analytical exercise in relation to the epistemological and theoretical puzzle to be solved can be conducted in the case of every theory or framework of policy change.
9. For example: the MSA sees policy entrepreneurs as a necessary prerequisite for change, albeit serendipitous. This means that the role of entrepreneurs should necessarily be an independent variable, whereas it is very often used (also by other approaches) to explain the more marginal aspects of change (which are generally explained by changes in structural factors). The same is true of the concept of the policy window: from the MSA viewpoint, this concept is conceived as a structural, albeit contingent and random, factor of change, while too often it is used simply to cover for what structural factors fail to explain (a kind of serendipitous post hoccism).
10. It may be no coincidence that in the last review of the state of Political Science (Katznelson and Milner 2002), not one of the work's 30 chapters is devoted to public policy theories and frameworks, even if many of those same chapters deal with policy processes and choices!

References

Alexander, Jeffrey C., 1982, *Theoretical Logic in Sociology: Positivism, Presuppositions and Current Controversies* (London: Routledge and Kegan Paul).
Axelrod, Robert and Cohen, Michael D., 2000, *Harnessing Complexity* (New York: Free Press).
Baumgartner, Frank R. and Jones, Bryan D. (Eds), 2002, *Policy Dynamics* (Chicago: University of Chicago Press).
Berger, Peter L. and Luckmann, Thomas, 1966, *The Social Construction of Reality* (New York: Doubleday).
Boudon, Raymond, 1986, *Theories of Social Change: A Critical Appraisal* (London: Polity Press).
Buckley, Walter (Ed.), 1967, *Sociology and Modern Systems Theory* (Englewood Cliffs, NJ: Prentice Hall).
Capano, Giliberto, 1996, Political science and the comparative study of policy change in higher education: theorico-methodological notes from a policy perspective. *Higher Education*, **31**(3), 263–282.
Cashore, Benjamin and Howlett, Michael, 2007, Punctuating which equilibrium? understanding thermostatic policy dynamics in pacific northwest forestry. *American Journal of Political Science*, **51**(3), 532–551.
Castaldi, Carolina and Dosi, Giovanni, 2006, The grip of history and the scope for novelty: some results and open questions on path dependence in economic processes, in: Andreas Wimmer and Reinhart Kossler (Eds) *Understanding change* (London: Palgrave), pp. 99–128.
Coleman, James S., 1986, Micro foundations and macrosocial theory, in: Siegwart Lindenberg, James S. Coleman and Stefan Nowak (Eds) *Approaches to Social Theory* (New York: Russell Sage Foundation), pp. 345–363.
Dansereau, Fred, Yammarino, Francis J. and Kohles, Jeffrey, 1999, Multiple levels of analysis from a longitudinal perspective: some implications for theory building. *Academy of Management Review*, **24**(2), 346–357.
David, Paul A., 1985, Clio and the economics of QWERTY. *American Economic Review*, **75**, 332–337.
DeLeon, Peter, 1999, The stages approach to the policy process, in: Paul Sabatier (Ed), *Theories of the Policy Process* (Boulder, CO: Westview Press), pp. 19–32.
Durant, Robert F. and Diehl, Paul F., 1989, Agendas, alternatives, and public policy: lessons from the U.S. foreign policy arena. *Journal of Public Policy*, **9**(2), 179–205.
Eldredge, Niles and Gould, Stephen J., 1972, Punctuated equilibria: an alternative to phyletic gradualism, in: Tom J. M. Schopf (Ed) *Models in Paleobiology* (San Francisco: Freeman & Cooper), pp. 82–115.
Eve, Raymond A., Horsfall, Sara and Lee, Mary E. (Eds), 1997, *Chaos, Complexity, and Sociology* (London: Sage).
Farazmand, Ali, 2003, Chaos and transformation theories: a theoretical analysis with implications for organization theory and public management. *Public Organization Review*, **3**(4), 339–372.
Gerlach, Luther and Hines, Virginia, 1973, *The Dynamics of Change in America* (Minneapolis: University of Minneapolis Press).
Gersick, Connie J. G., 1991, Revolutionary change theories: a multilevel exploration of the punctuated equilibrium paradigm. *Academy of Management Review*, **16**(1), 10–36.
Giddens, Anthony, 1984, *The Constitution of Society* (Cambridge: Polity Press).
Goldstein, Jeffrey A., 2000, Emergence: a concept amid a thicket of conceptual snares. *Emergence*, **2**(1), 5–22.
Gould, Stephen J and Eldredge, Niles, 1977, Punctuated equilibria: the tempo and mode of evolution reconsidered. *Paleobiology*, **3**(2), 115–151.
Hall, Peter A., 1993, Policy paradigms, social learning, and the state. *Comparative Politics*, **25**(3), 275–296.
Haydu, Jeffrey, 1988, Making use of the past: time periods as cases to compare and as sequences of problem solving. *The American Journal of Sociology*, **104**(2), 339–371.
Heclo, Hugh, 1974, *Modern Social Politics in Britain and Sweden: From Relief to Income Maintenance* (New Haven, CT: Yale University Press).
Hernes, Gudmund, 1976, Structural change in social processes. *American Journal of Sociology*, **82**(3), 513–547.
Hogwood, Brian W. and Peters, Guy B., 1983, *Policy Dynamics* (New York: St. Martin Press).
Howlett, Michael and Ramesh, M., 1992, Policy subsystem configurations and policy change. *Policy Studies Journal*, **26**(3), 466–481.
Howlett, Michael and Rayner, Jeremy, 2006, Understanding the historical turn in the policy sciences: A critique of stochastic, narrative, path dependency and process-sequencing models of policy-making over time. *Policy Sciences*, **39**(1), 1–18.

John, Peter, 1998, *Analysing Public Policy* (London: Cassell).
John, Peter, 2003, Is there life after policy streams, advocacy coalitions, and punctuations: using evolutionary theory to explain policy change. *Policy Studies Journal*, 31(2), 481–498.
Jones, Bryan D. and Baumgartner, Frank R., 2005, A model of choice for public policy. *Journal of Public Administration Research and Theory*, 15(3), 325–351.
Katznelson, Ira and Milner, Helen V. (Eds), 2002, *Political Science. State of the discipline* (New York: Norton & Company).
Kay, Adrian, 2005, A critique of the use of path dependency in policy studies. *Public Administration*, 83(3), 553–571.
Kingdon John W., 1984, *Agendas, Alternatives, and Public Policies* (Boston: Little Brown).
Kingdon John W., 1995, *Agendas, Alternatives, and Public Policies*, 2nd edition (Boston: Little Brown).
Knill, Christoph and Lenschow, Andrea, 2001, Seek and ye shall find!. Linking different perspectives on institutional change. *Comparative Political Studies*, 34(2), 187–215.
Laporte, Leo F. (Ed), 1982, *The Fossil Record and Evolution* (San Francisco: W.H. Freeman).
Ma, Shun Yun, 2007, Political science at the edge of chaos? The paradigmatic implications of historical institutionalism. *International Political Science Review*, 28(1), 51–78.
Mahoney, James, 2006, Analyzing path dependence: lessons from the social sciences, in: Andreas Wimmer and Reinhart Kossler (Eds) *Understanding Change* (London: Palgrave), pp. 129–139.
March, James G. and Olsen, Johan P., 1976, *Ambiguity and Choice in Organizations* (Bergen: Universitetsforlaget).
Mattausch, John, 2003, Chance and societal change. *The Sociological Review*, 51(4), 506–527.
Mawhinney, Hanne B., 1993, An advocacy coalition approach to change Canadian education, in: Paul A. Sabatier and Hank Jenkins-Smith (Eds) *Policy Change and Learning. An advocacy coalition approach* (Boulder, CO: Westview Press), pp. 59–81.
Mayr, Ernst, 1982, *The Growth of the Biological Thought: Diversity, Evolution, Inheritance* (Boston: Harvard University Press).
Merton, Robert, 1968, *Social Theory and Social Structure* (New York: Free Press).
Morgan, Glenn and Kubo, Izubi, 2005, Beyond path dependency? Constructing new models for institutional change: the case of capital markets in Japan. *Socio-econonomic Review*, 3(1), 55–82.
Nisbet, Robert, 1972, Introduction: the problem of social change, in: Robert Nisbet (Ed.) *Social Change* (New York: Harper and Row), pp. 1–45.
Pierson, Paul, 2000a, Increasing returns, path dependence, and the study of politics. *American Political Science Review*, 94(2), 251–267.
Pierson, Paul, 2000b, Not just what, but when: timing and sequence in political process. *Studies in American Political Development*, 14(1), 72–92.
Prigogine, Ilya, 1997, *The End of Certainty: Time, Chaos, and the New Laws of Nature* (London: The Free Press).
Ragin, Charles, 2006, How to lure analytic social science out of the doldrums: some lessons from comparative research. *International Sociology*, 21(5), 633–646.
Roberts, Nancy C., 1998, Radical change by entrepreneurial design. *Acquisition Review Quarterly*, 5(2), 107–128.
Sabatier, P. A. and Jenkins-Smith, H. C. (Eds), 1993, *Policy Change and Learning. An advocacy coalition approach* (Boulder, CO: Westview Press).
Sabatier, Paul A. and Jenkins-Smith, Hank C., 1999, The advocacy coalition framework: an assessment, in: Paul Sabatier (Ed), *Theories of the Policy Process* (Boulder: Westview Press), pp. 117–166.
Sabatier, Paul A. and Weible, Christopher, 2007, The advocacy coalition framework; innovations and clarifications, in: Paul A. Sabatier (Ed) *Theories of the Policy Process*, 2nd edition (Boulder, CO: Westview Press), pp.189–220.
Thelen, Kathleen, 1999, Historical-institutionalism and comparative politics. *Annual Review of Political Science*, 2, 369–404.
True, James L., Jones, Bryan D. and Baumgartner, Frank R., 2006, Punctuated-equilibrium theory. Explaining stability and change in policy-making, Paper presented at the ECPR Joint Sessions, Nicosia, Cyprus, April 25–30.

Van de Ven, Andrew H. and Poole, Marshall S., 1995, Explaining development and change in organizations. *Academy of Management Review*, **20**(3), 510–540.
Waldrop, Morris M., 1992, *Complexity: The emerging science at the edge of order and chaos* (New York: Simon and Schuster).
Wimmer, Andreas and Kossler, Reinhart (Eds), 2006, *Understanding Change* (London: Palgrave).
Zahariadis, Nikolaos, 2003, *Ambiguity and Choice in Public Policy* (Washington, DC: Georgetown University Press).
Zucker, Lynne G., 1987, Institutional theories of organization. *Annual Review of Sociology*, **13**, 443–464.

The Dependent Variable Problem in the Study of Policy Change: Understanding Policy Change as a Methodological Problem

MICHAEL HOWLETT and BENJAMIN CASHORE

ABSTRACT   *The new orthodoxy in studies of policy dynamics is that policy change occurs through a homeostatic process. "Perturbations" occurring outside of an institutionalized policy subsystem, often characterized as some type of societal or political upheaval or learning, are critical for explaining the development of profound and durable policy changes which are otherwise limited by "endogenous" institutional stability. These homeostatic assumptions, while useful for assessing many cases of policy change, do not adequately capture the historical patterns of policy development found in many sectors. The roots of this problem are traced back to the origins of the new orthodoxy in comparative policy research whereby different levels (orders) of policy making have been incorrectly juxtaposed, providing a parsimonious, but sometimes empirically incorrect, view of policy change. Revising existing taxonomies of policy levels provides a superior identification of the processes of change, and uncovers more than one mechanism through which significant policy change can occur. Three of these alternative mechanisms – a "neo-homeostatic" one in which paradigmatic changes occur through endogenous shifts in goals; a "quasi-homeostatic" in which exogenous factors influence changes in objectives and settings; and a "thermostatic" one in which durable policy objectives require that settings adapt to exogenous changes – are discussed.*

1. The Contemporary Study of Policy Dynamics: Moves Towards the Development of a New Orthodoxy in the 1990s

The contemporary study of policy dynamics owes a broad debt to two studies which appeared 30 years apart: Charles Lindblom's 1959 work on incrementalism and Peter Hall's 1989 study of policy paradigms. Both authors worked in a synoptic fashion, utilizing the insights of other scholars into aspects of politico-administrative behaviour – in Lindblom's case Herbert Simon's (1957) insights into organizational behaviour and in Hall's case Thomas Kuhn's (1962) ideas about the history of scientific advance – to propose and refine the notion that general patterns of policy development can not only be identified but predicted.

Hall's work served to break a long-term "old" orthodoxy in studies of policy change dominated by Lindblom-inspired incrementalism, one which argued that a single type of policy dynamics – marginal increments from the status quo – characterized almost all instances of public policy change (Hayes 1992, Howlett and Ramesh 2003). Since Hall's identification of a second pattern of change – the broad "paradigm" shift - scholars studying public policy dynamics have been involved in a 20 year process of attempting to reconcile the two patterns and their inter-relationships. This period has now witnessed the emergence of a new "post-incremental" orthodoxy as policy scholars have come to generally accept the idea – borrowed from paleo-biology (Eldredge and Gould 1972), and first put forward in the context of policy dynamics by Baumgartner and Jones in 1991 – that periods of marginal adaptation and revolutionary transformation are typically linked in a "punctuated equilibrium" pattern of policy change.

Research undertaken during this period has involved scholars in three related projects designed to understand better how incremental and paradigmatic patterns of policy change are related to each other. First, they have been interested in understanding exactly how longstanding policies which have tended to develop incrementally can become "punctuated" and shift toward a new "equilibrium" (Baumgartner and Jones 1991, 1993, 2002), after which policy making, though of a different content, settles back into a familiar incremental pattern. Second, they have been involved in investigating the manner in which enduring institutions structure policy dynamics, creating the "musts, mays, and must nots" of policy development (Steinmo *et al.* 1992, Clemens and Cook 1999). Thirdly, and relatedly, they have focused on understanding how changes in policy subsystems (Sabatier 1988, Hall 1993) interact with institutional characteristics and serve to, respectively, constrain and facilitate overall patterns of policy development.

The results of such efforts have been fruitful. The discipline now has a much stronger understanding about factors such as legislative "attention spans", "policy windows", and alterations in subsystem beliefs and membership that can result in certain issues coming to the fore on policy agendas, precipitating change by shaping what subsystem members deem to be appropriate types and modes of policy making (Hall 1989, Baumgartner and Jones 1993, 2002, Kingdon 1995, Leach and Sabatier 2005). It also has a much better understanding of the role played by macro, meso and micro institutions, formalization of issue discourses, and routinization of political and administrative affairs in shaping the mobilization of actors and restraining change in policy agendas and processes (Weaver and Rockman 1993, Thelen 2003, 2004, Deeg 2005). The well documented self-reinforcing, "path-dependent" effects of institutionalization on policy making (Pierson 1993, 2000, Mahoney 2000, Hacker 2004, Howlett and Rayner 2006, Kay 2006) have promoted the idea that paradigmatic policy change, given the role played by policy subsystems in this process, requires institutional destabilization through some kind of exogenous "shock".

While alluring as a synthetic construction, and certainly with the potential for great explanatory power in many empirical instances, most elements of the new orthodox punctuated equilibrium model have not been fully tested or proven (John and Margetts 2003). In what must be worrisome for followers of the new orthodoxy, some recent longitudinal studies have not found evidence of the exogenously driven change processes typically associated with it (Coleman et al. 1996, Cashore and Howlett 2007).[1] In these cases, researchers have found, dramatic policy change took place in the *absence* of institutional change and involved a more complex pattern of linkages and change among the levels or orders of policy identified by Hall (1993). Cashore and Howlett (2007), for example, found paradigmatic change in US Pacific Northwest forest policy making to have occurred in a process in which existing institutions prompted paradigmatic changes in logging practices, "thermostatically", in order to protect endangered species (Cashore and Howlett 2006, 2007). Similarly, Coleman *et al.*'s studies of agricultural policy changes in the EU, Canada and Australia over a two decade period revealed a pattern in which cumulative incremental changes in policy settings and instruments led, gradually, to paradigmatic change (Coleman *et al.* 1996, Skogstad 1998). Cashore *et al.* (2001) also found that massive fluctuation in the critically important policy of timber pricing in British Columbia (which resulted in multi-million dollar shifts in government revenue from one year to the next), was indeed the result of a highly durable institutionalized system for allocation of resource rents that embedded within it a historical compromise among business interests, unions and government revenues. This suggests either that some elements of the model have been misstated and/or that more than one overall model or process of policy dynamics exists and is at work in different policy-making circumstances (a possibility suggested by Mortensen 2005). These types of seemingly anomalous findings prompt the need for a reassessment of the foundations of the new orthodox view of policy dynamics.

2. Revisiting the Foundations of the New Orthodoxy

In re-examining the present orthodoxy it is important to note the four important methodological, epistemological, and causal elements of this model which have emerged from research over the last two decades:

- First, there is widespread acceptance that any analysis of policy development must be historical in nature and cover periods of years or even decades or more (Sabatier 1993).[2]
- Second, it has generally been agreed that political institutions and their embedded policy subsystems act as the primary mechanisms of policy reproduction (Clemens and Cook 1999, Botcheva and Martin 2001, Howlett and Ramesh 2003).

- Third, "paradigmatic" change, a process in which there is a fundamental realignment of most aspects of policy development, is generally understood to occur only when the policy institutions themselves are transformed. In the absence of such processes any policy changes are hypothesized to follow "incremental" patterns (Genschel 1997, Deeg 2001).
- Fourth, many scholars studying policy dynamics agree that paradigmatic transformations or "punctuations" usually result from the effects of "external perturbations" that cause widespread disruptions in existing policy ideas, beliefs, actors, institutions and practices (Sabatier and Jenkins-Smith 1993, Smith 2000, Thelen 2003, 2004).

Taken together, these elements provide the basis for the current "orthodox" view of policy dynamics: that is, (1) an expectation of a typical set of stability processes (path dependent institutionalization) in ongoing policy deliberations; (2) the expectation of a typical pattern of policy change ("punctuated equilibrium") resulting from the breakdown of an institutionalized "policy monopoly"; and (3) a typical explanation for why this occurs (alteration in subsystem beliefs and membership usually owing to some type of societal "perturbation").

The first and second elements raise several methodological concerns for scholars interested in policy dynamics; especially answering the question of whether or not a lengthy period of time must elapse before the direction of policy change can be discerned,[3] and also determining the exact mechanisms through which institutions affect policy outcomes (and vice versa). These are interesting questions, but more problematic are the third and fourth postulates, drawn from quite selective case and comparative studies on budgetary and economic policy making which have been the feature of punctuated equilibria studies, as they have difficulty explaining other sectors and cases. To address these challenges, we must revisit existing efforts designed to classify policy and characterize its change processes.

Hall's Formulation: The Basis of the Current Orthodoxy and Its Problems

Peter Hall's (1993) effort is undoubtedly the clearest single statement of the current orthodox position on policy dynamics and is the model and classification of policy change most often cited in the literature and applied in empirical studies.[4] Hall's work appropriately challenged the dominant view in existing scholarship that tended to conflate all the elements of a "policy" into a single dependent variable (Heclo 1976, Rose 1976) and to argue that all change was incremental in nature. Drawing on divergent cases of economic policy development in Great Britain and France, Hall argued that distinguishing between the means and ends of policymaking and between abstract and concrete policy decisions was necessary to gain new insights into processes of policy stability and development.

Such an approach, for Hall, revealed three principal elements or components of a policy which, he argued, could change at different rates (small-scale, typical, incremental and larger-scale, rarer, paradigmatic form) with different consequences for overall policy dynamics. "*First order*" changes occurred when the calibrations of policy instruments, such as increasing the passenger safety or automobile emissions requirements manufacturers must follow, changed within existing institutional and instrument confines. "*Second order*" changes involved alterations to dominant types of policy instruments utilized within an existing policy regime, such as switching from an administered emission standard to an emissions tax. *"Third order"* changes involved shifts in overall abstract policy goals such as, in the pollution example, the 1990s shift in many countries from a focus upon *ex post* end-of-pipe regulation to *ex ante* preventative production process design. More significantly, Hall linked each change process to a different specific cause agent and to a specific overall pattern of "punctuated equilibrium" policy dynamics. In his view first and second order changes were typically incremental and usually the result of activities endogenous to a policy subsystem while third order changes were "paradigmatic" and occurred as anomalies arose between expected and actual results of policy implementation. The events triggering anomalies and the response to them on the part of policy makers (such as contestation within a policy community on the best course of action to pursue, or the development of new ideas about policy problems and/or solutions) were linked to exogenous events, especially societal policy learning.

This model of change, which captures the current punctuated equilibrium orthodoxy, is a variant of what cybernetic theorists refer to as a *"homeostatic"* one; that is, one in which positive and negative feedback mechanisms allow a new equilibrium to be reached after stable system parameters have been altered by outside forces (Steinbruner 1974). This change process involves a system which, like a spinning top, is constantly undergoing some kinds of (incremental) changes as it spins, but remains in one place (equilibrium) until an outside force (a foot, for example, in the case of the spinning top analogy) moves it to a new location where, after this "punctuation", a new equilibrium is established (Steinbruner 1974, Mertha and Lowry 2006). Without exogenous shocks, in Hall's model, it would be expected that existing policy elements would tend to arrange themselves in a self-perpetuating or equilibrating order, allowing (unspecified but incremental) changes in settings and instruments to occur but without altering policy goals.

The recent analyses of long-term policy change in areas such as agricultural and natural resource policy making cited above, however, question the universality of this pattern and hence challenge the last two arguments in the now prevailing orthodoxy on the nature of policy dynamics. Revisiting the existing literature on policy change reveals two problems that require the reformulation of two of the basic building blocks upon which the current orthodoxy is constructed. First, existing taxonomies designed to measure policy conflate very different forms or elements of policy. Second, and related, classifications of the types of changes different policies can, and do, undergo has been both underdeveloped and limited. Failure to address these problems results in several erroneous conclusions being drawn by Hall and others about the factors underlying policy dynamics and their appropriate modelling.

Measuring the Dependent Variable: The Need to Precisely Disaggregate Different Elements of Policy in Order to Construct Accurate Models of Policy Dynamics

The first problem with the current orthodoxy which must be rectified concerns the widely accepted model of policy composition used to describe historical patterns of policy development. This is the "dependent variable problem" uncovered by research into social and welfare policy change (Knill 2001, Green-Pedersen 2004, Kuhner 2007). As Green-Pedersen (2004) put it in his work on social welfare policy change:

It is clear that the dependent variable problem is crucial for the entire debate, and that disagreement about the dependent variable is a major obstacle for cumulative knowledge about welfare state retrenchment ... To put it bluntly, the debate about explanations of variations in retrenchment cannot move beyond the stage of hypotheses before the dependent variable problem has been addressed, and the same goes for the debate about welfare state persistence or change. Addressing the dependent variable problem should have high priority within the retrenchment literature (p. 4).

Similarly, Paul Pierson (2001) has argued that "it is difficult to exaggerate" the obstacle the dissensus over the definition, operationalization and measurement of policy change creates for comparative research and theory construction into policy dynamics.

To date, the operationalization and measurement of the dependent variable in studies of policy dynamics – "policy change" – based mainly on Hall's "three order" model, has led many scholars to inadvertently conflate several distinct change processes present in specific elements of policy. Uncovering these "hidden" and more complex patterns of policy development challenges the rather blunt binary "paradigmatic" or "incremental" characterizations that permeate much of the literature (Howlett and Ramesh 2002, Lindner 2003, Lindner and Rittberger 2003).

An improved model of policy composition. Hall's work was path breaking in its linking of different overall policy development processes to changes in the order or level of policy in flux. Still, this initial conceptual effort at classification requires recalibration in light of its own logic, as well as in light of the empirical evidence gathered in many cases of policy change analyzed since Hall's work was first published.

That is, according to Hall's own emphasis on distinguishing abstract or theoretical/conceptual goals from specific programme content or objectives, and operational settings or calibrations, along with his distinction between the aims or "ends" of policy and its actual policy requirements ("means"), it is possible to discern six, rather than three, policy elements that can undergo change (see Figure 1).

The implication of this taxonomy is that every "policy" is in fact a more complex regime of ends and means related goals (more abstract), objectives (less abstract), and settings (least abstract) than was suggested by the use of Hall's original decomposition and definition of the elements of policy into three "orders". Paying attention to these regime differences, and how each element changes or remains stable over long periods of time, results in a much more complex picture of policy dynamics emerging than is usually found in the existing literature derived from Hall's work (Liefferink 2006).[5]

Reconceptualizing the number and type of policy elements found in Hall's model, however, has serious consequences for his (and the current orthodoxy's) linking of policy elements to specific drivers of policy change and for the consideration of the number and type of possible overall patterns of policy regime change. In particular, two implications result. First, the links between policy components and endogenous and exogenous sources of policy change are seen to be more complex than Hall suggested (Bannink and Hoogenboom 2007). Second, existing classifications of

Figure 1. A modified taxonomy of policy components following Hall (cells contain examples of each measure) (1993). Modified from Cashore and Howlett (2007)

			Policy Content		
		High Level Abstraction	*Programme Level Operationalization*	*Specific On-the-Ground Measures*
	Policy Ends or Aims	**GOALS** What General Types of Ideas Govern Policy Development? (e.g. environmental protection, economic development)	**OBJECTIVES** What Does Policy Formally Aim to Address? (e.g. saving wilderness or species habitat, increasing harvesting levels to create processing jobs)	**SETTINGS** What are the Specific On-the-ground Requirements of Policy? (e.g. considerations about the optimal size of designated stream-bed riparian zones, or sustainable levels of harvesting)
Policy Focus				
	Policy Means or Tools	**INSTRUMENT LOGIC** What General Norms Guide Implementation Preferences? (e.g. preferences for the use of coercive instruments, or moral suasion)	**MECHANISMS** What Specific Types of Instruments are Utilized? (e.g. the use of different tools such as tax incentives, or public enterprises)	**CALIBRATIONS** What are the Specific Ways in Which the Instrument is used? (e.g. designations of higher levels of subsidies, the use of mandatory vs voluntary regulatory guidelines or standards)

"paradigmatic" and "incremental" policy development must be revisited so that we can better capture the complex interplay of change processes among the six different policy components. That is, in addition to distinguishing six different levels of policy which can be used to generate more nuanced descriptions of historical patterns of policy development, it is equally necessary that the proper classification tools be available to assess the degree and overall type of policy change found in any such description (Kuhner 2007).

Characterizing Change Patterns the Dependent Variable Undergoes: Distinguishing Possible Patterns of Policy Development Based on More Accurate Models of Policy Decomposition

The effort to better distinguish possible patterns of policy development sensitive to a model with six regime elements rather than three requires revisiting widely accepted assumptions within policy studies that originated in Simon's (1957) and Lindblom's (1959) early works on the subject of satisfycing and incremental policy change. The general idea that emerged from these articles, which have influenced generations of scholars, including Hall, is that incremental change is associated with marginal changes in policy means and ends, and is treated as being synonymous with a pattern of relatively long-lasting policy stability (Hayes 1992, Bendor 1995). Paradigmatic change, on the other hand, has been treated as an abnormal, atypical, relatively unstable, and usually short-lived process associated with changes in policy ends (Lustick 1980, Sabatier 1988, Baumgartner and Jones 1991, 2002). The development of "punctuated equilibrium" models underlined the importance of understanding not just incremental or paradigmatic policy processes per se, but also the manner in which these two types of change are linked together and the propensity different sectors, issue areas, or policy subsystems have to undergo these processes at different points in time (Baumgartner and Jones 2002).

Applying such an appreciation of policy dynamics, however, requires both a clear definition of what constitutes "incremental change" so that it can be distinguished from "paradigmatic", and proof that these two modes of change are the only ones possible in any given policy area. But, as has been pointed out for some time, neither a clear definition nor an exhaustive taxonomy of change types currently exists, resulting in both incremental and paradigmatic change remaining under-specified entities (Kuhn 1974, Bailey and O'Connor 1975, Berry 1990, Capano 2003).

An example of the problems encountered to date with respect to defining and classifying modes of change can be found in Durant and Diehl's (1989) work which followed paleo-biological practice in arguing that policy change types could be distinguished according to their *mode* (incremental versus paradigmatic) and speed or *tempo* (rapid versus slow) (see also Hayes 1992). This generated four distinct types of change (see Figure 2).

Figure 2. A basic taxonomy of policy change by mode and speed (cells contain typical "modes" of change). Adapted from Durant and Diehl (1989)

	Tempo or Speed of Change	
Mode of Change	*Fast*	*Slow*
Paradigmatic	Classic Paradigmatic (one large step)	Gradual Paradigmatic (one large step but a slow moving one)
Incremental	Rapid Incremental (many small but fast steps)	Classic Incremental (many small and slow moving steps)

Such formulations are useful but this specific method of classifying types of change is problematic in that (1) it includes the same concept (mode of change) as both a dependent and an independent variable; and (2) in doing so it ignores or conflates a significant dimension of change – its *"directionality"* – while overemphasizing a concern for the size of the moves away from the status quo. That is, what is most important is not simply the number of moves away from the status quo which occur over time, but whether these changes are *cumulative*, i.e., leading away from an existing equilibrium toward another, or whether they represent a fluctuation consistent with an existing policy equilibrium (on directionality see Nisbet 1972), Reconceptualizing modes of policy change as the result of the interplay of tempo and cumulative directionality provides a superior model of policy dynamics to that found in earlier work focusing on mode and tempo.

Transcending the Current Orthodoxy: Thermostatic, Neo- and Quasi-Homeostatic versus Homeostatic Models of Policy Change

Advancing the study of policy dynamics beyond the current orthodoxy requires a new taxonomy of policy change processes which takes both the additional number of policy elements and the criteria of directionality seriously in re-aggregating shifts in those elements. The homeostatic model, as suggested above, is only one possible overall model or pattern of policy change (Mortensen 2005). Other arrangements of system elements and change drivers exist and should not be ruled out *a priori* as inappropriate templates for the forms of policy dynamics found in specific sectors or issue areas. For example, one obvious such alternative would be a Hall-type regime, but where changes in goals are driven endogenously, rather than exogenously, in a process of gradual paradigmatic change. Empirical evidence for this *"neo-homeostatic"* model can be found in Coleman *et al.*'s (1996) work on agricultural policy change cited above, and also in Capano's (2003) study of Italian administrative reform. In both cases small-scale changes in policy settings – in the agriculture case through the alteration of the level of subsides, and in the Italian administrative case through variations in hiring and personnel policies – built up over the years until the original goals of the overall policy were unrecognizable.

This variant on the homeostatic model does not in any way exhaust the number of possible overall patterns of change. Others would include a *"quasi-homeostatic"* pattern in which goals are stable but where exogenously driven changes in end or means related objectives can cause paradigmatic shifts to occur. This was what appeared to happen, for example, in welfare reform driven by international organizations or influenced by "lesson drawing" (Rose 1991, Ramesh and Howlett 2006, Lee and Strang 2006) in which efforts to re-order welfare programmes to make them more efficient and market oriented resulted in changes in policy goals (from "welfare" to "workfare"). Finally, as pointed out above and has been observed in the case of US Pacific Northwest forest policy cited earlier, a *"thermostatic"* model (Buckley 1968, Gell-Mann 1992) also exists in which goals are set broadly enough to allow, or simply do not figure in, paradigmatic change driven endogenously by major alterations in end-related objectives and settings (Wlezien 1995, Cashore and Howlett 2007).[6] In the Pacific Northwest forestry case durable objectives created an institutionalized "logic of appropriateness" (March and Olson 2004) in which policy settings are likely to follow a classic incremental pattern of development until such time as a built-in thermostatic mechanism is "tripped", resulting in classic paradigmatic change through changes in policy settings and objectives.[7]

3. Conclusion

Three findings and recommendations for current and future studies of policy change emerge from this analysis. The first is that scholars must be aware of the "dependent variable" problem in studies of policy dynamics and must develop taxonomies that disentangle the policies they are measuring and describing (Mortensen 1995, Robinson and Caver 2006, Robinson et al. 2007). Failing to distinguish between different levels of policy can improperly juxtapose several distinct types of policy development and present a misleading picture of the actual pattern of change present in an empirical case.

Second, and relatedly, assessments of policy dynamics must take the "direction" of change into account. That is, rather than focus on the "mode" of change in assessing possible change types, they should distinguish policy developments that move in slightly different directions over time but never deviate much from the status quo (policies in equilibrium), from those that move in the same (new) direction over time (cumulative change) (Goldstone 1998, Pierson 2000, Deeg 2001).

Third, broad-based theories of institutional and policy change need to be careful in attributing exogenous or endogenous sources of policy development. Path-breaking work by Hall on homeostatic models linking exogenous change in goals to changes in end and means related objectives and settings may need to be modified to take into account both the possible endogeneity of change processes and the different institutional structures that can permit change to occur in other ways: for example, through neo- or quasi-homeostatic means or in a thermostatic or progressive incremental fashion (Daugbjerg 1997, 2003, Braun and Benninghoff 2003).

In summary, the reconceptualization of the "dependent variable" in studies of policy dynamics undertaken above, and the subsequent identification of six levels of policy, has helped to uncover additional overall patterns of policy development often elided by the current punctuated equilibrium orthodoxy on policy change. While more research is required in order to determine if other patterns exist, and which patterns prevail in different circumstances and why, this is an essential reconceptualization if studies of policy dynamics are going to continue to progress.

Notes

1. In a related critique, Hacker (2004) found that studies finding significant changes in policy stasis failed to assess the changing impacts of institutional stability when the problem the policies were seeking to address were undergoing significant changes.
2. This observation is explicitly raised in every project by Baumgartner and Jones on punctuated equilibrium and in Paul Sabatier and Hank Jenkins-Smith's work on "advocacy coalitions", as well as being implicit in the broad field of historical institutionalism (Sabatier 1988, 1993, Sabatier and Jenkins-Smith 1993, Mahoney 2000, Lindner and Rittberger 2003).

3. Those that wish to apply the insights of explanatory scholarship towards real world environmental and social challenges will also be frustrated by the notion that a decade must pass before meaningful conclusions can be drawn.
4. Baumgartner and Jones' many works on the subject provided the empirical backing required to support the idea that incremental policy making was in fact routinely punctuated by dramatic change. Their focus on budgetary policy was not matched by the development of generalizable taxonomy for measuring policy dynamics in other spheres (Baumgartner and Jones 1993, 2002, Mortensen 2005, John 2003).
5. For similar models based on a similar critique of Hall, see Daugbjerg (1997) and Smith (2000). These six categories are inspired from much of the work on applied policy analysis that teaches students to break policy down into their "goals", "operationalized" objectives, and specific criteria and who likewise take pains to distinguish policy instruments from "on-the-ground" policy requirements (Weimer and Vining 1999). Such a distinction is also consistent with the work of Howlett (2000) who has hypothesized and empirically demonstrated the important and independent causal impacts of process (means) based policy instruments. Similarly, Sabatier's ACF distinguishes different causal influences on different measures of policy, theorizing that "core values" or ideas behind policy can rarely change in the absence of societal transformation, but that "secondary belief systems" can lead to changes in what we are defining as "means-oriented" policy objectives and policy settings, as advocacy coalitions undergo "learning" about causal mechanisms within the policy process (Sabatier 1988).
6. In the Pacific Northwest forest policy case, formalized policy objectives were very durable and survived changing or fluctuating policy goals. This type of change process involves a system in which policy objectives obtain "institutional status" and prevent or control the amount of change possible in policy settings. Whether such institutionalized objectives will prevent or require changes in policy settings depends on their internal logics. (Cashore and Howlett 2006, 2007).
7. Clemens and Cook's (1999) work shows that "institutions" can be seen as involving formal and informal rules, policies and standard operating procedures that bind and guide behavior. The "binding" aspect is important because not all institutions, even those emanating from constitutional sources, are enduring. They can be, rather "soft" institutions (Pollock *et al.* 1993, Giuliani 1999, Abbott and Snidal 2000) that quickly adapt to outside pressure and allow significant changes to occur in policy outcomes.

References

Abbott, Kenneth W. and Snidal, Duncan, 2000, Hard and soft law in international governance. *International Organization*, **54**(3), 421–456.

Bailey, J. J. and O'Connor, R. J., 1975, Operationalizing incrementalism: measuring the muddles. *Public Administration Review*, **35**, 60–66.

Bannink, Duco and Hoogenboom, Marcel, 2007, Hidden change: disaggregation of welfare regimes for greater insight into welfare state change. *Journal of European Social Policy*, **17**(1), 19–32.

Baumgartner, Frank and Jones, Bryan, 1991, Agenda dynamics and policy subsystems. *The Journal of Politics*, **53**(4), 1044–1074.

Baumgartner, Frank and Jones, Bryan, 1993, *Agendas and Instability in American Politics* (Chicago: University of Chicago Press).

Baumgartner, Frank R. and Jones, Bryan D. (Eds), 2002, *Policy Dynamics* (Chicago: University of Chicago Press).

Bendor, Jonathan, 1995, A model of muddling through. *American Political Science Review*, **89**(4), 819–840.

Berry, W. T., 1990, The confusing case of budgetary incrementalism: too many meanings for a single concept. *Journal of Politics*, **52**, 167–196.

Botcheva, Liliana and Martin, Lisa L., 2001, Institutional effects on state behaviour: convergence and divergence. *International Studies Quarterly*, **45**(1), 1–26.

Braun, Dietmar and Benninghoff, Martin, 2003, Policy learning in Swiss research policy: the case of the national centres of competence in research, *Research Policy*, **32**, 1849–1863.

Buckley, Walter, 1968, Society as a complex adaptive system, in: W. Buckley (Ed.) *Modern System Research for the Behavioural Scientist* (Chicago: Aldine Publishing Company), pp. 490–513.

Capano, G., 2003, Administrative traditions and policy change: when policy paradigms matter, the case of Italian administrative reform during the 1990s. *Public Administration*, **81**(4), 781–801.

Cashore, B. and Howlett, M., 2006, Behavioural thresholds and institutional rigidities as explanations of punctuated equilibrium processes in Pacific Northwest forest policy dynamics, in: R. Repetto (Ed.) *Punctuated Equilibrium and the Dynamics of U.S. Environmental Policy* (New Haven, CT: Yale University Press), pp. 137–161.

Cashore, Benjamin and Howlett, Michael, 2007, Punctuating which equilibrium? Understanding thermostatic policy dynamics in Pacific Northwest forestry. *American Journal of Political Science*, **51**(3), 532–551.

Cashore, Benjamin, Hoberg, George, Howlett, Michael, Rayner, Jeremy and Wilson, Jeremy, 2001, *In Search of Sustainability: British Columbia Forest Policy in the 1990s* (Vancouver: University of British Columbia Press), Chapter four: "Timber pricing: change as a function of stability".

Clemens, Elisabeth S. and Cook, James M., 1999, Politics and institutionalism: explaining durability and change. *Annual Review of Sociology*, **25**, 441–466.

Coleman, W. D., Skogstad, G. D. and Atkinson, M., 1996, Paradigm shifts and policy networks: cumulative change in agriculture. *Journal of Public Policy*, **16**(3), 273–302.

Daugbjerg, Carsten, 1997, Policy networks and agricultural policy reforms: explaining deregulation in Sweden and re-regulation in the European Community. *Governance*, **10**(2), 123–142.

Daugbjerg, Carsten, 2003, Policy feedback and paradigm shift in EU agricultural policy: the effects of the MacSharry reform on future reform. *Journal of European Public Policy*, **10**(3), 421–437.

Deeg, Richard, 2001, *Institutional Change and the Uses and Limits of Path Dependency: The Case of German Finance* (Cologne: Max Planck Institute fur Gesellschaftsforschung MPIfG).

Deeg, Richard, 2005, Change from within: German and Italian finance in the 1990s, in: Wolfgang Streeck and Kathleen Thelen (Eds) *Beyond Continuity: Institutional Change in Advanced Political Economies* (Oxford: Oxford University Press), pp. 169–202.

Durant, Robert F. and Diehl, Paul F., 1989, Agendas, alternatives and public policy: lessons from the U.S. foreign policy arena. *Journal of Public Policy*, **9**(2), 179–205.

Eldredge, N. and Gould, S.J., 1972, Punctuated equilibria: an alternative to phyletic gradualism, in: T.J.M. Schopf (Ed.) *Paleobiology* (San Francisco: Freeman, Cooper), pp. 82–115.

Gell-Mann, Murray (1992) Complexity and complex adaptive systems, in: J. A. Hawkins and M. Gell-Mann (Ed.) *The Evolution of Human Languages* (Redwood City: Addison-Wesley), pp. 3–18.

Genschel, Philipp, 1997, The dynamics of inertia: institutional persistence and change in telecommunications and health care. *Governance*, **10**(1), 43–66.

Giuliani, Mark, 1999, "Soft" institutions for hard problems: instituting air pollution policies in three Italian regions, in: W. Grant, A. Perl and P. Knoepfel (Ed.) *The Politics of Improving Urban Air Quality* (Cheltenham: Edward Elgar), pp. 31–51.

Goldstone, Jack A., 1998, Initial conditions, general laws, path dependence, and explanation in historical sociology. *American Journal of Sociology*, **104**(3), 829–845.

Gould, S. J. and Eldredge, N., 1977, Punctuated equilibria: the tempo and mode of evolution reconsidered. *Paleobiology*, **3**, 115–151.

Green-Pedersen, Christoffer, 2004, The dependent variable problem within the study of welfare state retrenchment: defining the problem and looking for solutions. *Journal of Comparative Policy Analysis*, **6**(1), 3–14.

Hacker, Jacob, 2004, Privatizing risk without privatizing the welfare state: the hidden politics of social policy retrenchment in the United States. *American Political Science Review*, **98**(2), 243–260.

Hall, Peter (Ed.), 1989, *The Political Power of Economic Ideas: Keynesianism across Nations* (Princeton: Princeton University Press).

Hall, Peter, 1993, Policy paradigms, social learning, and the state: the case of economic policymaking in Britain. *Comparative Politics*, **25**(3), 275.

Hayes, Michael, 1992, *Incrementalism and Public Policy* (New York: Longman).

Heclo, Hugh, 1976, Conclusion: policy dynamics, in: R. Rose (Ed.) *The Dynamics of Public Policy: A Comparative Analysis* (London: Sage), pp. 237–266.

Howlett, Michael, 2000, Managing the "hollow state": procedural policy instruments and modern governance. *Canadian Public Administration*, **43**(4), 412–431.

Howlett, Michael and Ramesh, M., 2002, The policy effects of internationalization: a subsystem adjustment analysis of policy change. *Journal of Comparative Policy Analysis*, **4**(3), 31–50.

Howlett, M. and Ramesh, M., 2003, *Studying Public Policy: Policy Cycles and Policy Subsystems* (Toronto: Oxford University Press).

Howlett, Michael and Rayner, Jeremy, 2006, Understanding the historical turn in the policy sciences: a critique of stochastic, narrative, path dependency and process-sequencing models of policy-making over time. *Policy Sciences*, **39**(1), 1–18.

John, P. and Margetts, H., 2003, Policy punctuations in the UK: fluctuations and equilibria in central government expenditure since 1951. *Public Administration*, **81**(3), 411–432.

Kay, Adrian, 2006, *The Dynamics of Public Policy: Theory and Evidence* (Cheltenham: Edward Elgar).

Kingdon, J. W., 1995, *Agendas, Alternatives and Public Policies* (Boston: HarperCollins College Publishers).

Knill, C. 2001. *The Europeanization of National Administrations: Patterns of Institutional Change and Persistence* (Cambridge: Cambridge University Press).

Kuhn, T. S., 1962, *The Structure of Scientific Revolutions* (Chicago: University of Chicago Press).

Kuhn, T. S., 1974, Second thoughts on paradigms, in: F. Suppe (Ed.) *The Structure of Scientific Theories* (Urbana: University of Illinois Press), pp. 459–482.

Kuhner, Stefan, 2007, Country-level comparisons of welfare state change measures: another facet of the dependent variable problem within the comparative analysis of the welfare state. *Journal of European Social Policy*, **17**(1), 5–18.

Leach, William D. and Sabatier, Paul A., 2005, To trust an adversary: integrating rational and psychological models of collaborative policymaking. *American Political Science Review*, **99**(4), 491–503.

Lee, C. K. and Strang, D., 2006, The international diffusion of public-sector downsizing: Network emulation and theory-driven learning. *International Organization*, **60**(3), 883–909.

Liefferink, Duncan, 2006, The dynamics of policy arrangements: turning round the tetrahedron, in: Bas Arts and Pieter Leroy (Eds) *Institutional Dynamics in Environmental Governance* (Dordrecht: Springer), pp. 45–68.

Lindblom, Charles E., 1959, The science of muddling through. *Public Administration Review*, **19**(2), 79–88.

Lindner, Johannes, 2003, Institutional stability and change: two sides of the same coin. *Journal of European Public Policy*, **10**(6), 912–935.

Lindner, Johannes and Rittberger, Berthold, 2003, The creation, interpretation and contestation of institutions – revisiting historical institutionalism. *Journal of Common Market Studies*, **41**(3), 445–473.

Lustick, Ian, 1980, Explaining the variability utility of disjointed incrementalism: four propositions. *American Political Science Review*, **74**(2), 342–353.

Mahoney, James, 2000, Path dependence in historical sociology. *Theory and Society*, **29**(4), 507–548.

March, James G. and Olsen, Johan P., 2004, *The Logic of Appropriateness* (Oslo: University of Oslo Centre for European Studies).

Mertha, Andrew C. and Lowry, William R., 2006, Seminal events and policy change in China, Australia and the United States. *Comparative Politics*, **39**(1), 1–20.

Mortensen, Peter B., 2005, Policy punctuations in Danish local budgeting. *Public Administration*, **83**(4), 931–950.

Nisbet, Robert, 1972, Introduction: the problem of social change, in: R. Nisbet (Ed.) *Social Change* (New York: Harper and Row), pp. 1–45.

Pierson, Paul, 1993, When effect becomes cause: policy feedback and political change. *World Politics*, **45**(4), 595–628.

Pierson, Paul, 2000, Increasing returns, path dependence, and the study of politics. *American Political Science Review*, **94**(2), 251–268.

Pierson, Paul, 2001, Coping with permanent austerity: welfare state restructuring in affluent democracies, in: Paul Pierson (Ed.) *The New Politics of the Welfare State* (Oxford: Oxford University Press), pp. 410–456.

Pollock, Philip H. III, Lilie, Stuart A. and Vittes, M. Elliot, 1993, Hard issues, core values and vertical constraint: the case of nuclear power. *British Journal of Political Science*, **23**(1), 29–50.

Ramesh, M. and Howlett, Michael, 2006, *Deregulation and Its Discontents: Rewriting the Rules in Asia* (Cheltenham, UK; Northampton, MA: Edward Elgar).

Robinson, S. E. and Caver, F. S. R., 2006, Punctuated equilibrium and congressional budgeting. *Political Research Quarterly*, **59**(1), 161–166.

Robinson, Scott E., Caver, Flou'say, Meier, Kenneth J. and O'Toole, Lawrence J. Jr., 2007, Explaining policy punctuations: bureaucratization and budget change. *American Journal of Political Science*, **51**(1), 140–150.
Rose, Richard, 1976, Models of change, in: R. Rose (Ed.) *The Dynamics of Public Policy: A Comparative Analysis* (London: Sage), pp. 7–23.
Rose, R., 1991, What is lesson-drawing? *Journal of Public Policy*, **11**(1), 3–30.
Sabatier, Paul, 1988, An advocacy coalition framework of policy change and the role of policy-oriented learning therein. *Policy Sciences*, **21**(2), 129–168.
Sabatier, P., 1993, Policy change over a decade or more, in: P. A. Sabatier and H. C. Jenkins-Smith (Eds) *Policy Change and Learning: An Advocacy Coalition Approach* (Boulder, CO: Westview), pp. 13–40.
Sabatier, Paul and Jenkins-Smith, Hank (Eds), 1993, *Policy Learning and Policy Change: An Advocacy Coalition Approach* (Boulder, CO: Westview Press).
Simon, Herbert A., 1957, *Administrative Behavior: A Study of Decision-Making Processes in Administrative Organization* (New York: MacMillan).
Skogstad, G., 1998, Ideas, paradigms and institutions: agricultural exceptionalism in the European Union and the United States. *Governance*, **11**(4), 463–490.
Smith, Adrian, 2000, Policy networks and advocacy coalitions: explaining policy change and stability in UK industrial pollution policy. *Environment and Planning C: Government and Policy*, **18**(1), 95–114.
Steinbruner, John D., 1974, *The Cybernetic Theory of Decision: New Dimensions of Political Analysis* (Princeton, NJ: Princeton University Press).
Steinmo, S., Thelen, K. and Longstreth, F. (Eds), 1992, *Structuring Politics: Historical Institutionalism in Comparative Analysis*, Cambridge Studies in Comparative Politics (Cambridge, Cambridge University Press).
Thelen, Kathleen, 2003, How institutions evolve: insights from comparative historical analysis, in: J. Mahoney and D. Rueschemeyer (Eds) *Comparative Historical Analysis in the Social Sciences* (Cambridge: Cambridge University Press), pp. 208–240.
Thelen, Kathleen, 2004, *How Institutions Evolve: The Political Economy of Skills in Germany, Britain, the United States and Japan* (Cambridge: Cambridge University Press).
Weaver, R. Kent and Rockman, Bert A. (Eds), 1993, *Do Institutions Matter?* (Washington, DC: The Brookings Institution).
Weimer, David L. and Vining, Aidan R., 1999, *Policy Analysis: Concepts and Practice*, 2nd edition (Englewood Cliffs, NJ: Prentice-Hall).
Wlezien, Christopher, 1995, The public as thermostat: dynamics of preferences for spending. *American Journal of Political Science*, **39**(4), 981–1000.

Mechanisms of Policy Change: A Proposal for a Synthetic Explanatory Framework

JOSÉ REAL-DATO

ABSTRACT *Since the early 1990s, the theoretical debate on policy change in the field of policy studies has been clearly dominated by three major reference approaches – the advocacy coalition framework (ACF), the punctuated-equilibrium theory (PET), and the multiple streams approach (MS). Their success led the reference approaches to evolve separately without explicitly establishing communication across theoretical boundaries. This has greatly limited the advance of the debate in order to get a better understanding of policy change. The three reference approaches have proved to offer widely contrasting and accepted accounts of policy change. They also present a number of shortcomings which render partial the explanations and limit their applicability. Starting from the analysis of these points, this article is devoted to the main purpose of presenting a synthetic theoretical framework that both profits from the strengths and commonalities of the three reference approaches – by emphasizing the complementarity of the causal explanations they devise – and solves the detected problems – through providing a more precise specification of theoretical relationships among the conceptual elements of the framework.*

Introduction

Since the early 1990s, the theoretical debate on policy change in the field of policy studies has been clearly dominated by three major reference approaches – the *advocacy coalition framework* (ACF) (Sabatier 1987, 1988, Sabatier and Jenkins-Smith 1993), the *punctuated-equilibrium theory* (PET) (Baumgartner and Jones 1993), and the *multiple streams* approach (MS) (Kingdon [1984] 1995). Along the years, these lenses have widely attracted the attention of policy scholars, generating (in particular, in the case of ACF and PET) authentic research programmes which have constituted fertile soil for a great deal of academic research (for a review, see Sabatier 2007a).[1]

Nevertheless, their success led the reference approaches to evolve separately without explicitly establishing communication across theoretical boundaries. This has greatly limited the advance of the debate in order to get a better understanding of policy change. In this sense, in 2003 Peter John asked an intriguing question: "[Was] there life after Policy Streams, Advocacy Coalitions, and Punctuations?" (John 2003). His answer was that, although the reference approaches had been subject to further development along the years (i.e. Jones 1994, 2001, Sabatier and Jenkins-Smith 1999, Jones and Baumgartner 2005, Sabatier and Weible 2007, True *et al.* 2007), "nothing [had] changed the direction of thinking in the same way that the cluster of books and articles at the beginning of the 1990s did" (John 2003: 481–482). As an alternative, John proposes an "evolutionary theory" of the policy process which he contends is implicit in the three reference frameworks. Nevertheless, the problems such an alternative implies are so many (Dowding 2000) that even John himself acknowledges that it may not add very much to conventional narratives and models (John 2003: 495).

The present article follows a different strategy. The three reference approaches have proved to offer widely contrasting and accepted accounts of policy change. Nevertheless, they also present a number of shortcomings which render partial the explanations and limit their applicability. Starting from the analysis of these points in the next two sections, the rest of this article is devoted to the main purpose of presenting a synthetic theoretical framework that both profits from the strengths and commonalities of the three reference approaches – by emphasizing the complementarity of the causal explanations they devise – and solves the detected problems – through providing a more precise specification of theoretical relationships among the conceptual elements of the framework.

Policy Dynamics in the Three Reference Approaches

The basis of the success of the MS, the ACF, and the PET is their commitment to providing true causal explanations of the policy process – in contrast to the until then predominant approach based on the stage-heuristics model. In this sense, the three reference approaches aim to uncover the underlying generative causal processes (Goldthorpe 2001) that constitute the drivers of policy dynamics (change and stability).

In the explanatory accounts provided by the three reference approaches there are a number of common elements that constitute the basic structure that will allow their further integration in a single framework. Firstly, they take the subsystem – the set of actors interested in a policy issue or problem that interact forming decisional systems – as the basic unit of analysis. Secondly, their explanatory accounts rest on the behaviour of rational-bounded actors who interact within the subsystem's boundaries. Finally, the three approaches emphasize the causal role played by ideational factors (that is, actors' interpretations, ideas, and beliefs about public policies).

Despite these common features, the explanations of the policy process the three reference lenses offer clearly differ. The MS focuses on the agenda-setting process – although it has subsequently been adapted to explain policy adoption (Zahariadis 1999, 1995b). Agenda change is presented by the MS as a result of the coupling of three independent "streams" – problems, policy alternatives and macro-political context. In broad terms, the coupling depends on the opening of opportunity windows for advocating actors to promote their pet solutions or issues, and on the skilfulness of policy entrepreneurs to exploit such opportunities. Regarding the PET, it applies to both agenda setting and policy adoption, aiming to explain both policy change and stability. The latter is a result of the joint action of institutional decision structures and constructed positive policy understandings (images), which contribute to maintain the monopolistic control over the issue by a set of dominant participants.

Policy change takes place when change proponents (entrepreneurs) manage to subvert the existing policy monopoly through the redefinition of the policy image and the subsequent expansion of the conflict outside the boundaries of the policy subsystem to attract previously uninterested allies in more favourable decisional venues. Finally, the ACF also aims to explain policy change and stability along dilated time periods (over 10 or more years). Since policies are conceived as mirroring participants' beliefs systems, policy dynamics are equated with the changes in such beliefs. These are structured in three levels – deep core of basic beliefs, policy core beliefs, and secondary aspects. Since deep core and policy core beliefs are closely tied to individual identities, these levels are extraordinarily resistant to change in the light of incoming information. That is why cognitive policy change as a consequence of learning only affects secondary aspects. Major policy change (affecting policy core beliefs) is mainly non-cognitive, and only takes place in case of external perturbations in the political or socio-economic environment altering the composition of the policy coalition and its power position, endogenous shocks affecting the policy subsystem, or from a negotiated agreement between participants in case of harmful stalemate.[2]

Shortcomings in the Three Reference Approaches

Notwithstanding their wide acceptation and success, these approaches have not been exempt from criticisms.[3] They can be grouped in three levels. The first level refers to the *incompleteness of generative causal processes* offered by the three approaches (John 2003). In this respect, two major "blind spots" have been identified by the literature. The first one refers to the scarce attention the three lenses pay to microlevel processes, that is, the way participants' actions affect the policy process. Both the MS and the PET overlook the problems of collective action and co-ordination among participants that arise during the process of policy change – this is particularly important regarding the PET, since mobilization processes associated with conflict expansion are considered central in this approach (Schlager 2007: 303). Only the ACF – after being the target of major criticisms to its first versions (Schlager 1995, 1999, Schlager and Blomquist 1996) – has dealt with the problems of collective action and coordination in advocacy coalitions in subsequent revisions (Zafonte and Sabatier 1998, Sabatier and Jenkins-Smith 1999, Sabatier and Weible 2007).

A second blind spot is the gross specification of the role of institutions. Since the early 1980s, political scientists have been aware of the need to take into account in their explanations the way institutions influence individual behaviour (Hall and Taylor 1996, Peters 1999). Here institutions are understood as "humanly devised constraints that shape human interaction" (North 1990: 3). Institutions include (formal and informal) *rules* – "shared prescriptions (must, must not, or may) that are mutually understood and predictable enforced in particular situations by agents responsible for monitoring conduct and for imposing sanctions" – and *social norms* – "shared prescriptions that tend to be enforced by the participants themselves through internally and externally imposed costs and inducements" (Ostrom 1999a: 37, see also McAdams 1997). In this respect, reference approaches offer a very limited treatment of the institutional constraints at work shaping participants' behaviour in the policy process. The MS deals with institutions unsystematically and at a gross level of specification, treating them as part of the political environment affecting coupling – putting them together with other non-agency factors such as personal turnover or focusing events. In its turn, institutional elements also play a secondary role in the ACF. They appear as the targets of the coalitions' strategic behaviour, similar to PET's *venue shopping* (Sabatier and Jenkins-Smith 1999: 142) or as contextual elements affecting policy change (i.e., constitutional changes as factors producing substantive policy change). As with collective action, institutions seem to have advanced their stance in this framework only recently (i.e., the influence of institutional opportunity structure on coalition's behaviour – Sabatier and Weible 2007), although deeper theoretical account is still needed. In any case, the ACF only considers institutions in depth when dealing with the characteristics of policy *fora* promoting policy learning. Finally, the PET also calls for a more detailed treatment of institutions. For instance, in explaining conflict expansion, it would be necessary to precise how institutional structures affect the receptivity of the new policy image, the formation of alliances, or how institutional structures facilitate or hinder the impact of exogenous factors within the policy monopoly. Recent versions of the PET offer an even more abstract use of institutions as factors affecting systemic information processing (Jones and Baumgartner 2005).

This misspecification of microlevel processes and institutional constraints reflects a third blind spot, namely the weak theoretical articulation of *boundary relationships*. On the one hand, this term refers to the relationships between policy subsystems and their environment, and particularly to the mechanisms through which causal influences traverse subsystem boundaries both inwards and outwards. This is an important point, since the three reference approaches consider environmental factors (institutions and other actors outside the policy subsystem) as key elements in explaining substantive policy change. In the MS approach environmental processes (those in the political stream) remain grossly characterized as more or less conjunctural opportunities that entrepreneurs must seize. Entrepreneurs are, then, represented in a basically expectant stance, waiting for the opening of opportunity windows, while more proactive behaviour (i.e., actively looking for more favourable institutional venues) is considered less important. Boundary relationships are also of most importance in the PET, as policy change is presented as a result of conflict expansion outside the subsystem's boundaries. Nevertheless, the account this approach offers of how external actors in favourable policy venues are attracted as allies – as a consequence of attention shift resulting from image redefinition – is incomplete, since it does not explain how redefined policy images influence external actors' incentives to get involved in previously unattractive policy issues. Regarding the ACF, in its first versions the relationship between exogenous factors and substantive policy change was mechanically presented (Mintron and Vergari 1996: 422, Nohrstedt 2005). Later revisions have introduced new elements in order to explain such connection – policy entrepreneurs, structures of opportunity, redefinition processes, or bias mobilization (Sabatier and Jenkins-Smith 1999: 147–149, Sabatier and Weible 2007). However, the process of transmission of exogenous influences (being institutional or not) still requires further specification regarding how they affect participants' behaviour.

On the other hand, boundary relationships also refer to the interactions among specialized decisional sub-units within the subsystem – which can present substantial overlapping with each other or, in the contrary, be quite distinct (Rayner *et al.*

2001: 320). The study of the interactions between these sub-units is clearly interesting in order to understand subsystem dynamics. Nevertheless, the reference approaches ignore such processes, with the exception of the treatment by the ACF of overlapping subsystems (Zafonte and Sabatier 1998).

The second level of criticism refers to the *limited explanatory scope* of the three reference approaches, in the sense that each one of them tends to favour a particular causal path of policy change (John 2003). This is particularly important since it contributes to reduce the ability of the different approaches to cope with the inherent complexity of policy change processes. The problem applies mainly to the MS and the PET. The former favours in explanation environmental factors outside the policy subsystem over other causal vectors, such as policy entrepreneurs' strategic behaviour (who usually limit themselves to keeping the policy alternative or issue warm in hope that the opportunity window will open) or policy learning (which takes place only within the policy community in the alternative selection stage, without influencing final policy change). In its turn, the PET emphasizes as the causal drive of substantive policy change entrepreneurs' strategic behaviour in mobilizing other participants, manipulating images, searching for policy venues, and expanding conflict outside the subsystem. In contrast, learning is left aside, even though it may be an important element in explaining why some subsystem participants become unsatisfied with the working of policy monopolies and cause conflict expansion. Regarding the ACF, it has been more prone to consider different causal paths of policy change. In its first versions, it favoured two causal paths: learning (only producing minor policy change) and shocks external to the subsystem (as responsible for major policy change). Along time, in subsequent revisions of the framework these causal paths have been developed in more detail. In addition, other causal paths to major policy change have been added, such as internal shocks affecting the subsystem and negotiated agreements among coalitions (Sabatier and Weible 2007).

Finally, the third level of criticism refers to *the problem of the explanandum*, that is, what changes when policy changes. The ACF associates policy change with change in dominant coalition's beliefs, ignoring the institutional structures and strategic dynamics that mediate between beliefs and the content of policy programmes (Schlager 1999: 252). In their turn, the MS and the PET focus on changes in the decisional agenda and the level of policy production (i.e. number of regulations or the size of the budget related to a given issue). However, none of them pays attention to the outputs of policy decisions, that is, the policy designs which are actually implemented (Hayes 2001: 96, John 2003: 489).

Conceptual Components of a Synthetic Framework for Explaining Policy Change

The three reference approaches clearly represent a major advance in the study and explanation of policy change, as is confirmed by their wide acceptance and utilization by policy scholars. However, the criticisms outlined in the previous section show that more theoretical work is needed in order to reach a more complete understanding of policy change (Sabatier 2007b). In this sense, the three approaches may constitute the starting point for elaborating a more comprehensive theoretical synthesis, which takes into account both their main advances and amends their critical points.

Regarding the problem of the *explanandum*, an alternative would be to focus on *policy designs* – defined as "observable phenomena found in statutes, administrative guidelines, court decrees, programs, and even the practices and procedures of street level case workers as they interact with policy recipients" (Schneider and Ingram 1997: 2) – as the main *output* of the policy process. Thus, policy change could be assessed by examining the variations along time of the different empirically observable components of policy designs.[4]

Together with the *explanandum*, such a theoretical synthesis would require to deal with the problems detected in the *explanans*, that is, the incompleteness of the generative causal processes. To that end, Ostrom and associates' institutional analysis and development framework (IAD) (Kiser and Ostrom 1982, Ostrom 1990, 1999a, 2005, Ostrom et al. 1994) seems to offer a suitable theoretic-conceptual baseline. Here, the concept of "framework" is used in its strict sense (Ostrom 1999a) – in contrast to those of "theories" and "models" – as a tool to identify the "set of variables and relationships that should be examined to explain a set of phenomena" (Sabatier 2007b: 322).[5] The IAD framework is particularly suitable to solve the abovementioned blind spots of neglected microlevel processes and gross specification of institutions, as it emphasizes social explanation based on actors' interactions within the limits established by the relevant institutional structures. In the field of public policy, the IAD has been used mainly to study how actors solve the problems related to the management of common-pool resources (Ostrom 1990, 1999b, Ostrom et al. 1994). Regarding policy change, the framework has been discarded by arguing that it mainly accounts for incremental policy change (Schlager 1999: 252, 2007: 309). Nevertheless, this assertion particularly applies mainly to the "common-pool resources theory", which presents policy-institutional change in the context of polycentric decision settings, and not to the general IAD framework, which is perfectly compatible with the explanation of substantive policy change. Table 1 summarizes the different conceptual elements of the IAD framework.

These elements constitute the conceptual skeleton from which to develop a more detailed account of the generative causal process behind policy change and stability. In such an account, the policy subsystem occupies a central position. In IAD terms, the policy subsystem will comprehend an action arena where actively interested actors in a problem or policy (*participants*) interact in order to influence implementation, day-to-day decisions (*operational level*) and/or policy designs (*collective choice level*). Participants may be classified in three main categories: public decision makers (state agents), insiders (actors and organizations with access to the decisional core) and outsiders (actors and organizations with limited access to the decisional core – Maloney et al. 1994, Page 1999). Patterns of interaction within the subsystem (action arena) vary depending on 1) the components of the action situation (participants, relative positions they occupy, actions, the range of possible results, information circulating within the action situation, benefits and costs they can obtain, and available resources), 2) the type of actors (with their preferences and beliefs over the action situation), and 3) external factors (formal and informal rules affecting the action situation, community attributes, and material conditions). Policy designs are a result of these patterns of interaction (Figure 1).

One of the advantages of using the IAD as a baseline conceptual framework is that it pays attention to the links existing between action arenas (Ostrom 2005: 57ff.).

Table 1. Elements of the IAD framework

Action arena	Social space where individuals interact (Ostrom 1999a: 42–43). Every action arena consists of: a) participants, and b) an action situation.
Participants	Bounded-rational actors; preferences influenced by shared culture and experiences; motivations ranging from material interests to normative orientations.
Action situation	"Whenever two or more individuals are faced with a set of potential actions that jointly produce outcomes" (Ostrom 2005: 32). Actions situations consist in: 1) *participants*; 2) *positions* they occupy; 3) set of *actions* available to participants; 4) *results* linked to actions; 5) *information* about the situation; 6) *costs and benefits* linked to actions and results; and 7) degree of participant's *control*.
Rules	"Shared understandings by participants about enforced prescriptions concerning what actions (or outcomes) are required, prohibited, or permitted" (Ostrom 2005: 18); rules structure action situations by affecting their different elements. They are classified in (in the order corresponding to the elements of the action situations they regulate): 1) boundary rules, 2) position rules, 3) choice rules, 4) scope rules, 5) information rules, 6) payoff rules, and 7) aggregation rules (Ostrom 2005: 190).
Exogenous factors	These are: 1) *Material or biophysical conditions* affecting the action situation; 2) *Community attributes* (generally accepted social norms, common understandings about the structure of action arenas, and the social distribution of preferences and resources).
Levels of analysis	Rules organized in three hierarchical ordered levels of analysis: 1) *operational level* (rules affecting participants' day-to-day decisions); 2) *collective choice level* (rules regulating decision making affecting the operational level); 3) *constitutional level* (rules regulating the making of collective choice rules).

This is important, since, as it has been stated above, policy dynamics are influenced by events occurring in other action arenas, both outside (other subsystems or macro-political action arenas) and within (specialized sub-units, organizational actors, actor's coalitions) the subsystem. The IAD thus allows a more detailed specification of the generative causal process accounting for policy change by incorporating *boundary relationships* into the analysis.

Specifying boundary relationships requires changing the scope of the unit of analysis from the subsystem to a wider *policy space* of analytically relevant policy interactions. In IAD terms, policy space may be defined as *the analytic whole formed by related action arenas which influence in a relevant way the final result of the considered policy process*. The boundaries of such policy space do not depend on substantive criteria – as it occurs, in contrast, with other concepts such as that of "policy domain"[6] – but on the relevance of the links among action arenas to the event to be explained. This is important to bear in mind, since relevant events affecting the policy process may not have substantive relationship with the policy issues at stake – as it occurs with some exogenous impacts (see below).

The concept of policy space allows generative causal processes involving elements from the subsystem's environment, actors and institutions in other action arenas, material conditions and community attributes, to be better specified. According to

Figure 1. Schematic representation of a policy subsystem (action arena)

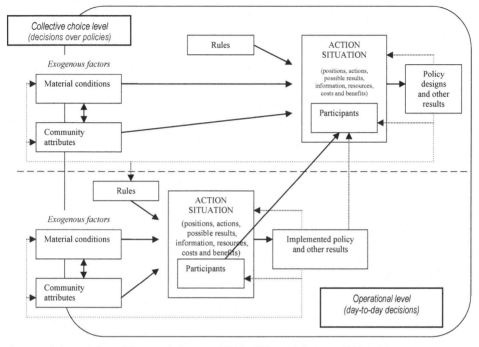

Source: Adapted from Kiser and Ostrom (1982: 207) and Ostrom (2005: 15).

the reference approaches (mainly the ACF and the PET), policy stability is directly related to a subsystem's autonomy – revealed by the maintenance of an internal equilibrium among subsystem participants and the ability of the subsystem's decisional core to be isolated from external influences. Such equilibrium is institutionally induced (Shepsle 1979) and it would mainly reflect the interests of dominant actors and/or coalitions of actors (Moe 1990, 2006). Subsystem rules would achieve two main tasks: 1) they would reduce co-ordination costs among subsystem participants by making predictable internal processes; and 2) they grant a subsystem's dominant actors control over policy design and implementation. This is done by limiting access to unacceptable actors (boundary rules); by assigning positions, alternatives for action, and control over decision making and veto points unevenly among participants (position, choice and aggregation rules); by controlling the available information and its flow within and outside the subsystem (information rules); by distributing unevenly costs and benefits among participants (payoff rules); and/or by establishing which outcomes are permitted or prohibited (scope rules). Besides, in accordance with the PET, the isolation of the subsystem's decisional core from external interference would also be a result of the ability by dominant participants to link this institutional design to a positive *image* of the policy at stake, connected to widely accepted social and political values. Such image would contribute to de-legitimate any attempt to alter the current institutional configuration of the policy subsystem.

In sum, the subsystem's institutional structure and the policy image would be the basis of the processes of *negative feedback* in charge of correcting potential deviations able to alter subsystem's internal equilibrium identified by Baumgartner and Jones (1993, 2002b). They would also contribute to favouring routine within the subsystem and, thus, policy continuity. But along this homeostatic function identified by the PET, institutions also contribute to policy stability through a *positive feedback* mechanism (Pierson 2004). As they are accepted and enforced, co-ordination among policy participants stabilizes on the incentive structure established by subsystem rules. Then participants and target populations must adapt their strategies to such incentive structure. Thus, institutional structure also promotes policy stability by shaping participants' preferences and behaviour along time (March and Olsen 1984: 739–740). Besides, as times goes by, policy change will be more difficult as participants' sunk costs increase (particularly if participants' adaptation requires periodical reinvestment), and if their gains from current policy status quo are of the increasing returns form (Pierson 2004: 142ff.). Here should be added the uncertainty of future benefits in case of policy change and the costs of surmounting the negative feedback mechanism protecting the current status quo.

In these situations where subsystems are autonomous, *the limits of the policy subsystem coincide with the analytical policy space*. Nevertheless, policy subsystems – even policy monopolies, those subsystems where rules completely exclude outsiders from decisions – are not in total isolation from their environment. On the one hand, changes in *material conditions* and the *attributes of the community* may affect their internal configuration. In situations of stability, these exogenous factors are included as given constants in the functioning of the action arena (this is represented in Figure 1 by the overlapping of the boxes containing these variables over the action arena). However, material conditions and community attributes are not under complete control. They may be affected by a subsystem's results – both at the operational and the collective choice level (this is represented in Figure 1 by the dotted feedback lines) – or they may change independently from the subsystem's inner dynamics.

Environmental influences may also transmit into the subsystem through the existing connections between the subsystem and other action arenas. This is called here *subsystem permeability* and it implies that, when influences go across a subsystem's boundaries, the limits of the analytical policy space expand too.

Relationships between the subsystem and other action arenas may be schematically grouped in two categories: *vertical* and *horizontal*. Vertical relationships involve the existence of a *hierarchical-institutional component*. External rules at higher analytical levels, as in the case of subsystems nested within wider action arenas, may affect subsystem structuring conditions (that is, its inner rules) or actors' behaviour (i.e., actors' organizational affiliations may make their preferences and strategies dependent on the orders and instructions they receive from their hierarchical superiors). In contrast, horizontal links *exclude such a hierarchical component*, implying that subsystem processes are influenced by the non-institutional results in other action arenas (and, sometimes, vice versa). Horizontal links may be based on *functional (inter)dependencies* affecting both/either the subsystem as a whole and/or specific participants (who overlap in both action arenas), or on existing *homomorphisms* (structural similarities) between action arenas. Here subsystem permeability depends on participants' cognitive predisposition and ability to interpret information from the environment. For instance, decisions taken in other structurally similar subsystems may give rise to feelings of inequality among participants or illustrate new policy alternatives. In any case, the co-existence in the policy process of formal and informal relationships may make both types of vertical and horizontal relationships converge simultaneously.

In sum, using the IAD as a baseline framework for the study of the policy process helps to surmount the problem of incompleteness that has been identified in the causal accounts of policy dynamics offered by the three reference approaches. The following section deals with the problem of their limited explanatory scope.

Mechanisms of Policy Change

As a result of their theoretical origins, the three reference frameworks have tended to favour particular causal paths in explaining policy change. For instance, the importance Baumgartner and Jones conceded to the process of mobilization of bias (Schaatschneider 1960), led them to assign a central role to such a process in the explanation of policy punctuations. In contrast, the MS owes much of its emphasis on serendipity in agenda setting to the inspiration provided by the "garbage can" model of decision making (Cohen *et al.* 1972). Finally, Sabatier and Jenkins-Smith's account of the limited influence of policy-oriented learning in policy change is derived from their interest in the role of technical information in the policy process (Sabatier and Weible 2007: 189). All in all, putting them together, the three reference approaches offer evidence that policy dynamics are driven by a multiplicity of contingent and complex causal paths.

The contention here is that it is possible to assemble these different causal paths or *mechanisms of policy change* in an integrated and coherent single explanatory framework that accounts for both policy change and stability. In recent years the concept of explanatory causal mechanisms has come to be of wide use among social scientists, mainly those discontent with statistical correlational causal approaches (i.e. Elster 1989, Hedström and Swedberg 1996, 1998, Goldthorpe 2001, McAdam *et al.* 2001, Abell 2004, George and Bennet 2005). Nevertheless, there is no consensus about what a mechanism is (for a review see Mahoney 2001, and Mayntz 2004). Here, the concept is used as a synonym of "generative causal process" (Goldthorpe 2001), that is, as the chain of logically related events (usually at a lower level of analysis) linking an initial state (policy design at moment t) to a final state (policy design at moment $t + n$).[7] The result is a typology of three different *mechanisms of policy change*: 1) endogenous change; 2) conflict expansion; and 3) exogenous impacts. This typology specifies analytically alternative causal paths that, in practice, may interact with each other producing complex sequences of policy change.

Endogenous Change

In autonomous subsystems policy change is endogenous, that is, is the exclusive result of the internal processes involving interactions among subsystem's participants (decision makers, insiders, and outsiders). In such contexts, policy participants promote policy change when they perceive that their actual or expected payoffs deteriorate as a consequence of a malfunction in one or more components of the policy design (policy failure).[8]

In order to reverse such detrimental situations, policy participants may resort, first of all, to the stored knowledge contained in causal theories underlying policy designs. In these cases, change in policy designs is the result of applying previously devised recipes (sometimes automatically) indicating what to do, which may be included within the set of rules governing the subsystem. If causal theories are not available or the existing ones prove to be ineffective, a second alternative is rethinking the causal reasonings underlying the policy design, which implies, thus, a process of *learning* – elaborating new policy usable knowledge.[9] It is necessary to distinguish policy-oriented learning from other types of knowledge production and utilization in the policy process. May's (1992) distinction between "policy learning" and "political learning" applies here. The former refers to learning through which political actors acquire a higher degree of sophistication in the prosecution and promotion of policy goals and ideas. In contrast, "policy learning" refers to the production of knowledge oriented towards a better understanding – even a redefinition – of the relationship between the configuration of components of policy designs and their consequences.[10] In some cases, this merely consists in improving existing causal theories while in others learning entails searching for new ones. In any case, learning involves the utilization of new ideas and knowledge in policy decisions (collective choice level) and implementation (operational level – Busenberg 2001, Meseguer 2005).

In order to grasp the causal role of learning, it is also necessary to distinguish it from policy change itself (Bennett and Howlett 1992: 290, Levy 1994: 289–290). Thus, learning may take place (new policy-relevant usable knowledge may be produced) without lessons being implemented. Indeed, learning may be used to reinforce the existing status quo.

Endogenous change would be, thus, the result of processing incoming information, which implies a number of intermediate steps – acquisition of information, distribution, interpretation, and storage (Huber 1991). This information may originate at different sources (Figure 2). A major source is policy results produced along time by policy designs at work in the subsystem. According to the ideal of rational policy making, the main stimulus to policy change would arise from decision makers' interest in overcoming policy failures and errors (Wildavsky 1987). This is particularly important when such errors are costly (Radaelli 1995, Popper and Lipshitz 1998). Subsystems' environmental conditions (material and community attributes) affecting policy effectiveness also constitute a source of informational input. In this sense, organization theorists have identified environmental uncertainty as a stimulus for organizational learning (Popper and Lipshitz 1998, 2000). Finally, relevant information may come from other action arenas the subsystem is related to (i.e. information from homomorphous or structurally similar subsystems is basic in policy transfer – Dolowitz and Marsh 2000).

Policy learning may take place in a variety of settings, *within and outside the subsystem* – so learning is not necessarily endogenous to the subsystem: it may occur in other action arenas. Such learning settings range from individual actors (citizens, opinion leaders, experts) (Dudley 2007), organizations (legislative bodies, mass media, interest groups ...) to the policy subsystem as a whole (Bennett and Howlett 1992, Adams 2004), both at the collective choice and the operative levels of action (Figure 2).

Figure 2. Endogenous policy change (learning)

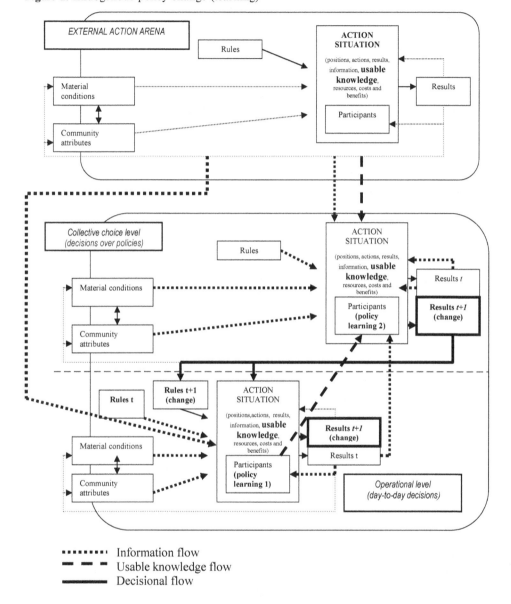

······· Information flow
– – – Usable knowledge flow
——— Decisional flow

The production of usable knowledge is, first of all, an individual process. Explaining how, what and why individuals learn is intimately associated with a particular model of individual information processing. Here, despite the three reference frameworks slant on a rational-bounded model of the individual, they present important differences regarding how information is processed and, in consequence, how learning takes place. For instance, the PET conception of the individual as a "selective attender" (Schlager 2007: 302, and see Jones 1994, 2001), implies that policy learning occurs when new information available makes salient previously unconsidered dimensions and consequences in existing policy designs. In its turn, the ACF emphasizes the existing limitations in the transformation of information in policy-usable knowledge, since individuals' core beliefs act as "cognitive filters" which tend to exclude from consideration all information that contradicts such beliefs. In the case of the IAD (see Table 1), the individual is conceived as a "rational-bounded updater", that is, she can improve her understanding of situations as new information is available, especially when situations repeat over time and they are not excessively complex – namely, learning depends more on the structure of the situation than on the individual characteristics (Ostrom 2005).

The production of usable knowledge may also take place as a result of collective efforts either in organizations[11] or at the subsystem level. In these contexts, learning appears when individual knowledge is incorporated and codified within collective routines and practices or, in other words, it is institutionalized within the collective entity (Simon 1991, Levy 1994: 287). In this sense, institutional arrangements oriented to promote such policy learning are of most importance (Busenberg 2001). Information rules influence the way and the extent informational inputs are transformed into usable knowledge to guide evaluation and the modification of the components of policy designs. They regulate the different steps of information processing: flows, which channels of information are authorized, the subject of communication, the criteria of accuracy and validity of information, who is obliged, permitted, or prohibited to communicate, or the required language to accept and transmit knowledge (Ostrom 2005: 206). Therefore, the probability of learning taking place is greatly increased by the existence of institutional elements (within organizations or at the subsystem level) designed to foster it, such as internal or external evaluations, consultative bodies, professional *fora*, information systems integrated in policy implementation procedures, etc.

Along with institutional structure, other elements in the actions arenas and their environment affect learning. Haas (1992) underlines how growing technical uncertainties and complexities of problems of global character promote the creation of epistemic communities. Elements in community attributes also influence the production of usable knowledge, such as the social constructions of issues (which may frame and bias actors' selection of information and/or its interpretation – Jones 1994, Schneider and Ingram 1997); or the presence of certain values in organizational culture – i.e. procuring full, undistorted and verifiable information, transparency (individuals' actions are open to inspection), issue orientation (opinions are judged according to their merits, not to the status of the proponent), and responsibility of actors for their actions (accountability – Popper and Lipshitz 1998).

As the result of past decisions, subsystem rules affecting information management and knowledge production are also influenced by political dynamics. Policy usable knowledge is socially constructed and, thus, it occupies a subordinate position regarding underlying social and political processes (Weiss 1983, Jenkins-Smith 1988, Bennet and Howlett 1992, Schneider and Ingram 1997: chap. 6). Information rules are part of the working rules in policy subsystems and, hence, respond to power equilibria existing within them. Consequently, policy learning may acquire a strategic character in helping policy participants to promote their respective policy interests and values (Majone 1989). Some scholars have emphasized the importance of the interaction between learning and the level of conflict within policy subsystems. In this sense, high consensual policy subsystems or those where participants with discrepant views are marginalized by participation and decision rules (such as in policy monopolies), are hypothesized to be less prone to promote policy learning (Capano 1996, Thomas 1999). The same applies to highly polarized subsystems – especially those divided around value charged issues, but also those where substantive material interests are at stake. In contrast, situations of moderate conflict may stimulate learning processes among subsystem participants (Jenkins-Smith 1988: 177–178, Jenkins-Smith and Sabatier 1993: 49).

In the conception of endogenous policy change presented here, the translation of usable knowledge produced within or outside the subsystem into changes in policy designs (that is, knowledge institutionalization) is mediated by institutional arrangements resulting from the balance of power within the subsystem. According to the PET (and, implicitly, to the ACF), in policy monopolies and closed policy subsystems information rules would be part of the set of rules preventing outsiders' influence and participation in decision making. In this type of subsystem, rules affecting the use of policy knowledge are biased to reflect the interests and values of those participants controlling the subsystem. This overrides the rational conception of learning within the policy process. Many sensible policy proposals (namely, adjusted to information accuracy and validity rules) are systematically discarded by decision makers (Gormley 2007). Under such institutional contexts, available knowledge is more likely to be used when it is produced or sponsored by the actors controlling the decision process, and it fits their interests and/or policy values (Hansen and King 2001). In contrast, more open subsystems (i.e., where decision makers are equidistant from other social participants' interests and values) are expected to be more receptive to different sources of usable knowledge. Besides, together with institutional factors, the translation of usable knowledge into policy change also depends on the conjunctural feasibility of the proposed alternatives (i.e. available technical or economic resources – Kingdon 1995).

Regarding the type of policy change associated with endogenous processes, it has been pointed out that organizations and, by extension, policy subsystems, only tolerate internal change as far as it does not affect the fundamental aspects of its internal working (and, consequently, of policy designs – Argyris 1976, Hall 1993, Argyris and Schön 1996). Policy change in this context will usually fit existing causal theories. In this respect, the ACF underlines how policy change resulting from learning (when present formulations of policy causal theories prove ineffective) only affects secondary aspects of belief systems, while knowledge questioning core beliefs is systematically ignored. Nevertheless, the possibility that learning produces substantive policy change should not be discarded. Accordingly, when the ineffective working of a policy endangers dominant participants' status (even their survival chances) it is likely that they promote a substantive review of policy designs (Weiss 1983: 233, Sabatier and Weible 2007).

Conflict Expansion

As in the endogenous change mechanism, in conflict expansion the policy change process is also triggered by subsystem participants who are discontented with some aspect of the internal working or with the policy results obtained in the subsystem. Given the costs that the activation of this mechanism has for change promoters, it is plausible to infer that subsystem participants will resort to conflict expansion in a subsidiary fashion – when they find it impossible to modify the perceived negative situation through endogenous change. In this sense, outsider participants are more likely to resort to conflict expansion than those with permanent access to decisions (insiders). Sometimes the issue of policy change runs parallel to the rise of new organized participants, representing new or previously ignored (because they were unorganized) interests in target populations or concerned publics. Newcomers usually find it difficult to get incorporated into the subsystem's decisional core since their policy interests may not coincide with those of decision makers and insiders and/or because their incorporation may alter the existing power equilibrium.

In such cases of denied access, the only alternative outsiders and newcomers have to promote policy change is expanding the subsystem's internal conflict beyond its boundaries, by involving other previously uninterested actors (Schaatschneider 1960). These external participants may alter the existing bargaining power relationships within the subsystem or induce a moving of the decision to other, more favourable, action arenas. In brief, conflict expansion consists basically in turning previously isolated arenas into connected ones, which entails an expansion of the analytical policy space outside the subsystem's boundaries (represented in Figure 3 by the external discontinuous line containing the subsystem and the external action arena).

Expanding conflict is a costly task. It demands the investment of a considerable amount of human and material resources greater than those required for endogenous change. Unless change promoters are endowed with the needed resources, conflict expansion depends on collective action processes. They range from the organization of groups of individuals within target populations to mass mobilizations oriented to get public attention. How policy proponents solve collective action problems – the free rider problem and the costs associated with organization and the maintenance of mobilization (Olson 1965, Hardin 1982, Taylor 1987, Kollock 1998) – is, therefore, a key part of this mechanism. Assessing how collective action problems are solved would require an examination of the range of participants and their action orientations (i.e. egoistic vs. altruistic – Scharpf 1997), the distribution of such orientations among the population of potential participants (Marwell and Oliver 1993), the way the structure of the action situation participants confront favours/hinders collective action (i.e. prisoners' dilemma vs. assurance game structures – Heckathorn 1996), the presence of skilled leaders willing to pay organizational start-up costs (Chong 1992), and the framing strategies organizational leaders use to promote a more favourable perception of the structure situation by participants (Benford and Snow 2000).

The strategies used by change promoters to expand conflict beyond subsystem's boundaries are those pointed out by Baumgartner and Jones in the PET: *venue shopping* and policy *image redefinition*. In the IAD terms, venue shopping can be reinterpreted as the attempt to move decision-making processes into the institutional agenda of external action arenas not controlled by the subsystem's dominant actors. The availability of such arenas depends on the formal institutional structure of the polity, and more specifically on the degree of concentration/dispersion of policy relevant authority among different decision-making units – i.e. polities with federal

Figure 3. Mechanism of conflict expansion

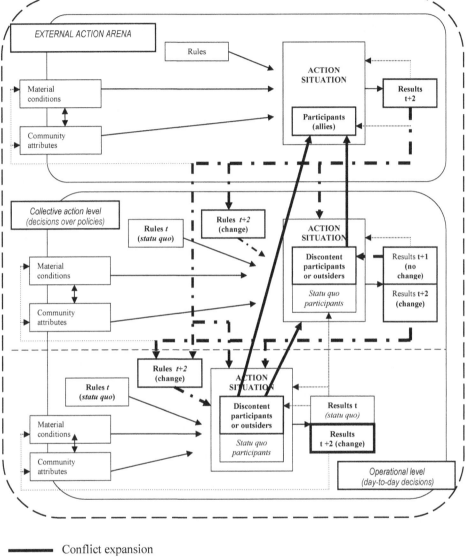

———— Conflict expansion

— · — Decisional flow

structures, separation of powers, and/or multilevel types of governances (such as in the European Union) offer more opportunities than unitary and centralized states (Baumgartner and Jones 1993: 239–240, Baumgartner *et al.* 2006).

Baumgartner and Jones present venue selection as a process basically guided by strategic calculus. However, ideological criteria may lead policy change promoters to favour certain venues over others (Pralle 2003). On the other hand, as potential allies' interest is frequently (mostly at the macro-political level) guided by general

Figure 4. Exogenous impacts mechanism

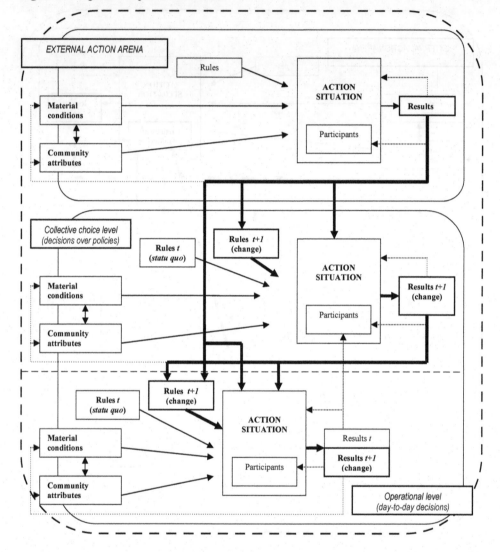

public attention, a great deal of the promoter's efforts will be directed to attract wider public support to their claims (i.e. by strategically targeting mass media or through mass mobilization – Cobb and Elder 1983). In such cases, for change promoters, failing to draw public attention to the issue is usually equal to losing the game.

Image redefinition is the other key process in the conflict expansion mechanism. It is inextricably related to venue shopping strategies. Provided that change promoters get potential allies' attention, redefined policy images are directed to show them previously not perceived (or underestimated) links between the actions arenas where they are regular participants and the subsystem. This is done through two mechanisms: a) by affecting potential allies' strategic calculations – redefinition shows them previously unperceived opportunities of benefit; b) by stimulating the "logic of appropriateness" (March and Olsen 1984, 1989) – new policy images activate normative orientations that make them "do the right thing". In any case, potential allies' adherence will be conditioned by their perception of the social legitimacy of the claims being made and/or the claimers, that is, the extent they adjust to socially accepted values and norms. Therefore, the effectiveness of image redefinition in attracting allies' support would depend on policy promoters' ability to combine in the narratives that form such new image elements pertaining to potential allies' discourse together with broader, socially accepted values and images (Hajer 1995). Such common elements will contribute to create a shared perception of the action situation (Ostrom 2005: 108) and to reinforce promoters' public stance.

Two issues should be borne in mind when considering the relationship between change promoters and allies. The first one refers to allies' commitment to the promoters' cause. When the alliance is constructed over strategic calculation, commitment is conditional upon the extent to which allies obtain the expected payoffs. Consequently, it is likely that in deciding to maintain their support allies take into account opportunity costs and discounting (namely, the gains they would obtain by devoting their time and attention to other issues). In contrast, when normative orientations are the glue of alliances, it is expected allies' commitment is more stable. In these situations, "policy champions" (allies that identify themselves with and are unconditional supporters of the promoters' cause) may play a major role in keeping the issue on the institutional agenda.

A second topic to consider when analysing the relationship between change promoters and allies refers to the concordance between their respective policy preferences. Both categories of actors may disagree regarding the dimensions of policy design that should be modified or the intensity of change. The incorporation of the promoter's preferences by allies will depend on the extent such preferences are acceptable for the latter in terms of costs-benefits (some changes are more costly to attain than others in terms of allies' efforts), their compatibility in normative terms with allies' policy beliefs, or their promotion is feasible according to the existing rules in the allies' action arena. Along with persuasion (the elaboration of more nuanced and persuasive policy arguments), promoters' ability to change allies' preferences may depend on their capacity to force an agreement (i.e. promoters may harm allies by publicly discrediting them after allies have compromised their support. Nevertheless, this is conditional upon the dependence promoters have on those particular allies and the relative cost these assign to the promoters' manoeuvre).

Once the issue is "uploaded" onto the institutional agenda at an external venue, the fate of promoters' alternatives depends on the inner dynamics within that action arena. The final result (that is, whether policy change is achieved and its extent) will depend, firstly, both on allies' leverage within the venue (the degree of influence and control they have over the decision-making process) and other participants' stand on the issue (in favour, contrary to, or neutral). When allies do not control the decision process, it is relevant whether they can obtain support from other participants. Here it is important whether the final definition of the issue (which may differ from that of promoters) is compatible with other participants' preferences and with general values within the action arena. In this respect, promoters' efforts should continue during this stage, in order to get the support of indecisive participants at the venue.

The rules at work are also important. They may influence, for instance, available courses of action (choice rules, i.e. in a legislature, the type of parliamentary proposal permitted), the degree of control participants have over the outcome (aggregation rules, i.e. the type of majority required to get the issue into the agenda to pass the proposal or to veto decisions), or results (scope rules, i.e. obliging policy change, or merely producing a recommendation to decision makers at the subsystem level).

The results of conflict expansion are also mediated by the possibility of *countermobilization* by subsystem participants or other actors opposed to policy change. In doing so, they may also resort to image manipulation (presenting promoters' redefinition in negative terms or reinforcing previous positive policy image), mass mobilization, and venue shopping (by looking for allies in other action arenas to maintain the status quo). The position within the subsystem's decisional core confers opponents structural advantages compared with proponents (Cobb and Ross 1997: 26) – legitimacy (derived from their control on decision making and the positive policy image they disseminate outside the subsystem), authority (in case of public decision makers), and greater control over relevant procedural and substantive information. Besides, opponents are usually endowed to a greater extent with other important resources, such as social capital (functional interdependencies with other actors in other action arenas), and organizational and economic resources. Thus, opponents find it easier to mobilize and to get access to other venues in order to stop conflict expansion and policy change.

Exogenous Impacts

The three reference approaches identify a variety of exogenous factors – events external to the subsystem not assumed in its internal working – which influence policy change. They include changes in material conditions (i.e. technology innovations, natural disasters), in the attributes of the community (socio-economic conditions, public mood), and in other action arenas linked to the subsystem, both at the macropolitical level (i.e. changes in governmental coalitions as a consequence of general elections, cabinet reshuffles, constitutional changes) and at other policy subsystems. However, further clarification is needed in order to understand the causal role of such exogenous factors in policy change. Reference approaches present exogenous factors as contextual elements in action situations. Hence, their influence in policy change is mediated by interaction processes within relevant policy arenas. In this sense, previous mechanisms would include the presence of such exogenous factors. For instance, focusing events have been underlined as a source for endogenous policy change (Busenberg 2000, Birkland 2004). Changes in material conditions or community attributes (i.e. changes in public mood over an issue through time) can also open opportunity windows for change promoters to expand conflict beyond the subsystem, by attracting the attention of external actors and opening venues.

However, there is also the possibility that exogenous factors directly trigger policy change. This is the essence of what here is called the exogenous impact mechanism. As changes in material conditions and community attributes are mediated by internal processes in action arenas, the exogenous impact mechanism mainly refers to those policy changes occurring as a consequence of events originated beyond the subsystem's boundaries in other action arenas it is related to. In contrast with the previous mechanisms, in the exogenous impact mechanism policy change occurs independently of internal processes within the subsystem (this is shown in Figure 4 by the fact that no causal arrow starts from the subsystem's action situation boxes). As in the conflict expansion mechanism, exogenous impacts imply the extension of the policy space outside the subsystem's boundaries.

As stated above, policy subsystems are usually hierarchically dependent on other action arenas. Then, through these hierarchical links, decisions taken in those external action arenas may result in changes in policy designs. Such external decisions may directly shape policy design elements when the subsystem's decisional core is bypassed and decision making goes up into a higher level, external, action arena. As in the conflict expansion mechanism, actors outside the subsystem get attracted by subsystem activities, but this time without the intervention of change promoters within the subsystem. In this respect, focusing events and/or increased public attention on the subsystem's working may redirect the attention of previously uninterested external actors. The reasons to get involved may also range from a pure "logic of expected consequences" (an opportunity for benefit) to the "logic of appropriateness" (external actors find it is their duty to intervene). In the external actors' search for available policy alternatives, the exogenous impact mechanism intersects with the other two mechanisms, as actors may take such alternatives either from the "pool" of ideas within the subsystem – opening an opportunity window for outsiders to promote their pet solutions – or from other structurally equivalent subsystems – turning themselves into potential vehicles of policy learning.

Decisions made outside the subsystem may also indirectly affect policy designs, by altering the different elements of the action situation at the subsystem level (rules, participants, the resources and position they occupy, action alternatives, payoffs, etc.). External causal effects reach the subsystem through the vertical and horizontal links it has with outside action arenas (subsystem permeability). Here the casuistic is too vast to exemplify all possible situations. Regarding vertical links, for instance, changes in governmental coalition or a cabinet reshuffle may entail changes in upper political-administrative levels responsible for policy decisions within the subsystem. New decision makers may bring with them new styles or priorities which could affect the continuity of the policy design. With respect to exogenous impacts transmitted horizontally it is common for policy designs in subsystems to take into consideration changes in other subsystems with which they maintain functional interdependence relationships (such as, for instance, between the energy and transport subsystems). This transmission is facilitated by the fact that overlapping membership may be a common feature in interdependent subsystems (Zafonte and Sabatier 1998).

As in the other mechanisms, counteracting elements may limit the influence of exogenous impacts. When such impacts threaten policy participants' interests or values (mainly those at the decisional core), it is likely they will try to limit the scope of the implied changes by directly persuading external decision makers or, in case argumentation fails, by turning to mobilization and conflict expansion.

Conclusion and Final Remarks

In sum, as stated in the introductory section, the proposed synthetic framework allows the theoretical advances in explaining policy change reached by the ACF, the

PET and the MS to be presented in a unified set of propositions and, in addition, it contributes to overcome the detected shortcomings in the three reference approaches. The key elements of this framework are, firstly, its emphasis on identifying the set of generative causal processes or mechanisms behind policy change – in contrast to the trend in the reference approaches to favour particular causal paths; and, secondly, the utilization of the IAD framework as a conceptual skeleton which allows the relevant theoretical relationships among basic conceptual elements (rational-bounded participants, resources, patterns of interaction, institutional constraints, ideas, material and cultural conditions, and policy outputs) to be better specified. In this sense, the proposed synthetic framework accomplishes what is supposed to be the main task of a framework in the strict sense, namely, to identify the set of relevant variables and relationships that should be examined in order to account for policy dynamics. In addition, it meets the criteria that make it acceptable from a theoretical point of view (Sabatier 1999: 8), that is, conceptual elements are clear, internally consistent and positive, it identifies clear causal drivers, and it is broad in scope. Besides, it is suitable for theoretical development, as it allows specific and falsifiable theoretical propositions that refer to the internal working of the different mechanisms to be generated (i.e. whether effectively institutional features make a difference in subsystem action arenas favouring endogenous change).

In addition, there are a number of additional remarks to be made in order to clarify some relevant aspects of the proposed synthetic framework. Concerning the scope of policy change, it is difficult to establish *a priori* definitions of what is substantive or minor (incremental) policy change. Focusing on policy designs as the proposed framework does calls for avoiding traditional clear-cut distinctions, such as that between substantive change associated with changes in goals or assumptions and incremental change linked to policy instruments (i.e. Hall 1993). Policy designs appear as configurations of elements where, for instance, instruments or implementation structures may be intertwined with basic assumptions or policy goals. Hence, looking closely at such relationships between the different components of policy designs allows the scope of change to be identified. This is related to the issue of the timing of policy change, since identifying whether a change in policy design is substantive or not is conditional upon the time span considered. In this sense, the proposed framework is compatible with explaining sudden and long term policy change.

Another remark must be made regarding the dichotomy "ideas vs. interests" as causal drivers of change. This is especially important, since the ACF considers that, in the long term, only ideas (beliefs) are relevant to understanding policy change. However, in principle, both elements must be taken into account. The proposed framework contends that participants can be motivated both by the logic of the expected consequences and the logic of the appropriateness. It is thus part of the tasks associated with empirical analysis to ascertain what kind of motivations guide participants' behaviour in action situations and how they combine.

Last but not least, the outlined generative causal processes or mechanisms are presented as "pure types". Nevertheless, in real situations it is common that such mechanisms combine and interact, forming complex patterns of generative causal processes (i.e. failed endogenous change may lead change proponents to expand conflict outside the subsystem's boundaries). This agrees with the widely acknowledged difficulty of drawing general explanations of policy change (Jones and

Baumgartner 2005), given the complex and contingent nature of the considered phenomenon. Policy dynamics are characterized by a great number of intervening factors making them statistically unmanageable, causal links between factors are neither unambiguous nor lineal, event sequence matters, and agents' decisions may decisively influence the final result (George and Bennet 2005: 211–212, Howlett and Rayner 2006). In this sense, the emphasis on causal mechanisms constitutes a more suitable explanatory strategy than the more traditional correlational-statistical explanation to deal with the contextual nature of policy dynamics. Besides, this does not dismiss the epistemological validity of an explanation emphasizing causal generative processes (Goldthorpe 2001). Causal mechanism based explanation is not mere narrative, thick description of the process that leads to a particular event. The mechanisms identified in the proposed framework allow the student to combine a certain degree of theoretical generality with the widely contextual character of policy dynamics. Finally, the focus on generative causal processes fits particularly well with the types of research designs that predominate in policy dynamics studies – small-n, qualitative comparative studies and case studies – where intensity of analysis prevails over generalization goals (Gerring 2004).

Acknowledgements

A preliminary draft of this paper was presented at the workshop organized by the editors of this Special Issue at the ECPR Joint Sessions held in Helsinki in May 2007. I wish to thank all the participants at that workshop for their helpful discussion and suggestions. I also extend my gratitude to the editors and three anonymous referees for their comments on a latter version, which have allowed me to substantially improve the paper. Of course, any errors are my sole responsibility.

Notes

1. The MS approach, although widely cited by policy scholars, does not equal the other lenses either in terms of further empirical applications or regarding theoretical development (Sabatier 2007b: 332, note 4).
2. These two later paths of change have been included in the last version of the ACF (Sabatier and Weible 2007).
3. Major criticisms of one or more of the three reference frameworks may be found in (among others): Mucciaroni 1992, Hajer 1995, Hann 1995, Schlager 1995, 1999, Zahariadis 1995a, 1999, Mintron and Vergari 1996, Schlager and Blomquist 1996, John 1998, 2003, Sabatier 1999, Sabatier and Jenkins-Smith 1999.
4. These components are: 1) policy goals and problems to be solved; 2) target populations; 3) agents and implementation structures; 4) policy instruments; 5) rules; and 6) rationales and assumptions (Schneider and Ingram 1997: 81–100).
5. In contrast, *theories* would provide "a denser and more logically coherent set of relationships [within a framework], including direction and hypotheses, that self-consciously seek to explain a set of phenomena" (Sabatier 2007b: 322). In its turn, *models* "make precise assumptions about a limited set of [framework] parameters and variables" (Ostrom 1999: 40).
6. "Policy domain" has been defined as "a component of the political system that is organized around substantive issues" (Burstein 1991: 328) or "a relatively self-contained political arena consisting of a core set of organizations that pay close attention to important substantive policy issues and problems" (Knoke 2004).

7. This is congenial to Elster's concept of explanation (1989: 3): "To explain an event is to give an account of *why it happened*. Usually, and always ultimately, this takes the form of *citing an earlier event as the cause of the event we want to explain, together with some account of the causal mechanism connecting events"* (italics added).
8. Thus, this mechanism excludes those changes resulting from alterations in the participants' bargaining power, since subsystem autonomy implies stability in participants' resources and positions.
9. The notion of learning used here agrees with that by Fiol and Lyles (1985: 810), who define it as "The development of insights, knowledge, and associations between past actions, the effectiveness of that actions, and future actions".
10. This definition of policy learning merges the two types of policy learning distinguished by May (1992): "instrumental policy learning" – referred to implementation instruments – and "social policy learning" – where learning affects other components of policy design such as rationales, goals, and objectives.
11. On organizational learning, see for example Cyert and March 1963, Huber 1991, Argyris and Schön 1996, Popper and Lipshitz 1998, 2000, Shipton 2006.

References

Abell, Peter, 2004, Narrative explanation: an alternative to variable-centered explanation? *Annual Review of Sociology*, **30**, 287–310.
Adams, David, 2004, Usable knowledge in public policy. *Australian Journal of Public Administration*, **63**(1), 29–42.
Argyris, Chris, 1976, Single-loop and double-loop models in research on decision making. *Administrative Science Quarterly*, **21**(3), 363–377.
Argyris, Chris and Schön, Donald A., 1996, *Organizational Learning II: Theory, Method, and Practice* (Reading, MA: Addison-Wesley).
Baumgartner, Frank R. and Jones, Bryan D., 1993, *Agendas and Instability in American Politics* (Chicago: The University of Chicago Press).
Baumgartner, Frank R. and Jones, Bryan D. (Eds), 2002a, *Policy Dynamics* (Chicago/London: The University of Chicago Press).
Baumgartner, Frank R. and Jones, Bryan D., 2002b, Positive and negative feedback in politics, in: Frank R. Baumgartner and Bryan D. Jones (Eds) *Policy Dynamics* (Chicago/London: The University of Chicago Press), pp. 3–28.
Baumgartner, Frank R., Foucault, Martial and François, Abel, 2006, Punctuated equilibrium in French budgeting processes. *Journal of European Public Policy*, **13**(7), 1086–1103.
Benford, Robert D. and Snow, David A., 2000, Framing processes and social movements: an overview and assessment. *Annual Review of Sociology*, **26**, 611–639.
Bennet, Colin J. and Howlett, Michael, 1992, The lessons of learning: reconciling theories of policy learning and policy change. *Policy Sciences*, **25**, 275–294.
Birkland, Thomas A., 2004, Learning and policy improvement after disaster: the case of aviation security. *American Behavioral Scientist*, **48**(3), 341–364.
Burstein, Paul, 1991, Policy domains: organization, culture, and policy outcomes. *Annual Review of Sociology*, **17**, 327–350.
Busenberg, George J., 2000, Innovation, learning, and policy evolution in hazardous systems. *American Behavioral Scientist*, **44**(4), 678–689.
Busenberg, George J., 2001, Learning in organizations and public policy. *Journal of Public Policy*, **21**(2), 173–189.
Capano, Giliberto, 1996, Political science and the comparative study of policy change in higher education: theoretical-methodological notes from a policy perspective. *Higher Education*, **31**(3), 263–282.
Chong, Dennis, 1992, *Collective Action and the Civil Rights Movement* (Chicago and London: The University of Chicago Press).
Cobb, Roger W. and Elder, Charles D., 1983, *Participation in American Politics: The Dynamics of Agenda-Building* (Baltimore, MD: Johns Hopkins University Press).
Cobb, Roger W. and Ross, Marc Howard (Ed.), 1997, *Cultural Strategies of Agenda Denial: Avoidance, Attack, and Redefinition* (Lawrence, KS: University Press of Kansas).

Cohen, M. D., March, J. G. and Olsen, J. P., 1972, A garbage can model of organizational choice. *Administrative Science Quarterly*, **17**, 1–25.

Cyert, Richard M. and March, James G., 1963, *A Behavioral Theory of the Firm* (Englewood Cliffs, NJ: Prentice-Hall).

Dolowitz, David P. and Marsh, David, 2000, Learning from abroad: the role of policy transfer in contemporary policy-making. *Governance*, **13**(1), 5–24.

Dowding, Keith, 2000, How not to use evolutionary theory in politics: a critique of Peter John. *British Journal of Politics and International Relations*, **2**(1), 72–80.

Dudley, Geoffrey, 2007, Individuals and the dynamics of policy learning: the case of the Third Battle of Newbury, *Public Administration*, **85**(2), 405–428.

Elster, Jon, 1989, *Nuts and Bolts for the Social Sciences* (Cambridge: Cambridge University Press).

Fiol, Marlene C. and Lyles, Marjorie A., 1985, Organizational learning. *Academy of Management Review*, **10**(4), 803–813.

George, Alexander L. and Bennet, Andrew, 2005, *Case Studies and Theory Development in the Social Sciences* (Cambridge, MA: MIT Press).

Gerring, John, 2004, What is a case study and what is it good for? *American Political Science Review*, **98**(2), 341–354.

Goldthorpe, John H., 2001, Causation, statistics, and sociology. *European Sociological Review*, **17**(1), 1–20.

Gormley, William T. Jr., 2007, Public policy analysis: ideas and impacts. *Annual Review of Political Science*, **10**, 297–313.

Haas, Peter M., 1992, Introduction: epistemic communities and international policy coordination. *International Organization*, **46**(1), 1–35.

Hajer, Maarten A., 1995, *The Politics of Environmental Discourse. Ecological Modernization and the Policy Process* (Oxford: Oxford University Press).

Hall, Peter A., 1993, Policy paradigms, social learning, and the state. The case of economic policymaking in Britain. *Comparative Politics*, **25**(3), 275–296.

Hall, Peter A. and Taylor, C. R., 1996, Political science and the three new institutionalisms. *Political Studies*, **44**, 952–973.

Hann, Alison, 1995, Sharpening up Sabatier: belief systems and public policy. *Politics*, **15**(1), 19–26.

Hansen, Randall and King, Desmond, 2001, Eugenic ideas, political interests, and policy variance: immigration and sterilization policy in Britain and the U.S. *World Politics*, **53**, 237–263.

Hardin, Russell, 1982, *Collective Action* (Baltimore: Resources for the Future/Johns Hopkins University Press).

Hayes, Michael T., 2001, *The Limits of Policy Change. Incrementalism, Worldview, and the Rule of Law* (Washington, DC: Georgetown University Press).

Heckathorn, Douglas D., 1996, The dynamics and dilemmas of collective action. *American Sociological Review*, **61**(2), 250–277.

Hedström, Peter and Swedberg, Richard, 1996, Social mechanisms. *Acta Sociologica*, **39**, 281–308.

Hedström, Peter and Swedberg, Richard (Eds), 1998, *Social Mechanisms. An Analytical Approach to Social Theory* (Cambridge: Cambridge University Press).

Howlett, M. and Rayner, J., 2006, Understanding the historical turn in the policy sciences: a critique of stochastic, narrative, path dependency and process-sequencing models of policy-making over time. *Policy Sciences*, **39**(1), 1–18.

Huber, George P., 1991, Organizational learning: the contributing processes and the literatures. *Organization Science*, **2**(1), 88–115.

Jenkins-Smith, Hank C., 1988, Analytical debates and policy learning: analysis and change in the federal bureaucracy. *Policy Sciences*, **21**, 169–211.

Jenkins-Smith, Hank C. and Sabatier, Paul A., 1993, The dynamics of policy oriented learning, in: Paul A. Sabatier and Hank C. Jenkins-Smith (Eds) *Policy Change and Learning* (Boulder, CO: Westview Press), pp. 41–56.

John, Peter, 1998, *Analysing Public Policy* (London: Continuum).

John, Peter, 2003, Is there life after policy streams, advocacy coalitions, and punctuations: using evolutionary theory to explain policy change? *The Policy Studies Journal*, **31**(4), 481–498.

Jones, Bryan D., 1994, *Reconceiving Decision-Making in Democratic Politics* (Chicago/London: The Chicago University Press).

Jones, Bryan D., 2001, *Politics and the Architecture of Choice* (Chicago: The University of Chicago Press).
Jones, Bryan D. and Baumgartner, Frank R., 2005, *The Politics of Attention* (Chicago: The University of Chicago Press).
Kingdon, John W., 1995, *Agendas, Alternatives and Public Policies*, 2nd edition (New York: Harper Collins College Publishers [1st edition 1984]).
Knoke, David, 2004, The sociopolitical construction of national policy domains, in: Christian H.C.A. Henning and Christian Melbeck (Eds) *Interdisziplinäre Sozialforschung: Theorie und empirische Anwendungen. Festschrift für Franz Urban Pappi* (Frankfurt: Campus), pp. 81–96.
Kiser, Larry L. and Ostrom, Elinor, 1982, The three worlds of action: a metatheoretical synthesis of institutional approaches, in: Elinor Ostrom (Ed.) *Strategies of Political Inquiry* (Beverly Hills, CA/London: Sage), pp. 179–222.
Kollock, Peter, 1998, Social dilemmas: the anatomy of cooperation. *Annual Review of Sociology*, **2**, 183–214.
Levy, Jack S., 1994, Learning and foreign policy: sweeping a conceptual minefield. *International Organization*, **48**(2), 279–312.
Mahoney, James, 2001, Beyond correlational analysis: recent innovations in theory and method (Review Essay). *Sociological Forum*, **16**(3), 575–593.
Majone, Ginadomenico, 1989, *Evidence, Argument, and Persuasion in the Policy Process* (New Haven, CT: Yale University Press).
Maloney, William A., Jordan, A. G. and McLaughlin, A. M., 1994, Interest groups and public policy: the insider/outsider model revisited. *Journal of Public Policy*, **14**(1), 17–38.
March, James G. and Olsen, Johan P., 1984, The new institutionalism: organizational factors in political life. *The American Political Science Review*, **78**(3), 734–749.
March, James G., and Olsen, Johan P., 1989, *Rediscovering Institutions. The Organizational Basis of Politics* (New York: Free Press).
Marwell, Gerald and Oliver, Pamela, 1993, *The Critical Mass in Collective Action. A Micro-Social Theory* (Cambridge: Cambridge University Press).
May, Peter J., 1992, Policy learning and failure. *Journal of Public Policy*, **12**(4), 331–354.
Mayntz, Renate, 2004, Mechanisms in the analysis of social macro-phenomena. *Philosophy of the Social Sciences*, **34**(2), 237–259.
McAdam, Doug, Tarrow, Sidney and Tilly, Charles, 2001, *Dynamics of Contention* (Cambridge: Cambridge University Press).
McAdams, Richard H., 1997, The origin, development, and regulation of norms. *Michigan Law Review*, **96**(2), 338–433.
Meseguer, Covadonga, 2005, Policy learning, policy diffusion, and the making of a new order, *Annals, AAPSS*, **598**, 67–82.
Mintron, Michael and Vergari, Sandra, 1996, Advocacy coalitions, policy entrepreneurs, and policy change. *Policy Studies Journal*, **24**(3), 420–434.
Moe, Terry M., 1990, Political institutions: the neglected side of the story. *Journal of Law, Economics, and Organization*, **6**, Special Issue, 213–253.
Moe, Terry M., 2006, Power and Political Institutions, in: Ian Shapiro, Stephen Skowronek and Daniel Galvin (Eds) *Rethinking Political Institutions. The Art of the State* (New York: New York University Press), pp. 32–71.
Mucciaroni, Gary, 1992, The garbage can model and the study of policy making: a critique. *Polity*, **XXIV**(3), 459–482.
Nohrstedt, Daniel, 2005, External shocks and policy change: Three Mile Island and Swedish nuclear energy policy. *Journal of European Public Policy*, **12**(6), 1041–1059.
North, Douglass, 1990, *Institutions, Institutional Change, and Economic Performance* (Cambridge: Cambridge University Press).
Olson, Mancur, Jr., 1965, *The Logic of Collective Action* (Cambridge, MA: Harvard University Press).
Ostrom, Elinor, 1990, *Governing the Commons* (Cambridge: Cambridge University Press).
Ostrom, Elinor, 1999a, Institutional rational choice. An assessment of the institutional analysis and development framework, in: Paul A. Sabatier (Ed.) *Theories of the Policy Process* (Boulder, CO/Oxford: Westview Press), pp. 35–71.
Ostrom, Elinor, 1999b, Coping with tragedies of the commons. *Annual Review of Political Science*, **2**, 493–535.

Ostrom, Elinor, 2005, *Understanding Institutional Diversity* (Princeton, NJ: Princeton University Press).
Ostrom, Elinor, Gardner, Roy and Walker, James, 1994, *Rules, Games, and Common-Pool Resources* (Ann Arbor: The University of Michigan Press).
Page, Edward C., 1999, The insider/outsider distinction: an empirical investigation. *British Journal of Politics and International Relations*, 1(2), pp. 205–214.
Peters, B. Guy, 1999, *Institutional Theory and Political Science. The "New Institutionalism"* (London: Continuum).
Pierson, Paul, 2004, *Politics in Time. History, Institutions, and Social Analysis* (Princeton, NJ: Princeton University Press).
Popper, Micha and Lipshitz, Raanan, 1998, Organizational learning mechanisms: a structural and cultural approach to organizational learning. *The Journal of Applied Behavioral Science*, 34(2), 161–179.
Popper, Micha and Lipshitz, Raanan, 2000, Organizational learning: Mechanisms, culture, and feasibility. *Management Learning*, 31(2), 181–196.
Pralle, Sarah B., 2003, Venue shopping, political strategy, and policy change: the internationalization of Canadian forest advocacy. *Journal of Public Policy*, 23(3), 233–260.
Radaelli, Claudio M., 1995, The role of knowledge in the policy process. *Journal of European Public Policy*, 2(2), 159–183.
Rayner, Jeremy, Howlett, Michael, Wilson, Jeremy, Cashore, Benjamin and Hoberg, George, 2001, Privileging the sub-sector: critical sub-sectors and sectoral relationships in forest policy-making. *Forest Policy and Economics*, 2, 319–332.
Sabatier, Paul A., 1987, Knowledge, policy-oriented learning, and policy change. *Knowledge*, 8, 649–692.
Sabatier, Paul A., 1988, An advocacy coalition framework of policy change and the role of policy-oriented learning therein. *Policy Sciences*, 21, 129–168.
Sabatier, Paul A., 1999, The need for better theories, in: Paul A. Sabatier (Ed.) *Theories of the Policy Process* (Boulder, CO: Westview Press), pp. 115–166.
Sabatier, Paul A. (Ed.), 2007a, *Theories of the Policy Process*, 2nd edition (Boulder, CO: Westview Press).
Sabatier, Paul A., 2007b, Fostering the Development of Policy Theory, in: Paul A. Sabatier (Ed.) *Theories of the Policy Process*, 2nd edition (Boulder, CO: Westview Press), pp. 321–336.
Sabatier, Paul A. and Jenkins-Smith, Hank C. (Eds), 1993, *Policy Change and Learning* (Boulder, CO: Westview Press).
Sabatier, Paul A. and Jenkins-Smith, Hank C., 1999, The advocacy coalition framework. An assessment, in: Paul A. Sabatier (Ed.) *Theories of the Policy Process* (Boulder, CO: Westview Press), pp. 115–166.
Sabatier, Paul A. and Weible, Christopher M., 2007, The advocacy coalition framework: innovations and clarification, in: Paul A. Sabatier (Ed.) *Theories of the Policy Process*, 2nd edition (Boulder, CO: Westview Press), pp. 189–220.
Scharpf, Fritz W., 1997, *Games Real Actors Play. Actor-Centered Institutionalism in Policy Research* (Boulder, CO: Westview Press).
Schattschneider, E. E., 1960, *The Semisovereign People. A Realist's View of Democracy in America* (London: Thomson Learning).
Shepsle, Kenneth A., 1979, Institutional arrangements and equilibrium in multidimensional voting models. *American Journal of Political Science*, 23(1), 27–59.
Schlager, Edella, 1995, Policy making and collective action: defining coalitions within the advocacy coalition framework. *Policy Sciences*, 28, 243–270.
Schlager, Edella, 1999, A comparison of frameworks, theories, and models of policy processes, in: Paul A. Sabatier (Ed.) *Theories of the Policy Process* (Boulder, CO: Westview Press), pp. 233–260.
Schlager, Edella, 2007, A comparison of frameworks, theories and models of policy processes, in: Paul A. Sabatier (Ed.) *Theories of the Policy Process*, 2nd edition (Boulder, CO: Westview Press), pp. 293–319.
Schlager, Edella and Blomquist, William, 1996, A comparison of three emerging theories of the policy process. *Political Research Quarterly*, 49(3), 651–672.
Schneider, Anne Larason and Ingram, Helen, 1997, *Policy Design for Democracy* (Lawrence: University Press of Kansas).
Shipton, Helen, 2006, Cohesion or confusion? Towards a typology for organizational learning research, *International Journal of Management Reviews*, 8(4), 233–252.
Simon, Herbert A., 1991, Bounded rationality and organizational learning. *Organization Science*, 2(1), 125–134.
Taylor, Michael, 1987, *The Possibility of Cooperation* (Cambridge: Cambridge University Press).

Thomas, Gerald B., 1999, External shocks, conflict and learning as interactive sources of change in U.S. security policy. *Journal of Public Policy*, **19**(2), 209–231.
True, James L., Jones, Bryan D., and Baumgartner, Frank R., 2007, Punctuated-equilibrium theory: explaining stability and change in public policymaking, in: Paul A. Sabatier (Ed.) *Theories of the Policy Process*, 2nd edition (Boulder, CO: Westview Press), pp. 155–187.
Weiss, Carol H., 1983, Ideology, interests, and information: the basis of policy positions, in: Daniel Callahan and Bruce Jennings (Eds) *Ethics, the Social Sciences, and Policy Analysis* (New York: Plenum Press), pp. 213–245.
Wildavsky, Aaron, 1987, *Speaking Truth to Power*, 2nd edition (New Brunswick: Transaction Publishers).
Zafonte, Matthew and Sabatier, Paul, 1998, Shared beliefs and imposed interdependencies as determinants of ally networks in overlapping subsystems. *Journal of Theoretical Politics*, **10**(4), 473–505.
Zahariadis, Nikolaos, 1995a, Comparing lenses in comparative public policy. *Policy Studies Journal*, **23**(2), 378–382.
Zahariadis, Nikolaos, 1995b, *Markets, Status, and Public Policies: Privatization in Britain and France* (Ann Arbor: University of Michigan Press).
Zahariadis, Nikolaos, 1999, Ambiguity, time, and multiple streams, in: Paul A. Sabatier (Ed.) *Theories of the Policy Process* (Boulder, CO: Westview Press), pp. 73–93.

The Matching Problem within Comparative Welfare State Research: How to Bridge Abstract Theory and Specific Hypotheses

SABINA STILLER and KEES VAN KERSBERGEN

ABSTRACT *This paper draws attention to the problem of matching abstract theory and specific hypotheses within welfare state research, which reinforces the dependent variable problem and entails methodological difficulties. We show that matching theory and hypotheses is a ubiquitous problem in the literature. We further elaborate and illustrate the argument with an empirical example from our research on structural welfare state reform. We observe two methodological problems: 1) the risk of drawing conclusions about one level of analysis using evidence from another; 2) the problem of translating causal mechanisms formulated at a high level of abstraction to a lower level.*

Introduction

Scholarly work on the welfare state is characterized by many theoretical and empirical schools. Recently, research attention has been redirected to explaining variation in welfare state *reform*. The conceptualization of the dependent variable "reform", however, has caused considerable theoretical, empirical and methodological confusion and, accordingly, scholarly debate, both within mainstream approaches and between the mainstream literature and other approaches (such as the regulation school with its focus on the changes in production regimes and issues of "workfare").

The debate on the dependent variable problem (see Green-Pedersen 2004, Kühner 2007), that is, the conceptual and operational ambiguity about how the explanatory problem of welfare state reform is formulated for research purposes, has considerably improved our understanding of reform. We now have sharper specifications of welfare state reform and its various *dimensions* (see Pierson 2001a and below), more valid operationalizations and more reliable measurements of crucial concepts (such as decommodification, see Allan and Scruggs 2004), better datasets (see the dataset collected by Allan and Scruggs: http://sp.uconn.edu/~scruggs/wp.htm), important debunking efforts of overly speculative theories (for example Swank 2002, Castles 2004) and promising methodological innovations (for example Jaeger and Kvist 2003, Vis 2007).

Part of the solution to the dependent variable problem surely lies in further improving the quality of the data, operationalizations, measurements and methods as well as disaggregating research attention to the programme level (Kühner 2007). But even if we would have perfect measures and operationalizations, we are still left with the problem that so many different and competing (explanatory) theories seem to fit the same data on welfare state reform. In order to explain welfare state reforms, a great variety of explanatory approaches has been formulated. This variety reinforces the dependent variable problem as different theories suggest different conceptualizations and operationalizations of the welfare state or reform as the dependent variable. In any case, these rival theories cannot all be correct at the same time. But how to test such competing theories empirically? We think that in research practice there has been insufficient awareness of the necessity, but also of the complexity and difficulty, of competitive hypothesis testing. It involves a comparison of types of explanation, for instance whether political or economic factors are driving welfare state reform. Next, one needs to establish the explanatory status of the theories involved. Does the theoretical model specify causes and effects in a correlational approach or does the theory mainly describe causal mechanisms linking cause and effect in a historical approach? Also, the level of analysis at which theories specify their hypotheses differ. For competitive testing, it matters whether one aims to explain changes *of* or *in* welfare state regimes or social policy programmes. Finally, there is the issue of the operational and empirical specificity of the hypotheses that can vary between theories and that may complicate comparison between theories with respect to their empirical validity.

In this paper we cannot hope to even start solving all these issues, but propose to focus on the operational and empirical specificity of hypotheses. The reason for this choice is that frequently the potential problems involved here are either not recognized or not well addressed. We believe that a better appreciation of the problem is critically important as different operationalizations tend to lead to different conclusions about the hypotheses that are deduced from the theory being tested. We define the issue as a problem of *matching*, which refers to the difficulty of matching propositions formulated at a high(er) level of abstraction with hypotheses than can be tested empirically. We call attention to this phenomenon, particularly as the matching problem tends to reinforce the dependent variable problem, a problem that is far better known and dealt with in the literature (Green Pedersen 2004, Clasen and Siegel 2007, Kühner 2007).

The structure of the paper is as follows. In the next section we present a short overview of recent welfare state research to provide the background for an identification of the problem of the dependent variable and the re-specification of welfare state reform in terms of different dimensions. In the third section we elaborate the matching problem, arguing that cause and effect tend to be specified on different levels of analysis, as a result of which the conceptualization and operationalization of the causal mechanism(s) and the dependent variable becomes complicated and the dependent variable problem is reinforced. By discussing examples using different analytical techniques, we show that matching is a problem of the field as a whole. Some circumvent the problem by remaining at a high level of abstraction and offer only loosely connected empirical illustrations. Others evade the problem by discarding theory and focusing on technically advanced quantitative tests of loosely connected (if at all) models that include variables from widely diverging theories. Most empirical researchers find practical solutions, for instance by combining a variable-oriented and a case-oriented approach, but still fail to make explicit how they have tried to match theoretical statements at one level with empirical statements at another level.

Our point is that we would like to raise awareness of the problem and spell out the intricacies involved. Instead of offering further detailed criticisms of other people's work, we present as a final example the work of one of us (Stiller 2007) to track in some detail how one travels from (abstract) theory, the level at which the causes of reform are formulated, to empirically testable hypotheses on causal mechanisms. In other words, to clarify better the matching problem and illustrate how to deal with it explicitly, we discuss one example of research practice in some more detail rather than present a sketchy discussion of a multitude of studies. Finally, the last section draws together the lessons of the foregoing discussion and ends with some recommendations on how to proceed from here.

Welfare State Reform: the Dependent Variable Problem

Until roughly 1990, the welfare state (its emergence and expansion) was routinely conceptualized in terms of welfare effort and operationalized as social spending. The literature of the early 1990s began to rethink what precisely welfare state theory should explain. The social spending variable was rightfully criticized for its loose correspondence to the theoretical issues of social democratization (Esping-Andersen 1990). Esping-Andersen argued that there was a striking conceptual indifference in the literature with respect to the dependent variable: the welfare state. Starting from the judgement that "expenditures are epiphenomenal to the theoretical substance of welfare states" (1990: 19), and the reflection that "it is difficult to imagine that anyone struggled for spending per se" (1990: 21), he suggested that the study of welfare states should focus on the quality of social rights, the typical patterns of stratification, and the manner in which the state, the market and the family interacted in the production of social welfare.

By looking beyond spending patterns, Esping-Andersen was able to distinguish three types of welfare state regimes: a social democratic, a liberal and a corporatist or conservative regime. These regimes differed with respect to the major institutions guaranteeing *social security* (the state, the market or the family); the kind of *stratification* systems upheld by the institutional mix of these institutions (the extent of status and class differentiation, segmentation and inequality typically implied in social security systems); and the degree of *de-commodification*, that is to say "the degree to which individuals, or families, can uphold a socially acceptable standard of living independently of market participation" (Esping-Andersen, 1990: 37). This inspired a whole new generation of research that focused on the explanation of variation between regimes, provoking discussion on the dependent variable "welfare state regime" and the correct typology to use as a suitable standard in comparative analysis.

Overlapping with this new way of looking at the welfare state, there was a gradual shift in the research attention away from "expansion" and "variation" of welfare state regimes towards "reform" and "retrenchment" (or their absence) of the welfare state as the main explanatory problem. A groundbreaking historical institutionalist study of welfare state *change* was Paul Pierson's (1994) *Dismantling the Welfare State?* His main finding was that, in spite of mounting pressures from liberal forces symbolized by the names of Reagan and Thatcher and in contrast to changes in the arenas of macroeconomic policy, industrial relations or regulatory policy, "the welfare state stands out as an island of relative stability" (1994: 5). Welfare states resisted change. In explaining this unexpected phenomenon, Pierson focused on institutional structures and electoral mechanisms. In his view, the former included networks of welfare bureaucracies and services in the policy areas of social housing, health care, education, public assistance and social security, the very existence of which was bound to the status quo in social policy and which therefore mounted powerful resistance against attempts of retrenchment. These professional networks were created by postwar welfare state development, and once established they were able to muster substantial veto power against reform efforts (Pierson, 1996: 147). Because these structures stood for path continuity, a weakening of the historical supporters of welfare state expansion (for example social democracy) did not necessarily translate into commensurate weakening of social policy.

Moreover, Pierson argued, "frontal assaults on the welfare state carry tremendous electoral risks" (1996: 178). While welfare expansion usually generated a popular politics of credit claiming for extending social rights and raising benefits to an increasing number of citizens, austerity policies affronted large groups of voters. Even "retrenchment advocates ... confront a clash between their policy preferences and their electoral ambitions" (Pierson, 1996: 146) and, as a rule, the latter prevailed.

In the literature on reform, there arose considerable confusion around the question "what is to be explained" and the specification of the dependent variable. Pierson (2001b) observed that there was a lack of consensus on welfare state outcomes, particularly with respect to the issue of how much welfare states had actually changed since the end of the Golden Age of growth, that is to say, roughly since the 1980s. The controversy over the dependent variable was first of all a result of the indistinctness of the concept of the welfare state itself. Too many and quite divergent phenomena were being discussed under the same heading. Welfare state research seemed to suffer from a weakness well known in comparative politics and comparative policy analysis: concept stretching. Related to this was the problem of which indicators to use for the operationalization of "the welfare state" or reform. Finally, Pierson also noticed theoretical weaknesses that concerned the implicit assumption in many studies that one could measure welfare state change on a single scale. He observed that there was a tendency to reduce the problem of welfare state retrenchment and reform to a dichotomy of "less" versus "more" and "intact" versus "dismantled", which was an unwarranted theoretical simplification.

Pierson proposed to solve the dependent variable problem and improve our understanding of welfare state change by looking at three dimensions:

(1) Recommodification: the attempt "to restrict the alternatives to participation in the labour market, either by tightening eligibility or cutting benefits" (Pierson 2001b: 422), that is to say, to strengthen the whip of the labour market;
(2) Cost containment: the attempt to keep balanced budgets through austerity policies, including deficit reduction and tax moderation;
(3) Recalibration: "reforms which seek to make contemporary welfare states more consistent with contemporary goals and demands for social provision" (Pierson 2001b: 425).

Making use of the strengths of Esping-Andersen's (1990, 1999) regime approach and the country and policy area studies he brought together in his edited volume, Pierson (2001b) inferred that each regime (social democratic, liberal or conservative) was characterized by its own specific "new politics" of welfare state reform. For instance, in the liberal regime voters are less likely to be attached to the welfare state than in the conservative or social democratic models. In this regime recommodification is the pivotal dimension of welfare state reform. In the social democratic welfare regime, voters are highly attached to, and dependent on, the welfare state. Recommodification is not so much on the political agenda of reform, but – if only because of the sheer size of the public sector – cost containment is. The conservative regime is probably the most ill-adapted model of the three worlds of welfare capitalism, as a result of which recalibration and cost containment are the two dominating dimensions of reform. Here, the issue is how to stimulate job growth in the underdeveloped service sector and how to contain the exploding costs of pensions, disability benefits, and health care.

Contemporary research seems to have taken seriously Pierson's suggestion of the multi-dimensionality of the dependent variable (see Wincott 2003). For example, the issue of *cost containment* and *retrenchment* (or *regress*, as Korpi 2003 calls it) is taken up, for instance, in the broad study by Huber and Stephens (2001) and by Green-Pedersen (2004). Olli Kangas' (2004) study of sickness benefits in 18 OECD countries indicates that – in spite of continuing institutional distinctiveness – cost containment and retrenchment in Scandinavia causes convergence towards the continental welfare states. Korpi and Palme (2003) have shown that retrenchment has become a significant phenomenon in many countries.

With respect to *recommodification*, one can find at least five different notions in the literature. First, as already noted, Pierson (2001b) defines recommodification as the effort to restrict the alternatives to participation in the labour market, either by tightening eligibility or cutting benefits. Second, there are scholars who link recommodification to changes in the international economy (Geddes 1994). Third,

Breen (1997) looks at recommodification from a risk and stratification perspective and argues that recommodification occurs whenever hedging institutions, mechanisms or arrangements are weakened. Fourth, Bonoli (1998) sees recommodification as the opposite of decommodification and analyzes measures that are intended to weaken the position of commodified workers. Finally, Holden (2003) holds that recommodification occurs when states withdraw from the field of social welfare.

Recalibration seems to be a much less studied topic, but there are scattered (mainly German) examples, such as Lamping and Rüb's (2004) study of the restructuring of the German pension system and Leibfried and Obinger's (2003) analysis of the direction of social policy reforms in Germany.

Finally, a dimension of welfare state reform that Pierson did not distinguish (probably because he saw it as an aspect of recommodification) concerns *activation* and (market-driven) *workfare*. There is a host of literature also on this dimension, particularly prominent in the regulation approach (for an overview see Vis 2007), but the issue also seems particularly "hot" among British social scientists who study welfare policies under New Labour in a comparative perspective (for example Clasen and Clegg 2003, Lindsay and Mailand 2004, Taylor-Gooby et al. 2004, Wright et al. 2004). Moreover, it has inspired studies of activation in cases such as Germany and Austria (Ludwig-Mayerhofer and Wroblewski 2004), the Netherlands (Van Oorschot 2004), and the Netherlands and Denmark (Van Oorschot and Abrahamson 2003).

Although Pierson considerably improved our understanding of welfare state reform, his analyses still suffered somewhat from a weakness that is inherent to the institutional approach. Institutionalist analyses are very well capable of explaining institutional *resilience*, but have much more difficulties with understanding institutional and policy *change* (see Taylor-Gooby 2002). There seems to be a growing awareness of this explanatory problem of institutionalist approaches.

The Matching Problem in Comparative Welfare State Research

Depending on the type of theory proposed, scholarly work highlights different aspects of welfare state reform, that is, of the dependent variable. Equally important is to note that there are various explanatory approaches that compete with each other, but nevertheless seem to fit the same empirical data. In other words, it seems exceedingly difficult to properly assess their theoretical and empirical value. We have already introduced four aspects of this issue that we now will briefly elaborate: the type of explanation; the explanatory status of the theory (in terms of the specificity of the underlying causal model); the level of analysis; and the operational and empirical specificity of the hypotheses.

Looking at *types of explanation* for welfare state reform, we find a) economic explanations, including studies of internationalization and globalization (for example Glatzer and Rueschemeyer 2005, Kemmerling 2005, Kittel and Winner 2005), b) institutional explanations (for example Pierson 2001a, Obinger et al. 2005), party-political explanations (Kitschelt 2001, Green-Pedersen 2002, Burgoon and Baxandall 2005), d) discourse and framing-related explanations (Béland 2005, Schmidt 2000, Schmidt et al. 2005), and e) hypotheses on how European level policies affect national welfare states (Ferrera and Gualmini 2004, Natali 2005).

Next, the *explanatory status* refers to the precise type of causal argument employed in a study. Macro-level quantitative analyses usually employ a correlation approach focusing on the relation between variables that represent cause(s) and effect(s) (for example Castles 2004). Meso-level studies usually study causal mechanisms in addition to specifying causes and effects (for example, the many case studies we find in the field; see for an overview Starke 2006). Rare but important are the studies that combine both, as Huber and Stephens (2001) do.

If we focus on the *level of analysis* we note that welfare state reform is usually either analyzed at the macro-level of the determinants of regime change via comparative case studies or cross-national (pooled) quantitative studies, or at the meso-level of the determinants of changes in single programmes, such as unemployment insurance, sickness benefits, pension benefits and so on (for example on pensions: Bonoli 2001, Immergut et al. 2007; or on unemployment: Clasen 2005).

The final category is the *operational and empirical specificity of the hypotheses*. This is the aspect we focus on further because it is all too often neglected or not properly addressed in the literature. Different operationalizations may lead to different conclusions about the hypotheses that are deduced from the theory that is being tested. Remember Esping-Andersen's (1990: 19) insight on the operationalization of the dependent variable: "Most ... studies claim to explain the welfare state. Yet their focus on spending may be misleading. Expenditures are epiphenomenal to the theoretical substance of welfare states." His operationalization remained closer to the theoretical substance in terms of the various qualitative dimensions of the welfare state. This not only opened up a whole new way of looking at welfare state development, but also in one stroke made redundant a whole series of theories that had focused on social spending alone.

The issue on which we focus is the matching problem: frequently, causes and effects are specified at different levels of analysis, which has consequences for the conceptualization and operationalization of the causal mechanisms and the dependent variable. The crucial point is that this matching problem reinforces the dependent variable problem. We believe that the matching problem is a general phenomenon in various welfare state research traditions. If we make a distinction between, on the one hand, the mainstream literature that uses welfare state regime theory as an analytical instrument, and, on the other hand, the regulation approach to political economy (see Vis 2007), we observe that – in spite of their different levels of abstraction – they struggle with the same matching problem.

One way of "solving" the problem is to circumvent it by remaining at a high abstract theoretical level. This implies that theory and hypotheses are not matched at all because no (clear) empirical test strategy is offered. Torfing (2001), for instance, takes up the difficulty of institutional analysis referred to above, namely how to deal with institutional and policy change. He posits that in four important areas change has occurred in the welfare state: 1) demand-side macro-economic policy has been replaced by a supply-side orientation; 2) there has been a shift from welfare to workfare; 3) the scale and level of social policy making has shifted because authority has been displaced away from the national level; and 4) decentralized governance networks have taken over hierarchical state intervention. His proposal is to recognize that change is evolutionary and the result of the interplay between path shaping and path dependency. He offers a well informed and refined comparison between various institutional approaches and discusses how to analyze institutional change. To this end, Torfing proposes new theoretical concepts such as dislocation and path shaping, embedded in a more general neo-Gramscian framework that stresses institution-building as hegemonic projects. He then speculates how path shaping and path dependency interact to produce change.

His theoretical position is formulated at a very high level of abstraction:

> The political answer of the social and political forces to the obstructing effect of the institutional context on both policy output and policy outcome is the development of self-reflexive strategies. These aim to reduce or eliminate the effect of path dependency by deliberately restructuring the institutional framework for adopting and implementing new policies. Such strategies involve second-order reflections, since the hegemonic forces are not concerned with the form and content of the new policy, but rather with the tactical question of what they can do in order to remove obstacles to their path-shaping strategy and to turn new conjunctural opportunities into institutionalized supports of a new policy path. (Torfing 2001: 291)

After a thoughtful discussion of how the various institutionalisms have employed the concept of path dependency, he restates his position at an ever higher level of abstraction:

> the premise for analyzing path dependency is that a dislocating event disrupts the structured coherence of a policy path and thereby creates room for an effective agency engaged in processes of disarticulation and rearticulation which are not determined by any structural necessity. The dislocation of the old policy path creates a space for inchoate decisions about how to shape future policy regulations. These decisions are taken against a background of institutional fluidity. Whereas a relative institutional unfixity is the condition of possibility for path-shaping strategies, a relative institutional fixity is the condition of possibility of path-dependent policy reform. (ibid.: 298–299)

The empirical part consists of an *illustration* of the theoretical account via a description of failed and successful attempts to reform the Danish welfare state. Torfing (2001: 306) concludes that the new institutionalisms and his own theoretical contribution "help us to explicate the mechanisms of path dependency". However, he does not offer an empirical operationalization of the theoretical notions nor does he specify any hypotheses. He gives no conditions of refutation nor does he reflect upon the research design, the case selection, the data, the sources, and so on. As a result, he circumvents the problem of matching his highly abstract notions with hypotheses. He seems quite aware of this feature of his work, but discards it as unproblematic when he concludes that the "arguments about path dependency prove their value even in a brief and sweeping analysis of social policy reform carried out at a high level of abstraction" (ibid.: 306). Our point is that no matter how valuable his theoretical reflections are, by entirely circumventing the matching problem Torfing offers us one narrative about welfare state reform among the many that are possible and cannot convince that his theoretical notions are of empirical relevance.

At the other extreme, we find another strategy of evading the matching problem, that is narrowly focusing on what King *et al.* (1994) have called the observable consequences of various theories. This strategy is most often applied in quantitative comparative studies. It boils down to bringing together various hypotheses present in the literature, and translating these into a single regression model in order to test these hypotheses competitively. The matching problem arises here, because no attempt is made to connect the theories to the hypotheses derived from them, even though one would need such information in the first place for specifying the hypotheses clearly and correctly. As a result, it is impossible to judge the consistency of the theories and the model that results from it. It is also impossible to see whether uncritically adopting variables from very different approaches into a single model actually makes theoretical sense for the problem (for example social policy reform) at hand. In short, in this approach, which has a long tradition in comparative public policy studies, especially social policy or welfare state studies (one early example is Wilensky 1975, a more recent one Castles 2004), researchers usually make quite an effort to explain empirical operationalizations, hypotheses, the conditions of refutation, research design, case selection, the quality of the data, sources, and so on. But their models consist of loosely connected (if at all) hypotheses that have been isolated from contrasting and even conflicting theoretical perspectives.

In this context, for example, Castles and Obinger's (2007) recent study of social spending trends sums up the main theoretical approaches to welfare state research in a single table by simply isolating the main variables, predicted outcomes, measurement procedures and data sources. They go about as follows. First, they formulate a baseline model of three variables (level of GDP per capita, average rate of economic growth, average degree of bourgeois party cabinet incumbency). Second, they include other variables from various approaches on top of the incumbency variable already taken from the power resources approach included in the baseline model. This then becomes a difficult to grasp mixture that has no real theoretical grounding. It includes the impact on social expenditure of social needs (taken from functionalist modernization theories), of the timing of welfare state consolidation (taken from path dependency theories), and of political institutions (taken from political institutionalism). Finally, they offer a best-fit model by eliminating the statistically insignificant variables.

The goal of such designs is usually to debunk widely held but empirically unsubstantiated beliefs or speculations about the impact of certain developments on the welfare state, for instance globalization (see especially Castles 2004). To the extent that the hypotheses tested are accurate matches of the theoretical intentions and to the extent that they are in fact rejected, debunking is an important result. But since no attention is paid to how theories and hypotheses are matched, it is difficult to judge whether the successful debunking effort is the result of a fair test or an artefact of the design. To give but one illustration, theories of socio-economic development or modernization are fairly complex and multifaceted accounts – rooted in the theory of structural-functional differentiation – of why and how industrialization and its social and cultural correlates, in interaction with democratization, lead to higher social spending. It is highly questionable whether such a theory can be characterized by simple correlations or causal statements such as "economic affluence leads to more expenditure" and "problem pressure leads to more spending" or that it can be operationalized in two key variables; GDP per capita and a social need index. Such operationalizations do not match the high level of abstraction at which modernization theory is formulated.

These are extremes of a continuum between which most empirical/analytical studies of welfare state development and change could be placed. Theoretically informed thick descriptions, for instance, would be closer to the Torfing approach discussed above. But those studies that provide a combination of variable-oriented quantitative comparisons and case-oriented qualitative studies (for example Huber and Stephens 2001, Swank 2002) or approaches that make use of the Qualitative Comparative method or fuzzy sets (for example Kvist 2007, Vis 2007) would be more in line with the Castles and Obinger example. Concerning the former group of studies, the use of method triangulation may serve to alleviate the matching problem, as the problems linked to very abstract quantitative studies may be addressed in the case study part. Concerning the latter, the chances of studies using set-theoretic methods to avoid the matching problem ultimately depend on the carefully and theoretically motivated choice of how to operationalize set memberships of causal conditions. It is important to note that all of these studies face the same matching problem, but that they do make serious efforts, although not always explicitly, to deal with it.

The main advantage of the case-oriented approach over the variable-oriented one is that the former seems better capable of dealing with the matching problem. This is because thick descriptions tend to remain much closer to the conceptual framework than when proper names have been turned into variables (Przeworski and Teune 1970). Let us illustrate the point. A widely accepted insight is that political institutions of federalism have tended to obstruct the growth of social solidarity. Federalism is commonly assumed to be an institutional design to make sure that some level of national unity is preserved by decentralizing power and thus allowing a larger extent of social, cultural, economic and political diversity between subnational territorial units than would normally be tolerated in a unitary state. The welfare state's function, by contrast, is normally argued to derive from the goal to ensure equal social rights for all citizens. Federalism and the welfare state, then, apparently have conflicting goals. The received wisdom is that federalism has considerably held back the development of social policy. As regards the politics of reform, the argument is that federalism has an impeding effect too, as the multiple veto points in federal systems make it extremely hard to overcome resistance against changing the status quo. Quantitative studies time and again reported this effect (see Obinger et al. 2005). But it seems questionable that such studies have matched the theory and the hypotheses adequately, because not only do comparative historical analyses indicate that under certain conditions federalism also encourages social spending, but also that the causal link between federalism and the welfare state runs both ways. In other words, the causal theory on the relationship between the two concepts becomes complicated and the demands on matching accordingly rise. The message here is that we need to become more conscious of how such problems of endogeneity, an all too common phenomenon in social science (see King et al. 1994), influence the problem of matching. Even in the light of lacking definite solutions, at least paying attention to such issues would be an improvement.

The best way to develop the feedback link between federalism and the welfare state is in careful studies of single country experiences. For instance, Keith Banting (2005) argues that the development of the welfare state has had a decisive effect on the centralization of the Canadian federation. Moreover, social programmes played a key role in establishing the constituent political communities of the federal state and their political identities. "Political identities are highly contested in Canada", writes Banting (2005: 90), "and social programmes have emerged as instruments of nation-building. For the central government, social policy has been seen as an instrument of territorial integration, part of the glue holding together a vast country subject to powerful centrifugal tendencies". But also the subnational units, most obviously Québec, used social policy to reinforce their own distinctive regional community and identity, based on culture and language. For both the federation and the regions, "social policy has been an instrument not only of social justice but also of statecraft" (ibid.). The equalization programme of the Canadian fiscal system through which resources are redistributed from the poorer to the wealthier regions are to enhance national unity. The point of the analysis is that federalism shapes social policy and social policy shapes federalism and reform of social policy reforms federalism. Here highly abstract theoretical concepts (such as territorial integration, political identity and nation-building) and their interconnections play a crucial role in the description itself. Theory and empirics are closely matched: the concepts have a descriptive function.

However, at some point researchers who prefer this type of theoretically informed descriptions of welfare state change will face the problem of generalization. If one does not try this, or if scope conditions have been formulated that exclude further generalization, one ends up with only description and little is learned about the dynamics of welfare state change. Many case studies for this reason refrain from generalization. However, if one does try to generalize the findings, then in fact a new theory is formulated that needs to be tested against new data and this posits the matching problem all over again. Yet, better to be bold in generalization and create a new challenge than to refrain from trying to improve the scope of one's theory.

In order to further substantiate our argument, we finally present an example taken from the work of one of the current authors, focusing on ideational leadership as a cause of welfare state reform. In the welfare state literature that focuses on historical institutionalism and regime theory, strong institutional and electoral forces prevent states from conducting far-reaching, that is structural (or institutional) reforms in social policy. Then, the question arises how such reforms occur at all. The composite concept of ideational leadership can help to explain why welfare states – despite the obstacles identified – *do experience* at least some far-reaching reforms (Stiller 2004). The dependent variable is defined as far-reaching or structural reforms (measured by shifts in the financing, benefit, or management structure of a policy area), and the independent variable is ideational leadership (IL) of key policy makers. IL is characterized by four aspects: a) rejection of the status quo, b) consistent legitimization of new policy principles, c) an appeal to reform critics to rethink their resistance against reform, and d) efforts to build political coalitions for reform without resorting to tactical "games". The claim is that the combination of these aspects leads to a substantial reduction in reform resistance, enabling the passing of structural reforms. According to the resilience literature, such an event presupposes the overcoming of institutional and electoral obstacles. The causal mechanisms linking the separate aspects and structural reform draw on insights from the literature on ideas in policy making, institutional change and policy change. In combination, these mechanisms create an "institutional break-out" situation that reverses lock-in effects and policy stickiness, phenomena implied by path dependency. Engineering an institutional break-out enables ideational leaders to adopt structural reforms that transform the policy status quo in any one social policy area.

The problem of matching occurs in the following way. Cause and effect are situated on different levels of abstraction: on the one hand, IL and its aspects concern the level of actors, as they relate to the communicative or political behaviour of individual policy makers. The effects of such behaviour are conceptually situated at a higher level of abstraction dealing with institutional structures, relating to institutional lock-in mechanisms surrounding individual policies. Institutional structures are underlined by the values and interests of those defending policy arrangements: for instance, political parties and interest groups (and their perception of switching costs when choosing alternative institutional arrangements). The causal mechanisms linked to the different aspects of IL are: a) policy failure or loss of effectiveness brings on the search for alternatives; b) creating insights into the logics of appropriateness and necessity behind the innovation help lowering switching costs and redefining values underlying old policies; c) reform-critical interest groups are made to "face the facts" or redefine (the perception) of their interest, lowering switching costs; and d) forging consensus based more on policy-seeking than power-seeking motives reduces switching costs.

These mechanisms should ideally bridge the gap between the independent variable, IL, its operationalization in concrete patterns of argumentation and behaviour of individual policy makers, and the much more abstract concept of "institutional break-out" that enables structural reform to materialize. Conceptually, this does not immediately cause major problems, but empirically it is problematic. The main question here is twofold: 1) how to operationalize and match causal mechanisms linking an explanation on the individual actor level with an outcome that is conditional on the loosening of institutional constraints on the meso level of structure, and 2) how to find data to illustrate the working of each of the theorized causal mechanisms. For instance, which data should one use to show the effect of a policy maker criticizing the status quo and credibly promoting innovative reform on the perception and re-definition of interest by some crucial opposition party or interest group? If such data are not available, an alternative would be to use data that indirectly support (or refute) the mechanism in question. For instance, a trade union changing its preference during the reform process may be assumed to have undergone a reconsideration of interests. Another alternative could be to illustrate the effect of IL by first demonstrating its existence with the help of several qualitative indicators, and subsequently show its role in the adoption of reform by excluding alternative actor-related strategies (that is concession making) of overcoming reform obstacles. However, it would be preferable to improve the quality of the argument by illustrating the causal mechanism that links IL to the acceptance of a reform proposal. The ideal strategy in evaluating the effects of IL would be first to look for indicators of its several aspects in empirical material and establish whether these aspects were all present in a specific case of reform. Second, suitable data could illustrate the connection between politicians' actions and the outcome of structural reform.

Empirical research on Germany has shown that demonstrating the link between the theorized causal mechanisms and a specific reform outcome often proves difficult. For instance, the case of the adoption of the unemployment insurance reform "Hartz IV" illustrates well the difficulties related to the matching problem. The central question was whether ideational leadership by the Minister of Labour Affairs contributed to the eventual adoption of this structural reform. When tracing the causal mechanisms elaborated above, the first such mechanism, concerning the link between policy makers qualifying the status quo as failure, was hard to prove. Notably, policy failure (of existing unemployment insurance arrangements) had already been acknowledged by the opposition parties before the government announced its "Hartz IV" reform plan. Regarding the effect of cognitive and normative arguments about the policy alternative on the eventual breakthrough (the second causal mechanism), it could be shown that some sceptics, especially in the governing coalition parties, had been convinced. However, it could not be directly shown that the parliamentary opposition gave up its policy position because of the government's efforts to argue for its centralistic solution for providing and administering the new benefit. Third, despite the minister's appeals to reform opponents to co-operate constructively and refrain from detrimental blockades (third causal mechanism), the appeals to give up reform resistance did not change the opposition's negative attitude so that a crucial agreement was only achieved in the parliamentary reconciliation procedure. Fourth, regarding the link between the minister's efforts of political consensus-building and the outcome of structural reform, the picture was different: there was abundant evidence of the minister actively seeking consensus with reform opponents during the agenda-setting and legislative preparatory phases. Even when, during a mediation procedure in the final negotiation phase, the minister's consensus-building efforts met institutional constraints, he remained centred on achieving a final compromise in order to avoid an outright failure of negotiations.

To sum up, the analysis focused on demonstrating the presence of indicators of IL rather than direct effects of IL on reform adoption. It did establish, by way of indirect argument, that the fourth aspect of IL contributed to the breakthrough of reform, while the effects of the remaining three indicators could not be demonstrated directly. This nicely illustrates the difficulties of finding appropriate data to demonstrate causal mechanisms, that is to bridge the gap between levels of analysis of various variables, related to the matching problem.

Conclusion

In this article, we have presented a brief overview of contemporary issues in comparative welfare state research and demonstrated that there has been real progress in our understanding of the multi-dimensionality of the dependent variable, that is, the conceptualization of welfare state change via various dimensions of reform. We also found that the debate on welfare state change and reform is not yet over. Specifically, we highlighted that the matching problem reinforces still unresolved issues with respect to the conceptualization and operationalization of the dependent variable. Moreover, we found that – in addition to identifying causes and effects – there are difficulties with specifying the causal mechanisms that link causes and effects. Furthermore, we have tried to demonstrate, by referring to several examples from the literature using different analytical techniques, that matching theory and hypotheses is a ubiquitous problem in the literature. As a final example, we further elaborated and illustrated the argument with an empirical example from our research on structural welfare state reform, observing two methodological problems: 1) the risk of drawing conclusions about one level of analysis using evidence from another; 2) the problem of translating causal mechanisms formulated at a high level of abstraction to a lesser level.

We identified the risk of committing either an ecological or an individualist fallacy as a result of the matching problem. These fallacies occur when inferences are drawn about one level of analysis using evidence from another, for example, when on the basis of an analysis of aggregate-level data inferences are drawn about the behaviour of individuals (ecological fallacy) or vice versa (individual fallacy) (Landman 2000: 53). In addition, the problem of "measuring" causal mechanisms has to do with difficulties of "translating" them to a lesser level of abstraction which might involve finding a whole chain of mechanisms that provide together a plausible link between the two variables. However, even if such a causal link can be plausibly made theoretically, data to illustrate its workings may be difficult to obtain or non-existent.

As a first step to deal with the matching problem, we propose that researchers pay more attention to the difficulty of bridging the difference in levels of analysis between the independent and dependent variables. Furthermore, we need to address the question of how to use an actor-centred account to explain changes of structure. The second and related problem concerns the conceptualization and operationalization of the causal mechanism between these variables. There may be evidence that ideational leadership is capable of overcoming institutional resistance against change. But how can we specify precisely how this works?

We believe that questions of this sort are relevant to welfare state scholars and policy analysts more generally, deserve more attention in the welfare state literature and certainly merit further discussion. Recognizing such questions and therefore showing awareness of the matching problem and related methodological difficulties would be a first step. We hope our paper will stimulate researchers to think about potential answers and ways to deal with the matching problem so that we can improve our theoretical and empirical understanding of mechanisms of welfare state change.

Acknowledgements

An extended version of this paper was first presented in the panel "Comparative analysis of welfare reform: the dependent variable problem", ESPAnet Conference 2005, University of Fribourg, Switzerland. We wish to thank Birgit Pfau-Effinger and Ian Bruff for their comments. We would also like to thank Christoffer Green-Pedersen and the members of the Working Group on International Relations at Radboud University for helpful criticism and suggestions. Furthermore, we are grateful to two anonymous reviewers for their constructive criticism.

Kees van Kersbergen wishes to thank the University of Konstanz's Centre of Excellence "Cultural Foundations of Integration", and especially its Institute for Advanced Study, for their generous hospitality and support.

References

Allan, James P. and Scruggs, Lyle, 2004, Political partisanship and welfare state reform in advanced industrial societies. *American Journal of Political Science*, **48**, 496–512.

Banting, Keith, 2005, Canada: nation-building in a federal welfare state, in: Herbert Obinger, Stephan Leibfried and Francis G. Castles (Eds), *Federalism and the Welfare State. New World and European Experiences* (Cambridge: Cambridge University Press), pp. 89–137.

Béland, Daniel, 2005, Ideas and social policy: an institutional perspective. *Social Policy & Administration*, **39**, 1–18.

Bonoli, Giuliano, 1998, Globalization, the welfare state, and recommodification. Round Table "Globalization and social governance in Europe and the US", Brussels.

Bonoli, Giuliano, 2001, Political institutions, veto points, and the process of welfare state adaptation, in: Paul Pierson (Ed.) *The New Politics of the Welfare State* (Oxford: Oxford University Press), pp. 238–264.

Breen, Richard, 1997, Risk, recommodification and stratification. *Sociology*, **31**, 473–489.

Burgoon, Brian and Baxandall, Phineas, 2004, Three worlds of working time: the partisan and welfare politics of work hours in industrialized countries. *Politics and Society*, **32**, 439–474.

Castles, Francis G., 2004, *The Future of the Welfare State: Crisis, Myths and Crisis Realities* (Oxford: Oxford University Press).

Castles, Francis G. and Obinger, Herbert, 2007, Social expenditure and the politics of redistribution. *Journal of European Social Policy*, **17**, 206–222.

Clasen, Jochen, 2005, *Reforming European Welfare States: Germany and the United Kingdom Compared* (Oxford: Oxford University Press).

Clasen, Jochen and Clegg, Daniel, 2003, Unemployment protection and labour market reform in France and Great Britain in the 1990s: solidarity versus activation? *Journal of Social Policy*, **32**, 361–382.

Clasen, Jochen and Siegel, Nico A., 2007, *Investigating Welfare State Change. The "Dependent Variable Problem" in Comparative Analysis* (Cheltenham: Edward Elgar).

Esping-Andersen, Gøsta, 1990, *The Three Worlds of Welfare Capitalism* (Cambridge: Polity Press).

Esping-Andersen, Gøsta, 1999, *Social Foundations of Postindustrial Societies* (Oxford: Oxford University Press).

Ferrera, Maurizio and Gualmini, Elisabetta, 2004, *Rescued by Europe: Social and Labour Market Reforms in Italy from Maastricht to Berlusconi* (Amsterdam: Amsterdam University Press).

Geddes, Mike, 1994 Public services and local economic regeneration in a post-Fordist economy. Towards a post-Fordist welfare state? in: Roger Burrows and Brian Loader (Eds) *Towards a Post-Fordist Welfare State?* (London: Routledge), pp. 151–176.

Glatzer, Miguel and Rueschemeyer, Dietrich, (Eds) 2005, *Globalization and the Future of the Welfare State* (Pittsburgh: University of Pittsburgh Press).

Green-Pedersen, Christoffer, 2002, *The Politics of Justification. Party Competition and Welfare-State Retrenchment in Denmark and the Netherlands from 1982 to 1998* (Amsterdam: Amsterdam University Press).

Green-Pedersen, Christoffer, 2004, The dependent variable problem within the study of welfare-state retrenchment: defining the problem and looking for solutions. *Journal of Comparative Policy Analysis*, **6**, 3–14.

Holden, Chris, 2003, Decommodification and the workfare state. *Political Studies Review*, **1**, 303–316.

Huber, Evelyne and Stephens, John D., 2001, *Development and Crisis of the Welfare State: Parties and Policies in Global Markets* (Chicago: The University of Chicago Press).

Immergut, Ellen M., Anderson, Karen M. and Schulze, Isabelle (Eds) 2007, *The Handbook of West European Pension Politics* (Oxford: Oxford University Press).

Jaeger, Mads Meier and Kvist, Jon 2003, Pressures on state welfare in post-industrial societies: is more or less better? *Social Policy and Administration*, **37**, 555–572.

Kangas, Olli, 2004, Institutional development of sickness cash-benefit programmes in 18 OECD countries. *Social Policy and Administration*, **38**, 190–203.

Kemmerling, Achim, 2005, Tax mixes, welfare states and employment: tracking diverging vulnerabilities. *Journal of European Public Policy*, **12**, 1–22.

King, Gary, Keohane, Robert O., Verba, Sidney, 1994, *Designing Social Inquiry: Scientific Inference in Qualitative Research* (Princeton: Princeton University Press).

Kitschelt, Herbert, 2001, Partisan competition and welfare state retrenchment: when do politicians choose unpopular policies? in: Paul Pierson (Ed.) *The New Politics of the Welfare State* (Oxford: Oxford University Press), pp. 265–304.

Kittel, Bernhard and Winner, Hannes, 2005, How reliable is pooled analysis in political economy? The globalization–welfare state nexus revisited. *European Journal of Political Research*, **44**, 269–294.

Korpi, Walter, 2003, Welfare-state regress in Western Europe: politics, institutions, globalization, and Europeanization. *Annual Review of Sociology*, **29**, 589–609.

Korpi, Walter and Palme, Joachim, 2003, New politics and class politics in the context of austerity and globalization: welfare state regress in 18 countries, 1975–95. *American Political Science Review*, **97**, 425–447.

Kühner, Stefan, 2007, Country-level comparisons of welfare state change measures: another facet of the dependent variable problem within the comparative analysis of the welfare state? *Journal of European Social Policy*, **17**, 5–18.

Kvist, Jon, 2007, Exploring diversity: measuring welfare state change with fuzzy-set methodology in: Jochen Clasen and Nico A. Siegel (Eds) *Investigating Welfare State Change. The 'Dependent Variable Problem' in Comparative Analysis* (Cheltenham: Edward Elgar), pp. 198–216.

Lamping, Wolfram and Rüb, Friedbert W., 2004, From the conservative welfare state to an "uncertain something else": German pension politics in comparative perspective. *Policy and Politics: Studies of Local Government and its Services*, **32**, 169–192.

Landman, Todd, 2000, *Issues and Methods in Comparative Politics: An Introduction* (London: Routledge).

Leibfried, Stephan and Obinger, Herbert, 2003, The state of the welfare state: German social policy between macroeconomic retrenchment and microeconomic recalibration. *West European Politics*, **26**, 199–218.

Lindsay, Colin and Mailand, Mikkel, 2004, Different routes, common directions? activation policies for young people in Denmark and the UK. *International Journal of Social Welfare*, **13**, 195–207.

Ludwig-Mayerhofer and Wroblewski, 2004, Eppur si muove? Activation policies in Austria and Germany. *European Societies*, **6**, 485–509.

Natali, David, 2005, Europeanization, policy arenas, and creative opportunism: the politics of welfare state reforms in Italy. *Journal of European Public Policy*, **11**, 1077–1095.

Obinger, Herbert, Leibfried, Stephan and Castles, Francis G. (Eds), 2005, *Federalism and the Welfare State. New World and European Experiences* (Cambridge: Cambridge University Press).

Pierson, Paul, 1994, *Dismantling the Welfare State? Reagan, Thatcher, and the Politics of Retrenchment* (Cambridge: Cambridge University Press).

Pierson, Paul, 1996, The new politics of the welfare state. *World Politics*, **48**, 143–179.

Pierson, Paul (Ed.) 2001a, *The New Politics of the Welfare State* (Oxford: Oxford University Press).

Pierson, Paul, 2001b, Coping with permanent austerity: welfare state restructuring in affluent democracies. in: Paul Pierson (Ed.) *The New Politics of the Welfare State* (Oxford: Oxford University Press), pp. 410–456.

Przeworski, Adam and Teune, Henry, 1970, *The Logic of Comparative Social Inquiry* (New York: Wiley-Interscience).

Schmidt, Vivien A., 2000, Values and discourse in the politics of adjustment, in: Fritz W. Scharpf and Vivien A. Schmidt (Eds) *Welfare and Work in the Open Economy, Vol. 1. From Vulnerability to Competitiveness* (Oxford: Oxford University Press), pp. 229–309.

Schmidt, Vivien A., 2005, *Public Discourse and Welfare State Reform. The Social Democratic Experience* (Amsterdam: Mets & Schilt).

Starke, Peter, 2006, The politics of welfare state retrenchment: a literature review. *Social Policy and Administration*, **40**, 104–120.

Stiller, Sabina, 2004, Operationalizing and refining ideational leadership: towards explaining institutional change in German pension policy. Paper presented at the NIG Annual Congress, Rotterdam, The Netherlands, October 29, 2004.

Stiller, Sabina, 2007, Innovative agents versus immovable objects. The role of ideational leadership in German welfare state reforms. PhD thesis, Radboud University Nijmegen.

Swank, Duane, 2002, *Global Capital, Political Institutions, and Policy Change in Developed Welfare States* (Cambridge: Cambridge University Press).

Taylor-Gooby, Peter, 2002, The silver age of the welfare state: perspectives on resilience. *Journal of Social Policy*, **31**, 597–622.

Taylor-Gooby, Peter, Larsen, Trine and Kananen, Johannes, 2004, Market means and welfare ends: the UK welfare state experiment. *Journal of Social Policy*, **33**, 573–592.

Torfing, Jacob, 2001, Path-dependent Danish welfare reforms. The contribution of the new institutionalisms to understanding evolutionary change. *Scandinavian Political Studies*, **24**, 277–310.

Van Oorschot, Wim, 2004, Balancing work and welfare: activation and flexicurity policies in the Netherlands 1980–2000. *International Journal of Social Welfare*, **13**, 15–27.

Van Oorschot, Wim and Abrahamson, Peter, 2003, The Dutch and Danish miracles revisited: a critical discussion of activation policies in two small welfare states. *Social Policy and Administration*, **37**, 288–304.

Vis, Barbara, 2007, States of welfare or states of workfare? Welfare state restructuring in 16 capitalist democracies, 1985–2002. *Policy and Politics*, **35**, 105–122.

Wilensky, Harold L., 1975, *The Welfare State and Equality: Structural and Ideological Roots of Public Expenditures* (Berkeley: University of California Press).

Wincott, Daniel, 2003, Slippery concepts, shifting context: (national) states and welfare in the Veit-Wilson-Atherton debate. *Social Policy and Administration*, **37**, 305–315.

Wright, Sharon, Kopac, Anja and Slater, Gary, 2004, Continuities within paradigmatic change, activation, social policies and citizenship in the context of welfare reform in Slovenia and the UK, *European Societies*, **6**, 511–534.

The Dependent Variable Problem within the Study of Welfare State Retrenchment: Defining the Problem and Looking for Solutions

CHRISTOFFER GREEN-PEDERSEN

ABSTRACT *Since the publication of Pierson's seminal work, a scholarly debate about welfare state retrenchment has emerged. One of the debated issues has been the "dependent variable problem": what is welfare state retrenchment and how can it be measured. In particular the pros and cons of different types of data have been discussed. The argument of this article is that the "dependent variable problem" is a problem of theoretical conceptualization rather than a problem of data. It is crucial to be aware that different theoretical perspectives on retrenchment should lead to different conceptualizations of retrenchment. Furthermore, different conceptualizations lead to different evaluations of the same changes in welfare schemes, just as the question of which data to use depends very much on the theoretical conceptualization of retrenchment.*

Introduction

Since the publication of Pierson's seminal work (1994, 1996), a scholarly debate about welfare state retrenchment has emerged.[1] This debate has several aspects: Pierson's work has provoked a discussion about the importance of economic, institutional, and political factors for explaining cross-national variation in retrenchment (Castles 2001; Ross 2000; Kitschelt 2001; Bonoli 2001; Green-Pedersen 2001). Furthermore, Pierson's work has started a discussion about differences in vulnerability to retrenchment of social security schemes (Alber 1998; Anderson 1998), as well as a debate about the persistence of the welfare state (Clayton and Pontusson 1998; Cox 1998; van Kersbergen 2000; Scarbrough 2000; Stephens *et al.* 1999).

This article addresses a fourth aspect of the retrenchment debate also sparked off by Pierson's work, namely what can be labelled the "dependent variable problem" (Pierson 1994, 1996, 2001; Clayton and Pontusson 1998; Alber 1996, 1998; Lindbom 1999; van der Veen *et al.* 1999). As the term suggests, the "dependent variable problem" is about defining the object of the entire retrenchment debate. This involves such questions as which changes to welfare states should be classified as retrenchment; how one can separate retrenchment from reform and reconstruction; and which data are most appropriate for empirical investigations of retrenchment outcomes.

It is clear that the dependent variable problem is crucial for the entire debate, and that disagreement about the dependent variable is a major obstacle for cumulative knowledge about welfare state retrenchment. As Pierson (2001) argues following Kitschelt (2001): "It is difficult to exaggerate the obstacle this dissensus creates for comparative research ... it is impossible to seriously evaluate competing *explanations* [original emphasis] when there is no agreement about the pattern of *outcomes* [original emphasis] to be explained". To put it bluntly, the debate about explanations of variation in retrenchment cannot move beyond the stage of hypotheses before the dependent variable problem has been addressed, and the same goes for the debate about welfare state persistence or change. Addressing the dependent variable problem should have high priority within the retrenchment literature.

At times, the debate about these issues has been rather heated, and several suggestions of "ground rules" for the study of retrenchment have been seen (Pierson 1994: 13–17; Alber 1996: 10–13). The first step forward in this debate must be to identify the nature of the dependent variable problem. This article argues the dependent variable problem to be a problem of theoretical conceptualization of retrenchment. Thus, it is not in the first place a question about the use of quantitative, especially expenditure data, versus "qualitative" data, which is often the impression left by the debate about the dependent variable (Pierson 1994, 1996; Clayton and Pontusson 1998; Alber 1996: 10–13). One should distinguish between two questions. First, *what* should be measured in empirical investigations? In other words, what should the theoretical definition of retrenchment be? Second, *how* can retrenchment actually be measured? This is a question identifying the most appropriate data for empirical investigations of retrenchment, that is, operational definitions. Both questions are clearly important. The first question is, however, more crucial in the sense that the question about the most appropriate data can only be answered when one knows exactly what to measure. The first question is theoretical since it can only be answered in light of each researcher's theoretical perspective and research question.

The argument may seem somewhat commonsensical, but as will be shown in the following much of the disagreement about the dependent variable actually originates from scholars having different theoretical perspectives and not always being fully aware of the implications of their theoretical approaches to welfare state retrenchment. Part of the problem also originates from disagreement about defining the welfare state notion in the first place.

This argument will be substantiated by taking three steps. The first section looks at the dependent variable debate within the study of welfare state expansion and especially the work of Gøsta Esping-Andersen (1990). The reason for including this is that Esping-Andersen's argument about the dependent variable is often used in the dependent variable debate in the study of welfare state retrenchment. The next section discusses one source of theoretical confusion, namely defining the welfare state notion. Different definitions of the welfare state notion have consequences when it comes to defining welfare state retrenchment. The third and main section discusses different conceptualizations of welfare state retrenchment and especially the work of Paul Pierson (1994, 1996, 2001). The section argues that one should keep two different conceptualizations of retrenchment apart, namely retrenchment as an unpopular cutback in people's entitlements, and retrenchment as a change in the institutional structure of different welfare states.

The Dependent Variable Debate in the Study of Welfare State Expansion

The scholarly debate about the expansion of the welfare state also had its dependent variable debate. Most of the research into the growth of the welfare state was based on aggregate expenditure data. Esping-Andersen (1990) challenged this by basing his analysis of the three worlds of welfare capitalism on, among other things, a measurement of the degree of decommodification resulting from different social security schemes.[2]

What is worth noticing about Esping-Andersen's reformulation of the dependent variable is not so much the fact that he used a different kind of quantitative data from that which had traditionally been used for research into the growth of the welfare state. The interesting point was Esping-Andersen's argument that the expansion of the welfare state should be analyzed as a question of higher levels of decommodification, not as a question of higher levels of social security expenditure. As Esping-Andersen (1990: 21) put it: "It is difficult to imagine anyone struggled for spending *per se*". What Esping-Andersen offered was in reality a "theory-internal" criticism of the dominating theoretical perspective within research into the growth of the welfare state, namely "power resources theory" (cf. O'Connor and Olsen 1998). If power resources theory is to be taken seriously, it is misplaced to focus on social security expenditure. Social democracy, which power resources theory sees as the driving force behind welfare state expansion, had struggled for the right of workers to uphold a living independently of the market, not for higher social security expenditure. The lesson to learn from Esping-Andersen's reformulation of the dependent variable is thus not so much that aggregate social security expenditure by definition is a bad way of conceptualizing and measuring welfare state expansion. The lesson is better formulated like this: when analysing the question of welfare state expansion from the power resources theory perspective, social security expenditures are inappropriate as a measure of expansion. In this way, Esping-Andersen underscored that the question about defining the dependent variable cannot be detached from a theoretical perspective and a specific research question. These are two sides of the same coin. From a different theoretical perspective and with a different research question, it may be perfectly justified to focus on the growth in social security expenditure.

What is the Welfare State?

Before turning to the question of defining welfare state *retrenchment*, it is worth focusing on defining the *welfare state* since disagreements about welfare state retrenchment often originate from different definitions of the welfare state notion.

Generally, definitions of the welfare state can be divided into policy definitions and outcome definitions. In the latter case, the welfare state is defined with reference to certain outcomes. For instance, Clayton and Pontusson (1998) challenged Pierson's conclusion (1994, 1996) about persistence of the welfare state by arguing that Pierson ignores rising social inequality and insecurity. Focusing on policy changes is not enough.[3] Other examples are Korpi and Palme (2001), who include full employment in their welfare state definition, and Cox (1998), who argues that, even though policy changes might not be dramatic, numerous minor cutbacks and changes have changed the conception of social rights away from citizens' rights towards more "achievement oriented" principles. Thus, the conclusion about the persistence of the welfare state does not cover its normative foundation. As argued by Korpi and Palme (2001), it may theoretically be justified to focus on such outcome since they, and not the policies, are the ultimate interest of political actors. However, there are several significant problems with outcome definitions of the welfare state. First of all, many factors other than the acts of governments influence outcomes such as equality and full employment. Therefore, interpreting changes in, for instance, equality and employment as a result of government action requires considerable caution. For instance, economists often argue that full employment can be achieved by decreasing the reservation wage through social security cutbacks, which could then be considered an expansion of the welfare state.

Policy definitions, where the welfare state means the benefits provided by the state in case of sickness, old-age, unemployment, and so forth, and services in the area of health, child care and so on, are the most commonly used The question with regard to policy definitions is which policies to include. Again, this is to some extent a question of theoretical interest. For instance, Schwartz (2001) defines the welfare state as social protection in the sense of sheltering income streams from market pressures. Following this definition, for instance, changes to regulatory arrangements protecting particular economic sectors are also retrenchments. However, when the welfare state notion is defined more broadly, one may be facing a staggering task when it comes to operationalizing the concept, especially in a way suitable for cross-national or policy area comparisons. As stated by Pierson (2001):

> Yet, as the concept of the welfare state, or welfare regime, "stretches", it becomes inevitable that quite distinct processes and outcomes will be joined together under the umbrella of a single master variable ... The complexity of this multi-faceted concept cuts against our attempts to generate the relatively parsimonious measures of outcomes that make a serious enterprise of comparative explanation possible.[4]

To sum up, no definition of the welfare state is a priori better or worse than others. However, when one moves away from the mainstream policy definition of the welfare state either by including certain outcomes or other policy areas, one changes focus considerably. What has happened to the welfare state understood as certain policies is a question quite different from asking what has happened to the welfare state understood as a commitment to equality. Therefore, even though it is interesting if studies based on "alternative" definitions of the welfare state reach different conclusions from the more mainstream studies, the possibilities of engaging in a debate with studies based on the mainstream definition may be limited and moving away from defining the welfare state as social transfers and services requires strong arguments.

Different Conceptualizations of Welfare State Retrenchment

Different ways of defining the welfare state notion is one part of the dependent variable problem. Yet, this is probably the most obvious part and thus the easiest to observe. The part of the problem relating to the consequences of different theoretical perspectives and different research questions is more delicate. What has not always been clear in the dependent variable debate is that even though the same policies are in focus, different research questions and theoretical perspectives should lead to different conceptualizations of retrenchment and consequently also to different measurements of it (cf. King *et al.* 1994: 55–63; Peters 1998: 218–219). There is no such thing as retrenchment *per se*.

Exactly this was the gist of Esping-Andersen's criticism of research into social democracy and the welfare state based on social expenditure data: Given the research question and the theoretical perspective, welfare state growth should be conceptualized in terms of decommodification, which cannot be measured by social security expenditure. When looking at the debate about welfare state retrenchment, two different theoretical perspectives on welfare state retrenchment are prominent, namely retrenchment as cutbacks in people's entitlements and retrenchment as institutional change. Even though the two conceptualizations are related, they are not identical and should lead to different conceptualizations of retrenchment.

Retrenchment as Cutbacks

From the first perspective, retrenchment is a question of cuts in people's welfare entitlements. By way of example, Green-Pedersen (2002: chap. 4) defines retrenchment as changes in social security schemes making them less attractive or generous to the recipients. Examples of such changes are cuts in benefit levels, stricter eligibility criteria or shorter duration of benefits. The theoretical argument behind focusing on such changes is an expectation of negative reactions from the electorate. Following Ross (2000: 157–158), such changes can be considered "constituencyless issues", where losses are imposed on concentrated groups while gains are spread to, for instance, all taxpayers. With a theoretical interest in how politicians avoid blame or are able to implement unpopular policies, focusing on such changes seems logical. Such a conceptualization of retrenchment is also implicit in many studies of retrenchment which more or less equate retrenchment with budgetary cuts.

With such a theoretical definition of retrenchment, there would from a theoretical perspective be no problem in using social security expenditure as the operational definition of retrenchment. However, a number of more practical problems make expenditure data problematic. First of all, expenditure data are outcome measures and other factors intervene between political decisions and actual outcomes such as expenditures. A standard problem is the power of bureaucrats when it comes to the implementation of public policies. With regard to welfare transfers such problems are probably limited, but with regard to welfare services, political decisions to retrenchment may, for example, be counteracted by bureaucrats not keeping budgets.

Another problem with expenditure is that expenditures on, for instance, unemployment benefits can rise due to more unemployed without any changes to legislation. Corrections can be made for such effects (cf. Siegel 2001), but if one, for example, corrects expenditure figures for changes in the number of claimants, one also neutralizes the effects of changes to the rules concerning eligibility.

A final problem with expenditure figures is the "time-lag" problem highlighted by Pierson (1994: 14). This refers to the fact that many retrenchments are designed to have gradual rather than immediate effects. Consequently, many enacted retrenchments are not yet visible in expenditures. The importance of this problem varies, but with regard to pension systems it is a very serious caveat against expenditure data as pension reforms are typically designed to work in the long run.

Another outcome measure of retrenchment understood as cutbacks in people's entitlements is average replacement rates in social security schemes as used by, for example, Korpi and Palme (2001) and Swank (2002). Compared to social expenditure, the advantage is that this measure is not affected by, for instance, changes in the level of unemployment. However, the time-lag problems still exist and the measure has other drawbacks as well. Retrenchments such as tightened eligibility and shorter duration are not captured by the measure. Finally, for instance, net replacement rates as used by Korpi and Palme (2001) are affected by wage development and the tax system as well and interpreting a drop in net replacement rates as a sign of government cutbacks in the welfare state is thus not straightforward.

An alternative to outcome measures such as expenditure data and replacement rates are output measures. Kitschelt (2001) suggests an index measuring changes made in social security in relation to the level of benefits, eligibility criteria and so forth. Thus, retrenchment could be measured by "micro-data", that is, data providing a quantitative measure of the degree of retrenchment implied by individual changes in social security schemes. An example of such "output data" is provided by Green-Pedersen (2002; cf. also 2000). The degree of retrenchment following from a change in a social security scheme is measured by its likely budgetary effects as a percentage of the total amount of cash spent on the scheme. This measurement is calculated using statistical information about the scheme and material from the parliamentary reading of the proposals. The strength of this measure compared to aggregate expenditure data is the minimization of the time-lag problem, and the provision of a measure for each individual change, hence giving a better idea of which changes have contributed to a certain degree of retrenchment of a scheme. The weakness of this method of measuring retrenchment is first of all the existence of some validity problems when calculating expected budgetary effects, especially when government documents are used. Second, it is a very time consuming exercise requiring language skills and so on. Thus, for one single researcher studying more than a handful of social security schemes in a few countries in this way is impossible.

Summing up, when defining retrenchment as entitlement cuts both output and outcome measures exist. Many of the problems with outcome measures sketched above disappear when an output measure is used, but at least the output measure discussed here is very time consuming to provide.

Retrenchment as Institutional Change

As a point of departure, the second theoretical perspective on retrenchment regards the above retrenchment definition as too narrow because it does not measure changes to the content or institutional structure of welfare schemes. Thus, Pierson (1996: 157) focuses on "reforms that indicate structural shifts in the welfare state". And further elaborates this into three criteria: (1) significant increases in the reliance on means testing; (2) major transfers of responsibility to the private sector; (3) dramatic changes in benefit and eligibility rules that signal a qualitative reform of a particular programme. Another example is Lindbom (1999), who investigates whether "the Swedish welfare state has lost its defining characteristics". Generosity is one of those characteristics, but there are others such as universalism. Finally, Clasen and van Oorschot (2002) investigate whether the basic principles of European welfare states, defined on the basis of Esping-Andersen's three welfare regimes, have changed.

The focus on institutional characteristics is very much inspired by Esping-Andersen's criticism of studies of welfare state expansion based on expenditure data. Yet, as outlined above, Esping-Andersen criticized such studies from the power resources theory perspective. Therefore, the question in relation to Pierson's definition of retrenchment, and other studies using Esping-Andersen's three welfare regimes as their point of departure, is why institutional changes such as increased means testing or privatization can be considered retrenchment. From the perspective of power resources theory, it is clear why especially increased means testing should be considered retrenchment. The labour movement has been striving exactly to avoid means testing. However, Pierson actually criticizes power resources theory, and it is therefore unclear why means testing should be considered retrenchment from his perspective. This does not imply that defining retrenchment as certain institutional changes is invalid. However, the point is that it requires theoretical arguments as to why certain institutional changes should be considered retrenchment. Referring to Esping-Andersen's criticism is only an argument in this regard, if one accepts *his* theoretical point of departure, namely power resources theory.

The focus on "institutional" changes is clearly also inspired by the new institutional wave within political science (cf. Hall and Taylor 1996; Peters 1999). Thus, both Pierson (1996), Clasen and van Oorschot (2002) and Lindbom (1999) emphasize an interest in retrenchment as qualitative changes, that is, a break with basic institutional principles. Again, this is of course perfectly valid. The point, however, is that it requires a substantial theory of the welfare state to single out the institutional features which are so central that changes in them can be considered qualitative change or structural shifts.

With regard to the operational definition of such institutional conceptualizations of retrenchment, it is important to note that the question is not one of quantitative versus "qualitative" data. Following Esping-Andersen's argument presented above, social security expenditure is a very problematic measure of retrenchment defined as institutional change. The reason is not so much the time-lag problem, but rather that social expenditure data do not measure institutional characteristics. However, Esping-Andersen's alternative was not "qualitative" assessments, but indices measuring decommodification and stratification, that is, quantitative data. Thus, there is no a priori reason why one should use "qualitative" assessment as the operational definition of "institutional" conceptualizations of retrenchment. Yet, where social expenditure data is a fairly straightforward operational definition of retrenchment conceptualized as cutbacks in entitlements, there is no similar straightforward operational definition of retrenchment conceptualized as institutional change. Therefore, there is probably a tendency to use "qualitative" assessments when retrenchment is conceptualized in this way. This may be fine in many cases, yet qualitative assessments are vulnerable to the kind of "fuzzy judgment" criticism launched by Alber (1996). Part of the problem is that the exact criteria for such assessments are often blurred and the evaluations can, therefore, be hard to reproduce by others. Thus, especially in studies comparing retrenchment across countries and social security schemes, "qualitative assessments" are often too flimsy.

The kind of data used by Esping-Andersen in the *Three Worlds of Welfare Capitalism* (1990) is one way of avoiding the problem. Another interesting way is to use the "fuzzy sets" idea developed by Ragin (2000). These ideas have, for instance, been used by Kvist (1999) to evaluate whether welfare state reforms have moved the Scandinavian welfare states away from the Nordic welfare model. In other words, there are quantitative ways of operationalizing institutional conceptualizations of retrenchment, but they are not always recognized.

Cutbacks or Institutional Change: Does it Make a Difference?

Above, the two different conceptualizations were discussed separately as part of the argument that they should be kept apart. A relevant question, however, is whether different conceptualizations of retrenchment make any difference for, say, evaluations of cross-national variation in retrenchment? The short answer to this question is yes, but how much depends on which institutional traits are in focus. If generosity is defined as the central institutional trait of a welfare state, the difference to the cutback in entitlements perspective is likely to be small. However, as soon as other institutional traits are in focus, evaluations of concrete changes can be markedly different depending on the conceptualization of retrenchment. Two small examples serve as evidence.

In 1982, a means testing of the basic amount of the Danish old age pension was carried through. Since the means testing was related exclusively to significant job earnings and only affected pensioners between the ages of 67 and 69, it only affected very few people's entitlements significantly. From an entitlement perspective, the change can be considered irrelevant (cf. Green-Pedersen, 2000: chap. 6). However, from the power resources theory perspective, the change can be seen as a significant break with the principle of universalism in the Danish old age pension, and consequently be considered an important retrenchment (Esping-Andersen 1985: 542, 545).

The second example is the privatization of Dutch sickness benefits in 1996. Sickness benefits from the government were abolished for most employees, but instead the new law stipulated that all employees were entitled to sickness benefits from their employer for the same time period and at the same level as they had been before (van der Veen and Trommel 1999). Thus, there were no changes to the entitlements of the employees, but according to Pierson's definition of retrenchment outlined above, this privatization is a significant retrenchment.

The general point here is that a significant cutback in entitlements is possible without changing institutional traits and vice versa. One could also imagine other changes which from an institutional perspective would be retrenchment, but not from an entitlement perspective. For instance, increased means testing could lead to higher expenditure. This could be intended from the side of policy makers in order to improve benefits for "needy" groups, but could also be the result of the way street-level bureaucrats administer the rules.

The above should not be taken as an argument that there is no relation between the two conceptualizations. One way is which they are connected is that institutional changes can be considered an indirect way of achieving cutbacks in entitlements. This idea is an offshoot of Pierson's work on retrenchment (1994, 1996). He argued persuasively that governments seek to retrench welfare states in indirect and obfuscated ways. Thus, one could argue that even though retrenchment is conceptualized as a question of cuts in entitlements, institutional changes are still very important (cf. also Bonoli and Palier 1998; Taylor-Gooby 1999). A good example is recent changes in the Danish disability pension (Christiansen 2000). Danish governments have transferred the authority to award disability pensions from independent boards, which had no financial interest in the number of pensions being awarded, to the municipalities. At the same time, the municipalities have been provided with a fiscal interest in keeping down the number of pensioners. The result of these changes is a significant reduction in the number of pensions being awarded (Christiansen 2000).

In other words, the argument that institutional changes in an indirect way may lead to cutbacks in entitlements is clearly convincing, yet the question is what implications it has for the conceptualization and measurement of retrenchment. One implication would be to collapse the two conceptualizations of retrenchment into one broad conceptualization. Certain institutional changes could be defined as retrenchment because they may lead indirectly to cuts in entitlements. However, at this point it is important to realize that arguing that such changes *may* lead to cuts in entitlement does not imply that they will *necessarily* do so. The effects of the institutional changes will often be rather uncertain and the risk is that institutional changes having no effects on entitlements are measured as cuts in entitlements. Therefore, as a research strategy it seems more sensible to measure separately direct cuts in entitlements and institutional changes possibly leading to the same result. Having focused on the direct cuts in entitlement, one can always investigate whether there is empirical evidence that institutional changes have actually led to or will in the future lead to cuts in entitlements (cf. Green-Pedersen 2000: chap. 6).[5]

A final argument about the connection between the two conceptualizations is that retrenchment as institutional change is the more general of the two and retrenchment as cutbacks should be seen as one type of institutional change. Again, there is nothing wrong about this argument, but the implications depend on one's research question. If the question is "what happened to the welfare state", then seeing cutbacks as one type of institutional change seems reasonable. This is close to what Pierson (2001) has recently suggested when he argues that one should distinguish between three dimensions of welfare state change, namely recommodification, cost containment and recalibration. He further argues that these dimensions have different relevance across the three worlds of welfare capitalism.

However, if the research question is reformulated slightly into "was the welfare state retrenched?" then it becomes important to keep the two different conceptualizations apart. As shown above, the same change may be evaluated differently from the two perspectives. Further, if the research is driven by the intention to test a theoretical argument about welfare state retrenchment, it becomes crucial which conceptualization is in line with the theoretical perspective.

Conclusion

Questions about definition and measurement of the dependent variable not being easy to answer are nothing special for the study of welfare state retrenchment. Identifying such phenomena as policy change and policy convergence is always difficult (cf. Hall 1993; Seeliger 1996). Such questions are, however, extremely important. It has already been argued that thorough investigation into defining and measuring retrenchment is crucial for further progress on the question about which factors cause variation in retrenchment, and for the discussion about change or persistence of the welfare state.

This article has not tried to offer the ultimate solution to the dependent variable problem. There is simply no such thing as the ultimate solution. Instead, the article has focused on determining the nature of the problem. Here, the problem is claimed to be more about theoretical ambiguity than about the pros and cons of different types of data. Different definitions of the welfare state notion is one theoretical problem, but more importantly, welfare state retrenchment can be conceptualized in two different ways, namely as either cuts in entitlements or changes in institutional characteristics. These two conceptualizations are not unrelated but the same changes may be evaluated very differently from the two perspectives and, therefore, they should be kept apart. Which conceptualization of retrenchment to use for a specific study is dependent on one's theoretical perspective. Thus, the main solution to the dependent variable problem is to be very clear-cut about one's theoretical perspective and research question. This should be helpful in deciding which of the two conceptualizations is most in line with one's theoretical interest.

In a way this conclusion sounds very commonsensical and the point about the importance of one's theoretical perspective may be found in any textbook about research methods. However, such basic points are often forgotten in substantial debates and the debate about welfare state retrenchment shows that the point deserves to be made again.

Questions about qualitative versus quantitative data and the use of expenditure data have taken up a very prominent place in the dependent variable debate. This article does not claim that debate to be unimportant. All forms of data have their specific drawbacks and limitations to which attention should always be paid. Yet, discussions about data have a theoretical side which has not always been sufficiently included. The question about the most appropriate data can only be answered once one knows exactly what to measure, and that is a theoretical question.[6] By way of example, expenditure data are much more appropriate, though still highly problematic, when retrenchment is conceptualized as cuts in entitlements than when conceptualized as institutional changes.

Notes

1. A survey of the retrenchment literature can be found in Green-Pedersen and Haverland 2002.
2. Decommodification means upholding a living independently of the market (Esping-Andersen 1990: 22).

3. Yet, as claimed by Lindbom (1999: 23), this is not really a justified criticism of Pierson, who explicitly argues that he is not addressing the question of inequality.
4. This problem of "conceptual stretching" (Sartori 1991) is of course aggravated when non-state provisions such as occupational pensions are included in the welfare state. Such definitions are the ones to which Pierson argument above actually refers.
5. The same argument relate to what Pierson (1994: 15–17) labels "systemic retrenchment". This refers to, for instance, a de-funding of the welfare state or a weakening of pro-welfare interest groups. Such contextual changes (van der Veen et al. 1999) may lead to retrenchment, yet it is not necessarily the case. Therefore, such changes should be kept apart from the ones which by definition imply cuts in entitlements.
6. Of course, it may for practical reasons be necessary to use data which are developed from a different theoretical perspective. Then it is of course important to be aware of what the data was originally intended to measure and what problem this may cause when they are used as a measure of something else.

References

Alber, Jens, 1996, Selectivity, universalism, and the politics of welfare retrenchment in Germany and the United States. Paper for the 92nd Annual Meeting of the American Political Science Association, August 1996, San Francisco.

Alber, Jens, 1998, Recent developments in continental European welfare states: do Austria, Germany and the Netherlands prove to be birds of a feather? Paper for the 14th World Congress of Sociology, July 1998, Montreal.

Anderson, Karen M., 1998, The welfare state in the global economy: the politics of social insurance retrenchment in Sweden 1990–1998. Doctoral dissertation, Seattle, University of Washington.

Bonoli, Giuliano, 2001, Political institutions, veto points, and the process of welfare state adaptation, in: Paul Pierson (Ed) *The New Politics of the Welfare State* (Oxford: Oxford University Press), pp. 238–264.

Bonoli, Giuliano and Palier, Bruno, 1998, Changing the politics of social programmes: innovative change in British and French welfare reforms. *Journal of European Social Policy*, **8**, 317–330.

Castles, Francis G., 2001, On the political economy of recent public sector development. *Journal of European Social Policy*, **11**, 195–211.

Christiansen, Flemming, 2000, Førtidspensionen: Økonomiske incitamenter og tilkendelser. *Samfundsøkonomen*, **2**, 19–25.

Clasen, Jochen and van Oorschot, Wim, 2002, Changing principles in European social security. *European Journal of Social Security*, **4**, 85–115.

Clayton, Richard and Pontusson, Jonas, 1998, Welfare state retrenchment revisited: entitlements cuts, public sector restructuring, and egalitarian trends in advanced capitalist societies. *World Politics*, **51**, 67–98.

Cox, Robert H., 1998, The consequences of welfare reform: how conceptions of social rights are changing. *Journal of Social Policy*, **26**, 1–16.

Esping-Andersen, Gøsta, 1985, Government responses to budget scarcity: Denmark. *Policy Studies Journal*, **13**, 533–546.

Esping-Andersen, Gøsta, 1990, *Three Worlds of Welfare Capitalism* (Cambridge: Polity Press).

Green-Pedersen, Christoffer, 2000, How politics still matters. Retrenchment of old-age pensions, unemployment benefits, and disability pensions/early-retirement benefits in Denmark and in the Netherlands from 1982 to 1998. Doctoral dissertation, University of Aarhus.

Green-Pedersen, Christoffer, 2001, Welfare state retrenchment in Denmark and the Netherlands, 1982–1998. The role of party competition and party consensus. *Comparative Political Studies*, **34**, 963–985.

Green-Pedersen, Christoffer, 2002, *The Politics of Justification. Party Competition and Welfare-State Retrenchment in Denmark and the Netherlands from 1982 to 1998* (Amsterdam: Amsterdam University Press).

Green-Pedersen, Christoffer and Haverland, Markus, 2002, The new politics and scholarship of the welfare state. *Journal of European Social Policy*, **12**, 43–51.

Hall, Peter A., 1993, Policy paradigms, social learning, and the state. The case of economic policymaking in Britain. *Comparative Politics*, **25**, 275–296.
Hall, Peter A. and Taylor, Rosemary C. R., 1996, Political science and the three new institutionalisms. *Political Studies*, **44**, 936–957.
King, Gary, Keohane, Robert O. and Verba, Sidney, 1994, *Designing Social Inquiry* (Princeton: Princeton University Press).
Kitschelt, Herbert, 2001, Partisan competition and welfare state retrenchment. When do politicians choose unpopular policies? in: Paul Pierson (Ed) *The New Politics of the Welfare State* (Oxford: Oxford University Press), pp. 265–302.
Korpi, Walter and Palme, Joakim, 2001, New politics and class politics in welfare state regress: a comparative analysis of retrenchment in 18 countries. Paper presented at the Annual Meeting of the American Political Science Association, 30 August–2 September 2001, San Fransisco.
Kvist, Jon, 1999, Welfare reform in the Nordic countries in the 1990s: using fuzzy-set theory to assess conformity to ideal types. *Journal of European Social Policy*, **9**, 231–252.
Lindbom, Anders, 1999, Dismantling the social democratic welfare model. Has the Swedish welfare state lost its defining characteristics? Paper for the ECPR, Joint Session of Workshops, 26–31 March 1999, Mannheim.
O'Connor, Julia and Olsen, Gregg (Eds), 1998, *Power Resources Theory and the Welfare State* (Toronto: University of Toronto Press).
Peters, B. Guy, 1998, *Comparative Politics* (London: Macmillan).
Peters, B. Guy, 1999, *Institutional Theory in Political Science* (London: Pinter).
Pierson, Paul, 1994, *Dismantling the Welfare State. Reagan, Thatcher, and the Politics of Retrenchment* (Cambridge: Cambridge University Press).
Pierson, Paul, 1996, The new politics of the welfare state. *World Politics*, **48**, 143–179.
Pierson, Paul, 2001, Coping with permanent austerity: welfare state restructuring in affluent democracies, in: Paul Pierson (Ed) *The New Politics of the Welfare State* (Oxford: Oxford University Press), pp. 410–456.
Ragin, Charles, 2000, *Fuzzy-set Social Science* (Chicago: University of Chicago Press).
Ross, Fiona, 2000, Beyond left and right: the new partisan politics of welfare. *Governance*, **13**, 155–183.
Sartori, Giovanni, 1991, Comparing and miscomparing. *Journal of Theoretical Politics*, **3**, 243–257.
Scarbrough, Elinor, 2000, West European welfare states: the old politics of retrenchment. *European Journal of Political Research*, **38**, 225–259.
Schwartz, Herman, 2001, Round up the usual suspects! Globalization, domestic politics and welfare state change, in: Paul Pierson (Ed) *The New Politics of the Welfare State* (Oxford: Oxford University Press), pp. 17–44.
Seeliger, Robert, 1996, Conceptualizing and researching policy convergence. *Policy Studies Journal*, **24**, 287–306.
Siegel, Nico A., 2001, Jenseits der Expansion? Sozialpolitik in westlichen Demokratien, 1975–1995, in: Manfred G. Schmidt (Ed) *Wohlfahrtsstaatliche Politik, Institutionen, Prozesse, Leistungsprofil* (Opladen: Leske + Budrich), pp. 54–89.
Stephens, John D., Huber, Evelyne and Leonard, Ray, 1999, The welfare state in hard times, in: Herbert Kitschelt, Peter Lange, Gary Marks and John D. Stephens (Eds) *Continuity and Change in Contemporary Capitalism* (Cambridge: Cambridge University Press), pp. 164–193.
Swank, Duane, 2002, *Diminished Democracy? Global Capital, Political Institutions, and Policy Change in Developed Welfare States* (Cambridge: Cambridge University Press).
Taylor-Gooby, Peter, 1999, Policy change at a time of retrenchment: recent pension reform in France, Germany, Italy, and the UK. *Social Policy and Administration*, **33**, 1–19.
van der Veen, Romke and Trommel, Willem, 1999, Managed liberalization of the Dutch welfare state: a review and analysis of the reform of the Dutch social security system, 1985–1998. *Governance*, **12**, 289–310.
van der Veen, Romke, Trommel, Willem and de Vroom, Bert, 1999, Institutional change of welfare states. Empirical reality, theoretical obstacles. Paper for the 11th SASE Conference, 8–11 July, Madison.
van Kersbergen, Kees, 2000, The declining resistance of welfare states to change, in: Kuhnle Stein (Ed) *The Survival of the European Welfare State* (London: Routledge), pp. 19–36.

Policy Innovation

Editor: AIDAN R VINING

Policy Innovations: Towards an Analytic Framework

SAMI MAHROUM

ABSTRACT *This paper argues that innovation in public policy arises within the general frameworks of public policymaking and implementation. Therefore, policy innovations can only be studied and understood in the context of public policy and public sector environments at large. To date, frameworks to analyse policy innovations in terms of type, scale and aim have been lacking. Accordingly, this paper uses two public policy analytic frameworks to create an integrated policy innovation analysis framework. The paper then makes use of four high-profile cases of public policies to operationalize the typology scheme seeking to achieve two things; a methodological verification of the usefulness of the mapping scheme as an analytic tool and how it may be used to generate and structure cross-case learning in the domain of policy innovation.*

Introduction

In general, public policy can be defined as government action (or inaction) with regard to a particular issue affecting the general population. Such issues might concern natural resources, technology, infrastructure, human capital and the environment/energy and, especially relevant, social problems (Nagel 1980). More specifically, a policy can be defined as a "relatively stable, purposive course of action or inaction followed by an actor or set of actors in dealing with a problem or matter of concern" (Anderson 2006: 6). A policy intervention is normally a subset component of a wider policy agenda, one that is aimed at delivering socially desired outcomes. While most government work is based on long-established tried and tested routines, government workers and policymakers nevertheless strive to decrease instances of failure and increase success through innovation. This is particularly so when routine practices have failed to produce the desired results (Sanger and Levin 1992). However, when it comes to defining the success and failure of government policies and practices, multiple dimensions of policymaking complicate the picture. This is particularly so when policy objectives are not well defined. Ambiguity and incoherencies between problem, goals and means may lead to confusion about the implementation of a policy and its eventual assessment (Matland 1995). Consequently, researchers, policy analysts and observers at large have found it difficult to agree on the characteristics of success and failure in policy (Ingram and Mann 1980; Boyne 2003; Marsh and McConnell 2010).

This difficulty in defining success in public policy extends itself to defining success in innovation in government and public policy, since whether a policy innovation has been successful or not is subject to different assessment criteria emanating from different perspectives. A policy innovation in itself represents a policy change that can take place at a number of levels. In a recent work, McConnell (2010) has suggested that the success or failure of policy can be observed as three different dimensions, namely the dimension of the policy process, the policy instrument and the political dimension. These are three different levels of policy change, where success and failure are defined differently. These dimensions are also, by extension, relevant to the understanding of policy innovations when they occur and when they are pursued. If policy success is largely measured by the effectiveness of a particular policy in bringing about a desired outcome (Mahroum 2012), and given that the desired outcomes for any given policy can vary from one group to another, success is then context specific. Since this paper focuses on innovations in policy, its aim is to advance thinking about policy innovations by providing a new schematic tool for analysing innovation in public policy where both success and failure can be located.

It is worth mentioning here that a common definition or understanding of what constitutes an innovative policy does not exist (Roste 2005). Nevertheless, some recent attempts have been made to define innovative policies along criteria similar to those in the private sector. For example, Mulgan and Albury (2003) defined policy innovation as "the creation and implementation of new processes, products, services and methods of delivery which result in significant improvements in outcome efficiency, effectiveness or quality". Furthermore, they distinguished between three main types of policy innovations – borrowing from Christensen (1997) – highlighting the following distinctions: incremental, radical and transformative (or systemic) innovations.

- Incremental Innovations. Innovations that represent minor or small changes to existing services or processes. The majority of public policy innovations are incremental in nature, consisting of those that do not attract headlines and rarely change how governments or organizations are structured or how inter- and intra-organizational relations are formed or managed (Dewar and Dutton 1986).
- Radical Innovations. Less frequent are innovations that develop new services or introduce fundamentally new ways of doing things in terms of organizational processes or service delivery. While such radical innovations do not alter the overall dynamics of a sector, they can bring about a significant improvement in performance for the innovating institution and alter the expectations of service users (Leifer 2000).

- Transformative or Systemic Innovations. Most rare are transformative innovations that give rise to new workforce structures and new types of institutions, transform entire sectors, and dramatically change relationships between organizations.

Another recent attempt at classification was undertaken in the context of a Nordic project entitled "Measuring Public Innovation in the Nordic Countries" (Bloch 2010). The classification here is also borrowed from the business world as stipulated in the OECD's *Oslo Manual* (2005), where four types of innovations are identified: product, process, organizational and communication innovations. These definitions refer more to public or government innovations and less to policy innovations.

An overarching definition, and eventually classification, that relates to the functional aspect of public policy innovation seems to be missing. For example, product or process innovations, whether incremental or radical, may exist in relation to achieving different types of outcomes and can emanate from different conditions and different contexts within the broader policy cycle. It is therefore not possible on the basis of these classifications to compare and contrast innovations in terms of function and purpose.

This paper aims, by providing a contextualized typology of policy innovations, to make available a framework for structured learning between different cases of policy innovations allowing the study of policy innovations in terms of both function and purpose. Such contextualization of policy innovation should enable learners to understand contexts that are unique to particular cases and those that are generically transferrable. I believe that this should help improve the chances of successful policy learning across jurisdictions, sectors and time.

The rest of the paper is designed as follows. The next section introduces two analytic frameworks for public policies and progresses to propose a typology of policy innovation that is based on a combination of these two frameworks. The third section introduces four policy cases to elaborate and operationalize the policy innovation scheme. The paper then discusses policy implications for policy diffusion and transfer; whilst the final section provides a set of conclusions.

Constructing a Typology for Policy Innovation

A typology scheme of two tiers is proposed here, from which four categories of policy innovation are later inferred. The two-tier scheme is based on Allan McConnell's (2010) policy dimensions framework and on Richard Matland's (1995) policy matrix ambiguity–conflict model. The rationale for this is that a policy innovation is still policy and hence needs be situated within the larger policymaking and policy cycle worlds. In order to understand a policy innovation, one needs to be able to locate it within the broader public policy dimension in which it exists. The two policy frameworks are introduced in the following sections.

Firstly, McConnell (2010) suggests that every policy has multiple dimensions upon which it may be evaluated. These are the policy process dimension, the programmatic dimension and the political dimension. McConnell suggests that the success and failure of policies may vary across the dimension of analysis. Figure 1 shows that success and failure, or the perception of these, may also be the result of overlaps between the various policy dimensions.

Figure 1. The three dimensions of policy success

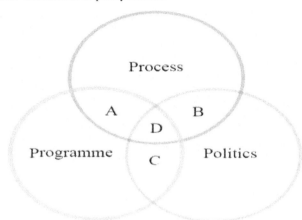

Source: McConnell (2010).

The policy process dimension represents the means through which policy decisions are reached, considering rationalistic-based approaches such as cost–benefit analysis, institutional and deliberative processes amongst others. This dimension of policy analysis can also be relevant to other dimensions such as the political. For example, a policy process that involves stakeholders may make a government politically more desirable among a targeted constituency and subsequently affect the political dimension of a policy positively.

The policy programme dimension is what government does after reaching a decision; it is an instrument of intervention, which can be financial, regulatory or fiscal. Here too this dimension can easily overlap with the two other dimensions as the rationalization approach taken and the choice of instruments are two different sets of analysis that can only be viewed together.

Finally, there is the politics or political dimension, which is the dimension where the relevance and impact of a policy on the political forces that stand behind it can be assessed, particularly with regard to whether it strengthens or weakens their position in the wider policy system. Here, the analysis may become more complicated as it relates to the often complex web of alliances and stakeholders that make up the policy environment.

We now shift focus to the second framework, Richard Matland's (1995) ambiguity–conflict model. Matland's matrix stipulates two conditions in particular that shape the successful implementation of policy, namely: ambiguity and conflict. The first refers to the levels of understanding and clarity that characterize any policy and the second refers to the levels of disagreement and inter-dependency that characterize the relationship between key stakeholders on a policy issue. Accordingly, a quadrant of policy circumstances emerges (see Figure 2).

The importance of Matland's matrix is that it helps position different policies within specific contexts. Matland suggests that the success and failure of policy implementation in particular depends less on whether policies were the result of a

Figure 2. Ambiguity–conflict matrix

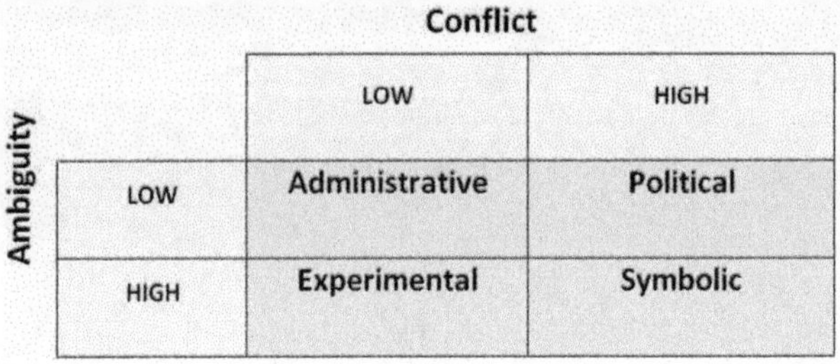

		Conflict	
		LOW	HIGH
Ambiguity	LOW	Administrative	Political
	HIGH	Experimental	Symbolic

Source: Matland (1995).

top-down process or a bottom-up process, but more on the levels of ambiguity and conflict that characterize them. Each of the circumstances in Figure 2 calls for a different form of policy management. For example, in the case of a policy that is characterized by low conflict and low ambiguity, policy management, which encompasses development, implementation and evaluation, becomes a matter of how best to administer it in the most efficient and effective matter. This is because there is already a high level of agreement on both resource distribution and the instruments needed to solve a problem. In contrast, in the case of high ambiguity and high conflict, a government will find it more difficult to manage a policy effectively and, according to Matland, in such a case a broad coalition comprising the different stakeholders in the matter will need to be formed. Ambiguity here is not necessarily a negative quality since policies are sometimes deliberately made vague so that some of the implementers have some discretion in interpreting them in an innovative fashion.

Matland (1995) suggests four categories of circumstances or conditions in which a policy implementation might exist, namely: (1) low conflict, low ambiguity; (2) low conflict, high ambiguity; (3) high conflict, high ambiguity, (4) high conflict, low ambiguity. He then introduces four categories of policies that result from these four conditions: Administrative and experimental when the level of conflict is low and political and symbolic when the level of conflict is high.

The administrative type of policies refers to the bureaucratic, operational and managerial aspects of public policy. A problem is considered administrative in nature if there is little political conflict around it and also clarity about its objectives. The experimental type of policy, however, refers to issues where conflict is also low, but ambiguity about a way forward is high. Finally, symbolic and political types refer to situations where there are high conflicts that require commanding political force to create coalitions or enforce implementation.

The Policy Innovation Mapping Model

Now that the two relevant analytic frameworks have been introduced, we move on to introduce our model for mapping policy innovations. The model is based on three tiers, each of which is generated by asking one question. The first tier is McConnell's

Figure 3. Policy innovation mapping scheme

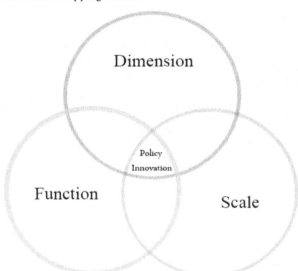

question: what type of a policy innovation is it? Process related, programme/instrument related or a policy related to a political dimension? The answer to this question helps direct further analysis of the case and allows for more focused inter-case comparative analysis to take place within the assigned category. In other words, if the policy innovation at hand is defined as a process type of policy innovation then it can be eventually compared with other cases in the same class or category.

Second we have Matland's question: where does the policy belong on the ambiguity–conflict quadrant? Subsequently, is it an administrative, experimental, political or symbolic policy? Matland's four scenarios may also be related to McConnell's three dimensions in the sense that within a policy or a programme dimension, ambiguity and conflict may apply themselves. The importance of Matland's question is that it allows us to define the policy innovation in accordance with its circumstantial conditions. As we will see later, policy innovations can be ascribed to attempts to find solutions to policy implementation in accordance with the ambiguity–conflict model.

Thirdly, we ask Mulgan and Albury's question: is it an incremental, radical or transformative innovation? The answer to this question helps us further sub-classify the innovation but in terms of its scale rather than nature. In other words, this tier of classification allows us to further describe the policy but it does not, on its own, allow us to evaluate the extent of its success or failure.

Policy innovations may then be defined and classified in accordance with a schematic system as presented in Figure 3.

In the next section, this schematic matrix is applied to structure an analysis of four successful cases of public policy. The aim of this analysis is twofold, firstly, to test the usefulness of the mapping scheme, and secondly, to use the resultant learning to further refine the scheme.

Case Studies

The cases analysed in this paper were selected on the basis of one of the following criteria: a policy that has been established as an outstanding success by a formal evaluation, a policy that has been taken up widely by other jurisdictions as a model of success, a policy that has gained international recognition, or one where there is a broad consensus among policy practitioners and researchers of its success. As has been established earlier in the paper, none of these criteria is necessarily a universal criterion for success. They have, however, been used as a pragmatic method for selecting policy instances that have generated interest from the wider policy community. Finally, it should be noted that none of our cases have been without their critics and none of them would be classified as an example of flawless success. Some of these cases have already been studied and subjected to a high level of scrutiny in both academic and policy circles.

The Japanese Top Runner Programme

The Japanese Top Runner (JTR) programme is an innovative policy instrument that has fast-tracked Japanese industry into "green manufacturing". The JTR programme was introduced in 1999 as a part of the revision of the Energy Conservation Law (Nordqvist 2006). Its objective was to improve the energy efficiency of various electrical and mechanical products produced by Japanese firms. As a result of the programme, Japan today has one of the most energy-efficient economies in the world and Japanese companies have developed competitive advantage in this regard. By 2004, environmental standard compliance was achieved by nearly all computers in the market and the levels of efficiency achieved by some models became substantially higher than the Top Runner standards. The success of the programme was also demonstrated by the fact that the standards set in the programme have been used as criteria for other policy instruments such as the Green Purchasing Law and green automobile tax scheme. The success of the programme is also seen in its expansion. At its launch in 1999, 11 product groups were originally included in the programme. Today, it has 21 product groups (Nordqvist 2006).

Traditionally, governments have set fixed standards on specific technological performance (energy use, emissions, sound levels, etc.) after consulting technical experts or conducting their own studies. The standards would then be communicated to the industry which would usually try to lobby for modifications. Furthermore, national standards often have to take into consideration standards and regulations imposed in other countries so that they do not impede the competitiveness of the local industries.

Dimension of Innovation. The JTR Programme was innovative in more than one policy dimension: Firstly at the policy process level, the companies themselves set the policy standards. Secondly, on the programme level, it set standards for product groups rather than industries and set dynamic standards with periodically moving targets for energy efficiency. These two aspects of the programme meant that firms could not hide energy-inefficient products among high-efficiency products and, in addition, the moving target meant that a race was sparked between firms to raise the bar for competition. The latter put corporations in charge of driving up efficiency standards with government playing the role of referee. This helped make the policy innovative in its third dimension, namely the political dimension. Primary stakeholders (the firms subject to the regulation) were themselves involved in setting targets. This meant that awareness and commitment levels were high. It has also ensured that targets were feasible and not overly ambitious. The benefits accrued from gaining recognition as an industry leader were sufficient to ensure continued buy-in from industry. Standard setting takes into account the potential for technological innovation and diffusion. This meant that, even when outstanding energy-efficient products existed, they would not become "standard setters" if they were too complicated.

Policy Type and Innovation. The JTR programme was a policy issue of potentially high conflict and high ambiguity. The programme succeeded in lowering both levels of conflict and ambiguity by its early involvement and engagement of stakeholders in the design of the content of a policy instrument. The programme used competition between firms as the driving force for the policy, thereby making it self-sustaining. The programme was created and implemented in a way that did not alienate the stakeholders. The result is similar to what Sabatier (1988) called the "advocacy coalition framework", where policymakers and stakeholders form together a coalition around a set of beliefs reflected in a set of targets. The advantage of such coalitions is that they make policy implementation more effective and the policy instrument more stable. They also allow for incremental changes to be made for the policy and its instrument over time.

Scale of Innovation. The JTR programme used an internal, self-perpetuating system of standards to ensure that the policy would be sustainable in the long run. In this respect, it may be described as a radical innovation on the programmatic dimension. Through a system of frequent reviews of industry products and by basing industry performance standards on the achievements of the best performer of the previous round of reviews, energy efficiency standards would continue to improve, but not outstrip the ability or capacity of the industry to achieve those standards. In this way, the JTR programme has been durable because it relied on progressive targets that were continuously pushed by the performance of the industry's own players. In this respect the policy has been a radical innovation in more than one respect: in the way it has been developed, in its design and content, as well as in the contexts it has forged between the different stakeholders involved. This policy innovation can be regarded as an innovative new version of an advocacy coalition framework policy process.

New Zealand Agri-reform of the 1980s

In the mid-1980s, New Zealand started an aggressive, unilateral policy of economic deregulation and liberalization. Prior to this in New Zealand, as in most mature economies, agriculture was highly regulated and protected, and there was an extensive regime of taxes, tariffs, subsidies and other protective measures in place. It was common economic policy to promote economic growth and prosperity through protection. The single biggest constraint faced by the government in implementing reform both across the economy and within the agricultural sector was social resistance. So the real policy challenge was the political dimension of policymaking, since this was the dimension where both potential conflict and ambiguity were high. Many people believed that a unilateral elimination of domestic support through subsidies and other forms of protection, without other countries doing the same, would surely lead to the imminent collapse of the economy. However, when compared to reform efforts in other markets such as the EU or the US, New Zealand's efforts at deregulation, particularly in the agricultural sector, are notable for their success. For example, although deregulation was rapid and extreme, it was not met with social unrest, industrial action or political upheaval.

The Labour government of 1984 came to office with a "wholesale deregulation" programme. Empowered with a fresh democratic mandate, it had enough powers to push through reforms across the economy. Reforms enjoyed political support from the Labour Party's traditional worker base as well from within the agricultural sector itself as many supporters in the sector regarded the situation as unsustainable and expected compensation through reforms elsewhere in the economy (Sandrey and Vink 2007). The 1980s were also the years when the EU market (then the Common Market) was being consolidated and New Zealand had to negotiate continued access to that market. In addition, GATT (General Agreement on Tariffs and Trade) and later WTO (World Trade Organization) membership requirements necessitated these reforms (Valdes 1994).

Dimension of Innovation. This policy case is best described as belonging to the political dimension as deregulation policy was applied across the entire economy and this prevented the surfacing of traditional resistance from farmers that is common in other countries. Furthermore, the agricultural sector, while subjected to rapid and extreme deregulation – assistance to the agricultural sector accounted for around 10 per cent of total public expenditure (Valdes 1994) – was not singled out but was selected as the first to go through the reform policy. This was an important component in the political dimension of the policy. Where New Zealand differs markedly from other countries that have deregulated is in the speed and "wholesale" approach within which it implemented this policy. The deregulation programmes were rolled out over a matter of months rather than years, and within five years government expenditure on assistance to agriculture as a proportion of total public expenditure dropped from a peak of around 10 per cent to less than 1 per cent. The universality of the reforms (affecting all sectors) had helped neutralize potential political conflict, since the policy was not seen as favouring one sector over the other, and the speed of implementation both denied potential serious conflict the time to build up and reduced the level of ambiguity that is often associated with anticipation (i.e. people did not have to speculate for long about the nature of the reforms).

Policy Type and Innovation. The policy issue at hand could be described as a potentially high-conflict/high-ambiguity type of policy. The innovation was political, particularly in pursuing reforms within a broader national reform agenda and doing so quickly. This led to a significant lowering of levels of both conflict and ambiguity. The policy was innovative primarily in its high level of political contextualization, particularly in how various domains of radical changes were linked to each other and subsequently systemic deep reforms were able to be delivered across the economy. The notion of "wholesale reforms" meant that no single group was made to bear the cost of economic reforms, something that has contributed significantly to lowering high levels of conflict and ambiguity. As a result, the potential resistance of political opponents was neutralized at least until after the reforms had been implemented. The speed of the implementation of the reforms reduced the level of ambiguity, which is often used by political opponents to resist or change a new policy (Winter 2003).

Scale of Innovation. The impact of the innovation was transformative in that it comprehensively changed the New Zealand economy. It shifted the system from one that was mired in bureaucracy and inefficiency to one that was critically driven by competition. Competition brought with it innovation and some of New Zealand's most profitable companies today were the direct product of this policy.

Feed-in Tariffs in Germany's Renewable Energy Policy

Germany's introduction of Feed-in Tariffs (FIT), through the Renewable Energy Sources Act (EEG), represented a fundamental shift in policy thinking in Germany and later across Europe. Although a similar programme had been implemented in the US some decades ago, that experience had limited success. Therefore, while the US experience was sub-optimal, the German version has seen lots of success. The programme led to the rapid emergence of a wind (and solar) energy industry, which has grown exponentially since the end of the 1990s and created a significant number of new jobs, especially within the EU. In 2008, wind energy companies in the EU employed over 100,000 people, representing a growth of 226 per cent in relation to 2003. More than 70 per cent of total employment in clean tech in the EU is generated in Germany, Spain and Denmark (Mostafaeipour 2010). Since first being tried, FITs have evolved into intricate public policy tools in both their content and purpose. FITs have proven to be one of the most effective policy instruments in overcoming the cost barriers to introducing renewable energy, thereby improving the economic viability of clean energy.

Dimension of Innovation. This policy can be described as a typical case to be analysed from the programmatic dimension. The FIT instrument owes its success to the adaptability and flexibility that are inherent in its content. There are two characteristics that are critical to the success of any policy innovation in an experimental domain (Matland 1995). Firstly, it allows for the use of a wide diversity of energy sources (solar, wind, wave/tidal, biomass, hydro- and geothermal power), which opened it up to a wider base of investors and made it a competitive investment vehicle. Secondly, through the supporting regulatory framework, utility companies were forced to adapt their distribution networks to guarantee access for these new sources of energy, such as power generated from home solar installations. This also had the secondary effect of making consumers and households part of the supply chain in that they could sell their surplus energy generation, which fast-tracked the diffusion of renewable energy technology and use. Thirdly, FIT pricing was based not on market prices of conventional fuels but on the basis of production cost and the price was guaranteed at a minimum level for a continuous 20-year term. This acted like a price floor and offered a guaranteed minimum return on investment.

Policy Type and Innovation. Renewable energy in Germany is a policy domain that can be described as low conflict but high ambiguity. It is a low-conflict policy issue given the broad support that renewable energy receives from both politicians and the public at large. It is high in ambiguity because the various solutions considered are still largely in the experimental phase and the effect of government policy remains highly ambiguous. Ambiguity therefore serves here as the main domain for potential conflict and resistance both at a political level and the level of implementation. The policy design of the FIT has served as an important hedge against risk and further shared the risk between the state and individual investors. For households this has cushioned the impact of the high initial investment costs associated with installing renewable energy technology at the household level. More importantly, the way the policy instrument was designed whereby consumers become part of the renewable energy supply grid has brought what Hull and Hjern (1987) described as "informal local networks" of actors into the policy implementation process. For the FIT programme to succeed, it was important to ensure that the lowest level of implementation, especially individual households, are brought into the scheme early on and have the infrastructure to benefit from the scheme.

Scale of Innovation. Introducing a regulation that forces utility companies to purchase all renewable energy produced is, on its own, a radical innovation. However, the use of regulation to force the application of a programme is not something new. I therefore opt to classify the German FIT programme as primarily a radical innovation in its programmatic component, since the process was ordinary while the instrument agreed was radical. In earlier versions, such as in the US, FIT lacked price stability (and hence had higher levels of ambiguity) and universal grid access eligibility. These changes, together with guaranteed purchase of supply, amounted to a radical form of content innovation. The overall result has been the fast-track adoption and diffusion of both renewable energy technology and the policy instrument itself.

Canada Research Chairs (CRC) Programme

The Canada Research Chair (CRC) programme was designed to help Canada resist and fight back against the brain drain from its universities to the US and elsewhere. In less than ten years, the programme has fast-tracked the state of science in Canada. Initially, the CRC programme had the goal of ensuring that 2,000 chairs would be occupied during 2007–08. The allocation of approved chairs had already reached this target by 2006–07. Ten years on from its set-up in 2000, 30 per cent (558) of chairs had been recruited from outside Canada and 357 of them were recruited from the US. The programme has been viewed as a model of success in the media and in various evaluation exercises and has been copied by several nations including South Africa, Portugal, Spain, New Zealand, Finland and France. Recently, the (Canadian) International Development Research Centre has established an

International Research Chairs programme modelled around the CRC and in partnership with it. Subsequent reviews of the CRC have come out strongly in praise of the programme (Picard-Aitken et al. 2010). Among the programme's major achievements, it has been pointed out, are the recruitment and retention of some of the world's most accomplished and promising researchers, one of the programme's main objectives. Another main outcome of the programme is raising the profile of otherwise non-prestigious universities and professors.

Dimension of Innovation. The policy fits largely within the programmatic dimension of analysis but can also be analysed politically. The content of the policy instrument was innovative in the way it linked different levels of policymaking and constituencies together, i.e. the federal with the provincial, the universities with the innovation strategy, the chairs with the universities and the funding agency the Canada Foundation for Innovation (CFI) with the CRC. The programme was rolled out as a bridge linking the macro level of implementation to the micro level (Berman 1978). According to Berman (1978), policy implementation takes place at two levels: macro and micro. At macro level, centrally located actors devise programmes and hand them down to the lower levels of administration for implementation. The micro level, however, is more diverse, as it involves not only intermediary and street-level government agencies but also the communities and stakeholders that are affected by these programmes. Most often policies become lost in translation as they move from the macro to the micro. The CRC was innovative in the ability of its design to minimize the chances for the policy to be lost in translation between the two levels of implementation.

Policy Type and Innovation. The policy issue was one of low conflict in the sense that there was a general consensus about the existence of a problem and that funding was a problem and ambiguity was low in the sense that there was a general expectation that increased funding would improve the situation. This low conflict–low ambiguity situation made the policy largely administrative and programmatic in nature. Thus, the CRC was designed to address the problem of quality directly by requiring universities to draw out strategic plans for their R&D activities and commit to better working conditions for the chairs. Government funds went into ensuring that both the infrastructure and salaries for scientists were very attractive. When submitting a nomination, a university must show the importance of the chair for the development of its strategic research plan. The examiners would then determine whether the candidate would fit with the university's strategic research plan and evaluate the way in which the candidate will help to achieve the university's objectives.

In addition to the financial allocation for the CRC, each university is provided with a CFI envelope for all of the CRCs it has been allocated. Accordingly, individuals who are nominated for CRCs are eligible to apply for a separate CFI grant to provide them with the infrastructure that they require to carry out their research programme. This partnership with the CFI helped strengthen the CRC programme in the hard sciences where access to expensive equipment is an important part of the incentive package. Chairs are also allocated for disciplines in line with the Canadian science and innovation strategy.

Scale of Innovation. While in the 1990s and early 2000s governments who were concerned with "brain drain" focused primarily on revamping their immigration and visa systems Canada realized that the problem had more to do with the quality of science and academic careers in Canada than an openness problem. The CRC can be considered a radical innovation among the traditional instruments of combatting brain drain, but also in bridging macro and micro level policy implementation in a domain that is laden with political sensitivity. Universities, as the main target community for this programme, are well known for carefully guarding their autonomy. Thus, for any government policy instrument to be effective within this community, it needs to strike a careful balance between macro policy objectives and the objectives of the individual university. In fact, the CRC was designed in a way that even departments within universities were tied up to the macro plan level.

Implications for policy diffusion and transfer

The four case studies show that on the whole policy innovations can be situated within the three McConnell dimensions – process, programme and political. Thus, it is possible to classify policy innovation as being process innovation, programmatic innovation or political innovation. Within this classification, it is possible to further sub-classify the policy innovations in terms of their scale, as suggested by Mulgan and Albury (2003), namely as incremental, radical and transformative. These two tiers of classification remain largely descriptive. They do not contribute much to understanding the underpinning dynamics or the functions of the innovations themselves within the wider policymaking system.

In this regard, the Policy Innovation Mapping Matrix (Figure 3). which was based on the McConnell and Matland frameworks, can be seen as a potentially useful analytic tool for defining and classifying policy innovations. After a policy issue has been classified as process, programmatic or political, the ambiguity–conflict matrix provides a tool to assess the context of, and the conditions surrounding, the policy issue and subsequently to either retrospectively assess the success of an innovation in contributing to a solution, or prospectively suggesting where an innovation might be needed.

Analysis of the previous sections also has implications for policy diffusion and transfer. In order to be effective, it is important to compare policy innovations at corresponding levels and within similar contexts. This is important because policy innovations often arise as a result of the efforts made by policy entrepreneurs who are embedded in their own administrative and political environments (King and Roberts 1987; Kingdon 1995; Mintrom 1997). For example, Berry and Berry (1999) have suggested that the processes of policy innovation in a particular jurisdiction are closely intertwined with the internal characteristics of a jurisdiction including economic, political or social conditions. Thus, the contexts, dimensions and circumstances under which these innovations are introduced should inform any comparative analysis undertaken between different cases of policy innovations for an effective diffusion to take place.

The typology provided in this paper helps the policy learner to make the necessary differentiations between dimensions, contexts and scale of policy innovations. For example, it helps us understand why New Zealand's case of innovative political (and agricultural policy) reform is difficult to replicate elsewhere, given the intricacies of the dimension, context and scale of the policy innovations involved. The lower levels of conflict meant that what was particularly needed was clarity over the way forward. This resulted in a policy innovation at a political level where speed and wholesomeness were the main hallmarks. Elsewhere, this approach to reform comes across as somewhat counter-intuitive where "muddling through" approaches to change are viewed more favourably. In France, where repeated attempts at agricultural reforms, and other reform, have met with failure, this policy innovation would have faced greater resistance given the level of comfort with the existing regimes and the high levels of conflict involved. In such a context, a different type of policy innovation would be required, one that would be aimed at generating broad coalitions instead in order to lower the level of conflict as well as ambiguity levels.

The German FIT was a successful innovation because it was applied in a situation characterized by relatively low conflict and low ambiguity. The Californian – original – version of it was less successful because it was characterized by high ambiguity and increasingly higher levels of conflict. The Canadian CRC was successful in the context of bridging macro and micro tiers of policy, but it might not be as successful if it was to be adopted to be implemented in a different jurisdiction where its implementation was delegated to the lowest levels of the policy system – i.e. street bureaucrats. The ambiguity of the programme would have increased and consequently the levels of conflict around it. Likewise, the Japanese Top Runner programme was successful because it aimed to reach accord between numerous players. However, the same programme might be less successful in a sector or jurisdiction where the number of players is too small or where there are traditionally high levels of conflict among industrial players or between them and government.

These examples of successful policies serve not only as examples of types of policy innovations, but also as guides to how and where policy innovators can intervene to make policy more effective.

Conclusions

A policy innovation is one that utilizes either new approaches or new design to initiate, launch and deliver a policy with a variety of declared and undeclared goals. This paper has argued that policy innovation arises within specific frameworks of public policymaking and implementation. Accordingly, the paper used two public policy analytic frameworks, namely those developed by McConnell (2010) and Matland (1995) to create an integrated policy innovation typology. The framework has proven to be useful as a descriptive and analytic tool to generate and structure new learning across case studies. This was made possible because as a framework it provided a structured way to differentiate between different types of policy innovations. The policy innovation typology scheme will benefit from more research and the inclusion of more case studies, but it has allowed us to create a new framework for cross-case learning of instances of very different policy innovations. In addition, the framework has provided a "map of targets" for potential policy innovators to think of potential solutions for policy challenges at the level of the politics, processes or programmes and across a combination of conditions, high and low levels of conflict and ambiguity and then to consider the level of change they should aim at.

References

Anderson, J. E., 2006, *Public Policymaking: An Introduction* (Boston, MA: Wadsworth).
Berman, P., 1978, *The Study of Macro and Micro Implementation of Social Policy* (RAND Corporation California).
Berry, F. S. and Berry, W. D., 1999. Innovation and diffusion models in policy research, in: P.Sabatier (Ed.) *Theories of the Policy Process* (Boulder, CO: Westview Press), pp. 169–200.
Bloch, C., 2010, *Measuring Public Innovation in the Nordic Countries* (Copenhagen: Danish Agency for Science, Technology and Innovation).
Boyne, G. A., 2003, Sources of public service improvement: A critical review and research agenda. *Journal of Public Administration Research and Theory*, **13**(3), pp. 367–394.
Christensen, C. M., 1997, *The Innovator's Dilemma* (Boston: Harvard Business School Press).
Dewar, R. D., and Dutton, J. E., 1986, The adoption of radical and incremental innovations: An empirical analysis. *Management Science*, **32**(11), pp. 1422–1433.
Hull, C., and Hjern, B., 1987, Helping small firms grow: An implementation analysis of small firm assistance structures, *European Journal of Political Research*, **10**(2), pp. 187–198.
Ingram, H. M., and Mann, D. E., 1980, *Why Policies Succeed or Fail* (London: Sage Publications Ltd).
Johnson, R.W.M., 2001, *New Zealand's Agricultural Reforms and Their International Implications* (London: Institute of Economic Affairs).
Kingdon, J. W., 1995, *Agendas, Alternatives, and Public Policies* (Boston: Little, Brown).
King, P. J. and Roberts, N. C., 1987, Policy entrepreneurs: Catalysts for policy innovation. *The Journal of State Government*, **60**(4), pp. 172–179.
Leifer, R., 2000, *Radical Innovation: How Mature Companies Can Outsmart Upstarts* (Boston: Harvard Business School Press).
Mahroum, S., 2012, *Innovation Policies and Socio-economic Goals: An Analytic-Diagnostic Framework.* INSEAD Working Paper no. 2012/35/IIPI.
Matland, R. E., 1995, Synthesizing the implementation literature: The ambiguity–conflict model of policy implementation. *Journal of Public Administration Research and Theory*, **5**(2), pp. 145–174.
Marsh, D. and McConnell, A., 2010, Towards a framework for establishing policy success. *Public Administration*, **88**(2), pp. 586–587.
McConnell, A., 2010, *Understanding Policy Success: Rethinking Public Policy* (Basingstoke: Palgrave Macmillan).
Mintrom, M., 1997, Policy entrepreneurs and the diffusion of innovations. *American Journal of Political Science*, **41**(3), pp. 738–770.
Mostafaeipour, A., 2010, Productivity and development issues of global wind turbine industry. *Renewable and Sustainable Energy Reviews*, **14**(3), pp. 1048–1058.
Mulgan, G., and Albury, D., 2003, *Innovation in the Public Sector* (London: Prime Minister's Strategy Unit/Cabinet Office).
Nagel, S. S., 1980, The policy studies perspective. *Public Administration Review*, **40**(4), pp. 391–396.
Nordqvist, J., 2006, *Evaluation of Japan's Top Runner Programme* (Brussels: AID-EE).
OECD, 2005, *The Oslo Manual: Guidelines for Collecting and Interpreting Innovation Data*, 3rd edition (Paris: OECD Publications).
Picard-Aitken, M., Foster, T., Labrosse, I., Caruso, J., Campbell, D., and Archambault, E., 2010, *Tenth-Year Evaluation of the Canada Research Chairs Program – Final Evaluation Report* (Montreal: Science-Metrix Inc.).
Roste, R., 2005, *Studies of Innovation in the Public Sector: A Theoretical Framework*. Publin Report No. D16.
Sabatier, P., 1988, An advocacy coalition model of policy change and the role of policy-oriented learning therein. *Policy Sciences*, **21**, pp. 129–168.
Sandrey, R., and Vink, N., 2007, The deregulation of agricultural markets in South Africa and New Zealand: A comparison. *Agrekon*, **46**(3), pp. 323–350.

Sanger, M. B., and Levin, M. A., 1992, Using old stuff in new ways: Innovation as a case of evolutionary tinkering. *Journal of Policy Analysis and Management*, **11**(1), pp. 88–115.

Valdes, A., 1994, Agricultural reforms in Chile and New Zealand: A review. *Journal of Agricultural Economics*, **45**(2), pp. 189–201.

Winter, S., 2003, Implementation perspectives: Status and reconsideration, in: B. G. Petersand, J. Pierre (Eds) *Handbook of Public Administration* (Sage Publications, London, UK).

Exploring the Concept of Governability

JAN KOOIMAN

ABSTRACT *In this paper a start is made in developing a conceptual model for the governability of a particular societal system based upon the (inter)active perspective on governance. Governability is seen as consisting of three main components, a system-to-be-governed (SG), a governance system (GS), and the interactions between these two (GI). The basis for conceptualizing the GS is the primary processes in which societal sectors specialize. These processes show characteristics by which they can be analyzed, such as their diversity, dynamics and complexity. The GS can be operationalized according to aspects of governance activities: elements, modes and orders of governance, and in the three major societal governance institutions: state, market, civil society and increasingly hybrid forms among them. The article also discusses the GI where one input is from the SG to the GS, defined as participatory interactions, and another from the GS to the SG which is seen as policy and management driven forms of interactions. Together these major governability components form a conceptual basis to analyze and eventually assess the governability of a particular societal sector, such as a fishery, a coastal zone or in fact any societal sector.*

Introduction

This paper grew out of a program directed at inter-disciplinary research on the governance of fisheries, and a subsequent project on the governability of fisheries, aqua-culture and coastal zones.[1] Central to these projects was addressing the question of what kind of factors have contributed to failure to slow depletion of the resource despite the great policy and management efforts by public authorities all over the world. Answers suggest that not only are policies usually inadequate, but that the institutions formulating and implementing these policies are weak or lacking and the value foundations of all these efforts are contradictory, to say the least.

These findings led to the realization that not only policy and management are at stake, but so also is governance of the fisheries system as a whole. In our terminology, the fishery system includes the system to be governed (SG – the fish chain from catching to consuming fish); the governing system (GS – state, market and civil society institutions governing this chain); and the interrelations between the two (GI – all interactions between those involved in the chain). All of these play a role in what we call governability, which, in the case of fisheries, has a weak capacity for governance (Jentoft 2007b).

The framework outlined in this paper is designed to facilitate the comparative assessment of the governance capacity of a societal sector such as fisheries; however, it can also be seen as a contribution to developing a conceptual context for policy analytical purposes. The paper aims at continuing a discussion as formulated in the "Introduction to a Symposium on Comparative Social-political Governance and Policy" in this Journal in 2003, in which my work was partly used, saying:

> There can certainly be little doubt that the socioeconomic, political, cultural, and natural environments that now prevail in most advanced liberal democracies are much changed from any that have existed before. All these societies have become more diverse, dynamic, and complex, so the role of governments have changed... The response has been a gradual transition away from traditional modes of governing towards new patterns of state-society interactions... When one considers the increased plurality of agents of government and civil society participating in the policy process, and the growing complexity of issues to be decided upon, it is perhaps not surprising that some contributors to this debate question whether modern societies are in fact governable. (Dixon *et al.* 2003: 101–102)

As stated this way, features of governance and governability become major contextual factors for policies and for policy connected concepts such as policy problems, policy processes, policy arenas, and may become even a part of a general conceptual framework for the policy sciences (Pielke 2004: 218).

The paper starts by establishing the relation between governability and its 'mother' concept governance. This is followed by a systematic discussion of its major components SG, GS and GI. In the conclusion the potential role of the framework for policy analysis is taken up again.

Governability

Background

Governability as a concept has several pedigrees. The first one has a somewhat dubious scholarly standing, notwithstanding the high status of its contributors, Crozier, Huntington and Watanuki (1975). The concept served as a carrier for a semi-political movement promoting the idea that modern democracies had become ungovernable because of an overload of public tasks. This did not contribute to its scholarly reception (Dahrendorf 1980). Its second lineage is in the German discussion on governance and governability under the title *Steuerung* and *Steuerungsdefizit* (governability failure). Luhmann and his followers attributed this failure to the basic *autopoietic* nature of societal (sub)systems, while Mayntz and her collaborators put the blame on the difficulty of governing the special dynamics of complex modern societies and the capacity of highly organized policy fields to resist political guidance

(Mayntz 1993, Luhmann 1995, Dunsire 1996). Most recently a third source for conceptualizing governability can be found in relation to democracy, in particular for Latin American countries (Figuerdo 2006). In all instances governability has been coupled in one way or another to the state as governance agency.

The ideas underlying the concept of governability pursued in this article by distinguishing a SG and a GS builds on the important discussion on *Steuerbarkeit*, governability, in the German context, as summarized by Mayntz (2005: 16–17) in a recent state of the art survey of governance research. She argues that the change in perspective from *Steuerung* to governance, in which the separation between *Steuerungsobjekt* and *Steuerungssubjekt* has disappeared, has made it much more difficult to address the *Steuerbarkeitsproblematik* in a systematic manner. This sophisticated discussion of governability, unfortunately hardly recognized elsewhere, is important and a far cry from the short-lived and ideological one of the 1970s.

The governability concept as sketched in this paper builds on this German contribution and my own earlier suggestions (Mayntz 1993, Kooiman 1993). My exploration of governance (2003) ended with a short conceptual note on governability. This paper takes that as a starting point and continues this exploration by extending it based upon the experiences with the governance of fisheries worked out in a number of papers, and applying it to fisheries, coastal zones and aqua-culture in a few settings in the South (see the examples below). These efforts show its potential capacity as a conceptual base for comparative research in different fields and as an element in a framework for comparative policy analytical purposes as suggested above.

The Concept

The idea of relating governability to qualities of the object of governance, to its subject and to the relation between these two led us to conceive governability of any societal system or entity as the propensity for its successful governance. Governors, the governed and the interactions among governors and the governed all contribute to governability, as do all kinds of external influences. Governability can therefore be defined as: "*the overall capacity for governance of any societal entity or system*".

Its conceptual starting point is to look at three major sets of variables contributing to governability of societal entities, including the natural resources valued by those entities: those entities themselves considered as system-to-be-governed (SG), those governing these entities labeled the governance system (GS), and the inter-relation between these two, worked out in terms of governing interactions (GI). All three add in varying degrees to governability.

Governability is always changing, depending on external and internal factors. What may be high governability at a given time may be low governability at another. Similarly, what may be effective governance in one place may be ineffective in another. Governability as a whole, or any of its components, can be influenced by acts of governance. However, many external factors influence governability as well, some of which can only be poorly handled in governance, or not at all. This often enhances uncertainty with respect to the governability of a societal system or entity.

As sources for variables for SG I use earlier work on complexity, diversity and dynamics and general literature on environment and natural resources to give a first global idea of the possibility to conceptualize the SG component of governability. The variables for GS are taken from my earlier work on governance as the emphasis there was on aspects of those responsible for governance. The variables for GI are a broadening of the interaction concept as developed earlier. Policy and participation literature are the main sources for this, as well as some classical ideas on pressure and some recent ones on impact assessment. For all three components the chosen variables can be considered as a conceptual middle way for on the one hand the richness of potential variables, and on the other to limit the number of them as the model serves as a basis for going into the field and assess governability in concrete situations.[2]

Interactive governance, in keeping with its basic assumptions, considers governability as a property of systems as wholes: that is, systems that are defined as the totality of inter-relations among given entities. Societal systems imply interactions, and interactions are conditions for the existence of those systems. In interactive governance, interactions and systems belong together (Kooiman 2003).

What a system looks like, how it can be broken down, and what its boundaries and other qualities might be, depends on the perspectives of its observers. The systems concept in this paper is to be considered as a heuristic tool, without any teleological, functional or reification connotations (Jervis 1997, Jentoft 2007b). Any system – societal, natural or combinations of the two – is part of a hierarchy of nested systems. Where in the hierarchy one wants to locate a particular system also exists in the eyes of its beholders. The more beholders with comparable ideas about a system, the stronger the concept becomes, for study and for practical purposes (see Figure 1).

This article describes the concept of governability as an integrated whole, while explaining that each of its components (SG, GS and GI) has a conceptual basis on its own. It might be held that only people (and not nature) "govern". However it can also be argued that, because of the nested hierarchy of systems, nature in the end

Figure 1. Integrated framework for governability

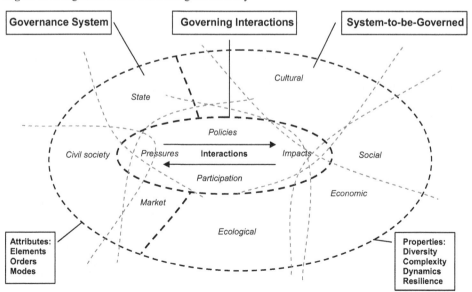

governs all societal governance. These are fundamental issues only a full-fledged study of governability can deal with in a serious manner. Here it is mentioned, because in operational terms what belongs to the GS or what to the SG might come up in an actual analysis of the governability of a particular societal-natural system, such as a fishery, or in fact any other societal entity.

Governability and the System-to-be-Governed (SG)

The key consideration with the SG is to determine which dimensions decide if a system is governable or not. On the one hand one would think that this is relatively simple because any societal activity in theory and in practice can be considered as an SG. On the other hand defining the SG is complicated because what we could consider as potentially relevant for governability is almost unlimited. By focusing on societal interactions as our prime conceptual tool we hope to make the analysis of SG workable. Interactions can be instrumental in ordering societal activities, and they can serve to – at least conceptually – limit the scope of what we need to look at.

Governability of SG and Societal Primary Processes

Societal subsystems as systems of interactions exist around specific societal activities. Such a basic undertaking can be labeled a "primary process": educating children, taking care of sick people, catching fish, producing bicycles, handling a bank account. All such processes have increasingly become more diverse, dynamic and complex and take place at different scales – not only quantitatively but also qualitatively. How this works out in fisheries is shown in Box 1.

Box 1. Scales in fisheries and governability

> The scales of capture fisheries can be described in many ways, for example, by the size of the resource (small local stock vs. large wide-ranging stock), the types of vessels used (small, inshore vs. large, ocean-going), the nature and state of technological development of fishing gear (manual, home-made vs. advanced electronic and hydraulic), and their administrative arrangements (small vs. large fisheries departments and national vs. regional and international administrations). These highly variable scales form the complex, multi-dimensional space in which fishers fish.
>
> Problems arise when aspects of capture fisheries are scaled up or down without careful consideration of the consequences for functionality. For example, some small developing countries have attempted to replicate large-country fisheries department capacity in small departments, with the result that few function effectively. A lack of fit between some fisheries' management practices and the scales at which they are applied can contribute to real or perceived failures. By taking different spatial, temporal, and organizational scales in capture fisheries into account, their governability might be greatly enhanced.

Source: Johnson *et al.* 2005.

Operationalizing factors to take into consideration in interaction systems around primary processes at different levels of abstraction is not a simple matter. Fortunately the impact assessment literature (Becker and Vanclay 2003) might help with this, as this is the field of research where occurrences having an impact are studied systematically. Social impact assessment, for example, maps people's way of life, their culture, their community, their political systems, their environment, their health and well-being, their personal and property rights, and their fears in a researchable manner. Recently this literature (Van Schooten *et al.* 2003) has also distinguished a wide variety of societal processes (i.e., interactions) that are useful for assessing a SG and its governability.

In our own research, the concept of the (fish) chain from ecosystem to the consumer, enabled analysis of ecological, social, economic, cultural, ethical and political aspects of fisheries systems by scholars from different disciplines and persons having different points of view (Kooiman *et al.* 1999, Kooiman *et al.* 2005).

Governability of SG and Common Properties

It is the inter-relationships and interactions among the economic, social, ecological and other components of a SG – often studied as individual components – that constitute the SG as a whole. Each of these components has specific major variables and terminology. For studying the systemic qualities of a SG by focusing on overlaps, linkages, interactions and interdependencies among its components, it is essential to find common concepts, descriptors and measures for the properties of the SG and these components. The interactive governance perspective considers diversity, complexity, dynamics and scale to be such commonalities.

To understand interactive governance and governability, in particular on the boundaries between its social, political and natural facets, one must recognize and confront their diversity, complexity, dynamics and scale (Kooiman 1993, 2003, Bavinck and Kooiman 2005). *Diversity* calls attention to the specific and varying qualities of actors and other entities in an SG, its GS and GI between them. It is a source of creation and innovation, but also carries the danger of disintegration. *Complexity* invites examination of societal structures, interdependencies and inter-relations and is a condition for combining interdependencies. The difficulty is how to reduce it in an effective and responsible manner. By introducing the *dynamics* of systems we call attention to the regularity or irregularity with which developments within and around systems take place. Dynamics create the potential for change, but can have disruptive consequences. *Scale* concerns their dimensions in space or time for a specific analytical or applied purpose. It represents the level at which the combined effects of diversity, complexity and dynamics can be best observed and analyzed. Governability as a component of societal systems is itself also diverse, complex and dynamic. They are features that emerge at different scales of those systems. The role of diversity, complexity and dynamics for governability in aquaculture is shown in Box 2.

Other common characteristics are also in use. Robinson and Tinker (1997) argue, for example, that a number of attributes apply to a greater or lesser extent to all three primary systems they look at (the biosphere, the economy and human society). They discuss attributes such as the capacity to change (with respect to) diversity, stability,

Box 2. The diversity, complexity and dynamics of aqua-culture

> Aqua-culture operations vary from homestead and farm ponds of less than 100 m^2 to cage, pen and pond farms covering hundreds of hectares. Small-scale aqua-culture, sometimes as a part-time occupation, makes large contributions to poverty alleviation in Asia. Cold-water aqua-culture (for example, trout and salmon farming) and warm-water aqua-culture (for example, tilapia farming) mirror the broad differences between temperate and tropical agriculture. Organic aqua-culture is also developing rapidly.
>
> Aqua-culture also has considerable complexity, largely because of the complex life histories of aquatic organisms and the complex technical requirements of providing for these in captivity. Farmed fish are bred in breeding programs, striving for genetic improvement of commercial traits. Fish hatcheries produce seed and fish nurseries grow those to juveniles of more viable size. Fish farmers then proceed to raising those juveniles to marketable size. Arrangements among hatchery, nursery, farming and post-harvest operations are complex because of seasonal and other shifts in supply and demand and the advent of new technologies and products.
>
> Inter-relationships among aqua-culture and other sectors are highly dynamic, especially those concerning land and water use, environmental impacts, farm workers health and safety, and farmed fish health, quality and safety for consumers. Aqua-culture is often risky. Unpredictable climatic conditions, operator error, equipment failure, and largely uncontrollable events such as toxic algal blooms, the spread of aquatic diseases and pollution all cause mass mortalities of farmed fish.

Source: Pullin 2005.

resilience and self-organization in response to stress. They also assert the existence of more or less inflexible outer limits for such properties beyond which a system will collapse. Using essentially the same kind of ideas on generic properties, Holling et al. (1998: 352) state that for natural resources management "Characteristically, problems tend to be systems problems, where aspects of behavior are complex and unpredictable and where causes, while at times simple (when finally understood), are always multiple".

Examples of common properties used across a wide range of disciplines are: capital, capacity, capability, function, chain, impact, resilience, sustainability, uncertainty, vulnerability, memory, and risk. Two examples show their usefulness for our purpose. Vulnerability might reveal the problematic side of governability, while resilience is symbolic of its opportunity side.

Resilience. Holling (1973) introduced the concept of resilience into ecology to facilitate assessments of ecosystem behavior in the face of disturbances and change. Resilience was initially conceived with the assumption of stable states – that is, an ecosystem returning to its original situation after a disturbance. Now it has become a more dynamic concept, allowing for changes taking place after a disturbance, and it has been broadened to include social and economic aspects as well as ecological ones. Key properties in recent studies of resilience are adaptive renewal cycles, emphasizing feedback loops, uncertainty and surprise, self-organization, learning and innovation (Berkes et al. 2003). Social resilience is also conceived of as a central category of analysis and is related to resource dependency and risk (Adger 2000).

A SG with higher resilience might be thought to have higher governability than one with lower resilience, because the former copes better with disturbances, is better at organizing (that is, governing) itself, and has a higher learning capacity, and so on. But are there direct and positive correlations between governability, self-governance and resilience? In the interactive governance perspective, it is assumed that most modern SGs are, in the face of a complex, dynamic and diverse world, characterized by mixes of three modes of governance, among which self-governance is only one (see the section on modes of governance). For a SG to be more governable, self-organizing is important but not entirely sufficient.

Vulnerability. Vulnerability is a concept used in ecology, economics and social science. It is a measure of weakness, often compared with and related to resilience as a measure of strength. From their conservation perspective, Wilson et al. (2005) define vulnerability as a threatening process, implying risk as a loss: the likelihood or imminence of bio-diversity loss to current or impeding threatening processes. They distinguish three dimensions of vulnerability: exposure, intensity and impact. Adger (1999: 249) approaches vulnerability from social and economic points of view, saying "[s]ocial vulnerability is the exposure of groups or individuals to stress as a result of social and environmental changes and disruption to livelihoods". In this approach, social as well as physical impacts are included. The distinction between individual and collective dimensions of vulnerability is also important, with separate determinants, consequences, and thus indicators, as hinted at in the example on coastal zones given in Box 3.

Governability and the Governance System (GS)

Governability from the point of view of the GS is the capacity to bring about, organize and carry out governing interactions in the face of societal and natural diversity, complexity and dynamics in terms of elements, modes and orders of governance as attributes (Kooiman 2003). This applies to all three of the major components, state, market and civil society, and to the hybrid forms among them. How do governing images, instruments and action elements used by governors contribute to governability? In which way do fact and value systems, resources and social capital contribute to the way governing images are formed, instruments developed and action potential employed? At the structural level are the three modes of governance, self-, co- and hierarchical governance, fully exploited? And are the three governing orders, problem solving/opportunity creation, care for institutions and meta-considerations complementary, or are they at odds, and thus is their contribution to governability low, medium, or high? Questions like this point to the combination of norms and practice in the governability aspect of the GS.

Box 3. Vulnerability of coastal zones

> The ecological, social and economic conditions of coastal zones are such that the chain of (natural and human) producers of various coastal products and services to consumer may be better described as "coastal webs". The intricacy of these webs is enhanced by a multitude of interactions: among living organisms in coastal ecosystems, among coastal stakeholders, and between humans and ecosystems. As systems become more vulnerable with alteration and extraction by natural and anthropogenic causes, an understanding of these interactions is required to increase governability of coastal zones. Such interactions also imply that coastal management goals may be short term and long term. Given their features and these multiple interactions, there are high risks associated with decision making for coastal zones. Managing coastal activities to minimize risk and damage to ecosystems, and controlling undesirable ecological, social and economic impacts, might be more attainable than trying to achieve ideal and holistic goals. Both reactive and proactive approaches can be applied in risk-management situations, however, particularly where coastal resources are highly vulnerable and the cost of damages may be too high.

Source: Chuenpagdee *et al.* 2005.

Governability and Attributes of GS

Elements. Governors govern in and through interactions, and in those interactions three elements can be distinguished: images, instruments and action. In every governance interaction all three play a role: images as sets of ideas where a governor wants to go, instruments giving these ideas substance, and action needed to let these instruments do their work.

Images constitute the guiding lights for the how and why of governance. Images come in many types: visions, knowledge, facts, judgments, presuppositions, hypotheses, convictions, ends and goals. They not only relate to specific issues but also contain assumptions about fundamental matters such as the relationships between society and nature, the essence of humankind, and the role of government (see Box 4). *Instruments* link images to action. Instruments are not neutral. Their design, choice and application frequently elicit strife. Instruments may be "soft" or they may be "hard" and their choice is not free: positions in society determine their available range. *Action* is the putting of instruments into effect. This includes the implementation of policies according to a set of guidelines. However, action may also consist of mobilizing actors in new and uncharted directions.

We should not forget that for governability structural conditions might be even more important than the actual governing interactions themselves. From which sources do images come? From what kinds of resources do instruments come, and which of those resources are limited and/or renewable? What kinds of action patterns belong to a particular political culture and which ones do not? Together these resources form the base on which governing entities can draw for actual use.

Box 4. The Tragedy of the Commons

> The Tragedy of the Commons is undoubtedly the most influential image governing fisheries (and maybe natural resources in general) as coined by Hardin (1968) explaining the inevitably of depletion of a natural resource if the exploitation is left to those using it. It is (economically) rational for all fishermen to individually catch more fish even when the harvest is already on the decline, thus causing a tragedy for all. One response is for the state to impose restraining measures; others, however, propose privatizing the commons, arguing that private ownership will provide sufficient incentive for restrained behavior. Both lines of argument have come under critique. The tragedy itself has been attacked because of its behavioral and other untested assumptions – thus it is not a tragedy but a tragicomedy. Governance regimes in between the two just mentioned options are promoted, for example co-management, as a more effective strategy against over-fishing in the long term.

Source: McGoodwin 1990: 89–96.

Modes of governance. Interactive governance recognizes three main modes: hierarchical governance, self-governance, and co-governance. Of the three, the hierarchical mode is the most familiar and classic mode of governance. Co-modes are emerging more and more and being experimented with, while societal self-governance is the subject of much misunderstanding, theoretical as well as political-ideological (see Box 5).

All societies not only demonstrate these three modes; they also require them. A considerable step forward in our knowledge about societal governability could be taken when governance qualities of societies would be considered as mixes of the three, and not as any one of these modes in particular. The limits of hierarchical governance we see every day around us, where more and more rules and regulations become less and less effective. Experiences with co-governance, such as co-management in fisheries governance, and public-private partnerships have become widely used to fill the gaps in hierarchical governance (see the section on Forms of Interactions). Self-governance is probably the most ubiquitous mode, but also the least well known and understood in its contribution to governability. Theoretical work and empirical research is needed to specify under which conditions what kinds of mixes of the three governance modes might contribute to societal governability or hamper it.

Orders of governance. Governing activities can focus on different sorts of things, and these can be categorized in three 'orders': first-order, second-order, and meta-governance.

First-order governance deals with day-to-day affairs. It takes place wherever people and their organizations interact in order to solve existing societal problems and to create new opportunities. Of course there are many other primary governing tasks, but these serve as examples of how other tasks can be conceptualized as well.

Second-order governance focuses on the institutional arrangements within which first-order governance takes place. Here, the term 'institution' denotes the

Box 5. Modes of governance in capture fisheries

> In capture fisheries, the three major modes of governance (self-, co- and hierarchical) all influence governability. *Self-governance* in fisheries has been common worldwide, with its basis usually in local communities. The main reason is the use of fisheries resources as a commons, and the need to regulate their use, for technical reasons and/or to avoid conflicts. In the North, this mode of governance in its purest form has become rare, though remnants are still in operation in some parts of southern Europe. *Hierarchical* governance in fisheries is also widespread, particularly in the North where interventionist interactions by the state are the order of the day. However, this involvement by the state is not unchallenged. Erosion of traditional self-governing modes and their replacement with state-run management systems often does not work well. Although hierarchical governance is mainly connected with the state, it is also common in the market sector, particularly by multi-national companies. In such cases, hierarchical governance by the state is replaced by hierarchical governance by the market. Co-management, as a form of *co-governance*, means that government agencies and fisher people share responsibility for resource management functions. It tries to steer a middle course between government regulation and community-initiated regulation. Co-management is not as informal as community-based management, it requires fishermen to establish organizations with formal leadership and an executive staff. But this leadership is participatory rather than hierarchical, and (where feasible) decentralized rather than centralized.

Source: author.

arrangements of agreements, rules, rights, and procedures applied by first-order governors to make decisions. One might say that state, market and civil society are high-level expressions of such institutional arrangements in a society.

Third-order or meta-governance feeds, binds, and evaluates the entire governance exercise. Many principles or criteria guide governance. Some are of a more 'applied' nature: such as rationality, efficiency, effectiveness or performance. Others may have a more fundamental or even ethical stance, such as equity, responsibility or justice. In meta-governance, governors and the governed alike take each other's measure in formulating the norms by which they want to judge each other and the measuring process itself.

With respect to governability, the three orders of governance (first-, second- and meta-) cannot survive without each other. If no problems are solved or no opportunities created, governing institutions become hollow shells. If institutions do not renew and adapt, they will hamper rather than help in meeting new governance challenges. If these two different sets of governing activities are not put against the light of normative standards in the long run they will become pillars without foundations, blown away or falling apart in stormy weather or chaotic times (see Box 6).

Box 6. Code of conduct for responsible fisheries

In response to recent developments and concerns in world fisheries, the Food and Agriculture Organization (FAO) of the United Nations developed a Code of Conduct for Responsible Fisheries (CCRF). The goal was to establish principles and international standards for responsible fisheries, defined in relation to the effective conservation, management and development of living aquatic resources, with due respect for the ecosystem and bio-diversity. The CCRF states that fisheries management should promote the maintenance of the quality, diversity and availability of fishery resources. The CCRF was shaped in conformity with the United Nations Convention on the Law of the Sea (UNCLOS). It applies to all fisheries, whether on the high seas, within the Exclusive Economic Zone (EEZ), in territorial waters or in inland waters. Its main target is the regulation of professional fisheries, though it also voices the intention to cover recreational fisheries.

Source: Bavinck and Chuenpagdee 2005.

Governability and Sub-systems of GS

States are still the most central and omni-present societal governance sub-systems.

They steer and control from the local to international levels in complex ways, and for all practical purposes the concept of a homogeneous societal institution, denoted as "the state" and governed by uniform rules, has to be replaced by other models, allowing variety and differentiation as well as certain degrees of independence and interdependence. Changes show the dynamics of the modern state, and "[w]hilst the state...may be in retreat in some respects, its activity may be increasing in others. And nowhere...has its key decision-making role been seriously undermined" (Müller and Wright 1994: 1).

Markets, as governance institutions, also consist of many mixes of interactions, each with their own diverse, complex and dynamic features. Williamson's (1975) view of governance, in which institutional economics provide the institutional framework, consists broadly of markets, hierarchies and mixed forms of these, through which transactions are channeled. This amounts to getting away from general economic laws explaining market interactions, but showing some of their governance aspects.

The governance roles of *civil society* can be conceived as a societal domain which is predominantly characterized by governing interactions that are rather spontaneous, semi-formalized, mainly horizontal, and non-interventionist. In principle, it is not the formal status of individuals or organizations, but rather the ways in which they interact with each other, that are decisive in deciding if they belong to civil society or not. Cohen and Arato (1992) have shown state and market as successful in institutionalizing their autonomy and task differentiation, civil society less so. The dynamics and balance between state and civil society are in constant flux such that "neither of the two can monopolize public life without provoking a reaction from the opposite realm to retain political space" (Biekart 1999: 36–37).

Hybrids between the three societal institutions such as public and private have always been present. Other hybrids where the state withdraws and leaves some of its servicing tasks to companies with private or mixed ownership are also common, often in the same countries. For governability this hybridization of institutions and the way they are institutionalized on the borderline between state, market and civil society are important and are challenging to assess (Van Tulder and Van der Zwart 2006).

Governability and Governance Interactions (GI)

Governing Interactions

Interactions between the SG and the GS are a basic element of governance, and important for assessing governability. Those governed, through their participation, try to exert influence on those governing. Governing entities try to influence those governed through their policies and management efforts. Recently, interactions of a more collaborative governance nature have become the order of the day (Box 7).

Power relationships and social-political cultural traditions find their expression in governance interactions. For example, it is often said that "Anglo-Saxon"

Box 7. Interactions in aqua-culture

> Aqua-culture operations and institutions depend upon multiple interactions with each other. These interactions are largely shaped by market forces. For example, fish breeding in government research stations and seed production in private hatcheries can function well as public-private partnerships. Expansion of aqua-culture has inevitable consequences for equitable sharing of natural resources. Small-scale fish seed producers and farmers cannot easily compete with larger operators. Aqua-culture has been the world's fastest growing form of food production for over 20 years (about 9% per year). It could not have achieved this without multiple interactions. However, the persistent image of aqua-culture as a special "thing in itself", still often administered as a sub-sector of fisheries, is limiting interactions that could further revolutionize food production.
>
> Moreover, many of the world's institutions are established in ways that limit interaction between conservation of bio-diversity and food production, in terms of policy making, administrative arrangements and budgets. The Convention on Biological Diversity (CBD) regards all wild and farmed organisms and their supporting ecosystems as bio-diversity. The fish that humans consume, as well as the agro-ecosystems from which more and more are derived through aqua-culture, are indeed bio-diversity. However, the interactions of aqua-culture do not yet reflect this well, because institutions are still fostering its separation from agriculture and its false alliance with capture fisheries. The score for the presence of governing interactions in aqua-culture is high.

Source: Pullin 2005.

social-political culture does not stimulate formal interactions between governors and governed, in contrast to the "continental" tradition, where those are enabled and often institutionalized. Such differences may also explain why co-governing interactions, such as co-management schemes as in fisheries, are more common in some political cultures than in others (Wilson *et al.* 2003). Scale may also be an important feature in governance interactions. Market parties, such as multinational companies may interact with NGOs at the global level, while at the local or national level they do not interact at all.

This points to an important analytical distinction in governance interactions: an action or intentional level and a structural or contextual level. This distinction, although the subject of heated social science debates, such as in terms of agency structure, is a useful one. Any conceptualization of the constituent actors in a governance interaction necessarily involves an idea of its structural and agency component. In the literature on interest groups there are at least five structural explanations for their role in modern policy making: pluralist, neo-pluralist, Marxist, neo-Marxist, elitist and corporatist or neo-corporatist (Granados and Knoke 2005). And a heated debate on the role of agency, structure or contextual levels of explanation for the effects of policy networks also shows that the distinction between more than one dimension of governance interactions might be a sensible one (Marsh and Smith 2000, 2001).

Modalities of GI

In the reality of modern governance an enormous variety in interactions can be observed. From the GI perspective they can be ordered in a few major types: participatory, collaborative and policy or management interactions (see Kooiman 2003 for the conceptual basis of this distinction).

For governability, it is important to know how social-political entities – such as individuals, organizations, groups, movements or other forms of collective action – *participate* in governing interactions. Where does such participatory action come from? Who acts and who reacts? The character of the interaction is determined by the responsiveness of those governing and what has been called the "repertory" of resources and activities which the governed command (Barnes and Kaase 1979). This repertory is wide, and varied: voting, letter writing and protesting in sit-ins and boycotts and participating in a movement or being a member of a focus or action group. I see participatory interactions as directed from the SG to the GS. Social movements are the classical example of this kind of spontaneous, loosely organized form of governance interaction.

The importance of *collaborative* forms of governance interactions is growing. Why, for governance purposes, are groups, organizations and authorities willing to share their activities and aim to do things together instead of doing them alone? Often mutual interdependencies are mentioned as the main reason for such collaborative or co-operative interactions. Partnerships between public and private entities are a popular form of such collaboration. But collaborative interactions between companies and NGOs can also be found, although their motives may differ. Companies seem to be compliance-, risk-, value- or opportunity-driven, while motives for NGOs are more in terms of funding, capabilities or mission (Austin 2006).

Policy and *management* interactions are the collective variables for all hierarchical interactions by GS aimed at having an impact on SG. Public authorities at all levels have numerous interactions, dressed in policy terms, at their disposal to bring about politically preferred societal changes (Mayer *et al.* 2005). Management is seen as a way to organize these interactions according to criteria of efficiency and effectiveness. Stakeholder identification, for example, has become a popular (interventionist) tool in this respect (Bryson 2004: 32–33).

Systems of GI

Interactive governance considers governance and governability as a property of societal systems. To understand what is going on in the governance of modern societal systems, and thus systems of GI, one must confront head-on issues connected with their diversity, complexity and dynamics. Too often, in more traditional approaches to governing, these features have been ignored or have lip-service paid to them. We can not solve all issues related to them, but we can at least put them at the center of our approach to governance and governability.

There is an important argument for taking the *diversity* of values, goals and interests of those involved in interactions into account. This points to processes of ordering and re-ordering of aspects of diversity. For example, such a process led Buanes *et al.* (2004) to test this diversity searching approach for stakeholders in coastal zones of Norway into several distinct categories.

More often than not, *complexity* is considered not to mean anything more than that something is difficult to understand, or complicated to handle. However, complexity is more than that: it is a basic aspect of the phenomena we deal with, and, as such, it has baffled practitioners and scholars alike. We assume that there are limits to the human capacity to know and to act. This means that, in coping with complexity, we have to follow the path of combined strategies (LaPorte 1975).

Dynamics can be seen as a composition of forces which sometimes turn into gradual developments, but more often result in non-linear patterns of change. Insights in societal dynamics have direct or indirect relevance for governance and an assessment of the role of the GI in governability. For example in his study of interactions between state and society De Vries (2005) distinguished four (macro) types of policy interactions between government and society in the Netherlands by crosstabulating (dis)parity of power and authority (vertical, horizontal) and perceived interests (antagonistic, congruent). These four types were characteristic only for a certain period during the last 50 years, and after some time changed into another system of policy interaction, a transition which expresses the dynamic nature of governance interactions.

Influence of GS on SG

Among the many controversies in political science, and to some extent in sociology, few can compete with the so-called "power or influence" debate that raged in the 1960s and 1970s. Although it has never ended in anything really satisfying, it resurfaces regularly, and understandably, because applying influence and bringing power into play are facts of life in general, not only in politics. However, the story of research on influence and its "ugly sister power", the term coined by Wootton (1970: 73), shows, as Baumgartner and Leech (1998: 3) state, that substantial progress has been made but serious gaps in our knowledge remain in the study of interest groups and their influence in politics. Influence, pressure and power remain, nevertheless, fascinating subjects for social science scholars; some of whom mourn their neglected status in areas such as fisheries governance (Jentoft 2007a).

Impact or Effect of GS on SG

A summary of the multiple interactions between the GS and the SG can be obtained by looking at the effects or impacts of these interactions on the SG. The concept of impacts enables us to bring order to the changes governors try to bring about in SG

Box 8. Sea tenure, social organization and power in South Indian fisheries

> Sea tenure systems present different ways of regarding and organizing the use of marine resources. They tend also to correspond to different modes of social and economic organization.
>
> Small-scale fisheries along the Coromandel Coast – as in most developing countries – are predominantly a rural affair, rooted in pre-colonial formations and in a village style of life. Here a fisher, if he has done well on a particular day, tends to stay home the next, as his family's needs have basically been met. Kinship and ties of residence structure social interactions and influence individual decision making. The division of labor is elementary and communities are egalitarian in nature. Religious attitudes permeate everyday life in many ways.
>
> The trawler fisheries of the region are quite dissimilar. Here the laws of capitalism color the dynamic. This is brought out by the pattern of fishing. As soon as craft have returned from a fishing trip, they are prepared for the next one – after all, time wasted is money lost. Every participant's ambition is to maximize returns. There is a high degree of labor differentiation, with boat owners, and the back-lying providers of capital, calling the tune. Here life has a raw flavor, and people largely have to fend for themselves.
>
> Power is an essential ingredient in both forms of social organization and sea tenure, and also plays an important role in the relationship between the fisheries sub-sectors. The Fisheries Department, as one arm of government, has deeply influenced the balance of power at sea, which already tends toward the party with the bigger craft and engine power. The Department lent essential support to trawler fishers particularly in the sub-sector's formative phase, rebutting the waves of anger and successfully deafening small-scale fishers' protest. But the Fisheries Department has not always sided with the trawler fishers, often striving to play a mediating role. This is motivated also by the fact that small-scale fishers constitute a substantial vote bank, and cannot be ignored politically.

Source: Bavinck 2005.

by means of their policy or management interactions. Impact analysis might help in operationalizing the effect of governing efforts by a GS on the SG (Boothroyd 1995, Becker and Vanclay 2003). Impact analysis or assessment looks at the effects or potential effects of such efforts. It has been applied in many areas, such as social, environmental, ecological, technology, and risk impact assessments, all with their own specialized methodologies and technical requirements.

Recently interest in building a common theoretical and conceptual basis for impact assessment has been growing, and it is this effort which fits best with our aim of using impacts as a variable in the governability model (Slootweg *et al.* 2003). The synthesis known as policy assessment (Boothroyd 1995) is particularly relevant to applying impact assessment analysis to the operationalization of governance efforts. Policy assessment is a combination of policy evaluation and impact assessment aimed at intended as well as unintended outcomes of policies. As such it deepens the systemic awareness of impact chains. These developments are significant because for designing analytical tools for assessing the impacts or effects of governing efforts by the GS on the SG we first need sound conceptual and, for preference, broad and interdisciplinary-oriented frameworks for them.

Conclusion

In this paper the conceptual contours of governability as part of an interactive governance perspective have been sketched. In principle, all societal systems or activities can be looked upon from the point of view of their governability. They can be characterized by variables such as the diversity, complexity and dynamics of their primary processes and by properties like resilience, vulnerability, risk and others. The same applies to variables describing the main qualities of the way they are governed by institutions such as state, market and civil society and other features describing their GS. GI is of special importance, because it is the part of governability of any system where the policy aspects of governance interactions find their place.

We may assume that not all societal systems are equally diverse, complex and dynamic, or show the same patterns of governing interactions or institutional involvement. The next step in working with the framework is to make it applicable for assessment and comparison purposes. For several variables like resilience and risk, policies and participation, and the governance role of institutions, sufficient literature is available for this task. Others like complexity, diversity and dynamics or modes of governance have to be adapted or even invented. Assessing and comparing will be a longer-term research task.

This brings me to a final point. In the Introduction a potential role of this governability framework for policy, policy analysis and comparative policy analytical work in this field was suggested. Since the basic features of the framework have been sketched now, it might be clearer what this role might be: a contextual one. As part of a "renaissance" in comparative policy analysis DeLeon and Resnick-Terry mention all kinds of possibilities for a new generation of comparative policy analysis, using new conceptual approaches and theoretical perspectives. "The concept that *context* counts has become a guiding principle in the second 'generation' of comparative policy analysis" (1999: 18; emphasis added). Governance theorizing, with its broad orientation to factors involved in policy and policy making is certainly a candidate for defining such a context. The link between governance and governability on the one hand and policy and comparative policy analysis on the other, may become a strong one if we keep in mind the call made by Geva-May (2002: 257):

> for a comparative research agenda that will look into (1) what variables are inherent in 'political cultures/cultural bias' or 'ways of life' that affect public policy analysis in various contexts; (2) what their common manipulable denominator is; (3) the ways in which these variables can be manipulated when normative policy analysis methodology is employed; and (4) how we can develop an awareness for culturally sensitive variables in policy arena interactions.

This comes close to aims of the governability framework as sketched above, and opportunities in establishing links between its further development and continuous work on comparative policy analysis certainly come to mind. Such a framework might create a conceptual and, eventually even a theoretical link between policy and governance or policy analysis and governability assessment, preferably in a comparative manner, links which so far have not received much attention. This paper is a modest step in filling this gap.

Acknowledgements

I would like to express my gratitude to members of the Fisheries Governance Network, to James Meadowcroft, and to the reviewers of JCPA for their comments on earlier versions of this paper, and to Roger Pullin and Derek Johnson for their editorial help.

Notes

1. The concept of governance presented in this paper is based upon, and a follow-up to the interactive governance perspective developed by Kooiman (2003), and applied to fisheries in Kooiman *et al.* (2005) as part of the work of Fisheries Governance Network (www.fishgovnet.org). Governability has been discussed in Kooiman (2003); applied to fisheries, aqua-culture and coastal zones in Chuenpagdee and Kooiman (2005) and used for assessing governability in three papers presented at the MARE Conference "People and the Sea", July 2005 in Amsterdam: Chuenpagdee, Kooiman and Pullin (2005), Mahon (2005), Bavinck and Salagrama 2005 (see: www.marecentre.nl). The cases in this article are derived from the work of this Fisheries Governance Network.
2. A proposal for a project with the purpose of continuing this work and assessing the governability of fisheries in four areas in the South has been filed with a potential donor.

References

Adger, W. N., 2000, Social and ecological resilience: are they related? *Progress in Human Geography*, **24**, 347–364.
Adger, W. N., 1999, Social vulnerability to climate change and extremes in coastal Vietnam. *World Development*, **27**, 249–269.
Austin J. E., 2006, Sustainability through partnering: strategic alliances between businesses and NGOs. Paper presented at the Royal Netherlands Academy of Arts and Sciences Colloquium: Partnerships for Sustainable Development. Amsterdam, June 6.

Barnes, S. H. and Kaase, M., 1979, *Political Action* (Beverly Hills, CA: Sage).
Baumgartner, F. R. and Leech, B. L., 1998, *Basic Interests* (Princeton, NJ: Princeton University Press).
Bavinck, M., 2005, Understanding fisheries conflicts in the south – a legal pluralist perspective. *Society and Natural Resources*, **18**, 805–820.
Bavinck, M. and Chuenpagdee, R., 2005, Current principles, in: J. Kooiman, M. Bavinck, S. Jentoft and R. Pullin (Eds) *Fish for Life: Interactive Governance for Fisheries* (Amsterdam: Amsterdam University Press), pp. 245–264.
Bavinck, M. and Kooiman J., 2005, The governance perspective, in: J. Kooiman, M. Bavinck, S. Jentoft and R. Pullin (Eds) *Fish for Life: Interactive Governance for Fisheries* (Amsterdam: Amsterdam University Press), pp. 11–24.
Bavinck, M. and Salagrama, V., 2005, Assessing the governability of capture fisheries in the Bay of Bengal. Paper presented at MARE Conference "People and the Sea", University of Amsterdam, Amsterdam July.
Becker, H. A. and Vanclay, F. (Eds), 2003, *The International Handbook of Social Impact Assessment* (Cheltenham: Edward Elgar).
Berkes, F. Colding, J. and Folke, C. (Eds), 2003, *Navigating Social-Ecological Systems* (Cambridge: Cambridge University Press).
Biekart, C. H., 1999, *The Politics of Civil Society Building* (Utrecht: International Books).
Boothroyd, P., 1995, Policy assessment, in: F. Vanclay and D. A. Bronstein (Eds) *Environmental and Social Impact Assessment* (Chichester: Wiley), pp. 83–125.
Bryson, J. M., 2004, What to do when stakeholders matter: stakeholder identification and analysis technique. *Public Management Review*, **6**, 21–54.
Buanes, A., Jentoft, S., Karlsen, G. R. and Søreng, A., 2004, In whose interest? An exploratory analysis of stakeholders in Norwegian coastal zone planning. *Ocean and Coastal Management*, **47**, 207–223.
Chuenpagdee, R. and Kooiman, J., 2005, Governance and governability, in: J. Kooiman, M. Bavinck, S. Jentoft and R. Pullin (Eds) *Fish for Life* (Amsterdam: Amsterdam University Press), pp. 325–350.
Chuenpagdee R., Kooiman J. and Pullin R., 2005, Exploring governability of capture fisheries, aquaculture and coastal zones. Paper presented at MARE Conference "People and the Sea", University of Amsterdam, Amsterdam, July.
Cohen, J. L. and Arato, A., 1992, *Civil Society and Political Theory* (Cambridge, MA: MIT Press).
Crozier, M., Huntington, S. P. and Watanuki, J., 1975, *The Crisis of Democracy: Report on the Governability of Democracies to the Trilateral Commission* (New York: New York University Press).
Dahrendorf, R., 1980, Effectiveness and legitimacy: on the governability of democracies. *The Political Quarterly*, **51**, 393–402.
DeLeon, P. and Resnick-Terry, P., 1999, Comparative policy analysis. *Journal of Comparative Policy Analysis*, **1**, 9–22.
De Vries, M. S., 2005, Generations of interactive policy-making in the Netherlands. *International Review of Administrative Sciences*, **71**, 577–591.
Dixon, J., Kouzmin, A. and Goodwin, D., 2003, Introduction to the Symposium: Comparative Sociopolitical Governance. *Journal of Comparative Policy Analysis*, **5**, 101–105.
Dunsire, A., 1996, Tipping the balance: autopoiesis and governance. *Administration and Society*, **28**, 299–334.
Figuerdo, D. S., 2006, Democratic governability in Latin America: limits and possibilities in the context of neoliberal domination. *Critical Sociology*, **32**, 105–124.
Geva-May, I., 2002, Cultural theory: the neglected variable in the craft of policy analysis. *Journal of Comparative policy Analysis*, **4**, 243–265.
Granados, F. J. and Knoke, D., 2005, Organized interest groups and policy networks, in: T. Janoski, R. Alford, A. Hicks and M. A. Schwarz (Eds) *The Handbook of Political Sociology* (New York: Cambridge University Press), pp. 287–309.
Hardin, G., 1968, The tragedy of the commons. *Science*, **162**, 1243–1248.
Holling, C.S., 1973, Resilience and stability of ecological systems. *Annual Review of Ecology and Systematics*, **4**, 1–23.
Holling, C. S., Berkes, F. and Folke, C., 1998, Science, sustainability and resource management, in: F. Berkes and C. Folke (Eds) *Linking Social Systems and Ecological Systems* (Cambridge: Cambridge University Press), pp. 352–378.
Jentoft, S., 2007a, In the power of power: the understated aspect of fisheries and coastal management. *Human Organization*, **66**, 426–437.

Jentoft, S., 2007b, Limits to governability? Institutional implications for ocean and coastal governance. *Marine Policy*, **4**, 360–370.
Jervis, R., 1997, *System Effects: Complexity in Political and Social Life* (Princeton, NJ: Princeton University Press).
Johnson, D., Bavinck, M. and Veitayaki, J. 2005, Fish capture, in: J. Kooiman, M. Bavinck, S. Jentoft and R. Pullin (Eds) *Fish for Life: Interactive Governance for Fisheries* (Amsterdam: Amsterdam University Press), pp. 71–92.
Kooiman, J. (Ed.), 1993, *Modern Governance* (London: Sage).
Kooiman, J., 2003, *Governing as Governance* (London: Sage).
Kooiman, J., Van Vliet, M. and Jentoft, S. (Eds), 1999, *Creative Governance: Opportunities for Fisheries in Europe* (Aldershot: Ashgate).
Kooiman, J., Bavinck, M., Jentoft, S. and Pullin, R. (Eds), 2005, *Fish for Life* (Amsterdam: Amsterdam University Press).
Laporte, T. R. (Ed.), 1975, *Organized Social Complexity* (Princeton, NJ: Princeton University Press).
Luhmann, N., 1995, *Social Systems* (Stanford, CA: Stanford University Press).
McGoodwin J. R., 1990, *Crisis in the World's Fisheries* (Stanford, CA: Stanford University Press).
Mahon, R., 2005, Governability of fisheries in the Caribbean Paper presented at MARE Conference "People and the Sea", University of Amsterdam, Amsterdam, July.
Marsh, D. and Smith, M., 2000, Understanding policy networks: towards a dialectical approach. *Political Studies*, **48**, 4–21.
Marsh, D., and Smith, M., 2001, There is more than one way to do political science: on different ways to study policy networks. *Political Studies*, **49**, 528–541.
Mayer, I., Edelenbos, J. and Monnikhof, R., 2005, Interactive policy development: undermining or sustaining democracy. *Public Administration*, **83**, 179–199.
Mayntz, R., 1993, Governing failures and the problem of governability: some comments on a theoretical paradigm, in: J. Kooiman (Ed.) *Modern Governance* (London: Sage), pp. 9–20.
Mayntz, R., 2005, Governance Theory als fortentwickelte Steuerungstheorie? in: G. F. Schuppert (Ed.) *Governance Forschung* (Baden-Baden: Nomos), pp. 11–18.
Müller, W. C. and Wright, V., 1994, Reshaping the state in Western Europe. *West European Politics*, **17**, 1–11.
Pielke, R. A. Jr., 2004, What future for the policy sciences. *Policy Sciences*, **37**, 209–225.
Pullin, R., 2005, Aquaculture, in: J. Kooiman, M. Bavinck, S. Jentoft and R. Pullin (Eds) *Fish for Life: Interactive Governance for Fisheries* (Amsterdam: Amsterdam University Press), pp. 93–108.
Robinson, J. and Tinker, J., 1997, Reconciling ecological, economic and social imperatives: a new conceptual framework, in: T. Schrecker (Ed.) *Surviving Globalism* (Houndmills: MacMillan), pp. 71–94.
Slootweg, R. F., Vanclay, M. and Van Schooten, M., 2003, Integrating environmental and social impact assessment, in: H. A. Becker and F. Vanclay (Eds) *The International Handbook of Social Impact Assessment* (Cheltenham: Edward Elgar), pp. 56–73.
Van Schooten, M., Vanclay, F. and Slootweg, R., 2003, Conceptualizing social change processes and social impacts, in: H. A. Becker and F. Vanclay (Eds) *The International Handbook of Social Impact Assessment* (Cheltenham: Edward Elgar), pp. 74–91.
Van Tulder, R. and Van der Zwart, A., 2006, *International Business-Society Management* (London: Routledge).
Williamson, O. E., 1975, *Markets and Hierarchies* (New York: Free Press).
Wilson, C. D., Nielsen, J. R. and Degnbol, P. (Eds), 2003, *The Fisheries Co-Management Experience* (Dordrecht: Kluwer Academic Publishers).
Wilson, K., Pressey, R.L., Newton, A., Burgman, M., Possingham, H. and Weston, C., 2005, Measuring and incorporating vulnerability into conservation planning. *Environmental Management*, **35**, 527–543.
Wootton, G., 1970, *Interest-Groups* (Englewood Cliffs, NJ: Prentice Hall).

The Role and Impact of the Multiple-Streams Approach in Comparative Policy Analysis

DANIEL BÉLAND & MICHAEL HOWLETT

ABSTRACT *John Kingdon's multiple-streams framework has been widely used since the publication of his book* Agendas, Alternatives and Public Policies *in 1984. The popularity of this agenda-setting framework in comparative policy analysis is especially interesting because the book focused exclusively on the United States. It is not clear, however, that a framework developed exclusively on the basis of the examination of a single, somewhat idiosyncratic national case should be able to generate insights useful in comparative research. This article discusses the nature of the multiple-streams framework and its impact on comparative policy analysis, before outlining its contribution to key debates in the field.*

Introduction

Appearing slightly more than 30 years after its first publication, this collection of articles on John Kingdon's multiple-streams framework (MSF) (Kingdon 1984; Zahariadis 1995, 2007) explores the ongoing applicability and relevance of the framework for comparative policy research. Although his 1984 book *Agendas, Alternatives and Public Policies* focused exclusively on the United States, comparative policy research has long engaged with the multiple-streams framework (Kingdon 1984).[1] For example, according to the Taylor & Francis search engine, over the years the book has been cited in more than three dozen *Journal of Comparative Policy Analysis* articles.[2] However, it is not clear that a framework developed exclusively on the basis of the examination of a single, somewhat idiosyncratic national case should be able to generate insights for comparative research (Cairney and Jones 2016). In this introduction, we discuss the nature of the multiple-streams framework and its impact on comparative policy analysis, before outlining the contributions of this collection to key debates in the field.

Multiple-Streams Framework: Basic Elements

Kingdon proposed a means of understanding public policy agenda setting based upon first-hand and secondary (see for example Walker 1977) examinations of agenda processes within the fragmented US political system (Kingdon 1984). As is well known, his particular explanation of how agenda setting worked in the United States focused on three categories of independent (and interdependent) variables that interact to produce "windows of opportunity" for agenda setting. These problem, policy, and political streams have the following characteristics:

- The *problem stream* is filled with perceptions of problems that are seen as "public" in the sense that government action is needed to resolve them. These problems usually reach the awareness of policy makers because of dramatic events such as crises or through feedback from existing programmes that attract public attention. People come to view a situation as a "problem" based upon its variance with their understanding of some desired state of affairs.
- The *policy stream* is filled with the output of experts and analysts who examine problems and propose solutions. In this stream, the myriad possibilities for policy action and inaction are identified, assessed, and narrowed down to a subset of ostensibly feasible options.
- Finally, the *political stream* comprises factors that influence the body politic, such as swings in national mood, executive or legislative turnover, and interest group advocacy campaigns.

According to Kingdon (1984), these three streams flow along different channels and remain more or less independently of one another until, at a specific point in time, a *policy window* opens. Only then do the streams cross.

Under certain circumstances, *policy windows* can be used by particular actors in a policy subsystem in order to advance the engagement of the issues they care about (Howlett 1998). As Kingdon (1984, p. 21) viewed agenda setting: "The separate streams of problems, policies, and politics come together at certain critical times. Solutions become joined to problems, and both of them are joined to favourable political forces". Only then does an issue become a recognized problem on the official (or institutional) agenda and the public policy process starts addressing it.

Kingdon (1984) suggested that window openings could sometimes be triggered by apparently unrelated external *focusing events*, such as crises, accidents, or the presence or absence of "*policy entrepreneurs*" both within and outside of governments. At other times, these windows are opened by institutionalized events such as periodic elections or budget deadlines (Birkland 1997, 1998). As Kingdon (1984, p. 21) argued:

windows are opened either by the appearance of compelling problems or by happenings in the political stream. ... Policy entrepreneurs, people who are willing to invest their resources in pushing their pet proposals or problems, are responsible not only for prompting important people to pay attention, but also for coupling solutions to problems and for coupling both problems and solutions to politics.

Policy Entrepreneurs play an important role in shaping the course of the three streams and their intersection by linking or "coupling" policy problems and policy solutions together with political opportunities. These policy entrepreneurs point to the central role of agency within the multiple-streams framework.

This framework and the streams metaphor in general has proved valuable in helping explain policy dynamics and envisioning the convergence of multiple societal phenomena to precipitate an "idea whose time has come" (Kingdon 1984, p. 1). And applying the concept of multiple streams has become common practice in policy sciences, including comparative analysis. For example, it was applied in the 1990s to US foreign policy making (Wood and Peake 1998); public enterprise privatization in Britain, France, and Germany (Zahariadis 1995; Zahariadis and Allen 1995); US efforts to combat illegal drug use (Sharp 1994); collaborative pollution control partnerships between business and environmental groups in the US and Europe (Lober 1997); and the wide-ranging dynamics of further policy reform and restructuring in Eastern Europe (Keeler 1993). Since then, over 300 cases have been examined using this framework (Jones et al. 2016; Zahariadis 2016).

Metaphors and Models

Academic policy analysis often relies on metaphors to simplify complexity and illuminate subtle policy dynamics (Black 1962; Edelman 1988; Stone 1988, 1989; Pump 2011). However, there is always the risk of confusing a metaphor with a model, which can constrain the development of testable theories and impede theoretical advances (Dowding 1995; Pappi and Henning 1998). Turning a metaphor into a model or, in the case of Kingdon (1984), a framework, requires careful development of key concepts and tenets and confrontation with evidence.

Kingdon's (1984) book is replete with vivid metaphors, such as the *primeval policy soup* and, most significantly for later work, the images of *policy streams* and *policy windows* discussed above.[3] However, the framework in itself is built upon and has generated a powerful metaphor for policy activity – the idea of several independent or quasi-independent "streams" of events and actors coming together to create opportunities for, and inform the content of, policy activity. This metaphor has, in turn, informed the development of the multiple-streams framework itself.

This framework originated in March and Olson's (1979; and see Cohen et al. 1972) earlier work on decision-making theory. Their metaphor of decision making as a "garbage can", informed Kingdon's work and has been used in many studies both as a metaphor for agenda setting, as Kingdon (1984) originally intended it, and as a larger framework to interpret policy making as a whole (Mucciaroni 1992).

Although metaphors such as "streams" and "windows" are very powerful and have great purchase, it is another question how far or in what circumstances they, and any framework developed from them, might apply. Mucciaroni (1992), for example, argued this was precisely the case with the original "garbage can" metaphor, which, he noted, was never intended by its originators to be used to describe events and processes outside of those situations characterized by fluid participants and decision "technologies" and practices. How and to what extent this is the case with the multiple-streams framework itself is an ongoing question which has not received as much attention in the comparative policy literature as it deserves.

Comparative Kingdon

As noted, Kingdon's book relied exclusively US examples, particularly in and around the distinctively American congressional system. Nevertheless, the book's concepts were soon embraced by others to explain the entire policy process (Zahariadis 1995; Barzelay 2006). This "multiple-streams" framework, and its variants, hence has yielded an ongoing analytical tradition that both describes policy making and seeks to explain it in terms of the confluence of key factors or variables at particular moments in time. Unfortunately, most of these scholars apply the framework somewhat mechanically or simply draw on isolated components (e.g. "policy entrepreneur" and "focusing event") while combining it with other related policy approaches, which may or may not be compatible with Kingdon's vision and original intent (Howlett et al. 2014).

The underlying concepts and variables developed on the basis of the US experience may not apply in comparative contexts with, for example, different legislative and law-making institutions, or where there may be greater efforts made at planning, or where there are limits or restrictions on the development and practices of policy entrepreneurship, among others.

The articles in this Special Issue address such key issues in comparative analysis, examining aspects of the multiple-streams framework including the role of ideas, the weight of formal political institutions, path-dependence and path-departing policy change, and the relationship between the multiple-streams framework and other approaches to policy making. The articles also discuss how Kingdon's framework applies across different countries and institutions.

This Special Issue

This collection of articles begins and ends with two broad theoretical contributions, which frame the two empirically grounded articles at its centre. As suggested, this combination of theoretical innovation and rigorous empirical research is necessary to both reassess and reinvigorate the multiple-streams framework in policy research. The discussion of the multiple-streams framework featured in our four main contributions includes not just policy theory but also reaches out to other crucial policy-relevant literatures: ideational analysis, historical institutionalism, and comparative policy analysis.

The collection starts with Daniel Béland's critical discussion of Kingdon's work, written from the perspective of ideational analysis in comparative spatial and historical research. It argues that scholars interested in the relationship between ideas and public policy can learn a great deal from the multiple-streams framework, whose ideational component remains largely underexplored in the comparative and international ideas literature. This neglect is particularly unfortunate because, as Béland's detailed analysis reveals, *Agendas, Alternatives and Public Policies* is a book devoted in large part to the study of policy ideas. Considering this, Béland argues that students of ideas and comparative public policy should pay more direct attention to the multiple-streams framework and, more specifically, to what Kingdon wrote about ideational processes, with regard to issues such as problem definition, policy formulation, and the work of policy entrepreneurs. Reading *Agendas, Alternatives and Public Policies* through an ideational lens provides invaluable insights into policy-making processes that too many comparative policy scholars have ignored. Béland demonstrates the power of the approach by formulating a new, Kingdon-inspired research agenda for the study of ideational processes in comparative policy research. This agenda stresses institutional factors also discussed in the next two contributions.

The article by Reimut Zohlnhöfer, Nicole Herweg, and Christian Huß takes an explicitly comparative perspective on the multiple-streams framework. Noting that the framework was originally formulated exclusively through the examination of US cases in the context of agenda setting in that country's somewhat unique political institutions, the authors discuss how institutions at the decision-making stage can be introduced into the framework. While the existing literature does not systematically integrate political institutions that structure the decision-making process into the MSF, the article suggests that distinguishing two distinct coupling processes, one for agenda setting and one for decision making, can help accomplish this. During the latter coupling, the main issue is the adoption of proposals – and formal institutions play an important role here. Political entrepreneurs can ensure the adoption of their bills under conditions of institutional pluralism by conceding concessions, proposing package deals or manipulating the severity or salience of problems.

Florian Spohr's article further develops these comparative insights into the general applicability of the Kingdon framework to comparative study, but does so in the context of its extension not across jurisdictions but across time to historical neo-institutionalism. The article shows how the multiple streams framework can shed light on the path-departing policy reforms which neo-institutionalist scholars typically struggle with in order to better understand and explain them. Empirically, the article focuses on labour market policies in Germany and Sweden to show how policy entrepreneurs can take advantage of new political windows and reframe their policy discourse to bring about path-departing change. Like the two first contributions, Spohr's article shows how comparative policy scholars directly gain from meshing the multiple-streams framework with aspects of institutional analysis. This is especially the case in the context of comparative policy analysis, in which taking into account key institutional differences between countries over time is a widely accepted research strategy. From this perspective, the comparative turn in multiple-streams research is largely an institutionalist turn.

In the final contribution, Michael Howlett, Alan McConnell, and Anthony Perl examine the strengths and weaknesses of the multiple-streams framework comparatively, but this time at the theoretical level. They ask whether it is possible to combine the policy streams framework with other approaches to policy making, such as the classic policy cycles approach and the Advocacy Coalition Framework (ACF), in order to provide a more realistic framework that can capture a wider range of diverse factors, including changing governance norms, detailed programme interventions, and the complexity of policy drivers which influence policy development. Their article suggests that combining elements of these frameworks, rather than viewing them as competing or zero-sum alternatives, provides a superior explanatory framework of policy making than any – including the multiple-streams framework – does individually (for a similar perspective see John 2003).

Conclusion

Taken together, the articles in this Special Issue bridge different theoretical and empirical perspectives to both reassess and reinvigorate a most influential approach in public policy analysis that deserves more than mechanistic applications and piecemeal conceptual borrowings. By comparing and combining the multiple-streams framework with existing policy theories and with influential bodies of literature, the articles endorse the use of the multiple-streams framework in comparative policy research, but also suggest important points in which it should be amended or combined with aspects of other approaches in order to provide a more accurate and more powerful depiction of policy-making reality (on combining insights from different theories see Cairney 2013).

Acknowledgements

The authors thank Leslie Pal for his comments and suggestions. Daniel Béland acknowledges support from the Canada Research Chairs Program.

Notes

1. Several editions of the book are now available but, in this Introduction, we only refer to the original, 1984 edition.
2. Recent examples include Agartan (2015), Jones (2014), and Kulczycki (2014).
3. He also used other less dynamic metaphors, such as "windows of opportunity" and "policy entrepreneurs".

References

Agartan, T. I., 2015, Learn, frame and deploy? Cross-national policy: Ideas and comparisons in Turkey's health reform. *Journal of Comparative Policy Analysis*. doi:10.1080/13876988.2015.1059657
Barzelay, M., 2006, Introduction: The process dynamics of public management policymaking. *International Public Management Journal*, **6**(3), pp. 251–282.
Birkland, T. A., 1997, *After Disaster: Agenda Setting, Public Policy and Focusing Events* (Washington, DC: Georgetown University Press).
Birkland, T. A., 1998, Focusing events, mobilization, and agenda setting. *Journal of Public Policy*, **18**(1), pp. 53–74. doi:10.1017/S0143814X98000038
Black, M., 1962, *Models and Metaphors: Studies in Language and Philosophy* (Ithaca: Cornell University Press).
Cairney, P. and Jones, M. D., 2016, Kingdon's multiple streams approach: what is the empirical impact of this universal theory? *Policy Studies Journal*, **44**(1), pp. 37–58. doi:10.1111/psj.12111
Cairney, P., 2013, Standing on the shoulders of giants: How do we combine the insights of multiple theories in public policy studies? *Policy Studies Journal*, **41**(1), pp. 1–21. doi:10.1111/psj.12000
Cohen, M., March, J. and Olsen, J., 1972, A garbage can model of organizational choice. *Administrative Science Quarterly*, **17**(1), pp. 1–25. doi:10.2307/2392088

Dowding, K., 1995, Model or metaphor? A critical review of the policy network approach. *Political Studies*, **43**, pp. 136–158. doi:10.1111/j.1467-9248.1995.tb01705.x

Edelman, M. J., 1988, *Constructing the Political Spectacle* (Chicago: University of Chicago Press).

Howlett, M., 1998, Predictable and unpredictable policy windows: Institutional and exogenous correlates of Canadian federal agenda-setting. *Canadian Journal of Political Science*, **31**(3), pp. 495–524. doi:10.1017/S0008423900009100

Howlett, M., McConnell, A. and Perl, A., 2014, Streams and stages: Reconciling Kingdon and policy process theory. *European Journal of Political Research*. doi:10.1111/1475-6765.12064

John, P., 2003, Is there life after policy streams, advocacy coalitions and punctuations: Using evolutionary theory to explain policy change? *Policy Studies Journal*, **31**(4), pp. 481–498. doi:10.1111/psj.2003.31.issue-4

Jones, M. D., Peterson, H. L., Pierce, J. J., Herweg, N., Bernal, A., Raney, H. L. and Zahariadis, N., 2016, A river runs through it: A multiple streams meta-review. *Policy Studies Journal*, **44**(1), pp. 13–36. doi:10.1111/psj.12115

Jones, S., 2014, Flirting with climate change: A comparative policy analysis of subnational governments in Canada and Australia. *Journal of Comparative Policy Analysis: Research and Practice*, **16**(5), pp. 424–440. doi:10.1080/13876988.2014.942570

Keeler, J. T. S., 1993, Opening the window for reform: Mandates, crises and extraordinary policy-making. *Comparative Political Studies*, **25**(4), pp. 433–486. doi:10.1177/0010414093025004002

Kingdon, J. W., 1984, *Agendas, Alternatives and Public Policies* (Boston: Little, Brown and Company).

Kulczycki, A., 2014, A comparative study of abortion policymaking in Brazil and South America: The salience of issue networks and policy windows. *Journal of Comparative Policy Analysis: Research and Practice*, **16**(1), pp. 62–78. doi:10.1080/13876988.2013.785669

Lober, D. J., 1997, Explaining the formation of business-environmentalist collaborations: collaborative windows and the paper task force. *Policy Sciences*, **30**(1), pp. 1–24. doi:10.1023/A:1004201611394

March, J. G. and Olsen, J. P., 1979, *Ambiguity and Choice in Organizations* (Bergen: Universitetsforlaget).

Mucciaroni, G., 1992, The garbage can model & the study of policy making: A critique. *Polity*, **24**(3), pp. 459–482. doi:10.2307/3235165

Pappi, F. U. and Henning, C. H. C. A., 1998, Policy networks: More than a metaphor? *Journal of Theoretical Politics*, **10**(4), pp. 553–575. doi:10.1177/0951692898010004008

Pump, B., 2011, Beyond metaphors: New research on agendas in the policy process. *Policy Studies Journal*, **39**, pp. 1–12. doi:10.1111/psj.2011.39.issue-s1

Schlesinger, M. and Lau, R. R., 2000, The meaning and measure of policy metaphors. *The American Political Science Review*, **94**(3), pp. 611–626. doi:10.2307/2585834

Sharp, E. B., 1994, Paradoxes of National Anti-Drug Policymaking, in: D. A. Rochefort and R. W. Cobb (Eds) *The Politics of Problem Definition: Shaping the Policy Agenda* (Lawrence: University Press of Kansas), pp. 98–116.

Stone, D. A., 1988, *Policy Paradox and Political Reason* (Glenview, IL: Scott, Foresman).

Stone, D. A., 1989, Causal stories and the formation of policy agendas. *Political Science Quarterly*, **104**(2), pp. 281–300. doi:10.2307/2151585

Walker, J. L., 1977, Setting the agenda in the U.S. Senate: A theory of problem selection. *British Journal of Political Science*, **7**, pp. 423–445. doi:10.1017/S0007123400001101

Wood, B. D. and Peake, J. S., 1998, The dynamics of foreign policy agenda setting. *American Political Science Review*, **92**(1), pp. 173–184. doi:10.2307/2585936

Zahariadis, N., 1995, *Markets, States, and Public Policy: Privatization in Britain and France* (Ann Arbor: University of Michigan Press).

Zahariadis, N., 2007, The multiple streams framework: Structure, limitations, prospects, in: P. Sabatier (Ed) *Theories of the Policy Process*, 2nd ed. (Boulder: Westview), pp. 65–92.

Zahariadis, N., 2016, Delphic oracles: Ambiguity, institutions, and multiple streams. *Policy Sciences*, **49**(1), pp. 3–12. doi:10.1007/s11077-016-9243-3

Zahariadis, N. and Allen, C. S., 1995, Ideas, networks, and policy streams: Privatization in Britain and Germany. *Review of Policy Research*, **14**(1–2), pp. 71–98. doi:10.1111/ropr.1995.14.issue-1-2

Differences That Matter: Overcoming Methodological Nationalism in Comparative Social Policy Research

SCOTT GREER, HEATHER ELLIOTT, & REBECCA OLIVER

ABSTRACT *Welfare states are often discussed as if they were territorially homogeneous state-wide institutions measurable by state-wide expenditure averages and explained by country-level variables. It is rare in comparative policy studies to investigate the role of territorial politics in the outcomes of even federal countries. This article argues, using social policy examples in the UK and US, that the impact of intergovernmental finance and division of labour profoundly shapes social investment and redistribution – producing almost as much expenditure variance within the US as within the OECD. The findings show the importance of incorporating territorial politics and intergovernmental arrangements into comparative welfare state and policy analysis.*

1. Introduction

Students of welfare state and public policy are well aware of the importance of territorial allocation of authority. No serious textbook of public policy in a federal or decentralised country fails to mention the roles of regional governments and their policy activities; in some countries, such topics merit their own professional journals and undergraduate courses. Yet the study of comparative public policy is strangely uncomfortable with the role of regional governments in explaining policy outcomes (Agnew 2013). Students of the detail of the policy sometimes fail to pay much attention to the constraints and politics of the precise government bodies formulating interesting policies. Comparativists, especially those focused on the welfare state, often become methodological nationalists (Chernilo 2006). Methodological nationalism is "the naturalisation of the equation of society, state, and nation" – the assumption that states are the best or only units of observation or analysis (Jeffery and Wincott 2010, p. 170). In comparative politics, policy, and welfare state studies, it amounts to the use of country-level data to characterise and explain welfare decisions.

Methodological nationalism poses problems for the analysis of welfare states. First, it is problematic because it defines distinctive regional welfare arrangements out of existence. Second, it substitutes state-level averages for more telling regional data, reducing the number of cases available. Causal analysis about the effects of a given variable might be better served by avoiding a once-removed analysis of aggregate data, and, instead, pursuing an inspection of the actual political units where the decision making takes place. A study of the effects of leftist government on education spending, for example, would be poorly executed through an analysis of aggregate spending data and political representation at the federal level if the actual spending levels were determined locally. Third, it oversimplifies the complexity revealed by the historical study of federalism and welfare (Obinger et al. 2005). Fourth and finally, it is a problem because it makes it much harder to study the interaction of nationalism, territorial politics, and the welfare state (McEwen and Moreno 2005; Wincott 2006; Béland and Lecours 2008; Greer 2009).

Methodological nationalism, we posit, is particularly likely to be a problem in the analysis of "new" social policy debates, such as those about the ways welfare states are handling demographic changes such as ageing populations, the decline of male-breadwinner households, and the challenges of long-term unemployment – broadly speaking, the debates surrounding new social risks. Unlike pension policies, the diverse policies aimed at women, youth, and the long-term unemployed all tend to be decentralised and depend on regional or local government finances, collaboration, and implementation. The scale of social investment or adaptation of the welfare state in these areas, with the large "footprints" of staff and programmes found in areas such as health or activation policies and the large role of regional governments, is particularly unlikely to be captured by state-wide averages.

Working with the cases of the United Kingdom and United States, in the perspective of data from the OECD countries, this article argues that analyses of the politics of important social policy developments are illuminated if we incorporate regions into comparative welfare state analysis. The following sections sketch a method for understanding regional welfare state effort and develop an example in the development of social policy in the United Kingdom and United States. We focus on two kinds of social policy, often associated with the discussion of new social risks: the relative age alignment of spending (Lynch 2001, 2006) and active labour market spending. The analysis finds substantial variation within the United States, especially if placed in juxtaposition with the heavily used OECD data, which stands as the basis for a large portion of current understandings of different welfare states. As a result we can see the effects of the different forms of decentralisation in the United States and United Kingdom on two key kinds of distributional concern, namely the extent to which risks associated with age are addressed by policy, and the extent to which the regional governments charged with much active labour market policy (ALMP) are acting to address the risks of long-term unemployment.

2. Regions in Comparative Welfare State Literature

There are two broad ways in which the existing literature handles the role of regions in comparative welfare state studies (Greer 2009). One emerges from the literature in comparative welfare state politics and macrosociology and treats decentralisation as a property of states. It regularly finds that decentralisation correlates with lower welfare state effort, argues that the problem is veto points, and is usually hostile to decentralised allocations of authority. This body of work converges with conservative public choice scholarship, which formulates similar arguments but applauds smaller welfare states and posits intergovernmental competition as a more important mechanism. The other broad way of handling territorial welfare states emerges from studies of individual regions, and often praises their policy experiments and higher welfare state effort.

2.1 Macro-Comparative Approaches

The traditional macro-comparative approach, practised equally in sociology and political science on both sides of the Atlantic, is to treat any decentralised allocation of authority as an attribute of the state. The units of analysis are states, and the allocation of authority is either a variable or part of a larger variable such as "fragmentation" (Hicks and Swank 1992; Hicks 1999; Lancaster and Hicks 2000; Huber and Stephens 2001; Swank 2001, 2002; Brooks and Manza 2007). Either way, decentralisation, like bicameralism or referenda, is an attribute found to a variable degree in countries. Almost every study with this premise finds that centralisation promotes welfare state growth, and decentralisation the reverse (Castles 1999; Stepan and Linz 2011). They tend to explain this pattern with a form of veto-players argument: federalism increases the number of obstacles to welfare-expanding legislation. Such a veto-players argument also seems like a plausible explanation for what appears to be relatively slower retrenchment of welfare states in decentralised countries; they are just slower to change (Simeon 2006).

Public choice scholars come to many of the same conclusions while employing a different analytical framework. They argue that mechanisms of competition keep governments from "overproviding" desirable things and thereby raising taxes too much or incurring too much debt, while competition and shorter principal–agency connections (e.g. greater proximity to voters) reduce waste and local rent-seeking (Weingast 1995, 2009; also discussed in Costa-i-Font and Greer 2013). While the logic focuses on competition rather than the veto points that interest macro-sociologists, and the normative commitment is to small government, it concurs with the comparative sociologists on one basic point: more decentralisation yields less welfare state expenditure.

Neither school of thought explores the possibility that variation within the state can produce higher or lower levels of expenditure on priorities in different places; both are narrowly focused on using stylised state-level institutional structures to explain state-level averages. But treating decentralisation only as a property of sovereign states reduces regional governments' activities to their participation in state averages. There are several problems with this approach.

First, regional governments may or may not play any role in determining welfare spending. If they lack decisive influence over the central government, why should they matter? Decentralisation is logically and practically independent of regional government vetoes over central government (Greer 2009) – self-rule is not the same thing as shared rule (Elazar 1987).

Second, state-level measures of welfare effort should decompose into state and regional welfare state effort. If the regions are dominant welfare providers and the central state plays little role then there might be considerable variation. Overall welfare expenditure will be an unrevealing average, as it often is in the United States.

Third, there is no theory of regional or state welfare politics in these accounts; it is not at all clear that even territorial decentralisation means anything on its own. It might be an unrevealing aggregate of more focused variables such as the structure of intergovernmental finance or the specific extent of regional government influence over central government actions. This is because the basic idea of "fragmentation" has no meaningfully specified mechanism associated with it.

Fourth, the endogeneity problem that afflicts all studies of territorial politics means that it is hard to see, at the state level, whether welfare state effort is a property of institutions, or whether both welfare state effort and institutions are effects of deeper social structures (Rodden 2004; Erk and Koning 2009). Insofar as the fragmentation runs deeper than the institutional level, there is a good chance that these structures are territorially differentiated and would be revealed in a territorially sensitive analysis, as studies have indeed found (Linz and de Miguel 1966; Snyder 2001). It is certainly the case that territory shapes the intense arguments about the distribution of government resources that are found in many countries (e.g. Beramendi 2011).

Fifth, the narrow concept of "decentralisation" obscures the very complex ways in which territorial politics and institutions shape welfare state priorities and expenditure. For example, areas of the Spanish and US welfare states that are the responsibilities of autonomous communities and states are under more fiscal pressure than areas in the hands of the central governments (Greer 2009). Gais (2009), accounting for the complex system of US welfare programmes, presents an intricate comparison of US state and local expenditures on cash assistance, medical assistance, and social services and discerns a decline in assistance and growing divergence in state spending depending on fiscal capacity. The historic roots of this differentiated American welfare state, other major scholars argue (Lieberman and Lapinski 2001; Katznelson 2013; Mickey 2013), involves precisely the exploitation of federalism in social policy design to preserve inequality in undemocratic racial enclaves in the South.

These problems more or less automatically flow from treating decentralisation as a property of countries in regression analyses. As Benz and Broschek (2013) conclude, "although many scholars have emphasized the dynamic character of federalism, there obviously is a shortage of informed studies on the topic". The next section reviews the main alternative.

2.2 Regional Agency

The alternative in a great deal of the literature is to focus on the activities of individual regional governments. This means writing about regional protagonism: what did a given region do, and why? This genre of work is predominantly case-based. It focuses on small numbers of regions, or regions in a given country, and explains what they did and what they were capable of doing in a theoretically informed way (McEwen and Moreno 2005; Béland and Lecours 2005, 2008). It encompasses studies that discuss, in varying degrees, the use of welfare policy as a nation- or region-building exercise as well as the development of distinctive welfare politics and policy in any given region. Work in this vein, as often as not, celebrates regional welfare states; it is fairly clear that the desire to defend a Scottish welfare state was a major driver of devolution (regardless of what scholars might say about the Scottishness of that desire, or that welfare state). In principle, this literature is complemented by the general public policy literature that exists for some regions (Keating 2005; McGarvey and Cairney 2008; Birrell 2009; Lodge and Schmuecker 2010) as well as by qualitative comparative studies which tend to find that the territorial politics of welfare is very complicated (Obinger et al. 2005).

This second approach has advantages over the standard macro-comparative account. It is more precise, connects better with relevant areas of comparative politics such as the study of parties, institutions, and intergovernmental relations, and is more theoretically fertile because it is not based on rough and nearly uninterpretable correlations. The problem is that it has been pursued through small-N studies. This creates difficulties in comparing specific studies as well as problems of case bias: many discussions of Catalan, Quebec, and Scottish policy, few studies of Valencian, Manitoban, and Northern Ireland policy.[1] There is a risk that a focus on the experiences of a handful of regions shapes the theory.

2.3 Regional Welfare State Effort

So long as comparative findings are derived from studies that use states as units and "federalism" or "fragmentation" as a variable, macro-comparative welfare state studies will continue to write regional governments out, fail to connect with case study and intra-country comparative literature, or slight decentralisation by lumping it into a single variable with other presumed enemies of the welfare state. Qualitative comparisons of policy variations within countries and case studies of divergent social policy approaches both have great merits but fail to straightforwardly respond to the macro-sociological or public choice claim that decentralisation impedes the development of the welfare state.

We propose that it is possible to compare the extent of divergence within countries, showing how different degrees of financial centralisation interact and shape policy (Agranoff 2004). We argue that decentralisation can allow or create substantial internal variation through greater or lesser redistributive spending across territory and financial integration. If this is true, then it should be possible to choose two countries with very different institutional forms and see substantially different levels of expenditure within them, comparing the role of regions within their systems, identifying the scale of territorial divergence within countries, differentiating divergence between countries. We undertake this endeavour in our study of the cases of United States and Great Britain, elaborating a cross-national comparative analysis of social policy questions that places territorial governance at the centre of the investigation.

3. Decentralisation and New Social Risks in the Federal United States and the Devolved United Kingdom

This section compares regional and welfare state spending in two countries with substantially different arrangements for allocating money, focusing on the way territorial politics shape two key aspects of the welfare state: the distribution of spending between young and old, and the extent and vigour of active labour market programmes. These are preoccupations of the literature on new social risks (Taylor-Gooby 2004; Armingeon 2007). As Bonoli (2005) summarises it, "new social risks" are risks that fall onto the young, long-term unemployed, single mothers, and others who are structurally vulnerable but not priorities of welfare states built on supporting full-time male wage earners. They are also preoccupations of the newer work on social investment (Morel et al. 2012). Simply put, ALMP is a key form of social investment. Spending on the young is more of an investment than spending on the old because of the longer term expected payoff due to longevity, and the actual spending on the young tends to be investment such as education.

Comparative analyses of new social risks, while folding new elements within the comparative cross-national analyses, share the common ground with previous studies in this vein comparing and grouping cases of social policy spending levels (Cameron 1978), degrees of de-commodification (Esping-Andersen 1990; Scruggs and Allan 2006), or tendency towards relatively high spending on the elderly (Lynch 2006).

3.1 Case Selection

Our cases were selected to provide a basic test of the thesis that the structure of territorial politics shapes the welfare state; they are therefore two countries with substantially different territorial politics and welfare states that are generally categorised in the same way, as liberal. The United Kingdom and United States are frequently classified as similar countries: English-speaking, liberal in Esping-Andersen's terms (1990), held up as paragons of neoliberalism, closely linked in politics and many policy debates, and with (broadly) residualist welfare states and low levels of employment protection. While the politics and policies of their welfare states still differ, their welfare states overall resemble each other much more than they do those of corporatist or Southern European countries. In terms of territorial politics, however, they are very different. The United States has long been a very decentralised federation (the states preceded and had to agree to the creation of the federal government), while the UK's modern experience as a politically decentralised state began in 1998[2] and the UK remains asymmetric, with England directly governed by the UK government while Northern Ireland, Scotland, and Wales have their own autonomous parliaments with responsibilities concentrated in the welfare state. The central government of the UK still substantially controls finances within the country, despite some recent liberalisation of the Scottish financial mechanisms (if not the underlying distributional formula).

This makes the two countries excellent cases to assess whether the given political institutions produce greater or lesser territorial variation in the welfare state. In countries such as the UK, where finances are substantially centralised, we should expect relatively limited variation. In the United States, the institutional and financial arrangements permit considerable variation and put much less effort into inter-territorial equalisation, and we should see it in the variation between states. The structure of territorial politics – centralised finance and responsibility in the UK, decentralised finance and responsibility in the US – should produce varying levels and kinds of inequality among residents of different territories.

3.2 Methodological Approach and Data

Conceptually, our approach reconstructs a standard international framework for measuring comparative welfare state effort by incorporating the division of governmental powers with regard to a specific function. Data on state-level spending in the United States was extracted from the United States Census of State and Local Governments, year 2009, and where available 2010, which reports expenditure data for the federal and state governments, and survey-based returns for local government. This data presents numerous advantages in terms of degree of detail but comes from a data series that has since been discontinued.[3] The United Kingdom data is from the Public Expenditure Statistical Analysis (PESA) series, produced by HM Treasury, for 2009 as well.

Coding is one of the biggest challenges for cross-national quantitative comparisons. Our approach was to rely on broad, largely comparable, budget categories: health, retirement income, primary and secondary education, higher education, and public assistance. We then translated the categories reported by each government into the larger categories. While it might be interesting to have more specific data on more specific policy areas, it becomes difficult to code coherently and comparatively below the level of those large categories. The least self-explanatory category, public assistance, consists of any form of benefits or income support excluding pensions. This includes cash benefits such as unemployment insurance as well as more distinctive benefits such as the Supplementary Nutritional Assistance Program (SNAP) in the United States.[4] The categories we use essentially follow the same categories as the UK PESA statistics.

The age-alignment spending ratio was calculated closely following Lynch (2006). This measure is calculated by dividing the total spending on pension and survival benefits by the number of individuals over 65 and then dividing this figure by the per capita spending on social expenditures for the population under 65.[5] With regard to the percentage of spending on active labour market programmes or close equivalents, the denominator, the calculated gross national product of each state or region, was calculated based on data from the US census data, Eurostat, and the OECD (Adema et al. 2011).

Calculations for the OECD countries drawn from the OECD Social Expenditures Dataset were made based on data from the OECD. As with Lynch (2001, 2006) we are obliged to exclude several types of direct expenditures from this measure given the problem with ascertaining the age of the recipients: incapacity-related benefits (notably, disability pensions), housing, and health spending. Spending included in the elderly category are the following: old-age pensions, survivors' pensions, services for the elderly, and early retirement pensions. Non-elderly expenditures include sums for unemployment compensation, severance pay, early retirement, family cash benefits and services (child allowances and credits, childcare support, income support during leave), ALMPs (OECD 2011), and other social assistance expenditures such as income maintenance as well as spending on education.

4. The United States

It is a commonplace of American politics that states vary widely in their wealth, taxes, welfare benefits, and political commitment to welfare. What is less widely studied is the extent to which this produces a distinctive welfare state in each state as a result of interaction between state politics and federal programmes. What is the interaction between state welfare policies and federal welfare policies and how does it shape the overall US welfare state?

Governments in the United States have many financial options and trade-offs. As a legacy of the country's age and long history of intergovernmental relations, practically every form of intergovernmental arrangement – and gaming – may be located in some place at a given point in time. State and federal spending are both conceptually simple: the state or federal government raises a sum of money and spends it in a given state. The more complex problems arise from federal grants and co-financing, which meld state and federal money by inviting states to participate in programmes that allow the federal government to match their expenditures for some reason. While the state governments have no formal representation in the government (they serve as electoral circumscriptions for the directly elected Senate), members of Congress are able to direct spending to the state governments in a variety of ways (Richardson 2009). When the federal government co-finances services, it often uses different matching formulae for different states; a higher matching rate means that a state gets more federal dollars for each dollar it spends (e.g. Thompson 2012). Negotiating this rate can have important consequences for state budgets.

Figure 1 shows the 2008 returns for spending numbers for state and federal governments from the Census. For simplicity, it only shows three categories: state spending out of own revenue; direct federal spending; and conditional grants – federal spending via grants to the states such as Medicaid. This excludes local government spending, which is especially important in education. Figure 1 uses the measure of per capita expenditure, which shows substantial variance, summarised in Table 1. A look at the relative weight of state, federal, and federal grant expenditure reveals that not only are there wide differences in American states' welfare expenditure but also divergences in the degree to which they affect federal grant outlays (e.g. Medicaid) but not direct federal expenditure (e.g. Medicare). For instance, the coefficient of variation for federal spending is 0.20 and for state spending it is 0.31, while the variation is much greater for federal via state per capita spending (0.82).

Based on a more detailed breakdown of per capita spending data (Data Appendix, Table A), there is substantial variation in states' share of welfare spending, less variation in federal spending via states (co-financing, i.e. Medicaid, Temporary Assistance for Needy Families (TANF), and the Children's Health Insurance Program (CHIP)), and still less in federal spending, as shown in Figure 1. Including covariates such as age and poverty rates would lessen the variation between expenditure by federal programmes in different states. The variation is therefore not just between states; it is between programmes. Programmatic areas such as higher education that have more state money have more variation in per capita expenditure than the paradigmatic example of a federal programme, old-age pensions. Where the federal government leaves space for states to vary (Béland et al. 2014), states will; when the federal government creates incentives for states to take, they vary greatly and the states take them at very different rates, as the coefficient of variation in Table 1 shows.

Further cross-state comparisons emerge based on measures of state spending presented in Figures 2 and 3. The first is the elderly–nonelderly spending ratio (ENSR), introduced in Section 3.2. A higher value reflects more spending directed at the elderly, controlling for populations. Crudely, in the US this maps onto a ratio between federal spending, directed at the elderly, and state spending, directed at the non-elderly. The considerable variation in ENSR shown in Figure 2 suggests substantial variation in state spending against a background of a federal welfare state more focused on the elderly.

The second dimension of social risks under analysis, active labour market programmes, are difficultly captured in the United States. We use one of the only schemes with an active job training programme, TANF, a federal block grant programme that provides

Figure 1. State, federal, federal via state per capita ($ Thousands) social spending in the United States (2009)

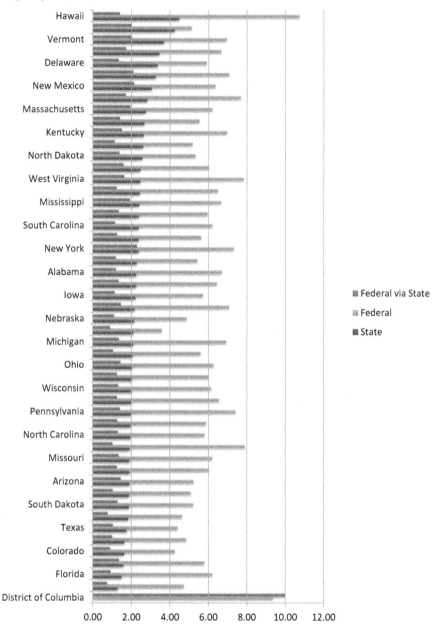

Notes: Per capita spending in thousands includes spending in the following areas: primary, secondary and higher education, old-age pension, public assistance with TANF and public assistance without TANF, health, housing, and local amenities. *Source*: Census Bureau, authors' calculations.

Table 1. Variation in US state, federal, and conditional spending ($ thousands per capita)

	State	Federal	Conditional grants from centre
Average	2.29	6.15	1.54
SDD	0.72	1.23	1.26
Coeff. of variation	0.31	0.20	0.82

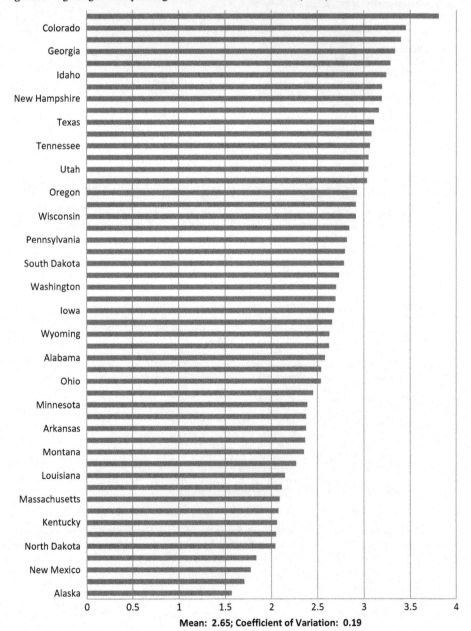

Figure 2. Age-alignment spending ratios in the United States (2009)

Mean: 2.65; Coefficient of Variation: 0.19

Figure 3. TANF spending in United States as a percentage of State GDP (2009)

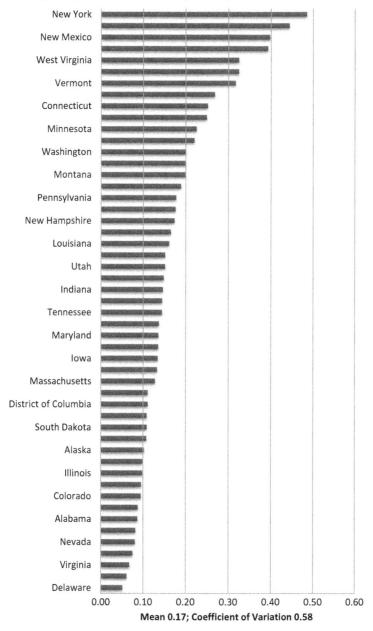

Mean 0.17; Coefficient of Variation 0.58

"assistance and work opportunities to needy families by granting States the Federal funds and wide flexibility to develop and implement their own welfare programs".[6] It might not be all that advocates of ALMPs would recommend, but it is a labour market policy with elements of activation in the American context,[7] and is classified as a component of

ALMPs by the OECD (OECD 2011). We report TANF as percent of state GDP to match OECD data.

Spending on TANF varies to a greater extent than the variation observed in the age-alignment ratio. As illustrated in Figure 3, the coefficient of variation for the TANF data indicates relatively high variance across states for this measure – 0.58, compared to that of the ENSR 0.17. In the case of the TANF data, 12 states are outside the range of the median plus or minus 50 per cent. With regard to the age-alignment orientation of spending in a given state (ENSR), there is some overlap between the top 15 states in terms of degree of age spending ratio and the lowest proportion of state-calculated GDP dispensed on TANF (New York, Ohio, Vermont).

For comparative welfare state studies, overall low US average welfare state effort is not very revealing. There are deep divergences between states that reveal different priorities, expenditure levels, and corresponding welfare states and effects on citizens' lives. The overall US programmatic bias towards age and medical care is in large part a function of the structure of federal government spending, though it seems help for the aged is largely parallel (run without reference to the states, except for Medicaid's role in long-term care for the elderly) and healthcare is largely additive, with states having the capacity and sometimes the will to expand healthcare spending beyond the apparent minimum of Medicaid and CHIP participation. The age profile of the US *federal* welfare state is biased towards the elderly (Lynch 2001); the extent to which states reduce that bias is in large part driven by state politics.

5. United Kingdom

If the decentralised finances and division of labour in the US seems to encourage interstate variation in some services (loosely those aimed at under-65s) and federalise benefits in others, the UK's centralised finances at devolution were geared to produce rough equality between residents regardless of their territories. UK debates tend to focus on the variation in per capita spending between England, Northern Ireland, Scotland, and Wales, and more sophisticated versions incorporate differences between spending in English regions as well (McLean 2005; Trench 2008; McLean et al. 2009). But compared to the United States, what stands out is the lack of variation and lack of scope for variation in welfare spending so far.

Devolution finance in the UK has two components. One is a block grant that allows the three devolved administrations (Northern Ireland, Scotland, and Wales) large sums of unrestricted money. The money given to devolved governments is calculated from a historic baseline, which traditionally gave them all higher per capita spending than England. Changes in the amounts budgeted then come via something known as the "Barnett formula". The Barnett formula stipulates that for each change in spending in England on services that are devolved in Northern Ireland, Scotland, and Wales, the devolved administrations each receive a pro-rata per capita share; so if an extra pound is spent on English services, an additional per capita share of that is given to the devolved administrations (about 11p for Scotland). There are a variety of significant loopholes (classifying some spending as UK rather than comparable, or manipulating local government taxation), but the system is relatively transparent. Devolution of specific tax bases could produce more variation in expenditure as the share of Barnett block grants shrinks relative to taxes that devolved administrations can vary.

Atop the block grant comes an arrangement being introduced in Scotland, which implements the recommendations of the Calman Commission (issued in 2009). The new Scottish system goes beyond the (unused) Scottish power to raise income tax slightly, and instead devolves taxes totalling approximately 30 per cent of its expenditure. The devolved taxes include some entire individual taxes, such as landfill tax and the "stamp tax" on real estate transactions, and a slice of the income tax. The taxes gained will be matched with a cut in the block grant to Scotland (that will match the revenue raised in Scotland each year). There are discussions of parallel reforms for financing in Northern Ireland and Wales. These arrangements are new and still being implemented as of 2015.

The devolved governments are then free to spend that money within their legal powers, which vary in form and extent but basically make them responsible for health, education, housing, and community amenities, and those aspects of public assistance involving personal social services. The bulk of devolved budgets go on the "comparable" welfare state services, i.e. ones that are overwhelmingly the responsibility of devolved governments or England-only departments in England. The UK government's all-UK social welfare responsibilities are mostly in old-age pensions and those areas of public assistance that involve cash transfers. Formally, the social security system in Northern Ireland is devolved, but it historically moves in lock-step with UK benefits and is paid by the UK for that purpose (meaning that, properly understood, it should cause no variation in spending per capita on the elderly).

Figure 4 shows the territorial breakdown of welfare state spending in the UK. It displays the well-established inequalities in spending by territory, inequalities that are actually much more substantial if we consider the large inequalities between English regions (McLean et al. 2009). Such comparisons often appear in discussions of whether the allocation of funding to one region or another is "fair". In the variation in the

Figure 4. UK social spending by region and area, 2009, per capita (£ thousands)

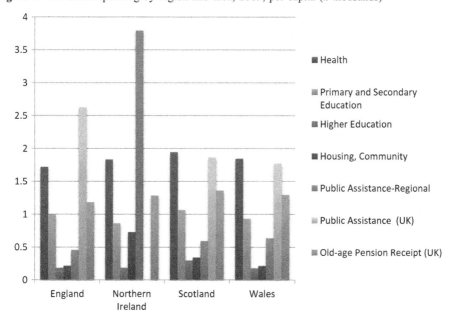

Source: Public Expenditure Statistical Analysis (PESA) series. See notes to Table 2 for discussion of Northern Ireland.

Table 2. Percentage of social expenditure by regional government (relative to total including regional and UK government)

	% Regional
England	48.40%
Northern Ireland	79.20%
Scotland	56.81%
Wales	50.82%

Source and notes: The United Kingdom data is from the Public Expenditure Statistical Analysis (PESA) series. Northern Ireland is formally responsible for social security, which accounts for its higher regional percentage, but as benefit levels are set in lock-step with overall UK social security and it receives a subsidy to maintain those levels the regional role is essentially administrative rather than policy making.

percentage of spending that is allocated by regional governments, we can see some effects of differences in formula funding, as well as different eligibility for UK benefits.

Table 2 presents the percentages of expenditure that are regional. For a Scot, about 56 per cent of the welfare state effort is regional. And for the UK overall, about the same percentage of the welfare state is "regional" – meaning spent by either a devolved administration or an England-only department such as Health. Apart from Northern Ireland, where the formally regional social security field is essentially part of the UK system, the variations are probably due to a mixture of devolved finance and the age profile of different parts of the UK. Compared to the US, what stands out is the uniformity of the percentages; the two categories of mechanism (central block grants to devolved regions and central programmes operated centrally) are in rough balance.

Table 1 and Figure 4 both show that the impact of regional welfare states depends substantially on the financing mechanism and degree of fiscal equalisation. Devolved governments in the UK do not have much freedom to change overall welfare effort. They have a block budget calculated primarily based on three major English services (health, education, and social care) and spend most of it on those three services in their jurisdictions. They have limited trade-offs between sectors and no meaningful trade-off with taxation levels, which also means their incentive to reorganise might be limited. It should be no surprise that the divergence in devolved policy is more in organisation than in levels of expenditure (Greer 2004; Birrell 2009; Lodge and Schmuecker 2010). For the UK, the future, with at least some greater degree of fiscal autonomy for Scotland, might allow greater variation.

6. Cross-National and Cross-Regional Comparisons

Standard analyses often mask the composition of the welfare state by hiding the substantial role of regional politics. Approximately one-third of US welfare spending is by state governments out of their own resources, with the effect that Connecticut and Kansas, or Texas and New York, can run welfare states with different priorities, eligibility, and services. To some extent they must; Connecticut is a much richer state than Kansas. To some extent they choose; Connecticut is also much more left-leaning than Kansas.

Approximately another 12 per cent of expenditure in the US is state spending of federal grants, in which they have some autonomy to treat their populations differently. Approximately half of UK welfare spending is by devolved administrations or England departments, with the devolved governments highly autonomous; the formula financing system means that they do not vary their spending much but the half of welfare that they expend does explain why the experience of the same welfare services in different parts of the UK might be quite substantially different.

This divergence raises an obvious question: is the divergence within at least some countries perhaps greater than the much more studied divergence between countries? Comparing Figures 2, 5, and 6 addresses this question. The coefficient of variance is designed to allow for the comparison of the degree of variance across samples of data without being sensitive to the measure utilised (calculated as the standard deviation divided by the mean). With regard to the age-alignment spending ratio, the coefficient of variation is 10.6 per cent greater for the sample of OECD countries when compared to the state ratios for the United States and 63 per cent greater than in the case of regions within the United Kingdom. Given the volumes of critical comparisons and theoretical groupings of OECD countries, it is surprising to consider that such a high degree of variation may be found within *a single case*. Moreover, in TANF, which the OECD considers to be the key American ALMP programme, the coefficient of variation is actually greater in the USA (0.58) than in the OECD overall (0.53) (compare Figures 3 and 7). The comparison is imperfect because TANF is a mixture of ALMP and straightforward income support, but as a statement about variable commitment to the labour market and life prospects of the poor, the extent of variance within the US is noteworthy. American states, many of which rival OECD member states in size, seem also to rival them in the divergence of their approaches to, and spending on, new social risks.

Figure 5. Age-alignment spending ratios in the United Kingdom (2009) (ENSR)

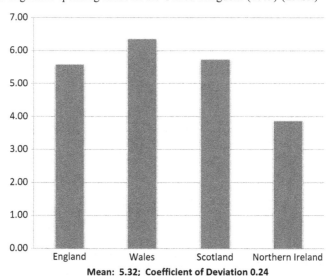

Mean: 5.32; Coefficient of Deviation 0.24

Source: The United Kingdom data is from the Public Expenditure Statistical Analysis (PESA) series.

Figure 6. Age-alignment spending ratio in the OECD

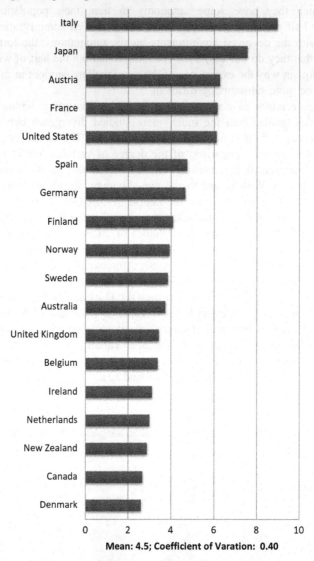

Mean: 4.5; Coefficient of Varation: 0.40

Source: The OECD countries in question are limited to those within a 33 per cent range of GDP per capita relative to the US. Data from OECD Social Expenditures and Population from OECD and OECD.stat, education and skills (primary, secondary, and tertiary education (excluding post-secondary non-tertiary education so as not to double-count spending on ALMPs and educational programmes)).

Second, the different patterns of spending have effects on the sustainability and nature of the policy. American states, for example, operate under balanced budget constraints. This makes them procyclical, along with any services they provide – they have more money to spend in good times and less to spend in bad times (when demands on the welfare state are likely to be higher). Thus, for example, it is no surprise that US higher education spending is procyclical: much of it is by states. Likewise, the large share of

Figure 7. OECD countries' ALMPs as a percentage of GDP (2009)

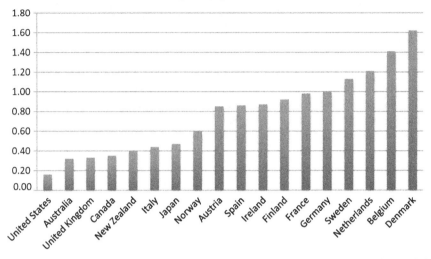

Source: Social expenditures OECD; employment and labour markets: Key tables from OECD (OECD 2011).

public assistance entrusted to states means that these are less effective as automatic stabilisers than might be thought. The United Kingdom, by contrast, achieves very similar welfare states because of its simple division of powers (98 per cent comparability is quite strikingly high compared to the US and probably most other states, where funding streams are much more mixed) and block budgets.

Third, the effect of breaking down spending by both programme and territorial level highlights the importance of institutions. The US federal government could in theory legislate universal single-payer healthcare or massively increase its higher education spending, so in that sense the variation and averages in state expenditure are a federal decision (though one attributable to fragmentation in Washington, not the existence of states). But given the well-established difficulties of passing comprehensive and coherent legislation in Washington, it seems more useful to appreciate the areas of state discretion and the effects of state discretion. This is especially so at the time of writing, when an historically unusually number of states are under one-party government are unsurprisingly diverging rapidly in many kinds of public policies including implementation of the 2010 Patient Protection and Affordable Care Act.

The United Kingdom has a party system and legal framework seemingly designed to promote divergence, but the financial system has substantially constrained it and produces what we have seen so far: divergence primarily in how things are done, not how much of them are done. Greater financial autonomy might produce variation not just in organisation but also in the priorities and levels of welfare spending.

7. Conclusion

If the groupings of liberal, conservative-corporatist, and egalitarian welfare states matter, and more literature than can possibly be contained in a bibliography argues that it does, then the finding, albeit modest, that in issues of social risk there is practically as much difference within a single country as there is between groups of countries falling into these pre-established ideal types is unnerving. Moreover, as Lynch (2006) showed, there is little doubt that the age orientation of a welfare state has tremendous distributional and policy implications. By this same token, the breadth of variation within a given country reveals important dynamics not only about the type of territorial politics but also about the differentiation of policy debates. In this article we showed how two superficially similar liberal states turned out to have very different territorial social politics with regard to both age and unemployment. Further, we hope we showed the extent of variation and its potential usefulness not just in domestic but in cross-national research. The variation permits a renewed evaluation of the usefulness of averages in comparative research as well as suggesting the need for a more sophisticated treatment of territorial politics in theories of welfare state politics.

Methodological nationalism and "mean-spirited thinking" (Snyder 2001, p. 98) afflict welfare state studies as much as any other part of comparative politics, and it probably explains why it has been so difficult to move beyond the old arguments that first divided centralisers and decentralisers at the dawn of the twentieth century. Decentralised states have lower welfare state efforts but we know neither why nor how; it is possible that the correlation is basically spurious. The main line of attack on such macro-comparative arguments has been to point out cases of regional mobilisation in defence of welfare states, or regions with higher welfare spending, or regions with distinctive welfare policies.

We went a step further and investigated the share of regional and central expenditure in the two countries by expenditure category. We have presented quantitative evidence of the scale of differentiation that is possible within countries, thereby questioning the basic value of methodological nationalist analyses that, for example, handle an average value for the United States and seek to explain it without examining its subnational territorial structure. The United Kingdom has much less variance in expenditure, reflecting its institutional structures, which means that the usefulness of averages is in itself a reflection of the structure and extent of decentralisation within the country.

The United States has almost as much internal variation as the OECD has between countries, which is a remarkable finding in itself. The causes are clear enough since in the US state spending is focused on social investment and protection against new social risk, while federal policies are mostly targeted towards the elderly. What is striking is how this division of labour, combined with the diversity of states, produces radically different age and ALMP orientations. The contrast with the United Kingdom illustrates the extent to which institutional variables can support a very different approach; while the division of labour between regions and the central state is quite similar, the financing of regions in our time period gave them almost no leeway to change the variance between their expenditure levels. Wales or Northern Ireland, simply put, had a guaranteed budget to spend on social services that US federal states cannot, or choose not to, have. Divergence happened either because of financial formulae or in-service organisation, not due to the financial decisions of the three devolved administrations (Birrell 2009). The result is that the United States has 50 different approaches to new social risks for the under-65s, as varied in their age profile as the whole OECD, while the UK jurisdictions vary in policies rather than expenditure levels.

At the present, the approach adopted in this article has some limitations. First, at this stage, the availability of data does not permit longitudinal comparisons. Moreover, our data shares the drawbacks of a spending variable in comparative welfare state studies. The internationally comparable data for any aspect of welfare state policy typically focuses on inputs – hence the phrase "welfare effort" – and therefore ignores all questions of the organisation and effectiveness of provision (see Jochen and Siegel 2007). The focus on expenditures distinguishes it from approaches that focus on the issue of benefits eligibility and its measurement (Scruggs 2006; Scruggs and Allan 2006). The argument for eligibility, as against expenditure, data has two legs. One is its political realism: as Esping-Andersen famously wrote, "it is difficult to imagine anyone struggled for spending per se" (Esping-Andersen 1990, p. 21). The other is the risk of spurious results – governments can cut back eligibility and benefit levels without decreasing expenditure if they do so when need is increasing (lower unemployment benefits can coexist with higher unemployment replacement expenditures in a recession).

Nevertheless, we opted for expenditure data. First, in territorially decentralised countries people do struggle for spending per se. Intergovernmental finance is the stuff of much intergovernmental relations (Rodden 2005; Trench 2006; Bednar 2009; McLean et al. 2009; Weingast 2009; Beramendi 2011). Second, we believe that many of the pitfalls (such as the unemployment insurance example) could be handled with covariates such as unemployment. Third, we see no way to collect region-level data on eligibility: not only would it be a very long and expensive process, it would also be nearly impossible in the case of eligibility standards for complex services such as healthcare or education.[8]

For scholars, the conclusion is that methodological nationalism obscures a great deal of important variation, and that disaggregating decentralised states reveals a much more complex and powerful set of explanations than the mere concept of fragmentation. For policy, the conclusion is that the design of intergovernmental relations, law, and finance is very important for the welfare state. Party politics in the UK diverge more than party politics in the United States, with explicit nationalists in government in Northern Ireland, Scotland, and Wales, and very different partisan configurations, but the financial structure limits their ability and need to vary overall expenditure.

In our specific cases, of policies to address "new social risks" in the United Kingdom and United States, we found that the structure of intergovernmental responsibilities and finance qualify for generalisations about both the role of decentralisation and about their approaches to new social risk. The United States federal welfare state's substantial bias towards the elderly means that states' expenditure decisions have dramatic effects on the distribution of resources between the under- and over-65s, contributing to substantial territorial variation in welfare state strategies. The programmatic design of the US welfare state focuses variation on services for the non-elderly, which depend more on state politics. By contrast, the UK legally permits much policy variation and, like the United States, focuses the activity of the central state on pensions, but the centralisation of finance and provision of under-65 income replacement at the level of the UK government combine to substantially harmonise expenditure on new social risks across the UK. In neither case has there been a simple federalism or decentralisation effect as public choice and macro-sociological accounts might suggest; rather, the specific allocation of responsibilities and funding responsibilities has deeply shaped the meaning of territory and federalism for citizens.

Supplemental data

Supplemental data for this article can be accessed at http://dx.doi.org/10.1080/13876988.2015.1060713.

Notes

1. The list of Spanish regions with distinctive social policies does not look much like the list of stateless nations (Gallego 2001; Gallego et al. 2002).
2. "State of Unions" that the UK is, the phrase must be qualified. It previously had an autonomous Northern Ireland government in its territory from 1921 until it was suspended in 1972 (see Mitchell 2009).
3. The PESA series is comparable across short periods, but periodic recalculations of the data mean that it is not comparable over more than about five years.
4. Data and detailed coding notes are posted at http://sph.umich.edu/faculty-profiles/greer-scott.html.
5. In line with Lynch (2006), housing is excluded from the equation.
6. http://www.hhs.gov/recovery/programs/tanf/tanf-overview.html (accessed May 2013). Under the welfare reform legislation of 1996, TANF has replaced the Aid to Families with Dependent Children (AFDC) programme, the Job Opportunities and Basic Skills Training (JOBS) programme, and the Emergency Assistance (EA) programme. More recent details on the changes to TANF in Schott and Pavetti (2011).
7. In line with categorisation of programmes within the OECD Employment Outlook (2011), Statistical Index, p. 273.
8. With regard to the TANF data, we note Gais' (2009) discussion of the pros and cons of using "State Spending on Cash Assistance, Per Poor Person" and decided against it since this method appears to pose greater difficulties when between-state comparisons are embedded within international comparisons.

References

Adema, W., Fron, P., and Ladaique, M., (2011), Is the European Welfare State Really More Expensive? Indicators on Social Spending, 1980-2012; and a Manual to the OECD Social Expenditure Database (SOCX). OECD Social, Employment and Migration Working Papers, No. 124, OECD Publishing. doi:10.1787/5kg2d2d4pbf0-en

Agnew, J., 2013, Territory, Politics, Governance. *Territory, Politics, Governance*, **1**(1), pp. 1–4. doi:10.1080/21622671.2013.765754

Agranoff, R., 2004, Autonomy, devolution and intergovernmental relations. *Regional and Federal Studies*, **14**(1), pp. 26–65.

Armingeon, K. (Ed), 2007, *The Politics of Post-industrial Welfare States: adapting Post-war Social Policies to New Social Risks* (Abingdon: Routledge).

Bednar, J., 2009, *The Robust Federation: principles of Design* (Cambridge: Cambridge University Press).

Béland, D. and Lecours, A., 2005, Nationalism and social policy in Canada and Québec, in: N. McEwen and M. Luis (Ed) *The Territorial Politics of Welfare* (London: Routledge).

Béland, D. and Lecours, A., 2008, *Nationalism and Social Policy: the Politics of Territorial Solidarity* (Oxford: Oxford University Press).

Béland, D., Rocco, P., and Waddan, A., 2014, Implementing health care reform in the United States: Intergovernmental politics and the dilemmas of institutional design. *Health Policy*, **116**, pp. 51–60. doi:10.1016/j.healthpol.2014.01.010.

Benz, A. and Broschek, J. (Eds), 2013, *Federal Dynamics: continuity, Change, and the Varieties of Federalism* (Oxford: Oxford University Press).

Beramendi, P., 2011, *Regions and Redistribution: the Political Geography of Inequality* (Cambridge: Cambridge University Press).

Birrell, D., 2009, *The Impact of Devolution on Social Policy* (Bristol: Policy).

Brooks, C. and Manza, J., 2007, *Why Welfare States Persist: the Importance of Public Opinion in Democracies* (Chicago: University of Chicago Press).

Cameron, D. A., 1978, The expansion of the public economy: A comparative analysis. *American Political Science Review*, **72**(1), pp. 1243–1261.

Castles, F. G.., 1999, Decentralization and the post-war political economy. *European Journal of Political Research*, **36**(1), pp. 27–53. doi:10.1111/ejpr.1999.36.issue-1

Chernilo, D., 2006, Methodological nationalism and its critique, in: G. Delanty and K. Kumar (Eds) *The Sage Handbook of Nations and Nationalism* (London: SAGE), pp. 129–140.

Costa i Font, J. and Greer, S. L., 2013, Health System Federalism and Decentralization: What is it, why does it happen, and what does it do? in: J. Costa i Font and S. L. Greer (Eds) *Federalism and Decentralization in European Health and Social Care* (Basingstoke: Palgrave Macmillan).

Elazar, D., 1987, *Exploring Federalism* (Tuscaloosa: University of Alabama Press).

Erk, J. and Koning, E., 2009, New structuralism and institutional change: Federalism between centralization and decentralisation. *Comparative Political Studies*, **42**(11), pp. 1–23.

Esping-Andersen, G., 1990, *The Three Worlds of Welfare Capitalism* (Princeton, NJ: Princeton University Press).

Gais, T. L., 2009, Stretched Net: The Retrenchment of State and Local Social Welfare Spending Before the Recession. *Publius*, **39**(3), pp. 557–579.

Gallego, R., 2001, La política sanitària catalana: La construcció d'un sistema universal de provisió pluralista, in: R. Gomà and J. Subirats (Ed) *Govern i Polítiques Públiques a Catalunya (1980-2000): Autonomia i Benestar* (Bellaterra: Universitat Autònoma de Barcelona), pp. 138–158.

Gallego, R., Gomà, R., and Subirats, J. (Eds), 2002, *Els Règims Autonòmics De Benestar* (Barcelona: Instit d'Estudis Autonòmics).

Greer, S. L., 2004, *Territorial Politics and Health Policy: UK Health Policy in Comparative Perspective* (Manchester: Manchester University Press).

Greer, S. L., 2009, How does decentralisation affect the welfare state? *Journal of Social Policy*, **39**(2), pp. 1–21.

Hicks, A., 1999, *Social Democracy and Welfare Capitalism: A Century of Income Security Politics* (Ithaca: Cornell University Press).

Hicks, A. M. and Swank, D. H., 1992, Politics, institutions, and welfare spending in industrialized democracies, 1960-82. *American Political Science Review*, **86**(3), pp. 658–674.

Huber, E. and Stephens, J. D., 2001, *Development and Crisis of the Welfare State: parties and Policies in Global Markets* (Chicago: University of Chicago Press).

Jeffrey, C. and Wincott, D., 2010, The challenge of territorial politics, in: C. Hay (Ed.) *New Directions in Political Science: Responding to the Challenges of an Interdependent World* (Basingstoke: Palgrave Macmillan), pp. 167–188.

Jochen, C. and Siegel, N. A. (Eds), 2007, *Investigating Welfare State Change: the 'Dependent Variable Problem' in Comparative Analysis* (Cheltenham: Edward Elgar).

Katznelson, I., 2013, *Fear Itself: the New Deal and the Origins of Our Time* (New York: Liveright).

Keating, M., 2005, *The Government of Scotland* (Edinburgh: Edinburgh University Press).

Lancaster, T. D. and Hicks, A. M., 2000, The impact of federalism and neo-corporatism on economic performance: An analysis of eighteen OECD countries, in: U. Wachendorfer-Schmidt. (Ed) *Federalism and Political Performance* (Abingdon: Routledge).

Lieberman, R. C. and Lapinski, J. S.., 2001, American Federalism, Race and the Administration of Welfare. *British Journal of Political Science*, **31**(2), pp. 303–329. doi:10.1017/S0007123401000126

Linz, J. J. and Amando, D. M., 1966, Within-Nation differences and comparisons: The eight Spains, in: R. L. Merritt and R. Stein (Ed) *Comparing Nations: the Use of Quantitative Data in Cross-National Research* (New Haven: Yale University Press).

Lodge, G. and Schmuecker, K. (Eds), 2010, *Devolution in Practice 2010* (London: IPPR).

Lynch, J., 2001, The age- orientation of social policy regimes in OECD countries. *Journal of Social Policy*, **30**(3), pp. 411–436. doi:10.1017/S0047279401006365

Lynch, J., 2006, *Age in the Welfare State: the Origins of Social Spending on Pensioners, Workers and Children* (Cambridge: Cambridge University Press).

McEwen, N. and Moreno, L. (Eds), 2005, *The Territorial Politics of Welfare* (London: Routledge).

McGarvey, N. and Cairney, P., 2008, *Scottish Politics: an Introduction* (Basingstoke: Palgrave Macmillan).

McLean, I., 2005, *The Fiscal Crisis of the United Kingdom* (Basingstoke: Palgrave Macmillan).

McLean, I., Lodge, G., and Schmuecker, K., 2009, Social citizenship and intergovernmenal finance, in: S. L. Greer (Ed) *Devolution and Social Citizenship in the United Kingdom* (Bristol: Policy).

Mickey, R., 2013, *Paths out of Dixie: the Democratization of Authoritarian Enclaves in America's Deep South* (Princeton, NJ: Princeton University Press).

Mitchell, J., 2009, *Devolution in the United Kingdom* (Manchester: Manchester University Press).

Morel, N., Palier, B., and Palme, J., 2012, *Towards a Social Investment Welfare State? Ideas, Policies and Challenges* (Bristol: The Policy Press).

Obinger, H., Leibfried, S., and Castles, F. G. (Eds), 2005, *Federalism and the Welfare State: new World and European Experiences* (Cambridge: Cambridge University Press).

OECD, 2011, *OECD Employment Outlook 2011* (Paris: OECD Publishing). doi:10.1787/empl_outlook-2011-en

Richardson, G., 2009, The truth about redistribution: Republicans receive, Democrats disburse. *The Economists' Voice*, **6**, pp. 10.

Rodden, J. A., 2004, Comparative federalism and decentralisation: On meaning and measurement. *Comparative Politics*, **36**(4), pp. 481–500.

Rodden, J. A., 2005, *Hamilton's Paradox: The Promise and Peril of Fiscal Federalism* (New York: Cambridge University Press).

Schott, L. and Pavetti, D., 2011, *Many States Cutting TANF Harshly Despite High Unemployment and Unprecedented Need* (Washington, DC: Center on Budget and Policy Priorities).

Scruggs, L., 2006, The generosity of social insurance, 1971-2002. *Oxford Review of Economic Policy*, **22**(3), pp. 349–364. doi:10.1093/oxrep/grj021

Scruggs, L. and Allan, J., 2006, Welfare-State decommodification in 18 OECD countries: A replication and revision. *Journal of European Social Policy*, **16**(1), pp. 55–72. doi:10.1177/0958928706059833

Simeon, R., 2006, Federalism and social justice: Thinking through the jungle, in: S. L. Greer (Ed) *Territory, Democracy, and Justice: regionalism and Federalism in Western Democracies* (Basingstoke: Palgrave Macmillan).

Snyder, R., 2001, Scaling down: The subnational comparative method. *Studies in Comparative International Development*, **36**(1), pp. 93–110. doi:10.1007/BF02687586

Stepan, A. and Linz, J. J., 2011, Comparative perspectives on inequality and the quality of democracy in the United States. *Perspectives on Politics*, **9**(4), pp. 841–856.

Swank, D., 2001, Political institutions and welfare state restructuring: The impact of institutions on social policy change in developed democracies, in: P. Paul (Ed) *The New Politics of the Welfare State* (Oxford: Oxford University Press).

Swank, D., 2002, *Global Capital, Political Institutions, and Policy Change in Developed Welfare States* (Cambridge: Cambridge University Press).

Taylor-Gooby, P. (Ed), 2004, *New Risks, New Welfare: the Transformation of the European Welfare State* (Oxford: Oxford University Press).

Thompson, F. J., 2012, *Medicaid Politics: federalism, Policy Durability and Health Reform* (Washington: Georgetown University Press).

Trench, A., 2006, Intergovernmental relations: In search of a theory, in: S. L. Greer (Ed.) *Territory, Democracy and Justice: Regionalism and Federalism in Western Democracies* (Basingstoke: Palgrave Macmillan), pp. 224–256.

Trench, A., 2008, Tying the UK together? Intergovernmental relations and the financial constitution in the UK, in: R. Hazell (Ed) *Constitutional Futures Revisited: Britain's Constitution to 2020* (Basingstoke: Palgrave Macmillan).

Weingast, B., 1995, The economic role of political institutions: Market-Preserving federalism and economic development. *Journal of Law, Economics and Organization*, **11**(1), pp. 1–31.

Weingast, B. R., 2009, Second generation fiscal federalism: The implications of fiscal incentives. *Journal of Urban Economics*, **65**(3), pp. 279–293. doi:10.1016/j.jue.2008.12.005

Wincott, D., 2006, Social policy and social citizenship: Britain's welfare states. *Publius*, **36**(1), pp. 169–189.

Europeanization as a Methodological Challenge: The Case of Interest Groups

SABINE SAURUGGER

ABSTRACT   *Europeanization studies has become a very prominent research agenda. However, the theoretical framework becomes problematic when one starts to look for methods to study Europeanization empirically. Three main problems can be identified: First, Europeanization is not a linear process, where European integration influences the national level. It is, on the contrary, a circular movement, where national actors, policies, ideas or structures influence European integration, which, at the same time, reflects clearly at the national level. Second, what precisely is "Europeanized" compared to what is influenced by "purely" domestic politics? Third, how can we measure change at the national level? The aim of this article is to articulate the implications of the main methodological challenges and to propose possible solutions in the context of Europeanization studies. I argue that in order to study Europeanization, two particular methodological choices must be made. It is first necessary to compare actors from different national backgrounds, but also from different policy fields based on a long-term analysis. Second, a test variable is needed to study the activities of these actors not only in the European Union, but also abroad.*

Introduction

Since the mid 1980s, European integration has been flourishing and producing new politics, policies and polities at the European Union level. At the same time, the process of European integration has induced important policy changes in the member states of the European Union. The study of these processes, generally called 'Europeanization', has become a very prominent research agenda. However, while the empirical and theoretical literature on this subject is abundant,[1] few scholars have addressed the methodological problems linked to Europeanization studies. An analysis of the literature identifies three main challenges:

1. Europeanization is not a linear process, where European integration influences the national level. It is, on the contrary, a circular movement, where national

actors, policies, ideas or structures influence European integration, which, at the same time, reflects clearly at the national level (Schmidt 2002). Transformation may occur on the basis of "a multitude of coevolving, parallel and not necessarily tightly coupled processes" (Olsen 1996: 271). The challenge is to model the impact of European integration at the domestic level, knowing that at the same time domestic politics is a major factor at work in EU integration. Therefore, determining the dependent from the independent variable becomes difficult. The boundaries between cause and effect are blurred.

2. What precisely is "Europeanized" compared to what is influenced by "purely" domestic politics? Political processes at the domestic level take place at the same time as those at the European level. It thus becomes difficult to distinguish clearly between them. The challenge here is to keep a clear distinction between these different elements, also known in more general terms as Galton's problem. It refers to the methodological difficulty of sorting out diffusion from other causes of variance in social systems (Peters 1998: 42).

3. How to measure the change induced at the national level? Is a change of national actors' discourse already a sign that the European level has influenced these actors? Or must there be a change in institutional structures or core values (Hall 1993, Sabatier 1998, Knill and Lenschow 2001). This problem becomes particularly relevant in the study of national actors. Whereas the Europeanization of national policies can be exclusively observed at the national level, as policies as such do not leave national territory,[2] actors, on the contrary, can. It becomes therefore relevant to observe their practices not only at the national level, where the reference to European integration can be a mere strategic usage but to analyse their behaviour also outside EU borders.

The aim of this article is to articulate the implications of these problems and to elaborate a methodological framework to tackle these challenges. I argue that these problems can be solved through two specific methodological choices.

In order to study Europeanization, it is *first* necessary to compare different national backgrounds as well as different policy fields during a long time period. Comparison of both is essential as it allows the methodological problems that are identified to be addressed. These problems are: complex interdependence and blurring of differences between national and European causes of change. Comparing different national systems and different policy fields allows an understanding of the situation of the policy sectors in different EU countries *before* European integration occurred. An in-depth knowledge of different national policy fields in different countries makes it possible to understand how actors participated in European integration and how European integration affected these actors in return. Thus, comparison makes it possible to measure the influence of European integration as compared to that of domestic variables. Change in national actors' behaviour can have domestic, European or international causes.[3]

Second, I argue in favour of a counterfactual research design, which takes into account the argument of a test variable. The most common denominator in Europeanization literature states that Europeanization means change. However, Europeanization scholars do not agree on the degree of change necessary to certify Europeanization. In-depth transformation of actions and structures is different from the sole usage of European discourses (Jacquot and Woll 2003). The measurement of the degree of transformation thus needs a test variable.

In order to illustrate this methodological framework, the article will concentrate on interest group behaviour in specific policy areas. Three different aspects of interest group behaviour will be analysed in particular: the relations between interest groups and political actors, interest group action repertoires[4] and, finally, the political legitimacy of interest groups.

The illustration is based on a study of German and French interest group behaviour in the fields of agriculture and nuclear energy in the framework of the Community's enlargement policy from 1989 to 1999. The choices are influenced by a very different research design (Przeworski and Teune 1970, Lijphart 1971, Eckstein 1975). I compare interest group behaviour in a policy sector where a specific European public policy exists (agriculture) with that of a policy field based on national competences (nuclear energy). The German and French national backgrounds are equally differentiated. While Germany is considered to be a neocorporatist system with strong sectoral traditions, France is characterized as a system with a centralist, technocratic bureaucracy and a political culture where "the state" is still widely appreciated as the essential public governance mechanism. With regard to interest representation, France is usually described as *"protestataire"* (protest) and *"dirigiste"* (statist) (Tilly 1984, Cohen 1992, 1996, Schmidt 1996, Wright 1997, Grossman and Saurugger 2004). The case study is constructed in an attempt to illustrate the methodological solutions rather than to test them. This limitation is only superficial however. My main point is that comparative methodology and the inclusion of a test variable are crucial elements to operationalize research based on the theoretical framework of Europeanization.

This article is structured in three parts. The first part will present the theoretical debates surrounding Europeanization and deepen the understanding of the inherent challenges of conducting research in this field. The second part will then look both conceptually and empirically at the problem of comparison and time period. This part will concentrate in particular on the question of complex interdependence in Europeanization studies. The third and final part will then look more in detail at the problem of the test variable. Based on empirical data of Western European interest group behaviour in enlargement policies both inside the EU and in Central and Eastern Europe, the paper will thus illustrate central methodological problems linked to the Europeanization debate and discuss in detail how to solve these problems.

Europeanization

In recent years, a large number of studies have been published on the definition of Europeanization (Ladrech 1994, Knill and Lehmkuhl 1999, Börzel and Risse 2000, Radaelli 2001, 2003, Caporaso *et al.* 2001, Featherstone and Radaelli 2003) as well as on specific case studies – the Europeanization of policies (Héritier *et al.* 2001; Irondelle 2003) as well as politics (Goetz and Hix 2001) or polities (Schmidt 2004).

A short review of the main definitions shows that the problem of complex interdependence and thus the difficulty in distinguishing clearly between the dependent and the independent variable is inherent to theoretical debates on

Europeanization. In short, what does Europeanization mean: the influence of the national level through European processes or the construction of European integration?

One of the first definitions was proposed by Ladrech (1994: 17): "Europeanization is an incremental process reorienting the direction and shape of politics to the degree that EC political and economic dynamics become part of the organizational logic of national politics and policy-making". Here it is clear that developments in the domestic arena become the dependent variable, whereas European integration is seen as the explanatory variable. In an equally clear manner, Goetz and Hix (2001) propose to distinguish between European integration and Europeanization. European integration thus becomes the explicative factor for changes taking place in national public policies. European integration is considered in this approach to be the independent variable, influencing the Europeanization of domestic policies. The main question here is not why and how member states produce European integration, but how the delegation of competences to the European level influences the policy-making processes in the national arena. Empirically, however, this clear-cut distinction is difficult to observe: both domestic and European level developments influence each other constantly.

This empirical problem is taken up by Caporaso et al. (2001: 3) in their conceptual debate on Europeanization. They propose to understand by Europeanization "the emergence and the development at the European level of distinct structures of governance, that is, of political, legal and social institutions associated with political problem solving that formalize interactions among the actors, and of policy networks specializing in the creation of authoritative European rules". According to these authors, Europeanization involves the evolutions of new layers of politics that interact with older ones. Europeanization is thus about the discrepancy between European and domestic politics, processes and institutions. However, this definition seems to see in Europeanization not the influence the EU exercises at the national level but rather the creation of distinct institutions and rules at the European level. Whereas the differentiation becomes less evident between European integration and Europeanization, to stick to Goetz and Hix's (2001) terminology, the Caporaso et al. definition brings the theoretical debate closer to empirical observation.

Radaelli (2001: 110) offers finally an overarching approach to Europeanization incorporating both its mechanisms and effects. He describes it as:

> processes of (a) construction (b) diffusion and (c) institutionalization of formal and informal rules, procedures, policy paradigms, styles, "ways of doing things" and shared beliefs and norms which are first defined and consolidated in the making of EU public policy and politics and then incorporated in the logic of domestic discourse, identities, political structures and public policies.

Here, Europeanization is linked on the one hand to the establishment of policies, politics and polities at the EU level (or "uploading" in Börzel's (2001) terminology) and their diffusion at the national level ("downloading"). This incremental definition clearly states the complex interdependence of EU and national levels and is, thus, in my view, the most useful one.

The problem of complex interdependence is inherent in different attempts to define Europeanization as we have seen. It becomes even more visible when concentrating on the literature dealing with mechanisms and consequences of Europeanization. With regard to "uploading", Bulmer and Radaelli (2004) consider negotiation as the main mechanism of Europeanization. The EU is in a constant state of negotiation across multiple policy areas in which large number of actors, and amongst them interest groups, participate. In each case where the EU takes a decision – whether legally binding or a mere declaration – it is the culmination of a processes of negotiation.

In the literature, three types of consequences relating to the downloading perspective of Europeanization can be identified (Börzel and Risse 2000, Radaelli 2001). First, the phenomenon of absorption, where member states incorporate politics and ideas developed at the European level. Secondly the process of accommodation in which member states adapt their politics, processes, discourses and institutions without however modifying their essential characteristics. And, finally, the deepest transformation whereby member states transform their national politics and national actors replace politics, processes and institutions by new and substantially different forms. Like many other observers (see Featherstone 2003: 4), they do not regard adjustment as necessarily bringing about harmonization.

However, the measurement of change is problematic. The vocabulary of absorption, accommodation and transformation is becoming very popular. But how does one know that there is mere accommodation and not transformation? Radaelli suggests applying the insights from the literature on learning in underlining the useful distinction between simple coping strategies and those of learning. In this context, coping strategies also refer to strategic usages of the European Union (Jacquot and Woll 2003). People may adopt the same language and talk in terms of the same criteria without necessarily taking the same decisions. The "linear causal relationship between the formation of a European ideational consensus and the local action" has also been questioned by projects on regional policy (Kohler-Koch 2002). A test variable will help to address this particular problem, as we will see in a moment.

While research on the representation of private interests at the European level has mushroomed since the 1980s, few have addressed the question of change in national interest representation through European integration (for exceptions see Ward and Lowe 1998, Green Cowles 2001, Perez-Solorzano 2001, Grossman 2002). Most scholars have rather implicitly argued that one can observe the emergence of a particular mode of interest representation at the European level.[5] In an attempt to rally this shortcoming, Balme and Chabanet (2002) identify four different consequences of Europeanization for interest groups at the national level. The first mode is that of internalization, in which one observes the development of local or national mobilizations around European policies. Concertation among national or local groups is very important in order to influence national or European policy making. The second mode of Europeanization of collective action is externalization. Here, national interest groups contact European political actors directly without passing through the national level in order to represent their specific interests. Supranationalization is the third mode of Europeanization and corresponds to the institutionalization of European confederations or federations of national interest groups at the EU level. Finally, transnationalization, the fourth Europeanization mode of collective action refers to a profound transformation of national actors which become transnational actors such as Greenpeace.

Whereas the first three modes of Europeanization are useful to identify the consequences of Europeanization for interest groups, the fourth mode is linked to internationalization or globalization rather than to the EU. All three modes can be observed as different strategies the same interest groups adopt when challenged by European decisions. They also are an illustration of the complex interdependence problem of Radaelli's definition of Europeanization: whereas internalization can be seen as mainly "downloading", externalization and supranationalization are both concerned with "uploading" as well as "downloading" mechanisms.

Now how do we tackle the main problems arising from these theoretical considerations of Europeanization: blurring the distinction between dependent and independent variables, the difficulty to distinguish clearly between domestic and European factors for change, and finally, the measurement of change? I argue that two methodological choices can help here: long-term comparison and test variables.

Long-term Comparison

Distinguishing between dependent and independent variables becomes problematic when analysing the Europeanization of processes and actors. Actors and national policies as well as discourses participate at the same time in the construction and institutionalization of formal and informal rules, procedures and policy paradigms, but are at the same time influenced by it. It is therefore not clear to define Europeanization as the influence of European integration at the domestic level, or to define it exclusively as the emergence of European political structures, institutions, norms and discourses at the EU level. The overarching approach is therefore central to Europeanization studies as shown for the public health sector (Steffen 2005) – the national level is a permanent actor in European integration and it is therefore crucial to study its participation in the construction process, but it is, at the same time, influenced by this European integration process. This is the classical chicken and egg problem. Caporaso et al. (2001) underline that careful process tracing and attention to time sequences between EU policies and domestic changes allow one to distinguish between the impact of Europeanization, on the one hand, and domestic politics on the other. With regard to comparative policy analysis, this means that we either start by the analysis of an existing European public policy, or the absence of it, and we then elaborate a comparative research design. Or, on the contrary, we start with a comparison of national policy areas over a long time, if possible, even before the European integration process started. In this article, I strongly argue for the second approach, as it allows for comparison over the long term (Peters 1998).

Test Variables

In general, the research designs regarding Europeanization are mostly limited to the analysis of "European effects" in certain areas of change at the national level but do not control for rival hypotheses. The serious risk is in prejudging the significance of

EU variables and to conclude that some form of change has taken place – be it absorption, accommodation or transformation. This is particularly true when analysing the Europeanization of actors' behaviour. As Jacquot and Woll (2003) have shown, the strong concentration of the Europeanization literature on institutional dynamics leads to an underestimation of the discretion and role of political actors in the process of change. While the emphasis on the importance of political actors in Jacquot and Woll's study is innovative, it nevertheless presents a serious fallacy. Their analysis is still concentrated at the territory of the European Union. The transformation of actors' practices may be felt at the national and the European level, but how does one distinguish between mere strategic usage of "Europe" and in-depth transformation? While the Europeanization of public policies must be observed at the national level, actors' behaviour can take place outside the EU. Interest group behaviour is particularly adapted to be analysed in this context. If in-depth transformation has taken place, we must be able to observe it inside the EU as well as outside the EU borders. My main argument here is that the focus on Europeanization can produce serious fallacies when it leads the researcher to adopt a top-down logic in which the only aim is to find out the domestic effects of independent variables defined at the EU level. If in-depth change has occurred in behaviour, we must be able to observe it outside the EU as well, which can be used as test variable in this particular case.

The two following parts of this article will propose methodological frameworks stemming from the theoretical debates on Europeanization: How to operationalize complex interdependence studies, and how to distinguish between "European" and "domestic" factors, and, finally, how to measure change.

Complex Interdependence: How to Solve the Problem?

In order to illustrate the challenge regarding the link between dependent and independent variables in Europeanization studies, it is first important to gain an in-depth understanding of the analysed policy. As Europeanization is a "process" it becomes crucial to isolate "change" and to measure it. With regard to the Europeanization of interest groups, we must thus start with an analysis of the relationships established between interest groups and political actors at the national level, if possible before the start of a European integration process.[6] This approach allows us to gain an in-depth understanding of the collective action system at the national level. This understanding makes it possible to observe changes and to distinguish clearly between European variables and domestic ones. We can see, for example, whether purely domestic factors might explain structural changes in some cases, with little or no independent effects from Europeanization.

However, it is crucial in this respect to engage in a long-term analysis which includes a micro-level method. If Europeanization is linked to change, as the main scholars indicate, then it is necessary to know the machinery of a policy field. With regard to the Europeanization of actors – and interest groups in particular – one of the main mechanisms of Europeanization is learning (Knill and Lehmkuhl 1999, Caporaso *et al.* 2001). However, the cognitive changes can only be analysed through micro-studies, that is studies of policy sectors concentrating on individual or collective actors.

Despite the advantages large-n studies provide with regard to the generalization problem, it poses huge disadvantages in Europeanization studies as the specific variables must be very general in order to create a comparative research design. For a single author presenting research in a single paper, it seems difficult to choose a large number of policy areas which can be compared with each other in all 25 or, for similarity reasons, at least in all 15 old EU member states. The result of such a research design would be very general typologies (Giuliani 2003).

Thus, in order to find out if a Europeanization of national collective action can be found, one must take into account sector-specific national styles of interest intermediation, which interact with the fragmentation of the EU's institutional system.

Long-term Comparison of Collective Action

Based on a case study of German and French interest group activities in the field of agriculture and nuclear energy in the framework of the Community's enlargement policy from 1989 to 1999, this article will propose an explanation of when and why different modes of interest representation occur. I have chosen the context of enlargement policies as it allows the variables to be kept constant: similar problems occur at similar times in both policy areas (see also Saurugger 2003). I argue that by looking systematically at the sector-specific characteristics of European policy making, we observe sectorally divergent styles of public–private interaction, which are mediated by the interaction style forged at the national level.

This two country–two sector comparison is thus based on a hypothesis that major differences do not only occur between national styles of interest representation but also among national sectors. This hypothesis is similar to the main claim made by Bovens *et al.* (2001), presenting a large-scale but nevertheless detailed study: national policy styles either do not exist or are outweighed by strong sectoral institutions and traditions of handling sectoral governance issues. Thus, inside national political systems, the relationship between interest groups and state actors can take different forms of networks.[7]

Agriculture: Policy Communities

The German and the French Farmers' Unions, DBV (*Deutscher Bauernverband*) and FNSEA (*Fédération nationals des syndicates d'exploitants agricoles*), have since the end of the Second World War both created a particularly tight relationship with their respective ministries of Agriculture (Hendriks 1991, Heinze 1992, Hervieu and Lagrave 1992, Marie 1994). While this relationship existed until recently in Germany,[8] it was profoundly modified in France after the new socialist government came into power in 1981. While the FNSEA still had very strong ties within the French Ministry of Agriculture, its representational monopoly has decreased, and the ministry as well as the government have started to establish a dialogue with other minor farmers' unions. The FNSEA is still the main farmers' union in France and is still integrated in a policy community with the ministry. Here two developments must be underlined. First, the FNSEA created a particular "vertical" form of unionism, organized by sub-sectors to counter the establishment of other "horizontal" unions (Hubscher and Lagrave 1993: 126). This led to relative independence for agricultural sub-sectors inside the FNSEA. These sub-sectors are part of the very powerful sub-sectoral French "*interprofessions*", interest groups consisting of producer groups and distributors, which often have their own independent representation offices in Brussels. The second evolution is the development of close contacts with other ministries, responsible for areas such as finance or economics. This situation contrasts with the German farmers' union DBV which is essentially a centralized organization where sub-sectors have very little existence and no interdependence from their parent organization. In the DBV, the powerful actors are the regional members who have built forms of policy communities with *Länder* ministries. The policy community established with the Ministry of Agriculture is therefore maintained and the relations with other ministries are rare. The centralized organizational structure makes it necessary for sectoral interests to convince the DBV's Präsidium (Board) to go ahead with a specific issue. This situation can be seen as a strength as the representation of an interest by the union as a whole is likely to have greater impact.

However, in the framework of the fragmented and sectorized environment in the context of the enlargement policies of the EU, this has had some particular consequences, as we will see later.

Nuclear Electricity: Issue Networks

In France and Germany, policy networks have existed since the 1950s in the field of nuclear energy. These networks include the electricity supply industry, the nuclear construction industry, scientific agencies and the political-administrative system (Kitschelt 1980, Radkau 1983, Lucas 1985, Rüdig 1987, Müller 1990). Nuclear power primarily concerns the major German utility providers, in particular the *Rheinisch-Westfälische Elektrizitätswerke* (RWE), *Bayernwerk* and *Preussenelektra*,[9] and the French EDF (*Electricité de France*), the main players in the field. Regarding nuclear industry as a whole, we find the German Siemens KWU (Siemens Power Generation Group), and the French firms Framatome and COGEMA, and in the field of independent scientific agencies the German GRS (*Gesellschaft für Anlagen und Reaktorsicherheit*) and the French IPSN (*Institut pour la protection de la sûreté nucléaire*). In France and in Germany, the networks established in this field were strongly affected by the interests and capabilities of the state institutions. But whereas in Germany, because of a greater number of actors, the relationship between the ministries responsible for nuclear energy and safety[10] (the Ministry for the Economy and the Ministry for the Environment, respectively) and the nuclear industries is similar to a rather tight issue network, the French situation is different. EDF is a monopolistic state-owned electricity producer whose relationship with the Ministry of Industry falls under the heading of "pantouflage". Civil servants leave the ministry to work for EDF and high-level leaders from EDF leave their jobs to work for the ministry. The same was true for the Framatome and COGEMA. Since the 1980s, the relationship between the industries and the government as a whole has changed. French industries have become more internationalized without cutting extremely tight ties with the French public authorities. This modification led, however, to a great adaptability of the industries, in particular as they can still count on their "pantouflage" relationship with the government.

Thus, in order to operationalize Europeanization analysis, it is important to understand the policy developments and structures which are historically established at the national level. Continuities and changes at the national level are the point of departure in order to understand which processes and structures were Europeanized and which were not. These public–private relationships were confronted at the European level with a policy problem never before encountered to that extent: EU enlargement. The enlargement process is an excellent example of the complex interdependence between a dependent and independent variable: national level actors participate very clearly in the policy formulation phase, when the policy problem is defined, but are, at the same time, influenced by their co-operation at the European Union level as well as by the impact the EU decisions in this field have at the national level.

Interaction at the European Level: Complex Interdependence

A research design with regard to Europeanization needs to elaborate a model of complex interdependence. Caporaso *et al.* (2001) have developed a three-step approach to Europeanization and domestic structural change (Figure 1). They first identify the relevant Europeanization processes – formal and informal norms, rules, regulations, procedures, and practices at the EU level. The second step identifies the "goodness of fit" between the Europeanization process, on the one hand, and the national institutional setting, rules and practices, on the other. This degree of fit constitutes what the authors identify as "adaptational pressures". The authors underline specifically that the very meaning of Europeanization might vary from country to country. A third step stresses, then, the importance of mediating institutions of formal and informal nature which leads finally to domestic structural change.

This chain causality model of Europeanization is extremely useful. It does, however, too clearly distinguish between dependent and independent variables – a proceeding empirically difficult to prove as national actors are not only influenced by European integration but clearly participate in the elaboration of European policies, politics and polities.

Figure 2 is inspired by Rochefort and Cobb (1994) and shows a complex causality model of Europeanization. Here, both European integration and domestic processes influence each other and together produce transformation on each level.

Figure 1. Chain Causality

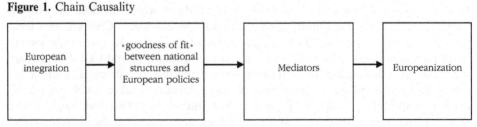

Source: Adapted from Risse *et al.* (2001: 6).

Figure 2. Complex causality

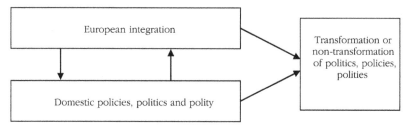

As we will see, interest groups interact at the same time with national actors and European bureaucracy. They experience adaptational pressure in particular at the EU level, as bureaucratic competition is high, but they also influence policy processes at the European level. An in-depth study shows, however, that this adaptational pressure does not always lead to change. National mediation structures are still a powerful factor in influencing interest group behaviour.

The following case studies thus show how European level negotiations influence and are at the same time influenced by national interest group behaviour. For both policy fields, agriculture and nuclear safety at the EU level, evidence of "bureaucratic competition" (Saurugger 2001) was strong during the enlargement process.

Adaptation vs Internalization as Results of Bureaucratic Competition

Three directorates general (DGs) dealt with questions arising in the field of agriculture regarding Central and Eastern Europe: the very powerful and resourceful DG VI, responsible for the management and the implementation of policies in the field of agriculture; DG I, responsible for international trade issues; and DG IA, responsible for the management of policies towards the Central and Eastern European countries (CEECs). While DG IA could be described as very much in favour of enlargement, the units responsible for international relations in DG VI had very strong relationships with the European farmers' unions, which feared the "invasion" of their European markets. DG I, on the contrary was characterized as very liberal by officials I have interviewed. These different attitudes towards enlargement made the management of agricultural issues a very complex situation.

Three directorates general share the few competences the Commission has in the field of nuclear energy and safety. DG XVII (Energy), DG XI (Environment, nuclear safety and civil protection) and DG IA, dealing mainly with PHARE and TACIS[11] aid programmes, which were, amongst other aims, supposed to support programmes in the fields of nuclear safety in the CEECs and the CEIs. DG II (Finance) decided on the viability and financial soundness of the relevant projects.

The degree of resource interdependence between the different actors was thus high, which imposes the idea of co-operation, despite the bureaucratic conflicts inside the Commission. According to Fritz Scharpf, this situation corresponds to an institutionalized "joint decision system", in which the actors must negotiate an agreement which satisfies a large number of actors, because unilateral action is forbidden and sanctioned.[12]

In 1994, the agricultural market situation in the European Union was severely disrupted by a high level of sour cherry imports from the CEECs. The German producers, for whom this sector is particularly important, raised the issue in the DBV; the board of the DBV subsequently decided to inform the Ministry of Agriculture and to demand action. The complex set of personal contacts between the board and the cabinet of the ministry made a rapid reaction possible. While the DBV raised the issue in the relevant committees at the European level linked to DG VI, the German minister of agriculture directly contacted the commissioner's cabinet and requested strict safeguard measures, if possible even an import ban. While DG VI was in favour of safeguard measures and proposed to introduce them, DG IA and DG I opposed these safeguard measures in informal meetings and an exchange of letters. A compromise was finally found among the commissioners at the highest level. The level of these prices were nevertheless very much below the prices called for by the German DBV. As a result, German sour cherry producers resorted to direct action: they dumped a load of sour cherries in Chancellor Kohl's garden. Parallel to pressures coming from the DBV's board and the German minister of agriculture, Chancellor Kohl's cabinet requested DG VI to publish a new regulation. The unit responsible for this question in DG I blocked the new regulation. This led to the personal intervention of two secretaries from the German chancellery at the level of a DG I director, a meeting which resulted in a change in DG I's position. The Commission decided in June 1994 to introduce a minimal price for imported sour cherries. This compromise was designed to prevent the EU market from collapsing, while assuring the supply of cherries.

All three DGs in question had a unit responsible for agricultural trade relations with the CEECs. These positions, based on very divergent attitudes towards the CEECs, had to be co-ordinated. While DG I put forward the interests of the processing industry, DG IA sought to support the CEEC exporting countries. Only DG VI seemed to be an ally for the German producers. However, instead of intervening at different levels, the DBV adopted a strategy which could be called "internalization" (Balme and Chabanet 2002), in the sense of a renationalization of its behaviour. In short, when confronted with bureaucratic politics at the European level the DBV turned its pressure upon the national ministry, demanding that it intervene more forcefully and thus politicizing the issue.

The agricultural case study regarding France concerns safeguard measures taken by the Czech government against EU imported apples in 1998. This issue was taken up by DG I and published amongst other market access distortions on its internal website, as well as in a report later in the year.[13] DG IA was opposed to this publication because, according to officials interviewed, it did not reveal the real difficulties the CEECs face in preparing themselves for accession. DG I and DG VI were informed of this distortion, on the one hand, by the official DG IA source, but also by the French interest group INTERFEL, consisting of French fruit and vegetable producers and distributors. The fruit and vegetable farmers' union, FNPF, is one of the members and was particularly concerned by the Czech safeguard measures as Czech apple imports consist mainly of French apples. INTERFEL, while being integrated in a policy community with DG VI, is very active in contacting and informing other DGs as well. This action repertoire is very similar to INTERFEL's attitude at the French national level, where interests are represented to different ministries. The fact that distributor's interests, which are not only concerned by the Ministry of Agriculture, are also present in INTERFEL is certainly an important intervening variable.

Despite the opposition of DG IA, countermeasures against the Czech safeguard measures were then decided by the relevant Central Europe Working Group in the Council. Proposed by DG VI, and supported by the French delegation, these measures were introduced in February. Only after long negotiations between the Czech government and the commissioner for agriculture were the safeguard measures and the countermeasures abandoned in June 1998.[14]

Thus, one observes the influence of the national model of interest representation at the European level, in particular when confronted with bureaucratic politics. In the field of agriculture, the French sectoralized representation mode can be adapted to the fragmented EU environment, contrary to the German one, which had to politicize the issue at the national level because the policy community relationship with DG VI did not allow it to exercise sufficient pressure.

Networks of Expertise

The accident which took place at the Chernobyl nuclear power plant in April 1986 was the first in a long series of events which caused concern over the condition of nuclear power plants in Central and Eastern Europe as well as in the Commonwealth of Independent States (CIS). In most cases, these plants did not satisfy the requirements of the international safety standards and practices. The Commission was thus confronted by a double challenge concerning the requirement made by the member states to develop strategies for nuclear safety in Eastern Europe. However, given the Commission's lack of technical and institutional competencies, responsibility for this sector was to remain with national governments.[15]

Confronted with the dangerous situation of the nuclear power plants in Eastern Europe, DG XVII and DG XI decided to approach the problem from a technical point of view. On this basis, DG XVII invited the operators of nuclear power plants first to establish ad hoc consultation committee in 1990 (see Pijnenburg 1997), which developed into industrial consortia bringing together European operators from France, Italy, Germany, Great Britain, Spain, Belgium and Sweden. The creation of the consortia set out to enable the operators of Western European nuclear power plants to co-operate and not to compete in the very fragile Eastern European market.

Politicians were highly mobilized on this issue and the College of Commissioners, under particular pressure from its president, Jacques Delors, decided that the question was of a purely political nature and that DG I/IA should be in charge of this problem. After the creation of the PHARE and TACIS programmes whose management was attributed to DG I, shortly after divided in DG I and DG IA, there was no doubt left about the centre of competence in this issue. This concentration on the political side had consequences for the relationship between nuclear sector interest groups and the Commission. The nuclear issue of Central and Eastern Europe was reclassified under the point of view of nuclear safety and no longer under "nuclear energy" as a whole. This approach has considerably weakened DG XVII in the power game, reinforced DG XI's position, without however according it new competencies, and created a pole of power inside DG IA. Instead of referring to their long-term relationship with DG XVII, interest groups need now to deal with a new, unknown, bureaucracy.

At first sight, the attitudes adopted by the French and German nuclear industries were very similar. Both accepted the new powerful actor DG IA without hesitation and represented their interests vis-à-vis DG IA as well as vis-à-vis DG XVII and DG XI. Their strategy was to present the highest level of expertise to the relevant DG in order to influence decision making in their favour. This influence was considerable as the Commission's formal powers and scientific knowledge in this field were very low[16] and it was having to deal with a new and very complex and issue.

A closer look at the field of nuclear operators, however, shows that the French operator adopted rather different behaviour, and imposed itself as the central actor in the field. Very few German operators were part of the consortia. This is due to a difference in the structure of the German and French electricity markets. Whilst engineering is a strong component of EDF, which can offer expertise in this sector, the German electricians have strong commercial competences, which have been of little use vis-à-vis the expertise-seeking Commission. To this technical knowledge gap one must add that the German situation in the nuclear sector is extremely hesitant. Thus, German operators were less active in the expertise-producing arena formed by the consortium TPEG. German technical expertise is more often found outside the electricity operator. In Germany, it is the universities[17] which offer technical knowledge, and not the electricity producers, whereas in France EDF has a large research and development division in different areas of electricity production. This situation has led to internal conflicts in the group resulting in German operators, and in particular RWE, criticized EDF for monopolizing knowledge and obtaining many more tenders, excluding the other members.[18] Other German industrial and administrative officials have repeated this, and underlined that EDF has "too" strong ties with the French government and French civil servants in the Commission.[19]

Regarding the relations between private actors and national administrations, a parallel concerning the relationships these actors had with the Commission services can be observed. Whilst EDF had particularly close relations with the French government, given its status as a monopolistic public enterprise in the electricity sector in France, one can observe that it had the same contacts with the European Commission. Even more so, as EDF, and also Framatome and Cogema, regularly sent a certain number of experts to the Commission where they obtained the status of "detached national expert". In contrast to France, the German operators and nuclear industries kept in permanent contact with the German ministries without, however, attaining the same degree of closeness. Consequently, the German and French interest representatives were not able to become detached national experts in the same way. It seems that one could echo Mazey and Richardson's (1993: 9) statement generally that "the 'procedural ambition' of many Commission officials to seek a stable and regular relationship with the affected interests might be seen as presenting a particular advantage to those lobbyists used to that type of policy style at the national level".

This in-depth micro-level analysis shows that Europeanization has both a horizontal and a vertical dimension. It is not sufficient to study solely the impact of European policy on the actor's behaviour. On the contrary, it is necessary to understand the specific national and sectoral structures in which interest groups act.

This understanding allows explanation of actors' behaviour in European negotiations. The analysis of the actor's participation in the EU level policy-making process allows observation of the horizontal dimension of the Europeanization process – the socialization between actors already takes place at this level. Europeanization is not a linear process whereby European integration meets the "goodness of fit" of national policies, politics or polities, is then mediated by national institutional structures and leads to different degrees of Europeanization. Instead, actors take part in European integration processes. The study of the interaction between national interest groups and the Commission's fragmented and sectorized bureaucracy has shown that sector-specific forms of national interest representation largely influence the attitudes of interest groups at the European level, leading to collective action in agriculture and nuclear safety. The two sector/two country comparison has shown that while there seem to be large differences between sectors in these countries, the difference between integrated (agriculture) and less integrated (nuclear electricity) policy fields does not play a significant role in the degree of Europeanization. Interest groups in both policy fields still feature very national forms of interest representation.

Introducing a Test Variable

This leaves us with the last of the methodological challenges identified: how to measure the degree of change interest group behaviour has experienced? Do they only use European discourse and access points without changing their representational structures and strategies or can we observe in-depth transformation? In order to avoid the danger of limiting the analysis to correctional arguments between European developments and domestic changes, as Checkel (2000) reminds us, I argue that by introducing a test variable this challenge can be met. The context of enlargement policy allows us to analyse Western European interest group behaviour not only at the EU level but also in Central and Eastern Europe. The ten Central and Eastern European candidate countries (CEECs) were not yet member states during the chosen time period, which offered the possibility to use the CEECs as "international" level. Thus, if the collective action repertoires of Western European interest groups active in the CEECs, and thus outside the EU borders, was transformed by the European integration process, that is if their action repertoires, public–private relationships and political legitimacy have been transformed and not only marginally adapted, then one can speak about the emergence of the Europeanization of interest representation. This particular challenge of the operationalization of Europeanization studies is generally ignored (see also Greenwood and Jaceck 2000). In both policy areas, agriculture and nuclear safety, the EU was faced with severe problems regarding the Central and Eastern European countries and in both fields Western European interest groups were active in the CEECs.

Exporting National Models

Regarding agriculture, the Western European interest groups have proposed supporting their Central and Eastern European counterparts in establishing new and efficient organizational structures as well as to create new relationships with political actors. The empirical study shows that these activities, while financed by the EU PHARE programme, led to a competition amongst national farmer's unions, members of the COPA, the Eurogroup charged with the implementation of these programmes.

Both the German farmers' union DBV and its French counterpart FNSEA wished to be active in Poland, the most important candidate country with regard to agriculture. At the end of the 1980s, 25 per cent of the active population worked in this sector, a percentage which is decreasing only slowly. The influence on the establishment of a specific organizational structure among the Polish farmer's unions can be considered as strategic: The new farmer's union would be a very powerful actor in the Common Agricultural Policy of the EU. If it can be modelled according to either the French or the German national model – and exclude in particular the neoliberal Dutch or Danish farmer's unions – a powerful ally in EU agricultural negotiations would be gained, and, at the same time, a very similar and therefore well known structure would be created. The French farmers' union finally won the game and was able to work closely with the existing Polish farmers' unions to reform their organizational structures.

The Influence of Domestic Action Models Abroad

In the field of nuclear safety, the EU financial programmes can be considered an important incentive for Western European interest groups to engage in the CEECs. However, a detailed empirical analysis shows a result similar to that in the agricultural policy field. No transformation of collective action could be observed regarding Western European interest groups active in the CEECs. Two case studies more clearly illustrate this influence of national structures among Western European nuclear electricity providers.

The construction of the Slovakian nuclear power plant in Mohovce began in 1984, but was suspended in 1991 due to lack of funds. In September of 1993, with the idea in mind to sell the electricity produced by Mochovce to the West, the French utility provider Electricité de France (EDF) and the German electricity producer Bayernwerk requested a loan from the European Bank of Investment and the European Bank for Reconstruction and Development (EBRD) to finance the completion of the construction of the reactor. In January of 1994, EDF concluded a joint venture agreement with the Slovakian electricity provider to construct and manage the two Mochovce reactors. The works, which were to be undertaken for the nuclear part of the facilities by the construction companies Framatome (French) and Siemens (German) in the context of the Consortium EUCOM (European Consortium Mochovce), were scheduled to begin in May or June of 1995. As such, the first unit would have been completed by the end of 1997, the second in 1998. Additional expertise would have been provided by RISK-AUDIT, a Franco-German nuclear safety organism. However, in February 1995, the European Parliament voted to suspend the funding for Mochovce until nuclear safety issues were resolved. The electricity producer Bayernwerk, contrary to its French partners, only wanted to participate in the project if Western safety criteria were respected and if the EBRD agreed to contribute to the financing of the project. The French company EDF asserted that if the West were to pull out, the reactors would be completed with the assistance of the Russian authorities, whose compliance with safety norms would be questioned.[20] Following the refusal of Slovakian officials to meet these conditions, Bayernwerk indeed withdrew,[21] while EDF continued to participate in the project. Given the sensitivity of the nuclear issue, the German government exercised indirect pressure on the nuclear operator, despite the formal independence of the latter from any political influence. Many have raised fears that German producers, prevented from constructing plants in Germany, would delocalize their power production to Eastern Europe. The safety standards of such installations would come into question.[22] Wishing to avoid domestic and international criticism, the German government as a whole convinced Bayernwerk executives to abandon the project.

The case of the nuclear power plant of Kozloduy is equally relevant as it shows how when there were contradictions among different German governmental officials regarding the question of nuclear power it became ever more difficult for German industries to decide on a clear strategy. This underlines the influence of the particular structural features of the German political system where bureaucratic fragmentation, ministerial autonomy and coalition governments make co-ordination a real but more difficult exercise. The Kozloduy nuclear power plant consists of six reactors, four of which (1–4) are operational. According to West European nuclear safety officials, the two remaining reactors (5–6), which are still under construction, could be modernized to bring them into line with Western safety standards. In 1991, Bulgarian authorities approached the International Atomic Energy Agency (IAEA) to request technical assistance. On the basis of the conclusions of the IAEA experts, the director of the IAEA demanded the immediate closing of the plant. Following the refusal of Bulgaria to do so given its dependence on this source of energy, the World Association of Nuclear Operators (WANO) decided to undertake the necessary works on the 1–4 reactors in order to ensure the continued, yet limited, functioning of the plant. Financial assistance was to be provided by the European Commission. The key actor in WANO is the French energy producer EDF, which supervised the modernization process. Early on in the project, a consortium between EDF and Siemens was created to undertake the completion of the works. On the European level, the European Commission continued to pressure Bulgarian authorities to close the reactor.

In 1995, EDF recalled its experts when an accident in the nuclear reactor was narrowly avoided. The respective reactions of French and German officials are highly instructive: whilst the French government, and the Ministry of the Environment in particular, congratulated EDF for its efforts to promote nuclear safety at Kozloduy and encouraged the firm to continue its efforts in Bulgaria, the German *Bundestag*, as well as the European Parliament, called for the reactor to be closed.

These empirical studies show that, despite the fact that European integration, in particular enlargement issues, changed interest group behaviour and specifically their discourse at the national level, their practices outside the EU were still very much influenced by national political structures. Thus, concentrating only on actors' practices at the national level might give a false impression of change due to Europeanization. This "change" might be due to strategic usages of European integration. Introducing a counterfactual research method is thus a possible solution to this problem.

Conclusion

While theories and concepts of Europeanization have become very prominent issues in a number of research agendas, the methodological challenges linked to these studies have been rather less considered. This article has identified three main problems: the problem of complex interdependence, the difficulty in distinguishing between "European" and "domestic variables" and the measurement of change. I have argued that two methodological choices need to be made when operationalizing a Europeanization research agenda in policy studies: a comparative research design linked to a long time period which leads to a complex interdependence model and the inclusion of a control variable.

With regard to comparative research design, the case studies presented in this article have shown that a long-term micro-study is necessary to understand the policy styles linked on the one hand to different national political systems and on the other to public policies. Ideationally, these long-term comparisons start before the beginning of European integration. It is then possible to show how national attitudes interact at the European level with institutional access structures summarized in a complex interdependence model.

The empirical analysis of Western European interest group behaviour outside the European Union territory has shown the importance of the usage of Europeanization made by interest groups and the importance of a control variable. The term usage covers both the strategic interaction of rational actors with European institutions and the more sociological effect of usage, understood as daily practice, on the interests and identities of the actors. In the context of this article, usages of Europeanization refer to the practices of interest groups which adjust and redefine themselves by seizing the European Union as a set of opportunities. Political opportunities, that is resources and constraints, provided by the European system offer the necessary conditions for interest group behaviour. However, interest groups need to seize these opportunities, as we have shown, in order to transform them into political practices. The importance of a control variable became evident in the operationalization process of Europeanization studies: the transformation of interest group behaviour in public policies through a European integration and socialization process must be shown in situations taking place outside the EU if one wishes to prove a transformation or adaptation process. The comparative research design used in this article has shown that in both policy fields national actors remain very much influenced by national relational as well as cognitive structures.

Europeanization research is very much institutionalized today, but still lacks a wide-ranging methodological debate suggesting how to tackle central difficulties regarding its operationalization, a debate this article has sought to open.

Notes

1. For an excellent overview on theoretical approaches and empirical case studies see Radaelli (forthcoming).
2. Policy ideas and models can 'travel' though (Keohane and Goldstein, 1993).
3. I this article I will not take international variables into account in order to limit the complexity of the demonstration.
4. As understood by Tilly (1984) as means used by groups to defend their interests.

5. Amongst others Greenwood *et al.* 1992, van Schedelen 1993, Pedler and van Schendelen 1994, Greenwood 1997, 2003, Claeys 1998, Greenwood and Aspinwall 1998.
6. As do Knill and Lehmkuhl (2002) in their study on the changing patterns of public–private governance.
7. The term 'network' is used in a purely heuristical way to describe different degrees of closeness between interest groups and public actors. It is not based on the use of the network literature initiated amongst others by Marsh and Rhodes 1992, Smith 1993, Marsh 1998, Marsh and Smith 2000).
8. The Minister of Agriculture appointed in January 2001 is, for the first time in German history, a woman, who has no ties with the agricultural world, has never been member of the DBV and is, furthermore, a member of the German Green Party, *Die Grünen*. This appointment, like the new social democratic government elected in September 1998, has significantly modified the relationship between the leaders of the DBV and the ministry's senior civil servants.
9. I use the company names as they were before the merger agreements, which started in 1999, and came into force in 2000. Since June 2000, when the European Commission authorized the merger between VIAG and VEBA, the two electricity groups in which Bayernwerk and Preussenelektra are parts, both electricity producers are parts of the holding company E-ON.
10. A relationship which became even looser, similar to the ideal type of issue networks, after the change in the government majority in 1998.
11. PHARE: Pologne-Hongrie Aide à la restructuration, later on enlarged to all the candidate countries. TACIS: Technical Assistance for the Commonwealth of Interdependent States.
12. Fritz Scharpf uses the notion of *joint decision trap* "to describe constellations in which parties are either physically or legally unable to reach their purposes through unilateral action and in which joint action depends on the (nearly) unanimous agreement of all parties involved" (Scharpf 1997: 143). This argument is very close to March and Olsen's (1989) analysis of the role of institutions. While competition amongst administrative units can be observed, the resulting polity is something different from, or more than, an arena for competition among rival interests. Interdependence does thus not exclude conflict, the actors know however, that a compromise is necessary to carry on the policy-making process.
13. MAAG-Doc.119-Final, *Central and Eastern European Countries. Report on Market Access*, September 16, 1998.
14. Europe agro, no. 22, May 29, 1998.
15. This situation is interesting as nuclear power is part of the founding treaties of the Community: the EURATOM Treaty of 1957.
16. The Euratom treaty specifies competences in the field of radioprotection, Title II, Chapter III.
17. The University of Aachen is a particular example.
18. Interview, Tractebel, October 28, 1999.
19. Which can be linked to the rather specific problems between German electricity producers and EDF after the liberalization of the electricity market in Europe.
20. Interview, EDF, December 4, 1998.
21. Interview, VIAG/Bayernwerk, February 2, 1999.
22. Interview, RWE, January 27, 1999.

References

Balme, Richard and Didier, Chabanet, 2002, Action collective et représentation des intérêts dans l'Union européenne, in: Richard Balme, Didier Chabanet and Vincent Wright (Eds) *L'action collective en Europe* (Paris, Presses de Sciences Po).

Börzel, Tanja, 2001, Pace setting, foot dragging and fence-sitting. Member state responses to Europeanization. *Queen's Papers on Europeanization* no. 4.

Börzel, Tanja and Risse, Thomas, 2000, *When Europe hits Home: Europeanization and Domestic Change*, RSC no. 2000/56, EUI Working Paper.

Bovens, Mark, t'Hart, Paul and Peters, B. Guy (Eds), 2001, *Success and Failure in Public Governance. A Comparative Analysis* (Cheltenham: Edward Elgar).

Bulmer, Simon and Radaelli, Claudio, 2004, The Europeanization of National Policy. *Queen's Papers on Europeanisation* no. 1.

Caporaso, James, Green Cowles, Maria and Risse, Thomas (Eds), 2001, *Transforming Europe. Europeanization and Domestic Change* (Ithaca, NY: Cornell University Press).
Checkel, Jeffrey, 2000, *Bridging the Rational Choice/Constructivist Gap? Theorizing Social Interaction in European Institutions.* ARENA Working Paper, 11.
Claeys, Paul-Henri (Eds), 1998, Lobbyisme, pluralisme et intégration européene. Lobbying, pluralism and European integration (Bruxelles: Presses interuniversitaires européenes).
Cohen, Elie, 1992, Dirigisme, politique industrielle et rhétorique industrialiste. *Revue française de Science politique*, **42**(2), 197–218.
Cohen, Elie, 1996, *La tentation hexagonale: la souveraineté à l'épreuve de la mondialisation* (Paris: Fayard).
Eckstein, Harry, 1975, Case study and theory in political science, in: F. I. Greenstein and N. W. Polsby (Eds) *Handbook of Political Science*, vol.7 (Reading, MA: Addison-Wesley).
Featherstone, Kenneth, 2003, Introduction: in the name of "Europe", in: K. Featherstone and C. M. Radaelli (Eds) *The Politics of Europeanization* (Oxford: Oxford University Press).
Featherstone, Kenneth and Radaelli, Claudio (Eds), 2003, *The Politics of Europeanization* (Oxford: Oxford University Press).
Giuliani, Marco, 2003, Europeanization in comparative perspective: institutional fit and national adaptation, in: K. Featherstone and C. M. Radaelli (Eds) *The Politics of Europeanization* (Oxford: Oxford University Press).
Goetz, Klaus. H and Hix, Simon (Eds), 2001, *Europeanised Politics? European Integration and National Political Systems* (London: Frank Cass).
Green Cowles, Maria, 2001, The TABD and domestic business–government relations, in James Caporaso, Maria Green Cowles and Thomas Risse (Eds) *Transforming Europe. Europeanization and Domestic Change* (Ithaca, NY: Cornell University Press).
Greenwood, Justin, 1997, *Representing Interests in the European Union* (London: Macmillan).
Greenwood, Justin, 2003, *Interest representation in the European Union* (Basingstoke: Palgrave Macmillan).
Greenwood, Justin and Aspinwall, Mark (Ed), 1998, *Collective Action in the European Union. Interests and the New Politics of Associability* (London: Routledge).
Greenwood, Justin and Jacek, H. (Eds), 2000, *Organized Business and the New Global Order* (Basingstoke: Macmillan).
Greenwood, Justin, Grote, Jürgen and Ronit, Karsten (Eds), 1992, *Organised Interests in the European Community* (London: Sage).
Grossman, Emiliano, 2002, L'européanisation des structures de représentation des intérêts: le cas des associations bancaires, *Politique européenne*, no. 7, 43–65.
Grossman, Emiliano and Saurugger, Sabine, 2004, Challenging French interest groups: the state, Europe and the international political system. *French Politics*, **2**(2), 203–229.
Hall, Peter, 1993, Policy paradigms, social learning and the state: the case of economic policy making in Britain. *Comparative Politics*, **25**(3), 275–296.
Heinze, Rolf G., 1992, *Verbandspolitik zwischen Partikularinteressen und Gemeinwohl – der Deutsche Bauernverband* (Gühtersloh: Verlag Bertelsmann Stiftung).
Hendriks, Gisela, 1991, *Germany and European Integration. The Common Agricultural Policy: An Area of Conflict* (New York, Oxford: Berg).
Héritier, Adrienne, Kerwer, Dieter, Knill, Christoph, Lehmkuhl, Dirk, Teutsch, Michael, Douillet, Anne-Cécile, 2001, *Differential Europe: the European Union impact on national policymaking* (Lanham: Rowman & Littlefield).
Hervieu, Bertrand and Lagrave, Rose-Marie, 1992, *Les syndicats agricoles en Europe* (Paris: l'Harmattan).
Hubscher, Ronald and Lagrave, Rose-Marie, 1993, Unité et pluralisme dans le syndicalisme agricole français. *Annales ESC*, no. 1.
Irondelle, Bastien, 2003, Europeanization without the European Union? French military reforms 1991–1996. *Journal of European Public Policy*, **10**(2), 208–226.
Jacquot, Sophie and Woll, Cornelia, 2003, Usage of European integration – Europeanization from a sociological perspective. *European Integration Online Papers*, EIOP, **7**(12), http://www.eiop.or.at/eiop/texte/2003-012a.htm.
Keohane, Robert and Goldstein, Judith (Eds), 1993, *Ideas and Foreign Policy: Beliefs, Institutions and Political Change* (Ithaca, NY: Cornell University Press).
Kitschelt, Herbert, 1980, *Kernergiepolitik: Arena eines gesellschaftlichen Konfliktes* (Frankfurt: Campus).

Knill, Christoph and Lehmkuhl, Dirk, 1999, How Europe matters: different mechanisms of Europeanization. *European Integration Online Papers*, EIOP, **3**(7), http://www.eiop.or.at/eiop/texte/1999-007a.htm.

Knill, Christoph and Lehmkuhl, Dirk, 2002, Private actors and the state: internationalization and the Chaing pattern of governance. *Governance*, **15**(1), 41–63.

Knill, Christoph and Lenschow, Andrea, 2001, 'Seek and Ye Shall Find?' Differing Perspectives on Institutional Change. *Comparative Political Studies*, **34**(2), 187–215.

Kohler-Koch, Beate, 2002, European networks and ideas: changing national policies. *European Integration Online Papers* (EIPO), **6**(6), http://www.eiop.or.at/eiop/texte/1999-007a.htm.

Ladrech, Robert, 1994, Europeanization of domestic politics and institutions: the case of France. *Journal of Common Market Studies*, **32**(1), 69–88.

Lijphart, Arend, 1971, Comparative politics and the comparative method. *American Political Science Review*, **65**, 682–693.

Lucas, Nigel, 1985, *West European Energy Policy. A Comparative Study* (Oxford: Clarendon Press).

March, James G. and Olsen, Johan P., 1989, *Rediscovering Institutions. The Organizational Basis of Politics* (New York: Free Press).

Marie, Jean-Louis, 1994, *Agriculteurs et politique* (Paris, Clefs: Montchrestien).

Marsh, David (Ed), 1998, *Comparing Policy Networks* (Buckingham: Open University Press).

Marsh, David and Rhodes, R. A. W. (Eds), 1992, *Policy Networks in British Government* (Oxford: Oxford University Press).

Marsh, David and Smith, Martin, 2000, Understanding policy networks: towards a dialectical approach, *Political Studies*, **48**(1), 4–21.

Mazey, Sonia and Richardson, J. J. (Eds), 1993, *Public Lobbying in the European Community* (Oxford: Oxford University Press).

Müller, Wolfgang D., 1990, *Geschichte der Kernenergie in der Bundesrepublik Deutschland. Anfänge und Weichenstellung* (Stuttgart: Shäffer Verlag für Wirtschäft und Stenern).

Olsen Johan P., 1996, Europeanization and nation–state dynamics, in: S. Gustavson and L. Lewin (Eds) *The Future of the Nation State* (Stockholm: Nerenius and Santerus Publishers).

Pedler, Robin and Schendelen, Marius P.C. van (Eds), 1994, *Lobbying the European Union: companies, trade associations and issue groups* (Aldershot: Dartmouth).

Perez-Solorzano, Nieves, 2001, Organised interests in Central and Eastern Europe: towards gradual Europeanization. *Politique européenne*, no. 3, 61–85.

Peters, B. Guy, 1998, *Comparative Politics. Theory and Methods* (Houndsmills: Macmillan).

Pijnenburg, Bert, 1997, Eurolobbying par des coalitions ad hoc: une analyse exploratrice. *Politiques et Management Public*, **15**(2), 97–121.

Przeworski, Adam and Teune, Henry, 1970, *The Logic of Comparative Social Inquiry* (New York: Wiley Interscience).

Radaelli, Claudio, 2001, The domestic impact of European Union public policy: notes on concepts, methods and the challenge of empirical research, *Politique européenne*, no. 5, 107–142.

Radaelli, Claudio, 2003, The Europeanization of public policy, in: K. Featherstone and C. M. Radaelli (Eds) *The Politics of Europeanization* (Oxford: Oxford University Press).

Radaelli, Claudio, forthcoming, Europeanization: a concept?, in: Michelle Cini and Angela Bourne (Eds) *The Palgrave Guide to European Studies* (Basingstoke: Palgrave).

Radkau, Joachim, 1983, *Aufstieg und Krise der deutschen Atomwirtschaft, 1945–75* (Reinbek: Rowohlt).

Risse, Thomas, Green Cowles, Maria and Caporaso, James (Eds), 2001, *Transforming Europe. Europeanization and Domestic Change* (Ithaca, NY: Cornell University Press).

Rochefort, David and Cobb, Roger (Eds), 1994, *The Politics of Problem Definition: Shaping the Policy Agenda* (Lawrence, KS: University Press of Kansas).

Rüdig, Wolfgang, 1987, Outcomes of nuclear technology policy: do varying political styles make a difference? *Journal of Public Policy*, **7**(4), 389–430.

Sabatier, Paul, 1998, The advocacy coalition framework: revisions and relevance for Europe. *Journal of European Public Policy*, **5**(1), 98–130.

Saurugger, Sabine, 2001, A fragmented environment? Interest groups and the European Commission's sectorisation. *Politique européenne*, no. 5, 43–68.

Saurugger, Sabine, 2003, *Européaniser les intérêts? Les groupes d'intérêt économiques et l'élargissement de l'Union européenne* (Paris, L'Harmattan, Collection Logiques politiques).

Scharpf, Fritz, 1997, *Games Real Actors Play: Actor Centred Institutionalism in Policy Research* (Oxford: Westview Press).
Schendelen, Marius P.C. van (Eds), 1993, *National public and private EC lobbying* (Aldershot: Dartmouth).
Schmidt, Vivien A., 1996, The decline of traditional state dirigisme in France: the transformation of political economic policies and policymaking processes. *Governance*, **9**(4), 375–405.
Schmidt, Vivien A., 2002, The effects of European Integration on National Governance: Reconsidering Practices and Reconceptualizing Democracy, in: Grote J. and Gbikpi (Eds) *Participatory Governance: Theoretical, Political, and Societal Implications* (Opladen: Leske and Budrich).
Schmidt, Vivien A., 2004, Europeanization of National Democracies: The Differential Impact on Simple and Compound Polities. *Politique européenne*, **13**, 113–140.
Schmitter, Philippe C., 1974, Still the century of corporatism? *Review of Politics*, no. 36, 85–86.
Smith, Martin J., 1993, *Pressure, Power and Policy Process. State Autonomy and Policy Networks in Britain and the US* (Pittsburgh, PA: Pittsburgh University Press).
Steffen, Monika (Ed), 2005, *Health Governance in Europe. Issues, Challenges and Theories* (London: Routledge).
Tilly, Charles, 1984, Les origines du répertoire d'action collective contemporaine en France et en Grande Bretagne. *XXe siècle*, no. 4, 89–108.
Ward, Stephen and Lowe, Philip, 1998, National environmental groups and Europeanization: a survey of the British environmental lobby. *Environmental Politics*, **7**(4), 164–185.
Wright, Vincent, 1997, Introduction: la fin du dirigisme? *Modern and Contemporary France*, **5**(2), 151–153.

How to Construct a Robust Measure of Social Capital: Two Contributions

GERT TINGGAARD SVENDSEN and CHRISTIAN BJØRNSKOV

ABSTRACT *How to construct a robust measure of social capital? This paper offers two contributions. The first is an attempt to establish a broad social capital measure based on four indicators, the Freedom House Index, an index of perceived corruption from Transparency International, and scores on civic participation and generalized trust. This measure is then applied by comparing the level of social capital in 25 countries from Western and Eastern Europe. Our nine-cluster analysis shows that Switzerland has the highest score, followed by the Netherlands and Scandinavia. At the other end of the continuum we find post-communist countries and southern Italy. The findings for this specific sample suggest that institutions matter for social capital and the relationship between decentralization and social capital emerges as a promising line of inquiry. Thus, the highest scoring countries in the sample may serve as institutional models for countries and regions aiming to increase their future level of social capital. More rigorous empirical research is needed within this field.*

Introduction

What is social capital, and how can it be measured? The broad standard definition of social capital is the ability of people to work together for common purposes in groups and organizations (Coleman 1988, Fukuyama 1995). It is, however, not easy to apply such a broad definition and measure 'the ability to cooperate'. A review of the literature reveals that the concept has yet to be measured in a satisfactory way, and that it has only been addressed in various rather ad hoc ways (Bjørnskov 2005).

Consequently, as we are still searching for a standardized way to measure social capital there is a strong need to develop a single reliable measure. This shortcoming poses a serious problem when formulating public policy that takes the social capital dimension into account. Dasgupta (1999) describes the sociological and economic background for the use and interpretation of social capital, and Paldam (2000) introduces 'the social capital dream': that an underlying 'rock' of social capital exists upon which all the various definitions of the concept rest. If this is so, the social capital concept will be robust to variation in definition and become a very useful tool for explaining a number of problems in the social sciences. Thus, we suggest a broad measure for 'the ability to cooperate' and apply it in a simple cross-country analysis. Note that our contribution is not to distinguish between the sources and the consequences of social capital but simply to categorize countries by applying cluster analysis.

A first question to be asked is what indicators a standard social capital measure ought to contain. First, social capital has been shown to be a causal factor of political freedom (la Porta *et al.* 1998, Knack 2002, Rothstein 2005, Svendsen and Svendsen 2005). Second, social capital is strongly correlated with corruption (Uslaner 2001, Bjørnskov 2003). At the *macro*-level, we therefore suggest that the formation of social capital can be measured indirectly by using two indicators, political freedom and level of corruption.[1]

Third, generalized trust at the *micro* level has been used as an indicator of the likelihood of being cheated by strangers (Gambetta 2000, Offe 2004). Generalized trust is measured as the percentage of a population answering 'Yes' to the question 'do you think that most people can be trusted, or can't you be too careful?' It can thus be said to measure the normal trust radius of a population. The higher the level of generalized trust, the lower the likelihood of being cheated, thus facilitating voluntary cooperation. Fourth, Putnam (1993) states that membership of voluntary organizations at the *meso*-level matters. The measured density of voluntary organizations has become known as Putnam's Instrument.

The inclusion of the four proxies for social capital described above (political freedom, corruption, civic participation and generalized trust) matches the main theoretical and empirical findings in the literature so far (Bjørnskov 2005). Bjørnskov and Svendsen (2003) have applied principal component analysis to these four indicators, showing that they all load powerfully onto a single underlying component and thereby suggesting that at the national level it may make sense to talk about 'social capital' as a unitary concept.

If a standardized methodology for measuring social capital can be developed, it will open the door to a whole range of new research approaches. For example, it will be a most useful tool for tasks like performing comparative studies, evaluating the integration of migrants (Thränhardt 2004, Nannestad *et al.* 2007), measuring the effect on economic growth (Knack and Keefer 1997, Whiteley 2000, Zak and Knack 2001), and measuring subjective well-being such as happiness (Helliwell 2001, Frey and Stutzer 2002, Bjørnskov 2003). Moreover, it will be a most useful concept in facilitating communication between all the social sciences that in one way or another have all addressed the same bedrock, where 'everything might be shades of and approaches to the very same basic phenomenon' (Paldam 2000: 641).

In the following, section two presents the four social capital indicators in more detail. Section three introduces our cluster analysis method. Section four reports the results of a cross-national analysis of 25 Western and Eastern European countries. Compressing existing social capital measures into one underlying factor enables us to rank and cluster these 25 countries in terms of their social capital level. Section five summarizes the results.

The Four Social Capital Indicators

Political Freedom

First, the macro-measure *political freedom* addresses the policies implemented by the government. Bad policies have been rampant in centrally planned economies where power is centralized in the hands of bureaucrats. Economically harmful redistribution in a society will lower trust in the macro-economic institutions in the populations, reducing social capital. Doig and Theobald (2000: 4) argue that everywhere the state is active in society presents an opportunity for rent seeking (see Tullock 1967). Because developing countries have relatively large public sectors compared to developed countries, bad policies and looting of the public treasury are probably more widespread in these countries (Svendsen 2003).

Freedom House (2002) publishes an annual assessment of political freedom in the world by assigning each country and territory a status of 'Free', 'Partly Free', or 'Not Free' by averaging their political rights and civil liberties ratings. Those with ratings averaging 1–2.5 are generally considered 'Free', 3–5.5 indicates 'Partly Free', and 5.5–7 'Not Free'. The dividing line between 'Partly Free' and 'Not Free' usually falls within the group with average ratings of 5.5. For example, countries that are rated 6 for political rights and 5 for civil liberties, or 5 for political rights and 6 for civil liberties, could be either 'Partly Free' or 'Not Free'. The total number of raw points is the definitive factor that determines the final status. Countries and territories with combined raw scores of 0–30 points are 'Not Free', those with 31–59 points are 'Partly Free', and those scoring 60–88 are 'Free' (Freedom House 2002). This index of political freedom is believed to capture both institutional quality and capacity. As such, we use it as a fully vertical element of social capital.

Corruption

Second, studies point to similar results concerning *corruption* and the resulting low level of trust between citizens and states. Centralization and monopoly on granting permissions for most activities encourage corruption because the few people that hold such powers can earn a lot by offering their services in return for bribes. The annual World Bank report (WDR 1996: 94) states that government credibility is low in Russia and Eastern Europe in general. Rose and Mishler (1998) found similar results. Their 'battery of questions' about society's trust in Russian macro-institutions indicated that most Russians distrust every major institution especially representative institutions of governance (see also Paldam and Svendsen 2000, Rose-Ackerman 2001, Schjødt and Svendsen, 2002).

This argument is proposed and investigated in further detail by Svendsen (2003) in the EU setting, while Fisman and Gatti (2002) show empirically in their cross-national studies that more decentralization leads to less corruption in a society. Corruption, in turn, affects social capital and vice versa. In the absence of corruption, we may expect a higher level of social capital and hence more economic growth. This is so because a low level of corruption implies strong enforcement of contracts, encouraging the voluntary accumulation of trust among trading parties (Rose-Ackerman 2001, Paldam and Svendsen 2002). If trading parties know that the formal rules are strictly enforced and everyone is equal before the law, they are more likely to cooperate without cheating and thereby build trust so that more and more informal transactions will take place over time. (See also Paldam (2001) and Treisman (2000) concerning institutional quality and the dynamics of corruption, which affect the economy negatively.)

To paraphrase Søren Kierkegaard, the 'leap of faith' involved in any transaction becomes shorter and hence more likely when strong and credible institutions are able to punish those who abuse other people's confidence. However, causality may run both ways. Uslaner (2001), using generalized trust as an indicator for social capital, found that the influence of trust on corruption was substantially stronger than the reverse causal link. For example, trust makes people more willing to engage in transactions with a greater diversity of people, which in turn creates increased competition for any corrupt practices. Finally, by using factor analysis both Narayan and Cassidy (2001) and Bjørnskov (2003) confirm the validity of including corruption as an indicator of social capital.

The Corruption Perceptions Index (CPI) is used to measure the level of corruption at the national level in the year 2000 (Transparency International 2001). The scores range between 10 (highly clean) and 0 (highly corrupt). So, high scores mean low corruption and low scores high corruption. Business people, risk analysts and the general public in 89 different countries were interviewed about their perceptions of the degree of corruption. Note that the index is based on subjective perceptions (how people think it is), and so does not necessarily give an accurate picture of the actual situation. Note also that the CPI index is really an honesty index, as low values show corruption and high values show honesty. The corruption index is used as a partly horizontal, partly vertical element of social capital in that it measures the relative honesty of individuals as well as institutions.[2]

Generalized Trust and Civic Participation

Third and fourth, we adopt the dictatorship theory of Paldam and Svendsen (2000, 2002). It simply hypothesizes that power centralization affects the level of social capital in terms of both *generalized trust* and *civic participation*. Thus, we suggest that power centralization such as communist dictatorship destroyed social capital at the micro-level because the state made all decisions and left no room for entrepreneurship and voluntary organizations.

The first straightforward way to measure the general level of trust is simply to ask people. This approach was pioneered by the team behind the World Values Survey (Inglehart *et al*. 1998), who asked people about their generalized trust in the following way: 'Generally speaking, would you say that most people can be trusted, or that you cannot be too careful in dealing with people?' The national percentage of people who respond in the affirmative to the question is recorded. The data are drawn from the European Values Survey (van Schaik 2002).

A second option to measure social capital is Putnam's Instrument, that is, the density of voluntary organizations of any type that capture the network element.

Here we use the density of civic participation from the World Values Survey with data from 1993 as a rough proxy for Putnam's Instrument (Inglehart et al. 1998). Respondents were asked whether they participated in various civic activities, that is, voluntary activities like (a) social welfare services for the elderly and deprived; (b) education, art and cultural activities; (c) local community affairs; (d) activities related to conservation, the environment, and ecology; and (e) work with youth. The density of civic participation is measured as the percentage of these civic activities in which an average respondent in a country is involved.

Both measures are relevant and may capture different aspects of social capital. For example, a person may not trust strangers but can still be extremely active in terms of participation in voluntary organizations where trust is built by observing the outcome of repeat interactions. However, membership of voluntary organizations implies that part of the population is excluded from this process, while those included stand to gain access to a variety of resources through the network (Stolle 2002). So the two indicators measure two types of social capital with different degrees of inclusiveness and different mechanisms. Moreover, organizations such as trade unions are built as hierarchical structures, which also serve to distinguish the two indicators on a scale of horizontality and verticality.

Cluster Analysis

The methodological approach we now apply is cluster analysis. It is a multivariate technique for grouping elements according to their characteristics on a pre-specified set of parameters. The purpose of the method is to develop a taxonomy in which individual observations are grouped in clusters. It should ideally exhibit minimum intra-cluster homogeneity and maximum inter-cluster heterogeneity. To achieve this, we use the non-hierarchical k-means technique.[3]

The four indicators thus capture different facets of social capital that can be jointly captured by our choice of equivalence analysis. By regressing an underlying factor on cluster membership dummies, Table 1 provides some statistics on the quality of the

Table 1. Taxonomy goodness-of-fit

Clusters	F	Δ F	R-squared	ΔR-squared	Min t-statistic	Ward variance	Δ Ward
2	46.601	40.8	0.655	−5.2	6.826	6577.8	19.4
3	27.588	−158.9	0.689	−30.3	1.872	5301.4	57.9
4	71.425	14.5	0.898	−1.2	5.200	2232.1	20.8
5	61.071	17.8	0.909	−0.2	5.925	1767.9	43.2
6	50.193	−12.9	0.911	−2.4	1.493	1003.9	28.5
7	56.659	−2.0	0.933	−1.1	1.339	717.6	−7.2
8	57.778	−43.4	0.943	−2.3	1.390	769.3	39.5
9	82.873	15.6	0.965	0.2	2.725	465.7	21.6
10	69.940	0.4	0.963	−0.3	2.655	365.1	8.0
11	69.668	13.7	0.966	0.2	2.788	336.0	9.8

Note: Column six reports the t-statistic of the last cluster to be added to the taxonomy. All differences are in percentages.

potential taxonomies that emerge when these indicators are used. This factor is obtained from a principal component analysis using the four indicators above and it confirms that all elements load powerfully onto the same underlying factor (see Bjørnskov and Svendsen 2003).

First, a taxonomy using only two clusters explains about 66 per cent of the variation in the factor scores. The F-value also seems adequate, indicating that it makes sense to operate with this taxonomy. Secondly, between nine and eleven clusters explain about 97 per cent and have a relatively low Ward variance. More specifically, a nine-cluster taxonomy maximizes the F-value, indicating that this is optimal. The table also demonstrates that moving below nine clusters seems to create a 'bad' cluster that is not significantly different from one of the other clusters. This may indicate that the cluster consists of potentially spurious differences in only one of the four parameters that determine the cluster formation process. The Appendix therefore reports the results of a series of robustness tests. The next section discusses the properties of taxonomies with either two or nine clusters.

Results

A Two-cluster Partition

As is evident from Table 1, the cluster analyses lend substantial support to the hypothesis in that approximately two-thirds of the variation in the factor scores can be explained by picking only two clusters. For instance, Europe could meaningfully be divided into two halves, north and south, as suggested by Bjørnskov and Svendsen (2003).[4] The details of this partition are reported in Table 2, while average characteristics of the clusters are reported in Table A1. Note that the distance between the cluster centres is 43.9, and hence the two clusters are quite disparate compared to the average within-cluster distances, which are 18.1 in the north and 13.4 in the south.

The differences in social capital are remarkable. The Northern European cluster scores about double as much as Southern Europe on generalized trust. The northerners score between 30 and 66 percent, while the southerners score between 15 and 29 percent; the northern cluster is far less corrupt (7.4–9.9 versus 3.2–7.8) and has populations that participate much more in civic society than the populations in the southern part of Europe (6–47 versus 3–10). These differences are reflected in the factor scores that are all negative in the southern cluster, while nine out of thirteen are positive in the northern cluster. The countries in the latter cluster are also richer and score slightly lower on the Freedom House Index, even though all European countries are estimated to be relatively free. An even more important point to note is that people in the countries in the northern cluster are much more satisfied with life than those in the southern countries. All differences are significant at $p < 0.01$. What all these numbers suggest is that Robert Putnam may be right in asserting that there are two 'social equilibria'. More specifically, it should be noted that northern and southern Italy have landed in different clusters as argued in Putnam (1993).

The reason for the substantial differences in Table 2 may have centuries-deep roots in the two groups of countries. For example, Reynolds (1984) provides convincing evidence that there were no substantial regional differences in the strength of

Table 2. A two-cluster taxonomy

Country	Cluster	Percentage reformed	Generalized trust	Factor score	Distance
Iceland	1	96.6	41.1	0.93	10.54
Northern Italy	1	0.4	45.4	−0.02	11.94
Netherlands	1	42.5	59.7	1.47	15.32
Ireland	1	4.0	35.2	0.47	15.72
Austria	1	6.5	33.9	0.43	16.15
Germany	1	46.4	34.8	−0.13	16.28
Norway	1	97.9	65.1	1.30	17.82
Spain	1	0.1	38.5	−0.24	18.20
United Kingdom	1	43.9	29.8	−0.15	18.55
Finland	1	93.2	58.0	1.34	18.70
Sweden	1	68.4	66.3	1.37	19.95
Denmark	1	95.3	66.5	1.46	22.19
Switzerland	1	43.4	42.6	1.77	34.33
Lithuania	2	5.0	24.9	−0.87	3.59
Slovenia	2	1.0	21.7	−0.75	4.32
Hungary	2	21.6	21.8	−0.89	4.71
Estonia	2	66.0	22.9	−0.74	7.13
Poland	2	0.1	18.9	−1.06	8.46
Czech Republic	2	4.6	23.9	−1.03	10.34
Slovakia	2	8.4	15.7	−1.22	13.48
Portugal	2	2.1	21.7	−0.08	14.03
Latvia	2	14.1	17.1	−1.22	15.68
Southern Italy	2	0.4	19.8	−1.25	17.25
France	2	2.4	22.2	−0.56	18.05
Belgium	2	0.1	29.3	−0.34	19.34

Note: Germany is divided into two equally large areas. The North is Protestant and the South is Catholic.

communities in Medieval Europe. Hence, it seems acceptable to claim that no systematic differences existed in the strength of local-level social capital at that time. Religious differences are often found to influence the level of corruption (Treisman 2000, Paldam 2001). The table illustrates that this relationship may be expanded to cover our broad definition of social capital by showing that the relatively poor south is almost exclusively Catholic, while the richer Northern European countries are both social capital-intensive and predominantly Protestant or Anglican.[5] As such, the religious reformation of Northern Europe could be taken as an important historical source of social capital. Potential mechanisms for this very long-term influence include the impact of a specific Protestant work ethic (Weber [1930]1992), an individualization of responsibility in Protestantism or, alternatively, it could be an outcome of the decentralization of religious power that accompanied the reformation, but the question remains open (see also Bjørnskov and Paldam 2002). The issue of decentralization nonetheless emerges once more when examining the fine-grained taxonomy.

A Nine-cluster Partition

The other partition that seems to explain a good deal consists of nine clusters, as reported in Table 3. Even though the partition becomes quite fine-grained, it is still

Table 3. A nine-cluster taxonomy

Cluster number	Country	Generalized trust	Corruption index	Freedom House index	Civic participation	Weight	Factor score
1	Switzerland	42.6	8.4	1.0	46.64	2.243	1.77
4	Netherlands	59.7	8.8	1.0	20.80	1.667	1.47
4	Denmark	66.5	9.5	1.0	11.35	1.484	1.46
4	Sweden	66.3	9.0	1.0	10.94	1.451	1.37
4	Norway	65.1	8.6	1.0	11.74	1.448	1.30
6	Finland	58	9.9	1.0	10.66	1.414	1.34
5	Iceland	41.1	9.2	1.0	11.35	1.273	0.93
	Luxembourg	25.9	8.7	1.0		1.088	
2	Ireland	35.2	7.5	1.0	8.04	1.067	0.47
2	Austria	33.9	7.8	1.0	5.97	1.011	0.43
2	Germany	34.8	7.4	1.5	9.39	1.075	−0.13
2	United Kingdom	29.8	8.3	1.5	7.01	1.005	−0.15
3	Northern Italy	45.4	7.4	1.5	6.00	1.063	−0.02
3	Spain	38.5	7.0	1.5	4.70	0.957	−0.24
7	Portugal	21.7	6.3	1.0	4.07	0.803	−0.08
7	Belgium	29.3	6.6	1.5	10.05	1.019	−0.34
	Malta	20.7		1.0		0.865	
7	France	22.2	6.7	1.5	6.08	0.856	−0.56
9	Estonia	22.9	5.6	1.5	5.45	0.801	−0.74
9	Slovenia	21.7	5.2	1.5	7.7[b]	0.839	−0.75
	Bulgaria	26.9	4.0	2.5		0.762	
9	Lithuania	24.9	4.8	1.5	3.70	0.736	−0.87
	Greece	19.1	4.2	2.0		0.721	
9	Hungary	21.8	5.3	1.5	2.41	0.695	−0.89
8	Czech Republic	23.9	3.9	1.5	3.50	0.687	−1.03
8	Poland	18.9	4.1	1.5	5.0[b]	0.698	−1.06
8	Latvia	17.1	3.4	1.5	4.42	0.640	−1.22
8	Slovakia	15.7	3.7	1.5	3.38	0.612	−1.22
8	Southern Italy	19.8	3.2	1.5	2.60	0.603	−1.25
	Romania	10.1	2.6	2.0		0.543	
	Turkey	10[a]	3.2	4.5		0.423	

Note: [a]The score is estimated from surveys; [b]the figure is from Inglehart *et al.* (1998).

surprisingly stable to the inclusion of other variables in the cluster formation process. For example, the inclusion of the Human Development Index (from WDR 1996) in the process has absolutely no consequences, while only very little changes if we include the Gastil index or measures of the degree to which the populations have materialist values (see Inglehart *et al.* 1998).

Four countries of interest have missing values on one or more of the parameters that enter the cluster formation process. By applying an alternative weighted average to supplement the cluster memberships we are able to create a more complete picture that includes three of the four countries. All European countries listed in Table 3 are thus ranked according to three criteria: cluster, individual factor scores, and average factor score within the cluster. Greece, Malta and Luxemburg are then put into the table according to their weighted averages of the three criteria above.[6] What becomes readily apparent in the table is that there are substantial differences between the clusters. Some clusters are fairly similar, while others are quite disparate. All inter-cluster distances are therefore reported in Table A1 in the appendix; cluster averages are reported in Table A2.

This more subtle taxonomy enables us to refine some of the thoughts arising from the two-cluster partition. First of all, Table 3 shows that the country with the highest social capital level in Europe is Switzerland. It must be stressed, however, that this result arises solely as a consequence of the very high level of civic participation generated by the Swiss canton system. The Netherlands and the Scandinavian countries, which all score substantially higher values of generalized trust, are ranked in the following places. Seven countries all have weights above 1.3 – Ireland comes in at number eight with a weight of 1.06. Taken together with the finding that these seven countries – except Iceland – all receive factor scores higher than one, the table clearly illustrates how markedly Scandinavia, the Netherlands, and Switzerland differ from the rest of Europe, a finding underlined by the robustness tests in the appendix. These findings support our theoretical model in the second section as its picture is replicated in Figure 1, which plots the scores against Gross National Income (GNI) per capita, and in Figure 2 listing the factor scores against a decentralization index.[7]

At the other end of the continuum, cluster number eight stands out as a group of countries that appear to be deficient in social capital and it consists almost exclusively of post-communist countries. The exception is southern Italy, which serves to underline both Putnam's (1993) conclusions and Banfield's (1958) original findings. In light of Paldam and Svendsen's (2000) dictatorship theory, their position as the European countries with the lowest level of social capital is hardly surprising as all have – or recently had – centralized systems that made for passive clients. It

Figure 1. Social capital and income

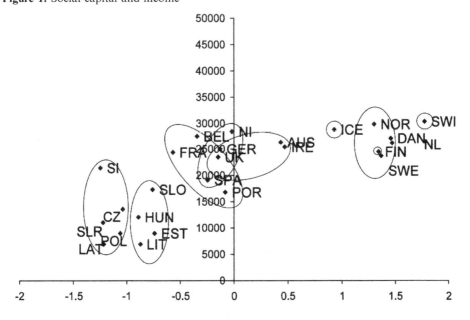

Figure 2. Social capital and decentralization

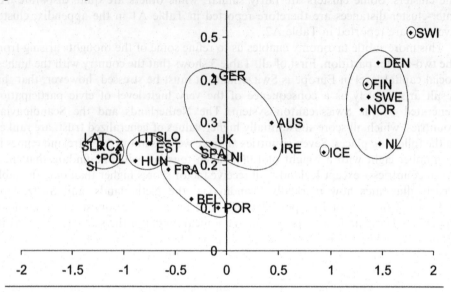

is an indisputable fact that these countries are doing quite poorly in terms of income and speed of transition.

In that sense, the members of cluster number nine are doing significantly better. This cluster consists of Slovenia, Estonia, Hungary, and Lithuania, which are often seen as the true front-runners of European integration.[8] They also appear to have more social capital than those in cluster eight, and are as such positioned remarkably close to cluster seven, a group consisting of three Western European countries with special characteristics. Besides illustrating that cluster nine is remarkably robust, Table A1 in the Appendix also suggests that the only real difference between clusters nine and seven is that nine has a slightly lower corruption score. Judged by the available information, this cluster should also include Greece and Bulgaria. The latter only scores 2.5 on the political freedom index, but seems to have corruption more under control than the countries in cluster eight and moreover exhibits a fairly high level of generalized trust.

The three countries in cluster seven – Portugal, France, and Belgium – stand out in Western Europe as those with the least social capital and very high degrees of centralization. Hence, as we hypothesized above, the centralized systems of these countries seem to have given rise to corruption and low levels of social capital. Surprisingly, this cluster is joined by Malta if a corruption score is imputed (not in figure).

The figures clearly depict the somewhat muddled middle of Europe, where clusters two, three and seven overlap in Figure 1, and cluster seven stands out in Figure 2.[9] Figure 2 in particular shows how close Western European cluster seven is to the predominantly post-communist cluster nine. The latter countries are all undergoing a successful transition process and will probably move in a north-easterly direction in Figure 1, implying that they will move into the 'circle' of cluster seven. In Figure 2, however, the movement will most likely be in a straight easterly direction, and hence cluster nine will move on top of cluster seven. Such movements will arise because the projected growth of these countries will in all probability lead to less corruption, and hence higher levels of social capital (see, for example, Treisman 2000, Paldam 2001, Bjørnskov and Paldam 2002).

The pictures painted by Figures 1 and 2 are rather clear. As mentioned above, the link between social capital and growth is currently being documented using a wide range approaches by, for instance, Whiteley (2000), Zak and Knack (2001), and Beugelsdijk et al. (2002). The relation suggested by Figure 2 can be further supported by econometric evidence since about 75 per cent of the social capital factor score in the present sample can be explained using a rather simple model. The results are reported below (t-statistics in parentheses). DECENT is the decentralization measure, REFORM is the percentage of the population belonging to either a Protestant or Anglican denomination, and TRANS is a dummy for transition countries.

$$SC = -0.819 + 3.714 * DECENT + 0.786 * REFORM - 1.164 * TRANS$$
$$(-2.714) \quad (2.955) \qquad\quad (2.042) \qquad\qquad (-5.004)$$

Our last remaining problem is that we lack sufficient data on six countries to enrol them in the cluster formation process. By using their weights instead, however, we can place them in approximately the right position vis-à-vis the rest of the European countries. First, Luxemburg should clearly be placed in cluster two with the United Kingdom as the closest country. Secondly, Romania is by far the most corrupt European country while – as the only country in the sample – Freedom House ranks Turkey as only 'partly free'. Hence, Turkey and Romania do not belong in the picture as their weights only amount to 0.41 and 0.36, respectively.[10]

In summary, we find several groups of European clusters when we distinguish between those elements of their institutions that are captured by the broad concept of social capital. The main result is that Switzerland, the Netherlands, and Scandinavia stand out as countries with much more social capital than the rest of Europe. Along institutional lines, these countries shine as bright as the northern lights. As indicated by the figures above, their success seems to have been achieved through having decentralized systems of government that leave little room for lobbying and corruption. These countries also score highest on measures of macro- and micro-level social capital, both of which probably make their economies run more smoothly. Below this leading group we find a large group of countries in the middle of the scale. These countries, including Luxemburg, the United Kingdom, Germany, Ireland, Austria, Spain, and the northern part of Italy, perform relatively well and thus achieve factor scores around zero. Three Western European countries stand out: France, Belgium, and Portugal form their own cluster, joined by Malta. Although they all belong to the richer half of Europe they perform poorly when measured along institutional lines. The evidence here indicates that their heavily centralized systems have contributed to the lack of social capital. It should further be noted that, based on available information, Malta lands within this cluster although we are unable to provide a satisfactory explanation for this.

In Eastern Europe, we found two clusters. Estonia, Slovenia, Lithuania, and Hungary perform significantly better than the remaining post-communist countries. They are joined by Greece and probably also by Bulgaria. Finally, judging by the available data, Turkey and Romania seem almost non-European on these counts. In other words, they are the furthest away from the Northern hemisphere. The findings from this exercise in categorization leads us to the following conclusions.

Conclusion

Social capital is becoming quite the buzzword in policy debates around the world, but this should not preclude the development of a more precise and detailed understanding of it as a concept; hence this paper. Our main question concerns how to establish a robust standard measure for the level of social capital within a country, which may not be trivial; there is a gap in the literature as a general method of measurement has yet to be established. It is nevertheless necessary to know whether one measure is as good as another, or if they in reality measure disparate phenomena.

We suggested that a standardized methodology for measuring social capital could be developed on the basis of four proximate indicators, namely political freedom, corruption, civic participation, and generalized trust. This measure was applied when ranking countries from both Western and Eastern Europe that are close to each other geographically as well as culturally and historically. This proximity lowers the risk of drawing spurious conclusions. Our nine-cluster analysis showed that the country with the highest social capital level in Europe is Switzerland due to its canton system and concomitant high level of civic participation. The Netherlands and the Scandinavian countries (Denmark, Norway, Sweden, and Finland) all scored substantially higher values of generalized trust. These six countries, followed by Iceland, hit the top in both the equivalence analysis and in terms of factor scores, emphasizing how markedly Scandinavia, the Netherlands, and Switzerland differ from the rest of Europe.

At the other end of the scale, cluster number eight stands out as a group of countries that appears to be deficient in social capital. This cluster consists almost exclusively of post-communist countries that are doing relatively poorly in terms of income and speed of transition. The cluster nonetheless also includes southern Italy, thereby underlining Putnam's original contribution. However, the four-country group of Slovenia, Estonia, Hungary, and Lithuania is doing significantly better than other post-communist countries. Judged by the available information, this cluster should also include Greece and Bulgaria. In fact, this group is positioned remarkably close to the group consisting of Portugal, Belgium, and France, countries that stand out in Western Europe as having the least social capital and very high levels of centralization. One accession country, Malta, joins this cluster.

These results may have wide-ranging implications for future research. A first question requiring further investigation in more detail is why the level of social capital differs across countries. One suggestion may be the level of political decentralization. A general observation from this study is that the centralized political systems in the former communist countries may have bred corruption and low levels of social capital. In contrast, the top-ranking countries of Switzerland, The Netherlands, Scandinavia, and Iceland are all characterized by the most decentralized political systems and, consequently, the highest levels of social capital and GNIs per capita. Overall, the findings for our specific sample suggest that institutions affect social capital. In addition, the relationship between decentralization and social capital has emerged as a promising line of inquiry, which, however, reveals the need for much more rigorous empirical research in this field.

A second question that needs to be addressed is why Nordic welfare states do so well in socio-economic terms. While it could be argued that the welfare state has created social capital by reducing inequality, the observed high stock of social capital could be also be an underlying explanation why people are both happy and rich and able to sustain a welfare state.

A third question could deal with the role of public policy. How can policy makers stimulate the accumulation of social capital in a society? What are the causal relationships with other variables such as corruption? What can we learn from Switzerland, which has the highest score? How, if at all, can the countries with the highest scores in the sample serve as institutional models for countries and regions aiming to increase their future level of social capital?

However, we must end on a note of caution. Even while our use of a sample of 25 countries within the same cultural family and the same geographical region yields benefits in terms of lowering the risk of having confounding variables drive our results, it may also prove a limitation. For example, Bjørnskov (2006) suggests, on the basis of a large data set covering up to 63 countries, that social capital may have more than one dimension. Thus, one important task for future research would be to investigate how and why countries in large samples congregate into the groups we see empirically. Secondly, both Bjørnskov (2006) and Fischer (2005) use somewhat different measures than those in this paper, both arguing that social capital is multidimensional. Hence, while our findings suggest that a one-dimensional indicator is viable for the present sample of countries, future research should probably look into how robust any measure – not only ours – is to changing statistical indicators and definitions. Answering all such questions will help establish the exact importance of social capital, not only in everyday life. It may also serve to clarify the role of the state.

Acknowledgements

We are grateful for comments from colleagues and the two anonymous referees of this journal. Also, we thank the World Bank and the Danish Research Centre for Organic Food and Farming (DARKOF III) for financial assistance.

Notes

1. Social capital arguably enhances economic growth as well (Hall and Jones 1999, Whiteley 2000, Zak and Knack 2001, Woolcock 2001). As social capital reflects the ease of cooperation, it lowers transaction and monitoring costs between agents, be it general or institutional (Coleman 1988). The costs to people of undertaking informal transactions are lower, and the state saves resources because of lower monitoring and enforcement costs. Informal self-enforcement of contracts may now be possible without third party enforcement (Ostrom 1990). Also, a growing economy may in itself induce positive feedback on the level of social capital because the economic results will convince citizens that the state is working in their interest (Farr et al. 1998). The presence of social capital can thus help alleviate prisoner's dilemma-like situations and become 'the glue that holds societies together', lubricating voluntary collective action, increasing income and hence serve as an additional production factor.
2. The use of Transparency International's Corruption Perceptions Index (CPI) as a proxy for social capital is not without costs to academics. If we proceed with this approach, we cannot estimate the effects of social capital on corruption, since the same index then measures both the dependent and the

independent variables. In addition, CPI is an indicator of corruption at the country level. Should a researcher undertake an analysis of social capital at the sub-national level, another measure of social capital would have to be developed (or the researcher should assemble a group of experts at the regional level in an attempt to replicate Transparency International's methodology). At the moment, such sub-national measures only exist for Italy and the United States.
3. For other applications of cluster analysis with more technical descriptions of the method, see the appendix in Diaz-Bonilla et al. (2000). A full technical account can be found in Hair et al. (1998).
4. Unfortunately, we lack sufficient data on Greece, Malta, Cyprus, and Luxembourg. They are therefore not included in the cluster analyses. However, all but Cyprus are included in Table 3 below by relying on information from average rankings.
5. The simple correlation between the social capital factor scores and the percentage of reformed Christians is 0.72.
6. The percentage of the sample average is calculated for each country on each indicator; for economic freedom, the average is seven minus the score. The weight in Table 3 is the average of these scores. The normal procedure in cluster analysis to correct for missing values is to replace the missing value with the average score. As the four parameters that enter the formation process are highly correlated this procedure would nonetheless skew our results, as countries with missing values would seem to be closer to the average than they are when evaluated using the available data.
7. The pictures are also clear in the data as the simple correlation between factor scores and decentralization is 0.61, and between factor scores and income is 0.76, both significant at $p < 0.01$. We use the decentralization data from Fisman and Gatti (2002). Using national account data from the IMF, they code the share of total government expenditures that is politically determined in lower-tier administrations such as regional governments and municipalities.
8. The regular reports on the progress towards accession prior to the actual accession in 2004 were in three of the four cases particularly positive (see EU 2001a, b, c). The exception was Lithuania, which nonetheless made good progress in the last few years (EU 2001d). See also EU (2002).
9. The differences become clear in Bjørnskov (2003), which examines the relationship between happiness and social capital. The paper shows the important difference that France and Portugal are less happy than the countries in cluster two due to their deficiency in social capital.
10. Running the cluster analyses without civic participation, which Turkey and Romania are devoid of, reveals that these two countries would be placed in their own cluster far removed from all other countries in this survey.

References

Banfield, E., 1958, *The Moral Basis of a Backward Society* (New York: Free Press).
Beugelsdijk, S., de Groot, H. L. F. and van Schaik, A. B. T. M., 2002, *Trust and Economic Growth* (Tinbergen Institute Discussion Paper, Tilburg University).
Bjørnskov, C., 2003, The happy few. Cross-country evidence on social capital and life satisfaction, *Kyklos*, **56**, 3–16.
Bjørnskov, C., 2005, Investigations in the economics of social capital, Ph.D. Thesis, Department of Economics (Aarhus: Aarhus School of Business).
Bjørnskov, C., 2006, The multiple facets of social capital, *European Journal of Political Economy*, **22**, 22–40.
Bjørnskov, C. and Paldam, M., 2002, Corruption trends. Paper presented at the Workshop on Corruption, Göttingen, 15–16 November.
Bjørnskov, C. and Svendsen, G. T., 2003, How to measure social capital? One underlying factor. Working Paper, Department of Economics, Aarhus School of Business.
Coleman, J. S., 1988, Social capital in the creation of human capital, *American Journal of Sociology*, **94**, Supplement, S95–S120.
Dasgupta, P., 1999, Economic progress and the idea of social capital, in: P. Dasgupta and I. Serageldin (Eds) *Social Capital, A Multifaceted Perspective* (Washington, DC: The World Bank).
Diaz-Bonilla, E., Thomas, M., Robinson, S. and Cattaneo, A., 2000, Food security and trade negotiations in the World Trade Organization: a cluster analysis of country groups. TMD Discussion Paper No. 59, International Food Policy Research Institute, Washington DC.

Doig, A. and Theobald, R., 2000, *Corruption and Democratisation* (London: Frank Cass Publishers).
EU, 2001a, Regular Report on Estonia's Progress towards Accession. 13 November (Brussels: Commission of the European Communities).
EU, 2001b, Regular Report on Hungary's Progress towards Accession. 13 November (Brussels: Commission of the European Communities).
EU, 2001c, Regular Report on Slovenia's Progress towards Accession. 13 November (Brussels: Commission of the European Communities).
EU, 2001d, Regular Report on Lithuania's Progress towards Accession. 13 November (Brussels: Commission of the European Communities).
EU, 2002, Towards the enlarged Union – Commission recommends conclusion of negotiations with ten candidate countries, IP/02/1443, available at http://europa.eu.int/rapid/start/cgi/guesten.ksh?p_action.gettxt=gt&doc=IP/02/1443|0|RAPID&lg=EN (accessed 9 October 2002).
Farr, W., Ken, L., Richard, A. and Wolfenbarger, J. L., 1998, Economic freedom, political freedom, and economic well-being: a causality analysis, *Cato Journal*, **18**(2), 247–262.
Fischer, C. S., 2005, Bowling alone: what's the score?, *Social Networks*, **27**, 155–167.
Fisman, R. and Gatti, R., 2002, Decentralization and corruption: evidence across countries, *Journal of Public Economics*, **83**, 325–345.
Freedom House, 2002, http://www.freedomhouse.org/ratings/index.htm (accessed 3 September 2002).
Frey, B. and Stutzer, A., 2002, *Happiness and Economics. How the Economy and Institutions Affect Human Well-Being* (Princeton, NJ: Princeton University Press).
Fukuyama, F., 1995, *Trust: the social virtues and creation of prosperity* (London: Hamish Hamilton).
Gambetta, D., 2000, Can we trust trust?, in: D. Gambetta (Ed) *Trust: Making and Breaking Cooperative Relations* (Oxford: Department of Sociology, University of Oxford), pp. 213–237.
Hair, J. H. Jr., Andersen, R. E., Tatham, R. L. and Black, W. C., 1998, *Multivariate Data Analysis*, 5th edition (New York: Prentice-Hall).
Hall, R. E. and Jones, C. I., 1999, Why do some countries produce so much more output per worker than others?, *Quarterly Journal of Economics*, **114**(1), 83–116.
Helliwell, J. F., 2001, Social capital, the economy and well-being, in: K. Banting, A. Sharpe and F. St-Hilaire (Eds) *The Review of Economic Performance and Social Progress. The Longest Decade: Canada in the 1990s* (Montreal: Institute for Research on Public Policy).
Inglehart, R., Basañez, M. and Moreno, A., 1998, *Human Values and Beliefs. A Cross-Cultural Sourcebook* (Ann Arbor: University of Michigan Press).
Knack, S., 2002, Social capital and the quality of government: evidence from the U.S. states, *American Journal of Political Science*, **46**(4), 772–785.
Knack, S. and Keefer, P., 1997, Does social capital have an economic payoff? A cross-country investigation, *Quarterly Journal of Economics*, **107**(4), 1252–1288.
la Porta, R., Lopez-de-Silanes, F., Schleifer, A. and Vishny, R., 1998, *The Quality of Government*, NBER Working Paper no. 6727 (Cambridge MA: National Bureau of Economic Research (NBER)).
Nannestad, P., Svendsen, G. L. H. and Svendsen, G. T., forthcoming 2007, Bridge over troubled water? Migration and social capital, *Journal of Ethnic and Migration Studies*.
Narayan, D. and Cassidy, M. F., 2001, A dimensional approach to measuring social capital: development and validation of a social capital inventory, *Current Sociology*, **49**(2), 59–105.
Offe, C., 2004, Political corruption, in: J. Kornai and S. Rose-Ackerman (Eds) *Building a Trustworthy State in Post-Socialist Transition* (New York: Palgrave MacMillan), pp. 77–96.
Ostrom, E., 1990, *Governing the Commons: The Evolution of Institutions for Collective Action* (New York: Cambridge University Press).
Paldam, M., 2000, Social capital: one or many? Definition and measurement, *Journal of Economic Surveys*, **14**(5), 629–653 (Special Issue on Political Economy).
Paldam, M., 2001, Corruption and religion. Adding to the economic model, *Kyklos*, **54**(2/3), 383–414.
Paldam, M. and Svendsen, G. T., 2000, An essay on social capital: looking for the fire behind the smoke, *European Journal of Political Economy*, **16**, 339–366.
Paldam, M. and Svendsen, G. T., 2002, Missing social capital and the transition in Eastern Europe, *Journal of Institutional Innovation, Development and Transition*, **5**, 21–34.
Putnam, R., 1993, *Making Democracy Work. Civic Traditions in Modern Italy* (Princeton, NJ: Princeton University Press).
Reynolds, S., 1984, *Kingdoms and Communities in Western Europe, 900–1300* (Oxford: Clarendon Press).

Rose, R. and Mishler, W., 1998, *Untrustworthy Institutions and Popular Response,* Studies in Public Policy No. 306 (Glasgow: University of Strathclyde).
Rose-Ackerman, S., 2001, Trust and honesty in post-socialist societies, *Kyklos,* **54**(2/3), 415–444.
Rothstein, B., 2005, *Social Traps and the Problem of Trust* (Cambridge: Cambridge University Press).
Schjødt, E. B. and Svendsen, G. T., 2002, Transition to market economy in Eastern Europe: interest groups and political institutions in Russia, *Nordic Journal of Political Economy,* **28**(2), 181–194.
Stolle, D., 2002, Social capital – an emerging concept, in: B. Hobson, J. Lewis and B. Siim (Eds) *Key Concepts in Gender and European Social Politics* (Cheltenham: Edward Elgar).
Svendsen, G. T., 2003, *Political Economy of the European Union: Institutions, Policy and Economic Growth* (Cheltenham: Edward Elgar).
Svendsen, G. L. H. and Svendsen, G. T., 2005, *The Creation and Destruction of Social Capital: Entrepreneurship, Co-operative Movements and Institutions* (Cheltenham: Edward Elgar).
Thränhardt, D., 2004, Immigrant cultures, state policies and social capital formation in Germany, *Journal of Comparative Policy Analysis,* **6**, 159–183.
Transparency International, 2001, http://www.transparency.org/sourcebook/index.html (accessed 3 September 2002).
Treisman, D., 2000, The causes of corruption: a cross-national study, *Journal of Public Economics,* **76**, 399–457.
Tullock, G., 1967, The welfare costs of monopolies, tariffs and theft, *Western Economic Journal,* **5**, 224–232.
Uslaner, E. M., 2001, Trust and corruption. Paper presented at the Conference on Political Scandals, Past and Present, University of Salford, 21–23 June.
Van Schaik, Ton, 2002, Social capital in the European Values Surveys. Prepared for the OECD-ONS International Conference on Social Capital Measurement, London, 25–27 September.
WDR, 1996, *World Development Report 1996. From Plan to Market* (Washington DC: The World Bank).
Weber, M., [1930] 1992, *The Protestant Ethic and the Spirit of Capitalism* (London: Harper Collins).
Whiteley, P., 2000, Economic growth and social capital, *Political Studies,* **48**, 443–466.
Woolcock, M., 2001, The place of social capital in understanding social and economic outcomes, *ISUMA – Canadian Journal of Policy Research,* **2**(1), 11–17.
Zak, P. and Knack, S., 2001, Trust and growth, *The Economic Journal,* **111**(470), 295–321.

Appendix

A number of tests consisting of excluding one of the parameters entering the cluster formation process were performed on the nine-cluster taxonomy to assess its robustness. The results are reported in Table A1, where column 1 reports the taxonomy used in the paper. It should be noted that the cluster numbers may shift between columns.

Table A1. Robustness tests

	Full process	Without corruption	Without economic freedom	Without generalized trust	Without Putnam's Instrument	Weight
Switzerland	1	7	1	1	5	2.243
Netherlands	4	8	4	3	4	1.667
Denmark	4	4	4	6	4	1.484
Sweden	4	4	4	4	4	1.451
Norway	4	4	4	4	4	1.448
Finland	6	6	6	6	4	1.414
Iceland	5	5	5	4	5	1.273
Luxembourg					10	1.088
Germany	2	1	2	8	1	1.075

(continued)

Table A1. (*Continued*)

	Full process	Without corruption	Without economic freedom	Without generalized trust	Without Putnam's Instrument	Weight
Ireland	2	1	2	8	1	1.067
Northern Italy	3	5	3	8	3	1.063
Belgium	7	2	7	7	7	1.019
Austria	2	1	2	8	1	1.011
United Kingdom	2	2	2	8	10	1.005
Spain	3	1	3	7	3	0.957
France	7	3	7	7	7	0.856
Slovenia	9	3	9	5	9	0.839
Portugal	7	3	7	7	7	0.803
Estonia	9	3	9	5	9	0.801
Bulgaria					6	0.762
Lithuania	9	3	9	9	9	0.736
Greece					6	0.721
Poland	8	9	8	9	6	0.698
Hungary	9	3	9	5	9	0.695
Czech Republic	8	3	8	2	6	0.687
Latvia	8	9	8	2	8	0.640
Slovakia	8	9	8	2	8	0.612
Southern Italy	8	9	8	2	8	0.603
Romania					8	0.543
Turkey					8	0.423

Table A2. Distances between cluster centres

Cluster	1	2	3	4	5	6	7	8	9
1		40.63	43.01	39.91	**36.22**	41.91	47.67	68.09	56.06
2	40.63		**10.39**	33.87	16.83	32.79	15.17	43.51	27.52
3	43.01	**10.39**		29.82	20.90	31.86	18.83	42.17	27.49
4	39.91	33.87	29.82		23.53	**11.65**	47.38	70.55	56.68
5	36.22	**16.83**	20.90	23.53		18.31	31.80	60.09	44.23
6	41.91	32.79	31.86	**11.65**	18.31		47.73	73.87	58.79
7	47.67	15.17	18.83	47.38	31.80	47.73		29.37	**13.31**
8	68.09	43.51	42.17	70.55	60.09	73.87	29.37		**16.13**
9	56.06	27.52	27.49	56.68	44.23	58.79	**13.31**	16.13	

Note: the average of the distances is 36.89. The minimum distance from a given cluster to any other is marked in bold.

Table A1 clearly shows that the main results are resistant to small changes in the cluster formation process. The Northern Lights group – Switzerland, the Netherlands, Scandinavia and Iceland – always remain together and with the exception of excluding corruption when northern Italy is clustered with Iceland, the group also remains closed. The same stability can be observed for southern Italy, Latvia and Slovakia which remain clustered in all cases, and for Estonia, Slovenia, Lithuania and Hungary which remain clustered except one case where Lithuania is removed. Hence, the clusters reported in the paper are satisfactorily robust.

Table A3. Cluster characteristics

Cluster number	GNI per capita	GDP growth	Openness	Generalized trust	Corruption index	Freedom House index	Decentralisation	Percentage reformed	Civic participation	Factor score	Weight	Life satisfaction	Intra-cluster Ward variance	Standard deviation of intra-cluster distance
1	30,350	1.6	63.7	42.6	8.4	1.0	0.51	43.4	46.6	1.77	2.63	86.0	0.0	0.0
2	25,085	4.2	72.2	40.2	7.8	1.3	0.30	25.2	7.6	0.16	1.04	72.3	74.1	1.77
3	23,766	1.8	21.9	40.8	7.2	1.5	0.23	0.3	5.4	−0.13	1.02	33.0	32.6	0.0
4	26,705	2.9	69.8	60.6	9.0	1.0	0.35	76.0	13.7	1.40	1.66	83.3	142.9	2.03
5	28,770	4.8	53.6	43.6	9.2	1.0	0.23	96.6	11.4	0.93	1.34	85.0	0.0	0.0
6	24,610	4.6	60.3	62.7	9.9	1.0	0.39	93.2	10.7	1.34	1.52	79.0	0.0	0.0
7	22,950	2.8	79.5	26.0	6.5	1.3	0.14	1.5	6.7	−0.33	0.85	67.0	63.6	1.27
8	12,411	2.8	69.0	23.9	3.7	1.5	0.23	5.5	3.8	−1.16	0.53	39.4	66.8	0.77
9	11,365	3.2	108.5	25.0	5.2	1.5	0.24	23.4	4.9	−0.81	0.70	45.0	46.0	0.80
South	14,697	2.9	87.8	24.8	4.9	1.5	0.21	10.5	4.9	−0.83	—	48.2	1904.9	5.43
North	26,032	3.3	60.7	48.7	8.4	1.2	0.33	49.1	12.7	0.77	—	72.2	4672.9	5.55
Average	20,042	3.5	76.4	37.6	6.7	1.3	0.26	30.6	9.0	0.00	1.00	65.4	—	—

Cultural Theory: The Neglected Variable in the Craft of Policy Analysis

IRIS GEVA-MAY

ABSTRACT *This article discusses the role of the craft of policy analysis in public policymaking and, relating to cultural theory, provides a causal explanation for differences and nuances in the craft of policy analysis. Two perspectives underlie this article: The first is the role of policy analysis in policymaking; the second concerns cultural theory and its contribution to policy analysis. While highlighting the role of culture in policy analysis, the article suggests that in order to improve policy analysis processes, policy analysis studies and policy analysis training should take into account cultural factors. Finally, in view of the scarcity of studies in this domain, this article suggests a rationale for studies that enhance the understanding of how political cultures interfere with normative policy analysis and proposes an agenda for research on policy analysis craft by cultural bias.*

Introduction

Capturing context is an important element in policy analysis and policy design. Yet literature fails to elaborate seminal ideas into a well-developed basis for culture-sensitive policy analysis craft. I claim that in the policy process one should adapt normative systematic methods (i.e., policy analysis) to context (i.e., culture) in order to maximize "social utility" and to increase "policy utility," to use Klitgaard's terms (1998a, p. 195), in given cultural conditions. Hoppe (1993) contends that policy analysis, like any form of political judgment, is a special form of mediation between universal principles and local particulars, which are inescapably culturally "biased." Bobrow and Dryzek (1989) argue that "the policy field is currently marked by an extraordinary variety of technical approaches" or frames of reference. They list analytic policy methods inspired by welfare economics, public choice, social structure, information processing, and political/legal philosophy. Arguing that each analytic policy frame of reference only works well in a particular type of "environment," they try to develop the beginning of a contingency theory of reasoned selection-in-context of analytic policy methods.

The aim of the present article is to start a dialogue on the subject and to propose a related research agenda. The article highlights policy analysis conceptualizations and cultural theory impacts and implications for the policy analysis process. The hypothesis is that a culturally tuned policy analysis provides more adequate solutions to policy problems. In today's global village, cultural awareness and an understanding of impacts on policy processes are needed to foster harmonization, convergence, and accommodation of different policymaking styles, integration of policies and regulations, efficient negotiation, or investment orientations. Identifying cultural biases interfering with the policy courses of action can allow us to propose ways of treating and manipulating these biases for the benefit of the policy process.

Policy analysis

Prevailing policy analysis theory maintains that although good policymaking may be based on good intuition and creativity, it should adhere to systematic approaches, namely, policy analysis methodology. While policy analysis implies intensive and professional filtering of data for systematic policy planning, policy analysis methodology and craft rely on the mainstream academic literature, which is mainly American. However, while the American market is replete with a range of established policy analysis models, very few of these are sufficiently sensitive to varying cultures and susceptible to delivery of culture-sensitive skills. For instance, these models have typically failed to address cultural plurality either within American policy analysis or within West- and East-European or Far Eastern topics or craft variations (Mac Rae and Wilde, 1979; Weimer and Vining, 1989; Patton and Sawicki, 1993; Dye, 1995; Bardach, 1996, 2001; Geva-May and Wildavsky, 1997, 2001). While policy analysis pedagogy has created an extremely large market for skills-related material, which is currently adopted at face value or not adopted at all, the market remains largely unsatisfied. Problem definition in Singapore, alternative choice in Central Europe, and argumentation in Canada differ conceptually, so the craft tools employed should be different from those prescribed by American experts. Readymade recipes are not necessarily the best solution for all in every national or institutional context or at any given time (Rotmans and de Vries, 1997; Klitgaard, 1998a, 1998b; Geva-May, 1998, 1999; Hoppe and Grin, 2000).

Political cultures and cultural bias

Clearly, culture is part of the database or contextual anatomy for policymaking. Landes in his renowned *Wealth and Poverty of Nations* (1998) attributes much of the causal impacts to culture; so does the special issue of the *European Journal of Political Economy* dedicated to Economic Consequences of Political Culture (Hillman and Swank, 2000). Management and related choices in policymaking, including policy analysis, cannot escape political cultures and related cultural biases. Thompson, Ellis, and Wildavsky argue that "an organizational act is rational if it supports one's organizational culture, one's way of life" (1990, p. 276). Cultural theory is the study of formal institutions and of the informal behavior that has inspired them (Thompson et al., 1992), and therefore, it explains cultural bias as the formation of preferences. Culture is part of a given social context and implies negotiation, consequence, and cause. Accordingly, the policy analysis craft aspects of policy analysis methodology should differ inherently in different contexts.

What is cultural bias and how should it be included in craft considerations? Why haven't applications of scientific models of culture or culture-by-policy interactions been tested and developed in policy studies? What is the impact of allowing culture to become a neglected variable in the policy analysis process? What policy analysis craft procedures are more vulnerable, and how can they be manipulated in various cultural contexts? These questions will be partly answered in this article and partly left open-ended for further discussion and inquiry.

Conceptual background: context and culture

Policy analysis

Although the craft of policy analysis is generally presented as a methodological pattern of spatial value for systematic policymaking (Weimer, 1993; Weimer and Vining, 1989; Patton and Savicky, 1989; Geva-May with Wildavsky, 1997/2001; Bardach, 1992, 1996, 2000; Behn, 1981, 1978; etc.), it is very much culture bound and should be adapted accordingly in different contexts. As much as craft patterns seek to provide objective tools, subjective experiences in the social context are bound to create different craft nuances. Majone (1989), Wildavsky (1979, 1989), and others, in reference to the skills of the policy analyst, assert that his/her craft relies heavily on personal judgment and interpretation, experience, and professional norms determined by the contextual culture. The "client," through his/her own prism of cultural dissemination, also requires solutions based on apt contextual norms and values. Hence, culturally feasible policy analysis processes are impacted by and should be sensitive to cultural bias in the process of using tricks-of-the-trade and relaying alternatives to policymakers. Feasible policy alternatives can be selected, and effective implementation venues can be determined, only if "nuances" or deviations in the craft of policy analysis induced by local culture are allowed for.

As long ago as the 1950s, Lasswell was adamant that "context mattered," but this viewpoint was largely discredited by behaviorists and economists. Culture fell into the category of a "variable not considered." This is probably the reason why Western-oriented analysis has not taken hold in countries outside the occidental orbit. Max Weber's long chapter on "'Objectivity' in Social Science and Social Policy" in his *The Methodology of the Social Sciences* discusses the "cultural sciences" and how culture influences what social scientists study, although not the scientific method itself. By analogy, culture influences what policy analysts may have to study and adapt within a certain context, although not the policy analysis method itself. Currently, debates with "postpositivists" who take a cultural perspective within the national context are ongoing. Class, sex, race, and other characteristics are seen as defining cultures that shape perceptions and "realities." Although some may argue against the postpositivist approach, considerations of culture are a valuable development in the overall outlook of policy studies.

In international development, examples of policy domains in which culture should have been taken into account are plentiful. According to World Bank reports, given the same economic input, some programs fail and others do not. Why do the same economic models and financial investments succeed or go amiss in different contexts? This question brings to mind Robert Solow's warning that "construct economics as an axiomatically based hard science is doomed to fail" (1986, p. 21). Along the same lines, Huddleston, in his *Public Administration Review* article on public administration consultancy in Bosnia, cautioned that "anatomy should be learnt before doing surgery" (1999). Clearly, culture is part of that contextual "anatomy." This recognition relates to Lasswell's (1971) belief in the importance of acquiring maximum rational judgment of the elements involved in policymaking and Hoppe's view that, in producing viable policy recommendations, the policy analysis process should "mobilize the best available knowledge" (in the) "desire to tackle problems on the political agenda successfully" (1999, p. 201).

True stories are readily available, and they all shed light on the involvement of cultural bias in policymaking and policy implementation and the omission of cultural concerns in policy considerations. One such story was related in November 1999 in Washington, D.C., by a World Bank official. It involves an investment policy in the Kosovo region in the 1999s aimed at raising the living standard of the people in that region. De facto, the development of the railway there actually reduced the employment level of the region's population, and welfare problems started to surface. Asked about this, the project leader who planned and implemented the work replied simply, "I am a railway engineer, not a social scientist."

According to *Euromoney*, February 1999, the "new scapegoat for the emerging market crisis is the Asian corporate which overborrowed cheap dollars/foreign currency and expanded too fast without considerations of the risks." Standard value-at-risk analysis was a completely missing element in most corporate treasuries; no account was taken of the likely impacts of devaluation, and the treasuries ran up unsustainable debts. Followers of the Mary Douglas or Wildavsky cultural theories may identify a risk-taking culture. Inversely, Jerome Booth, a director at ANZ Investment Bank, cautions that "what is incorrect is this idea that all emerging markets are the same and that there are universal rules that can be learnt from (the Asian) crisis."

In international development, we know of many evaluation projects attempting to assess the efficiency of programs or effectiveness of investments. Nevertheless, Klitgaard (1998a) asserts that such evaluations clearly become biased, and the assessment feedback invalid, if they ignore the fact that (1) programs' effects may be biased unless sociocultural settings are controlled for, (2) successful adoption of programs depends on tailoring the program to the social setting, and (3) receiving valid evaluation feedback depends on ways of eliciting local knowledge.

Klitgaard (1998a, 1998b) also presents a number of studies that shed light on the importance of considering the cultural context in policy analysis. One such case is the Kamehameha Elementary Education Program in Hawaii, where a literacy policy was carried out through a course of action (reading aloud) that conflicted with scolding patterns at home. Only later in the process was it discovered that indirect praise of a child and praise for the group were more effective than spotlighting by direct praise (as advocated in Western societies). Vogt, Jordan, and Tharp (1987; quoted in Klitgaard, pp. 139–140) argue that ethnographic research is needed in order to present appropriate alternatives and avoid "relatively narrow-range mismatches or incompatibilities between... national culture and the culture of the school."

Another example is recorded by Epstein (1988; cited in Klitgaard, 1998a, p. 27) and concerns the policy of the Agricultural Department in Karnataka, India, which targeted the introduction of new weeding tools. An understanding of the culture would have avoided policy failure. Farmers opposed the policy because tradition obliges them to provide their Harijan (Untouchable) clients with a minimal level of subsistence: even if one employed fewer people, one would still have to give them charity. The 1991 UNESCO report on a birth spacing policy introduced in the Kisli district of Kenya in the 1970s revealed that "inadequate attention had been paid to socio-cultural factors" (qouted in Klitgaard, 1998b, p. 196). While women became interested in the related program, their husbands and especially their mothers-in-law opposed the policy. Eventually it was learned that this opposition was based on the belief that "after death people enter the spirit world and hover over their living family members to protect and provide guidance." The document concludes that in family planning policies, cultural norms, i.e., approaching key family members, must be adopted.

A number of European studies shed light on the impact of culture on policy processes in a variety of settings. Richardson (1982) has shown the importance of national policy styles in Europe. In the Netherlands, Koppenjan et al. (1987) have documented the cultural differences between policy styles of national departments. In one Dutch department, Jeliazkova and Hoppe (1997) replicated Durning and Osuna's (1994) American study for the Netherlands. They observed systemically different conceptions of professional identities and roles and systemic differences in beliefs and attitudes, for instance, about argument presentation and policy advocacy. Most importantly, their subjects either appeared to be unaware of these differences or assumed that everyone looks at these topics from the same perspective. Hoppe and Grin (1999, 2000) have shown how technology assessment experts working for different national parliaments in Europe bend their analytic practices to political opportunity structures largely shaped by national political and scientific institutions and cultures. Ellis and Thompson (1997) edited *Culture Matters* and brought together a number of studies related to policy and culture.

From theory to practice: the craft of policy analysis and cultural bias

Policy analysis

Dunn (1994) formally defined policy analysis as an applied social science discipline that uses multiple research methods in a context of argumentation, public debate, and political struggle in order to create, critically evaluate, and communicate policy-relevant knowledge. Following well-established empirical theory about the practice of policy analysis (MacRae and Wilde, 1979; Mintzberg et al., 1976; Weimer and Vining, 1989; Patton and Sawicki, 1989; Geva-May and Wildavsky, 1997, 2000; Bardach, 1996, 2001), we distinguish a number of universal policy analytic routines or craft components: assessing the policymaking context; problem definition; modeling the problem area; selection of policy alternatives; policy argumentation, selection, and presentation; and implementation design.

Becker regards craftsmanship as a combination of knowledge and skills leading to expertise:

> One who has mastered the skills—an expert—has great control over the craft's materials, can do anything with them, can work with speed and agility, can do with ease things that ordinary, less expert craftsmen find difficult or impossible... [Although] the specific object of virtuosity varies from field to field... it always involves an extraordinary control of materials and techniques (1978, p. 865).

And, as long ago as 1989, Majone asserted that:

> ...analysis is best appreciated in relation to the craft aspects of the field while the craft skills of an analyst are a repertoire of procedures and judgments that are partly personal and partly social and depend as much on his own experience as on professional norms.and culturally determined criteria of adequacy and validity (p. 3).

According to this analysis, culturally good policy analysis processes should be sensitive to craft nuances. Moreover, policy analysis tricks-of-the-trade are "better ways of doing things" if "professional norms and culturally determined criteria of adequacy and validity" are allowed. The importance of craft mastery is even greater in policy analysis than in other areas of inquiry because its conclusions cannot be proved correct or incorrect according to any axiomatic standards; instead, it must satisfy generally accepted criteria of adequacy in relation to stages, procedures, and heresthetics (Majone, 1989, p. 3). To meet these criteria, craft procedures should be sensitive to inherent cultural bias.

Despite this conceptualization, while recent policy analysis literature has been concerned with the meaning of "good analysis" and has indicated craft aspects of policy analysis (Bardach, 1996, 2001; Weimer, 1993, 1992; Weimer and Vining, 1989; Wildavsky, 1979; etc.), de facto, very few studies or materials are concerned with deviations due to cultural bias and intervening cultural variables in professional policy analysis. Studies by MacRae (1979), Majone (1989), Wildavsky (1979, 1993), Meltsner (1976), Weimer (1992, 1993), Lynn (1998), and others certainly endorse Becker's statement cited above, but do not go a step further to provide methodological guidelines. Geva-May with Wildavsky (1997, 2000), who presented a methodology based on the prevailing policy analysis' chief principles of the last 30 years, concur with Majone's (1989) view of policy analysis craft aspects but conclude that there is not a clear conception of the skills or craft.

Craft prototypes provide the analyst with devices for various purposes and at varying levels of sophistication: classification of concepts and approaches, of tools, data, argumentation, recommendations, and others. Yet much is left to the style of the craftsman in determining his analysis. Craftsmanship comprises the cultural biases in which the policy analyst has been immersed as well as awareness of the cultural context. In support of this assumption, Thompson et al. (1990) assert that the "cultural premise is that rational people support their way of life" and so "... given the premises involved in defining that social environment, certain distinctive values and belief systems will follow as necessary for the legitimation of actions taken within it" (p. 247). Moreover, if we accept the assumption that "the interaction of individual subjects produces a public cosmology capable of being internalized in the consciousness of individuals, if they decide to accept and stay with it..." (p. 200), then the way analysts determine their analysis is closely related to their use of reason, their perceptions, their craft preferences, the way they eventually create problems or choose alternatives, and their interactions with politics, clients, and recipients in order to support the way of life in which they are immersed.

Long ago, Meltsner (1972, 1976) differentiated the technician and expert from the politician with regard to policy analysts' skills, roles, and values. Ideal-type models followed, advocated by Jenkins-Smith (1982), Cook and Vaupel (1985), Torgerson (1986), Jennings (1987a), Weimer and Vining (1992), and Durning and Osuna (1994). Scholars have constantly sought to present guidelines for policy analysis methodology leading to expertise. Definitions of policy analysis found in the literature relate to courses of action or inaction, namely, positions, stances, or political decisions that stress goals, means, values, and practices (Cochran and Malone, 1995; Dye, 1995; Lasswell and Kaplan, 1970; Pal, 1992).

The very terminology used to define policy analysis implies that policy analysis involves biases.

According to Lindblom's first allusion to policy analysis, this process has been regarded as "a type of quantitative analysis involving comparisons and interactions of *values* and politics" (1958, p. 298). Wildavsky termed it *"creating* problems that can be solved" (1979, p. 1), and MacRae and Wilde regarded it as "the use of *reason* and evidence *to choose* the best policy among a number of alternatives" (p. 14). Whether the definition is "a problem-solving process" (Bardach, 1992, p. 1) or "client-oriented advice relevant to public decisions" (Weimer and Vining, 1989, p. 1), the process of policy analysis is closely dependent on cultural bias, since values, reasoning in the creation of problems, or problem-solving strategies are wide open to cultural interference.

Especially the first step, policy problem identification and definition, is by no means an objective operation, but rather a projection of frames of reference onto the negotiated reality around which action is taken.[1] These references are bound not only to personality but also to cultural bias. Likewise, the stage of choice of alternatives and implementation relates to projected alternatives chosen to address the given existent or conceived problem. Approaches to argumentation, or adherence to types of models, cannot escape the test of context feasibility. This test is inherently locus and culture bound. For instance, approaches to policy analysis in some U.K. contexts today increasingly start with the assumption that all voices should be heard. This assumption implies "clumsy solutions" but ones that would harness the constructive engagement of those voices. This craft approach has been currently instituted by Britain's Health and Safety Executive and acknowledged by the British Government Cabinet.

Examples of the need for divergent approaches in policy analysis methodology at its various stages (Problem Definition, Modeling and Criteria Choice, Alternative Choice, Argumentation, and Implementation) clearly show that, at each stage, reactions differ in different cultural contexts. These may be, but need not be, nationality related. Problem definition in the United States would be market oriented; in Vietnam, it would be ideology oriented. Alternative choice in certain FSU (former Soviet Union) states or South America would be influenced by a pinch of corruption and/or would not permit recommendations that would threaten the status of the corrupt organization leaders. In Cuba, one cannot recommend alternatives that would hint at criticism of Fidel Castro. The mullahs in Iran would not consider Western policy analysis recommendations that contradict their interpretation of Koran and Sharia. In Japan or China, clients would shy away from expressing their opinions about the problem and would be adverse to confrontational and argumentative discussions. In certain Western and Central European and South American languages, there is no word for "policy." A key concept such as policy analysis would be rendered by the French as *analyse politique*, which has completely different connotations and implications. How can the "normative" craft of policy analysis be applied to nonexistent conceptual entities? How can craft methods be transferred or adapted to missing concepts?

Indeed, in Europe, policy analysis methodology has not as yet succeeded in finding its way, de facto, into policymaking processes. Cultural differences arising from European pluralism play a vital role. French ENA-trained policy professionals excepted, most European governments do not recruit academically trained policy analysts but rely rather on "sectorial experts," who learn the policy analytic tricks of the trade on the job. Thus, more than in the United States, European policy analysis rests on a mix of mystery and mastery transferred on the job from one generation of analysts to another. This situation does not mean that policy analysis is not undertaken in Europe; rather, for most European policy analysts, knowledge and professional skill are on an unarticulated, tacit level of experience. Cultural factors loom large in such "knowledge." Biases are obvious. European scholars warn us that

> This character of policy analytic knowledge, skills and craft-aspects and the policy analysis styles are an irreproducible mixture of mystery and mastery learnt on the job, and influenced by cultural bias and most often not fully recognized by the other member states, is bound to affect Europe's image as capable of good governance and steering (Hoppe, 2000).

Cultural theory

Culture is not an inexplicable deus ex machina free of social context. The newly arising interest in political cultures is leading to awareness that institutions are not divorced from preferences, values, and beliefs; that social relations differ and become meaningful through shared beliefs and values; and that they are tied to norms and modes of perception (Douglas, 1982; Eckstein, 1988; Ellis and Thompson, 1997; Inglehart, 1988; Schwartz and Thompson, 1990; Thompson et al., 1990, 1992; Wildavsky, 1989; Klitgaard, 1998a, 1998b; Hoppe, 2000; etc.). Cultural theory explains formal institutions and the informal behaviors that keep them going through preference formation (Thompson et al., 1992). In explaining preference formation and its operational outcomes in general, and in policy-making in particular, an important aspect is the conception that societies are composed of multiple cultural categories. The characteristics of these cultural categories and/or amalgam affect rationality in decision-making. When political power contests are involved at the policymaking level, culture implies negotiation, consequence, and cause (Hall, 1986, p. 34; Thompson et al., 1992.)

Unlike Almond and Verba (1963) or Banfield (1958), who in their classic works regard culture as a causal force upon institutions, Barry (1970) views political culture as the direct by-product of living under democratic institutions. So does Pizzorno (1966) in his criticism of Banfield's work. In this context, the widely accepted definitions of political cultures regard culture as consisting of values, beliefs, norms, and assumptions, namely, "mental products" (Pye, 1968, p. 218).

In this context, the conceptualization of political culture ranges from "national character" (Benedict, 1934, 1946; Gorer, 1948, 1955; Mead, 1942, 1953) and classifications of parochial, participant, and subject typologies at the level of nation-states (Almond and Verba, 1963) to the myths of life and group-grid theory advocated by Mary Douglas (1970, 1982) and taken up by Thompson et al. (1990). These authors regard political cultures not only as mental products but also as values "justifying relationships indissolubly bound together" (Thompson et al., 1990, p. 508), i.e., "political" or "power" struggles. While political culture is not passed down through the generations without change and is constantly negotiated, societies represent a composition of multiple cultural categories that are not necessarily related to country or nation (Dogan, 1988; Douglas and Wildavsky, 1983; Thompson et al., 1992). For instance, the way people perceive, accept, or reject anger, risk, technology, etc., implies cultural biases that are not necessarily nation bound. "There are more similarities in the beliefs of a French and German social democrat than between a French socialist and a French conservative..." (Dogan, 1988, p. 3). These beliefs influence political culture, i.e., the framework for the formation of preferences. Therefore, political cultures are "patterns of orientation to political action" (Thompson et al., 1990, p. 216) and imply power relations. These may range over orientation towards government, casting an economic vote, child-parent or employer-employee exchanges, etc.

I prefer to adhere to the definition of culture coined by Mary Douglas (1970, 1982) and adopted by Thompson et al. (1990, 1992) because this article is concerned with how cultural factors impact policy analysis procedures (the six policy analysis stages and their craft routines or craft components, see Figure 1). A multiple-case comparison across policy sectors and across countries and institutional policymaking styles can be achieved only by using a cultural theory that can lend itself to comparative study and analysis. Grid-group cultural theory[2] is judged by many to be a promising attempt at formulating a nomothetic cultural theory, that is, a theory regarding general regularities of culture, irrespective of time and place (Douglas and Wildavsky, 1983; Thompson, Ellis, and Wildavsky, 1990; Thompson and Ellis, 1997; Hood, 1997; Mamadouh, 1999). Since it allows for change and for degrees of intensity varying with role and time, grid-group cultural theory provides a useful approach to the comparison of policymaking styles. Its four ideal-typical ways of life are hypothetical candidates for the formal universale in a general theory of culture (Eckstein, 1997). Group-grid cultural theory specifies cultural biases that are not necessarily nation specific. National political cultures and policy styles, rather, are conceptualized by group-grid cultural theory as path-dependent configurations of universal cultural types. Thus, group-grid cultural theory and its cultural prototypes offer good opportunities for cross-sector and cross-national comparative cultural analysis (Hood, 1997).

Culture, according to this conceptualization, is a way of life and cultural biases that are dictated by sets of shared norms, symbols, beliefs, and behaviors, and are constantly being negotiated and probed by individuals (Thompson et al., 1990, p. 1) or stable orientations to action (Eckstein, 1988, p. 790) or dispositions/habitus (Bourdieu, 1998, p. 6). Cultural bias is "an array of beliefs locked together into relational patterns...The beliefs must be treated as part of the action and not separated from it..." (Thompson et al., 1990, p. 199). Like all cultural theories, group-grid cultural theory anchors cultural bias in fundamentally different myths of nature and the (gendered) body[3] and human nature. The group and grid matrix is constituted according to the interaction of the ways of life of the individual, his/her group, and the surrounding social environment. This interaction, according to the theory, creates four main cultural categories, namely individualist (Thompson et al., 1990, pp. 34–35), fatalist (Schmutzer, 1994; Douglas, 1996, pp. 183–187), hierarchist (Douglas and Wildavsky, 1983, pp. 90–92), and egalitarian (Douglas, 1986, pp. 38–40).

	Range of Hierarchical bias	Range of Egalitarian/ enclavist bias	Range of Individualist bias	Range of Fatalist's bias
Policymaking context/setting				
Problem identification and definition				
Modeling the problem area and criteria choice				
Policy alternatives and feasibility implications				
Policy advocacy and argumentation				
Implementation design				

Figure 1. Policy analysis by cultural bias. This figure was initially submitted to PIRL, 1999, and was presented at Carleton University Colloquia, Ottawa, in 1998 and at the Canadian Studies Conference, Jerusalem, in 2000.

Corresponding to these four types of social relationships—group-grid cultural theory's fundamental claim—are *cultural biases* (in our case, affecting policy analysis processes):

> The guiding assumption is that judgments of value emerge as justifications of distinctive forms of organization...Furthermore, that there are only a limited number of possible organizations, and also that each develops its own cultural set, a cognitive and moral bias that contributes to reflexivity to the social organization, affects conceptions of time and space, and the functioning of memory (Douglas, gridgroup. listserv, March 10, 1998).

Similarly, Thompson (1990, p. 276) regards the rationality of organizational acts as the degree to which those acts support organizational culture, and Coyle suggests that "... the match between organization[s] and the environment is the key issue... " (1997, p. 65).

Culture, policy analysis and organizational arrangements

Hence, when a policy analyst makes a certain choice, at any stage of the policy analysis process, his/her use of analysis strategies, conceptualization of policymaking strategies, use of tools and techniques, and attitude toward opportunity and political forces are sustained, justified, and legitimized through immersion-related beliefs and values. These will vary according to the prisms through which ideas of nature and related ways of life are filtered and adopted by the analyst in a given environment (Geva-May, 1999). Therefore, it can be claimed that culture, through the distinctive features that support a certain way of life, makes a major impact on who interprets what, when, and why, and on how these factors affect policy analysis and related decision-making. In this context, ways of life have a distinctive cultural bias that justifies a distinctive pattern of social relations (Douglas, 1970, 1982; Douglas and Wildavsky, 1983; Thompson et al., 1990) and policy interpretations. This conclusion, in turn, demonstrates that customs, perception, conceptualization, and craft depend on cultural affiliation, namely, on attitudes toward various ways of life as frames of reference that may be, but need not necessarily be, nationality related.

Let's take the Israeli case. As long ago as 1968, Dror asserted that the lack of strong public administrative institutions in Israel, especially norms of systematic policy accountability and planning, could be attributed to the troubles that beset the new state, to the lack of an administrative tradition, and to culture. Pragmatism; the limited influence of experts and academia; the politicization of public service, including political appointments; and norms formerly present in the various Jewish agencies prior to the establishment of the state of Israel, i.e., "getting around" the law, "helping" one's friends, "naive socialism" (Weinshall and Kfir, 1994), improvisation, and ambiguity (Sharkansky, 1997), all became part of the so-called public administration and policymaking patterns (see Dror, 1971; Downs and Larkey, 1986; Nachmias and Rosenbloom, 1978; Galnoor et al., 1998; Geva-May, 1999).

R.D. Putnam's *Making Democracy Work* (1993) provides another example, one that evidently supports an argument that northern and southern Italy are culturally distinct. His study on Italy's experience in the 1970s regarding the decentralization of government functions found that a predictor of good governance was provinces' civic *culture*, expressed by civic attitudes, voting behavior, civic associations, etc. Furthermore, historical data on the nature and density of those associations permitted a longitudinal analysis that showed that causation ran from civic culture to economic growth to effective local government (Klitgaard, 1998a, p. 136). Similarly, Gow et al. (1989), with reference to economic development projects, comment on the compatibility of the project with the sociocultural environment into which it is introduced.

From the public administration/management point of view, and as a part of a "way of life," institutional arrangements are inherent parts of the interrelational triangle of policymaking, political cultures, and institutional arrangements. This association is almost axiomatic, since institutions are not divorced from values and beliefs, and policies are made within and by institutions. Institutions are shaped by culture and shape culture in return, while policies and contextual systems adapt to culture and culture to contextual systems. While interdependent and interrelated, each undergoes its own dynamic of change and imposes changes on the other (see Figure 2).

What are institutional arrangements? They are entities that may include constitutional/political/organizational arrangements, i.e., cameral/bicameral legislatures, review chambers and separation of powers, or executive dominance of the policy process, or unitary/federal systems diffusion of policymaking nodes. Electoral/voting systems within these frameworks, for instance, imply proportional representation, which creates coalition governments. Legal/judicial arrangements, for example, promote judicial review of administrative decisions, freedom of information, and judicial policymaking. At the

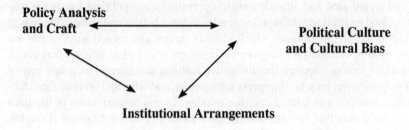

Figure 2. Interrelations of policy, political cultures, and institutional arrangements. This figure is based on a presentation given at Carleton University, Ottawa in 1998.

organizational level, executive-branch policymaking style may be "combative" or "consensual." These conditions are clearly influenced by sociopolitical culture (e.g., perception of government as benign rather than intrusive), by bureaucratic orientation (e.g., cultures of secrecy, accountability, performance, or career, whether apolitical or partisan-nepotistic), by civil-service organizational culture (service delivery or policy development orientation), or by a local accountability culture (e.g., cultures of secrecy or varying degrees of open accountability.) It is implicit that the nature of these conditions is shaped by and will shape cultural conceptualizations and will influence and will be influenced by policies.

The spread of rationality in the modern world accords with demands that institutions account for their actions and prove reliable (Hannan and Freeman, 1984; Weber, 1968), whether, for instance, in Canada, the United Kingdom, or Japan. Policy analysis plays a major role within the rationality, reliability, and accountability norms of institutional arrangements. Systematic planning and accountability aided by policy analysis are especially intense, for instance, when organizations produce symbolic products (e.g., education; see diMaggio and Powell, 1983) or when substantial risks exist (e.g., Medicare, economic investments), when long-term employee-organization relations muddle through, or when an organization's role is highly political (Weber, 1968). Hence, officials and executives, whether in North America, Europe, or Asia, are increasingly concerned with effective management and systematic policymaking procedures. Policy analytic skills are imperative in a highly competitive and increasingly flexible and dynamic global market. But, as noted, craft features promoted by conventional academic literature pay scant attention to cultural bias interference and its affect on policy analysis tricks-of-the-trade.

Why a neglected variable in policy research?

Unfortunately, cultural bias and the cultural impact on policy processes, particularly policy analysis, is a long-neglected variable. True, in recent years several scholars have become more actively engaged in this discussion (Thompson, Ellis, and Wildavsky, 1992; Douglas and Wildavsky, 1993; Ellis and Thompson, 1997), and to a limited extent in cultural assessment studies in different contexts (Grenstaad, 2001) or in the development of assessment tools for cultural measurement (Wildavsky, 1994; Cornell and Kalt, 1993). Still, little research on either the theoretical or the practical level has been done on culture or on the way it affects the conceptualization and the implementation of policymaking, economic planning, or political proceedings. Applied research on cultures and their application to actual social science practice, such as policy analysis, has not been undertaken. Bloch, cited in Houtman (1988, p. 19) and in Klitgaard (1989a), remarks in this respect that anthropology "is of as much use in practical problems as almost any other social-science..." Alas, so far his views on "applied anthropology" have not proliferated.

Why have anthropology and other fields that study culture made such a meager practical contribution? Why haven't applications of scientific models of culture or culture-by-policy interactions been tested and developed? Klitgaard, in his unique studies (1998a, 1998b), raises a number of highly valid reasons. They include (1) differences in the conceptualization of culture within academia— between theorists and applied scientists, anthropologists and economists, or scientists and humanists; (2) the sheer scientific difficulty of specifying the ways that cultures and policy choices interact; (3) the misguided notion of policy analysis, whereby projects magically materialize through study and systematic planning; and (4) fear of misuse, i.e., that taking culture into account will lead to oversimplification, discrimination, or omission, which are more damaging than the sins of omission (of culture) (1998b, p. 194).

Moreover, referring to the analogous problem of the search for aptitude-by-treatment interactions in psychology as an instructive guideline, Klitgaard believes that the problem of culture-by-policy-analysis studies lies in the difficulty of teasing out interaction effects and in the relatively high feasibility of measurement errors. The main reason for these difficulties is that culture is subject to change, and therefore evaluating policy by sociocultural interactions is elusive and difficult. Data on culture and cultural bias are hard to collect, and the measurement of errors makes it difficult to discover interaction effects. Statistical simulations may show interactive effects where none exist or may mask them when they do exist. Singling out interactive effects is complicated; random assignment of policies across sociocultural settings is not possible, and if the data obtained are too voluminous or too simplistic, they become meaningless. Finally, the social soundness of analyses has hardly any effect on the success of a project's implementation (Klitgaard, 1998a, pp. 139–140).

A study agenda

This article is not intended to provide a list of craft differences influenced by cultural bias or to provide examples of culturally tuned "best practices." These are components of a proposed study agenda and will include analyses of practices and cultural bias effects. Works by Dipak Gyawuli and Ajaya Dixit (1991) on energy and water management in Nepal and India, Steven Ney (2000) on pension reform in Europe, and Steve Rayner (1992) on climate change point to the increasing interest in such investigation and are a good source of studies lending themselves to cultural analysis.

It is obvious that to produce viable and implementable policies, policy analysts should be aware of their own cultural biases, should be able to recognize sensitivities, and should be willing to address them. Of particular interest in this discourse is a comparative research agenda that will look into (1) what variables are inherent in "political cultures/cultural bias" or "ways of life" that affect public policy analysis in various contexts; (2) what their common manipulate denominator is; (3) the ways in which these variables can be manipulated when normative policy analysis methodology is employed; and (4) how we can develop an awareness for culturally sensitive variables in policy arena interactions.

The author has designed such studies for Canada, involving several federal ministries, and for Europe, involving a number of European Union countries and comparable policy-making institutions. Once the design and tools are piloted, the study may also be undertaken in other regions. The individual studies will promote awareness of policy analysis methods and styles and will serve as a springboard for comparative analysis.

The Canadian proposal (SSHRC, 2002)

The Canadian proposal is based on the observation that Ottawa bureaucrats note among Ministries large differences in policy analysis/policymaking processes, seemingly attributable to organizational political culture. The main objective of the Canadian study is to enhance knowledge regarding systematic policymaking processes, to examine political cultures/cultural biases affecting policy analysis and policy planning in various Canadian policy-making institutional contexts (i.e., federal government departments), and to provide tools for adapting systematic policy analysis procedures to these contexts. The questions addressed will mainly be the following: What is the institutional culture of the investigated policymaking contexts? How are national policy styles accommodated in the Canadian regulatory arena? How do they take advantage of and adapt existing policy analysis methodology? How can awareness of these questions be heightened in the decision-making context for policy systematization and harmonization purposes?

Following well-established empirical theory about the practice of policy analysis, we distinguish a number of universal policy analytic routines or craft components, including (1) assessing the decision-making setting, (2) problem definition, (3) modeling the problem area, (4) selection of policy alternatives, (5) policy advocacy or argumentation, and (6) implementation design (Figure 1). At the level of policy analysis, we will use the methodology presented in Geva-May with Wildavsky (1997/2000) for a consensual approach to policy analysis.

Since we are interested in cultural factors impacting these routines, and since the proposed research design is a multiple-case comparison across policy sectors, the study opts for the relatively new group-grid cultural theory (Douglas, 1986; Thompson, Ellis, and Wildavsky, 1990) as a comparative framework for cultural differences because it allows for comparative cross-sector and cross-national cultural analysis (Hood, 1998).

Based on Mary Douglas's anthropological theory, there are four cultural biases/four ideal-typical ways of life lending themselves to formal universale in a general theory of culture (Eckstein, 1997).[4] If we present the craft elements in policy analysis as rows, and the four cultural ideal-types as columns, the matrix (Figure 1) abstractly represents the theoretical framework guiding our empirical research. In so doing, and by thus analyzing these cases, we will be interested not only in the cultural bias(es) impacting on any single policy analysis craft component but also in constructing so-called cultural-policymaking process-profiles. We regard the cultural policy analysis process profile as the set of cultural biases shaping (1) the organizational arrangements (i.e., in this case, federal government departments) within which policy is decided upon and (2) the (sequence of the six) craft components typical for the policymaking process as one possible type in a cultural morphology of such" processes. In this respect, a policy analysis cultural process profile is the independent variable leading to a particular output, i:e., a successful or nonsuccessful policy proposal.

The study will consider cases of "outrageous failure or success," since we expect consensus on "outrageous" cases. Such selection will allow us to estimate how much consistency and variation exists within each category across Canadian institutions/ministries as regards policy analysis processes and how much variation across ministries can be attributed to institutional cultural differences. The ministries proposed are (1) immigration, (2) health, and (3) environment, since these are policy areas high on the national and international agenda and are susceptible to issues of coordination, collaboration, and harmonization. They particularly demonstrate the complexities of policy formulation in areas of Canadian divided jurisdiction. These are areas in which international expectations and constraints and a range of domestic and transnational stakeholders play an important role in shaping policy formulation and assessment.

The study proposes to (1) identify institutional/contextual political cultures as well as policy analysis and policymaking strategies and processes within those contexts, (2) study the cultural influences affecting policy analysis and policy planning processes in national/institutional contexts, and (3) identify a number of policy analysis variables on which cultural biases act in order to determine how they can be manipulated.

A detailed study design has been submitted to SSHRC. Questionnaires, interviews, and content analysis of related documents (memos, minutes, bills, reports) will be used for categorization of each ministry's political cultures as assessed through the scheme of group-grid cultural theory and its impacts on policy analysis and policy planning practices. Respondents will be offered an adapted L/C *Berkeley Cultural Bias Questionnaire* (1993) in order to identify the contextual culture. The interviews with a variety of participants in the policymaking loci will shed light on narrations and judgments about any given policy decision and will reflect individual differences in many factors, including personality, vested interests, role in the decision, amount of available information, and distortions of memory. A core methodology from *Grounded Theory* (Glaser, 1972, 1998) will be used to validate views about policymaking activities. Due to the large number of numerical indicators from a relatively small number of participants, and since standard inferential statistical techniques will be of limited use, we adopted an evidential statistical approach to analyses, relying on *Ordinal and Nominal Pattern Analysis* (Thorngate, 1986a, 1986b, 1992; Thorngate and Carroll, 1986) and standard bootstrap/resampling techniques to examine the robustness of patterns in our data.

The data obtained will shed light on the use of policy analysis craft components in a respective policymaking context, will explain variations, will point to variables in the policy process that are more or less susceptible to cultural influences, and will allow for recommendations of systematic policy analysis methodology in the Canadian policy planning context.

The European proposal—"Policy Analysis and Cultural Pluralism: Towards European Union Harmonization of Public Policymaking"

The goal of this study is to enhance cross-European knowledge and awareness regarding systematic policymaking processes (policy analysis and planning) and to examine political cultures/cultural biases affecting policy analysis/policy planning within the European Union. The main purpose of the study is to contribute to the harmonization of the national policy styles that need to be accommodated in the European Union regulatory arena and to foster development of awareness and understanding of other policy styles and political cultures, accommodation of different policymaking styles, and integration of different regulations and policies in different European Union countries with different political cultures. By enhancing these components, the study proposes to present guidelines that allow for consensual and smoother implementation of European Union policies concerning social, economic, and public issues, and through awareness, removal of obstacles to change and to collaboration.

The project intends to bring together a group of leading European experts in the area of policy studies, public administration and cultural theory. The team will (1) identify, summarize, and compare local political cultures and current policymaking strategies and processes in several main policy areas such as immigration, healthcare, and higher education in several European Union countries (see the Canadian research proposal for study design); (2) lay the basis for communication and exploitation of findings towards guidelines for action at the policy level for cross national awareness, promotion, and harmonization of common and national interests; (3) allow for information exchange among the study's network members; and (4) allow for dispersion of knowledge regarding policy processes and affecting cultural interferences and providing guidelines for European Union policies harmonization.

The research design is similar to the Canadian study. It applies to each participating country respectively. Similar policy areas and institutions will be approached across the participating countries. Since each of the countries represented in the project team exercises different policies for key social fields and may employ different policy analysis and policy planning strategies and tools, the multinational/multicultural character of this project will allow for a comparative policy analysis study leading to "academia-practice transfer" of guidelines for enhancing awareness, reduction of frictions, and economic growth through effective collaboration in related European policies.[5]

The topic and nature of the two research agendas described above make it useful to disseminate the results beyond the usual academic circles and will be offered as findings and guidelines to public policymakers.

Conclusions

This article asserts that there is no one craft recipe for all and that policymaking and policy analysis are inherently affected by ways of life and cultural biases, which should be studied, taken into account, and adopted in craft considerations. While supporting the call for systematic policy analysis leading to institutional action, this article argues that the craft of policy analysis ought to consider prevalent cultural biases and "ways of life." These are not necessarily related just to national differences but also to fractions or groups within those wider groups.

Since the use of cultural frames of reference in craft considerations is missing from the policy analysis literature, I argue that only when these are included can policy analysis expand the meaning of "craft" and increase "policy utility." In order to do this and to maximize the added value of suggested policy alternatives, one should adapt normative systematic methods, i.e., policy analysis, to context, i.e., culture. Culturally tuning policy analysis implies effective implementation, an understanding of actual needs, speaking the cultural language of the interested parties, and allowing for awareness and policy bridging.

This article has sought to open the discussion on what policy analysts do in various settings, how and why they do it, and which competencies, skills, and attributes they need in order to be effective within the framework of their respective cultures. Moreover, it has presented a research agenda and research design that may allow for further comparative policy analysis and cultural theory study. It is hoped that further inquiry on this subject will contribute to a shift in the ongoing discussions on craftsmanship in policy analysis. The maturing field of policy analysis can no longer leave the neglected variable, culture, out of craft considerations. While benefiting from it, policy analysis can be an especially ripe field for applied cultural theory.

Notes

1. Concerning what we regard as truth and the rules of the game for discovering and inventing these projections, the European social psychologist Gergen Shotter would say that truth is subject to social influence.
2. For a sum-up of the theory, see Robert Hoppe's "Cultural Theory's Gift for Policy Analysis," the introduction to this Special Issue. See also Thompson, Ellis, and Wildavsky, 1990.
3. Myths of nature relate to nature benign, perverse/tolerant, fragile, and capricious (Schwarz and Thompson, 1990; Thompson et al., 1990, pp. 25–29); the (gendered) body and human nature relate to man as self-seeking and unmalleable, born sinful but redeemed by institutions, intrinsically good but malleable, or simply unpredictable (Thompson et al., 1990, pp. 33–37). For the idea of the "embodiment of thought," i.e., that the root metaphors we live by are based on our common experience of our bodies in motion and space, see Lakoff (1980, 1987).
4. For a detailed explanation of these ways of life, see Hoppe's introductory article in this issue. See also Thompson et al., 1998.
5. See European Union Community's social policy objectives (Fifth Program 2001).

References

Almond, G.A. and S. Verba. (1963). *The Civic Culture: Political Attitudes and Democracy in Five Nations.* Princeton, NJ: Princeton University Press.
Almond, G.A. and S. Verba. (1980). *The Civic Culture Revisited.* Boston: Little Brown & Co.
Banfield, E.C. (1958). *The Moral Basis of a Backward Society.* New York: Free Press.
Bardach E. (1992). "Problem Solving in the Public Sector." Berkeley: UC Berkeley, GSPP, 1.
Bardach, E. (1996). *Policy Analysis: A Handbook for Practice.* Berkeley: Berkeley Academic Press.
Barry, B. (1970). *Sociologists, Economists, and Democracy.* London: Collier-Macmillan.
Becker H.S. (1978). "Arts and Crafts." *American Journal of Sociology* 83(4), 865.
Behn, R.D. (1981). "Policy analysis and policy politics." *Policy Analysis* 7(2), 199–226.
Behn, R.D. (1978). "How to Terminate a Public Policy: A Dozen Hints for the Would-Be Terminator," *Policy Analysis* 4(3), 393–413.
Behn, R.D. (1976). "Closing the Massachusetts Public Training Schools." *Policy Sciences* 7(2), 151–171.
Benedict, R. (1934). *Patterns of Culture.* Boston: Houghton Mifflin.
Benedict, R. (1946). *The Chrysanthemum and the Sword: Patterns of Japanese Culture.* Boston: Houghton Mifflin.
Bobrow, D.B. and J.S. Dryzek. (1989). *Policy Analysis by Design.* Pittsburgh, PA: Pittsburgh University Press.
Bourdieu, P. (1998). *Practical Reason: On the Theory of Action.* Cambridge: Polity Press.
Caplen, B. (1999). "Where Will the Mud Stick? Emerging Market Crisis." *Euromoney*, Feb.
Cochran, C.L. and E.F. Malone. (1995). *Public Policy Perspectives and Choices.* New York: McGraw-Hill.
Cook, P. and J. Vaupel. (1985). "What Policy Analysts Do: Three Research Styles." *Journal of Policy Analysis and Management* 4(3), 427–428.
Cornell, S. and J.P. Kalt. (1993). "Culture and Self Government: American Indian Reservations." In "Cultural Assessments." Report on a workshop supported by the Rockefeller Foundation with support from the World Bank, New York.

Coyle, D.J. (1998). "A Cultural Theory of Organizations." in Richard J. Ellis and Michael Thompson (eds.), *Culture Matters, Essays in Honor of Aaron Wildavsky.* Boulder, CO: Westview Press.
diMaggio, P. J. and W.W. Powell. (1983). "The Iron Cage Revisited: Institutional Isomorphism and Collective Rationality in Organizational Fields." *American Sociological Review* 48, 147–160.
Dogan, M. (ed.). (1988). *Comparing Pluralist Democracies: Strains and Legitimacy.* Boulder, CO: Westview Press.
Douglas, M. (1970). *Natural Symbols: Explorations in Cosmology.* London: Barrie & Rockliff.
Douglas, M. (1982). "Cultural Bias." In *The Active Voice.* London: Routledge & Kegan Paul.
Douglas M. and A. Wildavsky. (1983). *Risk and Culture.* Berkeley: UC Press.
Downs, J. and P. Larkey. (1986). *The Search for Government Efficiency: From Hubris to Helplessness.* New York: Random House.
Dror, Y. (1971). *Design for Policy Sciences.* New York: Elsevier.
Dunn, W.N. (1994). *Public Policy Analysis: An Introduction.* Englewood Cliffs, NJ: Prentice-Hall.
Durning, D. and W. Osuna. (1994). "Policy Analysts' Roles and Values Orientations: An Empirical Investigation Using Q Methodology." *Journal of Policy Analysis and Management* 13(4), 629–657.
Dye, Thomas R. (1995). *Understanding Public Policy*, 8th ed. Englewood Cliffs, NJ: Prentice Hall.
Eckstein, H. (1988). "A Culturalist Theory of Political Change." *American Political Science Review,* 82(3), 789–804.
Ellis, J.R. and M. Thompson, (eds.). (1997). *Culture Matters, Essays in Honor of Aaron Wildavsky.* Boulder, CO: Westview Press.
Erickson, R.S., J.P. Melver, and G.C. Wright. Jr. (1987). "State Political Culture and Public Opinion." *American Political Science Review* 81, 797–814.
European Union Commission. (2001). European Union Commission, Fifth Program.
Galnoor, I., D. Rosenbloom, and A. Yraoni. (1998). "The Reform in the Israeli Public Management." *Economics Quarterly* 45, 83–108 (in Hebrew).
Geva-May, I. (1998). "Cultural Theory and Policy Analysis." Paper given at the Faculty of Public Affairs, Carleton University, Ottawa; submitted to PIRL.
Geva-May, I. (1999). "Reinventing Government: The Israeli Exception. The Case of Political Cultures and Public Policy Making." *International Management Journal* 2(3), 112–126.
Geva-May, I. with A. Wildavsky. (1997/2000). *An Operational Approach to Policy Analysis: The Craft. Prescriptions for Better Analysis.* Boston: Kluwer Academic Publishers.
Glaser, B. (1972). *Theoretical Sensitivity: Advances in the Methodology of Grounded Theory.* Mill Valley, CA: Sociology Press.
Glaser, B. (1998). *Doing Grounded Theory: Issues and Discussions.* Mill Valley, CA: Sociology Press.
Gorer, G. (1948). *The American People: A Study in National Character.* New York: Norton.
Gorer, G. (1955). *Exploring English Character.* New York: Criterion.
Gow, D. et al. (1989). *Social Analysis for the Nineties: Case Studies and Proposed Guidelines.* Bethesda, MD.: Development Alternatives, Inc.
Grendstad, G. (2001). "Culture." *Journal of Comparative Policy Analysis: Research and Practice* 3(1), 5–30.
Gyawuli, D. and A. Dixit. (1991). "Water and Politics." *The Economist* 319(7712), 38–40.
Hall, P. (1986). *Governing Economy: The Politics of State Intervention in Britain and France.* New York: Oxford University Press.
Hannan, M.T. and J. Freeman. (1984). "Structural Inertia and Organizational Change." *American Sociological Review* 49, 149–164.
Heineman, R., W. Bluhm, S. Peterson, and E. Kearny. (1990). *The World of the Policy Analyst.* Chatham, NJ: Chatham House.
Hillman, A. and O. Swank, (eds.). (2000). "Economic Consequences of Political Culture." *European Journal of Political Economy* 16(1), 1–4.
Hood, C. (1998). *The Art of the State.* Oxford: Oxford University Press.
Hoppe, R. (1999). "Policy Analysis, Science and Politics: From "Speaking Truth to Power" to "Making Sense Together." *Science and Public Policy* 26(3), 201–210.
Hoppe, R. (2000). "Political Cultures and Problem Definition." Paper presented at the Jerusalem International Conference in Canadian Studies; *JCPA* 4(3).
Hoppe, R. and J. Grin. (2000). "Traffic Problems Go Through the Technology Assessment Machine: A Cultural Comparison." In N. Vig and H. Paschen (eds.). (2000). *Parliament and Technology: The Development of Technology Assessment in Europe.* Albany: SUNY Press, pp. 273–324.

Huddleston, M.W. (1999). "Innocents Abroad: Reflections of a Public Administration Consultant in Bosnia." *Public Administration Review* 50(2), 147–159.

Inglehart, R. (1988). "The Renaissance of Political Culture." *American Political Science Review* 82, 1203–1230.

Jeliazkova, M.I. and R. Hoppe. (1997). "Criteria voor beleidsdocumenten; een empirisch onderzoek onder beleidsfunctionarissen bij een department" ("Criteria of Judging Policy Document Duality: An Empirical Study Among Departmental Policy Analysts"). *Beleidswetenschap* 1, 3–24.

Jenkins-Smith, H. (1982). "Professional Roles of Policy Analysts." *Journal of Policy Analysis and Management* 2(1), 88–100.

Jennings, B. (1987). "Policy Analysis: Science, Advocacy or Counsel?" *Research in Public Policy Analysis and Management*, vol. 4. Greenwich, CT: JAI Press, pp. 121–134.

Klitgaard, R. (1998a). "Including Culture in Evaluation Research." Rand Reprints/RP-695 Santa Monica: RAND, pp. 137–146.

Klitgaard, R. (1998b). "Applying Cultural Theories to Practical Problems." Reprinted from *Culture Matters. Essaysin Honor of Aaron Wildavsky,* 1997. Rand Reprints/RP-694. Santa Monica: RAND, pp. 191–202.

Koppenjan, J., W. Kickert, and E. Klijn. (eds.) (1997). *Managing Complex Networks: Strategies for the Public Sector.* Thousand Oaks, CA: Sage Publications.

Lakoff, T.R. (1990). *Talking Power: The Politics of Language in Our Lives.* New York: Basic Books.

Landes, D.S. (1998). *The Wealth and Poverty of Nations: Why Some Are So Rich and Some So Poor.* New York: WW Norton.

Lasswell, H.D. (1971). *A Pre-View of Policy Sciences.* New York: Elsevier.

Lasswell, H.D. and A. Kaplan. (1970). *Power and Society.* New Haven, CT: Yale University Press.

Lindblom, C.E. (1958). "Policy Analysis." *American Economic Review* 48(3), 298–312.

Lynn, E.L Jr. (1998). *Teaching and Learning with Cases.* New York: Chatham House.

Lynn, L.E. Jr. (1987). *Managing Public Policy.* Boston: Little, Brown and Co.

MacRae, D. Jr. (1979). "Concepts and Methods of Policy Analysis." *Society* 16(6), 17.

MacRae, D. Jr. and J.A. Wilde. (1979). *Policy Analysis for Public Decisions.* Belmont, CA: Duxbury Press.

Majone, G. (1989). *Evidence, Argument and Persuasion in the Policy Process.* New Haven, CT: York University Press.

Mamadouh, V. (1999). "Grid-Group Cultural Theory: An Introduction." *GeoJournal* 47, 395–409.

May, P.J. (1989). "Hints for Crafting Alternative Policies." *Policy Analysis* 7(2), 227–244.

Mead, M. (1942). *And Keep Your Powder Dry: An Anthropologist Looks at America,* New York: Morrow.

Mead, M. (1953). "National Character." In A.L. Kroeber (ed.), *Anthropology Today: An Encyclopedic Inventory.* Chicago: Chicago University Press.

Meltsner, A.J. (1972). *Political Feasibility and Policy Analysis. Public Administration Review* 32, 859–867.

Meltsner, A. J. (1976). *Policy Analysis in the Bureaucracy.* Berkeley, CA: UC Press.

Mintzberg, H. (1976). *The Structuring of Organizations: A Synthesis of the Research.* Englewood Cliffs, NJ: Prentice-Hall.

Nachmias, David and David H. Rosenbloom. (1978). *Bureaucratic Culture: Citizens and Administrators in Israel.* New York: St. Martin's Press.

Ney, S. (2000). "Are You Sitting Comfortably... Then We'll Begin...Three Gripping Policy Stories About Pension Reform." *Innovation: The European Journal of Social Sciences* 13(4), 341–372.

Pal, L.A. (1992). *Public Policy Analysis: An Introduction, 2nd ed.* Scarborough, Ontario: Nelson.

Patton, C.V. and D.S. Sawicki. (1993). *Basic Methods of Policy Analysis and Planning.* Englewood Cliffs, NJ: Prentice Hall.

Pizzorno, A. (1966). "Amoral Familism and Historical Marginality." *International Review of Community Development* 15, 55–60.

Putnam, R. (1993). *Making Democracy Work: Civic Traditions in Modern Italy.* Princeton, N J: Princeton University Press.

Pye, L. (1968). "Political culture." in D.L. Sillis (ed.), *International Encyclopedia of the Social Sciences.* New York: Macmillan and Free Press.

Pye, L. (1988). *The Mandarin and the Cadre: China's Political Cultures.* Ann Arbor, MI: University of Michigan Press.

Rayner, S. (1992). "Global Environmental Change: Understanding the Human Dimensions." *Environment* 34(7), 25–29.

Richardson, J.J. (ed.). (1982). *Policy Styles in Western Europe.* London: Allen and Urwin.

Rotmans, J. and B. DeVries. (eds.). (1997). *Perspectives of Global Change: The TARGETS Approach.* Cambridge: Cambridge University Press.

Schmutzer, M.A.E. (1994). "*Ingenium and Indivíduum.*" *Eine sozialwissenschaftliche Theorie von Wissenschaft und Technik.* Wien/New York: Springer Verlag.

Schwartz, M. and M. Thompson. (1990). *Divided We Stand: Redefining Politics, Technology, and Social Choice.* Hemel Hempstead: Harvester-Wheatsheaf.

Sharef, Z. (1962). *Three Days.* London: W.H. Allen.

Sharkansky, I. (1997). *Policy Making in Israel. Routines for Simple Problems and Coping with the Complex.* Pittsburgh: Pittsburgh University Press. Solow, R.E. (1986). "Economics: Is Something Missing?" In William N. Parker (ed.), *Economic History and the Modern Economist.* London: Basil Blackwell, pp. 21–29.

Thompson, M., R. Ellis, and A. Wildavsky. (1990). *Cultural Theory.* Boulder, CO: Westview Press.

Thompson, M., R. Ellis, and A. Wildavsky. (1992). "Political Cultures." In *Encyclopedia of Government and Politics.* London: Routledge.

Thorngate, W. (1986a). "The Production, Detection and Explanation of Behavioural Patterns." In J. Valsiner (ed.), *The Individual Subject and Scientific Psychology.* New York, NY: Plenum, pp. 271–293.

Thorngate, W. (1986b). "Ordinal Pattern Analysis." In W. Baker, M. Hyland, H. van Rappard, and A. Staats (eds.), *Current Issues in Theoretical Psychology.* Amsterdam: North Holland, pp. 345–364.

Thorngate, W. (1992). "Evidential Statistics and the Analysis of Developmental Patterns." In J. Asendorpf and J. Valsiner (eds.), *Stability and Change in Development: A Study of Methodological Reasoning.* Newbury Park, CA: Sage, pp. 63–83.

Thorngate, W. and B. Carroll. (1986). "Ordinal Pattern Analysis: A Method of Testing Hypotheses about Individuals." In J. Valsiner (ed.), *The Individual Subject and Scientific Psychology.* New York: Plenum, pp. 201–232.

Torgerson, D. (1986). "Between Knowledge and Politics: Three Faces of Policy Analysis." Policy Sciences.

Weber, M. (1968). *Economy and Society: An Outline of Interpretive Sociology.* New York: Bedmeiser.

Weinshall, T. and A. Kfir. (1994). "The Socio-Cultural System in Israel: Characteristics and Side Effects in Public Administration." In A. Shenhar and A. Yarkoni (eds.), *Administrative Culture in Israel.* Tel Aviv: Tcherikover (in Hebrew).

Weimer, D.L. (1992). "The Craft of Policy Design: Can It Be More than Art?" *Policy Studies Review* 11(3/4), 370–387.

Weimer, D.L. (1993). "The Current State of the Design Craft: Borrowing, Tinkering, and Problem Solving." *Public Administration Review* 53(2), 110–120.

Weimer, D.L. and A.R. Vining. (1989/1992). *Policy Analysis Concepts and Practice.* Englewood Cliffs, NJ: Prentice Hall.

Wildavsky, A.B. (1979). *The Art and Craft of Policy Analysis.* London: Macmillan.

Wildavsky, A.B. (1989). "Frames of Reference Come from Cultures: A Predictive Theory." In M. Freilich (ed.), *The Relevance of Culture.* New York: Bergin & Gamey, pp. 58–74.

Wildavsky, A.B. (1993). "On the Construction of Distinctions: Risk, Rape, Public Goods, and Altruism." In M. Hechter, L. Nadel, and R.E. Michod (eds.), *The Origin of Values.* New York: Aldine De Gruyter.

Yanow, D. (1995). "Built Space as Story: The Policy Stories that Buildings Tell." *Policy Studies Jounal* 23(3), 407–423.

Cultures of Public Policy Problems

ROBERT HOPPE

ABSTRACT *This article is an essay about the construction of a culturalist theory of problem definition in the public domain. Using grid-group Cultural Theory and a typology of the structures of policy problems, questions are posed such as the following: Why do some policymakers prefer to define problems as overstructured and not understructured? May one predict that policymakers who adhere to different ways of life will prove to be more adept in solving some problem types rather than others? Renowned policy science research work suggests how each way of life corresponds to a particular problem definition strategy. Hierarchists will impose a clear structure on any problem, no matter what the cost. Isolates see social reality as an unstable casino in which any privileged problem structure jeopardizes chances for survival. Enclavists (or egalitarians) will define any policy problem as an issue of fairness and distributive justice. Individualists will exploit any bit of usable knowledge to improve a problematic situation. These four focal strategies are part of repertoires of problem definition strategies, where each cultural solidarity type disposes of a differentially composed set of secondary strategies. Finally, it is suggested that the links between group-grid Cultural Theory and policy problem types may serve the practitioner as analytic tool for active and (self-) critical problem structuring and (re)framing.*

Introduction

In the mid-1990s, the Dutch government was pondering the future of civil aviation in its economy. The focal point of the debate was what should happen to Schiphol Airport Amsterdam, Europe's fourth largest airport in passengers and freight. To support Cabinet decision-making, the government organized a "societal dialogue" with some 80 participants from a wide range of backgrounds, including representatives from departments, local governments, the airport authorities, related industries, employers, trade unions, and environmental movements, as well as inhabitants of residential areas in Schiphol Airport's vicinity.

From the end of 1996 until July 1997, this heterogeneous stakeholder forum was to discuss the policy problem, as phrased by the Cabinet: "Should further growth of civil aviation be accommodated; and if so, how?" (TNLI, 1997, p. 8) Five problem frames emerged. Some participants framed the problem as one of international economic competition and argued that expansion of the civil aviation infrastructure was a sheer necessity. Others framed it as a public budget problem and argued the opposite, by claiming that expansion would be a squandering of public funds. Yet others viewed the problem as one of essentially regional accommodation of expanding airport facilities, or as an ecological modernization of the civil aviation sector, or as finding sustainable solutions to growing demands for mobility. From these perspectives, the "yea/nay" dilemma of the former two problem frames, logically implied in the government's phrasing of its policy problem, was superseded by more innovative answers. When the chips came down, the Cabinet chose to continue the policies of the previous 30 years to conditionally tolerate the airport's expansion. Obviously, it ignored the richer problem definitions (Van Eeten, 1999, pp. 113–142; Van Eeten, 2001).

Explaining policymaking histories like this one has become the challenge of an emergent subfield of public policy studies (PPS), namely, the *politics and analysis of problem definition*. It deals with "what we choose to identify as public issues and how we think and talk about these concerns" (Rochefort and Cobb, 1994, p. vii; Bovens and 't Hart, 1996). As in the aviation debate, PPS scholars frequently observe that "at the regime or macro-level of discussion and analysis there are remarkably few alternatives actually under debate" (Bosso, 1994, p. 184). Also, as in that debate, the explanation is hardly a deliberate elite influence or interest-group pressure but rather "received culture" (Bosso, 1994, p. 199).

One way of seeing policy problems is as cultural and political constructions. Culture is "the variable and cumulatively learned patterns of orientations to action in societies" (Eckstein, 1997, p. 26). Culture economizes action by relieving people of the impossible task of interpreting afresh every situation before acting. Culture also renders interactions between people, sometimes complete strangers, predictable through conventions, habits, rules, routines, and institutions. Thus, a culturalist approach to problem definition claims that rules for inventing and imposing closure on problem definition are primarily cultural.

Yet policy scientists have not taken the logical next step: if a policy problem is a cultural phenomenon, one should construct a theory of problem definition on a systematic culturalist approach to a politics of meaning (Sederberg, 1984; Stone, 1988; Hoppe, 1993) and symbolic power (Bourdieu, 1991). Granted, we have Gusfield's 'The *Culture of Public Problems: Drinking-Driving and the Symbolic Order* (1981). Gusfield uses anthropological and literary concepts like dramaturgy, ritual, and rhetoric to interpret how the history of collective problematic situations gives rise to political definitions of problems. We owe to Gusfield the insight that the *structure of public problems* is always composed of three symbolic elements (Gusfield, 1981, p. 6ff.): *problem ownership*, or who claims a say in defining a problem; *causality*, or which theory of causes and consequences of the problem is publicly espoused; and *accountability*, or who is praised or blamed for solving (failing to solve) the problem.

But later theoretical development is absent. Rochefort en Cobb's book (1994) offers a good example, in spite of its richness in empirical illustrations. And like so many pathbreaking "research essays" even Gusfield's study is based on just one single case, in one part of the U.S.A., in the 1970s and 1980s. Yet its title speaks of "the" culture of public problems and "the" symbolic order. In this contribution, I challenge this premature generalization. Gusfield's merit is in his way of conceptualizing the problem. Leaning on his work, I will complement it by reinterpreting empirical and theoretical work from the policy sciences on the taxonomy and typology of policy problems. I will demonstrate that we should speak of several cultural styles in policy problem definition, with each style featuring its own typical problem structure in Gusfield's sense of the term. Not singularity, but plurality rules.

The first policy problem typology to gain ascendancy was Lowi's (1972) distinction between regulatory, distributive, and redistributive policy issues. Since then, many others have tried their hands at building issue or problem typologies (see overviews in Parsons, 1995, pp. 132–134; Nelson, 1996). Pursuing a culturalist approach, I will elaborate upon an issue typology used by Douglas and Wildavsky (1983, p. 5; Hoppe, 1989; Hisschemöller and Hoppe, 1996; see also Thompson and Tuden, 1959) in their book on risk and political cultures. Douglas and Wildavsky's work is probably the first book-length public policy study in which *grid-group cultural theory* (gg-CT) was ever applied. It is surprising that Mary Douglas, the "founding mother," and Aaron Wildavsky, intellectual founder of Berkeley's school of public policy analysis and later lead user and promoter of gg-CT in political science, did so little to link up this theory to PPS (but see Geva-May, 1997, p. xiii). This is a pity because, at first glance, gg-CT is a promising starting point.

Within a culturalist approach, one may distinguish between the attitudinal and the inclusive approaches to the study of culture. The *attitudinal approach* uses a restrictive definition *of culture* as *mental products*, i.e., meanings, values, norms, and symbols. In research, culture is operationalized as the aggregate of individual attitudes, thereby exploring and mapping the nature of meanings, values, ideals, and so forth for a particular group, nation, or organization. In this approach, *culture* is different from *institutions*, as some who espouse an institutionalist approach to politics are never tired of pointing out (John, 1998). The *inclusive approach* defines culture more comprehensively, in two respects. First, it defines culture as ways of world making, or ways of creating conceptual order and intelligibility through labels, categories, and other principles of vision and division (Bourdieu, 1991). Second, culture is not set apart as mental product but studied as part and parcel of a way of life. This study includes man-man, man-artefact, and man-nature interactions. In the inclusive approach, it is configurations of beliefs, interactions, and behavioral strategies that count; one is looking for "matching" relationships between cultural, social, and technological systems. Gg-CT belongs in the inclusive camp. The group and grid dimensions of human transaction[1] are constructed as the ultimate causal drivers in ordering social relations. These give rise to cultural biases as justifications for particular social orders. As justifications and sets of available orientations to action, the cultural biases influence behavior by making it patterned.

For purposes of theory construction, gg-CT has three distinct advantages. First, the inclusive definition of culture as

$$\text{types of social relations} + \text{cultural bias} + \text{behavioral strategy} = \text{a way of life}$$

promises a *more encompassing theory*. For example, in the inclusive approach, institutions are not analytically distinct from but rather express culture (e.g., Lockhart, 1999, p. 868), since values cannot be extricated from the social relations they justify. Second, the two-by-two typology of ways of life resulting from crossing the grid and group dimensions provides a neat system of four basic orientations, working like an orientation to orientations, or a sufficiently variable, yet limited set of meta-orientations. Equally constructivist in studying social reality as the numerous interpretive theories within the inclusive approach (see Denzin and Lincoln, 1994), gg-CT's *constrained relativism* is more suitable for theory construction directed at conceptual ordering of the many proto-, small, and middle-range theories scattered over the domain of the politics and analysis of problem definition. Third, scholars claim that progress in this field depends on comparative studies of problem definition (Bosso, 1994, pp. 193, 201). Gg-CT represents a promising attempt at cultural nomothesis, i.e., the discovery of general regularities in culture. Its four ideal-typical ways of life are hypothetical candidates for the formal universale in a general theory of culture (Eckstein, 1997, p. 28ff). Thus, gg-CT should offer ample opportunities for *cross-sector and cross-national comparative research* into problem types and the dynamics of problem definition.

As I will show, gg-CT can enrich problem typologies by giving clues about puzzles like the following: Do some politicians and policy analysts prefer to define a problem as Type A rather than Type B, and why? Can policy actors adhering to different ways of life, i.e., hierarchy, enclavism, individualism, and isolationism,[2] be predicted to have differential skills in coping with different problem types? More generally, can some or all types of problems be plausibly matched with gg-CT's ways of life?

My argument will unfold in three steps. In the next section, I will explain and briefly illustrate the problem typology. The core of this article is in the middle section, which attempts to sketch a culturalist approach to problem definition built on gg-CT. The last section evaluates the results in terms of both theory and, more briefly, the potential for the practice of policy analysis.[3]

Types of policy problems

What is a *problem'?* Standard definitions speak of an unacceptable gap between normative ideals or aspiration levels and present and future conditions. It follows that a *problem* is an analytical compound of three elements straddling the fact-value distinction: (1) an ethical standard; (2) a situation (present or future); and (3) the construction of the connection between standard and situation as a gap that should not exist. Policymakers can (dis)agree on any of these elements. Concerning standards, one may distinguish between those with much and those with little acceptance. Regarding situations (and their future development), some are based on highly certain and some on highly uncertain knowledge. Regarding the relationship between standard and situation, people may disagree about the political sense—whether or not to construct it as an intolerable gap in need of mending.

To simplify, I use only two dimensions—degree of certainty about knowledge, and degree of acceptance of relevant standards—to distinguish four types of problems (Hoppe, 1989, based on Douglas and Wildavsky, 1983; see also Thompson and Tuden, 1959). Figure 1 also features some illustrations.

Structured problems are characterized by high degrees of certain knowledge and consent. Road maintenance and (in The Netherlands) the application of rules for the allocation of social housing facilities are some obvious examples. Dealing with such problems belongs to the routine of daily administration. Moderately structured problems come in two distinct forms. In one variation *(moderately structured problems/ends)*, agreement on relevant standards is high—i.e., relevant values and appropriate ends are not contested. But policy-makers cannot agree on the effectiveness and efficiency of the means to be

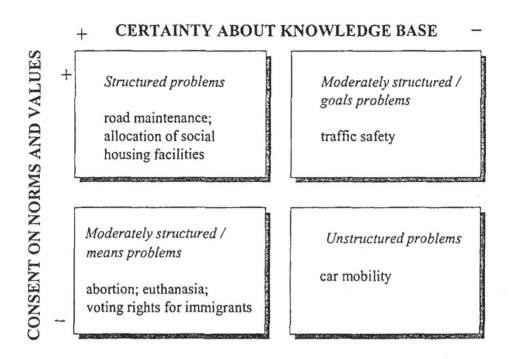

Figure 1. Types of policy problems. Sources: Hoppe (1989), Hisschemöller and Hoppe (1996).

used and the (financial) resources to be allocated. Many traffic safety problems belong in this category. Even though everybody sincerely supports the goals, neither experimental research nor pilot projects nor negotiations can usher in a definitive solution. The other variation *(moderately structured problems/means)* features substantial agreement on certain knowledge but sometimes intense disagreements about values at stake and ends to be pursued. Examples here are abortion, euthanasia, and voting rights for foreigners. We can easily enact policy for all these issues, but disagreement about the ethical desirability or acceptability of the values and goals continues and intensifies.

Finally, there are those problems where both the knowledge base and the ethical support remain hotly contested. The most urgent and virulent political problems, unfortunately, frequently belong to this category. Such problems remain ill-defined, "wicked," "messy," "ill-structured,"—or *unstructured*, a term I prefer. The technical methods for problem solving are inadequate; there is uncertainty about which disciplines, specialities, experts, and skills to mobilize; conflicts over values abound; and many people get intensely involved, with strong but divisive opinions. An example is car mobility problems, which frequently belong to this type of *unstructured problem*. Traffic jams are a permanent battlefield of value conflict: road pricing mechanisms increase costs versus equal access to car mobility, also for lower income groups; or the need for cheap road transport facilities as a basis for regional or national economic competition versus the accompanying rise in transport volume, which may clog major transport arteries. The knowledge base for choosing among policy instruments is weakly developed. High uncertainty continues about the effectiveness of policy measures due to inseparable interaction effects in field experiments, the long maturation time for effects to become visible and measurable, and disturbing influences from other policy domains and international developments.

The typology above has two obvious uses in empirical research. First, in a given policy formulation and adoption process, we may observe whether or not a (group of) policymaker(s) display(s) consistently patterned problem definition behavior. For example, is it true that the Foundation for Scientific Research on Traffic Safety (in Dutch: Stichting Wetenschappelijk Onderzoek Verkeersveiligheid, or SWOV) consistently presents a particular traffic problem as *structured*, whereas the Association of Car Dealers (in Dutch: Bond van Autobedrijven en Garageondernemers, or BOVAG) insists that the same problematic situation should be defined as a *moderately structured/ends* problem? Second, focusing on government policymakers, an analyst could try to establish whether official problem definitions remain stable over time (in the framework of one particular formulation/adoption process, or over several such processes in a decade, say). The typology functions as a conceptual canvas on which the historical trajectory of problem definitions may be mapped out. Pursuing this line of empirical research, the "normal" assumption that, during the same governmental formulation/adoption process, problem definitions always move from unstructured to more structured has to be discarded, at least for environmental policies (Hisschemóller, Hoppe, Groenewegen and Midden, 2001) The dynamics of problem definitions turns out to be very complex and should become the object of much more empirical research (cf. Bosso, 1994, p. 200).

Towards a culturalist theory of problem definition

What "value added" can be gained from bringing gg-CT to bear on the problem typology? Can we say anything about how policymakers or analysts belonging to each of the four ways of life or solidarities[4] would cope with different problem types? I will divide this overall question into subquestions, which follow the logic of the problem typology. First, can we predict the *primary* orientation of an adherent of a particular solidarity who must frame a problematic situation as a particular type of problem? Second, what can we say about that adherent's dispositions and skills in coping with the remaining types? In answering these questions, I will present the starkest contrasts first. I start with the hierarchist policymaker or analyst, who is an expert in framing and then solving structured problems. Then I will contrast him[5] with the frequently overlooked isolate policymaker or analyst, who sees unstructured problems everywhere and identifies solving them with personal and organizational survival. Finally, I will come to enclavists, who see value conflicts as the root cause of every problem and overcoming these as the precondition to any solution; and individualists, who want to move away from problems, if only by a few inches.

Hierarchists: "Structure it!"

Policymakers and analysts working in *complex bureaucracies* are exposed to strong hierarchical social relationships and interaction patterns. These organizational structures express a cultural bias or disposition in their worldview that can be characterized as paradigm protection (Thompson and Wildavsky, 1986, pp. 280–281) or as a belief in *"strong" theories or methods*—those certified by science, or more traditionally, those founded in religion. Although science and religion are often believed to be mutually exclusive, in a modern handbook on socio-cybernetic policy analysis (Rastogi, 1992, p. 12), we find them both, side by side.[6] Rastogi professes that any effort at problem solving begins with an ordered knowledge base, generated by a scientific methodology and an interdisciplinary theoretical language fit for complexity (Rastogi, 1992, p. 12).

Regarding long-term, lasting solutions, Rastogi (1992, p. 16) opines that the root causes of social problems are "the abnormal or disturbed emotions/motives of the social actors participating or involved in the problem situations." To "nullify" these, we need a belief system of "super-rational values":

"The only basis on which the intrinsic nature of moral values may be posited and *all* human beings may naturally and harmoniously relate themselves together is their common identification with the **Divine**. (...) This framework of truth, love, inner serenity, and righteous action... is *rational in an absolute and universal sense*. It provides the basis for eliminating the polluting symptoms of horror in social problems. It makes possible a lasting and steady state solution to the malfunctioning of social systems" (Rastogi, 1992, pp. 114, 117).

Given this orientation in worldview, the hierarchist's *rationality is functional and analytic*. It is functional in the sense of starting from a supposedly agreed-upon objective, on the basis of which the most effective and efficient means is worked out. It is analytic in the sense that problem solving is considered an intellectual effort best left to experts. In his *Administrative Behavior*, Simon (1947) has shown how this type of rationality, exactly because it does not deny but rather actively uses the inevitable boundaries on our intellectual capacity as a building block in organizational design, can be systematically applied to create complex bureaucratic structures in which everyone expertly solves his partial problem within the decision parameters of the organization's leadership. The whole idea presupposes that problems come neatly packaged; and if they don't, they can be made to turn out that way. *"Structure it!"* is the hierarchist's primary orientation to the definition of problems.

How does a hierarchist policymaker or analyst define a problem (cf. Dery, 1984. pp. 21–27; Hoppe, 1989, pp. 23–24)? Three rules for problem shaping and bringing closure to problem definition appear to be typical. The first and foremost condition for structuring any problem is decomposability: the problematic situation must be able to be broken down into relatively independent problem parts. This done, one may then define the most important or salient variables or causes of these problem parts (Rastogi, 1992, p. 120). The second condition is that the problem should be viewed from an interventionist perspective; the government must be presented as in control, i.e., in a position and endowed with resources to remedy the problem. This condition means two things. First, the hierarchist policymaker/analyst should know precisely what the goal is, i.e., he should know how to specify what the solution to the problem looks like. Our exemplary hierarchist analyst, Rastogi (1992, p. 56), speaks of determining the "goal state" of the system by observing the "viability" or effectiveness of variables in relation to "a system's 'health.'" Second, it means the identification of manipulable variables and major constraints from the regulator's or governmental perspective:

"Cybernetic methodology also provides additional insights toward policy identification. They are based on the identification of the most significant *control, constraint*, and *change lever* factors in a problem's multi-cycle structure. Control factors are those variables, which exercise a major controlling influence on the internal interactions within a problem's dynamic structure. Constraint factors are those variables, which constitute the major impediments in efforts to change the problem's behaviour. Change lever factors are those variables of fundamental importance which determine the strategy for long-term change in the problem's state and course" (Rastogi, 1992, pp. 64–65).

The third condition is the translation of these factors into custom-made action plans for a given organization or set of organizations. In addition to distinguishing between short-and long-term measures, this condition means developing an analytic capacity to differentiate between the relative importance of policy alternatives in relation to the relative urgency of problem dimensions. The practical implication is that, from the regulator's perspective, some problem parts are not worth solving. All the rules for hierarchist policymakers for creating a structured problem effectively lead to an inversion of the commonsense logic of a one-to-one relation running from problem to solution. What counts as problem in fact depends on the chosen, elaborated solution (Rittel and Webber, 1973, p. 161; Hoppe, 1989, p. 17).

Where does this leave the hierarchist policymaker or analyst in dealing with the other three problem types? Evidently, he will consider every problem structured until proven otherwise. Consider the way the Dutch government chose to ignore the more promising but less structured problem frames for the civil aviation problem. Consider also the way that hierarchistically inclined policymakers and analysts in agencies for parliamentarian technology assessment in European countries structure the car mobility problem (Hoppe and Grin, 2000). Although there are many more ways of framing the car mobility problem—to be discussed later—hierarchists desire an orderly, reliable and manageable transportation system. In their view, congested roads and traffic jams are problematic because they create chaos and stagnation. This means the system has no "slack," or does not efficiently use available capacity to channel traffic streams through existing traffic infrastructure. Essentially, then, the problem is a systems capacity problem, solvable in principle by capacity expansion—unless this solution proves technically absolutely infeasible to meet the demand for mobility and transportation. Because hierarchists by definition choose a "helicopter" or systems perspective, car mobility is reduced to a partial problem in an overall problem of transport mode selection and substitution. Because they can be implemented by experts, favorite hierarchist solutions have a large-scale and high technical-fix character—fast trains, underground transportation systems, mainports, and so forth.

Because hierarchists can only deal comfortably with problems whose valuative dimension is not openly contested, and because they are used to imposing their values on others, they are ill disposed to treat moderately structured problems/means. They will ignore rival value/goal clusters—like the one that prioritizes accessibility to different transportation modes over meeting an excessive demand for car mobility. Instead, they will implicitly impose their own values, or, if this cannot be done—another hierarchy may be too powerful—they will avoid dealing with such problems or problem parts. Hierarchists will only reluctantly deal with moderately structured problems/ends, where the knowledge and technology base for problem solving is either insufficient or contested. California's zero emission mandates for cars provides an example. By imposing a zero emission target, California forces the car industry to speed up its R&D efforts for producing zero- or extremely low emission vehicles. This forcing of technology corresponds to a hierarchist policymaker's preference for improving the problem's knowledge base. Simultaneously, it keeps open the possibility for wielding his preferred policy instrument, namely, law enforcement.

Isolates: "Surviving without resistance"

Isolates experience themselves as outcasts, subjected to a fate determined by dark forces or faraway ruling circles. "God is high, and the King is far" is a good expression of the isolates' state of mind. We may think of the isolate as belonging to the contemporary underclass—those who, at the margins of modern society, live a life of exclusion. This way of life is not expected to be seen and heard in policymaking circles. This is why, in many policy studies applying gg-CT, only the three "active" voices—hierarchy, enclavism, individualism—are heard, and the passive isolate is absent.

Isolates perceive the institutional settings in which they find themselves in one of two different ways. It is inherent in their worldview to see the world as a *lottery* and risk absorption as the only way of coping with this "fact of life" (Thompson and Wildavsky, 1986, p. 280). In their social, organizational, and political relations, they see the world as an *unstable casino*. Dror (1986, p. 168) gives a dramatic description of these conditions,

> "where not playing is itself a game with high odds against the player; where the rules of the game, their mixes of chance and skill, and the payoffs change in unpredictable ways...; where unforeseeable forms of external 'wild cards' may appear suddenly...; and where the health and life of oneself and one's loved ones may be at stake; sometimes without knowing it."

If isolates believe the unstable casino is ruled by mere randomness, they may define the institutional environment as *anarchy*. For example, an isolate belongs to an anarchic organization beset with garbage can-like decision processes. His organizational function, competence, status, access to decision-making arenas, and relationships to colleagues is continuously ambiguous, in flux, and unpredictable; and so are the organization's relations to its wider environment (March and Olsen, 1976). Alternatively, in a fatalist variation, he could define the institutional situation as a *barracks*, if he believes the unstable casino is actually run by an all-powerful but unpredictable human despot or tyrant. He belongs to a highly rule-bound organization; but the rules are changing, as are the conditions under which they apply and the consequences of breaking them. Examples would be soldiers at the mercy of a whimsical drill officer, students dealing with stern but unpredictable teachers,[7] or bureaucrats serving an autocratic ruler, be he of a traditional monarchical, revolutionary religious, or military *caudillo* type (Heady, 1991, p. 31 Off).

The rationality of the isolate and/or fatalist is a gaming or gambling one. According to Dror (1986, pp. 168–169), under conditions of adversity, isolate policymakers resort to "fuzzy gambling." In its extreme, fatalist form, any decision-making is senseless. Surprise dominates life, better intelligence cannot improve ignorance, having goals and values is a luxury, and nondecisions or incremental decisions make no sense because experience and past performance have lost their anchoring functions in a highly volatile environment. In an effort to make the best of it, fatalist policymakers or analysts could gamble to maximize their chances for maximum gain, or use a maxmax strategy, or, alternatively, try the policy principle of minmin-avoidance, i.e., choose a strategy that prevents the worst outcome or at least minimizes the damage (Dror, 1986, p. 10).

The isolate, whether fatalistically inclined or more optimistic, will be predisposed to define any problem as unstructured. Believing that the world is a lottery and the social world is an unstable casino, he will be extremely reluctant to impose any definitive framing on a problematic situation. "Survival" and "resilience" are the isolate's watchwords (Schwarz and Thompson, 1990; Hood, 1998), and they proscribe him from having any fixed ideas, let alone theories and methods, about the nature of the problem and how to solve it. Instead, he must be totally flexible and keep his options open in order to be maximally resourceful and alert at every opportunity to escape fate and grab the lucky number. However, it is recognized that this approach can lead to successful radical innovation (Schmutzer, 1994; March and Olsen, 1976, p. 69ff; Dror, 1986, p. 174).

Given their primary disposition to define problems as unstructured, isolationist and/ or fatalist policymakers and analysts turn a blind eye to the occurrence of structured and moderately structured problems. Hence, they will rely on random search behavior, inspiration, maxmax gambling, or minmin-avoidance[8] as coping strategies for problems. By imposing this frame on problematic situations, isolates produce self-fulfilling prophecies when confronted by adherents from rival solidarities. The result is exclusion from, or marginalization in, the halls of power.

In the preceding section, issues of car mobility were mentioned as typical examples of an unstructured problem, and in the previous subsection I showed how hierarchist policymakers nevertheless frame these issues as a structured problem of transportation infrastructure capacity. Senior policymakers in complex bureaucracies, for obvious reasons, resist the self-image of "gambling professionals," let alone admit "fatalist" problem definition behavior (Dror, 1986, p. 172). But Dutch environmental policymakers came close, some years ago and for a limited time. They declared, first, that the increasing *number of* traffic jams was beyond rational policy intervention; and, second, that allowing traffic jams to grow and multiply was their only hope of making the problem go away by itself! After these policymakers went on record with these surprising policy alternatives, politicians, not amused, and concerned about their own public image, summoned them back to more hierarchist (see above) and individualist problem definitions (see below).

Enclavists: "It's not fair!"

When one prefers a way of life permitting only relations with like-minded people and as little interference as possible from outsiders, one joins a *clan, club,* or *commune*. In group-grid CT, such people are called *enclavists*. They choose to inhabit an enclave encircled by a hostile world. The worldview of enclaves is best described as *enlarged groupthink*.

In PPS, this phenomenon of combined inside moralism and outside criticism is well known as a threat to high-quality decision-making in small groups at the top of the pyramid of hierarchist organizations (Janis, 1982). When groups consist of members with homogeneous social and ideological backgrounds, have no tradition of impartial leadership, and perceive their context as threatening or crisis ridden, symptoms of groupthink may occur. What is overlooked in such psychological analyses of organizational behavior is that an enclavist way of life institutionalizes itself by systematically instilling the groupthink cultural bias in most of its adherents. Guarding the group boundaries by picturing the outside world as evil and mean is the principal way of keeping a society of enclavists together, and this is exactly what the enlarged groupthink symptoms achieve. If they fail, expulsion, always disgraceful and sometimes violent, is the enclavist's means of last resort.

The worldview of enlarged groupthink is imbued with a *communicative* form of *value rationality*. It is communicative because verbal means of persuasion, from public debate to speeches to propaganda campaigns, are the only allowed means of creating consent among equals. It is value rational, in the sense of normative standards and goal-finding being the major issue of problem-solving efforts, because the mix of inside moralism and outside criticism makes enclavists never miss an opportunity to point out the value conflicts between "us" and "them." The major route to a solution is that "they" give up their "wrong" values and change their ways accordingly. Enclavists proselytize, and outsiders should convert to the enclavist's values and life style.

This assumption of ubiquitous value conflicts leads enclavist policymakers and analysts to structure problems as moderately structured/means. The valuative problem dimension is emphasized. This does not mean that enclavist policymakers and analysts scrupulously survey all relevant values: opposing "our" values to "theirs"—frequently on the basis of stereotypes—is sufficient. The same logic breeds close monitoring of differences between groups in society, particularly differences in treatment by government. Thus, frequently, the value conflict is shaped as an issue of distributive justice, equality, or (broadly understood) *fairness*.[9] As an example, since the 1980s, the environmental movement's and citizen protesters' major complaint in the Schiphol Airport expansion issue is that government weighs fragmented benefits to the population as a whole and concentrated benefits for the aviation-related business interests higher than the concentrated costs accruing to resident groups in the airport's vicinity. In doing so, the fairness problem frame spills over into a problem of trust in the sphere of interaction and institutions. The enclavist policymaker's weak spot for the value dimension of a problem comes at the cost of its cognitive aspects. Poor information search, incomplete search for alternatives, and underestimation of risks of a preferred choice are typical defects triggered by groupthink symptoms (Janis, 1982, pp. 243–245). With excessive attention given to values, there is a distinct tendency to let ends justify means, irrespective of the effectiveness, efficiency, and even counterproductive side effects of those means. Criticism of "their" knowledge base and repertoire of policy instruments is frequently mistaken for a policy alternative of equal standing. A good illustration is the fixation on the growth/no-growth alternatives in the civil aviation controversy, which may be attributed to the clash between hierarchist and enclavist problem definition strategies.

What about the remaining two problem types? Regarding moderately structured/ends problems, I would predict that enclavists frame these as distributive justice or fairness issues of who gets what, when, and how. Invoking Rawlsian rules like "favor the most disadvantaged group," enclavist negotiators may comfortably, but not very powerfully, participate in public policymaking.[10] Given their inclination to critique, which brings with it a natural aversion to nonshared value aspects and strong doubts about the validity of any knowledge base, enclavists would also not be unhappy to share the isolate's or fatalist's attraction to unstructured problems. After all, gg-CT sees egalitarian enclavists as the natural allies (as defenders) of fatalist isolates (as victims) on the negative group-grid diagonal (see also note 13).

The way the car mobility problem was framed by several technology assessment agencies working for national parliaments in Europe (Hoppe and Grin, 2000) offers an example of the enclavist's preferred problem definition strategy. The enclavist-egalitarian perspective defines the real issue at stake as equal access to public space for all. Car mobility is a partial problem of excessive demand, over-expanded infrastructure, pollution of public space, and violation of health, ecological balance, and quietude of residential areas. Ultimately, the problem is one of control and cutting back on demand for car mobility, and substitution with more friendly, low-tech, small-scale transport modes such as bicycles and light, zeroemission (electrical) vehicles.

Individualists: "Let's make things better!"[11]

In the low group/low grid cell, we find the individualist way of life. In terms of interaction patterns, adherents prefer freely chosen exchange relations to other people. Except in the institutional domains of *markets*, they find and (re)create these relations in social *networks*. In networks, individuals socialize with partners, which results in a flurry of networking activity, with persons continuously moving in and out and between networks as they see fit. In networking, they live out their worldview of *seizing opportunities* for individual benefit. The individualist type of rationality is *functional and strategic*. It is functional in the sense that the individualist searches for usable knowledge, i.e., data and information, which help him maximize his utility, or at least satisfice at the self-selected aspiration levels (Simon, 1947). It is strategic in the sense that individualists are adept in getting usable knowledge by exploiting their personal networks. Their approach is about "shifting the really vital discussions away from the formalized information-handling system and on to the informal old boy net. We characterize this strategy as individualist manipulative" (Thompson and Wildavsky, 1986, pp. 280–281). The individualist's basic orientation to problems and problem solving is *"Let's make things better, let's get usable knowledge."*

What is the proper definition of a policy problem for an individualist policymaker or analyst? Essentially, problems are *opportunities for improvement*.[12] Defining a problem means framing it as a choice between two or more alternative means to seize that opportunity (Dery, 1984, p. 27). This approach implies some strict rules of closure—so strict, actually, that individualist policymakers frequently appear outright indifferent about many undesirable and bridgeable gaps between given and valued situations (Dery, 1984, p. 26). To begin with, individualists emphasize means over goals. The individualist policymaker does not reason from goals to means but from means to goals Only those goals are worth considering for which effective means are available—organizationally, technically, and financially. The principal but negative task of the policy analyst is to point out constraints and determine the (in)feasibility of a policy proposal (Majone, 1975).

Individualists don't care much for explicit value search and goal formulation anyway. They actually resist political rhetoric, because they do not express what actually moves people. Preferences develop through experiencing particular situations over some time period—which means that preferences change and are hard to predict. Rather than deducing unambiguous criteria from lofty but shaky ideals, individualist policymakers express "concern" about "threats" or "ills from which to move away rather than goals towards which to move" (Braybrooke and Lindblom, 1963, p. 102). In part, this ameliorative attitude to the valuative dimension of problems depends on an individualist understanding of the nature of policy problems as "an extremely complex adjustment-of-interests situation. ... all that can at best be defended as a right 'solution' is that a series of conciliatory moves be made" (Braybrooke and Lindblom, 1963, p. 55).

Always taking present conditions as an evaluative baseline, individualists limit their preferences to comparisons of incremental change (Braybrooke and Lindblom, 1963, p. 85). In this way, the individualist believes he can safely forgo the vicissitudes of goal formulation and priority setting. His continuous incremental comparisons have implicit, contextually shifting policy preference rankings as a side product. This largely implicit, ameliorative way of treating values and goals fits the individualist networking style of political interactions hand-in-glove. Being casual about political ideology and explicit policy values allows individualist policymakers to identify shared interests, concerns, and threats easily—even with potential opponents (cf. Sabatier and Jenkins-Smith, 1993, pp. 223–225). Likewise, preference aggregation among many individualist policymakers comes about as an epiphenomenon of the ongoing partisan mutual adjustment in policy networks (Braybrooke and Lindblom, 1963, p. 15; Lindblom, 1965).

On the cognitive side of problems, the individualist policymakers' and analysts' instrumental outlook logically values know-how over know-that. Individualists need usable knowledge (Lindblom and Cohen, 1979), irrespective of its source. Sometimes the source is scientific or professional inquiry. But individualists rely as much or more on common sense and practical knowledge. Here again, their interaction style helps them mobilize the usable knowledge or "intelligence of democracy" (Lindblom, 1965) implicitly stored in their networks.

It follows that the individualist policymaker clearly prefers defining a problem as *moderately structured/ends*. But how does he deal with the other problem types? As soon as he is convinced a problem is worth solving, and the knowledge base permits, he will not resist defining a problem as structured. As in cost-benefit and to a lesser degree in cost-effectiveness analysis, in collaboration with hierarchist analysts he may even be at pains to elaborate algorithms and standardized calculation methods that help him perform his incremental comparisons between means by determining their monetized costs and benefits (Weimer and Vining, 1989). But unstructured and moderately structured/means problems are clearly not worth the individualist's precious time. They tie him up in unproductive value talk or equally unproductive debates about the misery of the human condition. He'd rather avoid both as obstacles to making things better—if only by a little bit.

Technology assessment studies of the car mobility problem also provide us with examples of typical individualist problem framing (Hoppe and Grin, 2000). They all define the car mobility problem as threatening free access to roads, and thus to the individual's right of freedom of movement. Thus, the car mobility problem is a lack of space, a shortage of passable roads, and a lack of useful traffic information. It is a loss of valuable personal time—ultimately, given the *total* demand for car mobility, the problem is undersupply of transport possibilities per car owner. As a choice-of-means problem, individualist policy analysts try to find out which alternative road pricing schemes will rebalance supply and demand.

Conclusions

Figure 2 summarizes the results achieved by bringing gg-CT to bear on one particular problem typology. It shows that there is a straightforward match between cultural ideal-types and policy problem types. Each solidarity corresponds to one focal problem-definition strategy. This focal strategy is part of a repertoire of problem definition strategies, with each solidarity matching a differential set of affinities to nonfocal or secondary strategies.

For further theory construction and testing, the secondary strategies are as important as the focal ones. In politically and ideologically plural societies, it is difficult to imagine that politicians and policymakers of just one cultural disposition could hold a monopoly on a policy domain. In order to turn a static problem typology into a dynamic theory of the process of problem analysis, the affinities to the secondary strategies in a problem definition repertoire determine the possibilities and constraints on building credible advocacy coalitions (Sabatier and Jenkins-Smith, 1993) or productive discourse coalitions (Hajer, 1996) with adherents of other ways of life. But to link the problem typology to types of policymaking (see Hisschemöller and Hoppe, 1996, for an example), and to find out whether or not gg-CT's postulates about the viability and durability of cross-cultural hybrids hold, is yet another empirical and analytical puzzle.[13] Hood (1998, pp. 233–241) has shown for public management strategies that gg-CT is up to the task of accurately describing and analyzing mixes and hybrids. Let it suffice here to remark that, as far as problem types and problem definition strategies go, gg-CT has done a remarkable job in theoretical integration. Theories and frameworks usually not treated within the covers of one book, let alone in one journal article, have been brought together in an intelligible way. At the least, this exercise has not refuted the expectation that gg-CT is a suitable candidate for a meta-theory for organizing the field of PPS studies.[14]

This conclusion may be strengthened by returning to Gusfield. His analysis stresses three elements that structure each public policy problem: problem ownership, causality, and accountability. Our theoretical analysis and empirical illustrations allow the proposition that at least four types of such structures will be identifiable. Hierarchically inclined policy analysts will opt for the government or for officials as problem owners; they will select the theory of causality with the highest academic credentials; and they will prefer an accountability system that reflects the "one for all" principle (Bovens, 1998). In contrast, policy analysts predisposed to isolationist or fatalist ways will consider everybody, but nobody in particular, as a problem victim; every causal theory will be rejected as "not of this world" and will thus be discarded in favor of stories about good and bad luck; and on the basis of both previous beliefs and attitudes, it follows that when, fully according to expectations, things go awry, nobody can be held accountable.

Enclavistically predisposed policymakers will claim problem ownership for the people, the citizens, or those who demonstrably belong to a deserving target group; a malfunctioning system always is the root cause of the problem, and in support for this claim, enclavists will appeal to both cognitive authority (counterexpertise) and lay knowledge; self-evidently, it is "they" who are accountable, meaning either evil outsiders or neglectful superiors—i.e., government officials or other authority figures who represent the collective (Bovens, 1998). For an individualistically programmed policymaker, the problem owner simply is someone who happens to have the highest stakes in solving the problem; he prefers usable knowledge of whatever kind, which frequently means—contra Gusfield—that causal knowledge counts for little; and those individuals—not groups or collectivities—are held accountable who were in a position to prevent bad results and damage but failed to do so (Bovens, 1998). Note that gg-CT not only complements Gusfield's analysis by pointing out predictable differences between four types of problem structure but also implies an amendment, by stressing that causal knowledge is less important than Gusfield predicts. After all, for isolationist and individualist policymakers and analysts, knowlege of causes and effects is unnecessary.

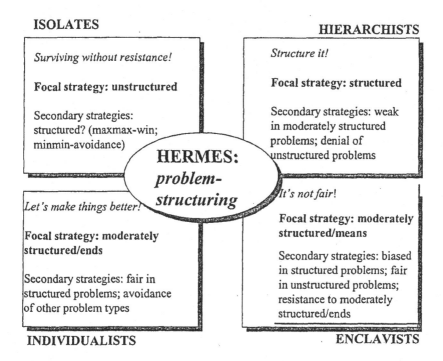

Figure 2. Cultural bias and problem definition.

Is the theory relevant for what-to-do and how-to-do-it questions of policy analysis? The special problem of defining the nature of the problem was recognized in policy analysis a long time ago, quite independent of gg-CT. More important, gg-CT teaches analysts which problem definition strategies to expect. It also gives them clues about which types will confront each other in policy arenas, and which hybrid strategies are likely and less plausible. This is usable knowledge. Elsewhere I have argued why deliberate cognitive *problem structuring* by analysts and *reasoned problem choice* by democratically accountable politicians are indispensable to avoid policy controversies and break deadlocks (Hisschemöller and Hoppe, 1996; reprinted in Hisschemöller et al., 2001). These approaches involve the confrontation, evaluation, and integration of as much contradictory information as possible.

Apart from many social and political conditions, problem structuring requires forensic policy analysts endowed with skills of problem reframing or "the capacity to keep alive, in the midst of action, a multiplicity of views of the situation" (Schôn, 1983, p. 281). The forensic policy analyst considers it his task to use the differences between problem frames to forge an innovative policy design from a combination of plausible and robust arguments ("frame-reflective analysis"), or to test and bolster some frames ("frame-critical analysis"). Knowledge about different types of problem frames, and different repertoires of problem definition strategies, is a basic element in building a best practice or craft of forensic analysis (for an excellent example, see Mamadouh in this issue).

Precisely at this point, gg-CT offers a valuable contibution. Thompson et al. (1990) have defended the thesis that at the intersection of grid and group on the sociocultural map sits a fifth ideal type. They call this type the "hermit," because of this type's self-conscious withdrawal from commitment to and involvement in the other four ways of life. Schmutzer (1994) stresses another aspect of aloofness from the four solidarities, i.e., free access and movement between them. He therefore interprets the fifth ideal type as a *Hermes*, the fast-running messenger and clever translator, the god of commerce and traffic of the Greeks. Policy analysis needs Hermes-like problem structuring to become an accepted and feasible, teachable tool of the trade. That is gg-CT's real contribution to policy analysis.

Acknowledgment

Previous versions of this paper have been presented and discussed at the Joint Sessions of Workshops of the European Consortium for Political Research, Workshop "Plural Rationality and Policy Analysis," Mannheim, 26–31 March, 1999; the Symposium on "Theory, Policy and Society," Leiden University, Leiden, 24–25 June, 1999; the 8th Biannual Jerusalem Conference in Canadian Studies of the Isreal Association for Canadian Studies and the Halbert Centre for Canadian Studies of the Hebrew University, Jerusalem, 25–29 June, 2000; and the APPAM Research Conference, Washington D.C., 1–3 November, 2001.

Notes

1. *Grid* refers to rules that relate one person to another on an ego-centered basis; it has heteronomy and autonomy as its two extremes. *Group* refers to the experience of belonging to a bounded social unit; it has the solitary individual and the "collectivized groupie" as opposites.
2. In gg-CT there are four ideal-typical biases: (1) low grid/low group: active *individualism* (Thompson et al., 1990, pp. 34–35); (2) high grid/high group: pattern-maintaining *hierarchy* (Douglas and Wildavsky, 1983, pp. 90–92); (3) low grid/high group: dissident *enclavism* (Douglas, 1986, pp. 38–40; Sivan, 1995, pp. 16–18), and (4) high grid/low group: *isolationism* (Schmutzer, 1994; Douglas, 1996, pp. 183–187). These terms are intended to be as neutral and ahistorical as possible in order to facilitate dispassionate comparisons across regions and time. Unfortunately, it is logically impossible to jump over one's own constructivist shadow and find a terminology that is at once technically correct, easily understandable, and not burdened (for some readers) by unintended historical, political, or contextual connotations (cf. Douglas, 1996, p. 175).
3. Ultimately, my knowledge interest is in finding out whether or not gg-CT does a satisfactory job in conceptually organizing the scattered and fragmented field of PPS (see Dunn and Kelly, 1992, and Parsons, 1995, for good overviews). Exploring the "value added" of gg-CT for one problem definition typology is part of this larger project (Hoppe, 1999a). Similar projects have been undertaken for organization studies (Coyle, 1997) and public management studies (Hood, 1998). All this contributes to an encompassing culturalist and argumentative approach to public policy studies within the framework of a politics of meaning (Hoppe, 1993; Parsons, 1995, pp. 151–153).
4. Some cultural theorists prefer *solidarities*, because by organizing *preferred* social relations, they represent different types of solidarity between people. This is true even for "isolates," who implicitly or explicitly choose this way of life, if only temporarily, like voluntary soldiers or students. It is perhaps less appropriate for the forced isolationism of the truly marginalized and outcasts, who are indeed condemned to the fatalist ways of life. Nevertheless, I will use *way of life* and *solidarity* interchangeably as synonyms.
5. Needless to say in this article he/him everywhere can also be read as she/her.
6. Of course, Rastogi is eccentric, but honest, in founding his normative position on religion. Policy analysts usually take either a cognitivist or a noncognitivist meta-ethical stance. Cognitivism in policy analysis is frequently identified with Brecht's Scientific Value Relativism (or Alternativism). Scientists cannot scientifically determine whether or not something is valuable; but given an ultimate value, they can use their scientific methods to clarify the implications and consequences of adhering to this "given" value. Most policy

analysts, e.g., cost-benefit analysts and pragmatic incrementalists, adhere to some form of emotive noncognitivism, i.e., they deny ethical statements any cognitive status beyond emotional expressions of ephemeral and temporary preferences. The only thing scientists may do is observe people's preferences as manifested in their behavior, and adopt these observed preferences as normative lodestars. Paradoxically, these more frequent meta-ethical positions, in practice, amount to the same hierarchical bias as Rastogi's in favor of experts who claim the right to force-feed their "scientific" interpretations and "empirical" indicators for values to politicians, policymaking officials, and citizens (Van de Graaf and Hoppe, 1989, pp. 141–157; Fischer, 1990).

7. Schmutzer (1994), an Austrian scholar, views schools and other educational institutions as the typical isolationist organization. Interestingly, March and Olsen (1976) use American and Norwegian universities and faculties to illustrate their theory of anarchic organizations and garbage can-like decision-making processes.
8. Some might argue that maxmax gambling and minmin avoidance can be viewed as strategies for structured problems.
9. So strong is this tendency that in many versions of gg-CT, enclavists are called *egalitarians*.
10. This may be the reason why, at face value, interest groups are always drawn into using enclavist-like rhetoric in advancing their cause. Still, there is not necessarily any positive relationship between the two. After all, interest groups may hold very different cultural biases. A labor union or an interest group representing the physically challenged may, indeed, espouse egalitarian beliefs. But a Chamber of Commerce or Rotary Club representative will more likely embrace individualist beliefs. The impression of a one-to-one connection actually derives from stolen rhetoric. The contemporary media demand strong policy statements, packaged as sound bites. This type of communication of group interests will always stress the group's cause at the expense of everything else, thereby lending such statements the semblance of pure enclavism.
11. Any similarity to an advertisement slogan of a multinational company is wholly intentional.
12. The Pareto optimum in cost-benefit analysis—choose the alternative(s) that make at least one person better off, and nobody else worse off—is the algorithmic form of the individualist position.
13. Douglas (1996) and Thompson et al. (1990) hypothesize that individualist/hierarchist hybrids are more stable than any other. They are on the *positive diagonal*, where socialization is based on instrumental rationalities, and they share affirmative attitudes toward power and authority, albeit different ones. Enclavists and isolates are on the *negative diagonal*, where socialization is based on emotive and communitarian values, which passively and actively resist all types of power and authority. Therefore, according to the gg-CT argument, they will be weaker in their efforts to establish and sustain power/authority structures of their own. In this article, due to space limitations I cannot pursue this intriguing line of thought in connection with problem definition strategies.
14. To an anonymous reviewer I owe the intriguing suggestion that the problem definition strategies are linked to the major disciplinary backgrounds in a multidisciplinary approach to policy analysis. The idea is lent some plausibility in Bobrow and Dryzek's (1987) list of approaches to doing policy analysis; by Schmutzer's (1994, p. 408) distinctions between clan science, market science, and bureaucratic science; and by my own historical sketch of the development of policy analysis (Hoppe, 1999b). In my view, hierarchy, then, would correspond to analycentric policy analysis based on economic assumptions (rational man, optimistic information processing); individualism corresponds either to eclectic, relativist, incremental, and pragmatic policy analysis inspired by assumptions of bounded rationality and pluralism in political science, or to institutional analysis and design inspired by political philosophy and public choice reasoning in economics; enclavism/egalitarianism would have its policy analytic homeland in sociologically inspired forms of critical, deliberative, or participatory modes of doing analysis; and, finally, isolationism/fatalism would be manifest in the fuzzy gambling or garbage can-like styles of "dirty analysis" inspired by history and anthropology. Hermit policy analysis, then, is the mul-tiparadigm, frame-critical, and frame-reflective mode of policy analysis advocated by authors like Mason and Mitroff (1981), and Rein and Schön (1994).

References

Bobrow, J.D. and J.S. Dryzek. (1987). *Policy Analysis by Design*. Pittsburg, PA: Pittsburg University Press.
Bosso, C.J. (1994). "The Contextual Bases of Problem Definition." In D.A. Rochefort and R.W. Cobb (eds.), Tile *Politics of Problem Definition: Shaping the Policy Agenda*. Lawrence, KS : University Press of Kansas, pp. 182–203.
Bourdieu, P. (1991). *Language and Symbolic Power*. Cambridge: Polity Press.
Bovens, M. (1998). *The Quest for Responsibility: Accountability and Citizenship in Complex Organizations*. Cambridge: Cambridge University Press.
Bovens, M. and P. 't Hart. (1996). *Understanding Policy Fiascoes*. New Brunswick, NJ: Transaction Publishers.
Braybrooke, D. and Ch.E. Lindblom. (1963). *A Strategy of Decision. Policy Evaluation as a Social Process*. New York: Free Press
Coyle, D. (1997). "A Cultural Theory of Organizations". In R. Ellis and M. Thompson (eds.), *Culture Matters*. Boulder, CO: Westview Press.
Denzin, N.K. and Y.S. Lincoln (eds.). (1994). *Handbook of Qualitative Research*. Thousand Oaks, CA: Sage.
Dery, D. (1984). *Problem Definition in Policy Analysis*. Lawrence, KS: University Press of Kansas.
Douglas, M. (1986). *How Institutions Think*. Syracuse, NY: Syracuse University Press.
Douglas, M. (1996). *Thought Styles: Critical Essays on Good Taste*. London: Sage.
Douglas, M. and A. Wildavsky. (1983). *Risk and Culture*. Berkeley, CA: University of California Press.
Dror, Y. (1986). *Policymaking Under Adversity*. New Brunswick, NJ: Transaction Books.
Dunn, W.N. and R.M. Kelly (eds.). (1992). advances *in Policy Studies since 1950. Policy Studies Review Annual* 10. New Brunswick, NJ: Transaction Publishers.
Eckstein, H. (1997). "Social Science as Cultural Science, Rational Choice as Metaphysics." In R. Ellis and M. Thompson (eds.), *Culture Matters*. Boulder, CO: Westview Press.
Ellis, R. and M. Thompson (eds.). (1997). *Culture Matters*. Boulder, CO: Westview Press.
Fischer, F. (1990). *Technocracy and the Politics of Expertise*. Newbury Park: Sage.
Geva-May, I. (1997). *An Operational Approach to Policy Analysis: The Craft. Prescriptions for Better Analysis*. Boston: Kluwer Academic Publishers.
Goodin, R.E. and H.-D. Klingemann (eds.). (1996). New *Handbook of Political Science*. Oxford: Oxford University Press.
Gusfield, J.R. (1981). *The Culture of Public Problems*. Chicago: Chicago University Press.
Hajer, M.A. (1996). *The Politics of Environmental Discourse*. Oxford: Clarendon Press.
Heady, F. (1991). *Public Administration. A Comparative Perspective*, 4th ed. New York: Marcel Dekker.
Hisschemôller, M. and R. Hoppe. (1996). "Coping with Intractable Controversies: The Case for Problem Structuring in Policy Design and Analysis." *Knowledge and Policy: The International Journal of Knowledge Transfer and Utilization* 8(4), 40–60. Reprinted in M. Hisschemôller et al. (eds.), *Knowledge, Power, and Participation in Environmental Policy. Policy Studies Review Annual* 12. New Brunswick, NJ: Transaction Publishers.
Hisschemôller, M., R. Hoppe, P. Groenewegen, and C. Midden. (2001). "Policy Networking or Problem Structuring: Knowledge Use and Political Choice in Dutch Environmental Policy." In M. Hisschemôller et al., *Knowledge, Power, and Participation in Environmental Policy. Policy Studies Review Annual* 12. New Brunswick, NJ: Transaction Publishers.
Hisschemôller, M., R. Hoppe, W.N. Dunn, and J. Ravetz. (eds.). (2001). *Knowledge, Power, and Participation in Environmental Policy, Policy Studies Review Annual* 12. New Brunswick, NJ: Transaction Publishers.
Hood, Chr. (1998). *The Art of the State. Culture, Rhetoric, and Public Management*. Oxford: Clarendon Press.
Hoppe, R. (1989). Hef *beleidsprobleem geproblematiseerd*. Muiderberg: Coutinho (inaugural address at the University of Amsterdam).
Hoppe, R. (1993). "Political Judgment and the Policy Cycle: the Case of Ethnicity Policy Arguments in The Netherlands." In F. Fischer and J. Forester, *The Argumentative Turn in Policy Analysis and Planning*. Durham, NC: Duke University Press, pp. 77–100.
Hoppe, R. (1999a). "Cultural Theory and the Study of Public Policy." Paper prepared for the Symposium "Theory, Policy & Society." Leiden University, June 24–25 (unpublished).
Hoppe, R. (1999b). "Policy Analysis, Science, and Politics: from 'Speaking Truth to Power' to 'Making Sense Together.'" *Science and Public Policy* 26(3), 201–210.

Hoppe, R. and J. Grin. (2000). "Traffic Problems Go Through the Technology Assessment Machine: a Culturalist Comparison." In N.J. Vig and H. Paschen, *Parliaments and Technology. The Development of Technology Assessment in Europe*. Albany: State University of New York Press, pp. 273–324.

Janis, I.L. (1982). *Groupthink. Psychological Studies of Policy Decisions and Fiascoes*, 2nd ed. Boston: Houghton Mifflin Company.

John, P. (1998). *Analysing Public Policy*. Pinter London and New York.

Lindblom, Ch.E. (1965). *The Intelligence of Democracy*. New York: The Free Press.

Lindblom, Ch.E. and D.K. Cohen. (1979). *Usable Knowledge*. New Haven, CT: Yale University Press.

Lockhart, Ch. (1998). "Cultural Contributions to Explaining Institutional Form, Political Change, and Rational Decisions." *Comparative Political Studies* 32(7), 862–893.

Lowi, T.J. (1972). "Four Systems of Policy Politics and Choice." *Public Administration Review* 32, 298–310.

Majone, G. (1975). "The Feasibility of Social Policies." *Policy Sciences* 6(1), 49–69.

March, J.G. and J.P. Olsen. (1976). *Ambiguity and Change in Organizations*. Bergen: Universitetsforlaget.

Mason, R.O. and I.I. Mitroff. (1981). *Challenging Strategic Planning Assumptions. Theory, Cases, and Techniques*. New York: John Wiley and Sons.

Nelson, B. (1996). "Public Policy and Administration". In G.E. Goodin and H.-D. Klingemann (eds.), *New Handbook of Political Science*. Oxford: Oxford University Press, pp. 5–592.

Parsons, W. (1995). *Public Policy. An Introduction to the Theory and Practice of Policy Analysis*. Aldershot and Brookfield: Edward Elgar.

Rastogi, P.N. (1992). *Policy Analysis and Problem-Solving for Social Systems. Toward Understanding, Monitoring, and Managing Complex Real World Problems*. New Delhi: Sage.

Rein, M. and D.A. Schön. (1994). *Frame Reflection: Towards the Resolution of Intractable Policy Controversies*. Durham, NC: Duke University Press.

Rittel, H.W.J, and M.M. Webber. (1973). "Dilemmas in a General Theory of Planning." *Policy Sciences* 4, 155–169.

Rochefort, D.A. and R.W. Cobb (eds.). (1994). *The Politics of Problem Definition. Shaping the Policy Agenda*. Lawrence, KS: University Press of Kansas.

Sabatier, P.A. and H. Jenkins-Smith (eds.). (1993). *Policy Change and Learning: An Advocacy Coalition Approach*. Boulder, CO: Westview Press.

Schmutzer, M.A.E. (1994). *Ingenium und Indivíduum. Eine sozialwissenschaftliche Theorie von Wissenschaň und Technik*. Wien/New York: Springer Verlag.

Schön, D.A. (1983). *The Reflective Practitioner*. New York: Basic Books.

Schwarz, M. and M. Thompson. (1990). *Divided We Stand*. New York: Harvester Wheatsheaf.

Sederberg, P.C. (1984). *The Politics of Meaning. Power and Explanation in the Construction of Social Reality*. Tucson, AZ: University of Arizona Press.

Simon, H. (1947). *Administrative Behavior*. New York: Wiley and Sons.

Sivan, E. (1995). "The Enclave Culture." In M.M. Marty (ed.), *Fundamentalism Comprehended*. Chicago: Chicago University Press.

Stone, D.A. (1988). *Policy Paradox and Political Reason*. Glennview, IL: Scott, Foresman.

Thompson, M. and A. Wildavsky. (1986). "A Cultural Theory of Information Bias in Organizations." *Journal of Management Studies* 23(3), 273–286.

Thompson, M., R. Ellis, and A. Wildavsky. (1990). *Cultural Theory*. Boulder, CO: Westview Press.

Thompson, M., G. Grendstad, and P. Selle (eds.). (1999). *Cultural Theory as Political Science*. London: Routledge.

Thompson, J.D. and A. Tuden. (1959). "Strategies, Structures, and Processes of Organizational Decision." In J.D. Thompson et al. (eds.), *Comparative Studies in Administration*. Pittsburgh: Pittsburgh, University Press.

TNLI. (1997). *Hoeveel ruimte geeft Nederland aan de luchtvaart. Integrate beleidsvisie*. Den Haag: SDU.

Van de Graaf, H. and R. Hoppe. (1989). *Beleid en Politiek. Een Inleiding in de Beleidswetenschap en de Beleidskunde* (1996, 3rd ed.). Bussum: Coutinho.

Van Eeten, M.J.G. (1999). *Dialogues of the Deaf. Defining New Agendas for Environmental Deadlocks*. Delft: Eburon Publishers.

Van Eeten, M.J.G. (2001). "Recasting Intractable Policy Issues: The Wider Implications of the Netherlands Civil Aviation Controversy." *Journal of Policy Analysis and Management* 20(3), 391–414.

Weimer, D.L. and A. Vining. (1989). *Policy Analysis: Concepts and Practice*, 1 st ed. Englewood Cliffs, NJ: Prentice-Hall.

Toward Cultural Analysis in Policy Analysis: Picking Up Where Aaron Wildavsky Left Off

BRENDON SWEDLOW

ABSTRACT *To generate policy alternatives and offer policy advice, the policy analysis and planning literature counsels analysts to assess the values and beliefs of policy actors, as well as the organizational and political contexts in which an analyst's proposed solution will have to be enacted and implemented, but does not further specify what these values, beliefs, and contexts might be. Analysts can anticipate the kinds of political values and the kinds of beliefs about human nature, the environment, and the economy that are likely to be associated with different forms of social organization by relying on Mary Douglas and Aaron Wildavsky's theory of culture. Additionally, this form of cultural analysis will allow analysts to deduce which policy problems are most likely to arise, which policy solutions are most likely to be feasible, and which policy advocacy coalitions are most probable in different cultural contexts.*

Introduction

Among the most pressing of the late Aaron Wildavsky's last projects was his desire to develop guidelines for policy analysis informed by British anthropologist Mary Douglas's brand of cultural analysis (Douglas, 1982, 1994; Douglas and Wildavsky, 1982). Indeed, within only two weeks of completing what has become the seminal refinement of Douglas's cultural theory (Thompson, Ellis, and Wildavsky, 1990), Wildavsky told one of his coauthors that their next book should provide "precepts for policy analysis" (Thompson, 1997, p. 203). Shortly before his death, Wildavsky and another coauthor had compiled a nearly exhaustive collection of precepts culled from the literature on policy analysis and planning, but Wildavsky never got a chance to take the next critical step of specifying what *cultural precepts for policy analysis* might look like or add to these existing precepts (Geva-May with Wildavsky, 1997/2001, xiii).[1]

In this article, I try to suggest how Douglas's form of cultural analysis might give further direction to analysts relying on the precepts that Geva-May and Wildavsky found in their wide-ranging, comprehensive review. My discussion frequently compares political cultural with political economic approaches to policy analysis, both to ground the unfamiliar in the pervasive and to suggest the value added by this cultural approach. Except as otherwise indicated, I do not assume the task of addressing or assimilating developments in cultural theory that have occurred since Wildavsky's passing (see Thompson, Grendstad, and Selle, 1999, and the present issue of this journal for examples of recent developments). I simply attempt to take a few more steps on the path Wildavsky was traveling, as described in the foregoing abstract.

Existing precepts for policy analysis, according to Geva-May and Wildavsky

The literature on policy analysis and planning explicitly recognizes the importance of cultural analysis to policy analysis when it advises analysts to "[d]iagnose the general political culture context before proposing alternatives for possible implementation [because that]... will help [analysts] anticipate possible resistance, and be able to assess the chances of implementation of [their] program" (p. 12; unless otherwise indicated, all citations in this section are to Geva-May with Wildavsky, 1997/2001). But cultural analysis can potentially contribute much more to policy analysis than this. As a significant source of "values, beliefs, related rituals and symbols, assumptions and behavioral norms (p. 12)," political culture influences all aspects of planning, policy analysis, and policymaking. That is why political culture is potentially such a powerful source of understanding, explanation, and prediction.

For example, while it is salutary for policy analysts to "consider the general values" that give rise to a policy problem (pp. 99, 128), as the policy analysis and planning literature counsels, it would be much better to be able to specify what these general values are before a problem even arises. Similarly, if analysts should "strive to develop a better understanding of organizational and political decision-making contexts" (p. 13), their efforts might bear greater fruit if at the outset they had an idea of the types of decision-making contexts they were likely to confront. Likewise, if the "motivations, beliefs, biases, and political resources" of various policy actors are important (pp. 13, 56), and decision-making arenas have distinct "rules and unique political features" (p. 58), it should be very useful to know that these tend to take several predictable forms. More controversially, if policy models are supposed to be deliberately biased by being grounded in a "mental meta-model" composed of the analyst's "subjective judgments" (pp. 75–76), and/or if "problems of interpretation might have biased [the analyst's] data" (p. 34), it would be helpful to know what some recurring sources of subjectivity and bias are. Douglas and Wildavsky's theory and conception of culture can help specify all of the foregoing contingencies.

If varying values not only define problems and possible solutions, as the policy analysis and planning literature has it, but also help determine political and administrative feasibility (pp. 127–128); and if "evidence and argument" have to be selected with "particular audiences" in mind (p. 15); and if "the same conclusions might have to be justified differently in different contexts (p. 15)," it should help to have an idea beforehand of what those varying values, particular audiences, and different contexts are. Similarly, if "political or problem windows" create special opportunities for policy advocacy (p. 164), and if altering the dimensions of debate, or coopting or compromising with opponents, is a way to avoid losing entirely (pp. 157–158), then it cannot hurt to have prior knowledge of the nature of likely windows of opportunity or dimensions of debate, and of the conditions under which cooptation and compromise are possible. Finally, if a proposed policy requires something as significant as "a change in institutions" (p. 136), analysts should like to know beforehand what kinds of institutions and therefore what kinds of institutional change are possible. Again, Douglas and Wildavsky's conception and theory of culture can help specify all of these contingencies.

Douglas and Wildavsky's cultural approach to policy analysis

Dimensions of social life: the extent of collectivization and individual autonomy[2]

Douglas and Wildavsky make the extent of individual autonomy and the extent of collectivization in social and political organizations[3] into independent dimensions rather than poles on a continuum, as is customary. This conceptual shift allows analysts to account for four rather than two patterns of social relations. People in *individualistic* and *fatalistic* social relations are *not* part of a collective undertaking, but individualists retain their autonomy, while fatalists do not. People in *egalitarian* and *hierarchical* social relations, meanwhile, *are* part of a collective undertaking, but egalitarians retain much more of their autonomy than hierarchs. Hierarchical social relations are highly structured, with everyone and everything having his, her, and its place—represented by a pyramid here. Individualistic social relations, by contrast, are highly fluid, and are subject to individual choice, represented by a network. Fatalistic social relations, meanwhile, are tenuous and unreliable, driven by the "whim and caprice" of others—represented by atomized individuals. Egalitarian social relations retain their autonomy by giving all members an equal voice in (and thus the power to veto) collective decisions. This "wanting to have it all" is represented by something that looks like a chocolate chip cookie (this paragraph adapted from Swedlow, 2001, p. 336).

This shift in conceptualization of social relations is where cultural theory makes its greatest contribution to policy analysis. Finally, there is a simple, theoretically coherent way to characterize organizational and political decision-making contexts, and therefore a way to map institutional locations and transformations. The contrast with political economy approaches to characterizing social relations usefully illustrates the value added by cultural analysis to policy analysis. Political economists assume a world populated by rational, self-interested, utility-maximizing individuals. With this much, cultural theorists agree. But they do not follow political economists in their further deduction that rational, self-interested individuals will necessarily seek to maximize the creation and consumption of material wealth. This deduction is only warranted in individualistic cultural environments, which teach people to think of themselves as autonomous entrepreneurs and sovereign consumers.

Of course, not all political economists deduce that self-interested, utility-maximizing individuals will seek to maximize the creation and consumption of material wealth. Many recognize that not all individuals will define the maximization of self-interest in these terms (Mansbridge, 1990). In fact, individuals may do the exact opposite: maximizing the material well-being of others at their own immediate expense. But political economists do not have a good way to explain why this occurs nor to predict when it will occur (Riker, 1991, as discussed in Wildavsky, 1994, 1998a). Cultural theorists, by contrast, explain such apparently altruistic behavior as the consequence of being embedded in a collectivist pattern of social relations. People in such cultural environments, which also occur in many places in the West, view it as in their self-interest to undertake other-regarding behavior because they view the self as dependent on others (Wildavsky, 1991, 1998a; Chai and Wildavsky, 1994, reprinted in Wildavsky, 1998a; Lockhart and Wildavsky, 1998).

Political economists recognize hierarchy as a pattern of social organization distinct from individualism. However, not only do "states and markets" insufficiently characterize the range of institutions in which these patterns are found (Lindblom, 1977; Williamson, 1975) but also political economists frequently treat bureaucrats and other state agents as though they were the self-interested, materialistic utility maximizers found in markets. Consequently, political economists have difficulty understanding that collectivist hierarchical and egalitarian social environments inculcate in individuals the desire to sacrifice their own material well-being for others and that they expect other people to do the same.

While there are irreducible problems of coordinating collective activity regardless of one's attitude toward collective enterprises—what political economists call "collective action problems"—surely one's attitude (and aptitude) makes a difference in the success of collective action. Because of these differences, one might expect (predominantly) individualistic Americans to have greater difficulty acting collectively than the (predominantly) egalitarian Danes or hierarchical Japanese, who have been socialized to do their part for the collective well-being (for evidence of cultural variation in Western Europe and discussion of some of its causes and consequences, see Grendstad, 1999, and Mamadouh, 1999a, 1999b; for the consequences of cultural variation for successful policy design in Japan, see Weare and Smolensky, 2000). Such communitarians do not have collective action problems; they have "individual initiative problems." Lacking the entrepreneurial qualities of individualists and the community support of collectivists, fatalists in many places (southern Italy, for example) have both individual initiative and collective action problems. (For more on the varying constructions placed on human nature by the cultural types, see Thompson, Ellis, and Wildavsky, 1990; Wildavsky, 1994; Enzell and Wildavsky, 1998; Lockhart and Wildavsky, 1998; Grendstad and Selle, 2000.)

Aspects of cultural bias: political values associated with dimensions of social life

As the foregoing discussion already indicates, different patterns of social relations have different consequences for behavior and for the values that people in those patterns hold. The need to justify and legitimate a pattern of relations places some boundaries on the views that will be acceptable. Only a certain range of views will serve the function of allowing people in a pattern of relations to justify that pattern to each other. Rather than assuming that self-interested individuals seek to maximize material acquisitions, cultural theory allows analysts to anticipate a wider range of motivations, preferences, values, and behaviors from the different patterns of social relations in which individuals are embedded.

Cultural theory's four patterns of social relations are hypothesized to be functionally related to four patterns of values and beliefs, including beliefs about human nature, the environment, and the economy.[4] These values and beliefs, or ideologies, are also called "cultural biases." Thus, hierarchs value order, propriety, and whatever collectivity gives them their station; egalitarians value equality (of result), and freedom to the extent that it can be reconciled with community; individualists value liberty, autonomy, and personal space; and fatalists value good luck while hoping merely to survive.[5] The central political values associated with each pattern of social relations are represented in Figure 1.

By specifying the political values that help rationalize particular patterns of social relations, cultural theory can provide much more helpful, concrete guidance to policy analysts than merely telling them to "consider the general values" that give rise to a policy problem before proposing solutions. With cultural theory, analysts know what values to consider.

Moreover, they know that these values are tied to particular patterns of social relations, and that they will be tied to particular views of the economy and environment. These and other entailments of political values help suggest the shape of acceptable policy solutions. In specifying these nonobvious relationships, cultural theory again breaks new ground, offering a unique analytical tool. Political economic approaches to policy analysis do not even attempt to provide such tools, yet they implicitly assume that human nature, the economy, and the environment have certain characteristics.

Aspects of cultural bias: beliefs about the environment

In cultural theory, individualistic business interests are hypothesized to construe nature as resilient or even robust because such a construction allows them the greatest scope for action, including the production and sale of property, unencumbered by regulation. Egalitarian environmentalists are hypothesized to construe nature as fragile because such a construction helps them criticize and limit business activities and build an alternative society that values smaller scale egalitarian community. Meanwhile, hierarchical government regulators are hypothesized to construe nature as complex—sometimes fragile, sometimes robust or resilient—because such a construction justifies a role for experts to sort it all out, and this need for experts in turn justifies the large bureaucratic organizations that produce and sustain them. Fatalists, finally, are hypothesized to construe nature as unpredictable because such a view helps them make the best of social relationships that they also experience as unpredictable (this paragraph is adapted from Swedlow, 2002).

Environmental beliefs that are functional for the different patterns of social relations are represented by a ball in a landscape in Figure 1. In the individualistic construction, the ball is in a deep pocket, difficult to knock out: this represents nature as resilient or robust. The egalitarian construct is most nearly the opposite of this: the ball is perched precariously on top of a pinnacle, and the slightest disturbance will send it downhill permanently: this represents nature as fragile or ephemeral. The hierarchical construct of nature combines these two constructs: the ball is in a shallow pocket, where small disturbances will not dislodge it, but large ones will: nature is construed as resilient within limits, beyond which it becomes fragile or unpredictable. In the fatalistic construction of nature, the ball is on a flat surface and can roll any which way: this represents the unpredictability of nature—sometimes resilient, sometimes fragile, without rhyme or reason. For more on the environmental biases of the cultural types, see Douglas and Wildavsky (1982), Thompson, Ellis, and Wildavsky (1990), Schwarz and Thompson (1990), Dake and Wildavsky (1990), Wildavsky (1994d), Coyle (1994), Jenkins-Smith and Smith (1994), Grendstad and Selle (1997/2000), Ellis and Thompson (1997), and Ellis (1998).

These constructs of nature of course do not exhaust the environmental views that people hold or that are functional for the different patterns of social relations. People frequently take the more straightforward approach of anthro-pomorphisis: projecting their views of human nature and social relations onto animals, plants, and even inanimate objects. Nature is made homologous or isomorphic with society. Recent efforts to preserve old-growth Douglas-fir forests in the Pacific Northwest, for example, have been driven in part by the view that these forests constitute distinct ecosystems or biological communities. This view resonates with collectivists both hierarchical and egalitarian, but particularly with egalitarians because, as in the human communities they are trying to create, all members of the biological community are presumptively equally important to the preservation and functioning of the whole. These recent egalitarian efforts at preservation contrast dramatically not only with the hierarchical conservationist movement they displace (which had been institutionalized in the U.S. Forest Service) and the "rugged individualists" who settled the American frontier but also with the Save the Redwoods League, dating from the 1920s.

League members were social hierarchs, i.e., patricians, religious romantics, and eugenicists, who viewed the redwoods as victors in the same evolutionary struggle for survival that led some individuals, i.e., the industrialists of turn-of-the-century America, and some races, i.e., northern Europeans, to dominate other people like these trees that tower over other plants (Swedlow, 2002).

Aspects of cultural bias: political economy revisited

Varying views of human nature and the environment are hypothesized to coalesce to generate views of economics that are also functional for these varying patterns of social relations. Cultural theorists predict that different cultures will have different ideas about how to make ends meet, because they perceive natural resources and human needs differently. Hierarchs believe in sustainable economic development, where the rate and type of growth, and control and allocation of resources, human and natural, are within the purview of the state, and its experts and authorities. Egalitarians, meanwhile, think that economic growth is constrained by natural resources, which are finite—a situation that is all well and good because humans uncorrupted by "consumer capitalism" have very simple needs anyway. Individualists, for their part, think that there is no limit to economic growth, since there are no limits to human wants that human ingenuity, the ultimate renewable resource, cannot satisfy. Finally, fatalists, unable to control needs or resources, can only hope for an alignment between them—that they have few needs or many winning lottery tickets. For more on the economic "theories" of the cultural types, see Thompson, Ellis, and Wildavsky (1990), Malkin and Wildavsky (1991), Wildavsky (1994d), and Fogerty, Jeanrenaud, and Wildavsky (1998) (this paragraph adapted from Swedlow, 2001, p. 349).

"Cultural auditing" to discover existing and potential policy advocacy coalitions

The only precept for policy analysis informed by cultural analysis that Wildavsky had a chance to suggest was that it should begin with "cultural auditing," by which he meant "[a] set of measures...to gauge the relative proportions of hierarchists, individualists, egalitarians, and fatalists in a population" (Wildavsky, 1994, p. 159). The relative proportion of cultural types in a population was important, he reasoned, because the cultural context in which policies were pursued mattered. Only certain cultural types would support certain policies. Economic development, for example, in his view depended on having many individualists and some hierarchs and egalitarians:

> For economies to grow... there must be diverse sources of capital and opportunity to bid resources away from existing holders. Evidently competition [promoted by

individualists] is the key process. But there must also be sufficient stability [provided by hierarchs] to maintain rules for competition—without collection of debts, for example, there can be no borrowing—and sufficient criticism of inequality [by egalitarians] to prevent the rise of monopolies that would eventually kill competition (Wildavsky, 1994b, p. 146).

Extending a metaphor used by Robert Putnam, Robert Klitgaard has emphasized that analysts must assess the "cultural soil" in which policies are planted if they expect their recommendations to take root and flourish (Putnam, 1993; Klitgaard, 1995). A number of cultural theorists have performed such "soil assessments" using public opinion surveys much in the same way that Wildavsky suggested doing cultural audits (see, for example, Dake and Wildavsky, 1990; Boyle and Coughlin, 1994; Jenkins-Smith and Smith, 1994; Grendstad and Selle, 1997; Ellis and Thompson, 1997; Coughlin and Lockhart, 1998; Grendstad and Selle, 2000). Others, myself included, have focused more on the cultural commitments of political elites in explaining the social construction, i.e., the framing and choice, of policy problems and solutions (see, for example, Schwarz and Thompson, 1990; Coyle, 1993, 1994; Hendriks, 1994; Hoppe and Peterse, 1993; Swedlow, 1994, 2001).

Auditing the general population to determine the proportion of cultural types, as Wildavsky suggested, would be important for any policy such as economic development that is likely to require widespread support and participation to be successful. The refinement of this idea that I want to suggest here is that the basic unit for cultural auditing should be what Paul Sabatier and Hank Jenkins-Smith call "policy advocacy coalitions" rather than an undifferentiated public (Sabatier and Jenkins-Smith, 1999). These coalitions can include various elites—scientists, journalists, and administrators, for example—that coalesce to advocate the enactment and implementation of policies. Analysis of policy advocacy coalitions should begin with (1) a cultural self-audit by the analyst, followed by (2) a cultural audit of the analyst's employer and (3) a cultural audit of the client, if different from the employer, and then (4) a cultural audit of the environment in which the proposed policy is to be enacted, and finally (5) implementation.

Analysts should then focus on identifying potential cultural policy coalitions and "shift points" or "windows of opportunity" for leadership and persuasion by policy entrepreneurs (on "shift points" or "punctuated equilibria," see Baumgartner and Jones, 1993, and True, Jones, and Baumgartner, 1999; for "policy windows" see Kingdon, 1995, and Zahariadis, 1999). To the extent that the creation of "policy windows" is beyond the client's control, analysts can identify the confluence of political cultural factors that is more or less likely to result in policy opportunities and constraints. This kind of information should in turn allow the refinement of models, analysis, and policy advice that can help clients build and maximize their leverage in the policy process.

Cultural theorists can contribute a great deal to this kind of analysis because they have a set of hypotheses about cultural constraints on policy choice—about how values, beliefs, and social relations bound each other, making some policies desirable, others possible, and many impossible without fundamental shifts in those values, beliefs, and social relations. Cultural theorists can help suggest when policy change requires cultural change and when cultural change makes policy change likely. They can help indicate which policies are likely to reproduce and reinforce existing cultural configurations and which are likely to challenge and reshape them.

From political economy to political culture: the policy analyst's role in satisficing cultural utilities

What I am suggesting here further reworks and recasts a vision of policy analysis as cultural analysis proposed by Klitgaard, which may make particular sense to policy analysts who are economists by training, as Klitgaard is:

> We have, metaphorically, a complicated set of simultaneous equations, in which "culture" enters in three ways. It shapes the utility function; in other words, it determines in part what a society will aspire to or desire. It conditions the production function (various kinds of them) for desired goods and services of many kinds, ranging from education to economic growth to artistic activities. And culture itself changes, meaning that as we try to estimate culture's impact and its interaction with policy choices, we are estimating a moving, dynamic, indeed living "variable".
>
> Imagine we had God's help and for a given society at a particular time could specify these complicated simultaneous equations and their dynamics. In other words, suppose we were divinely gifted social scientists. How could we then use this wonderful cultural theory to make decisions? The economist's answer is to maximize social utility given cultural conditions. We would maximize the value added of various choices given the moderating effects of the social cultural setting and taking into account how our choices in turn would affect the social cultural setting overtime (Klitgaard, 1997, p. 195).

While Klitgaard devotes his subsequent analysis to delineating some problematic implications of "the economist's answer," he is probably right that knowledge of the social utilities of various policies would allow analysts to suggest which policies maximize (or at least satisfice) social utility under given cultural conditions. But there are at least three other problems with the inference that analysts would be able to suggest the best policy path based on such cultural analysis.

First of all, maximizing social utility represents a value choice, whether those utilities are conceived in economic, political, or cultural terms. Adam Smith taught us that the world is composed of individuals who will bid and bargain for each others' goods and services until there are no more gains to be realized from trades, i.e., to the point at which no one will receive more of value to him- or herself by making a trade than by abstaining from one. Jeremy Bentham and John Stuart Mill transposed this idea to the political arena by suggesting that the best governmental policies were those that promoted the greatest good of the greatest number (but see Lockhart and Wildavsky, 1993, 1998). Economists further developed these and other ideas to create the field of social welfare economics that has been so influential in policy analysis.

But why should the greatest good of the greatest number, as determined by the individuals involved, be our guiding value? To put it another way, would people in hierarchical or egalitarian cultural environments agree that we should be maximizing social utilities so conceived? Hierarchs embrace the premise that all individuals do not equally know what is best for themselves and that it is more important to satisfy the utilities of "more important" people than of "less important" people. Egalitarians, meanwhile, are not likely to be happy with policies that merely satisfy the greatest good of the greatest number because such policies may not provide anything considered good by the lesser number or minority. For egalitarians, as for the Three Musketeers, policies should be "all for one and one for all" or not be pursued at all.

Second, even if we could envision maximizing social utilities so conceived— so that in individualistic cultural environments we would seek to satisfy the greatest good of the greatest number, while in hierarchical cultural environments we would ascribe different utilities to different classes of people, and in egalitarian cultural environments we would see to it that policies promoted equality—we could not impose this vision as analysts without undermining the very utilities we were trying to maximize, except in hierarchical cultural environments (under conditions specified below). For individualists, only the "revealed utilities" of people engaging in actual trades can determine their utilities for various goods and services. Analysts' attempts to use records of production and consumption to predict future supply and demand make individuals slaves to their own histories rather than masters of their fate with each new choice they confront. For egalitarians, everyone should have a hand in crafting the policies pursued by a community; that is, everyone should participate in policy analysis, enactment, and implementation. Egalitarians' utility for participation is so high that analysts who don't become part of this process de-legitimate policies that otherwise would be acceptable to the community.

Only in hierarchical cultural environments does the analyst have the opportunity to maximize social utility by imposing his policy vision on others. The realization of that opportunity depends on the analyst being given the role of knowing what's best for others, as policy analysts often have been in our society. To the extent that this role is reserved for or assumed by others in an hierarchical cultural environment—Brahmins in America, chiefs or shamans in tribal societies—analysts will be viewed as usurpers, and their advice will be correspondingly ignored or appropriated without credit.

The first two problems with maximizing social utilities conceived as varying cultural utilities are compounded by a third problem: societies and social subgroups and institutions are frequently multicultural. Consequently, maximizing the social utility of one cultural type will often mean minimizing the social utility of the other cultural types. Cultural conflict is in some ways an unavoidably zero-sum game: people can simultaneously maximize their preferred degrees of individual autonomy and collectivization only at the expense of people with different preferences. However, people can simultaneously maximize their values along one of these dimensions: hierarchs and egalitarians can together maximize collectivization, and individualists and egalitarians can together maximize individual autonomy. The shared values on these dimensions help suggest which policies will be supported by which cultural coalitions. There are also circumstances where a three-way cultural coalition is possible in support of a policy (Coyle and Wildavsky, 1987).

Cultural theorists also think that the cultural types cannot be maximized in isolation from each other but exist in a cultural system, where one relies on the other. While the beliefs and values of each culture are functional for that culture up to a point, the argument goes, they are dysfunctional beyond that point, at which point the beliefs, values, and institutions of other cultures become functional for them instead (Thompson, Grendstad, and Selle, 1999; see also this issue). For example, as Wildavsky argued above, maintaining markets depends not only on individualists for a competitive, entrepreneurial spirit (and behavior) but also on hierarchs to enforce contracts and on egalitarians to protest monopolies. Wildavsky developed a similar argument with respect to the proportions of cultures that strengthen and weaken democracy (Wildavsky, 1993, 1994; both essays are reprinted in Wildavsky, 1998; see also Lockhart and Franzwa, 1994). To the extent that such cultural interdependences exist, they suggest that maximization of cultural utilities cannot be an entirely zero-sum game. Individualists may reduce the overbearing Nanny State to a minimalist Nightwatchman State, for example, but to go further invites the collapse of individualism into Hobbesian anarchy and fatalism (Enzell and Wildavsky, 1998). If hierarchs grow the Nanny State to become an Authoritarian or Totalitarian State, however, they will kill the innovation and initiative of individualists and with them the goose that lays the golden egg of economic growth, without which no state can thrive.

There is no doubt that people with hierarchical cultural propensities—who are well-represented among policy analysts and planners and among their employers and clients—will find especially in this latter version of cultural theory a tempting inducement to build a Platonic society composed of the correct proportions of cultural types. Attempts to maximize social utility in the way suggested by Klitgaard will then focus on promoting multiculturalism of one kind or another. Yet even if the cultural interdependencies hypothesized by Thompson and Wildavsky exist, there is still plenty of room for basic cultural preferences to express themselves, as Dennis Coyle argues (1994). Hierarchs and individualists may concede that they need each other, placing the totalitarian state and anarchy off-limits as policy options, for example, but that still leaves plenty of room for disagreement about whether it is better to have a Nanny or a Nightwatchman State.

While it is foreseeable that hierarchical types will try to use cultural theory to displace democratic politics and market processes with central planning, as they have attempted to do in relying on social welfare economics, there is nothing inherent about cultural theory that disproportionately empowers hierarchs. Egalitarian and individualistic analysts can equally use cultural theory to game out areas of policy conflict and coalition and to figure out how to maximize their values in a multicultural setting. Moreover, to the extent that there are distinct proportions of cultures that support markets and democracies, not everyone will equally value markets and democracies, and it would be fairly antithetical to these institutions (and probably unfeasible) to try to impose such cultural change through central planning. People with different cultural commitments, it must be remembered, often value means as much as ends, although they share a human propensity to let ends justify means.

A final obstacle to using cultural theory to impose one's vision of the good life on society, an obstacle faced by proponents of all versions of the good life at one time or another, is that the social and natural worlds resist our cultural constructions, resulting in "the natural destruction of culture." The fact that not all cultural constructions are created equal—that at any given time and place, some "stipulated worlds" are in greater alignment with the "actual world" than others (Thompson, Ellis, and Wildavsky, 1990, pp. 69–81)—generates plenty of opportunities for cultural change that cannot be controlled by policymakers, whether central planners, politicians, or the public. In fact, windows for policy change will in part be constructed from events beyond the control of policymakers, and a big part of the policy analyst's job will be to analyze these events in ways that specify how they can be used to effect policy change that is also cultural change. At any given time and place, one cultural construction of human nature, the environment, and the economy is likely to get a better purchase on external realities than the other cultural constructions do. Appropriate policy analysis and advice should vary accordingly.

Conclusion: the promise and problems of this cultural approach to policy analysis

To paraphrase an oft-cited Wildavsky article on planning, if political culture is everything, then maybe it is nothing (Wildavsky, 1973). That is, if political culture permeates everything and is everywhere, then it cannot explain anything without reference to itself, creating unenlightening tautologies. That is why it is important to disaggregate culture into its constituent elements, to conceptualize culture as covariation among specific values, beliefs, and patterns of relations. Moreover, only by allowing for variation in these covarying packages of values, beliefs, and relations can other forms of variation in policies be accounted for by political culture. Only something that varies can explain other things that vary. Douglas and Wildavsky's cultural theory specifies different types of political cultures and so opens the door to using political culture to understand and predict the different types of values, beliefs, and forms of social organization that are likely to be associated with different kinds of policies.

As we have seen, Douglas and Wildavsky derive their types of political cultures from two dimensions of social organization (creating cultural types that are mutually exclusive and jointly exhaustive of the social possibilities.) The types and dimensions are sufficiently abstract and general so that they "travel" across space and time with a minimum of conceptual "stretching" (on conceptual "travel" and "stretching," see Sartori, 1970; Collier and Mahon, 1993; Swedlow, 2001). At the same time, Douglas and Wildavsky's characterization of the values, beliefs, and forms of social organization that constitute their political cultures are sufficiently specific to generate falsifiable hypotheses about their relationships to many other social phenomena, including public policies. This combination of characteristics makes their cultural concepts ideally suited for comparative policy analysis both within and among countries. Thus, the same concepts can be used to analyze and explain policy developments inside and across national, subnational, or supranational political organizations. Different mixes of cultural types can be used to explain the variety of political organizations, permitting their comparison, rather than allowing cultural types to multiply with the number of organizations, simply reproducing their variation, while driving out comparison, explanation, predictability, and the accumulation of knowledge.

Despite the promise of policy analysis as cultural analysis, its potential does not mean the approach is free of problems. For one thing, cultural theorists need a more discriminating, systematic understanding than they presently have of how individuals interact with institutions to reproduce a cultural pattern or shift to a new one (Lockhart, 1997; Coughlin and Lockhart, 1998). Studies of public opinion and voting behavior find that only politically sophisticated elites hold the well-developed, multifaceted ideologies that are functional for different patterns of social relations. More recent studies of public opinion and voting behavior indicate that political sophistication can take a variety of forms, including issue specialization and reliance on reference groups, including political elites, for policy cues (Brady and Sniderman, 1985; Luskin, 1987; Zaller, 1992; Sniderman, 1993; Elkins, 1993; Popkin, 1994; Lupia and McCubbins, 2000; Kuklinski and Quirk, 2000). These findings suggests that cultural theorists need to rethink the ways that they have attempted to measure culture in surveys of the general public. As cultural analysis is further specified by selective synthesis with insights generated by other kinds of studies of individuals, groups, and institutions, it will be able to inform policy analysis even further (for efforts by cultural theorists to pursue such syntheses with political economic and rational choice approaches, see Wildavsky, 1991, 1992, 1994c, reprinted in Wildavsky, 1998a; Lockhart, 1997, 2000; Lockhart and Coughlin, 1992, 1998; Chai and Wildavsky, 1994, 1998; Chai, 1997, 2001).

Acknowledgments

Many thanks to Eugene Bardach, Frank Baumgartner, Ray Bromley, Charles Lockhart, Iris Geva-May, Gunnar Grendstad, Rob Hoppe, Chandra Hunter, Helen Ingram, Robert Klitgaard, Perri 6, Eugene Smolensky, Michael Thompson, Marco Verweij, and the anonymous reviewers for their many helpful comments on earlier drafts of this article. Remaining inadequacies are my responsibility.

Notes

1. At a World Bank conference on culture and development that Wildavsky attended shortly before his death, "he speculated that a 'cultural audit' in Africa would be a baseline from which culture-by-policy interactions might be discovered" (Klitgaard, 1997, pp. 191–192).
2. The following description of Douglas and Wildavsky's cultural theory tracks that found in Thompson, Ellis, and Wildavsky (1990) fairly closely. However, I have relabeled their dimensions to make their theory "translate" better into terms that policy analysts and social scientists already understand. Thus, the extent of collectivization in a social organization corresponds to the extent of "group" in their formulation, while the extent of individual autonomy corresponds (inversely) to the extent of "grid." As Thompson, Ellis, and Wildavsky (1990, p. 5) explain, "*Group* refers to the extent to which an individual is incorporated into bounded units. The greater the incorporation, the more individual choice is subject to group determination. *Grid* denotes the degree to which an individual's life is circumscribed by externally imposed prescriptions. The more binding and extensive the scope of prescriptions, the less of life that is open to individual negotiation (emphasis in original)." Hierarchs are high and individualists low on both group and grid. Fatalists are high on grid but low on group, experiencing many constraints on individual autonomy that are not compensated for by being part of a group (Ellis, 1994). Egalitarians attempt to manage the tricky task of reconciling individual autonomy with group solidarity by requiring consensus decision-making. When their groups grow in size, consensus becomes harder to attain, leading to coercion, demonization of outsiders, and schism, as hidden hierarchies of decision-making develop (Ellis, 1998).
3. By the extent of collectivization, I mean the extent to which a relational pattern is defined by an external group boundary. By the extent of individual autonomy, I mean the extent to which individuals in a pattern of social relations are free from coercion and are free to act as they please; individual autonomy implies some personal power or efficacy. For current attempts to relate cultural theory to the literature on organizations and public administration, see Flentje (2000), Hendriks (1999), Hood (1998), Coyle (1997), and Wildavsky (1990, 1998b, 2001, forthcoming).
4. When I say that relations, values, and beliefs are functionally related, I mean that they are mutually compatible in a way that other combinations of relations, values, and beliefs would not be. In my view, such functional relationships can be—and frequently are—the result of intentional behavior by people who are aware of the compatibilities (and incompatibilities) of particular relations, values, and beliefs. Thus, I do not share the view that the validity of functional explanations hinges on meeting Jon Lister's criteria for

functional explanation, including lack of intentional action, as others have argued (see Grimen, 1999). Questions of what range of values and beliefs will be functional for a pattern of social relations, and exactly how the interrelationships among values, beliefs, and relations will manifest themselves, have not been adequately answered (or even asked) by cultural theorists. (For a significant disconfirmation of the hypothesized coincidence between constructs of human nature and the environment among members of Norwegian environmental groups, see Grendstad and Selle, 2000.)

5. In speaking of hierarchs, egalitarians, individualists, and fatalists, I am resorting to a shorthand for pattern-maintaining behavior for which functionally related beliefs and values may be internalized to different degrees (or not at all) by individuals moving through the pattern. That is, just because people act in a way that maintains a pattern of behavior, it does not automatically follow that they will develop or hold beliefs and values that are functional for the pattern, particularly if they are not spending a lot of time in the pattern and/or if they have strongly held beliefs and values from prior socialization experiences.

References

Baumgartner, Frank and Bryan Jones. *(1993). Agendas and Instability in American Politics.* Chicago: University of Chicago Press.
Boyle, Richard P. and Richard M. Coughlin. (1994). "Conceptualizing and Operationalizing Cultural Theory." In Dennis J. Coyle and Richard J. Ellis (eds.), *Politics, Policy, and Culture.* Boulder, CO: Westview Press.
Brady, Henry E. and Paul M. Sniderman. (1985). "Attitude Attribution: A Group Basis for Political Reasoning." *American Political Science Review* 79, 1061–1078.
Coughlin, Richard M. and Charles Lockhart. (1998). "Grid-Group Theory and Political Ideology: A Consideration of their Relative Strengths and Weaknesses for Explaining the Structure of Mass Belief Systems." *Journal of Theoretical Politics* 10(1), 33–58.
Chai, Sun-Ki. (1997). "Rational Choice and Culture: Clashing Perspectives or Complementary Modes of Analysis?" In Richard J. Ellis and Michael Thompson (eds.), *Culture Matters: Essays in Honor of Aaron Wildavsky.* Boulder, CO: Westview Press.
Chai, Sun-Ki. (2001). *Choosing an Identity: A General Model of Preference and Belief Formation and Its Application to Comparative Development.* Ann Arbor, MI: University of Michigan Press.
Chai, Sun-Ki and Aaron Wildavsky. (1994). "Culture, Rationality, and Political Violence." In Dennis J. Coyle and Richard J. Ellis (eds.), *Politics, Policy, and Culture.* Boulder, CO: Westview Press. Reprinted in Aaron Wildavsky (1998), *Culture and Social Theory* (Sun-Ki Chai and Brendon Swedlow, eds.). New Brunswick, NJ: Transaction Publishers.
Chai, Sun-Ki and Aaron Wildavsky. (1998). "Cultural Change, Party Ideology, and Electoral Outcomes." In Aaron Wildavsky (eds.), *Culture and Social Theory* (Sun-Ki Chai and Brendon Swedlow, eds.). New Brunswick, NJ: Transaction Publishers.
Collier, David and James E. Mahon, Jr. (1993). "Conceptual 'Stretching' Revisited: Adapting Categories in Comparative Analysis." *American Political Science Review* 87(4).
Coyle, Dennis J. and Aaron Wildavsky. (1987). "Requisites of Radical Reform: Income Maintenance Versus Tax Preferences." *Journal of Policy Analysis and Management* 7, 1–16.
Coyle, Dennis J. (1994a). "'This Land is My Land, This Land is Your Land': Cultural Conflict in Environmental and Land Use Regulation." In Dennis J. Coyle and Richard J. Ellis (eds.), *Politics, Policy, and Culture.* Boulder, CO: Westview Press.
Coyle, Dennis J. (1994b). "The Theory That Would Be King." In Dennis J. Coyle and Richard J. Ellis (eds.), *Politics, Policy, and Culture.* Boulder, CO: Westview Press.
Coyle, Dennis J. (1997). "A Cultural Theory of Organizations." In Richard J. Ellis and Michael Thompson (eds.), *Culture Matters: Essays in Honor of Aaron Wildavsky.* Boulder, CO: Westview Press.
Dake, Karl and Aaron Wildavsky. (1990). "Theories of Risk Perception: Who Fears What and Why?" *Daedalus,* Spring, 41–60. Reprinted in Brendon Swedlow (ed.), *Applying Cultural Theory,* forthcoming. New Brunswick, NJ: Transaction Publishers.
Douglas, Mary. (1982). "Cultural Bias." In Mary Douglas (ed.), *In the Active Voice.* London: Routledge & Kegan Paul.
Douglas, Mary and Aaron Wildavsky. (1982). *Risk and Culture: An Essay on the Selection of Technological and Environmental Dangers.* Berkeley, CA: University of California Press.

Douglas, Mary. (1986). *How Institutions Think*. Syracuse, NY: Syracuse University Press.
Douglas, Mary. (1994). *Risk and Blame: Essays in Cultural Theory*. London: Routledge.
Elkins, David J. (1993). *Manipulation and Consent: How Voters and Leaders Manage Complexity*. Vancouver: UBC Press.
Ellis, Richard J. (1994). "The Social Construction of Slavery." In Dennis J. Coyle and Richard J. Ellis (eds.), *Politics, Policy, and Culture*. Boulder, CO: Westview Press.
Ellis, Richard J. (1997). "Preface: Remembering Aaron Wildavsky, the Cultural Theorist." In Richard J. Ellis and Michael Thompson (eds.), *Culture Matters: Essays in Honor of Aaron Wildavsky*. Boulder, CO: Westview Press.
Ellis, Richard J. and Fred Thompson. (1997). "Culture and the Environment in the Pacific Northwest." *American Political Science Review* 91 (4), 885–897.
Ellis, Richard J. (1998). *The Dark Side of the Left: Illiberal Egalitarianism in America*. Lawrence, KS: University Press of Kansas.
Enzell, Magnus and Aaron Wildavsky. (1998). "Thomas Hobbes and His Critics: Interpretive Implications of Cultural Theory." In Aaron Wildavsky (1998), *Culture and Social Theory* (Sun-Ki Chai and Brendon Swedlow, eds.). New Brunswick, NJ: Transaction Publishers.
Flentje, H. Edward. (2000). "State Administration in Cultural Context." In John J. Gargan (ed.), *Handbook of State Administration*. New York: Marcel Decker.
Fogerty, David, Claude Jeanrenaud, and Aaron Wildavsky. (1998). "At Once Ubiquitous and Elusive, the Concept of Externalities is Either Vacuous or Misapplied." In Aaron Wildavsky (1998), *Culture and Social Theory* (Sun-Ki Chai and Brendon Swedlow, eds.), New Brunswick, NJ: Transaction Publishers.
Geva-May, Iris with Aaron Wildavsky. (1997/2001). *An Operational Approach to Policy Analysis: The Craft: Prescriptions for Better Analysis*. Kluwer Academic Publishers.
Grendstad, Gunnar and Per Selle. (1997). "Cultural Theory, Postmaterialism, and Environmental Attitudes." In Richard J. Ellis and Michael Thompson (eds.), *Culture Matters: Essays in Honor of Aaron Wildavsky*. Boulder, CO: Westview Press.
Grendstad, Gunnar. (1999). "A Political Cultural Map of Europe. A Survey Approach." *Geojournal* 47, 463–475.
Grendstad, Gunnar and Per Selle. (2000). "Cultural Myths of Human and Physical Nature: Integrated or Separated?" *Risk Analysis* 20(1), 27–39.
Grimen, Harald. (1999). "Sociocultural Functionalism." In Michael Thompson, Gunnar Grendstad, and Per Selle (eds.), *Cultural Theory as Political Science*. New York: Routledge.
Hendriks, Frank. (1999). *Public Policy and Political Institutions: The Role of Culture in Traffic Policy*. Cheltenham, UK: Edward Elgar.
Hood, Christopher. (1998). *The Art of the State*. New York: Clarendon Press.
Hoppe, Rob and Aat Peterse. (1993). *Handling Frozen Fire: Political Culture and Risk Management*. Boulder, CO: Westview Press.
Jenkins-Smith, Hank C. and Walter K. Smith. (1994). "Ideology, Culture, and Risk Perception." In Dennis J. Coyle and Richard J. Ellis (eds.), *Politics, Policy, and Culture*. Boulder, CO: Westview Press.
Kingdon, John W. (1995). *Agendas, Alternatives, and Public Policies*, 2nd ed. New York: Harper Collins.
Klitgaard, Robert. (1994). "Taking Culture into Account: From 'Let's' to 'How.'" In I. Serageldin and J. Taboroff (eds.), *Culture and Development in Africa*, Volume I. Washington, D.C.: World Bank.
Klitgaard, Robert. (1995). "Including Culture in Evaluation Research." In Robert Picciotto and Ray C. Rist (eds.), *Evaluating Country Development Policies and Programs: New Approaches for a New Agenda*. From *New Directions for Evaluation by American Evaluation Association*, No. 67, pp. 135–146, Jossey-Bass Publishers. Also available as a reprint from RAND at www.rand.org.
Klitgaard, Robert. (1997). "Applying Cultural Theories to Practical Problems." In Richard J. Ellis and Michael Thompson (eds.), *Culture Matters: Essays in Honor of Aaron Wildavsky*. Boulder, CO: Westview Press. Also available as a reprint from RAND at www.rand.org.
Kuklinski, James H. and Paul Quirk. (2000). "Reconsidering the Rational Public: Cognition, Heuristics, and Mass Opinion." In Arthur Lupia, Mathew D. McCubbins, and Samuel Popkin (eds.), *Elements of Reason: Cognition, Choice, and the Bounds of Rationality*. New York: Cambridge University Press.
Lindblom, Charles. (1977). *Politics and Markets: The World's Political-Economic Systems*. New York: Basic Books.
Lockhart, Charles and Richard M. Coughlin. (1992). "Building Better Comparative Social Theory Through Alternative Conceptions of Rationality." *Western Political Quarterly* 45, 793–809.

Lockhart, Charles and Aaron Wildavsky. (1993). "The 'Multicultural' Mill." *Utilitas* 5(2), 255–273. Reprinted in Aaron Wildavsky (1998), *Culture and Social Theory* (Sun-Ki Chai and Brendon Swedlow, eds.). New Brunswick, NJ: Transaction Publishers.

Lockhart, Charles and Gregg Franzwa. (1994). "Cultural Theory and the Problem of Moral Relativism." In Dennis J. Coyle and Richard J. Eilis (eds.), *Politics, Policy, and Culture*. Boulder, CO: Westview Press.

Lockhart, Charles. (1997). "Political Culture and Political Change." In Richard J. Ellis and Michael Thompson (eds.), *Culture Matters: Essays in Honor of Aaron Wildavsky*. Boulder, CO: Westview Press.

Lockhart, Charles and Aaron Wildavsky. (1998). "The Social Construction of Cooperation: Egalitarian, Hierarchical, and Individualistic Faces of Altruism." In Aaron Wildavsky (1998), *Culture and Social Theory* (Sun-Ki Chai and Brendon Swedlow, eds.). New Brunswick, NJ: Transaction Publishers.

Lockhart, Charles and Richard M. Coughlin. (1998). "Foreword." In Aaron Wildavsky (1998), *Culture and Social Theory* (Sun-Ki Chai and Brendon Swedlow, eds.). New Brunswick, NJ: Transaction Publishers.

Lupia, Arthur and Mathew D. McCubbins. (2000). "The Institutional Foundations of Political Competence: How Citizens Learn What They Need to Know." In Arthur Lupia, Mathew D. McCubbins, and Samuel Popkin (eds.), *Elements of Reason: Cognition, Choice, and the Bounds of Rationality*. New York: Cambridge University Press.

Luskin, Robert. (1987). "Measuring Political Sophistication." *American Journal of Political Science* 31(4), 856–899.

Malkin, Jesse and Aaron Wildavsky. (1991). "Why the Traditional Distinction Between Public and Private Goods Should Be Abandoned." *Journal of Theoretical Politics* 3(4), 355–378. Reprinted in Aaron Wildavsky (1998), *Culture and Social Theory* (Sun-Ki Chai and Brendon Swedlow, eds.). New Brunswick, NJ: Transaction Publishers.

Mamadouh, Virginie. (1999a). "National Political Cultures in the European Union." In Michael Thompson, Gunnar Grendstad, and Per Selle (eds.), *Cultural Theory as Political Science*. New York: Routledge.

Mamadouh, Virginie. (1999b). "A Political-Cultural Map of Europe. Family Structures and the Origins of Differences Between National Political Cultures in the European Union." *Geojournal* 47, 477–486.

Mansbridge, Jane J. (ed.). (1990). *Beyond Self-interest*. Chicago: University of Chicago Press.

Popkin, Samuel. (1994). *The Reasoning Voter: Communication and Persuasion in Presidential Campaigns*. Chicago: University of Chicago Press.

Putnam, Robert (with Robert Leonardi and Raffaela Nanetti). (1993). *Making Democracy Work: Civic Traditions in Modern Italy*. Princeton, NJ: Princeton University Press.

Riker, William H. (1991). "The Political Psychology of Rational Choice," unpublished manuscript.

Sabatier, Paul A. and Hank C. Jenkins-Smith. (1999). "The Advocacy Coalition Framework: An Assessment." In Paul A. Sabatier (ed.), *Theories of the Policy Process*. Boulder, CO: Westview Press.

Sartori, Giovanni. (1970). "Concept Misformation in Comparative Politics." *American Political Science Review* 64, 1033–1053.

Schwarz, Michiel and Michael Thompson. (1990). *Divided We Stand: Redefining Politics, Technology, and Social Choice*. London: Harvester Wheatleaf.

Sniderman, Paul M. (1993). "The New Look in Public Opinion Research." In Ada W. Finifter (ed.), *Political Science: The State of the Discipline II*. Washington, D.C.: The American Political Science Association.

Swedlow, Brendon. (1994). "Cultural Influences on Policies Concerning Mental Illness." In Dennis J. Coyle and Richard J. Ellis (eds.), *Politics, Policy, and Culture*. Boulder, CO: Westview Press.

Swedlow, Brendon. (2001). "Postscript: Aaron Wildavsky, Cultural Theory, and Budgeting." In Aaron Wildavsky, *Budgeting and Governing*. New Brunswick, NJ: Transaction Publishers.

Swedlow, Brendon. (2002). *Scientists, Judges, and Spotted Owls: Policymakers in the Pacific North-west* Ph.D. Dissertation, Department of Political Science, University of California, Berkeley.

Thompson, Michael, Richard Ellis, and Aaron Wildavsky. (1990). *Cultural Theory*. Boulder, CO: Westview Press.

Thompson, Michael. (1997). "Rewriting the Precepts of Policy Analysis." In Richard J. Ellis and Michael Thompson (eds.), *Culture Matters: Essays in Honor of Aaron Wildavsky*. Boulder, CO: Westview Press.

Thompson, Michael, Gunnar Grendstad, and Per Selle (eds.). (1999). *Cultural Theory as Political Science*. London: Routledge.

True, James L., Bryan D. Jones, and Frank R. Baumgartner. (1999). "Punctuated Equilibria Theory: Explaining Stability and Change in American Policymaking." In Paul A. Sabatier (ed.), *Theories of the Policy Process*. Boulder, CO: Westview Press.

Weare, Christopher and Eugene Smolensky. (2000). "Winners, Losers, and Efficiency: Achieving Multiple Goals in Japan's Financial System Reforms." *Journal of Comparative Policy Analysis: Research and Practice* 2, 9–37.

Wildavsky, Aaron. (1973). "If Planning is Everything, Maybe It's Nothing." Policy Sciences 4(2), 127–153.

Wildavsky, Aaron. (1990). "Administration Without Hierarchy? Bureaucracy Without Authority?" In Naomi B. Lynn and Aaron Wildavsky (eds.), *Public Administration: The State of the Discipline*. Chatham, NJ: Chatham House. Reprinted in Aaron Wildavsky (forthcoming), *Applying Cultural Theory* (Brendon Swedlow, ed.). New Brunswick, NJ: Transaction Publishers.

Wildavsky, Aaron. (1991). "Can Norms Rescue Self-interest or Macro Explanation be Joined to Micro Explanation?" *Critical Review* 5(3), 301–323. Reprinted in Aaron Wildavsky (1998), *Culture and Social Theory* (Sun-Ki Chai and Brendon Swedlow, eds.). New Brunswick, NJ: Transaction Publishers.

Wildavsky, Aaron. (1992). "Indispensable Framework or Just Another Ideology: Prisoner's Dilemma as an Antihierarchical Game." *Rationality and Society* 4(1), 8–23. Reprinted in Aaron Wildavsky (1998), *Culture and Social Theory* (Sun-Ki Chai and Brendon Swedlow, eds.). New Brunswick, NJ: Transaction Publishers.

Wildavsky, Aaron. (1993). "Democracy as a Coalition of Cultures." *Society* 31 (1). Reprinted in Aaron Wildavsky (1998), *Culture and Social Theory* (Sun-Ki Chai and Brendon Swedlow, eds.). New Brunswick, NJ: Transaction Publishers.

Wildavsky, Aaron. (1994a). "Cultural Pluralism Can Both Strengthen and Weaken Democracy." *Research on Democracy and Society* 2. Reprinted in Aaron Wildavsky (1998), *Culture and Social Theory* (Sun-Ki Chai and Brendon Swedlow, eds.). New Brunswick, NJ: Transaction Publishers.

Wildavsky, Aaron. (1994b). "How Cultural Theory Can Contribute to Understanding and Promoting Democracy, Science, and Development." In I. Serageldin and J. Taboroff (eds.), *Culture and Development in Africa*, Volume I. Washington, D.C.: World Bank.

Wildavsky, Aaron. (1994c). "Why Self-Interest Means Less Outside of a Social Context: Cultural Contributions to a Theory of Rational Choices." *Journal of Theoretical Politics* 6(2), 131–159. Reprinted in Aaron Wildavsky (1998), *Culture and Social Theory* (Sun-Ki Chai and Brendon Swedlow, eds.). New Brunswick, NJ: Transaction Publishers.

Wildavsky, Aaron. (1994d). "Accounting for the Environment." *Accounting, Organizations, and Society* 19(4/5), 461–481. Reprinted in Aaron Wildavsky (1998), *Culture and Social Theory* (Sun-Ki Chai and Brendon Swedlow, eds.). New Brunswick, NJ: Transaction Publishers.

Wildavsky, Aaron. (1998a). *Culture and Social Theory* (Sun-Ki Chai and Brendon Swedlow, eds.). New Brunswick, NJ: Transaction Publishers.

Wildavsky, Aaron. (1998b). *Federalism and Political Culture* (David Schleicher and Brendon Swedlow, eds.). New Brunswick, NJ: Transaction Publishers.

Wildavsky, Aaron. (2001). *Budgeting and Governing* (Brendon Swedlow, ed.). New Brunswick, NJ: Transaction Publishers.

Wildavsky, Aaron, (forthcoming). "From Political Economy to Political Culture, or Why I Like Cultural Analysis." In Brendon Swedlow (ed.), *Applying Cultural Theory*. New Brunswick, NJ: Transaction Publishers.

Williamson, Oliver. (1975). *Markets and Hierarchies, Analysis and Antitrust Implications: A Study in the Economics of Internal Organization*. New York: Free Press.

Zahariadis, Nikolaos. (1999). "Ambiguity, Time, and Multiple Streams." In Paul A. Sabatier (ed.), *Theories of the Policy Process*. Boulder, CO: Westview Press.

Zaller, John. (1992). *The Nature and Origins of Mass Opinion*. Cambridge, England: Cambridge University Press.

Metachoice in Policy Analysis

AIDAN R. VINING and ANTHONY E. BOARDMAN

ABSTRACT Many national governments now mandate some form of ex ante evaluation of policy alternatives. But, evidence suggests that both policy analysts and their political and bureaucratic clients have difficulty doing this form of policy analysis evaluation. To conduct effective ex ante evaluation of alternatives, analysts and decision-makers must first choose the choice method class – metachoice. This paper presents an explicitly normative metachoice framework to assist them decide on a policy choice method. We propose that the metachoice decision depends on two factors: (1) goal orientation and breadth, and (2) willingness to monetize efficiency impacts. This results in four choice method classes: (comprehensive) Cost–Benefit Analysis, Efficiency Analysis, Embedded Cost–Benefit Analysis and Multi-Goal Analysis. These four method classes embrace a more extensive set of specific methods. Efficiency Analysis, which is the least well understood method class, is described in detail.

The Choice of Choice Method: Metachoice

Both policy analysts and clients have more difficulty dealing with ex ante evaluation of alternatives than with other stages of the policy analysis process (Hahn and Sunstein 2002). The need for a better understanding of the conceptual basis of prospective, or ex ante, evaluation is increasing because governments in many countries are demanding it. Recent legislation in the United States, including the *Unfunded Mandates Reform Act* and the *Government Performance and Results Act* broadly mandates ex ante analysis. Other countries have done the same. For example, the Government of Canada's recent Regulatory Policy requires cost–benefit analysis of regulatory changes (Privy Council Office 1999). Article 130 R of the Single European Act now requires that proposed environmental policies consider "the potential benefits and costs of action or lack of action" (Navrud and Pruckner 1997). The United Kingdom government has been a leader in mandating, and publishing "how to" guidance on, ex ante analysis (usually called project appraisal) (HM Treasury 2003; DFP 2003).

Even though a variety of laws and regulations in a number of countries now require evaluation of policy alternatives, none that we are know of specify when and how an evaluation methodology should be selected. At least within North America, regulations simply require an assessment of "costs" and "benefits", but do not elaborate on the meaning of these terms or whether any specific evaluation method should be used. In order to conduct effective evaluation, analysts must first decide *how* to compare policy alternatives – they must make a metachoice. In practice, metachoice decisions are frequently implicit, sometimes because of a lack of understanding of the issues involved. (Of course, metachoice decisions are often made for purely political or tactical reasons.) This lack of understanding is one contributor to the variable quality of analyses (GAO 1998; Hahn *et al.* 2000). As there is relatively little guidance on metachoice decisions, the purpose of this paper is to present an explicitly *normative* metachoice framework.

We argue that the metachoice decision can be informed by explicitly addressing two factors: (1) goal orientation and breadth, and (2) willingness to monetize efficiency impacts. Doing so results in four policy choice classes: (comprehensive) Cost–Benefit Analysis, Efficiency Analysis, Embedded Cost–Benefit Analysis and Multi-Goal Analysis. Both Cost–Benefit Analysis and Multi-Goal Analysis classes are described in detail elsewhere. We describe the methods within Efficiency Analysis in some detail because, in our experience, they are less well understood.

The Metachoice Framework

In deciding on a choice class, policy analysts face two important questions. First, what are the policy goals of the analysis? As Figure 1 shows, we dichotomize the response into "Single Goal of Efficiency" or "Multiple Goals Including Efficiency" (as explained below, we posit that efficiency should always be a goal in policy analysis). Second, is the analyst willing to monetize all of the *efficiency* impacts of the alternatives? We dichotomize the response into "Comprehensive Monetization of Efficiency Impacts" or "Less-than-Comprehensive Monetization of Efficiency Impacts". The resulting four method classes are: Cost–Benefit Analysis (NW quadrant), Efficiency Analysis (SW quadrant), Embedded Cost–Benefit Analysis (NE quadrant), and Multi-Goal Analysis (SE quadrant).

Goals

Goal selection is probably the most important task in public policy analysis. Obviously, this can be a source of considerable controversy. However, there is some agreement that, where possible, the allocation of resources should be efficient (achieve the maximum difference between social benefits and social costs relative to the alternatives, including the status quo) – the legislation described above clearly requires at least a primacy emphasis on efficiency in this sense.

A key decision for policy analysts is when to treat allocative efficiency as the *only* goal. Many economists argue that allocative efficiency should often be the only relevant goal in many policy contexts (Vining and Weimer 2006). However, equity is also a legitimate policy goal in many policy contexts (e.g., Myers 2002). Equity has been codified in US Federal regulatory practice as a goal. The most recent version of the United Kingdom *Green Book* (HM Treasury 2003) also now explicitly requires that equity be considered (and quantified) "as much as possible". It suggests that this not only be conducted for different income groups, but for different age, gender, health-status and ethnic groups as well as by location.

Figure 1. Metachoice framework

	Single Goal of Efficiency	Multiple Goals Including Efficiency
Comprehensive Monetization of Efficiency Impacts	Cost-Benefit Analysis	Embedded Cost-Benefit Analysis
Less-than-Comprehensive Monetization of Efficiency Impacts	Efficiency Analysis	Multi-Goal Analysis

The revenue impact on government of a policy may also be a legitimate policy goal. Both the US General Accounting Office (GAO) (1998) and the Congressional Budget Office (CBO) (1992) posit three goals in most of their analyses: efficiency, equity and impact on government revenues. One rationale for the latter goal is that, although government has the power to increase revenues through taxes, many governments are not permitted to run deficits. Thus, increases in government revenues or reduction of expenditures are often relevant impacts in terms of this goal. Ethical behavior is nearly always an implicit goal or constraint. Maximizing allocative efficiency alone *in specific contexts* may be morally objectionable (Adler and Posner 1999). Where ethics is a potential concern (for example in many developing country projects) it is useful to explicitly include ethical behavior as a goal.

Political feasibility is often an appropriate goal of analysts because all major decisions require cooperation or approval by political actors (Webber 1986). Analysts may well wish to take this reality into account in choosing between policy alternatives. There may be other legitimate goals in addition to the ones described above that mean a policy problem must be treated as a multigoal problem.

Monetization

Monetization means attaching a monetary value (e.g., dollars) to each efficiency impact. It goes beyond quantification. For example, quantitative measures of impacts, such as the number of lives saved by a highway improvement project, are monetized by multiplying them by the value of a life saved. Monetization makes different kinds of impacts commensurable (Adler and Posner 1999). Comprehensive monetization requires the analyst to attach values to *all* efficiency impacts. But sometimes public decision makers and policy analysts are unwilling to explicitly monetize all efficiency impacts, even when the only goal is efficiency. The UK government has recently increased the emphasis on monetization for project appraisal and now requires "wherever feasible, attributing monetary values to all impacts of any proposed policy, project and programme ..." (HM Treasury 2003).

Quite a few analysts wish to substitute "uncertainty" for "monetization" as a second axis. We recommend against this because metachoice is a normative exercise. The decision to monetize is just that, a *decision*. Uncertainty is a (variable) *state of nature*. Of course, they tend to be correlated in practice – analysts are usually more willing to monetize predictions where there is less uncertainty. However, the correlation is by no means perfect. Retaining monetization as the focus of the choice exercise maintains the focus on the normative aspect of metachoice.

Choice Methods

The four choice methods are "classes" because there are quite wide variations within some of them.

(Comprehensive) Cost–Benefit Analysis

Cost–Benefit Analysis (NW quadrant, Figure 1) requires both prediction *and* valuation of all efficiency impacts through monetization. (When there is only one alternative to the status quo, Cost–Benefit Analysis can be thought of as a single row goal-by-alternative matrix.) "Cost–benefit analysis has reemerged as a widely used technique available to the public policy analyst" (Nagel and Teasley 1998: 516). The parameters of Cost–Benefit Analysis are well known and do not need to be repeated. It now plays an important role in policy areas where it traditionally had little influence, such as social policy (e.g., French *et al.* 2000) and welfare policy (e.g., Gueron and Pauly 1991).

The major value of Cost–Benefit Analysis is that if used in policy decision making it can move society toward more efficient resource allocation. But Cost–Benefit Analysis is often costly and difficult. Some legislative mandates imply they do not require this full-blown commitment of resources and that more limited forms of efficiency analysis would be sufficient. On the other hand, some other legislative mandates imply that Cost–Benefit Analysis is not enough; whether implicitly or explicitly, they ask for Embedded Cost–Benefit Analysis or Multi-Goal Analysis. In some cases, the courts have also mandated methods that go beyond efficiency alone.

Efficiency Analysis

Here (SW quadrant in Figure 1), efficiency is still the only goal, but not all impacts are monetized. Figure 2 summarizes a number of versions of Efficiency Analysis, depending on how costs and benefits are included and the degree to which they are monetized. Costs and benefits are measured more inclusively as one moves from the top-left corner to the bottom-right: (1) costs or benefits are not included at all, (2) only the government agency's costs or benefits included, (3) agency costs or benefits are included and, as well, some (but not all) non-agency costs or benefits are included, (4) all social costs or benefits are included, but not all of them are monetized, and (5) all social costs or benefits are included *and* monetized.

Figure 2. A typology of efficiency analysis methods

		"Benefits" Inclusion and Monetization				
		No "Benefits" Included	Agency Revenue Only	Some Non-Agency Benefits also Included	All Social Benefits Included, but Not All Monetized	All Social Benefits Included and Monetized
"Costs" Inclusion and Monetization	No "Costs" Included	No Efficiency Analysis	Revenue Analysis	Effectiveness Analysis	Effectiveness Analysis	
	Agency Costs Only	Cost Analysis	Revenue-Expenditure Analysis	Cost-Effectiveness Analysis, MNBA	Hybrid	MNBA
	Some Non-Agency Costs also Included	Incomplete Social Costing	MNBA	Cost-Effectiveness Analysis, MNBA	Hybrid	MNBA
	All Social Costs Included, but Not All Monetized	Incomplete Social Costing	Hybrid	Hybrid	Qualitative CBA/ MNBA+	Qualitative CBA/ MNBA+
	All Social Costs Included and Monetized	Complete Social Costing	MNBA	Cost-Effectiveness Analysis, MNBA	Qualitative CBA/ MNBA+	CBA

Notes: Lightly shaded cells indicate hybrid methods are used in this situation; medium shaded cells indicate cost-effectiveness is used in this situation; dark shaded cells indicate qualitative CBA (and MNBA+) is used in this situation.

In the top left-hand cell, efficiency is not considered as neither costs nor benefits are included – the analysis is based on other goals, such as political goals. In the bottom right-hand cell *all* efficiency impacts are included and monetized. This cell corresponds to Cost–Benefit Analysis and the analysis is equivalent to the NW quadrant of Figure 1 (it is also shown in Figure 2 for comparison purposes). Figure 2 identifies eight specific Efficiency Analysis methods: Cost Analysis, Social Costing, Revenue Analysis, Effectiveness Analysis, Revenue-Expenditure Analysis, Cost-Effectiveness Analysis, Monetized Net Benefits Analysis and Qualitative Cost–Benefit Analysis. All of these methods measure efficiency to some degree, but they differ on the manner in which "costs" and "benefits" are included and valued.

Cost Analysis (CA) measures the monetary cost *to the agency* of a policy. CA is used by virtually all agencies to some extent. The performance of an agency can be assessed by comparing the agency's costs to those in other jurisdictions or examining changes in costs over time. Marginal cost is usually the appropriate cost measure for policy analysis purposes. A fundamental problem with using CA is that, even for government impacts, the agency's costs may not reflect the opportunity costs of the resources used.

Social Costing (SC) includes at least some non-agency costs, in addition to agency costs. SC may include all social costs or not include, or not monetize, some social costs. It is almost always useful to know the cost of a policy or the social cost of a problem (e.g., Anderson 1999). Of course, both CA and SC do not consider program benefits.

Revenue Analysis (RA) measures the monetary benefits to the agency of a policy. We do not know of any written examples, but this method is often stressed in verbal contexts. The problem with it is that revenues are not a good measure of the social value of the good that the agency produces. Indeed, to the extent that high revenues represent monopoly pricing, they are more appropriately categorized as a cost or a transfer.

Effectiveness Analysis (EA) goes beyond RA to include benefits to other members of society, usually the public or taxpayers. It focuses on the outcomes of programs – for example, the effectiveness of garbage collection may be measured by the number of tons of garbage collected. EA has two major weaknesses; there may be secondary impacts that are not measured and no consideration is given to the cost of the inputs used to generate the outputs. Thus, EA is a very limited form of Efficiency Analysis.

Revenue-Expenditure Analysis (REA) measures both agency costs and agency revenues and takes the difference between them to compute the net agency revenue or net agency cost of a policy or project. It is sometimes called budget impact analysis. Although it is very different from Cost–Benefit Analysis, policy makers quite often treat it as being equivalent. Furthermore, agencies are increasingly being pushed to adopt a "business case" approach, which also encourages a revenue-expenditure orientation. REA does include *some* measure of both costs and benefits. However, REA suffers from many of the same problems as CA and RA analysis. For example, it commonly omits important social impacts (e.g., customer waiting time); it measures budgetary costs rather than opportunity costs; it measures revenues rather than willingness to pay, and it often excludes non-agency costs.

Cost-Effectiveness Analysis (CEA). In standard CEA, there is a single non-agency benefit (or effectiveness) impact category, such as lives saved, and only agency costs are included in terms of costs. CEA computes the costs–effectiveness ratio to determine the unit cost of some outcome, for example, a measure in terms of average dollar cost per life saved. CEA is most useful where there is only one major benefit category and the analyst is only prepared to quantify, not to monetize, that impact category, such as lives saved. On the cost side, it is common to include only agency budgetary costs (or net budgetary costs) and ignore non-agency social costs. In Figure 2, CEA applies to the three cells with medium-density shading. Obviously, as the range and importance of omitted costs or benefits increase, the usefulness of CEA as an evaluative mechanism decreases.

Monetized Net Benefits Analysis (MNBA) can be applied where there are some efficiency impacts that can be monetized relatively easily and other efficiency impacts that are more difficult to monetize. In these (common) circumstances, it often makes sense to perform MNBA which computes the net present value (NPV) of those efficiency aspects that can be monetized.

Qualitative Cost–Benefit Analysis entails the prediction of all of the efficiency impacts of each alternative, but not all impacts are monetized. As all efficiency impacts are included, qualitative cost–benefit analysis applies to the dark-shaded cells near the bottom right-hand corner of Figure 2. A great deal of non-comprehensive, cost–benefit analysis or so-called "economic policy analysis" is of this type. Some of these analyses can be thought of as MNBA+ analysis, where the + sign denotes the inclusion of all efficiency impacts in the analysis. Arrow *et al.* (1996: 8) are presumably referring to MNBA+ analysis when they say analysts should "give due consideration to factors that defy quantification but are thought to be important".

When there are *multiple* non-monetized (intangible) efficiency impacts the analytic problem is more complex. As Nijkamp (1997: 147) argues, "[t]he only reasonable way to take account of intangibles in the traditional cost–benefit analysis seems to be the use of a balance with a debit and credit side in which all intangible project effects (both positive and negative) are represented in their own (qualitative or quantitative) dimensions". Sometimes analysts perform some variant of analysis that lies between MNBA and MNBA+. Such hybrid analyses are shaded lightly in Figure 2.

Embedded Cost–Benefit Analysis

Embedded Cost–Benefit Analysis (NE quadrant, Figure 1) is appropriate where there are other goals in addition to efficiency. Embedded Cost–Benefit Analysis is a hybrid method where efficiency impacts are monetized; therefore, it includes an NPV calculation. In addition, however, at least one other goal is posited as being relevant – typically equity or impact on government revenues (see above). The non-efficiency goal or goals may be assessed using either a quantitative measure (e.g., "a 10 per cent increase in equity") or a qualitative measure (e.g., "politically infeasible"). Hahn and Sunstein (2002: 6) point out that government agencies do use this method: "There may also be cases in which an agency believes that it is worthwhile to proceed even though the quantifiable benefits do not exceed the quantifiable costs …". This can be interpreted as either Embedded Cost–Benefit Analysis or MNBA+.

Two common forms of Embedded Cost–Benefit Analysis are *Distributionally-Weighted Cost–Benefit Analysis* (DW-CBA) and *Budget-Constrained Cost–Benefit Analysis* (BC-CBA). DW-CBA is found in policy areas where the distributional impact on target populations is important (Boardman *et al.* 2006: 488–506). Some scholars argue that its use should be limited to specific governmental levels, for example, to Federal government analyses (e.g., Wasylenko *et al.* 1997: 50). Others argue for much more widespread use (Buss and Yancer 1999). More rigorous statistical techniques that produce empirically robust estimates of the distributional consequences of programs now make estimation more feasible. DW-CBA is quite common in health policy (Wodon and Yitzhaki 2002) and educational policy (Currie 2001).

One useful version of DW-CBA simply reports costs, benefits and net benefits for "participants" and "nonparticipants" (the rest of society) in addition to the aggregate NPV (e.g., Long, Mallar, and Thornton 1981). In practice, the implications of using DW-CBA will differ from those of using CBA when a policy either (1) passes the efficiency test (i.e., has a positive NPV), but makes disadvantaged people worse-off or (2) fails the efficiency test (i.e., has a negative NPV), but makes disadvantaged individuals better-off.

Most agencies face a budget constraint. BC-CBA can be used to choose among alternative projects when efficiency is the goal and there is a budget constraint. When the policy alternatives have similar purposes, one simply selects the project with the largest efficiency that satisfies the budget constraint. BC-CBA can also be used where the alternatives have different purposes or come from different agencies. In such circumstances, the analyst computes the ratio of the net social benefits (i.e., the NPV) to the net budget cost for each project. Projects will be ranked in terms of this ratio, which is equivalent to ranking them in the order of their benefit–cost ratios. Projects are selected until the budget constraint becomes binding. In practice, BC-CBA is used frequently, but less formally than we have described. For example, analysts simply exclude alternatives that require large government expenditures.

Multi-Goal Analysis

In Multi-Goal Analysis (SE quadrant, Figure 1), there are multiple goals, and efficiency is not monetized. There are many quantitative versions of Multi-Goal Analysis (MGA). Other versions of MGA are purely qualitative. Herfindahl and Kneese (1974: 223) make the case that a qualitative analysis is the only feasibly appropriate approach in some circumstances: "a final approach is that of viewing the various possible objectives of public policy as being substantially incommensurable on any simple scale and therefore necessitating the generation of various kinds of information, not summable into a single number, as the basis for political decision". Dodgson *et al.* (2001) provide a comprehensive overview of these methods, while Hrudey *et al.* (2001) describe the various ways that multigoal, or multi-attribute, decision-making methods can be actually used. MGA generally has three characteristics. First, it provides a clear distinction between alternatives and goals. Second, it clarifies the distinction between prediction and valuation. Third, the analysis is both explicit and comprehensive. One tool that forces comprehensiveness in MGA is a goals-by-alternatives matrix, sometimes also called a performance matrix (Dodgson *et al.* 2001).

Most explicit multi-goal valuations apply linear, "compensatory" schemes to attribute scores (Davey, Olson, and Wallenius 1994); non-compensatory rules are not useful for evaluating policy alternatives as they rarely yield dominant alternatives. The implementation of compensatory rules has become relatively simple with the advent of goal programming software. Such rules enable a higher score on one goal to compensate for a lower score on another goal. Probably the most commonly used rule is simple "additive utility", where the decision is based on a summation of all utilities for each alternative policy. The policy alternative with the highest total score is selected (Svenson 1979). Another commonly used rule is the "highest product of utility".

Some decision makers argue that multi-goal matrices are overly mechanistic. However, in discussion it often emerges that their concerns are not so much with the selected decision rule as a desire to add new goals (or criteria) or to add more complex policy alternatives. Prediction, valuation and evaluation then form part of an iterative policy choice process. An advantage of MGA is that it generates discussion among decision makers. Decision makers can engage in a debate about the impacts of each alternative and the weights that should be attached to each goal.

Conclusion

Figure 3 summarizes the specific methods that fall within the four method-classes. It provides a detailed expansion of Figure 1.

Figure 3. Sample goals/criteria for metachoice alternatives

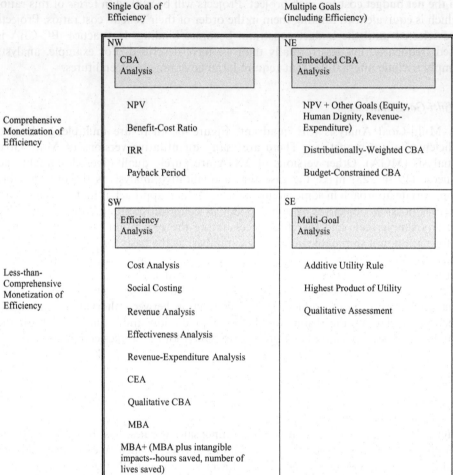

The four method classes can be summarized as follows:

- Cost–Benefit Analysis. Efficiency is the only goal and all dimensions of efficiency are monetized.
- Efficiency Analysis. Efficiency is the only goal, but not all dimensions of efficiency are monetized. Other dimensions of efficiency may be quantified and some may be expressed in qualitative terms.
- Embedded Cost–Benefit Analysis. All efficiency impacts are monetized. Thus, there is an embedded CBA. In addition, other goals, such as equity or impact on government revenue, are also taken into account.

- Multi-Goal Analysis. There are multiple goals, including efficiency. Not all dimensions of efficiency are monetized. Other goals are described quantitatively or qualitatively.

An understanding of metachoice is a useful step in improving one aspect of public sector policy analysis. Of course, metachoice clarity is by no means a panacea. Policy actors can, and will, ignore analysis, and some will engage in strategic behavior when conducting analysis (De Alessi 1996) or deliberately use idiosyncratic definitions of impacts. There are many claims that a Cost–Benefit Analysis is being performed, for example, when the reality is very different (Boardman, Vining, and Waters 1993).

References

Adler, Matthew D. and Posner, Eric A., 1999, Rethinking cost–benefit analysis. *Yale Law Journal*, **109**(2), 165–248.

Anderson, David A., 1999, The aggregate burden of crime. *Journal of Law and Economics*, **42**(2), 611–642.

Arrow, Kenneth J., Cropper, Maureen L., Eads, George C., Hahn, Robert W., Lave, Lester B., Noll, Roger C., Portney, Paul R., Russell, Milton, Schmalensee, Richard, Smith, V. Kerry and Stavins, Robert N., 1996, *Benefit–cost analysis in environmental, health and safety regulation: a statement of principles* (Washington DC: American Enterprise Institute for Public Policy Research).

Boardman, Anthony, E., Vining, Aidan R. and Waters, William, III, 1993, Costs and benefits through bureaucratic lenses: example of a highway project. *Journal of Policy Analysis and Management*, **12**(3), 532–555.

Boardman, Anthony, E., Greenberg, David H., Vining, Aidan R. and Weimer, David L., 2006, *Cost–Benefit Analysis: Concepts and Practice*. 3rd edition (Upper Saddle River, NJ: Prentice Hall).

Buss, Terry F. and Yancer, Laura C., 1999, Cost–benefit analysis: a normative perspective. *Economic Development Quarterly*, **13**(1), 29–37.

Congressional Budget Office (CBO), 1992, *Auctioning Radio Spectrum Licenses* (March, Washington, DC: CBO).

Currie, Janet, 2001, Early childhood education programs. *Journal of Economic Perspectives*, **15**(2), 213–238.

Davey, Anne, Olson, David and Wallenius, Jyrki, 1994, The process of multiattribute decision making: a case study of selecting applicants for a Ph.D. program. *European Journal of Operational Research*, **72**(3), 469–485.

De Alessi, Louis, 1996, Error and bias in benefit–cost analysis: HUD's case for the wind rule. *Cato Journal*, **16**(1), 129–147.

Department of Finance and Personal (DFP), Northern Ireland, 2003, *The Northern Ireland Practical Guide to the Green Book (DFP's Guide to the Appraisal, Evaluation, Approval, and Management of Policies, Programmes and Projects)* (Bangor, County Down: Economic Appraisal Branch, Department of Finance and Personnel).

DiNardo, John and Tobias, Justin L., 2001, Nonparametric density and regression estimation. *Journal of Economic Perspectives*, **15**(4), 11–28.

Dodgson, John, Spackman, Michael, Pearman, Alan and Phillips, Lawrence, 2001, *Multi-Criteria Analysis: A Manual* (London: Department of the Environment, Transport and the Regions (DTLR) and Office of the Deputy Prime Minister (ODPM)).

French, Michael T., Salome, Helena J., Krupski, Antoinette, McKay, James R. Donovan, Dennis M., McLellan, A. Thomas and Durell, Jack, 2000, Benefit–cost analysis of residential and outpatient addiction treatment in the state of Washington. *Evaluation Review*, **24**(6), 609–634.

General Accounting Office (GAO), 1998, Regulatory reform: agencies could improve development, documentation, and clarity of regulatory economic analyses. Report to the Committee on Governmental Affairs, US Senate, GAO/RCED-98-142, May.

Gueron, Judith and Pauly, Edward, 1991, *From Welfare to Work* (New York: Russell Sage Foundation).

Hahn, Robert W., Burnett, Jason K., Chan, Yee-Ho I., Mader, Elizabeth A. and Moyle, Petrea R., 2000, Assessing regulatory impact analyses: the failure of agencies to comply with executive order 12,866. *Harvard Journal of Law and Public Policy*, **23**(3), 859–885.

Hahn, Robert W. and Sunstein, Cass R., 2002, A new executive order for improving federal regulation? Deeper and wider cost–benefit analysis. *University of Pennsylvania Law Review*, **150**(5), 1489–1552.

Herfindahl, Orris C. and Kneese, Allan V., 1974, *Economic Theory of Natural Resources* (Columbus, OH: Charles Merrill).

HM Treasury, 2003, *Green Book: Appraisal and Evaluation in Central Government* (London: TSO).

Hrudey, Steve E., Adamowicz, Vic., Krupnick, Alan, McConnell, John, Renzi, Paolo, Dales, Robert and Lippmann, Morton, 2001, *Report of an Expert Panel to Review the Socio-Economic Models and Related Components Supporting the Development of Canada-Wide Standards for Particulate Matter and Ozone to the Royal Society of Canada* (Ottawa, ON: Royal Society of Canada).

Long, David, Mallar, Charles D. and Thornton, Craig V., 1981, Evaluating the benefits and costs of the jobs corps. *Journal of Policy Analysis and Management*, **1**(1), 55–76.

Myers, Samuel L., 2002, Presidential address – analysis of race as policy analysis. *Journal of Policy Analysis and Management*, **21**(2), 169–190.

Nagel, Stuart S. and Teasley, C. E., 1998, Diverse perspectives for public policy analysis, in Jack Rabin, W. Bartley Hildreth and Gerald M. Miller (Eds) *Handbook of Public Administration*. 2nd edition (New York: Marcel Dekker), pp. 507–533.

Navrud, Stale and Pruckner, Gerald J., 1997, Environmental valuation – to use or not to use? A comparative study of the United States and Europe. *Environmental and Resource Economics*, **10**(1), 1–26.

Nijkamp, Peter P., 1997, *Theory and Application of Environmental Economics* (Amsterdam: North-Holland).

Privy Council Office (PCO), 1999, *Government of Canada Regulatory Policy* (Ottawa, ON: PCO).

Svenson, Ola, 1979, Process description of decision making. *Organizational Behavior and Human Performance*, **23**(1), 89–92.

Vining, Aidan R. and Weimer, David L., 2006, Efficiency and cost–benefit analysis, in B. Guy Peters and Jon Pierre (Eds) *Handbook of Public Policy* (Thousand Oaks, CA: Sage, forthcoming).

Wasylenko, Michael, Bartik, Timothy, Duncan, Harley T., McGuire, Teresa J. and Ady, Robert M., 1997, Taxation and economic development: the state of the economic literature. *New England Economic Review* (March/April), 37–52.

Webber, David J., 1986, Analyzing political feasibility: political scientists' unique contribution to policy analysis. *Policy Studies Journal*, **14**(4), 545–564.

Wodon, Quentin and Yitzhaki, Shlomo, 2002, Evaluating the impact of government programs on social welfare: the role of targeting and the allocation rules among program beneficiaries. *Public Finance Review*, **30**(2), 102–123.

Introduction: The OECD and Policy Transfer: Comparative Case Studies

LESLIE A. PAL

ABSTRACT *The six articles in this issue examine the role of the OECD in policy transfer. Two articles (Kudrle on international tax agreements, and Legrand and Vas on Australia's vocational and educational training policy) conclude that the OECD has been influential, albeit in a grinding and lengthy way. Two others (Clifton on the OECD's "enhanced engagement" policy with five G-20 countries, and Eccleston and Woodward on tax transparency) find the OECD's influence either patchier or even dysfunctional. Carroll's article provides a novel analysis of policy transfer through accession processes, while Alasuutari explores transfer in terms of a comparative analysis of policy rationalizations that refer to the OECD as a "standard." A common theme of all six articles is the way in which policy transfer is driven by exogenous pressures and crises, and how international governmental organizations like the OECD exploit these pressures to protect and expand their global relevance.*

Though there are antecedents, the scholarly interest in policy transfer can be conveniently dated from Rose's book on "lesson-drawing" (1993). It is surprising that the concept took that long to incubate – with the beginning of the Cold War governments were feverishly trying to "transfer" their policy models to their respective blocs. As various crises hit the West in the 1970s and 1980s (stagflation, oil embargoes, recession) there was a greater if grudging need to coordinate responses, and hence compare policy models. Since Rose's book, of course, the pace of globalization, interdependence, and lesson-drawing has only grown in scale and pace, and the scholarly interest accordingly has enjoyed a resurgence as well (Dolowitz 2006; Evans 2009). The basics of policy transfer are straightforward. On the demand side, governments "puzzle", they search for solutions, they seek "best practices", they wish to be leaders rather than "laggards", they need resources and will accept conditions (i.e. changing their policies) if necessary. On the supply side, the hawkers are almost endless: NGOs, think tanks, corporations, unions, citizens' movements, movie stars, individual governments, regional governmental associations (think EU), and of course international organizations like the ever-clucking World Bank and ever-stern IMF. Even the Pope has climbed on board, urging a new evangelicalism that will surely translate into Catholic-inspired movements to temper the excesses of Wall Street (and thereby borrow more inflexible financial regulatory tools) (Pope Francis 2013).

Understanding contemporary public policy means understanding how policy models are spread, by whom, why, how they are received, and how they compare once in action. The topic is vast, and we can only feel parts of the elephant at any given time. The articles in this special issue address the question of policy transfer by international governmental organizations (IGOs), and, in this case, specifically from the Organisation for Economic Co-operation and Development (OECD), though with some comparisons to other IGOs. The rationale for this focus is two-fold. First, of all the "hawkers" of policy transfer, IGOs are among the most important: they typically have more resources than NGOs, their members are typically governments, they can claim special expertise and prestige, and they sometimes can carry a big stick in the form of conditionalities attached to aid and loans (Barnett and Finnemore 2004). For example, it would be impossible to understand policy developments in Central and Eastern Europe after the collapse of communism without understanding the role of the World Bank, the European Union, and the OECD, to name a few. The developing world has also been especially fertile ground for the transfer of public policy models across the spectrum of policy fields and management (Common 2001; McCourt and Minogue 2001; Evans 2004; Larmour 2005; Desai and Snavely 2007; Karini 2013), even if the efficacy of that transfer is increasingly brought into question (Easterly 2006; Moyo 2009). Second, the OECD represents an almost pure case of an international organization advising on policy transfer and best practices (though it resists using this terminology) without the big stick, and with only the power, more or less, of persuasion and research instead. The articles in this issue therefore make an important contribution to our understanding of the OECD as an organization, to the way in which it urges policy models on its members and non-members, the subtle dynamics of that transfer, and its success. We do not claim that the OECD is the most powerful of IGOs or that it can force its ideas on recalcitrant governments. Far from it. Yet understanding the OECD as an "ideational artist" in a global policy-making world helps us understand the role of research, persuasion, modeling, peer-review, and a host of other tools which, while not unique to the OECD, are used by other IGOs to spread the word.

Special Issue Focus

The articles in this special issue stem from two panels organized for the World Congress of the International Political Science Association held in Madrid, July 2012, on the OECD and aspects of policy transfer. They underwent a rigorous double-blind review process, and I am grateful to the reviewers and the editorial team of the *Journal of Comparative Policy Analysis: Research and Practice* for making this project possible.

The six articles in this issue can be viewed as thematic pairs: two are quite positive about the OECD's success in policy transfer; two are more skeptical; and two step somewhat outside the conventional categories of the policy transfer literature to raise some fresh considerations.

The two positive pieces are Robert Thomas Kudrle, "The OECD and The International Tax Regime: Persistence Pays Off", and Tim Legrand and Christopher Vas, "Framing the

Policy Analysis of OECD and Australian VET Interaction: Two Heuristics of Policy Transfer". Kudrle examines the OECD's role in developing an international regime around tax transparency (another article, by Richard Eccleston and Richard Woodward, does the same, but with somewhat more critical conclusions, so the two pieces are useful comparators on this question). He distinguishes between "vertical diffusion", as when the US became (and lobbied for) the template for the OECD's adoption of the Model Tax Treaty and its diffusion among member states, and "horizontal diffusion", as when the OECD itself worked through the G-20's Global Forum on taxation to encourage the spread of Tax Information Exchange Agreements. Kudrle agrees with critics that the Global Forum's approach of "information on request" is, in principle, weak when compared with obligatory models. However, in examining some key proposals for such models, he finds that they fall short of a standard of rational institutional design. By that same standard, the OECD's work through the G-20 over the years has successfully "incubated" a global scheme of tax cooperation. "The Forum appears to involve precisely the combination of consultation and information-sharing with scant formal power that marks the maximum institutionalization allowed by current political constraints."

In "Framing the Policy Analysis of OECD and Australian VET Interaction: Two Heuristics of Policy Transfer", Tim Legrand and Christopher Vas focus on a single country case study, the redesign of Australian Vocational Education and Training (VET) policy. They argue that the OECD was influential in that redesign, principally because it serves as an epistemic community that mobilizes and privileges some policy options over others, and because its mechanism of peer review induces both competition among members (and non-members) and ultimately some degree of conformity. VET in Australia has been the poor cousin to post-secondary education, and moreover is complicated by the jurisdictional divisions of a federal state (states and territories have primary responsibility for program delivery, but the Australian government has a coordinating and funding role through its responsibility for national economic development). Legrand and Vas point out that the OECD has been crucial to Australia as a source of policy ideas in this field, particularly in a 17-country study that led to the 2010 report *Learning for Jobs*. Australia participated vigorously, and took the OECD's study of its own policy regime seriously. The OECD report was used by Australian policy advocates as another source of pressure. The results took several years, but the authors nonetheless point to the symmetry between OECD recommendations and country policy results.

Judith Clifton and Daniel Díaz-Fuentes' "The OECD and 'The Rest': Analyzing the Limits of Policy Transfer", and Richard Eccleston and Richard Woodward's "Pathologies in International Policy Transfer: The Case of the OECD Tax Transparency Initiative", have more pessimistic assessments of the OECD's role in policy transfer. Clifton points out that the OECD was well aware through the 1990s and 2000s that its global influence was waning, not least because its members collectively were representing less and less of total global economic production. It launched a program of "Enhanced Engagement" focusing on five G-20 countries: Brazil, China, India, Indonesia, and South Africa. Clifton closely examines the strategy, and finds that it was relatively successful with South Africa and Brazil, but went nowhere with China. Why? While China did accept some OECD advice on taxation reform, this was purely pragmatic. The problem is that the OECD, despite these efforts, is still a "Western" organization in its approaches, models, and even its personnel. "The Rest" is the wider world of different policy traditions and cultures, increasing assertive and skeptical of "made in Paris" solutions. Clifton argues that it is not too late for the OECD, but that it will have to adapt more vigorously to this new global set of players.

Eccleston and Woodward, like Kudrle, examine the OECD's work around tax transparency, but through the lens of what they call "dysfunctional policy transfer". This is an important reminder, since there is an almost unconscious reflex among analysts to rate a transfer of policy from an IGO to a state as a "success" if the transfer actually occurred. Of course, the "what" and the "how" of the transfer may in fact be negative, detrimental, and even dysfunctional. The specific dysfunction that they focus on is a bureaucratic one – the OECD, like other IGOs, is a bureaucracy with organizational interests in survival and prominence. In some cases, IGOs will prefer weak or "lowest common denominator" international agreements simply in order to claim success and put something in the policy window. The OECD's "success" in promoting Tax Information Exchange Agreements has drawn criticism because it actually confers legitimacy on jurisdictions that meet an empty standard but flout the larger purpose of tax transparency. Nonetheless, the article points out that the somewhat surprising OECD endorsement of stronger transparency standards in 2012 suggests a counter-dynamic: IGOs also need to demonstrate their efficacy over time, rather than just forging empty agreements. If one takes into account the "long game" that IGOs need to play, it might be that what appears at first as failure (i.e. an empty or insipid agreement) is actually a deliberate stepping stone to stronger regime formation along the way.

In his article "Policy Transfer and Accession: A Comparison of Three International Governmental Organisations", Peter Carroll steps somewhat outside the conventional framework of examining the transfer of single policies, to the transfer of what might be called "bundled policies" through accession. Based on archival work and interviews with staff from all three IGOs, his cases are accession to the WTO, the EU, and the OECD in three phases: pre-accession, accession, and post-accession. Carroll finds that there has been an increase in the extent of pre-accession transfer (adopting policies in order to be "ready"), earliest in the case of the EU. Formal accession is more complex, as one would assume, and has interesting characteristics: (1) the degree of "opting out" permitted (the EU is the most restrictive); (2) increasing degree of transfer; (3) increasingly detailed accession processes over time; (4) increasing provision of technical assistance during all stages of the accession process (most by the EU, least by the OECD); and (5) a trend toward parallel accession processes. One would think that accession was the end of the story, but Carroll suggests that the post-accession phase includes implementation and transfer, as well as continued bargaining over at least some items in the original accession agreement. Carroll concludes that accession means substantial policy transfer, but with variations linked to the required range of transfer, the pre-existing isomorphism between the recipient and the IGO, and a host of possible opt-outs, temporary reservations and derogations, technical assistance, and IGO capacity to monitor compliance.

Pertti Alasuutari's "Following the Example of Other Countries? Policy Analysis of New Legislation in Canada, the United Kingdom and the United States" also applies a distinct lens to the question of policy transfer. He takes the interdependence of decision making in a world polity as given, and asks the deceptively simple question of how it actually occurs. His focus is recorded (and hence searchable) legislative debates and documents in Canada, the UK, and the US from 2001 to 2011. How do national parliaments take account of other governments' policy models in drafting new, national legislation? Do the states differ in their modes of discourse? With a unique methodology,

Alasuutari grounds his understanding of policy transfer in terms of policy argumentation, making the point that policy transfer is not only about institutions and laws, but also about rationalizations, justifications, and argument. Among his findings are that in all three countries the modes of general policy justification are similar: the national interest, existence and gravity of the problem, and rationality and acceptability of the proposed reform. When it comes to international comparisons (again a common feature of policy argumentation in all three countries) he finds five types of references: international comparison, international treaties or norms, exogenous policy models, models considered as something that other countries should adopt, and the nation's reputation. While these five types are common, he does find differences in their use. As would be expected, Canada and the UK are broadly similar, while in the US the frequency of references to international norms or standards is significantly lower. In this, Alasuutari finds support for the persistence of a sense of American exceptionalism: "Overall, the US political culture does not seem to favor arguments that justify a policy by referring to its success in other countries."

This special issue casts new analytical light on both the OECD and on the macro- and micro-dynamics of policy transfer. Though the authors were not explicitly asked to consider this variable, it emerges as a thread that binds all the articles, notwithstanding their differences: the combination of organizational entrepreneurship and global crisis. We learn, for example, that governments typically search for external models/help when they are in some trouble: China with its tax system, Australia with vocational training, the US with tax transparency after 9/11. At the same time, most of the articles point out that the OECD was well aware of rival IGOs, the declining influence of its core (Western) membership, the need to be relevant, and the strategic challenges of pushing policy agendas on the global stage. In short, it would seem that policy transfer frequently occurs because a crisis has generated an appetite for new solutions, and international organizations like the OECD are waiting in the wings to offer them, not only for national or global benefit, but to further their organizational interests. This is a potentially fertile field for future inquiry.

References

Barnett, M. N. and Finnemore, M., 2004, *Rules for the World: International Organizations in Global Politics* (Ithaca, NY: Cornell University Press).
Common, R., 2001, *Public Management and Policy Transfer in Southeast Asia* (Aldershot: Ashgate).
Desai, U. and Snavely, K., 2007, Technical assistance for institutional capacity building: The transferability of administrative structures and practices. *International Review of Administrative Sciences*, **73**(1), pp. 133–146. doi:10.1177/0020852307075694
Dolowitz, D., 2006, Bring back the states: Correcting for the omissions of globalization. *International Journal of Public Administration*, **29**(4-6), pp. 263–280. doi:10.1080/01900690500437162
Easterly, W., 2006, *The White Man's Burden: Why the West's Efforts to Aid the Rest Have Done so Much Ill and so Little Good* (New York: Penguin).
Evans, M., 2009, New directions in the study of policy transfer. *Policy Studies*, **30**(3), pp. 237–241. doi:10.1080/01442870902863810
Evans, M., 2004, *Policy Transfer in Global Perspective* (Aldershot, England: Ashgate).
Francis, P., 2013, *Apostolic Exhortation Evangelii Gaudium of the Holy Father Francis to the Bishops, Clergy, Consecrated Persons and the Lay Faithful on the Proclomation of the Gospel in Today's World* (Rome: Vatican Press).
Karini, A., 2013, Aid-supported public service reform and capacity development in post-communist Albania. *International Journal of Public Administration*, **36**(7), pp. 469–481. doi:10.1080/01900692.2013.772634

Larmour, P., 2005, *Foreign Flowers: Institutional Transfer and Good Governance in the Pacific Islands* (Honolulu: University of Hawai'i Press).

McCourt, W. and Minogue, M. (Eds), 2001, *The Internationalization of Public Management: Reinventing the Third World State* (Cheltenham, UK: Edward Elgar).

Moyo, D., 2009, *Dead Aid: Why Aid Is Not Working and How There Is a Better Way for Africa* (New York: Farrar, Straus and Giroux).

Rose, R., 1993, *Lesson-Drawing in Public Policy: A Guide to Learning Across Time and Space* (Chatham, N.J: Chatham House Publishers).

Learning Transferable Lessons from Single Cases in Comparative Policy Analysis

AMANDA WOLF & KAREN J. BAEHLER

ABSTRACT *Policy exemplars offer potential value to policy professionals seeking new ideas. Realizing that value typically assumes a learner who is both equipped with a well-specified policy or process objective and able to model causal connections to extract lessons. Yet there is a gap in explicating how, exactly, policy professionals find ideas worth pursuing. This article draws on the concepts of abduction and phronesis – broadly a flash of insight and practical judgement, occasioned by an observation – to fill that gap. The natural capabilities associated with abduction and phronesis rely on noticing what stands out, making analogical connections, and discerning which connections merit following up. With attention to these capabilities, policy professionals can extend their learning of transferable lessons from single cases.*

Introduction

Comparison lies at the heart of all policy analysis. Initially, policy students may learn how to compare different policy interventions in theory and in application to a specific problem. Analysing "what should be done" to improve situations involves applying specialist techniques to project (based on trends), predict (based on theory) and conjecture (based on expert judgement) (Dunn 2011), in order to estimate the degree to which policy options might satisfy selected criteria, thereby enabling a systematic comparison of trade-offs (Weimer and Vining 2011; Bardach 2012). In many policy settings at present, policy professionals are urged to derive "robust" or "scientific" evidence through cost–benefit analyses, policy experiments and other rigorous predictive and projective methods (Banks 2009; Gluckman 2013). Expert judgement in this analytic framing refers not to analysts deploying their own expertise, but to gathering and processing technical or other advanced knowledge using techniques such as policy

Delphi or scenario planning (Dunn 2011). Evidence "hierarchies" place such evidence near the bottom of the ranks (in Leigh 2009, it is last).

In practice, however, such comparison of estimated outcomes faces limitations. Evidence-based decision making requires that "the nature and dimensions of the problem being addressed are known, measurable and unambiguous, and that appropriate monitoring will show the success of policy measures" (Wesselink et al. 2014, p. 340). It is widely recognized that scientific evidence is rarely sufficient, and must be complemented by political and field-based practical judgement (Head 2008). Compounding the challenge, Bardach asserts (2012, pp. 47–48) that analysts' reluctance to "guess" may interfere with estimating uncertain futures.

Analysts' reluctance to apply their own judgement outside of strictly cordoned technical tasks and the limitations of evidence can be mitigated if a similar policy to the one being estimated has already been implemented somewhere else. This is where the concepts and practices of policy transfer and policy learning enter. Instead of having to analytically construct a hypothetical future state of affairs from theory, trends and others' guesses to compare with the status quo, the analyst can study an actual exemplar: *looking can (partly) substitute for guessing or making other leaps to conclusions from available evidence*. Based on what they see in the other case, analysts can update their understanding of their own policy situation, revisit key criteria, refine policy designs and better estimate outcomes.

There is virtually unlimited scope for policy professionals to learn directly, comparatively, interactively and over time about policy "cases". Cases, unlike "scientific" evidence, are contextually rich, specific to a time and place, and conveyed through formats such as extended narratives, images and personal profiles that seek to convey the case holistically. To take a few examples, well-resourced repositories such as the Rockefeller Foundation-sponsored 100 Resilient Cities (http://www.100resilientcities.org/#/-_/) and the International City/County Management Association (ICMA) (http://icma.org/en/international/about) exchange programmes support city-to-city learning. Developing country implementation features in the World Bank's Global Delivery Initiative (http://www.globaldeliveryinitiative.org/).

Informal and professional networks also link professionals for case exchanges. One study of city transportation policy learning found that officials "rely on their trusted networks of peers for lessons" and may gather information "informally and sometimes quite randomly" (Marsden et al. 2011, pp. 501, 508). In addition to finding out about another's policy (Wolman and Page 2002), networks support a "social process built around curiosity, exchange and trust" (Marsden et al. 2011, p. 511).

The claim that policy analysts routinely, confidently and effectively learn from policy cases elsewhere appears to be so obvious as to merit little attention: it is simply what policy professionals do, and they do it better as they gain experience. Hence, it goes unremarked when those interested in addressing central city traffic congestion are drawn to the apparent success of Stockholm's congestion charge system (Börjesson et al. 2012) or when those concerned about hard-to-reach homeless people take an interest in New York City's efforts to convert disused hotels into residences with on-site social services for formerly homeless people ("A Place to Call Home" 2001; Parsell et al. 2014).

Our intent in this article is to probe the taken for granted assumption that experienced policy professionals know how to use a Stockholm or New York case to inform their own policy work with congestion or homelessness. The contribution we point to is not something new to policy practice, but addresses a methodological gap in the theory of transferring lessons by making explicit *how*, exactly, an analyst's *own* attunement to a learning need and expert judgement operate in discovering or generating transferable lessons from one policy context for application in another. Our examination draws on the concepts of abduction (a flash of insight) and phronesis (practical judgement) occasioned by an observation. Our aim is to help improve the ratio of poor lessons and transfers to effective ones. In favouring a continuous everyday learning-from-experience frame, our analysis may accord more closely with policy professionals' experience than a technical–analytic "problem solving" framing, with its heavier reliance on scientific evidence.

However, before proceeding, it is necessary to acknowledge that despite enthusiasm for learning from cases, the prospect of unavoidable learning failures can dampen the exercise of single-case learning. A principal cautionary note derives from the work of Kahneman and Tversky. Their research has shown that people tend to base their conclusions on a dominant example or a subset of examples. This phenomenon is known as the "availability heuristic" (Tversky and Kahneman 1974) because people tend to rely on – and, we might say, learn from – those examples that come most readily to mind (due to cognitive availability), which often means either the most recent or nearby examples, the most dramatic ones, or the ones that they have heard repeatedly. When alerted to the risks of cognitive bias, some policy professionals may further distrust their experience and judgement and concentrate on becoming more sophisticated and specialized users of the types of methods featured in most policy analysis textbooks, particularly methods that project and predict outcomes.

For those who persevere in seeking to learn from a single case, Kahneman's later work (2011) suggests that policy professionals may be able to use their heuristics and biases more prudently, in particular by exposing some "fast-brain" conclusions to a second, "slow-brain" test. Our adoption of the concepts of abduction and phronesis directs a narrow focus on the fulcrum between fast-thinking-like flashes of insight and initial conclusions on one hand, and slow-thinking-based due consideration of them on the other. Explicit attention to abduction and phronesis can, like Kahneman's distinctions or Schön's sketches of "reflective practitioners" (1983), alert policy professionals to the benefits of further cultivating their judgemental capabilities, whether they are already highly adept or still developing, in their work with single-case lesson drawing for transferable applications. Specifically, we suggest that an essential aspect of lesson drawing – gaining a new, plausible idea – draws on policy professionals' natural capability to iterate between cases that supply transferable lessons and cases to which those lessons might be best applied.

Method

The article proceeds as follows. First we describe a stylized learning scenario, and establish terms for learning transferable lessons by comparing an existing case and a prospective case. In the base scenario, a policy learner in a city in need of a congestion solution looks at congestion charges in Stockholm. We then sketch two variants, one to reflect non-case-centred analysis using case evidence and one to illustrate an occasion for unexpected learning from a case.

Following this, we examine the literature on learning transferable lessons from single cases, with an emphasis on Rose (2005) and Barzelay (2007), who offer methods to guide policy professionals and researchers in using existing policy programmes or processes as cases for "lesson drawing" and "vicarious learning", based on the congruence between studied cases and prospective decisions. Notwithstanding the persuasiveness of these methods, deeper examination of lesson-drawing methods and their limits for practice has attracted little explicit focus to date. We argue that many, if not most, accounts of policy transfer assume that the policy learner knows of, or can find, an instance of a relevant policy solution in place elsewhere. The result is a lack of adequate scholarly attention to the set of intuitive, judgement-based mechanisms that include spotting a promising case exemplar and sparking "fresh thoughts" about the future as a result of case encounters. The same gap is noted in the broader policy learning and policy transfer literatures, which adds weight to our claim that the nature of the learning "moment" is scarcely addressed.

To begin addressing the identified gaps, we expand on the concepts of abduction and phronesis and examine their potential for advancing understanding of how policy learners settle on a fresh thought worth pursuing. We then examine the functions of these concepts in aiding policy professionals to learn in the base-scenario context. Although abduction and phronesis cannot be broken into steps or standardized easily for purposes of training policy professionals, several principles can be identified that point the way toward good practice in drawing lessons from single cases. The article highlights how policy professionals might weave these principles into their single-case lesson-drawing practice.

Stylized Learning Scenarios

A stylized transferable lesson-drawing situation establishes our comparative focus and some terminology. The base scenario depicts the process of learning about one's home case from a similar case elsewhere. To support parts of the argument, we also sketch two variants of the scenario. In the first, much of the case context is jettisoned in favour of selected, discrete evidence. The second variant illustrates the serendipitous and unexpected emergence in the midst of the base scenario of a different "case".

Base Scenario: Finding Exemplary Instance, Studying It, Extracting Lessons, Using Lessons in New Instance

A big city (A) faces significant traffic congestion. Based on earlier analysis, the city is ready to embark on in-depth work on the merits of introducing congestion charges, which would be a first for the country. Quite naturally, an analyst assigned to the work starts by looking around for congestion charge systems in operation. Stockholm seems to provide an exemplary case (B), and the analyst decides to study it in detail, extract lessons from it and apply those lessons to develop the city's new charge system.

More abstractly, a status quo "receiving environment" or home case (A) is defined by locality, context and the learner's policy objective (for example, to reduce congestion). The learner seeks to design a policy to introduce in A that is informed by a relevant policy elsewhere, such as Stockholm's congestion charge system (B). We designate as a "prospective case" (A') the receiving environment, A, at time $t + 1$, in which policy based on lessons from B is in place and producing impacts, for better or worse. Thus, the most relevant comparison is between B (current/recent past) and A' (future), with A (current/recent past) as conditioning background.

Variant 1: Using Selected Evidence from a Case

The base scenario starts when City A has already decided that congestion charging is the preferred policy option. However, to get to this point, analysts have examined congestion charges as just one option among others, such as subsidizing public transport. Congestion charges are assumed to reduce traffic volume. Accordingly, analysts may look to an evaluation of the Stockholm policy (such as Börjesson et al. 2012) to find robust grounds for modelling traffic reductions in City A and thus provide an estimate for that outcome in A'. Skilled technical experts may combine data from Stockholm with data from other cities, with no need for details specific to those cities.

Variant 2: Noticing a Chance or Surprising Observation that Can Form the Basis for an Unanticipated Lesson

The water office is next door to the traffic office in City A, and the analysts often meet informally. A water official perks up when a traffic official casually comments that "Stockholm really knows how to turn around hostile public attitudes" (Börjesson et al. 2012). Public hostility has created significant hurdles to implementing a comprehensive flood protection initiative in the city, prompting the water official's curiosity about Stockholm's experience as a case of "turning around the public".

Learning for Transfer from the Single Case

Learning theorists identify some general components of "learning", which in their generality may be expected to be at least implicit in literature on policy learning: a learner prepares to learn by activating existing knowledge in the context of a learning need; selects or receives information and engages with it in some way; and applies the outcomes of that engagement (Hermans 2011; Ettelt et al. 2012; Bengtsson and Hertting 2014; Botma et al. 2015). Policy learning lies at the heart of the impulse to look elsewhere for bright ideas (Sabatier 1987; Rose 1991; Bennett and Howlett 1992; May 1992). For a policy professional, preparing to learn is taken to precede the consideration of another case, the case is studied to extract information, the value of which is considered in view of its application in practice.

The literature includes work that looks at learning from single cases (with numerous examples) and various arguments for and against case evidence for policy making. The scholarly focus to date has extended to considerations of learning from experience, anticipating the future, and more, all of which entail at least an implicit construction of the comparison between cases B and A'. Many comparative studies *of* policy reinforce the primacy of measuring policy performance and developing theories of how policies are made (Schmitt, 2013). However, explicit consideration of the particular learning *for* policy making in the unique single-case, future-focused transfer context is rare.

The case study literature might be expected to contain answers to how, exactly, learners extract insights and form them into transferable lessons from other potentially fertile instances. Yet few studies consider case learning *practices* on the ground, apart from scholarly methods associated with the case study method of research. Academic researchers aiming to compare cases in order to explain policymaking or build theory about it are well served by outstanding case study methodological guidance,[1] but such methods may not be enough when comparisons are undertaken for the purpose of guiding policy adoption and action.

Perhaps due in part to academics' uneven and sometimes overzealous efforts to achieve rigour in methodology, including case study methodology, policy practitioners have reported that they find much of the existing policy research literature too "academic", too piecemeal, biased, or of unclear quality (Marsden et al. 2011, p. 501). The gap between the existing literature and what officials want points to limited understanding of the ingredients and mechanisms in the early stages of the case learning process. When seeking to learn for purposes of *doing* rather than studying policy transfer, we postulate that a policy professional must be able to "case" a learning situation (B, such as Stockholm's response to traffic congestion) in the very act of being exposed to it. Without that capability and the opportunity to exercise it, according to this argument, the policy professional cannot determine if the case at hand (B) is worth pursuing in the first place. Such determination may involve examining reports and case documentation, conversing in person or otherwise at networking meetings or observing policies in action during site visits. Whatever the setting and tools used, the process appears to involve the rough-and-ready construction of a prospective case, A′, based on available information, however scant or impressionistic, about B, and knowledge of what is "unsatisfactory" in the current case, A. When done effectively, A′ is fully and creatively constructed as a prospective case to serve a comparative learning purpose.

Existing literature sheds some light on learning in this setting, but more is needed. We build on the work of Rose (1991, 2005) and Barzelay (2007), both of whom combine lesson drawing for practice with what are, essentially, case methods. Rose and Barzelay provide the fundamentals for learning a transportable lesson from elsewhere (B) and applying it to a parallel case in the learner's own policy environment (A). Importantly, they speak more directly to policy professionals than to the curious reader *of* comparative policy analysis or policy transfer. We look closely at these contributions, and then more broadly to the various other literatures that can aid in weaving together the components of learning for comparative policy analysis from the single-case exemplar.

Rose's method requires a learner to be dissatisfied with the policy measures in some policy domain currently in place in the "home" environment; unwilling or unable to get traction with untried ideas; able to extract and understand the strengths and weaknesses of measures operating in a policy programme elsewhere through journalistic investigative techniques; and able to encompass that understanding in a cause–effect model, to "re-conceptualize" it for application, and then to consider its hypothetical future along a number of dimensions (Rose 2005). Thus, it is necessary that policies that focus on the same problem creating dissatisfaction at home can be accessed elsewhere, and that the lesson can be transferred through a cause–effect model.

In a nutshell, Rose envisages a learner who can get fresh thoughts by looking outward, and draw from them practical lessons to improve policy at home (Rose 2005, p. 4). Rose's premise is persuasive. If the learner's own experience is stale and the existing stock of evidence no longer reveals ideas worth trying, there is reason to go searching. But where? Which policy destinations offer enough novelty to spark new insights without overwhelming the learner with contextual differences? Rose largely sidesteps these complications by emphasizing examples where "fresh" is both easy to detect and relatively uncomplicated. His approach to lesson drawing is most straightforward when policies are essentially similar in numerous instances, such as tax systems.

Barzelay (2007) presents guidelines for extracting public management lessons from a source case (B) and translating them to a target case (A), with cases defined as event trajectories that bound complexity. This method relies on identifying social mechanisms that explain the trajectories and performance impacts found in the source case; building causal narratives based on these mechanisms; and then designing an intervention for the target case that activates the mechanisms found in the source case. The process requires ingenuity on the part of the designer since the target case's setting and available levers nearly always differ in meaningful ways from those of the source case. Barzelay essentially advocates studying the process of moving from a previous B to a current B', and comparing that, in our terminology, to a prospective case trajectory from a current A to a future A', rather than comparing the snapshots of B and A'.

Barzelay (2007) focuses on management practices, not on lessons in the form of a recommended new policy (Rose 2005). Following Bardach (2004), Barzelay (2007, p. 528) envisages learning focused on the design of a functional system, which in turn leads to the desired outcomes: "Craft contrivances with the intention of activating the same configuration of social mechanisms in the target site as that which were activated in the design exemplar and are believed to explain its outstanding performance characteristics". Although Barzelay mentions reverse engineering, he emphasizes a second track, in which the learner "requires theoretical insight into *how* observed practices actually mobilize human action and bring about substantively significant effects" (Barzelay 2007, p. 522, emphasis in original). Thus, like Rose, Barzelay (2007, p. 523) insists on causal understanding of mechanisms and their outcomes, according to which "actors use their minds to envision how the causal process involved in the exemplar's functioning could be made to occur within their own undertakings". By studying event trajectories that cumulate in performance effects of interest (Barzelay 2007, p. 525), a learner can consider how the effects hypothetically would apply in another situation. The learner's mind thus enters a "dialectical engagement" with theory literature (Barzelay 2007, p. 526).

While in Barzelay's approach similarity between source and target cases is not required at the ground level, it is a necessary feature of the social mechanisms. Thus, Barzelay establishes a second-order field for transfer. It is not the solution itself that provides ingredients for the lesson, but explanatory theories of change that are stimulated by the design exemplar.

Rose (2005) and Barzelay (2007) occupy a corner of a vast literature in comparative policy analysis, policy transfer and policy learning. Based on an extensive review, Schmitt (2013) characterizes research on policy learning and lesson drawing with attention to how policy actors perceive and make use of policy experiences elsewhere, and how they approach the learning process. The learning orientation has been systematized in the widely used framework of Dolowitz and Marsh (2000), who urge attention to why actors engage in policy transfer and the bases for their selection of the learning exemplars from which lessons are drawn, noting that policy transfer exemplars can be local, national and/or international. However, in Dolowitz and Marsh's framework, the actual extraction of lessons is approached only obliquely, with attention to eight discrete categories of transferred lesson – policy goals, policy content, policy instruments, policy programmes, institutions, ideologies, ideas and attitudes and negative lessons – and four modes of transfer – copying, emulation, combinations, or inspiration (another jurisdiction may inspire a policy change but the final outcome does not actually draw upon the original idea).

Bennett and Howlett (1992, p. 289), also widely cited, establish three descriptive components of policy learning: who learns, what is learned and what effects on resulting policies emerge as a result of learning, with respect to three "highly complex processes: learning about organizations, learning about programs, and learning about policies". A third influential piece explicitly considers networks in learning. Stone (2004, pp. 546–547) observes that the public policy literature has tended to concentrate on the transfer of knowledge, policy instruments and practices, with a focus on decision-making dynamics. But networks deserve attention as important frameworks and "transfer mechanisms" for learning. In a comprehensive table, Stone (2004, pp. 562–563) looks at 15 variables applied to "modes of policy transfer", adding richness to previous treatments.

Throughout the fulsome literature on policy transfer, prescriptions abound (such as "beware of being trapped in a frame"; Argyris and Schön 1996, p. 197), at the expense of methods, and we cannot readily detect attention to the moment of insight and fresh thinking that constitutes learning about the future – A'. In one partial exception, Wolman and Page (2002, p. 493) found that "assessment" was in terms of a "local official's own sense of what sounds right"; yet they envisage such assessment only in terms of an analytic "critical evaluation". This is consistent with accepting that analysts exercise professional judgement in the conduct of their tasks, such as described in the first scenario variant, and also consistent with Dolowitz and Marsh's (2000) lesson categories.

Abduction and Phronesis in Policy Transfer Learning

The review of Rose's method raises some questions: from within a flow of observations when a learner engages in case B, in what form does a fresh thought present itself? How does the learner receive and recognize it? Which fresh thoughts are suited to drawing lessons? And from Barzelay, what exactly goes on when learners use their minds to "see" how a causal process that resulted in a desired trajectory from B to B' might unfurl in a prospective case? Barzelay (2007, p. 526) is alert to the risk that "extrapolation-oriented case research design" may be "wholly arbitrary and idiosyncratic". The solution he offers is to engage with the literature. But does such engagement provide sufficient guidance to what case-specific details can be stripped away as non-essential and what should be retained when devising a transportable cause–effect model? What is the role of the learner's prior knowledge and experience? Further, both Rose and Barzelay premise their methods on similarity between source and target cases and privilege causal–analytic lesson drawing. Yet given the richness and complexity of cases, lesson learning may arise from unexpected directions, and create re-casing opportunities, as in the scenario variant 2.

We offer the beginning of an answer to these challenges based on the phenomena of abduction and phronesis, which offer conceptual resources for understanding what happens in the various moments of learning. In the context of single-case learning, abduction and phronesis potentially offer opportunities to learn through an everyday, unstructured and non-specific process of learning, which may involve narratives of policy experiences, such as may arise informally in networks, or observation of policies in practice. In case learning, abduction centres precisely on the detection and initial evaluation of the freshness of an idea, while phronesis fills the need for a high degree of professional judgemental expertise. Both can be applied alongside standard analytic approaches to policy work.

Clarifying the Concepts

Abduction occurs in both everyday contexts and scientific reasoning (Douven 2011, p. 1), drawing on an initial, surprising perception, and leading, often immediately, to a plausible explanation that can be tested. Sherlock Holmes makes abductive inferences from observations such as the dog that didn't bark in the night, and parents develop an ability to infer the reason a baby is crying. In a foreign policy context, decisions about how to manage a delicate situation such as North Korea's nuclear threats involve abduction from fragments of information about regional tensions, attitudes of allies and enemies, and Kim Jung Un's goals, intentions, proclivities and state of mind, all of which must be woven into plausible hypotheses about how the various players will react to different possible US actions and to other players' reactions in turn. In the case of relieving traffic congestion, abduction might take the form of fresh insights into motivating millennials to use public transportation and helping them spread their habits to other generations. Such insights may depend on formulating plausible hypotheses about people's likely transportation choices in response to policy changes. Those hypotheses, in turn, depend on deeper insights about why individuals with different characteristics facing different circumstances make the transportation choices that they do. Such insights may be informed by survey research and modelling of past behaviour, but with a gaze turned toward the future, new, creative ideas about the problem are more likely to arise from stories, analogies and case-like encounters.

When convincing explanations for an autocrat's behaviour or a subpopulation's transportation choices are deemed lacking in theory, and when there are limited explanations from well-matched prior situations, the way is open for new explanations to be generated. Abduction – in the form of noticing followed quickly by the leap to an (informed) guess – may be possible if the leaper is already equipped with some raw materials for supplying a plausible solution to the general question, "what is this that I am noticing"? Plausible explanations may be selected from an existing database (in the manner of a clinician settling on a likely diagnosis fitting a presenting patient's unusual symptoms) or they may be historically new (Hoffman 2010, p. 583). Hoffman illustrates the latter through Aldo Leopold's realization that he had to "think like a mountain" in order to be able to manage an ecosystem as a multi-dimensional configuration, not as simple causal relations, thereby achieving a "perceptual shift" for ecosystem management.

Bajc, an ethnographer, describes how abduction arises in her case learning context as she is "able to play with the data freely and let this process lead to a surprising discovery and insight" (Bajc 2012, p. 73). Tavory and Timmermans (2014) emphasize that data must be brought into loose connection with what the researcher is predisposed to discover (as in the case of an experienced clinician), counterpoised at the same time with existing theories and conversations with members of one's intellectual community. Noticing surprises and deriving plausible explanations is more than pure guessing; tacit knowledge (Polanyi 1966) and "clues, or strong intuition about what the data are communicating" (Bajc 2012, p. 82) serve an important role.

For researchers in the Tavory and Timmermans and Bajc tradition, abduction contributes to the scientific aim to iteratively improve theories and understanding of the social world. More like clinicians, however, policy learners need to learn in order to recommend policy action. It may not be feasible to iteratively consider all plausible explanations, but rather there may be pressure to select and proceed with one. In situations in which a large number of plausible explanations compete, McKaughan (2008) offers the criterion of "pursuitworthiness": "abductions yield *recommendations about what courses of action to pursue* given our values and given the information and resources at our disposal" (McKaughan 2008, p. 454; emphasis in original).

Pursuit, for policy professionals, means selecting explanations to more systematically investigate for their merits in addressing a policy challenge. Where researchers may turn at this point to theory and an intellectual community, or to a causal model (following Rose's or Barzelay's method), policy professionals also have recourse to their networks, their analogical reasoning and their own judgement. When learners embedded in a network talk through their ideas, others' reactions help them filter hypotheses, and further connect with their repertoire of policy experiences.

When gauging the usefulness of plausible explanations, learners naturally use analogical reasoning. In analogical reasoning, a comparison is made between two domains that highlights similarities and supports a hypothesis pertaining to something as yet unobserved in the second domain, but observed in the first (Bartha 2013). As Holyoak and Thagard (1995, p. 7) write, the "act of making an analogy creates new connections between [the two analogues] even when they at first seem unrelated".

Finally, the Aristotelian concept, phronesis, underscores the quality of discernment or practical wisdom in judging explanations worth pursuing (or not) for policy purposes. Phronesis, as described by Thomas (2011, p. 24, drawing on others), is "a combination of knowledge, judgement and taste, together producing a discernment ... emerging out of our experience". Coupling abductive reasoning to phronesis, as Thomas (2010, 2011) does, provides a compelling explanation for learning from a single case. Thomas writes, drawing on the work of the philosopher Hans-Georg Gadamer:

> there is a need to move toward the *"exemplary* knowledge" of abduction and phronesis.... I am talking about example viewed and heard in the context of another's experience – another's horizon, in Gadamer's terms – but used in the context of one's own, where the horizon changes: The example is neither taken to be representative or typical nor is it exemplary in the sense of being a model to follow. Rather, it is taken to be a particular representation given in context and understood in that context. However, it is interpretable only in the context of one's own experience – in the context, in other words, of one's phronesis, rather than theory. (Thomas 2010, p. 578)

Together, abduction and phronesis demonstrate aspects of "learning as meaning making" (Zittoun and Brinkmann 2011, p. 1809), which maintains that people actively engage in making sense of situations, "drawing on their history of similar situations and on available cultural resources" to generate coherent accounts of the past and future. Accordingly, a policy exemplar (B) occasions in a person a means to both notice and discern in its "image" the ideas, connections and possibilities for creating a corresponding image for the prospective case, A' (or, indeed, to add to a growing repertoire that may be drawn on in some other, dissimilar, situation). The same policy exemplar also may create a focal point around which individuals from different personal and organizational perspectives can discover shared interests, concerns and bases for cooperative action. Both realizations may come as surprises to the actors involved.

Toward More Beneficial Lessons and Transfers

Because the phenomena of abduction and phronesis play important roles in policy learning and transfer (whether acknowledged or not), a question naturally arises about how they might be mobilized to improve the quality of policy work in its many diverse manifestations (Colebatch 2015). Abduction's dual role in generating new hypotheses for analytic testing in conventional models and sparking fresh insights in less well-structured learning situations provides sufficient reason to work on developing its contributions to policy learning. Phronesis' capacity for assessing the products of abduction against professional experience and *nous* makes it, too, worthy of extension and development in the sphere of practice.

Both concepts resist codification, however, and neither fits comfortably in the usual toolbox-oriented approach to training policy analysts and advisers. They cannot be broken down into steps, which makes them difficult to teach. They do not involve repeated, standardized activities or behaviours, which makes them difficult to rehearse. Abstracted from any particular context, they do not qualify as definable skills or talents per se, although some people may be more adept than others at fresh thinking or exercises of professional judgement.

In lieu of an abduction and phronesis manual, a few basic principles can be identified, aligned to the general learning components (preparing, getting information and considering its applicability), which will improve policy professionals' ability to learn effectively and efficiently from a single case. As a precondition, the potentially large and significant benefits of single-case lesson transfer need to be acknowledged within the fields of policy studies and policy analysis – not as substitutes for larger-n studies, but as complements. Renewed enthusiasm for single-case learning as a mode of policy analysis is then likely to motivate further study of abduction and phronesis as key features of the modality.

First, to prepare for learning from the case, B, learners need to define a "need" that results from some challenge in A that will be resolved in A'. In the manner of "looking before leaping", learners can ready themselves by activating their existing relevant knowledge (of what is, in A, and what is desired, in A'). This establishes a mental field in which any subsequent plausible ideas may be hypothetically examined. Such readying is analogous to a crime detective undertaking explicitly to tune in to what may be available upon first arriving at a crime scene. Preparation cues a wiser use of case content and the analogies it may trigger. Preparation, thus, is not merely a necessary springboard for analysis proper, but a choice to be ready to discern creative possibility, involving the preparer personally, and establishing a specific "horizon" for learning.

Second, once so readied, policy professionals need to open up to a new case by exploring it freely with as few preconceptions as possible. Like a detective, a clinician facing a challenging case or an engineer attempting to understand a post-earthquake building collapse, the learner may start mentally to try out a number of possible explanations. Here, the practice of abduction functions as curiosity, motivating the natural propensity of sensory perceptions to settle into the form of plausible explanations of the specific resources (data) available to "play around" with in the hypothetical learning space. Phronesis adds in relevant professional expertise. Starbuck (2006) refers to a similar practice as "disturbing oneself"; Schön (1983) recommends reflection.

Thomas (2010, pp. 579–580, drawing on Bruner) expands on the skills of discerning and practices for "entering into" a case. Examples are enabling "a spirit of inquisitiveness … not extinguished in a search for generality", "putting together related information to make a story" in a relaxed setting (imagine Sherlock Holmes musing in a darkened theatre) and "noticing change … and its correlates and sequelae". Learners can intentionally engage their ability to see anomaly, to actively draw analogies, to listen around the edges of stories and mull over not just what people do but what they think and feel. At least speculatively, learners can consider how the experiences of the case actors have influenced their reported interpretations. These devices assist learners to enter into the case as any visitor can, to see what is highlighted in their own horizon and to increase the likelihood that viewing and reflecting on what is reported will prompt the expertise or experientially grounded hunch that develops into a transferable lesson.

A third principle encourages the learner to assemble a picture, as seen from the prepared horizon, using observations gleaned from entering into the case openly. That is, while ostensibly looking at B, the learner can strive to "see" as through a two-way mirror, A transposed to A'. These pictures are fresh thoughts, some of which will be judged worth pursuing. Considering Stockholm's congestion charges, for example, thoughts may stem from how prices affect the aggregate of drivers' utility calculations, but may also be sparked by observing the impacts of the policy change on public attitudes about multiple modes of transportation, land use, siting of residential and commercial real estate, telecommuting and other flow-on issues. The learner reflects on plausible ideas in light of their implications for action (via phronesis), rather than their fit with any posited pattern, such as a theory or diagnostic category (Thomas 2010). At this stage, the learner will have the broad elements of a new narrative in place. It will take the form of a comparison between B and A': "They did *this and that* there (B), and we might do *such and so* here" (introduce in A in order to get A'). This is not the counterfactual analysis of historical case researchers, but (being hypothesized for the future), a counter-scenario prospective exercise drawing on the discernment of phronesis. Ultimately, the story may be expressed as a middle-range theory – a somewhat abstract simplification as in the "lesson" in Barzelay's (2007) method – which carries idea content rather than empirical detail but is recognizable in new contexts (Tsoukas 2009; Thomas 2010). It is built up from data, not down from causal theory.

As the learner enters into the design phase of policy transfer, sifting through accumulated ideas for ways to improve a potential policy (whether sourced from generic lists of instruments or through abduction), emerging policy lessons can be further scrutinized in light of contextual constraints and opportunities in A, including political dynamics, existing policies at various levels of government, availability of resources, local values, and so on. During this process, more conventionally analytic approaches, such as modelling and cost–benefit analysis, may work alongside more freely flowing exercises of abduction and phronesis – such advice generates a fourth principle of good practice.

Fifth and finally, as often as possible and at every stage of learning, as outlined in the preceding principles, policy professionals probably should be encouraged to make site visits in person, or at least to talk on the phone or skype with experienced individuals in case destinations. Interacting directly with knowledgeable individuals cultivates situated social learning in which knowledge is understood not as a "possession of the individual" but as "held in relationships" of "co-constructed understanding" (Waite and Pratt 2015, pp. 5–6). Professional networks play important roles in facilitating interpersonal exchanges of knowledge leading to more opportunities for brainstorming, creativity and fine-tuning of professional antennae.

Conclusion

Methods that seek analytically to extract causal mechanisms for policy transfer, based on comparing a source policy exemplar (B) to a target case (A'), can be usefully complemented by methods that support abductive leaps and the exercise of expert judgement based on the discernment of phronesis. Our investigation has made explicit how, in the midst of a rich, complex undertaking to compare a single exemplar and a prospective case, a learner can activate these contributions to transferable lesson drawing.

Abduction and phronesis – noticing something that stands out and judging it in the context of a presenting need – are integral to all learners. Although they are not conventional skills that can be taught, they can be developed and enhanced. More adept experts can coach and mentor the less adept, and arguably must: clinicians and engineers do not learn all they need to know from books, and nor, of course, do, or should, policy professionals.

All of us – professionals, academics, stakeholders and members of the public – can reflect and build in more attention to the exercise of abduction and phronesis throughout the policy learning and transfer process. For the policy professional at the centre of a transfer, attention is essentially comparative: a receptive and attuned learner acquires and judges plausible lessons from B for application in A to achieve A'. The field of learning includes the "unexpected" in the initially seen policy case, B, thus opening up vast opportunities for lesson drawing. Comparative case learning can be enhanced in the dialogic interaction in network exchanges between the source and target case actors, the memories of the past and prospective images that are presented, triggered and created in the course of those interactions. The two-pronged capacity for abduction and phronesis, expertly harnessed for single-case learning, holds considerable promise given its affinity with natural and everyday learning practices.

Notes

1. See, for example, (Bennett and Elman 2006; Hall 2006; Tsoukas 2009; Vogel and Henstra 2015). For reviews and discussions, as well as texts, see Stake (1995) and Yin (2014).

References

"A Place to Call Home", 2001, Nov 15. *Chronicle of Philanthropy*, **14**(3), pp. 23–24.
Argyris, C. and Schön, D., 1996, *Organizational Learning: Theory, Methods, and Practice* (Reading, MA: Addison-Wesley).
Bajc, V., 2012, Abductive ethnography of practice in highly uncertain conditions. *The ANNALS of the American Academy of Political and Social Science*, **642**, pp. 72–85. doi:10.1177/0002716212438197
Banks, G., 2009, *Challenges of Evidence-Based Policy-Making* (Canberra: Australian Government Productivity Commission, speech delivered as the ANZSOG/ANU Public Lecture Series), Feb 4.
Bardach, E., 2004, Presidential address—The extrapolation problem: How can we learn from the experience of others? *Journal of Policy Analysis and Management*, **23**, pp. 205–220. doi:10.1002/pam.20000
Bardach, E., 2012, *A Practical Guide for Policy Analysis: the Eightfold Path to More Effective Problem Solving* (4th ed) (Los Angeles: Sage/CQ Press).
Bartha, P., 2013, Analogy and analogical reasoning, in: E. N. Zalta (Ed) *The Stanford Encyclopedia of Philosophy (Fall Ed.)* (Stanford, CA: Center for the Study of Language and Information, Stanford University). http://plato.stanford.edu/archives/fall2013/entries/reasoning-analogy/
Barzelay, M., 2007, Learning from second-hand experience: Methodology for extrapolation-oriented case research. *Governance*, **20**(3), pp. 521–543. doi:10.1111/gove.2007.20.issue-3
Bengtsson, B. and Hertting, N., 2014, Generalization by mechanism: Thin rationality and ideal-type analysis in case study research. *Philosophy of the Social Sciences*, **44**(6), pp. 707–732. doi:10.1177/0048393113506495
Bennett, A. and Elman, C., 2006, Qualitative research: recent developments in case study methods. *Annual Review of Political Science*, **9**, pp. 455–476. doi:10.1146/annurev.polisci.8.082103.104918
Bennett, C. and Howlett, M., 1992, The lessons of learning: Reconciling theories of policy learning and policy change. *Policy Sciences*, **25**, pp. 275–294. doi:10.1007/BF00138786

Börjesson, M., Eliasson, J., Hugosson, M. and Brundell-Freij, K., 2012, The Stockholm congestion charges—5 years on. Effects, acceptability and lessons learnt. *Transport Policy*, **20**, pp. 1–12. doi:10.1016/j.tranpol.2011.11.001

Botma, Y., Van Rensburg, G. H., Coetzee, I. M. and Heyns, T., 2015, A conceptual framework for educational design at modular level to promote transfer of learning. *Innovations in Education and Teaching International*, **52**(5), pp. 499–509. doi:10.1080/14703297.2013.866051

Colebatch, H. K., 2015, Knowledge, policy and the work of governing. *Journal of Comparative Policy Analysis: Research and Practice*, **17**(3), pp. 209–214. doi:10.1080/13876988.2015.1036517

Dolowitz, D. and Marsh, D., 2000, Learning from abroad: The role of policy transfer in contemporary policy-making. *Governance: an International Journal of Policy and Administration*, **13**(1), pp. 5–23. doi:10.1111/gove.2000.13.issue-1

Douven, I., 2011, Abduction, in: E. N. Zalta (Ed) *The Stanford Encyclopedia of Philosophy (Spring Ed.)* (Stanford, CA: Center for the Study of Language and Information, Stanford University). http://plato.stanford.edu/archives/spr2011/entries/abduction/

Dunn, W. N., 2011, *Public Policy Analysis* (5th ed) (London: Routledge).

Ettelt, S., Mays, N. and Nolte, E., 2012, Policy learning from abroad: Why it is more difficult than it seems. *Policy & Politics*, **40**(4), pp. 491–504. doi:10.1332/030557312X643786

Gluckman, P., 2013, *The Role of Evidence in Policy Formation and Implementation* (Auckland: Office of the Prime Minister's Chief Science Advisor).

Hall, P. A., 2006, Systematic process analysis: When and how to use it. *European Management Review*, **3**, pp. 24–31. doi:10.1057/palgrave.emr.1500050

Head, B. W., 2008, Three lenses of evidence-based policy. *The Australian Journal of Public Administration*, **67**(1), pp. 1–11. doi:10.1111/j.1467-8500.2007.00564.x

Hermans, L. M., 2011, An approach to support learning from international experience with water policy. *Water Resources Management*, **25**, pp. 373–393. doi:10.1007/s11269-010-9705-x

Hoffman, M. H. G., 2010, "Theoric transformations" and a new classification of abductive inferences. *Transactions of the Charles S. Peirce Society*, **46**(4), pp. 570–590. doi:10.2979/trancharpeirsoc.2010.46.4.570

Holyoak, K. X. and Thagard, P., 1995, *Mental Leaps: Analogy in Creative Thought* (Cambridge, MA: MIT Press/Bradford Books).

Kahneman, D., 2011, *Thinking, Fast and Slow* (New York: Farrar, Strauss and Giroux).

Leigh, A., 2009, What evidence should social policymakers use? *Economic Roundup*, **1**, pp. 27–43.

Marsden, G., Frick, K. T., May, A. D. and Deakin, E., 2011, How do cities approach policy innovation and policy learning? A study of 30 policies in Northern Europe and North America. *Transport Policy*, **18**(3), pp. 501–512. doi:10.1016/j.tranpol.2010.10.006

May, P., 1992, Policy learning and failure. *Journal of Public Policy*, **12**(4), pp. 331–354. doi:10.1017/S0143814X00005602

McKaughan, D. J., 2008, From ugly duckling to swan: C. S. Peirce, abduction, and the pursuit of scientific theories. *Transactions of the Charles S. Peirce Society*, **44**(3), pp. 446–468.

Parsell, C., Fitzpatrick, S. and Busch-Geertsema, V., 2014, Common ground in Australia: An object lesson in evidence hierarchies and policy transfer. *Housing Studies*, **29**(1), pp. 69–87. doi:10.1080/02673037.2013.824558

Polanyi, M., 1966, *The Tacit Dimension* (Chicago: University of Chicago Press).

Rose, R., 1991, What is lesson drawing? *Journal of Public Policy*, **11**, pp. 3–30. doi:10.1017/S0143814X00004918

Rose, R., 2005, *Learning from Comparative Public Policy: A Practical Guide* (London and New York: Routledge).

Sabatier, P. A., 1987, Knowledge, policy-oriented learning, and policy change: An advocacy coalition framework. *Knowledge: Creation, Diffusion, Utilization*, **8**(4), pp. 649–692. doi:10.1177/0164025987008004005

Schmitt, S., 2013, Comparative approaches to the study of public policy-making, in: J. Araral, J. Eduardo, S. Fritzen, M. Howlett, M. Ramesh and X. Wu (Eds) *Routledge Handbook of Public Policy* (London/New York: Routledge), pp. 29–43.

Schön, D., 1983, *The Reflective Practitioner: How Professionals Think in Action* (New York: Basic Books).

Stake, R. E., 1995, *The Art of Case Study Research* (Thousand Oaks: SAGE).

Starbuck, W., 2006, *The Production of Knowledge: the Challenge of Social Science Research* (Oxford: Oxford University Press).
Stone, D., 2004, Transfer agents and global networks in the 'transnationalization' of policy. *Journal of European Public Policy*, **11**(3), pp. 545–566. doi:10.1080/13501760410001694291
Tavory, I. and Timmermans, S., 2014, *Abductive Analysis: Theorizing Qualitative Research* (Chicago and London: University of Chicago Press).
Thomas, G., 2010, Doing case study: Abduction not induction, phronesis not theory. *Qualitative Inquiry*, **16**(7), pp. 575–582. doi:10.1177/1077800410372601
Thomas, G., 2011, The case: Generalisation, theory and phronesis in case study. *Oxford Review of Education*, **37**(1), pp. 21–35. doi:10.1080/03054985.2010.521622
Tsoukas, H., 2009, Craving for generality in small-N studies: A Wittgensteinian approach towards the epistemology of the particular in organization and management studies, in: D. A. Buchanan and A. Bryman (Eds) *The SAGE Handbook of Organizational Research Methods* (London: SAGE), pp. 285–301.
Tversky, A. and Kahneman, D., 1974, Judgment under uncertainty: Heuristics and biases. *Science*, **185**, pp. 1124–1131. doi:10.1126/science.185.4157.1124
Vogel, B. and Henstra, D., 2015, Studying local climate adaptation: A heuristic research framework for comparative policy analysis. *Global Environmental Change*, **31**, pp. 110–120. doi:10.1016/j.gloenvcha.2015.01.001
Waite, S. and Pratt, N., 2015, Situated learning, in: N. J. Smelser and P. B. Baltes (Eds) *International Encyclopedia of the Social & Behavioral Sciences*, (2nd ed) (Amsterdam: Elsevier), Vol. 22, pp. 5–12.
Weimer, D. and Vining, A., 2011, *Policy Analysis: Concepts and Practice* (5th ed) (Boston: Longman).
Wesselink, A., Colebatch, H. and Pearce, W., 2014, Evidence and policy: Discourses, meanings and practices. *Policy Sciences*, **47**, pp. 339–344. doi:10.1007/s11077-014-9209-2
Wolman, H. and Page, E., 2002, Policy transfer among local governments: An information-Theory approach. *Governance*, **15**(4), pp. 477–501. doi:10.1111/gove.2002.15.issue-4
Yin, R. K., 2014, *Case Study Research: Design and Methods* (5th ed) (London: SAGE).
Zittoun, T. and Brinkmann, S., 2011, in: N. M. Seel (Ed) *Learning as Meaning Making, Encyclopedia of the Sciences of Learning* (Boston: Springer), pp. 1809–1811.

Index

Note: Page numbers followed by "n" denote endnotes.

abduction 401, 403–404, 408–413
abstraction level 138–139
ACF *see* advocacy coalition framework (ACF)
achievement oriented principles 215
action arena 173–176, 178, 182, 185–188
active individualism 364n2
active labour market policy (ALMP) 268, 272–273, 277–278, 281–284
actor-related strategies 206
Adachi, Y. 3, 82
Adams, D. 32, 178
adaptation *vs.* internalization: case study 300; DG I 300; DG IA 300; DG II 299; DG VI 300; DG XI 299; DG XVII 299; directorates general (DGs) 299; FNPF 300; INTERFEL 300; resource interdependence 299
Administration & Society 84
advocacy coalition framework (ACF) 5, 20, 22, 51, 130, 134–135, 139, 141–143, 145–146, 164, 168–172, 175, 180–181, 187–188, 231, 264; epistemological point of view 145; structuralist point of view 146; theoretical point of view 145; transformation in external factors 146
AFDC *see* Aid to Families with Dependent Children (AFDC)
Agartan. T. I. 265n2
age-alignment spending ratio 273, 276, 281–282
agenda change 169
agenda-setting literature 63
agenda-setting process 23, 169
agricultural department 332
agriculture 296; DBV 296; DBV's Präsidium 297; FNSEA 296; policy community 297
Aid to Families with Dependent Children (AFDC) 286n6
AIDS: policy case 105; prevention agency 117–118
Alasuutari, P. 395, 398–399
Alber, J. 212–213, 219
Albury, D. 225, 229, 236

Almond, G. A. 336
ALMP *see* active labour market policy (ALMP)
ambiguity–conflict model 226–227, 229
American policy researchers 34
American Political Science Association 32
anthro-pomorphisis 372
ANZ Investment Bank 332
APPAM *see* Association for Public Policy Analysis and Management (APPAM)
aqua-culture 246; cold-water 246; interactions 252; organic 246; small-scale 246; warm-water 246
Arato, A. 251
Argyris, C. 181, 190n11, 408
Aristotle 14, 51
Army Corps of Engineers 71
ASEAN *see* Association of South East Asian Nations (ASEAN)
Aspinwall, M. 307n5
Association for Public Policy Analysis and Management (APPAM) 48, 364
Association of South East Asian Nations (ASEAN) 99
attitudinal approach 351
Australian Vocational Education and Training (VET) 397
authority-based instruments 20
autocrat's behaviour 409
availability heuristic 403
Avrami, S. 94

Baehler, K. J. 5
Baldwin, P. 107
Balme, R. 293, 300
Banfield, E. C. 319, 336
Banting, K. 205
Bardach, E. 402, 407
Barnett formula 278
Barry, B. 336
Barzelay, M. 403, 406–408, 412
baseline model 203
basic taxonomy 161

418 INDEX

Baumgartner, F. R. 144, 155, 163n2, 164n4, 176–177, 182–183, 255
Bavaria 115
Bavarian CSU party 115
Bavinck, M. 257n1
Bayer, R. 126n12, 297, 304–305, 307n9
Bayernwerk 297, 304–305, 307n9
BC-CBA *see* Budget-Constrained Cost–Benefit Analysis (BC-CBA)
Béland, D. 94, 263–264
beneficial lessons and transfers 410–412; assemble a picture 412; learners 411; middle-range theory 412; potential policy 412; preparation 411; single-case learning 411
Benito, B. 94
Bennett, A. 413n1
Bennett, C. 178, 405, 407
Bentham, J. 375
Benz, A. 270
Berman, S. 16
Berman, P. 235
Berra, Y. 32
Berry, F. S. 94, 236
Berry, W. D. 94, 236
Berry, W. T. 161
Beveridgian type 108, 122, 124
Bismarckian type 108
Bjørnskov, C. 311–312, 314, 316–317, 321, 323, 324n9
blind spots 170–171, 173
Blomquist, W. 170, 189n3
Blount, R. 40n2
Boase, A. 7
Bobrow, D. B. 329
Bobrow, J. D. 365n14
Bonoli, G. 200, 272
Boudon, R. 149
boundary relationships 171, 174
boundary rules 174–175
Boushey, G. 7
Bovens, M. A. P. 52, 77n7, 78n10, 296
Brans, M. 94
brass plaque institutionalism 77n5
Brecht's Scientific Value Relativism 364n6
Breen, M. 6
Breen, R. 200
Britain's Health and Safety Executive 335
British Government Cabinet 335
Broschek, J. 270
Bruff, I. 208
Brusca, I. 94
Buanes, A. 254
Budget-Constrained Cost–Benefit Analysis (BC-CBA) 390–391
Bulmer, S. 293
bundled policies 398
Burkhauser, R. 102

CA *see* Cost Analysis (CA)
CAFÉ *see* Corporate Average Fuel Economy (CAFÉ)
Cairncross, F. 40n6
California's zero emission 356
Californian–original–version 237
Calman Commission 278
Campbell Collaboration 55
Canada Foundation for Innovation (CFI) 235
Canada Research Chairs (CRC) Programme 234–235
Canadian fiscal system 205
Canadian proposal 342; anthropological theory 342; Canadian institutions/ministries 343; cultural policy analysis process profile 342; objectives 342; study proposes 343
Capano, G. 4, 7, 129, 162
Caporaso, J. 291–292, 294, 298
capture fisheries 244, 250, 252
Carothers, T. 40n3
Carroll, B. 343
Carroll, P. 398
case selection 272; English-speaking 272; Scottish financial mechanisms 272; territorial politics 272
case-oriented approach 197, 204
Cashore, B. 136, 154, 156, 160
Cassidy, M. F. 314
Castles, F. G. 203–204
causal mechanism 135, 139–140, 142–143, 146, 148, 164n5, 177, 189, 190n7, 196–197, 201, 206–208, 412
CBD *see* Convention on Biological Diversity (CBD)
CBO *see* Congressional Budget Office (CBO)
CCRF *see* code of conduct for responsible fisheries (CCRF)
CEA *see* cost-effectiveness analysis (CEA)
CEECs *see* Central and Eastern European candidate countries (CEECs)
Central and Eastern European candidate countries (CEECs) 299–300, 303–304
Central Europe Working Group 301
ceteris paribus 69
CFI *see* Canada Foundation for Innovation (CFI)
Chabanet, D. 293
Chernobyl nuclear power plant 301
chicken and egg problem 294
children immunization 67
Children's Health Insurance Program (CHIP) 274, 278
CHIP *see* Children's Health Insurance Program (CHIP)
chlorofluorocarbons (CFCs) 37
choice methods: cost–benefit analysis 387; efficiency analysis 387–390; Embedded Cost–Benefit Analysis 390–391; Multi-Goal Analysis 391

Christensen, C. M. 225
Chuenpagdee, R. 248, 251, 257n1
CIS *see* Commonwealth of Independent States (CIS)
civic participation 311–312, 314–315, 318–319, 322, 328
civil society 240–241, 247, 250–252, 256
Claeys, P.-H. 307n5
Clasen, J. 218
classical dichotomy 136
classics of comparative policy analysis: and institutions 6; comparative policy sectors 7–8; inter-regional studies 6–7; methodology 5–6; theory 5–6
Clayton, R. 214
Clemens, E. S. 156, 164n7
Clifton, J. 395, 397
Clinton, H. R. 33, 36
cluster analysis 315–316; factor scores 316; maximum inter-cluster heterogeneity 315; minimum intra-cluster homogeneity 315; non-hierarchical k-means technique 315
co-governance 249–250
co-management 250; *see also* co-governance
co-modes 249
coastal webs 248
Cobb, R. W. 66, 298, 350
code of conduct 251
code of conduct for responsible fisheries (CCRF) 251
coding 81, 87, 89, 273
Cohen, J. L. 251
cold-water aqua-culture 246
Coleman, J. S. 138
Coleman, W. D. 156, 162
collaborative GI 253
collective choice level 173–174, 176, 178
common pool resources 15, 35; theory 173
Commonwealth of Independent States (CIS) 301
Community's enlargement policy 291, 296
comparable policy problem, construction of: comparative results and interpretation 119–124; homosexual couples, legal recognition of 109; selected country stories, sex education at school 109; typical policy content, typical policy timing 112–113
comparative administration group 84
Comparative Agendas Project 21
comparative analysis 7, 13–14, 36–38, 45–46, 49, 57n2, 94–95, 100–101, 105–107, 198, 229, 236, 262–263, 271, 342
comparative avenues 51
comparative health policy analysis 125n1
comparative inter-regional policy analysis studies 6–7; analysis 7; policy differences 7; typologies 7
comparative logic *vs.* problem logic 99–103; agenda setting 103; complex policy issues 99; cross-national policy learning 102; empirical observations 100; interpretation of results 100; limited space 103; major international data collection systems 102; methodological approaches 101; national models 100; national policy-making system 101; non-governmental organizations 100; on health care policy 102; policy elaboration 100; policy framing 103; public health policies 101
comparative policy analysis: access 87; articles in EBSCO academic complete database 92; articles in EBSCO Academic Database 88–93; comparative renaissance, traces 34–38; content analysis study of JCPA 88–93; countries studied 90, 93; cross-national problems 87; development of 82–85; economic path dependence 87; ethnography and interview 92; growth of field of 89; importance and limitations of 85–88; learning transferable lessons from single cases 401–412; methodology and theory 90–91, 93; policy areas studied 89–90, 92; qualitative research 91; quantitative analysis 91; survey created for this research 92; textual and content analysis 91; theory and framework pieces 91
comparative policy analysis and institutions 6; governance 6; institutions 6; policy variation 6; scope 20
comparative policy analysis and linkages: approaches and relationship to policy 14; best practice 21; comparative methodologies and policy 23–24; comparative political economy 19; comparative politics, role of 19–20; cross-fertilization 14; development studies 18; generalizations 14; governance 18–19; institutionalism 14–16; interest intermediation 17–18; knowledge of actors 13; low level of connection 22; methodological individualism and public policy 22; to other comparative domains 13–14; policy analysis outputs 13; public policies 13; public policy studies 19–20; quantitative analysis of 14
comparative policy analysis studies 3; beginnings, the 45–47; Cyr and deLeon alternative arguments 44; facing globalization 48–49; policy analysis grows and diversifies 47–48; policy analysis methods 54; policy ideas 52–53; policy process research 51; policy research 53–54; policy transfer 54–56; policy-relevant research 52; possible avenues 50–51; as profession 49–50; in US policy analysis 45
Comparative Policy Process, The (Smith) 32
comparative policy research 23, 33–34, 39–40, 49–50, 56, 83, 154, 260, 264–265
comparative policy sectors 7–8; absence of papers 8; federalist regimes 8; immigration 7; policy domains 8; technology 7

comparative political studies 89
comparative politics 3–4, 7, 13–24, 32, 37–38, 81–84, 86, 103, 198, 268, 271, 284; role of 19–20
comparative public administration 83–84; decline of literature in 84
comparative public policy 3–4, 7–8, 14, 18, 21–22, 24, 32, 46, 82–84, 87–89, 94–95, 100, 203, 264, 267
comparative renaissance, traces 34–38; analysis strength 38; cross-fertilization 36; economic competition 35; electronic communications 35; European-style urban planning concepts 36; Harrison's analysis 37; incorporate cultural variables 36; informal international consortium 35; national environmental policies 36; natural resource issue 37; pollution taxes 37; urban policy evaluation 36
comparative research agenda 257, 341
comparative results and interpretation 119–124; beneficiary participation 123; (de)centralization factor 122; decision-making and implementation systems 122; exception in France 124; HIV infection prevalence 119; national/local relationship 122; policy patterns 123; policy-building capacity 123; political consensus-building 122; political rhetoric 123; practical policy construction 123; public health risk 123
comparative welfare state research: matching problem in 200–207; welfare state reform 197–200
complex interdependence 295–298; adaptational pressures 298; bureaucratic competition 299; European integration 298; Europeanization processes 298
complex policies, comparision: addicts 109; aim 107; basic features of political system 108; Catholic tradition 109; centralized public policy system 108; comparable policy problem, construction of 109–113; comparative case study 107; comparative results and interpretation 119–124; consensus building and co-ordination 115–117; decentralized public policy system 108; epidemiological transmission models 109; French epidemic 108; government involvement 113–115; health and sex education 117–119; health care sector 108; historical comparative studies 107; HIV-positive population 108; individual and collective dimensions 106; institutional organization of health sector 108; international statistics 107; medical profession, role 106; militant organizations 107; national cases included 108; North/South, differences 109; policy initiation 113–115; private life issues 106; Protestant tradition 109; public health issues, successful management 106; selecting country cases 107–109, 113; social solidarity 106; transmission models of epidemic 108; typical policy content 110–113; Western Europe, differences 109
comprehensive monetization of efficiency impacts 385
conceptual stretching 222n4
configurative dimensions 139–140
conflict expansion 181–186; action arenas 182; allies' leverage 185; change promoters and allies, relationship 185; countermobilization 186; image redefinition 182; mechanism of 183; newcomers 182; orientations 182; outsiders 182; policy champions 185; strategic calculus 184; venue shopping 182
congestion charges systems 402–405
Congressional Budget Office (CBO) 386
consensus building and co-ordination 115–117; AIDS prevention 117; comprehensive prevention strategies 116; French case, specificity 116; French Parliament 115; harm reduction strategies 116; Henrion Commission 117; in France 115; in Germany 115; Italian Parliament 115; left promoted risk reduction strategies 116; methadone provision to IDUs 116; methadone treatment 116; political opposition 117; screening debate 115
constituencyless issues 216
consumer capitalism 373
contemporary study of policy dynamics 155–156; attention spans 155; Lindblom-inspired incrementalism 155; paradigm shift 155; path-dependent effects 156; policy windows 155; post-incremental orthodoxy 155; punctuated equilibrium 155
Convention on Biological Diversity (CBD) 252
Cook, J. M. 164n7
Cook, P. 334
Corporate Average Fuel Economy (CAFÉ) 75
corporatism 17
corruption 313–314; causality 314; factor analysis 314
Corruption Perceptions Index (CPI) 314, 323n2
Cost Analysis (CA) 388
cost-effectiveness analysis (CEA) 361, 388–389
cost–benefit analysis 227, 365n12, 384–385, 387–390, 392, 412
Cox, R. H. 215
Coyle, D. J. 338, 372, 377, 379n3
CPI see Corruption Perceptions Index (CPI)
craft components 333, 337, 342–343
craft mastery 334
craft prototypes 334
craft skills 54
craftsmanship 334, 345

cross-national and cross-regional comparisons 280–283; breaking down spending, effect 283; coefficient of variance 281; different patterns of spending 282; divergence 281; of OECD countries 281; welfare spending 281
Crozier, M. 241
Cullingworth, J. B. 36
cultural analysis in policy analysis: cultural auditing 373–374; Douglas and Wildavsky's cultural approach 370–373; existing precepts 369; from political economy to political culture 375–378
cultural auditing 373–374
cultural bias, aspects of: beliefs about environment 372–373; political economy revisited 373; political values associated 371–372
cultural biases 371
cultural foundations of integration 209
cultural theorists 370, 373, 374
cultural theory: conceptual background 331–333; culture/policy analysis/ organizational arrangements 338–340; from theory to practice 333–338; gift for policy analysis 345n2; grid-group 337; mental products 336; neglected variable in policy research 340–341; policy analysis 330; political culture 336; political cultures and cultural bias 330–331; social relations, patterns of 371; study agenda 341–344
Culture Matters (Ellis and Thompson) 333
culture/policy analysis/organizational arrangements: analyst 339; bureaucratic orientation 340; civil-service organizational culture 340; electoral/voting systems 339; Israeli case 339; Italy's experience 339; public administration/management point of view 339; rationality, spread of 340; sociopolitical culture 340
Cyert, R. M. 190n11
Cyr, A. 40n1, 44

Dake, K. 372
Danish disability pension 220
Danish old age pension 219
Danish welfare state 202
Dasgupta, P. 312
debunking 196, 203
decentralisation 268–271, 284–285, 328
de-commodification 198, 272
deep core of basic beliefs 170
de facto comparisons 86
degree of agreement 65
degree of interdependence 75
deLeon, P. 3–4, 31, 40n1, 44, 82, 256
Delors, J. 301
Department of Defense analysts 46

Department of Health and Human Services 75
Department of Homeland Security 78n14
dependent variable 4, 6, 19, 22–23, 139, 154, 195–201, 205, 207–208, 212–214, 216, 221, 292
dependent variable problem 197–200; activation 200; contemporary research 199; cost containment 199; de-commodification 198; recalibration 199, 200; recommodification 199; retrenchment 199; social security 198; stratification systems 198; welfare state regimes 197; workfare 200
dependent variable problem 159; case studies 230; cutbacks or institutional change 219–221; different conceptualizations 216; in Study of Welfare State Expansion 214; retrenchment as cutbacks 216–217; retrenchment as institutional change 217–219; Welfare State 214–215
development studies and public policy 18
De Vries, M. S. 254
Diaz-Bonilla, E. 324n3
Díaz-Fuentes', D. 397
Diehl, P. F. 161
Dierkes, M. 83
dimension of innovation 230–232, 230–235
disconnected linearity 134
dissident enclavism 364n2
Distributionally-Weighted Cost–Benefit Analysis (DW-CBA) 390
diverse policies 268
divisibility: distributive politics 72; economic concern and distinction 72; form of intervention 73; politics 72
Dixit, A. 341
Dodgson, J. 391
Doig, A. 313
Dolowitz, D. 407–408
domestic action models abroad 304–305
Douglas, M. 332, 336–337, 342, 351, 365n13, 368–370, 372, 378, 379n2; cultural bias, aspects of 371–373; social life, dimensions of 370–371; theory 369
Dror, Y. 34, 46, 339, 357
Dryzek, J. S. 329, 365n14
durable solutions 66
Durant, R. F. 161
Durning, D. 333–334
Dutch government 356
Dutch sickness benefits 219
DW-CBA *see* Distributionally-Weighted Cost–Benefit Analysis (DW-CBA)
dynamic metaphors: policy entrepreneurs 265n3; windows of opportunity 265n3
dynamics of development: adaptation 134; descriptive reconstruction 134–135; reconstructive description 134; revolutionary process 134
dysfunctional policy transfer 398

EA *see* Effectiveness Analysis (EA)
EBRD *see* European Bank for Reconstruction and Development (EBRD)
EBSCO *see* Elton B. Stephens Co. (EBSCO)
Eccleston, R. 395, 397–398
eclecticism 145
economic consequences of political culture 330
economic development 373
economic explanations 200
economic policy 18–19, 68, 157; economic policy analysis 389
Economist, The 35, 40n5, 40n6
EDF *see* Electricité de France (EDF)
EEG *see* Renewable Energy Sources Act (EEG)
EEZ *see* Exclusive Economic Zone (EEZ)
Effectiveness Analysis (EA) 389
efficiency analysis 385, 387–391; cost analysis 388; cost-effectiveness analysis 389; effectiveness analysis 389; monetized net benefits analysis 389; qualitative cost–benefit analysis 389; Revenue Analysis 389; revenue-expenditure analysis 389; social costing 388–389; typology of 388
egalitarian environmentalists 372
egalitarians 365n9, 373
egalitarian social relations 370
elderly–nonelderly spending ratio (ENSR) 274
Eldredge, N. 150n1
Electricité de France (EDF) 304
Ellis, J. R. 330, 333, 345n2, 372–373, 379n2
Elton B. Stephens Co. (EBSCO) 82; analysis, results 93; articles per country 93; articles published in common policy areas 92; methodology 93
Embedded Cost–Benefit Analysis 385, 390–391; BC-CBA 390–391; DW-CBA 390
emergentist 138
enclavists 358–360; communicative 359; Rawlsian rules 359; weak spot 359
endogenous change 177–181; cognitive filters 180; information processing 180; policy failure 178; policy knowledge 181; policy-oriented learning 178; subsystems 178
Enhanced Engagement 397
enlarged groupthink 358
ENSR *see* elderly–nonelderly spending ratio (ENSR)
environmental issues 67
environmental policy 64
Escobar, O. 95
Esping-Andersen 197, 199, 201, 214; argument 214; reformulation 214; *Three Worlds of Welfare Capitalism* 219
Esping-Andersen, G. 213
EU *see* European Union (EU)
EUCOM *see* European Consortium Mochovce (EUCOM)
EURATOM Treaty 307n15

Eurogroup 304
European Bank for Reconstruction and Development (EBRD) 304
European Bank of Investment 304
European Consortium Mochovce (EUCOM) 304
European effects 295
European Journal of Political Economy 330
European policy 71; analysis of 336
European proposal 343–344; leading European experts 344; national policy styles, harmonization of 343–344
European social policy 67
European Union (EU) 99
Europeanization 7, 89; absorption 293; accommodation 293; complex interdependence 293; concertation 293; coping strategies 293; deepest transformation 293; disadvantages in 296; European integration and 292; externalization 293; fallacies 295; in-depth transformation 290–291; interest group behaviour 291; internalization 293; literature 295; mechanisms and effects 292; methodological problems 290; of public policies 295; supranationalization 293; theoretical framework 291; transnationalization 294
Europeanization as methodological challenge: complex interdependence 295–298; interaction at the European level 298–303; long-term comparison 294; test variables 294, 303–305; evidence-based policy 83
evidence-based policymaking 6
evolutionary theory 169
Exclusive Economic Zone (EEZ) 251
exogenous impacts 186–187; at macropolitical level 186; mechanism 186; new decision makers 187; at policy subsystems 186
exogenous influences, transmission 171
exogenous policy models 399
explanandum 130, 173; problem of 172
explanans 130, 173
explanatory accounts 169
explanatory variables 139–140
external perturbations 157

FAO *see* Food and Agriculture Organization (FAO)
fatalistic social relations 370
fatalists 372–373
Federal Ministry of Health 114
Federal Reserve Board 68
federalism 204
Feed-in Tariffs (FIT) 233
Fiol, M. C. 190n9
Fischer, C. S. 323
Fischer, M. 94
fisheries and governability, scale 244
fisheries department 255

fisheries governance network 257n1
Fisman, R. 313, 324n7
FIT *see* Feed-in Tariffs (FIT)
Flentje, H. E. 379n3
Fogerty, D. 373
Food and Agriculture Organization (FAO) 251
Ford Foundation 47
formal accession 398
Foundation for Scientific Research on Traffic Safety 354
four social capital indicators: civic participation 314–315; corruption 313–314; generalized trust 314–315; political freedom 313
fragmentation 149, 269, 270, 271, 285
Freedom House Index 315
Freeman, G. P. 8
Freeman, R. 102
French centralized Fordist model 100
French epidemic: drug abuse 108; heterosexual 109; homosexuality 109
functional (inter)dependencies 176
fuzzy judgment criticism 219

G-20's Global Forum on taxation 397
Gadamer, H.-G. 410
Gais, T. L. 270, 286n8
GAO *see* General Accounting Office (GAO)
garbage can model 177, 262
GATT *see* General Agreement on Tariffs and Trade (GATT)
Gatti, R. 313, 324n7
General Accounting Office (GAO) 386
General Agreement on Tariffs and Trade (GATT) 232
generalized trust 312, 314–315
generative causal process 177
generosity 218
German decentralized consensual model 100
German green party 307n8
German pension system 200
Germany's renewable energy policy 233
Gerring, J. 87
Gersick, C. J. G. 150n2
Geva-May, I. 3, 13, 8n2, 52, 81, 257, 329, 334, 342, 368–369
GI *see* governing interactions (GI)
global village 34
global warming 71
globalization 62, 89
GNI *see* Gross National Income (GNI)
Goetz, K. 292
Golder, B. 96
Goldhamer, H. 45; *The Adviser* 45
Goodsell, C. T. 22
Google Books N-gram search 84–85
Google Million 84–86
Gormley, W. T. 65
Gornick 8

Gould, S. J. 150n1
governability and attributes of GS 248–250; action 248; elements 248; images 248; instruments 248; modes 249; orders of 249–250
governability and governance interactions (GI) 252–256; governing interactions 252–253; impact/effect of GS on SG 255–256; influence of GS on SG 254–255; modalities 253–254; systems 254
governability and sub-systems of GS 251–252; hybrids 252; markets 251; states 251
governability concept, exploring: and governance interactions (GI) 252–256; and governance system (GS) 247–252; and system-to-be-governed (SG) 244–247; background 241–242; concept 242–244
governance and public policy 18–19; goal specification 18; governance capacity 19; third-generation policy analysis 19
governance system (GS) 242; governability and attributes (*see* governability and attributes of GS); governability and sub-systems (*see* governability and sub-systems of GS)
governing interactions (GI) 242; modalities 253–254; systems 254; variables 243
Government Performance and Results Act 384
government policymakers 354
Gow, D. 339
Green Book 385
green purchasing law 230
Green-Pedersen, C. 5–6, 158, 199, 208, 212, 216–217, 221n1
Greenwood, J. 307n5
Greider, W. 40n4
Grendstad, G. 372
grid 364n1, 379n2
grid-group cultural theory 337
Grin, J. 333
gross national income (GNI) 319
grounded theory 343
group-grid cultural theory 337
GS *see* governance system (GS)
Gunn, L. A. 48, 83
Gusfield, J. R. 350–351, 362
Guy, P. B. 3, 59, 102
Gyawuli, D. 341

Hacker, J. 163n1
Hajer, M. A. 189n3
Hall, P. 157–163
Hall's formulation 157–158; classifications 158; first order changes 157; incremental changes 158; literature on policy change 158; policymaking 157; second order changes 157; third order changes 158
Hann, A. 189n3
Harrison, K. 36–37

Hartz IV reform plan 207
Haverland, M. 221n1
hawkers 396
health and sex education 117–119; Catholic Church's monopoly 118; condom use 118; in France 118; gay organizations 117; in Germany 118; homosexuality 117; in Italy 118; methodological lesson 119; militant volunteers 118; policy problems 119; religious instruction at school 119; religious practice 119; sexually transmitted diseases, prevention 119; women campaigners 118
health education authority 118
health insurance system 108
health maintenance organizations 33
Heclo, H. 32
Heidenheimer, A. J. 32
Henrion Commission (1995) 117
Heron 8
Herweg, N. 264
heterosexual transmission 109
hierarchical governance 249
hierarchical social relations 370
hierarchical-institutional component 176
hierarchist policymaker or analyst 355
hierarchists 354–356
historical institutionalism 15
Hix, S. 292
Hjern, B. 234
Hogwood, B. 48, 83, 136
Holling, C. S. 200, 246
Holyoak, K. X. 410
homomorphisms 176
homosexual transmission 109
Hood, C. 362, 379n3
Hoornbeek, Dr. J. 77n1
Hoppe, R. 6, 329, 333, 345n2
horizontal diffusion 397
Houtman 341
Howlett, M. 4, 52, 154, 156, 160, 260, 264, 407
Hrudey, S. E. 391
Huber, E. 190n11, 199, 201
Huddleston, M. W. 332; Public Administration Review 331
Hull, C. 234
human development index 318
Huntington, S. P. 241
Huß, C. 264

IAEA *see* International Atomic Energy Agency (IAEA)
ICMA *see* International City/County Management Association (ICMA)
ICPA-Forum *see* International Comparative Policy Analysis Forum (ICPA-Forum)
ideal-type models 334
ideal-typical classification 131
ideational leadership (IL) 205

IDUs *see* intravenous drug users (IDUs)
IGOs *see* international governmental organizations (IGOs)
Imbeau, D. M. 35
implementation problem 47
inclusive approach 351
incompleteness of generative causal processes 170
incremental *vs.* paradigmatic 161
incremental/radical 136–137
individualistic social relations 370
individualists 360–361, 373; car mobility problem 361; intelligence of democracy 361; rationality 360; resist political rhetoric 360
industrialized democracies 70
inferential felony 23
informal local networks 234
Ingram, H. 35, 60
insiders 111, 173, 182
institutional analysis and development framework (IAD) 173; boundary relationships 174; elements of 174; environmental influences 176; horizontal links 176; negative feedback 176; participants 173; patterns of interaction 173; policy space 174; policy subsystem 175; positive feedback 176; subsystem rules 175; vertical relationships 176
institutional break-out 206
institutional explanations 200
institutional structures 206
institutionalism and public policy 14–16; comparative study 16; historical institutionalist literature 15–16; literature public policy 16; logic of appropriateness 15; presidential *vs.* parliamentary governments 16; rational choice literature 15; stepping stones for implementation 16; veto point argument 15; with Aristotle 14
institutions 170; formal rules 170; informal rules 170
instrumental policy learning 190n10
interactive governance 243, 249, 254
interdependencies 75–76; agriculture policy 76; educational policy 76; instrument choices 76; political push 76
interest intermediation and public policy: corporatism 17; governance networks 17; micro-corporatism 17
International Atomic Energy Agency (IAEA) 305
International City/Ccounty Management Association (ICMA) 402
International Comparative Policy Analysis Forum (ICPA-Forum) 82
International Comparative Policy Association 52
international governmental organizations (IGOs) 396
International Library of Policy Analysis 52
International Research Chairs programme 235
International treaties or norms 399

intravenous drug users (IDUs) 115
isolates 357–358; Dutch environmental policymakers 358; radical innovation 358; rationality of 357; unstable casino 357
isolationism 364n2

Jacquot, S. 295
Japanese Top Runner (JTR) programme 230, 237
Jeanrenaud, C. 373
Jeliazkova, M. I. 333
Jenkins-Smith, H. 177, 189n3, 334, 372, 374
Jennings, B. 334
Job Opportunities and Basic Skills Training (JOBS) 286
John, P. 141, 168, 189n3
Johnson, D. 257
Johnson, L. 46
joint decision trap 76
Jones, B. D. 63, 177, 179, 182–183
Jones, C. 68, 144, 176, 177, 265n2
Jones, M. D. 265n2
Jordan 332
Journal of Comparative Policy Analysis (JCPA) 3, 21; acceptance rate (2016) 82; aim 5–6; aims and scope statement of 87; appearance of 48; Capano contributes 4; comparative politics 4; contributors 3; cross-fertilization 4; founding editors of 3; number (%) by type 44; political science 4; public administration 4; scholarship 3
Journal of European Public Policy, The 89

Kahneman, D. 403
Kaldor-Hicks criteria 83
Kamehameha elementary education program 332
Kangas, O. 199
Kapur, D. 94
Kassimeris, C. 95
Kierkegaard, S. 314
Kim Jung Un 409
Kingdon, John 260, 261
Kisli district of Kenya 333
Kitschelt, H. 213, 217
Klitgaard, R. 329, 332, 341
Knack, S. 321
Knill, C. 307n5, 307n6
Kohl, C. 300
Kooiman, J. 240, 257n1
Koppenjan, J. 333
Korpi, W. 199, 215, 217
Kozloduy nuclear power plant 305
Kudrle, R. T. 395, 397–398
Kuhn, T. S. 155
Kulczycki, A. 265n2
Kuttner, R. 40n4
Kvist, J. 219

labour government (1984) 232
Ladrech, R. 292
Lamping, W. 200
Landes, D. S. 330
landfill tax 279
Lasswell, H. D. 13, 31, 33, 50, 83, 87, 332; public policies 13; *The Future of the Comparative Method* 83
learning as meaning making 410
learning for transfer from single case: Barzelay's approach 407; case learning practices 405; comparative studies of policy 405; craft contrivances 407; determination 406; dialectical engagement 407; dissatisfied with policy measures 406; existing literature 406; lesson drawing 407; policy learning 407; transfer mechanisms 408
Leech, B. L. 255
Lehmkuhl, D. 307n5, 307n6
Leibfried, A. 200
Leopold, A. 409
lesson drawing 4–5, 395, 403
light rail transit system 36
Lillard, D. 102
limited explanatory scope 172
Lindblom, C. 83, 155, 161
Lindbom, A. 218, 222n3
linear policy development 133
linear/combinative-conditional causality dichotomy 139
Lipshitz, R. 190n11
Lister, J. 379n4
logic of appropriateness 15, 163, 187
logic of expected consequences 187
logic of veto points 15
lowest common denominator 398
Lowi, T. J. 32, 77, 351; typology 7
Luedtke, A. 7
Luhmann, N. 241
Lyles, M. A. 190n9
Lynch, J. 273, 284, 285n5
Lynn, L. E, Jr. 3, 8n2, 82, 334

McConnell, A. 225–229, 236–237, 264
McKaughan, D. J. 409
McKinlay, R. 35
MacRae, D., Jr. 3, 82, 334
macro-comparative approaches 269–270; decentralisation 269–270; endogeneity problem 270; fragmentation 270; politics 270; veto-players argument 269; welfare effort 270
macro-economic policy 201
macro-level quantitative analyses 201
Maggetti, M. 94
Mahon, R. 257n1
Mahoney, J. 147
Majone, G. 68, 331, 334
Malkin, J. 373

Maloney, W. A. 173
March, J. G. 22, 190n11, 262, 307n12, 365n7
MARE Conference 257n1
marginal cost 34, 388
Marmor, T. R. 55–56, 102
Marsh, D. 307n6, 407, 408
Maslove, A. 82
Mason, R. O. 365n14
matching 196–197
Matland, R. 225–229, 236–237; matrix 227
May, P. J. 178, 190n10
Maybin, J. 95
Mayntz, R. 241–242
Mazey, S. 302
mean-spirited thinking 284
means-oriented policy 164n5
medical care state 106
mega-policy sciences 34
Meltsner, A. J. 334
mental meta-model 369
meso perspective 139
metachoice 384–385; framework, goals 385–386; monetization 386–387
methadone 111
methodological approach and data 273
methodological individualism and public policy: citizens attitude 22; dominant approach 12; role of 22
methodological nationalism in comparative social policy research 268; cross-national and cross-regional comparisons 280–283; decentralisation 271–273; new social risks 271–273; regions 269–271; United Kingdom 278–280; United States, the 273–278
methodologies and policy 23–24; experiments 24; policy scholars 23; policy studies 23; statistical methods, use of 23
Methodology of the Social Sciences, The 331
Meyer, P. B. 36
micro-corporatism 17
Mill, J. S. 83, 87, 375; A System of Logic 83; A Theory of Logic 87
Minister of Labour Affairs 207
Mintron, M. 189n3
Mishler, W. 313
Mitroff, I. 365n14
MNBA see Monetized Net Benefits Analysis (MNBA)
model tax treaty 397
modified taxonomy 160
monetarization 73–74; capacity of government 73; divisible problems 73; EU issue 74; indivisible problems 73
monetization 386–387
Monetized Net Benefits Analysis (MNBA) 389
Montefrio, M. J. F. 96
Montreal Convention (1987) 37

motors of change 135
MSA see Multiple Streams Approach (MSA)
Mucciaroni, G. 189n3, 263
Mulgan, G. 225, 229, 236
mullahs (Iran) 335
Multi-Goal Analysis 385, 391; advantage of 391; characteristics 391; compensatory rules and schemes 391
multiple causation 69
multiple goals including efficiency 385
Multiple Streams Approach (MSA) 130, 141–144, 168; adaptive system 141; basic elements 261–262; with chaos theory 141; comparative Kingdon 263; epistemological point of view 141–143; metaphors and models 262–263; on policy change 144; special issue 263–265; theoretical choices 142–143

NAFTA see North American Free Trade Agreement (NAFTA)
Narayan, D. 314
National AIDS Commission 114
National Front's anti-AIDS crusade 115
National Health Service (NHS) 33, 114
national health system 108
national models 100
national models, exporting 303–304; Danish farmer's unions 304; French counterpart FNSEA 304; French farmers' union 304; German farmers' union DBV 304
naturally occurring experiments 88
NE quadrant 385; see also Embedded Cost–Benefit Analysis
negative diagonal 365n13
neglected variable in policy research: applied research 341; culture-by-policy-analysis 341; Klitgaard studies 341
negotiated agreement path 146
neo-Gramscian framework 202
neo-homeostatic model 162
neophyte analysts 54
net present value (NPV) 389
networks of expertise 301; France EDF 302; German electricians 302; German operators 302; nuclear industries 302; nuclear power plants 301; politicians 301
new institutionalism 15, 35, 202
new orthodoxy foundations 156; characterizing change patterns 161–162; dependent variable, measuring 158–159; Hall's formulation 157–158; policy composition, improved model 159–160; transcending the current orthodoxy 162–163
new public management literature 84
New Zealand agri-reform (1980s) 231–232
Ney, S. 341
NHS see National Health Service (NHS)

Nijkamp, Peter P. 390
nine-cluster partition 318–322; DECENT 321; REFORM 321; social capital level 319; TRANS 321
nine-cluster taxonomy 316
non-elderly expenditures 273
normalization 126n14
North American Free Trade Agreement (NAFTA) 78n15
North Korea's nuclear threats 409
Northern European cluster 316
NPV *see* net present value (NPV)
nuclear electricity 297; enlargement process 298; French firms Framatome and COGEMA 297; French IPSN 297; German GRS 297; German Siemens KWU 297
nuclear energy 301
nuclear power plant (Kozloduy) 305
NW quadrant 385; *see also* Cost–Benefit Analysis

Obinger, H. 200, 203
OECD *see* Organisation for Economic Co-operation and Development (OECD)
Office of Economic Opportunity (OEO) 78n14
Okma, K. 102
Olsen, J. P. 22, 307n12, 365n7
Olson, D. 262
Oorschot, W. van 218
open method of coordination 71
operational level 173
operationalizations 201
operationalizing factors 245
optimism 46
orders of governance: first-order 249; meta-governance/third-order 250; second-order 249–250
ordinal and nominal pattern analysis 343
organic aqua-culture 246
Organisation for Economic Co-operation and Development (OECD) 90, 396; and policy transfer: special issue focus 396–399
Ostrom, E. 15, 35, 39, 51, 150n7, 175
Osuna, W. 334
output data 217
outsiders 173
overarching approach 294

Pacific Northwest forestry case 162
Page, E. 408
Pal, L. A. 4–5, 265
Paldam, M. 312, 314, 319
Palme, J. 199, 215, 217
participatory GI 253
partisan analysis 78n12
party government models 141
path dependency framework (PDF) 130, 147; feature of 147; irreversibility clause 147; scholars 147
path dependent institutionalization 157
Patient Protection and Affordable Care Act 283
pattern-maintaining hierarchy 364n2
patterns of interaction 173; action situation, components of 173; external factors 173; type of actors 173
Pattyn, V. 94
payoff rules 175
PDF *see* path dependency framework (PDF)
Pedler, R. 307n5
PEF *see* Punctuated Equilibrium Framework (PEF)
pensions 67
Perl, A. 264
Perrow, C. 65
perturbation 157
PESA *see* Public Expenditure Statistical Analysis (PESA)
Petracca, M. P. 63
Pew-MacArthur Results First Initiative 55
phronesis 403
Pierson, P. 159, 198–199, 212, 214–215, 217–220
pinching ideas 35, 88
Pizzorno, A. 336
pluralism 17
pluralist theories 141
policy advocacy coalitions 374
policy agenda project 144
policy analysis 5, 22, 24n1, 45, 57n2; as profession 49–50; metachoice in 384; professional training in 54; scholars 50
Policy Analysis for the Real World (Hogwood and Gunn) 48
policy analysis grows and diversifies 47–48; analysts 47; staffs 47
policy analysis methods 20, 51
policy analytic studies 5
policy change as epistemological and theoretical problem: abstraction and structure/agency dilemma, level of 138–139; advocacy coalition framework 145–146; causal mechanisms 139–140; configurative dimensions 139–140; dynamics of development 134–135; epistemological choices 131–135; explanatory variables 139–140; frameworks 140–150; grasping reality 148–149; motors of change 135; multiple stream approach 141–144; output of change 137; path dependency framework 147; policy development and change 135–136; Punctuated Equilibrium Framework 144–145; theoretical choices 135–140; type of change 136–137; way of event progression 133–134

policy change as methodological problem: contemporary study of policy dynamics 155–156; revisiting the foundations of new orthodoxy 156–163
policy change, mechanisms 177; conceptual components 172–177; conflict expansion 181–186; endogenous change 177–181; exogenous impacts 186–187; three reference approaches 169–172; policy dynamics in 169–170; shortcomings in 170–172
policy convergence 7
policy core beliefs 170
policy cycle models 20
policy Delphi or scenario planning 402
policy design 59, 173; efforts 69
policy development and change 135–136
policy diffusion 20; and transfer, implications for 236–237
policy domain 189n6
policy durability 67
policy entrepreneurs 172, 261
policy formulation and adoption process 354
policy framing 63
policy ideas 51–53; abstraction of 53; analysts 53; diffusion of 53
policy initiation and government involvement 113–115; in Germany 114; in Italy 114; in UK 114; regional and municipal health agencies 114
policy innovation mapping matrix 236
policy innovation mapping model 228–229
policy innovations 226–228
policy instruments and design: characteristics of 61; contingentists 61; layering of 70; political nature of 60; study of 60
policy learners 409
policy learning 172, 178
policy monopoly 157
policy or management GI 253
policy pinching 36
policy problem identification 335
policy problems: characteristics of 65; complexity 68–70; divisibility 72–73; interdependencies 75–76; monetarization 73–74; question of scale 70–72; scope of activity 74–75; solubility 66–68; policy instruments and design 60–61; social problems, changing nature of 61–62; stage one 63–64; stage two 64–65
policy process dimension 227
policy process research 51–52
policy research 53–54; comparative approaches 53; narrow approach 53; predictions 53
policy scholars 148–150
policy sciences 44
policy shocks 146

policy streams 261–262; frameworks 22; model 20
Policy Studies 89
policy styles: active vs. reactive policymaking 21; consensus vs. imposition policymaking 21; study of 21
policy subsystem 173
policy transfer 5, 20, 51; comparative pinching 55; cross-national comparisons 55; Marmor's rules 55–56
policy transfer learning: abduction and phronesis in 408; clarifying the concepts 408–410
policy type and innovation 231–232, 234–235
policy utility 329
policy window 261, 374
policy-relevant literatures: comparative policy analysis 263; historical institutionalism 263; ideational analysis 263
policy-relevant research 51–52
political complexity 68
political consensus-building 207
political culture 369
Political economists 370–371
political economy and public policy, comparative 19
political economy to political culture 375–378; analysts 376; economists 375; egalitarians 375; hierarchs 375; nanny state 377; obstacle by proponents 377; platonic society 377; social utilities 375; three-way cultural coalition 376
political feasibility 386
political freedom 313; economically harmful redistribution 313; free 313; not free 313; partly free 313
political identities 205
political science 51
political stream 261
political systems 21
Politics & Policy 89
Pontusson, J. 214
Poole, M. S. 131–132
Popper, M. 190n11
Portland planners 40n7
position/choice/aggregation rules 175
positive diagonal 365n13
post-accession phase 398
postpositivists 331
potential mechanisms 317
poverty 71
power resources theory 214, 218
power/influence debate 254
powers system 46
PPBS see program budgeting and systems analysis (PPBS)
PPS see public policy studies (PPS)
pragmatism 339

Pressman, J. L. 15
primary orientation 354
primary process 244
primary stakeholders 231
primeval policy soup 262
primeveral soup 143
problem stream 261
problem-solving process 335
program budgeting and systems analysis (PPBS) 46
programmatic complexity 69
project organizers 52
public assistance 273
Public Expenditure Statistical Analysis (PESA) 273
public hostility 405
Public Policies 264
public policy 86; arenas of power 140; ideational forums 140; influence of political institutions 140; institutions 140; sets of networked relationships 140
public policy problems, cultures of: towards a culturalist theory 354–361; types of 352–354
public policy studies (PPS) 19–20, 350
public policy theory 139
Pullin, R. 257n1
punctuated equilibrium 155, 157, 161
Punctuated Equilibrium Framework (PEF) 130, 144–145; institutions 145; policy making 145
punctuated-equilibrium theory (PET) 52, 144, 168
Putnam, R.D. 312, 316, 319, 339; instrument 312, 314; *Making Democracy Work* 339
Puttman 23

qualitative assessments 219
qualitative comparative method 204
qualitative cost–benefit analysis 389
quasi-homeostatic pattern 162
question of scale 70–72; disaggregation 71; European policy 71; poverty 71; space program 71

RA *see* Revenue Analysis (RA)
Radaelli, C. M. 292–294
Radin, B. 3, 7, 82, 84; Policy Analysis Reaches Midlife 82
Ragin, C. C. 4, 219
Rastogi, P. N. 354–355, 364n6
rational choice theory 140
rationalistic-based approaches 227
Rayner, S. 341
REA *see* Revenue-Expenditure Analysis (REA)
Reagan 198
reductionism 136, 138
Redwoods League 373

regional agency 270–271; macro-comparative account 271; welfare policy 270
regional agglomeration 7
regional welfare state effort 271
regulatory intervention 74
Reich, R. 35, 40n4; The Next American Frontier 35
Rein, M. 63, 365n14
Renewable Energy Sources Act (EEG) 233
Renn, O. 36
resilience 246–247
Resnick-Terry, P. 256
Reuters, T. 8n1
Revenue Analysis (RA) 389
Revenue-Expenditure Analysis (REA) 389
reversibility/irreversibility 137
Reynolds, S. 316
Rhodes, R. A. W. 307n6
Richardson, J. J. 302, 333
Riggs, F. W. 84
Rimmerman, A. 94
Rivlin, A. 46
Rizova, P. S. 94
Robinson, J. 246
Robust measure, construct:cluster analysis 315–316; four social capital indicators 313–315; results 316–322
Rochefort, D. A. 63, 66, 298, 350
Rockefeller Foundation 402
Rockman, A. 17
Rose, R. 87, 25n11, 313, 403
Ross, F. 216
rugged individualists 373
Russian Federation 126n2
Russian macroinstitutions 313

Sabatier, P. A. 136, 164n2, 177, 189n3, 231, 374
safer sex 117
Salagrama, V. 257n1
Saurugger, S. 5, 102, 289; Europeanization 102; methodological treatment 102
SC *see* Social Costing (SC)
Scale of Innovation 231, 233–234, 236
Scharpf, F. W. 15, 76, 299, 307n12
Schiphol Airport expansion issue 359
Schlager, E. 189n3
Schmitt, S. 407
Schmutzer, M. A. E. 365n7
Schneider, A. 35, 60
Schon, D. A. 63–64, 71, 190n11, 365n14, 403, 408, 411
Schulman, P. 71
Schwartz, H. 215
Schwarz, M. 372
scientific theory 131

scope of activity 74–75; economic incentives 75; government regulation 74; in environmental policy 75; nuclear energy facilities 74; soft law 75
scope rules 175
Scott, C. 82
SE quadrant 385; *see also* Multi-Goal Analysis
sea tenure systems 255
selected country stories: consensus building and co-ordination 115–117; health and sex education 117–119; policy initiation and government involvement 113–115
self-governance 249
Selle, P. 372
semi-political movement 241
SG *see* system-to-be-governed (SG)
shared prescriptions 170
Shaw, C. L. 36–37
Sheingate, A. D. 7–8
shift points 374
Shipton, H. 190n11
Simon, H. A. 155, 161, 355; *Administrative Behavior* 355
Single European Act 384
single goal of efficiency 385
single payer system 33
Slovakian nuclear power plant 304
small-scale aqua-culture 246
Smith, A. 164n5
Smith, T. A. 32
SNAP *see* Supplementary Nutritional Assistance Program (SNAP)
social analysis 4
social and political development 132
social capital 312
social construction 374
Social Costing (SC) 388–389
social democracy 214
social impact assessment 245
social policy 61
Social Policy and Administration 89
social security program 68
social unit 4
social utility 329
socialist capitalism 34
societal systems 243
soft law 75
soil assessments 374
Solow, R. E. 331
South American market union (MERCOSUR) 99
special issue 263–265
spending 273
Spohr, F. 264
stamp tax 279
standard setters 231
Starbuck, W. 411
state agents 173

Steffen, M. 99, 105; AIDS epidemic, management 101
Stephens, J, D. 199, 201
Stockholm 404; congestion charge system 402
Stockholm policy 405
Stone, D. A. 407
structural ambiguity 141
structural reform 207
structural-functional differentiation 203
structuration 139
structure/agency dilemma 138–139
structured problems 352
stylized learning scenarios 404–405
sub-attributes 66
substantial policy transfer 398
subsystem permeability 176
supplementary nutritional assistance program (SNAP) 273
Svendsen, G. L. H. 311–314, 316, 319
Svendsen, G. T. 311–314, 316, 319
SW quadrant 385; *see also* Efficiency Analysis
Swank, D. 217
Swanson, G. 86
Swedish welfare state 218
Swiss canton system 319
syringes sale 126n15
system-to-be-governed (SG) 242, 244; and common properties 245–246; and societal primary processes 244–245; resilience 246–247; vulnerability 247
systematic pinching 54
systemic retrenchment 222n5

Talbott, S. 40n3
TANF *see* Temporary Assistance for Needy Families (TANF)
Tavory, I. 409
tax information exchange agreements 397–398
tax policy 72
tax system (China) 399
tax transparency after 9/11 (US) 399
teleological social development 133
Temporary Assistance for Needy Families (TANF) 274; coefficient of variation 278
territorial integration 205
Thagard, P. 410
Tharp 332
Thatcher, R. 198
Thelen, K. 147
Theobald, R. 313
theory-internal criticism 214
thermostatic model 162
Thomas, G. 410
Thompson, J. D. 65, 330, 333–334, 338, 372
Tilly, C. 306n4
time-lag problem 217
Timmermans, A. 60

Timmermans, S. 409
Tinker, J. 246
Torfing, J. 201–202
Torgerson, D. 334
tragedy of commons 249
tricks-of-the-trade 334
Tsbelis 15
Tuden, A. 65
Tversky, A. 403
two-by-two typology 351
two-cluster partition 316–317
two-cluster taxonomy 317
two-tier scheme 226
typical policy content: comprehensive health systems 111; condom use, promotion of 111; drug use, prevention 111; for marginalized groups 111; health statistics, adaptation of 110; hemophiliacs' legal struggle 112; methodological options 110; political responses to AIDS 110; political–administrative decentralization 111; prevent social stigmatization 110; prevention and compensation 111; promoting solidarity 110; sexual practices, prevention 111; social work, re-medicalization of 111; sterile syringes, public provision of 111; substitutive medications 111
typical policy timing 112–113; initial phase 112; medical care institutions 113; policy debate and controversy 112; prevention campaigns, France 112; public health institutions 113

UNAIDS *see* United Nations Program on HIV/AIDS (UNAIDS)
uncertainty 387
UNCLOS *see* United Nations Convention on the Law of the Sea (UNCLOS)
unemployment insurance 273
UNESCO report (1991) 332
Unfunded Mandates Reform Act 384
United Kingdom: decentralised finances 278; in Northern Ireland 279; social expenditure 280; taxes 279
United Nations Convention on the Law of the Sea (UNCLOS) 251
United Nations Program on HIV/AIDS (UNAIDS) 107
United States 274; active labour market programmes 274; CHIP 278; direct federal spending 274; elderly–nonelderly spending ratio 274; federal governments 274; local government spending 274; medicaid 278; programmatic areas 274; state governments 274
University of Bristol's Policy Press 52
unstructured problem 353

value rationality 359
Van de Ven, Andrew H. 131–132, 134
Van Nispen, F. 3, 82
Van Waarden, F. 25n8
Varma, R. 94
Vaupel, J. 334
venue shopping 171
Verba, S. 336
Vergari, S. 189n3
vertical diffusion 397
VET *see* Australian Vocational Education and Training (VET)
veto players theory 150n7
vicarious learning 403
Vining, A. R. 334
vocational training (Australia) 399
Vogel, D. 39
Vogt 332
voluntary organizations 315
vulnerability 247; dimensions of 247; of coastal zones 248

WANO *see* World Association of Nuclear Operators (WANO)
war on poverty 78n14
warm-water aqua-culture 246
Washington State Institute 55
Watanuki, J. 241
water pollution control 69
way of event progression 133–134; adaptive learning 133; characteristics 133; functionalism 133; linear policy development 133; non-linearity 133; social constructivism 133; teleological social development 133
Wealth and Poverty of Nations (Landes) 330
Weaver, R. K. 16
Weber, M. 331
Weberian theory 102
Weimer, D. 3, 82, 334
welfare effort 285
Welfare State 21, 25n3
welfare state consolidation 203
welfare state policies 125n1
welfare transfers 216
Whiteley, P. 321
Whizz Kids 46; *see also* Department of Defense analysts
wholesale approach 232
wholesale reforms 233
Wildavsky, A. 15, 24n1, 25n10, 25n12, 83, 330, 331, 332, 334, 351, 372; cultural bias, aspects of 371–373; social life, dimensions of 370–371; theory 369
Williams, G. 96
Williamson, O. E. 251
Wilson, J. Q. 72, 77

windows of opportunity 374
Wolf, A. 5
Woll, C. 295
Wolman, H. 408
Woodward, R. 397
Wootton, G. 255
World Association of Nuclear Operators (WANO) 305
World Bank report 313
World Bank's Global Delivery Initiative 402
World Values Survey 314

Zahariadis, N. 189n3
Zak, P. 321
Zakaria, F. 33
Zohlnhöfer, R. 264